A Day in the Lives of a City's Police

A patrolman stares at the Mayor as His Honor bends over the hospital bed where an ambushed policeman lies dying . . . A "cool" Police Commissioner turns ice cold with rage when he hears the full extent of corruption among his men . . . A bearded detective with torn clothes and an earring stakes out a pusher . . . Another plainclothesman in an expensive suit and using a French accent waits for a beautiful hooker to put the make on him . . . A patrol car in a ghetto is surrounded by a mob howling for blood . . . The most respected man on the Force is ordered to hand in his resignation . . .

Robert Daley spent over 365 days like that with the New York Police Department in a position where he could see the total picture, from bottom to top. That was as much as he could take. Now he has written a book that for the first time gives the full story. Here it is, all of it—and it just may be as much as you can take, too.

TARGET BLUE

An Insider's View of the N.Y.P.D.

by Robert Daley

A DELL BOOK

Published by
DELL PUBLISHING CO., INC.
1 Dag Hammarskjold Plaza
New York, New York 10017

Portions of this book originally appeared in
New York Magazine and *Cosmopolitan*

They were killed because of their color,
which was neither black nor white,
but blue.

WILLIAM MORIARITY, SGT., N.Y.P.D.
following the assassinations of
Patrolmen Foster and Laurie, January 1972

This book is dedicated to the
New York Police Department

Book One / WINTER

1 / The Job

To be admitted into his presence was like entering the offices of certain Hollywood moguls of long ago. I was led through a series of doors—the walk seemed endless. The last was a double door, and his office seemed as huge as the Police Commissioner himself was small. The office was ornate: high, decorated ceiling, walls paneled in dark carved oak, brass chandelier, red velvet drapes. Above the marble fireplace hung a portrait of Police Commissioner Theodore Roosevelt, who went from this room to the White House. The new commissioner received me from behind Roosevelt's huge desk, sitting in a leather swivel chair whose back seemed taller than he was. He stood up to shake hands, allowing me to gaze full length on the number one crime fighter in the world today. He was a small man in shirtsleeves. His hair was thin and gray, and drooping eyebrows nearly hid his pale-blue eyes. The most significant thing about him did not show: he stood at the head of 32,000 armed men, a force larger than most of the armies of recorded history, an army big enough, until not very long ago, to conquer a country, or the world. He had three times as many agents as the FBI, six times as many as a city the size of Detroit, which was where he had just come from. His budget this year was 626.6 million dollars—more, probably, than the budgets of the five largest film companies combined. As might have happened in Hollywood too, my interview with him was interrupted several times by the entrance of one of his secretaries. He had about twenty, I was to learn, almost all of them detectives in shirtsleeves, each with a gun on his hip. They were part of his army. No starlets here.

While he spoke with one or the other in a voice so low I could not hear the words, I gazed about the ornate office. Later I would become as familiar with this place as with my own living room, but I did not know this then. I had never been a policeman, and never expected to be. I was there to write an article about the Police Commissioner because he seemed something new: a liberal cop, a man who had declared that he meant to stamp out police corruption while also introducing modern business techniques to the New York Police Department.

At one time or another, usually in other cities, he had made the following statements:

"The policeman is the most important social worker we have. Often it is far better to settle an argument or disperse a crowd and move on than to make an arrest."

"The police today aren't sufficiently trained, they aren't adequately educated, and they clearly aren't doing enough research into problems like improving patrol tactics."

"Every time police salaries go up, entrance and promotion standards ought to go up, too."

"There can be no effective police work without the cooperation of the community. If the people do not trust the police, if they don't come forward with information, if they're unwilling to stand as witnesses in trials, then the police themselves are virtually helpless."

The Police Commissioner had other appointments after mine, to which I accompanied him in his car, a gleaming black Mercury provided by the city. A Hollywood mogul might have been proud of it, though it was not a Cadillac. The Mayor and the five district attorneys were assigned Cadillacs, and the Police Commissioner was often reminded that they outranked him when he saw their cars. His two chauffeurs, who worked alternate days, were detectives who lived near his red brick, high-rise ranch-style house, on Staten Island. Of course they served as his bodyguards also.

The first stop was the 5th Precinct station house in Chinatown. As he came through the door somebody cried, "A-ten—hut!" Men sprang erect like rakes that had been stepped on and stood there rigid, almost quivering.

The building itself dated from well back into the last century. I glanced around, amazed at how shabby and dilapidated it was. Later I was to learn that a great many of the city's 75 station houses resembled it; crime was shabby too, but why did it have to be fought out of such shabby places?

I was trying to notice everything, without taking my eyes off the Police Commissioner.

Presently we were in a traffic jam in the street outside.

The Police Commissioner said, "Give them a little of the siren, Dave."

The gleaming black Mercury erupted into noise, surprising everyone on the street, though not the little man beside me on the back seat. He had command also, whenever he wished, of the flashing red lights concealed in the grill. In the glove box was a concealed radio with three different mikes operating on different frequencies. One was a confidential band on which the Police Commissioner, half the city away, sometimes gave orders to his secretaries back in headquarters.

He had a luncheon date that day. After ordering the chauffeur to take me anyplace I wanted to go, he stepped out onto the sidewalk, and we left him.

The chauffeur began to boast that no one could "make" this car. Sometimes traffic cops even came over and shouted into it before realizing their—ahem—mistake.

I wrote in my notebook: The car no more looks like a police car than the small man in the back seat looks like a policeman.

I did not know then that I was to spend a hundred or more hours beside him in the back seat of this car, both of us nearly invisible from the sidewalk, moving day by day through the city. Except for the confidential frequency, the radio would always be turned off. The Police Commissioner, I would learn, was not titillated by listening to police calls, and he had no intention of speeding to the scene of any crime or disaster. Crime as an expression of social pressures, to be controlled by the techniques of a skilled police administrator—he would always refer to himself as a police administrator—interested him greatly, but crime as crime interested him not at all. Though his wife sometimes read murder mysteries, he would tell me once, he himself did not.

I would come to the conclusion that crime—this may sound odd—bored him.

When he came out of the restaurant the chauffeur and I were waiting at the curb.

That day he was to present a plaque in the Municipal Building to two firemen who had aided in an important arrest. As we entered the crowded lobby, men called out his name, and in the elevator, the operator shook his hand. I saw that he glad-handed everybody. A politician could not have done it better: "Hello, how are you? How are you doing?"

I knew his name: Patrick V. Murphy. He did not know mine, though it must have been written on his appointment schedule back at headquarters, for now he introduced me to a group of officials as Mr. Ryan. Nevertheless, as I moved to step out of his car at the end of the afternoon, he suddenly asked if I would send him a résumé.

Résumé? Was he offering me a job?

"I don't know if you'd be interested," he said.

I stared at him in surprise.

"But if you would be interested, I'd appreciate having a résumé."

I had ridden with him most of the day, firing questions. Most he had answered vaguely, in a quiet, droning voice. There was no passion in this voice, though the subjects being discussed were armed robbery, racial tension, police corruption. His ideas had sounded new to me, his thinking incisive. But somehow I had expected a different kind of man. The number one crime fighter in the world today should perhaps have been big, tough, loud, brave. In the movies the part would have been played by John Wayne. The small, soft-spoken 50-year-old New Yorker in the back of this car would, in the movies, have played the part of the branch manager of a bank.

"You will send a résumé?"

I was not interested in becoming a policeman.

"Yes, of course," I said, adding, "I'll need another interview or two." The important thing was to assure his cooperation until my article was finished.

He agreed to future interviews.

Puzzled, I watched the black Mercury disappear in traffic. What had made him ask for my résumé? What exactly was he offering?

About two weeks later I concluded the final interview, and again was about to step out of his car.

"I thought you were going to send me your résumé," he said.

"Yes, well . . ." I said. After a moment I said, "I wondered what you wanted it for. What did you have in mind?"

He was a man given to speaking in broad, general terms. I had been striving—and failing—to worm specific answers out of him for days.

He did not say much that was specific now, either. I would have the rank of Deputy Commissioner. I would serve as an adviser and communications expert. My principal job would be to try to win back the people for the police.

"I don't know if you're interested . . ." he said. "If you are, I'd like to have a résumé."

I was trying to fathom his motives. Why me? What did he know about me?

He knew I had grown up in the 34th Precinct, for I remembered mentioning it in passing one day. Perhaps I had told him that I'd done all of my schooling in New York City—I wasn't sure. Had I told him that I had served for six years in Europe and North Africa as a foreign and war correspondent for *The New York Times*?

Did he realize that I was a close friend of Sergeant David Durk, whom Murphy perhaps considered the number one nemesis of the Police Department and of his own administration? Did he realize that I was a friend also of Patrolman Frank Serpico, another nemesis? The answer to both questions presumably was no.

I doubted he had read any of my books.

I had seen grim events, and been shot at, and later I would never see anything as a policeman that would surprise me very much, but he didn't know that.

When I went home that day I had no intention of sending any résumé, but despite myself I kept brooding about him, and one day I typed out three quarters of a page, a résumé of sorts, and mailed it to him, together with one of my books. I did not sign the book. Murphy did not strike me as the type of man who would be impressed by an autographed book nor the type of man who would ever read it, signed or not.

That winter I had a good many contracts and assignments to fulfill, and after I had completed the article on Murphy I forgot about him.

But when spring came Murphy would summon me back to headquarters and offer me the job, and to my surprise I would accept it. I who had never been a policeman before would suddenly have line authority over the police force of the city of New York. I would carry a gold shield and a .38-caliber Smith and Wesson. I would be thoroughly trained in the use of that gun both at the Police Academy, and on the outdoor range at Rodman's Neck. Though I never expected to use it, I would respect it, and practice regularly.

I was to head a staff of 33 cops ranging in rank from deputy inspector to patrolman, plus a civilian woman who would be my secretary. I would have a car assigned 24 hours a day, and alternating chauffeurs—patrolmen—to drive me. The car would have two radios and would receive transmissions on nine different frequencies. It would transmit on only one.

It was to be my job to serve in the Police Commissioner's cabinet. I would give him a civilian view. Three of the six other deputy commissioners also had never been cops; two were lawyers who worked only on legal matters, the third handled only administration.

Everyone else would be a career policeman. At times this imbalance was to lend my lone civilian voice rather more weight than perhaps it should have had; and at times, rather less.

If my advice was to have any worth, it seemed to me I would have to go out into the streets with cops. If I was to win the people back for the cops, then I would have to see what cops did, and be there when they did it. So I would ride in radio cars in Harlem, I would go up onto rooftops on prowler runs, I would go out on narcotics buys. Once I was to get caught in a stickup. One gunman was dead and I went through the building with cops looking for the other, not because I was a hero, but because I happened to be there, and this seemed no time to let cops think the brass was afraid. I was to go in with raiders who hit after-hours bars in Greenwich Village. I was to lead raids on junkyards that received stolen cars, and on massage parlors on Eighth Avenue. I would interrogate criminals, witnesses to murder, and once a murderess. I would be involved in a great many arrests, and receive one commendation.

I would look down at the bodies of a number of victims.

I would serve as Deputy Police Commissioner during

one of the most traumatic times in the Police Department's history.

But I was unaware that winter that the future held any of this. Spring seemed a long way off. In the meantime I was a writer with strange friends. Reality was the slush piled against the curbs, and the late-at-night phone call from Durk.

"Serpico's just been shot."

"Oh, no."

2 / Serpico

The bullet entered Serpico's head just beside the left nostril and tried to come out his right ear, but failed, barely. That was at about 10 P.M. Sometime later, he lay inside a square of curtains in a ward in Greenpoint Hospital, and his eyes, opening weakly, focused on Sergeant Durk, former friend, who stood beside his bed.

Together, with help from nobody and despite threats of what would happen to them, Durk and Serpico had forced into existence the Commission to Investigate Alleged Police Corruption—the so-called Knapp Commission—which was expected to hand down its findings later in the year. Together Durk and Serpico, the one only a detective sergeant, the other only a plainclothes patrolman, had caused convulsions within the police department and within the city government as well. An incumbent police commissioner had already been driven out. But their struggle, which had consumed four years, had also consumed their friendship. Not in weeks had they seen each other, and their last cordial words were further back than that.

But now Serpico took Durk's hand and held on to it. A nurse and a reporter watched Durk trying to free his hand. "Hey," said Durk. "What's Susan going to say?" Susan was Serpico's girlfriend.

There was a commotion in the hall; the curtains were swept back to reveal the new Police Commissioner, Patrick V. Murphy, accompanied by much of the top brass of the police department. This crowd gazed down on Serpico.

"You're looking fine, young fella."

"He looks fine, doesn't he?"

"Are you getting all the care you need?"

These were men who had responded to the bedsides of many wounded policemen, though seldom as promptly or in such numbers as now. They peered down on Serpico; so this was the guy. It was the first time most of them, including the Police Commissioner, had ever seen him.

As the group departed, an intern with a red sweater under his white coat remarked, "What's all the fuss about? It's just another cop who got plugged."

Removed later that day to Brooklyn Jewish Hospital, Serpico was placed in a private room, with round-the-clock uniformed cops ordered to guard his door against possible attempts on his life.

In the hallway, one guard relieved another.

"Don't talk to that guy," the guard said.

"Why not?" asked the other cop.

"Just don't talk to him."

"But I already did."

"I'm telling you what they told me at the precinct. Don't talk to that guy. You're here to guard him. No one said you had to talk to him."

The bullet had entered the sinus cavity, severed a facial nerve and possibly an auricular nerve as well, for one ear was deaf. The bullet had broken into fragments on the jawbone. One fragment had ruptured the cerebral membrane, and then stopped. Another was lodged in the ear canal. The wound had been judged inoperable.

Meanwhile a police investigation was under way to determine if Serpico had been gunned down in the ordinary course of events, or set up to be killed.

What the police called Manhattan North was, principally, Harlem. The newly assigned Inspector Paul Delise looked over the 30 plainclothesmen he had just been assigned to command. He knew none of them personally, and his first glimpse of Frank Serpico shocked him.

"He was standing in the corner, all by himself. None of the other plainclothesmen would go near him or speak to him. He was being ostracized, but I didn't know that at the time. I looked down at him and I thought: that can't be a policeman. That must be one of their informants here. Serpico had this long unkempt hair, a scroungy beard, and he had an earring in one ear. He wore some kind of army bush jacket, and sandals with no socks, and he carried this kind of khaki field pack over his shoulder. In the field pack were his guns. He never had less than two guns. The reason he was being ostracized is, he had just locked up some policemen in the Bronx.

"Two days later he came over and introduced himself. Meeting him, it was like a breath of fresh air. I knew him by reputation of course. Here was a man I could rely on. Not that I couldn't rely on the other men too, but when you're new in a new office you don't know who you can rely on. But I knew Serpico was somebody with a moral code who would stick up for what he believed in. He wouldn't bend to the traditions of the department and the traditions of the men. The other men wouldn't talk in the office when he was there. They were more sympathetic to their friends up in the Bronx."

Delise and Serpico spent much of that winter crouched on rooftops or standing at the windows in condemned buildings observing and photographing through long lenses gambling operations taking place across streets and courtyards. As an additional disguise, Serpico would munch on grapefruit halves all day. What gambler would find menace in a hairy young man whose attention seemed concentrated on a grapefruit?

Because no one else wanted to partner Serpico, Delise often did, and there were times that year when the middle-aged inspector would follow a trail of grapefruit rinds across rooftops to find the bearded young loner. Most men of Delise's rank and age did not go on rooftops anymore, but Paul Delise enjoyed it. For this reason, and because he would not take bribes, Delise was known in the Police Department as St. Paul.

Once he and Serpico trailed a Harlem gambling syndicate to an abandoned store where payoffs were being made. Because a lookout was posted out front, Delise and Serpico came at the store over the rooftops and then down the stairs from the roof. The store had a side door onto a hall-way, which was where Delise waited; presumably Serpico would flush them into his arms. Serpico came out the front door onto the sidewalk, and then tried to stroll back into the store. But the lookout had given a signal, and the door was slammed in his face and barred.

So Serpico heaved a garbage can through the plate-glass window and went in after it. Holding four men at bay, Serpico let Delise in the side door. But the crowd that now gathered in the street was angry, for policy gambling was a way of life in Harlem, and most citizens there did not want the gambling laws enforced. This crowd began calling threats in the gaping window. They had guns, some voices claimed, and when the two cops came out they would be shot. The prisoners began to make threats too, and this was an especially tough street in West Harlem. Delise had a walkie-talkie and was trying to call in help, but wasn't getting through.

The public perhaps supposed that the police radio system was fantastically efficient, but there were many "dead" areas in the city where radio signals simply disappeared, and this apparently was one of them. During the next hour and a half, trapped with the prisoners inside that aban-doned store, Delise exhausted the battery in the radio. But no one came to their aid and no reply was heard. The size of the crowd out front had diminished somewhat, but it was still there, still in an ugly mood, when Serpico sudden-ly slipped out the side door, raced for the roof, and escaped. From a pay phone several streets away, he called in the radio cars.

"He was a unique-type individual," said Delise. "He was very persistent, very serious. He always did the dangerous thing."

When I first met Frank Serpico the beard was temporari-ly gone, but the hippie haircut and the earring remained. This was at a party at Durk's house. Serpico came in pack-ing two guns, one of them a 14-shot automatic that, stuffed in his belt, looked like it weighed ten pounds not to men-tion the pain it must have given him in his side. As he en-tered this room (and all other "friendly" rooms I was to see him enter) he would lay the automatic on a bookshelf and hitch his belt two notches tighter. Only then would he smile and shake hands.

Serpico, after a number of years in gambling enforcement, had recently been reassigned to the pussy posse. The job of the pussy posse was to lock up prostitutes. The law said the girl must explicitly solicit a man, and must either touch him lewdly or promise sexual acts, if the arrest was to be legal. But the girls were extremely wary, they smelled cop from a great distance, and so most cops assigned to the pussy posse would simply leap out of the cars, grab the girls off the street corners, and then testify in court to a criminal solicitation that never took place.

Not Serpico. He had to get the girl legitimately, or not at all.

The quota was one girl a night. Easy duty, unless you worked at it. Serpico went out each night furnished with foreign airline tickets, a foreign accent, and having even sewn foreign labels in his clothes. One night he would be Pierre, the diamond merchant from Antwerp. The next night he would be José, the Madrid dealer in heavy machinery. Each night he would circle in on a girl and admit that he had just made a business killing, that it was his first time in New York, and that he wanted a little fun.

Still, the girls, relentlessly harassed by cops, were wary.

At Durk's party, Serpico began to tell how he had picked up a girl outside the Barbizon. In a heavy French accent, he had invited her into the bar for a drink.

A New York policeman must be armed at all times, whether on duty or off.

"She squeezed up close to me, bumping me with her hip, and her hands accidentally brushed me, trying to feel my piece."

But Serpico had left his service revolver elsewhere, and carried only a slim automatic in his pants pocket.

The girl made no overt sexual advances. Despite Serpico's beard, his earring, and his accent, despite no apparent gun, she was obviously suspicious.

"You are Belgian," said the girl.

"Zat iz right."

"They speak French in Belgium."

"Zat iz right."

Suddenly the girl said, *"Vous parlez français, alors?"*

After a brief hesitation, Serpico said, *"Oui, je parle français. Vous parlez français?"*

"Oui."

It was like a tennis serve so beautifully returned that the girl couldn't decide what to try next.

"Oh, what lovely small feet you have," probed the girl. "What size shoes?"

They were size 11s bought in New York. Bought in Belgium they would be size—

"Size 44," said Serpico without hesitating.

"Could I see your passport?"

Serpico had no Belgian passport. Pointing out that he wore the order of Lenin in his buttonhole, and "Ze party is not popular in zis country," Serpico added, "tzerefore I do not like zat people examine my papers too closely."

Apparently convinced at last, the girl suggested they repair to Serpico's hotel. Fine, but she still hadn't mentioned price or an explicit sexual act, nor even touched him lewdly. It was true she had checked him out for a revolver, but this, according to Serpico's code, she had a right to do.

"It will cost you something," the girl said.

"Not too much I hope."

"One hundred dollars."

"I do not wish to purchase you, only rent you for a little while."

"Quality is expensive."

"What you do, how we say, special?"

"Would you like a little *soixante-neuf?*"

An explicit sexual offer at last. Serpico planned to write it up just that way: *soixante-neuf.* He couldn't wait to get to court to hear the judge holler, "What the hell is *soixante-neuf?*"

By now they were in a taxi aimed toward the Americana. At this point Serpico withdrew his shield and in the same thick accent said, "Zis has gone far enough. I am, how you say, a policeman, and you are, how you say, under arrest."

The girl fixed him with a cold, cold eye. Then she said, "You're dirty, but you're good."

Serpico had all of us laughing, except Durk, who said, "What accent are you going to entrap prostitutes with tomorrow night, Serpico? Are you going to play Fritz the Austrian? Sven the Swede? Or haven't you decided yet?"

"What's the matter with you, Durk?"

"That disguise, that skill, could be used to trap muggers."

"If they told you to bust prostitutes, you'd bust prostitutes."

"Nobody has to serve on that squad. That's considered good duty. All you have to do is ask to be taken off, and they'll take you off."

Yes, assigning him, shorn and shaved, minus earring, minus his 14-shot automatic, right back into uniform on patrol. Plainclothes duty was a step up the career ladder, the only one Serpico, who had flunked the sergeant's examination, had made. Of course they both knew this. But without mention of it by either fanatic, the argument grew in intensity.

"Frank, listen to me. You hate that job and you don't even know it. Why do you sew those foreign labels in your clothes? Why do you use all those phony accents. I'll tell you why, Serpico. It's because Frank Serpico hates the job so much he has to pretend he's somebody else to do it. It isn't Frank Serpico who busts prostitutes every night. It's Fritz from Austria."

"Well let me tell you something, Durk. Every time you flash that gold shield you become someone else too. You're not David Durk anymore, you're the New York Police Department."

"It isn't your shield that busts prostitutes, Serpico. It's you, Frank Serpico. Meanwhile, what about real crime? What about the pushers and the muggers, and the people trying to corrupt cops? Frank, listen to me."

Once, when we were alone, Serpico confessed that he had indeed hated busting prostitutes. "It was one of the saddest periods of my life. I was always late for work. Every night. I had to go out on the street and misrepresent myself to someone, and as a result that someone would lose trust in another human being. Sure, she was only a prostitute. Sure. It was sad."

But he would never admit anything like this to Durk. By now they were fighting with each other, shouting at each other, nearly every time they met.

It was partly ego. Durk was already celebrated, while Serpico was unknown outside the New York Police Department, though solidly hated inside. Durk was far more celebrated even than the new Commissioner. Durk had been
the subject of a *Life* magazine profile I had written, a front
page *New York Times* article, and other articles and TV
shows. He was a young man with vibrant new ideas and he
seemed to be in the process of turning on a generation of
college boys and perhaps turning upside down the police
departments of the nation.

It was Durk's notion that the police could attract to their
ranks the brightest elements of the educated class, that the
New York Police Department could add a corps of hard-
core college graduates and that society would be the better
for it. He had won a grant of money from the National Institute of Law Enforcement and Criminal Justice, the research agency of the Justice Department, and had begun to
tour the college campuses, asking students what they wanted to be when they grew up, and suggesting that they ought
to become policemen.

The site would be Yale or Harvard or Princeton or
Union Theological Seminary, or even N.Y.U. I went into
some of these places with him. Durk would stand in front
of the blackboard and tell the students, "The secret's out.
I'm really after your body."

This always drew a laugh. But Durk wasn't kidding: "If
you really want to do good, if you really want to help people, become a cop. To be a cop is worthy of you. The easi-
est way to change the system is, You become the cop. You
are now the man. Let yourself dare to think about it. It
isn't VISTA, it isn't the Peace Corps. It isn't $2000 a year
chanting folk songs around a campfire in Ghana. It's
$10,000 a year to start. It's a real job, dealing with real
people and real problems. If you really want to get involved, if you really care, become a cop.

"You want the cop on the beat to be a responsible guy,

right? You want him to care about people, right? You don't object to him being there; you just want your scale of values applied, right?

"Being a cop is a socially critical job. I think it's the best graduate course you could possibly take. Cops can't afford to make believe and play all the quiet games we all play. The cop is out there among the people. As a cop your juices are flowing. You have a feeling you're on the front lines.

"Listen, it's an absolutely succulent job. I was bored out of my skull. Then I became a cop. I love being a cop. It isn't bank holdups, it's family fights. It's taking pushers and muggers off the street. It's showing compassion when people are in trouble. And it's fun. That siren and those red lights are fun. It's a job where altruism merges with fun.

"If you believe that all is lost and the next step is the barricades, this job is not for you. If you see social progress as a mass movement with you as the director, this job is not for you. But if individuals count, become a cop."

Throughout that school year Durk had moved through a dozen or more colleges, principally in the Northeast, recruiting students. Several hundred of them agreed to take the tests for the New York Police Force and a number actually did take and pass all tests, and they had gone onto the waiting list. When he spoke at Amherst, his alma mater, Durk signed up 16 out of 29 boys, or, he reckoned, every eligible student present, because "you have to rule out that white Black Panther in the back of the room and the guys with the real thick glasses." He signed up 20 students at Yale, who then began to sign up classmates until the total reached more than 45.

The response of the students astonished even Durk: "Most of these kids considered the cops worse than Dow Chemical. I wouldn't have been surprised if the SDS had organized to throw stones at me. But there was no resistance from the kids at all. They looked at me as if I had the power to dub them cops." Durk moved through Harvard, Princeton, Yale, saying, "I'm a cop; I want to talk to you."

Durk, the son of a New York doctor, grew up on New York's upper West Side, attended public schools there, and then went on to Amherst, where he majored in political science, intending to become a lawyer. He actually did go to Columbia Law School for a year; but that wasn't what he wanted, so he quit and drifted into a business that imported African carvings. He was married, with one small daughter (another would be born later) when, at the age of 28, he abruptly joined the police force.

In his class at the Police Academy on East 20th Street, there were no doubt a number of other young men with college backgrounds, though no other doctors' sons, and no one else from Amherst. But Durk was six feet tall, slender, wiry. He could do more push-ups than most other recruits, and the first time he ever shot a pistol, he outshot most of them too. So they made room for him. He graduated as a probationary patrolman and went out onto the streets of New York.

It was for Durk as if he had never seen the city before. He stared wide-eyed and open-mouthed, and then he embraced this new city with delight.

He found that there were a great number of great cops. Most were short on his type of education, but they had a street sense that he could not match and knew he would never be able to match: "There were cops who could see a guy on the street and say, 'That's a wrong guy,' and go up and take a loaded gun off him."

Durk watched them and gauged them. He came to the conclusion that almost all cops had joined the police force for reasons of idealism—to help their fellow man—though few would admit it. The vast majority wanted to do the right thing, but got very little reinforcement; not from their superiors, not from the system itself. The vast majority cared initially, but after two years or so of frustration, became cynical. Even so, Durk rated about 10 percent of cops incorruptible whatever happened. Another 10 percent would certainly go wrong. The 80 percent in between could go either way.

Durk had been assigned to the 18th Precinct—midtown —but being a rookie, he "flew," meaning he often was sent into short-handed precincts. He worked in precincts adjacent to his own; he worked in Harlem. He was a patrolman on patrol, and he saw what all patrolmen see. Very little of it was dangerous. He never fired his gun on duty. He did take one or two knives away from his fellow citizens. Once, chasing a burglar on a rooftop at night, he was shot at, but not hit. Most of his time was spent helping people. He helped the sick, and the injured, and the lost, like all patrolmen. There was a night when he came upon a man who had collapsed in a doorway. It was winter and snow was falling, and the man did not speak English. He looked up at the hulking patrolman in the big blue coat, and in his eyes there was terror. When he realized that Durk was trying to help him, he began to cry, and he grabbed Durk's hand and kissed it. Durk stood there in his blue coat with the brass buttons, while the big, beautiful snowflakes came down upon them, and there were tears in Durk's eyes too.

Durk learned that, as he put it, "The stereotypes are valid. Most hoods do look like hoods." He learned that all cops dread coming upon a dead body, whether murdered or otherwise, because the paper work connected with corpses is staggering, and there was one story cops told wherein the first step in the investigation of a homicide was to toss the body over the park wall into the next precinct.

Durk considered that he was a cop 24 hours a day, and there were cops who derided him for it. One night Durk was off duty and on his way home when he came upon a white prostitute being beaten up by four black pimps. They stood in front of a certain hotel, and the streetlight shone down on the electric blue-green suits of the pimps. They were trying to force the girl into a canary-yellow Cadillac that was double-parked. The girl had blood on her face and was fighting and screaming when Durk, who was wearing a dark suit, with button-down collar and tie, ran up.

"Police. Take your hands off her," cried Durk.

"She's my wife," said one of the pimps.

"I'm not his wife. They're going to kill me."

The second pimp called Durk a number of vicious names, while the first calmly maintained, "This is my wife, man."

"You only interfering 'cause she white," said the third pimp.

"She my wife, man. You take your hands off my wife."

"Why don't we both take our hands off her?" said Durk.

A crowd had gathered; four more pimps shouldered

through the crowd and edged close to Durk and the girl, who by now were backed against a parked car. In an aside to the girl, Durk muttered, "Start moving. Let's get out of here. Walk."

But the girl stared at him, unable to move. The semicircle of pimps edged closer. Durk searched the crowd for help, but no one moved. A number of voices began to mutter imprecations about cops in general, and about this cop in particular.

"Let's see the pig get himself out of this one."

"What's the matter with you people?" cried Durk. "Do you really think I'm abusing them? Look at the girl. Look at the blood."

But the faces were unsympathetic, and no one moved to help.

"Let's get him," said one of the pimps.

Durk dropped his shield into his pocket and drew his gun, which he let hang against his leg. The pimps recoiled slightly. The crowd fell silent. Now came the first sounds of police sirens. In a moment the first radio car squealed to a stop and a middle-aged uniformed captain said to Durk, "What you got, kid?"

Durk explained.

"But she's just a pross," said the captain.

"I know she's a pross," responded Durk.

"These guys are pimps," said the captain.

"I know they're pimps."

"The pimps congregate in that hotel."

"I know that."

"So what did you get involved for?" asked the captain. "What's the point?"

"But that *is* the point," said Durk. "Just because she's a prostitute, she didn't forfeit her life."

Durk now turned to the girl, on whose face the blood had begun to dry. "If you'll press charges," he pleaded with her, "I'll go all the way with you. There's nothing to be afraid of. I won't abandon you."

Now the cops began dispersing the crowd. Durk was still pleading with the girl. "If you'll sign a complaint, I'll go all the way with you. I won't abandon you."

But the girl refused, and presently she got into the yellow

Cadillac with the first four pimps, and the other four went back into the hotel.

"My advice to you," said the captain, "is next time don't get involved."

From the yellow Cadillac the girl called, "Thank you."

Durk thanked the newsboy on the corner who had called in the radio cars, then walked home and began to return the telephone calls that his wife had taken for him that day —there were always dozens of them. Then perhaps he began to cook himself an elaborate omelet. Durk was something of a gourmet, and a better than average cook, and, slim as he was, he could find an outlet from frustration in food.

Durk, still unknown, began to cultivate informants. This meant that he was nice to his prisoners. They would look at him in fear, expecting to be abused—if not beaten to a pulp—and Durk would say, "You didn't give me a hard time. The food in jail stinks. Come on, I'll take you out to dinner. You can have a last meal on me. But if you try anything, you prick, I'll shoot you."

One prisoner, whom Durk treated to a Chinese dinner, responded by giving information on two homicides, eight muggings, and by revealing the location of a stash of stolen IBM machines.

On occasion, Durk would give an informant money out of his own pocket, saying, "That's so you don't do anything to get busted tonight, because I need you tomorrow." One informant, temporarily out of prison, came to Durk looking for a job. Durk told him, "I can get you a fee if you will lecture to my class at N.Y.U. All you have to do is tell them what life is like for a guy like you." He did not add, "who is, by profession, a vicious mugger." He made sure the mugger understood that if he lied, Durk would see to it that they didn't pay him anything.

It was safe to say that the ambition of every patrolman in the New York Police Department, or any other police department, was to become a detective. In New York, detectives got to carry a gold shield, instead of a silver one. A third grade detective was paid about $1500 per year more than a patrolman, a second grade detective received sergeant's pay, and the pay of a first grade detective was equal to that of a lieutenant. Detectives, of course, operated in civilian clothes, and their prestige, compared to that of a patrolman, was enormous. Even the best patrolmen had to wait many years to be made detectives, and most patrolmen vainly waited out their entire careers. But Durk was a detective within three years of going out onto the street, and within six years he was a sergeant.

Durk's wife, Arlene, a graduate of Barnard College and the Columbia School of Social Work, was a psychiatric caseworker. They lived in a West Side apartment. One wall was floor to ceiling with books on psychology, economics, urban affairs, politics. The complete works of Sigmund Freud took up part of a shelf. Durk subcribed to *Commentary, The Public Interest, The American Scholar,* and he once wrote an article for the *Atlantic.* In this apartment the phone rang all day, and sometimes all night, for Durk was a cop, was he not, and all his friends and neighbors knew it. Eventually Durk ordered a phone replete with buttons, to handle multiple incoming calls and outgoing calls at once.

Arlene tried to screen these calls, but Durk accepted nearly all of them.

"David, my wife's maid hasn't shown up today."

"Yes?"

"Well, my wife is very fond of her, you know, and, well, er, maybe some foul play has occurred."

"Foul play?"

"Well, it's possible that her lover has killed her."

"I'll see what I can find out."

An hour later the phone rang again. "Er, David, she just came in."

One time the phone rang at 3 A.M. It was a friend who wanted to report that he was locked inside a garage, and this was his last dime. What should he do? Could the police or David get him out of the garage?

There were calls from Durk's informants. A number of times Durk would agree to meet an informant on a deserted street in the middle of the night. He knew well enough the danger; perhaps the informant was setting him up. Sometimes he paced his apartment. Should he go? Of course he always went. One night, back in the Durk apartment, it became 2:30 A.M., with no word from David, and

Arlene paced the floor talking to herself. She knew the phone number of another cop who lived nearby and was a close friend. She could call him, but she would wake his wife too. She knew he'd be very understanding. She knew he'd come right over. But did she have the right to call and wake him? If she called, David would be furious with her. At 2:45 in the morning, David walked in the door and said, "What's the matter with you?"

The Durks had moved in liberal intellectual circles before David became a cop, and now they began to be invited to all the ultra chic parties. Within a few minutes of entering rooms crowded with people he did not know, Durk was usually able to assign roles to everyone: "That's the way the hostesses planned the parties. This guy was the psychiatrist. That guy was the poet. I was the cop. I went to a literary critic's house for a dinner party, and Robert Lowell was there." Durk was one of the few cops in the city who knew any literary critics, or that Lowell was considered the poet laureate of America. "When Lowell heard I was a cop, he literally started to twitch, like I was the enemy."

Always at these parties, people would come forward who wished to complain about their aches and pains with regard to the criminal justice system in New York.

"Oh, I must tell you about my burglary."

Durk understood how a doctor felt when asked to look down someone's throat at a dinner party.

Then there were the gun nuts.

"I favor a shoulder holster myself," a psychiatrist said.

"You gotta be kidding," said Durk.

"I'm not putting you on, I love guns."

"You're really amazing."

"I have a friend in Texas. There they *really* carry guns. The first night I had my gun, I shot out the radiator. For the longest while they wouldn't give me a gun permit. I don't know why; I'm a very stable man."

And always there were the liberals who, learning that Durk was a cop, turned hostile. This was where Durk evolved the arguments which he would later use to recruit students for the police department.

"Well, how do you justify your existence, friend? You only have one life. What are you doing with it? You think you're doing wonderful things, that is to say, you're making money. You long ago sold your soul for a certain life style. You say you're interested in true justice? You say you're a liberal? Well this is what liberalism comes down to. What are you contributing to society?"

David Durk by nature was a priest, and his role was to preach the conversion of unbelievers. The New York Police Department was oriented toward organized religion; there were more official chaplains than deputy commissioners, and every single police ceremony began and ended with a formal invocation by one or more of the several chaplains inevitably on hand. The Police Department contained also a great number of so-called line organizations, and although some of these were based solely on rank (the Sergeants' Benevolent Association, the Detectives' Endowment Association, etc.) or on national origin (the Steuben Society, the Hispanic Society, etc.), a number of others were based on religion; and the biggest of these by far was the Holy Name Society, whose annual communion breakfast some years drew 4,000 or more cops. Cops tended to be religious men, who grew up in religious families; many of them had sisters and brothers scattered throughout the Archdiocese as priests and nuns. For instance, Patrick Murphy, who had resigned from the Department to accept a job in Washington just as Durk and Serpico entered plainclothes school in 1966—and who would be police commissioner when the Knapp Commission came crashing down around all their heads in 1971—had been one of eight children; three of the boys became cops, two of the girls entered the convent.

And so priests were as normal in and around the New York Police Department as on the campus of a Jesuit University. Yet David Durk, the Jewish college boy, often seemed more priest than any of them. Serpico was his acolyte.

4 / Plainclothes

One day I asked Serpico if he had ever shot anyone, and he launched into a speech about young cops who made good arrests, only to have credit for those arrests stolen from them by the detectives in their own precincts. This had happened to him a number of times in the early days; he would bring someone into the station house in handcuffs, and the detectives would write up the arrest as their own.

Then he told the following story.

"On this particular night I was on post on the borderline between two precincts, and a man came running over to me and asked could I please help him, because his place was being burglarized. So I left my precinct and I went into the next precinct.

"I looked in through the window and I could actually see this guy still burglarizing the apartment. The window to another room was open, so I went in through the window, and he must have heard me because he switched the lights out in the room he was in. I got involved in a struggle with him, and he hit me with this wrought-iron candlestick holder. He knocked me down and he escaped out the back window. It was in the back alley. Automatically I pulled my revolver out, and I fired. And I heard him sort of go 'oooh' and then I didn't see him anymore.

"I ran around the corner rather than go over fences, because it was dark and there were a number of fences there; and when I went completely around the block, all I saw was this blood, and there was some other substance on the floor there, and I couldn't find him.

"That night it was soon time to go to the precinct because it was the end of my tour, and I was waiting on the line to sign out, and my fellow officers were saying things like 'I thought you were supposed to be such a good shot, and here you let one get away.' And another guy said, 'Yeah, you're fooling around in another precinct and there's a guy upstairs that got his balls cut off. Some guy robbed him. How come you let that happen on your post?'

"So I immediately ran upstairs and there was the perpetrator, the guy I had been struggling with. He was sitting on the floor with his groin just hanging out.

"I said, 'That's the guy. That's the guy I was struggling with.'

"They said, 'So that's the story. He was trying to tell us that somebody robbed him and without any reason ripped his groin out.'

"So they said. 'Well, now we know the story. Give us a little salt. We'll fix him.'

"They were going to salt his groin for him, in the raw.

"I immediately called up the other precinct, because the detectives had responded there, and I had fired my shot, and they always make an investigation when shots are fired, and the detectives from that precinct responded immediately, and they said, 'This guy—we have a warrant for his arrest.'

"I said, 'What for?'

"They said, 'He's wanted for rape.'

"And then one guy said, 'Well, he won't be raping anybody anymore.'

"I said I was going in and take off my coat and stuff, because I was sort of tired and sweaty; and when I came back in the squad room, the guy was gone; the detectives from the other precinct had actually kidnapped him on me, and I never got credit for arresting him for the crime.

"That was the first and last time I shot anybody. When I first saw where my shot had hit the guy I felt pretty bad, but when I heard what he was wanted for I thought it was poetic justice."

After more than six years on the street in uniform, Serpico was sent to plainclothes school, and it was there that he met David Durk, who had been assigned to the same class. The course lasted a month. These were eight-hour days replete with a lunch break and coffee breaks, during which the students, who had been collected from units all over the city, got to know each other.

Corruption was on everybody's mind, because once the course had ended, most of the cops in attendance would be assigned to the public morals division, which, as its name implied, had jurisdiction over the enforcement of those laws (many of them enacted generations ago, or even a century ago) designed to safeguard public morality.

In New York this meant principally gambling enforcement, and it was possible for a plainclothesman assigned to gambling enforcement to earn $1000 a month or more, over and above his police pay. This was no secret and conversations about it were frequent, not only in plainclothes school but everywhere policemen congregated. There were cops who took gambling graft and those who didn't. There were those who thought gambling graft amusing, or unimportant, or exaggerated, or negligible, or deplorable; and there were those like Durk and Serpico, talking to each other between classes, who were fanatically opposed.

Selection to plainclothes school was the first step toward the detective division and therefore an enviable assignment on that ground alone. Detectives were thought to have all kinds of power they didn't have. Detectives in fact did not have any special power at all. They were not superior officers. They bossed nobody. Technically even a first grade detective was only a patrolman designated by the police commissioner to act as a detective and to receive special pay for it, and unlike the "hard" civil service ranks of sergeant, lieutenant, and captain, which were guaranteed by law, any detective could be busted back to uniform on a moment's notice without any formal charges being filed. Nonetheless, their role was admired and envied. Cops wanted to become detectives.

The plainclothes classes were fascinating enough. Patrolmen were taught, among other tricks, how to move in close to an operation—it was sound police practice to saunter down a suspicious alley sipping a container of hot coffee, or to enter a suspect bar wearing bedroom slippers and leading a poodle. This immediately established one as being from the neighborhood. In addition, new plainclothesmen were instructed in the intricate laws that it would now be their principal duty to enforce. In addition to the gambling laws, these included laws governing prostitution, unlicensed bars, and narcotics.

At no time were the cops instructed in the difference between clean money and dirty money, for the official position of the Police Department had always been that all graft was dirty. However, the feeling of the cops themselves was beginning to change, or perhaps it already had changed, and the distinction between clean and dirty graft was dying out. To take money from pimps or whores was no longer considered very dirty, and there were those who could defend even graft paid by narcotics pushers who wanted to avoid arrests, and/or the confiscation of their fabulously valuable merchandise. On the subject of gambling laws and unlicensed liquor laws, there never had been any question as far as general police morality was concerned: this money was clean.

The reason it was clean was that every cop in New York realized that the citizens he served did not want the gambling laws enforced. The Police Department had something like 600 men assigned solely to the enforcement of the gambling laws. The Department had men on rooftops, men on fire escapes, men peering down through skylights—and Serpico would soon be one of these—whose sole function was to arrest professional bookies or professional policy operators, or the youths and housewives and derelicts who worked as numbers runners in their communities. In addition, in every precinct station house in the city there were bulletin boards in the back room to which were pinned the photos and vital statistics of every known gambler who operated in that precinct. There were no similar bulletin boards bearing the photos of prominent muggers, robbers, or rapists. Known gamblers, KG's, as the cops called them, would have seemed to any outside observer the principal quarry of every cop in the city. The cops were pouring gambling arrests toward the court system at the rate of about 10,000 cases per year. Only about a third of these defendants were ever convicted, and most years less than 100 defendants were sentenced to short prison terms seldom exceding three months. There were known gamblers operating out of the same store front for nearly 30 years. There were known gamblers who had been arrested over 100 times, but who were still doing business.

In other words, to the young cop joining the police force, the number one priority of the department often seemed the suppression of gambling. A great many eager young cops rushed to arrest every KG they saw, only to find that the district attorneys were not going to prosecute these people, or that if the DA's did prosecute, the courts would impose ludicrous sentences. The young cops' frustration too often blossomed fast. After only a year or two on the job, he was an old cop, and the next time a KG offered to put him on the pad—that is, to guarantee regular payoffs—the cop possibly said to himself, "What the hell."

And so the system had perpetuated itself for decades.

It was easy enough for the cop on the beat to justify letting the gamblers operate in peace. After all, the gamblers hurt nobody. If the two fanatics, Durk and Serpico, saw graft as wrong anywhere and always, this was principally because it corrupted a cop's respect for himself and his job, and because moral muscle, once weakened, too often couldn't stand up to any pressure at all. Too many cops who had taken money to permit gambling could not be relied upon to refuse money from the same or other persons who were now dealing in narcotics.

Serpico was now an undercover man, and he began to grow his bushy black beard. In the evenings, Durk and Serpico would walk from the Police Academy up to 23rd Street together to catch the crosstown bus. As patrolmen they could ride free by showing their shields. Durk would leap aboard with his shield openly displayed. Serpico, his shield cupped so that only the bus driver could see it, would even pretend to drop money in the box, before slipping his shield covertly into his pocket. He would then upbraid Durk.

"There may be a wrong guy on this bus. How do you know who's on this bus? You may have just blown your cover."

Durk and Serpico stopped off at a shop where Serpico's motorcycle was being repaired. Serpico had already been clipped there once, and had asked Durk to come with him this time.

"Show the guy your shield," suggested Durk.

"What for?" asked Serpico.

"Because if he knows you're a cop, maybe he won't screw you on the price."

Serpico refused to do this.

"Why did you ask me to come with you, anyway?" asked Durk, and he walked over to the repairman and flashed his shield.

Serpico was furious. "That's corruption too, Durk," said Serpico.

Upon graduation Serpico was assigned to public morals enforcement, working out of the 90th Precinct in Brooklyn. Durk, the elite cop, was soon assigned to the elite Department of Investigation Squad, and within six months he was a detective. The Department of Investigation was staffed by about 20 detectives, and five or six civilian investigators; their job was to investigate corrupt people or practices in any and all city departments. They investigated backgrounds of nominees to high city office. They investigated possible kickbacks on contracts. They investigated building inspectors, sanitation inspectors, and the like. They had the authority to investigate corruption within the Police Department too, but this had rarely been exercised. At first the job seemed tailor-made for the eloquent Durk. As his immediate superior, Lieutenant Lawrence Dempsey, said, "People see something wrong, but don't want to testify. They fear for their lives or their jobs. Most people don't relate too well to cops, but very often they didn't even know David was a cop, and when they found out, a lot of them didn't believe it. David knew how to persuade such people to commit themselves, to perform their civic duties. David had really uncommon dedication. He was an aggressive officer; his honesty was without question. His personal bravery was also without question."

But the job's enchantment did not last. Durk wanted to nail crooked judges and district attorneys. Instead he worked on petty probes. A traffic department sign painter was accused of having painted his house with two gallons of stolen yellow traffic paint. Durk was sent to Yonkers to chip paint samples off the wall for the police lab to analyze; the painter was brought in, questioned, forced to sign a statement, and reduced to tears. But his job and pension were saved when Durk angrily told the attorney involved that if this was the way the game was to be played, Durk would do his best to lock up Department of Investigation attorneys who took home legal pads and pencils.

Another time, a building inspector was alleged to have accepted $10 three years before. Durk was sent out to interview an 82-year-old senile man in Coney Island whose wife was threatening to beat him up while Durk interviewed him. "That case got a big number, files, and reports," Durk later noted disgustedly.

There had to be more to corruption investigations than this. And corruption had to be extirpated from the Police

Department that Durk loved. The city needed scrupulously honest cops, and the cops needed to be given their honor back.

But nobody was doing anything.

Meanwhile, Serpico, a plainclothesman at last, found himself being offered money. During six years in uniform he had heard all the rumors. He now knew they were true. Looking around him, he had no idea who was accepting the payoffs and who wasn't.

No plainclothesman was offered money the first day he turned up in his new precinct. Graft was, after all, illegal. Therefore, a useful length of time was allowed to pass before the newcomer was offered his share of the monthly pad. It might be one month or three months, or even longer. The approach, when at last it was judged that the newcomer could be trusted, usually was made by whichever cop knew him best, on the grounds that however righteous the newcomer might turn out to be, he wouldn't turn in a friend. In Serpico's case, nearly six months went by before another plainclothesman handed Serpico an envelope containing $300 and said it was from a gambler known as Jewish Max.

Serpico didn't know whom he could trust, or where to go.

So he went straight to David Durk.

It was the case Durk had been waiting for. At last he had something to work with.

Durk took Serpico first to Captain Philip Foran, who at that time headed the Department of Investigation Squad. Foran, after hearing Serpico out, remarked that unless Serpico wanted to end up at the bottom of the East River, he should keep his mouth shut. Durk took Serpico to Jay Kriegel, right-hand man to the Mayor. Durk counted Kriegel, who had also gone to Amherst, a friend; they knew each other well. It was Sunday. Kriegel had his feet on his desk in his office in the basement of City Hall. Kriegel jotted down what Durk and Serpico hoped were notes. He said he had heard such allegations but had never before known a policeman to come forward with actual evidence. Kriegel then talked of priorities. It was important not to upset the police. Possibly the Mayor should sit down with Durk, Serpico, and one or two others and discuss police corruption face-to-face.

But the months went by and nothing was done.

Serpico gave the $300 back to his sergeant, because he didn't know what else to do with it.

"I don't need the money and I don't want to get involved," said Serpico. The sergeant thanked him, removed the money from the envelope, and rammed it in his pocket.

Presently, Serpico was transferred to a plainclothes squad in the Bronx, where he found corruption even more widespread than in Brooklyn.

Via Inspector Neal Behan, Serpico's tale was brought before John Walsh, First Deputy Commissioner, the number two man in the Police Department, whose office controlled investigations into internal corruption.

But more months went by and still nothing happened. Serpico wanted to quit; the system was too corrupt.

Durk insisted, "If you dare to test the system, you win either way. You either force it to respond, or you expose it."

Durk took Serpico to see Arnold Fraiman, Commissioner of Investigation. Fraiman seemed interested, and had several schemes. A surveillance truck might be bugged, or Serpico himself might wear a recording device. But again nothing was done. Durk would walk into Fraiman's office and attempt to talk to him on the subject. Fraiman would pick up his binoculars, spin his chair around, and peer out the window at the boats going by in the river. This meant that the interview was over. Once Fraiman dismissed Durk's arguments, saying, "Serpico's a psycho."

Durk dragged Serpico everywhere. It was Durk's belief that what Serpico had was a normal small-time police corruption story. What made it into something special was the fact that they couldn't get anybody to act on it. They went to Burton Roberts, District Attorney of the Bronx. After several meetings, Roberts suggested a grand jury probe, if Serpico would agree to testify against eight fellow policemen. Serpico agreed.

Roberts at this time had 60 or 70 assistant district attorneys working for him and about the same number of New York City policemen and detectives assigned to him as investigators. Some of these people were ordered to work actively on the Serpico case, meaning that the secret was out, it could not be kept. Serpico stood revealed as willing to send other policemen to jail, Durk as the moral force behind him. To an armed hothead, both might seem equally guilty, equally attractive as targets.

Durk went to David Burnham, the police reporter on *The New York Times.* "This is going to sound like a B-movie," Durk said. "But if anything should happen to me, there is certain information I want you to have."

And Durk laid out for Burnham not only all of the evidence that Serpico would put forth to the grand jury but also all additional names, dates, and places, much of it detailing narcotics corruption in Harlem, which Durk had collected in the past two years. Burham took this information down and locked it away.

On the night before Serpico was to testify, he was frightened. While he was out of the room, Durk said to District Attorney Roberts and his people, "Frank's doing this for you; now what are you going to do to protect Frank?"

Someone answered, "He's got a gun, hasn't he?" Someone else suggested that Serpico stay in Manhattan or the Bronx, and then no matter what happened, even if he had to kill somebody, they could control who had access to the facts of the case and the identities of the people involved.

As the trial neared, Serpico became convinced he was being followed.

Durk began to tail him down dark streets to prove that Serpico's fears were imaginary.

Eight cops were indicted.

An assistant district attorney now informed Serpico that he had best shave off his beard. Here were eight clean-cut police officers about to go on trial, and the only witnesses against them were some Puerto Rican policy runners and Frank Serpico, beard and all.

"It really galled me," said Serpico. "What he was saying was that the only police witness was this freak with all this hair on his face. A guy like that must hate the law and was probably a revolutionary besides."

A day later Serpico phoned the DA and admitted that the idea of shaving had some merit.

"Great, Frank."

"But don't expect too much."

Serpico turned up the next day with his beard trimmed down to a goatee and huge mutton chops.

"Christ, come on, come on," said the DA.

Serpico appeared on the stand clean-shaven. "But it really galled me, this idea that I could tell the truth better without my beard."

There were in fact a number of trials, and they went on for a long time. The immediate results did not impress Serpico very much: two cops convicted, two sentenced after pleading guilty, three acquitted, one case pending. Durk was not too impressed either. Why was nobody questioning higher-ups? Why was nobody indicting the system itself, which made such large-scale corruption possible?

Durk continued to badger Commissioner Fraiman and Jay Kriegel, the only important officials to whom he had ready access, but nothing happened. He talked to Burnham and to other reporters he knew, but no exposés appeared in print. The trials in the Bronx had partially drained the abscess, and people were patting Durk and Serpico on the back, telling them that the patient looked fine now. Durk kept pressuring Kriegel. Kriegel replied that the Mayor was up for reelection and that first priority at this time must go to that.

5 / Things Are Different Because I'm There

Durk's crusade against police corruption apparently ended there. Frustrated, he now decided to mount a different crusade entirely, for his Justice Department grant had just come through, and he began rushing from one college campus to another urging college seniors to take the test for the New York City Police Department.

"You're trying to blur the face of the enemy," shouted a 22-year-old youth at N.Y.U. "The real role of the police is to beat up kids with long hair. The system has its own momentum, which perpetuates itself; and if we go in they will find some way to screw us. And as for you, you'll never get promoted. If they're on to what you're saying here today, forget it."

"Well, I've been promoted," Durk shouted back. "It's a

safe, comforting feeling to believe you can do nothing. But either you are going to do it, or nobody's going to do it. Maybe you plan to join some conglomerate, planning once you get to the top to throw off your mask, saying, 'Shazam, it's me, good guy.' But sometimes you find the mask fuses with your face."

Students accused him of being a lone crusader.

"There are other guys in the department who feel as I do. Not many. We're not even a significant minority. If you come in, there will be more. You can create another model on the street. You can show the ordinary cop that it's not unmanly to be concerned, to show compassion."

At Harvard a 25-year-old divinity student asked, "What heat are you getting? Maybe you're on your way out, and this is your way of going out."

The answer was that Durk had been allowed a leave of absence. Otherwise the Police Department gave him no help whatsoever. Nor did the Lindsay administration.

The highest cop who would talk to me of Durk officially was a Captain Paul Glazer in the office of public information. Later Glazer would serve as my chief of staff, but at this time we had never met. "We don't oppose Durk's idea," Glazer told me. "We don't oppose it."

Durk wanted more than that, and he had a number of meetings at police headquarters but never succeeded in winning the endorsement of anybody.

Soon Durk had more than 200 college seniors panting to take the entrance examination for the New York Police Department; and in response to an official request from Harvard, the department did agree to give its next exam there. But this examination was later canceled.

Those students who had taken and passed the earlier exam faced a wait of at least 18 months. Qualifications for the police force in New York were so low, and the pay so relatively high, that 48,292 men had applied the year before for 3137 appointments. Of these, 24,640 had taken the test and 14,224 had passed it. As a result the waiting list for appointments contained at this time about 9000 names, and the Civil Service laws prevented any man, whatever his qualifications, from being shoved in front of those at the head of the line. A New York cop was required to be five foot seven, have good vision, and a high school equivalency certificate, and that's about all. "His motivation," Durk kept telling the college boys, "is not a factor, and that's scary."

Washington was expanding its force by 1300 men at this time. Durk went down there to see if they would accept his college boys, and they did in fact take in a number; but the officials that Durk confronted were highly suspicious of him personally. I interviewed some of these people myself. One, the then Director of Personnel, said, "We're not sure of Durk's motives. If Durk's got these kids all turned on, he needs a place where he can put them. I would be very worried that maybe he's trying to infiltrate the force here."

Durk was telling the students about crime and criminals in words they had never heard used quite that way before.

"It's nice to believe that everybody was born to be a beautiful fellow," he would tell them. "But at any given moment in time, it isn't so." He spoke of "the low threshold of the poor, the glorious release of inhibitions" when a poor and downtrodden individual committed a crime of violence.

"The average cop believes that the public can hurt you. Don't get involved. But you college guys won't be so vulnerable. You can get a better paying job any time. The average cop would hesitate to take action against the guy wearing a cashmere coat or sitting in a Cadillac. But you and I know those things don't mean anything. One time I locked up a landlord, and the diamond on his pinky was twitching.

"Imagine having good-guy observers in the station house 24 hours a day. You're going to come out and open your mouths, and you're going to have credibility. You're also going to discover that it's a heady feeling to be able to say to yourself, 'Things are different because I'm there.'"

At N.Y.U. a 22-year-old student said, "Name me a cop who's ever read Oscar Lewis. It's scary. When I came in here today, I knew what I wanted to be when I grew up." He gave his name and phone number to Durk, adding, "When you call, don't tell my mother who you are."

Meanwhile, two other policemen in Brooklyn were shaking down Serpico's brother, who kept his little grocery opened on Sundays. As Serpico said at the time, "Everybody knows that any store that's open on Sundays has to make a donation to the local precinct if they wish to remain open without being harassed."

The two cops demanded two dollars per Sunday from Serpico's brother. "Hey," said the grocer, "my brother's a cop."

"I don't give a crap who you have for a cop," explained the two police officers. "You'll pay like anybody else, and we don't have to kiss your ass." So they gave him a summons and walked out. The brother had violated no ordinance; it was not against the law to open on Sundays, or even to sell bread and milk and such. The violation was to sell canned goods and other nonperishable items.

"So I went to Brooklyn to have a talk with them," said Serpico. "They were quite arrogant."

What he did was to put on his lederhosen, stuff a tape recorder into his knapsack along with his guns, and to pedal his bicycle across the Brooklyn Bridge to the precinct house.

"I don't care who you are," Serpico was told. "Your brother will pay just like everybody else, or he'll get a summons every Sunday." And the cop began explaining which cops were in on the racket and which weren't—most weren't, in fact, and some of these were causing trouble by giving summonses to stores that had paid their protection money.

After a departmental trial both cops were dismissed, and later they were indicted.

The way most of New York's 32,000 cops saw this incident was that Serpico had locked up two brother officers over two dollars.

It was this precinct that later sent men to stand guard outside his hospital room.

6 / Birth of the Knapp Commission

Durk's abortive crusade to rid the Police Department of corruption had not hurt Durk, who had already been a detective and who soon took and passed the Civil Service exam for sergeant, but it had earned his acolyte Serpico the undying hatred of most cops. Serpico was still a patrolman, and would remain so, and everyone knew why.

Serpico traveled with a succession of girlfriends, the latest a lovely young stewardess; but Durk had a wife and two beautiful daughters, and Serpico loved to be invited to Durk's house where he would clown around with the little girls and make them laugh. He treated Arlene with respect, almost with awe, and invariably got into an argument with David before the evening ended.

Serpico was a college graduate too—he earned a B.S. degree from City College long after he became a cop—but City College was not Amherst. The two men were the same age, sure, but Serpico's parents still spoke with Italian accents and he was somewhat ashamed of them. Still, he had taken Durk out to Brooklyn to meet them. One day when they were returning to Manhattan, they had interrupted a street robbery. "There we were," Durk remembered. "We had these two guys up against the wall, each of us with his gun to a guy's head, and suddenly we looked across at each other, and both of us sort of grinned at each other." It was a special moment, which neither ever mentioned to the other afterward.

There was a time when Durk was invited to address a group in another city. He brought Serpico along. Durk was unarmed, Serpico was wearing all his guns, including the 14-shot automatic which Durk always referred to somewhat derisively as "Serpico's big gun." It had great penetrating power, Serpico claimed, and he was always entering dangerous places and situations. Furthermore, there wasn't a cop in the city who liked Frank, and every single one carried a gun.

Durk began telling people that the real reason Serpico carried all those guns was because it turned on girls, and that most times Serpico allowed the girls to imagine that he was not a cop but a gangster.

But Durk also told me once that if he were in charge, his first act would be to make Frank Serpico a first grade detective with city-wide jurisdiction, and turn him loose.

The priest now returned to the scene of his first crusade,

police corruption—Durk went back to David Burnham of *The New York Times*. Would the *Times* have the guts to print Durk's view of police corruption? Durk must have seemed far more formidable to Burnham and the *Times'* editors, and his story more substantial, than when he had first told it to Burnham almost two years before. The interviews which now began lasted over a period of months, and Durk brought in Serpico, Inspector Delise, and two other cops to substantiate his charges and to add their own.

Burnham, 37, was something of a priest himself—a small, baldish, tightly wired former paratrooper, who had later worked for the President's Crime Commission as a public relations officer. It was said of Burnham that he had no sense of humor, that he tended to see things in black and white (mostly black), that he believed the worst of every man—and that he was ferociously honest. He tended to check the facts of his stories over and over again; and if this meant squeezing the juice out of them, too bad. He would hold a story back for weeks to get it right. Burnham introduced Durk to Arthur Gelb, 45, metropolitan editor of the *Times*. Gelb was shocked to hear Durk's story, and he cautioned Burnham to check it out carefully. Burnham would have done this in any case, for it was the way he worked.

Before long it seemed that Durk and Serpico were living permanently in Gelb's small office on the third floor. Durk, tall and dark, his black hair already turning gray, wore conservative Brooks Brothers suits and button-down shirts. Serpico wore mod clothes and a wild head of hair. His beard, one *Times* man later reported, was as shaggy as a bird's nest. As the editors and reporters talked to him, their eyes kept turning involuntarily to the automatic jammed like a cutlass into Serpico's belt. Durk didn't look like a cop; he looked—and spoke—like a lawyer. Serpico didn't look like a cop, either. He looked like a pirate.

Other editors were brought in to grill Durk, Serpico, Delise, and the two other cops. At last Gelb and Burnham brought in the managing editor, A. M. Rosenthal. It was Rosenthal who gave the official go-ahead. Burnham would write a three-part exposé of police corruption.

All through February, March, and April the interviews

had continued. Paranoia had set in. Serpico was convinced that his telephone was tapped. So was Burnham. Durk was sure his wasn't, or was he? The three of them began to start telephone conversations talking in code. Sometimes Serpico would make an appointment, and then not show up, convinced that if he reported to the rendezvous point he would be killed.

The project stayed secret for most of the three months. But by late in April, word was all over town, and Mayor Lindsay, in the perfect tradition of public servants, announced the appointment of his own special committee to investigate police corruption. This would take the sting out of the *Times* exposé when it finally appeared. The Mayor would be able to announce casually, "Oh yes, we've already taken care of that."

The Mayor's committee was called the Rankin Committee, after J. Lee Rankin, the corporation counsel of the City of New York, a public official; and it included, among others, the incumbent Police Commissioner, Howard Leary. It was formed on Thursday, April 23, 1970. Burnham's exposé was still not ready, but Gelb summoned him, for the *Times* would have to go with the story at once. Two other reporters and David Durk helped Burnham hammer his story into final shape. It was published in the Saturday morning *New York Times*. As a courtesy, Gelb had sent copies of the story over to the Mayor's office on Friday afternoon, neatly trapping the Mayor into making comments that could be reported alongside Burnham's exposé in the Saturday morning paper.

"This government must root out corruption and wrongdoing with every means at its command," Mr. Lindsay said, after he had met for 90 minutes with the city's top law enforcement officials, including seven high-ranking police officers. Lindsay added that his Rankin Committee would look into all the allegations contained in the *Times* survey and would recommend appropriate action.

Burnham's story contained this paragraph: "The names of the policemen who discussed corruption with the *Times* are being withheld to protect them from possible reprisals." That is, neither Durk nor Serpico were anywhere mentioned by name. However, Fraiman, by then a state supreme court justice, was accused of refusing to look into charges that Bronx gamblers were paying policemen between $800 and $1000 a month: "Mr. Fraiman learned about the case during a three-hour conversation with two policemen in his Park Avenue apartment on May 30th, 1967."

Kriegel, still Mayor Lindsay's staff assistant for law enforcement, was accused of having told a policeman early in 1968 that the administration "could not act on charges of police corruption because it did not want to upset the police during the possibly turbulent summer ahead."

Mayor Lindsay's formal statement continued: "Police Commissioner Leary has advised me that many of the allegations in this story came from one particular patrolman." The heat was on, and it was clear that Lindsay, Leary, Fraiman, Kriegel and the rest had chosen to aim the blame in one direction only: Serpico.

Justice Fraiman immediately issued an angry statement: "The information this individual furnished about police corruption was extremely general in nature. No specifics ever were given."

As a patrolman on active duty, Serpico looked like an easy target. Although the fine hand of David Durk could be discerned in the background, Durk was presently on leave of absence. His college recruiting scheme had received a great deal of publicity, and he must have seemed, for the moment, invulnerable.

Burnham's story outlined in some detail organized gambling corruption, the single most regular and most lucrative source of police graft. But Burnham also described many other areas of corruption. The story closed with this quote by a Brooklyn policeman: "I remember one time we went on a call. A girl had tried to commit suicide by taking an overdose of pills. Three patrol cars responded, and there were six of us standing around this little one-room apartment, the girl lying there, just breathing. One of the guys walked over to her dresser and scooped up a large handful of subway tokens and dropped them in his pocket. No one said a word. It killed me, but there was nothing to do. There was no sense telling the sergeant, because he was part of the club."

This exposé was like a basketball dropped from a great height, for it rebounded nearly as high the second day, and again on the third. Burnham's second-day story concentrated mostly on gambling payoffs, but on Monday he went where many observers felt that the real malaise lay: the effects of police corruption on the morale of policemen. How could cops be proud and dedicated and honorable men when, as the cops themselves put it, they knew the job wasn't on the level?

The newly formed Rankin Committee every member of which owed primary political allegiance to the Lindsay administration, impressed nobody; and within a month it had voted itself out of existence, recommending that the Mayor appoint an "independent" commission to investigate alleged police corruption. His hand forced, the Mayor now did so.

To head the new commission Mayor Lindsay appointed Percy Whitman Knapp, a mild-mannered, 61-year-old Wall Street lawyer. Knapp said, "It's one of these jobs that makes you want to say no just because it's so tremendous." Knapp would have to get to know the four fellow members of his commission, then figure out how much money he needed, then win a pledge of that money, $325,000, from the city council, then win six months of subpoena power for his commission, then find a chief counsel, and then collect a staff of agents and lawyers and at last start the investigation.

For a while it was not clear whether the Knapp Commission was serious, much less competent. First the Board of Estimate failed to vote any funds at all and had to be reconvened the next day by the Mayor, who forced through the money allocation on a simple majority vote under altered parliamentary circumstances. After that, a group of police sergeants announced that they would institute suits against the use of the Commission's subpoena power. Which meant that although the Commission could subpoena police witnesses, they weren't going to appear until the courts ordered them to, and this wasn't going to occur for months.

Knapp hired Michael Armstrong, a corporate lawyer, as chief counsel; and it was Armstrong, a good-looking, well-educated tough guy, who now began to run the show. It was Armstrong's idea to recruit undercover agents from the Police Department's own ranks and send them out into the city to entrap crooked cops. The Police Department, and especially Commissioner Leary, did not like any of this. *The New York Times* was in possession of a tape-recorded conversation between Supervising Assistant Chief Inspector Joseph McGovern, the three-star chief in charge of investigating internal corruption, and a second police officer. Asked what his unit had accomplished, McGovern replied proudly, "I think I have done a damn good job protecting the Commissioner against the onslaughts of outside agencies." It was also known that four years before, when the President's Commission on Law Enforcement and Administration of Justice wanted to conduct corruption surveys in the slums of New York, Chicago and Washington, Leary had refused to cooperate, and Boston was later chosen to replace New York.

For five or six weeks Leary had complained to Lindsay regularly about the Knapp Commission. It was Leary's belief that any outside corruption investigation would smear the Police Department with unsubstantiated allegations of widespread corruption. "It would be McCarthyism all over again," Leary said. But Lindsay was stuck with the Knapp Commission now, and could do nothing.

So one day Howard Leary walked away from his desk and did not come back. One Sunday the story broke. Howard Leary had resigned. There was no letter of resignation from Leary, who had already been gone several days; no public statement of any kind. He simply wasn't there anymore. Lindsay released a letter extolling Leary's qualities and announcing that he would go down in history as one of the great police commissioners, and that was that. Three days later Howard Leary sailed to Europe. Three days after that, Patrick V. Murphy, former New York patrolman, now Police Commissioner of Detroit, appeared at a press conference with Mayor Lindsay and was presented to the citizens of New York as Howard Leary's successor. Murphy said all the right things: He was against corruption; rooting it out of the New York Police Department would be the number one goal of his administration.

Burnham's exposé was submitted for all the journalism

prizes, and he would win a number of them in the months to come, though not the Pulitzer he coveted and perhaps deserved. There was some talk that Serpico should be rewarded too, and some pressure exerted to make him a detective. But he stayed a patrolman. Serpico would never get the gold shield while he was Commissioner, Leary had remarked privately, for Serpico had embarrassed the Department. But now a new man was Police Commissioner.

Still no gold shield for Frank Serpico.

I went to see him. He lived in a tiny, cluttered, dirty apartment in Greenwich Village. The place was as dark and as crowded as a closet, and he did not like to invite friends there. He shared the place with two dogs, one of them an enormous English sheep dog, two gurgling goldfish bowls, and sometimes a girl. A real Bohemian pad.

There was a sleeping alcove barely bigger than the bed, and a bathroom; and the main room (which contained a kind of kitchen in one corner) measured in all about fourteen feet by twelve. A smallish room, it contained, in addition to the animals and fishes, a sofa, one armchair, four tables, a bicycle, a shopping cart, a TV set on a coffee table, and a desk with shelves above it; on the floor two stacks of records, one of them 20 inches high, the other 16, a good-sized cardboard box, a suitcase, a camel saddle, a hi-fi, bookshelves full of books, a firescreen and fire tools in front of a fireplace with ashes in it. A guitar leaned against one wall. The telephone on a long cord obstructed access to the middle of the floor. Almost no light came through the two grimy windows. On the mantel were a tall antique clock, an African mask, an antique fowling piece, and a pair of horns from a long-dead longhorn steer. On one wall was an enormous painting of a dreamlike nude, and a kind of Chinese screen blocked off the view of the kitchen sink.

Serpico seemed closed in on himself during this period, more and more a loner. So far, he had not received any public applause whatsoever. As he saw it now, Durk had grabbed all the headlines, all the bravos. He began to feel that Durk had manipulated him, and from time to time he accused Durk of treating him like a puppet.

On the few occasions when reporters sought him out,

Serpico tried to give his own theories for rebuilding and renewing the Police Department. Each time, he first would try to downgrade Durk's notions. To bring in college boys at the bottom wouldn't work, Serpico said, for they would merely be converted and perverted by the existing system. The system had to be thrown out first. The entire hierarchy of the Police Department had to be driven out of headquarters like a herd of cows, to be replaced by honest, honorable younger men.

Of course Durk learned of Serpico's new ideas. The arguments between Durk and Serpico now became shouting matches.

Serpico's newest fad was scientology. Durk wasn't interested. Serpico accused Durk of being close-minded and anti-intellectual.

"Becoming an intellectual isn't like putting on a disguise, Serpico. You have to read some books. Would you try reading a book once in a while, Serpico? Yeah, I know, books are long."

On the night of February 3, Serpico and three other plainclothesmen closed in on a narcotics operation in a tenement at 778 Driggs Avenue, Brooklyn. Serpico was carrying no less than three guns. "What are you expecting, a revolution?" someone had asked him at the station house.

"You go up and see if you can see the guy selling," one of his three partners said to Serpico.

"Yeah, you speak Spanish, Serpico," said another. Serpico loved learning languages, loved communicating with people he shouldn't have been able to communicate with. He spoke Italian from childhood and had since added good-enough Spanish, and considerable French. While in Korea in the Army he had studied Japanese, and at this time he was trying to learn Russian.

The vote was three to one that Serpico should go in and try to see the guy selling, so he went up the stairs and hid in the dark hallway.

A man knocked on a certain door and asked for Mambo. Some money was handed inside the door, and a bag of junk was handed out to the buyer.

Serpico followed the buyer downstairs and arrested him.

Then, with two of the three officers, Serpico reentered the building to arrest Mambo. Mambo was believed to have a shotgun up there, and so no one was anxious to rap on his door.

Serpico was wearing his old army fatigue jacket, dungarees, and his unkempt beard. With a partner on either side of him, he knocked and called out in Spanish, "Tell Mambo I want to make a buy."

The door opened a crack; it was on a chain. A face peered out—the voice that went with it summoned Mambo from another room.

Now Serpico shouldered into the door, breaking the chain. "Police, you're under arrest," he cried. Mambo came running up. Serpico had his head and one arm inside the door; the two men were trying to force the door shut on him. Serpico's gun was in his hand and cocked.

The two other plainclothesmen simply stood there, frozen.

Serpico turned to shout, "For God's sake, what are you waiting for? Give me a hand."

Serpico's attention was diverted only an instant. As his head spun forward again, he was looking down the barrel of Mambo's pistol. Mambo shot him in the face. There was a second explosion—Serpico's gun had fired too.

Serpico fell. He lay on his right side, both feet inside the door. So the door could not be closed and nothing impeded pursuit. Inside the apartment a woman was screaming. Mambo and the other man went out the back window and escaped. There was no pursuit by Serpico's partners.

"I can only tell you," a high-ranking police official said later, "that when word came in that Serpico had been shot, this building shook. We were terrified that a cop had done it."

Mambo was caught the next day, for he left a trail of blood everywhere. Serpico's reflex shot had apparently pierced Mambo's wrist. Mambo, whose name was Edgar Echevaria, had a long record. Narcotics men wearing bulletproof vests cornered him in a nearby apartment and shot him in the stomach. For a time he and Serpico lay in the same hospital, one floor apart.

For the next month Serpico was treated in Brooklyn

Jewish Hospital. Hundreds of cards and letters praised him, but one called him a "rat bastard. "Another called him a "scumbag" and said he should have been killed. "Scumbag" was a cop's word. His semideafness was pronounced permanent. Phlebitis developed in one leg. The phlebitis, he said, was more painful than getting shot in the face. There was no risk of infection from the bullet fragments in his head; a bullet traveled at such speed and got so hot that it sterilized itself totally while en route to its target.

Various police officials visited Serpico. One said cheerfully, "We're speeding up your commendation."

"What did I do?" said Serpico, undiplomatic as always. "I got shot by a junkie."

His two partners were getting commendations too. "What for?" he wanted to know. "For letting Mambo escape out the back window?"

Serpico was being named for various other hero awards as well, which interested him not at all, and the rumor was that Commissioner Murphy was about to give him his gold shield at last. But Serpico didn't believe this would happen, and as the months began to pass, it didn't.

When he got home the tiny apartment was more crowded than ever, for now a wheelchair had been added to all that clutter. When the day came that he didn't need it anymore, he so informed the Police Department, and two armed policemen and a truck came to take away one empty wheelchair.

As spring began, Serpico used to limp down toward the river and out onto the pier, accompanied usually by his girlfriend Susan and the two dogs. Some days I went with them. Serpico would sit in the sun and wait to become stronger. He always wore a long black coat and a black fedora. He limped along on a black cane, and with his bushy black beard he looked not like a wounded cop but like a Hasidic rabbi. He carried his khaki field pack over his shoulder, and when I asked what was in it, he said, "My artillery."

He didn't mind talking about getting shot. If you've ever done any boxing and caught a real hard punch right on the nose, then you know exactly what it felt like, he said. If you were to stick your head in a barrel, and somebody tossed a firecracker in there, then you would know exactly what the noise was like.

He never passed out. Lying on the floor, he thought, Is that all there is? Is that the end of it? He then remembered his partners, who seemed to be doing nothing at all, and he thought, What the hell are they waiting for? Are they just going to let me die? He was fighting to hold on to consciousness, because he believed that if he passed out he would never wake up. Later a priest gave him the last rites. He started to say, "Please leave," then decided, What have I got to lose?

"Every time you're on one side of a door, you wonder what's on the other side," he said. He had been through doors just like this one more than 20 times and had never been shot before, and as he got stronger he realized that he would soon have to make an evaluation. "You start to have a sense of immortality, because no one likes to believe he will get killed the next day, or that night. When I have time to reflect, I'm going to have to decide: No, I'm not immortal. Or else, well, you see, I am immortal."

He said that he was through with the New York Police Department, that to struggle against the system any longer was impossible. He couldn't go on with it. He was getting out as soon as he was whole again—or as whole as he would ever become. "It's like when I was in the Army in Korea, waiting to go home," he said. "I'm counting the days."

Meanwhile, not a single one of Durk's candidates had been accepted into the Police Department, and it began to seem that none would be.

7 / Murphy

In New York that first day, there was an excitement that seemed almost glee. The probable savior of the Police Department, if not the city itself, stood beside the Mayor in the Blue Room in City Hall, and the savior's name was Murphy.

Behind him in Detroit all was gloom. Carl Parsell, pres-

ident of the Detroit Police Officers' Association, said that
cops on the street there were very resentful. "We had a
man come in here and listen to our problems for nine
months," he said. "Then, just as we thought we had them
solved, he goes and flies out of here like a bird." The mayor
of Detroit, Roman Gribbs, was distraught, for he had had
the man everybody else wanted; but either he, or Detroit itself, had proved inadequate. Their beloved had walked out
of the house and wasn't coming back. Mayor Gribbs
looked embarrassed, even humiliated. Politically, this
would cost Gribbs.

In New York, Murphy told me the day I first met him,
"Ray Gribbs is just a great, great guy. I think so much of
Ray Gribbs. But Ray was his usual gracious self when he
saw what an opportunity this was for me. He said I had a
lot to contribute, and that where I could make the best
contribution was the only important thing to consider
here."

At City Hall, the Blue Room was jammed by at least a
hundred reporters and TV technicians. Some nine cameras
were turning at once and the lights were blinding. Mayor
Lindsay called Murphy a "take-charge commander who
gives his men and the public strong and decisive leadership."

The temperature under the lights must have been a
hundred and ten degrees. "Policemen don't dream about
becoming President, governor, or even mayor," Murphy
said. "But being Police Commissioner of New York is a
common dream." Now his eyes seemed to fill up with tears,
and he said, "I want to reduce crime. I want to reduce
fear."

His emotion lasted only a moment. Then he recovered,
and his soft scholarly voice seemed as cool and aloof as always.

His build was slight, and he looked almost frail. He was
a career Irish Catholic cop off the streets of New York, but
he didn't look it or sound it. He stood out as a kind of law-
and-order liberal, a strange new animal, an important addition to the city's zoo. He recognized crime as a result of social problems, not as mere antisocial aberration existing in
a vacuum. As Murphy saw it, the society would have to

understand and remove the underlying causes of crime, while at the same time strengthening and reforming its entire system of criminal justice: "It's not a question of either/or, and it is not going to be done overnight."

Mayor Lindsay walked out of the Blue Room with a bounce to his step, convinced he had found the best man in America. He had certainly found the most experienced: this would be the fourth city in which Patrick Vincent Murphy had bossed the police department. There were 40,000 police departments in the United States that year, and almost every single one of them was led by a somewhat narrow man who had never served a moment in any city except his own. If Murphy was to display stunning new ideas, this is where they would come from: Murphy had been around. No less important would be his demonstrated ability to coexist with politicians and political pressures.

Had he not once served as the first and also last Public Safety Director—a kind of super police chief—of Washington, D.C.? Had he not repeatedly been summoned to Capitol Hill to testify before the House District Committee, presided over by reactionary old John McMillan of South Carolina, about what his police department was doing or not doing? The District of Columbia was about 70 percent Negro, and the attitude of some of the Congressmen who ruled it, and also the attitude of a good many white citizens, was that the way to control Washington was to bust a few of them "niggah haids." This wasn't the way Murphy saw it, and he survived only nine months, but that he survived such political pressure at all seemed something of a miracle. When he left, the job was abolished behind him—Congress specifically removed it from the D.C. budget. "Law enforcement and politics do not mix," said Murphy, though he knew they always did, and had to.

In the midst of a soaring crime wave, Murphy was taking over a demoralized police force which he would now march confidently through the shredding machine of two separate corruption investigations, for New York State too had announced a commission to hold hearings in a few months. As if the looming Knapp Commission threat were not terrible enough.

But surely Murphy would know how to handle all that.

Today, three weeks before he would take office, he had admitted both that police corruption existed and that stamping it out would be his number one goal. So that was a plus. And the last plus was this: Murphy was one of their own. Surely the New York cops would welcome him with open arms.

New York was a city that had loved its cops in the old days, but mocked or feared them now. Ten times as many cops would be bitten that year as the year before. Twice as many would be kicked. There would be double the number of bomb threats and a 12.7 percent increase in reported major crimes: homicide, rape, armed robbery, and the like. Forty-five cops would be shot and seven murdered before Christmas, and ten more would be cut down before Murphy had completed twelve months in office.

New York policemen would make a quarter of a million arrests that year. Over 120,000 people would pass through the city's 13 jammed jails. There were fewer than 100 judges, who accorded each case an average of two and a half minutes. For a misdemeanor the average miscreant spent 35 days in jail awaiting trial, for a felony the average was five months. Despite the vast numbers, there were only 552 felony trials in the entire city that year. The rest was fallout, due to plea bargaining, dropped charges, failures of witnesses to show up or testify.

There was a massive imbalance of the criminal justice dollar: 80 percent went to the police, only 20 percent to pay for the courts, the jails, the virtually nonexistent rehabilitation programs. About 80 percent of the criminals in New York's jails had been there before. The courts and jails turned them out fast, because there was no room. Mayor Lindsay compared crime to glue: You touch it and your hands get gluey and nothing happens to the glue.

This glue was now the new Commissioner's domain. Patrick Vincent Murphy, one hesitates to say it, was now to have his chance to do what was right for New York.

In some ways Murphy was a typical cop. He was married with eight kids, the last of them born when he was 46 years old. He was a devout Catholic who received communion always at the funerals of slain Catholic cops, and on Sundays as well, and he sometimes read to the congregation from the pulpit during Mass. Although he had two university degrees, he had received the first at age 34 and the second when he was 40.

His rise through the ranks of the Police Department had been slow and painful, and his many relatives on the force —in addition to two brothers these included an uncle and a nephew—were unable to help him because he intended to go much further than they. Although he was a sergeant within five years, he stayed a lieutenant for nine, and he was 42 before he became a captain.

For one who had chosen always to stand in a violent arena, his life had been surprisingly devoid of violence. Trained as a bomber pilot in the Navy during World War II, he had never bombed anyone. As a cop on the beat in New York, he preferred always to use his soft, calm voice rather than his nightstick.

He was not a physical person. Like all patrolmen, he was called often to intervene in family fights, and he entered each one knowing, as any cop did, that family fights were dangerous; a great many cops have been killed by husbands and wives trying to get at each other. Called one day, Murphy stepped into the tiny kitchen of a tenement—and found himself face-to-face with an irate, drunken, six-feet-eight-inch husband. There was no room to wield the nightstick, and Murphy chose not to draw his gun. Instead he began talking soothingly, and after about five minutes, calmed the man down. As Commissioner, he later remembered this as the most dangerous encounter of his 25 years as policeman.

"It was my experience then, and I have believed it ever since, that if a policeman can identify with the people in the neighborhood where he works, it makes all the difference in the world. It makes all the difference to him too, as well as to the kind of job he can do for the Police Department. The rewards in police work are tremendous if you feel you've helped a family come through a crisis, rather than have it collapse with somebody being arrested."

There was only one other dangerous incident that he could remember at all. One day he stepped out onto a building ledge four stories high that was only eight inches wide, to bring in a young woman threatening to jump. Clutching the sill, he offered her his other hand. After a time she took it, and he coaxed her inside. That soft, calm voice was the best weapon he had, and he knew it. Although as Commissioner he still owned two of his guns, he had never used either of them in heat: "Thank goodness I never had to shoot anyone."

In 1954, when he was 34, Murphy at last found the "hook" that all cops, cynical or not, believe is essential, if a man is to progress upward into the police hierarchy. Frank Andrews, first of the reform commissioners, came to power that year, and he set Mike Murphy, a captain, in charge of the Police Academy. Mike Murphy chose two brothers unrelated to him, Pat and John Murphy, both lieutenants, as his deputies.

Mike Murphy was a forward-thinking officer for his day, and he later became a forward-thinking commissioner—for his day. Pat Murphy started off as his protégé and then became his idea man; and everywhere Mike Murphy went, Pat went. "Give me some ideas," Mike Murphy would say. Pat Murphy had a hundred of them. The trouble was, Mike Murphy accepted very few. Nonetheless, in 1963 Commissioner Mike Murphy allowed Pat to accept a job as police chief in Syracuse, even promoting him from captain to deputy inspector just before he left, as a kind of farewell present, and when Pat came back to New York 18 months later, Mike Murphy jumped Pat Murphy two more ranks, from deputy inspector to deputy chief, skipping the intervening rank of inspector, which put a great many police noses out of joint.

When Mike Murphy resigned as commissioner, Pat thought the successor should be himself—no one ever said he wasn't ambitious. But the choice went elsewhere and so Pat Murphy quit and went to Washington to work for the Justice Department, taking with him his New York police pension of almost $10,000 a year, which from now on would raise almost any job he took to the level of great comfort.

The trouble was, Pat Murphy wasn't interested in comfort, much less in money. He wasn't interested in good books—he never read for pleasure. He read books on police theory and sometimes he read the *Reader's Digest* and he always read every word written about himself. He wasn't interested in music—show tunes once in a while, otherwise he hardly knew what he was listening to. He wasn't interested in good food or good drink, or idle conversation. He was interested in his family: He trimmed his kids' fingernails, read to the little ones at night, and spent hours playing basketball with his boys in school yards. For the rest, he was single-minded. All he knew and cared about was law enforcement. This was his career, he meant to get to the top of it, and the top of it was New York.

He had had one supremely good break, the Syracuse job in 1963—after that he could make his own breaks. A state commission had uncovered widespread police corruption in Syracuse, and Elliott Lombard, a lawyer on Governor Rockefeller's staff, had been asked to find and recommend a man who could reform the Syracuse force. Lombard's search focused on the unknown Patrick Murphy, still only a captain in New York, who was described to him as an idea man who was frustrated and dissatisfied. They talked in the rain inside the fogged-up windows of Captain Murphy's car. Lombard found him, "an extraordinary kind of man in terms of police thinking. He wasn't a dramatic person. He was more of a quiet thinker. It wasn't his personality that impressed me, but his ideas. There were a lot of things he wanted to try. He wasn't parochial about the police. He saw the police as part of the larger system."

Murphy believed in management, in tight control of subordinates, and in public relations: In Syracuse, in command for the first time, he spoke at literally scores of luncheons and dinners and appeared on scores of radio and TV shows, which never took place too early or too late for him to appear. He also ordered the cops to get out of their cars and do part of their patrolling on foot. He said, "We gave our patrolmen cars and radios, which they need, and this increased their mobility and their communication. But at the same time it depersonalized them. The policeman became something riding by in a car. We've got to change that. The police have got to get back in touch with the people."

Years later, when he took command in Washington he pushed this idea one step further, inaugurating the pilot precinct project in the predominantly black 13th Precinct there. An elected board of local citizens became the official consultative body for the police in that area. The board met regularly with the police, and also operated family counseling services and the like. They had no police control, but they did become a kind of lobby—a force for the Force to reckon with.

Moving on to Detroit, Murphy ordered policemen in black areas to attend dances, clubs, church socials, to get to know the people they were there to serve. This grew into the Beat Commander idea, which he first installed there and planned soon to install in New York: The sergeant in charge of a specific sector became in effect the neighborhood police chief and was responsible for his sector 24 hours a day.

In the Justice Department, where he had briefly headed the Law Enforcement Assistance Administration under President Johnson, it was Murphy's function to distribute money and new police ideas to small-town police chiefs across the country, but it is possible that he took in more information than his visitors were willing to take away with them. One of those he impressed was Henry Ruth, whose Justice Department office was four doors down the hall, and who later, as head of New York's Criminal Justice Coordinating Council, recommended Murphy to Mayor Lindsay.

"In the world of police chiefs you won't find anything like Murphy," said Ruth to Lindsay, and also later to me. "In the fifties he was saying things about police work that people didn't start to pick up until the mid or late sixties— he was that far ahead of his time. He is quiet and soft-spoken but extremely forceful. The history of policing is that whatever the police chief says, goes. Where Murphy is different is that he likes to float ideas, and get people to come back to him with reactions, and then he makes up his mind and does it, and makes sure it's done in a very forceful way, although a very quiet way. For instance, in Detroit, when he announced the phasing in of the need for college credits for promotions, he just announced it. This is it. And it was."

At this time there was no proof that Murphy's revolutionary ideas worked or didn't work. His pilot projects in other cities were just that, pilot projects; and although there were those who claimed that pilot projects in themselves were a force for change, this was not, in the police world, strictly speaking, true. In order to survive in the police world, a pilot project had to become institutionalized—to reach the status of being mindlessly manned, paid for, obeyed; otherwise, once its backers left, it tended to fade away. Murphy had not been police chief anywhere long enough to institutionalize his own pilot projects. In the past eight years he had had nine jobs in four different cities.

He had quit as Syracuse police chief because his wife hated the deep snow, and it was a dead-end job anyway. He had quit as commander of the New York Police Academy when he wasn't named commissioner. He had quit his first Justice Department job to become Washington's Public Safety Director, and he quit that after only nine months because President Johnson and Attorney General Ramsey Clark offered him a new and enormous agency to head. He went to Detroit to get back to where the action was, and he quit there after only nine months because Detroit was only Detroit, whereas New York was capital of the world. It was true that Murphy had once waited around for nine years as a lieutenant. But these days he concentrated on moving on and up, and he waited no place very long.

His public personality seemed clear. In Detroit, cops had seemed to be shooting and killing too many suspects, and the city was tense. Murphy ordered that every time a policeman used his gun, a report had to be made out and reviewed at every level, from sergeant to police commissioner. Each commander had to endorse each report, and to recommend, if the case required it, either retraining or disciplinary action. The shootings fell off.

In Washington, during the riots that followed the death of Martin Luther King, Murphy had ordered his cops not to shoot looters. He limited mass police confrontations with crowds and concentrated instead on dispersing the mobs rather than detaining individuals. Bloodshed during those riots were minimal.

No question about it, in liberal New York in 1970, Murphy's credentials seemed extraordinary.

Whitman Knapp later said, "When he came back to New York, Murphy should have asked the Mayor to disband the

Knapp Commission at once. He should have said, 'You want me to reorganize and revitalize the force. I can't do this work with the Knapp Commission hanging over my head. Get rid of it.' " Knapp added, "I was certain that the appointment of Murphy meant the end of our commission. I was certain that all he had to do was ask. That's what I would have done in his place. But Murphy didn't do anything, and I was surprised."

Twenty-five years before, after only five months as a foot patrolman, Murphy had got the dream assignment other cops waited years for: He had been made a plainclothesman and sent out to enforce the gambling laws. Murphy said later, "In those days there was organized protection of gambling, and it was very obvious to me immediately that I was not going to be comfortable in that kind of assignment. I told the commander, and he said, 'That's fine. If you don't think you like the assignment you can go back to a precinct.' So I never served for any period of time in gambling or narcotics or kinds of enforcement duties where the temptations were at their worst."

Murphy's tour in plainclothes ended after three weeks. Of course there was other graft available for precinct patrolmen, and Murphy walked a beat in Brooklyn for 18 months, but he got out of that assignment too, as soon as he could, and went into emergency service, where he spent his time giving oxygen to heart attack victims and picking up the pieces of people who had jumped under subway trains or dived off buildings.

When he would talk about this work later, he never chose to fill in the gory details, and he never seemed particularly moved by any of these experiences, except when he spoke of removing one little boy who had climbed onto the roof of an elevator and ridden it all the way up to the top and halfway through the grillwork that closed off the shaft.

Almost all the rest of Murphy's 20 years as a policeman in New York was spent either at the graftless Police Academy or in equally graftless headquarters staff assignments.

And so as Murphy came back to New York from Detroit as Police Commissioner, his knowledge of police corruption in the city where he was born was theoretical rather than personal. He himself had chosen always to work in areas where it wasn't being offered. Nonetheless, as he now began to plan his purge of the New York Police Department, he was somewhat vulnerable to charges that he himself had known about corruption for decades, but had done nothing. Forced to respond, he said, "No one has any responsibility to begin a crusade. It's easier to shake the tree when you're at the top."

Murphy's appearance was perhaps of some importance, for two things had to be understood about cops. First, that their idea of a great leader was the hero cop, almost any hero cop. And secondly, a cop was used to judging people very quickly on very little evidence. On the street this ability helped him to stay alive.

And so New York cops had made their snap judgments about Murphy the minute they heard his name. Oh, you mean Chief Murphy from the Police Academy? This Murphy had never fired his gun on duty—no hero cop here. He had begun mentioning police corruption in New York even before he left Detroit. Did he hate New York cops, or what? He came bearing a mandate for change—and cops were conservative people, not overly enthusiastic about change, any change.

About this time, some reporter wrote that Murphy was "a certified member of the Irish ascendancy." But except for the fact that he was New York's fourth Commissioner Murphy (none of them related) since 1900 (can any man named Murphy be all bad?), this was nonsense. In 20 years Murphy had made no close friends inside the department. No one had known what his hopes were, nor what made him laugh. He had never had time or inclination to stand with other cops in a bar. He was no easy mixer. He had put in his eight hours each day and gone home. He had no intimates outside his immediate family, and if he had any close friends at all, no one knew who they were.

It was as if he had spent a lifetime carefully hiding his cards, waiting for this one job. As he took command, no man could presume upon his friendship. He could be ruthless if it suited him. He owed loyalty to no one. His style was cool and detached. In a somewhat repressive profession, he seemed a liberal, though he had some rigid standards. He considered formal education essential; street knowledge was not enough. He liked to speak of ideas, but only those that fit within the narrow realm of police administration. No, he was not and never had been a cop's cop.

Not that he lacked what passes in our time for political skill. He was quick with a handshake, quick with "How are you, how are you doing, good to see you," when people, some of them strangers, approached him. He looked into people's eyes when he spoke to them, and also when listening. His voice and manner seemed warm. He paid attention to whomever he was with; he just never thought to ask if his companion was married, if he had children, if he enjoyed tennis. The result was that no one could make any small talk with Murphy either. Reporters found he would talk endlessly on police subjects but would never reveal any of his own emotions or feelings, not one.

I myself spent hundreds of hours with him in all sorts of circumstances and never heard a minute's gossip. If we happened to be stalled in traffic he might stare out the window or at the back of the chauffeur's head. At formal lunches with businessmen or with newspaper or TV executives, he usually sipped a sweet sherry beforehand and remained politely aloof, while the idle chatter with which the ice is usually broken at such affairs ranged over sports or entertainment or politics or the stock market. I never once heard him utter a word about baseball or the movies or money or anybody's kids. including his own. He was interested in police business only. Once the food was served and the conversation got serious, he would talk about law enforcement for an hour, and never notice what he was eating.

Although he seemed friendly, all warmth on the outside, there was something forbidding about him, or perhaps only dignified, and intimate questions were never asked him. He captivated quite a few people on first acquaintance, for on his one subject he was fascinating, and some he impressed more and more through repeated meetings, but no one ever felt he was getting any closer to the essential Murphy. Still, he shook a thousand hands during those first days and weeks, threw a million smiles this way and that; a politician running for office could have done no better.

The trappings of power came with the job. He could

enter the station house in any of his 75 precincts, and every cop in the place would snap immediately to attention. The Police Commissioner could summon a subordinate to that gorgeous ornate office, and the man would appear instantly, perhaps trembling, whether guilty or not. As one cop once remarked about the Police Commissioner, "Guys who would walk into gun battles quiver before him, they forget their names."

So quite apart from the big office, the gleaming black car, the armed chauffeurs, the six Police Department helicopters which he could ride in or dispatch on any errand he chose, the Police Commissioner was, himself, within the Police Department, as capable as any Arabian pasha of instilling instant fear.

But what about power itself?

Outside the Police Department it was nothing much. Murphy had been appointed by the Mayor to fill Howard Leary's term. When this ended in five months, Murphy would be appointed to a term of his own, no question about it, and this term would be of five years' duration; the document would say so.

The fine print was not on that document but on another: According to the City Charter the Police Commissioner was dismissable by either the Mayor or the Governor, and it was sufficient for either to announce only that this dismissal was in the best interests of the city. No charges needed to be preferred. No reason needed to be given. The Mayor therefore believed himself, and was in fact, the number one law enforcement official of New York City, for the Police Commissioner served only at his pleasure. In addition, in each of the five counties composing the city, there stood an elected district attorney; each of them considered himself the first and last word in law enforcement within his own jurisdiction.

Although the elected mayor and the five elected DA's could technically be removed for gross malfeasance, such ponderous proceedings had never been invoked. These were men responsible only to the voters the next time an election came around. But the Police Commissioner could be dismissed at any time with a wave of the hand. If in some ways he flew higher than any of them, he was correspondingly easy to shoot down; it had happened often enough in the past. The Police Commissioner was and always had been the most vulnerable high official in the city. His five-year appointment was a joke. He had to hold his job from one day to the next, and if anybody started sniping at him, anybody at all—a DA, a congressman, a borough president, an influential citizen, the newspapers—his chance of survival was slight. Howard Leary, who had not finished out his five-year term, had exceeded in longevity every Police Commissioner appointed in this century except two.

And so Murphy's power outside the Department was an illusion. Murphy seemed to know exactly how little power he had at the start, and he set about to inflate it out of all proportion to its base. His plan was to proceed along several fronts simultaneously.

First he meant to establish his personality, his popularity—in short, his influence—within the city. This meant speeches and speeches and speeches. This meant interviews late at night with everyone from Caspar Citron for FM radio, to David Frost in prime time nationwide TV. The one interview reached millions, the other only a few dozen. Murphy didn't seem to care. His energy was boundless. The chauffeurs some days were picking him up at 6 A.M., as he proceeded from station house to breakfast meeting, to luncheon speech to TV interview to dinner speech, with interviews with other reporters along the way in the back of his car.

However, in the course of these early interviews, he said almost nothing that was not dull, and a great many of the articles about him were rejected by editors because the articles, like the Police Commissioner himself, appeared too bland.

Murphy seemed to realize this, but there wasn't much he could do about it yet. He could not afford to seem inflammatory yet, and he was being so careful that he was sometimes merely uninteresting, and other times boring.

The New York Times Magazine made three tries at a profile of Murphy before printing one, and *New York* magazine sent a parade of writers, four in all, over a period of about eight months. When Tom Buckley of the *Times*

Magazine appeared, I, the newly appointed deputy commissioner, warned, "Murphy is the hardest assignment you've ever had; to get him to say something dramatic is like pulling teeth." But no sooner had Buckley stepped into the Police Commissioner's car than Murphy began denouncing J. Edgar Hoover. I remember looking at Murphy in astonishment. So he had brooded over why profiles of himself often did not get into print. I was too new in my job to have talked this over with him yet, and he had not asked my advice. Nonetheless, the new Murphy, outspoken, opinionated, had just been born before my eyes. Later, Murphy even talked quite frankly to Buckley about one of his brothers who had a drinking problem.

About this time also, Murphy began to invite occasional reporters to sit in on high-level conferences with his top commanders. Murphy would enter the conference room and with veiled eyes introduce the reporter. Murphy would then conduct the meeting as if the reporter didn't exist. But nothing like this had ever happened before, and the commanders couldn't take their eyes off the reporter. However, not only was nothing said either in Murphy's presence or out of it, but during such meetings the commanders even seemed to avoid his glance—lest he read disapproval from their resolutely blank expressions.

But to Murphy, articles meant stature, stature meant power. Power is illusory. If people think you have it, you have it. Murphy wanted people to think he had plenty.

Within the Police Department he was solidifying his power somewhat faster, not much. He had taken over a gigantic bureaucracy, six times bigger than any he had handled before; his fingers were groping for the monster's throat. He dared not alarm it, lest it lash back and kick him to death. The risks were serious, for the various pockets of power within the Department—the Detective Bureau, for instance—were rooted in the structure of the Department itself, and each was virtually self-sustaining, with powerful political friends, a protective wall. The men commanding these individual fiefdoms had all been policemen many, many years, some of them longer than Murphy himself. All were imbued with the Civil Service mentality. Their permanent rank of captain was guaranteed by law, and their eagles and stars were guaranteed by tradition. Most of these men saw no need to make any changes in a department that was already the finest. Murphy wanted to break down all these pockets of power. Murphy had a hundred ideas he wanted to try out. Murphy wanted to drag the Police Department kicking and screaming into the 1970s.

But he could do none of this by himself. He had to make these men want to cooperate, though their tendency would be to wait, to watch his exertions from a distance, asking each other, "How long is Murphy going to last?" Some of them had seen a dozen commissioners come and go. If they didn't like what Murphy was doing, they could drag their heels, misplace their surveys, their studies and reports, and this would sabotage the Police Commissioner as effectively as a bomb under his desk. Murphy would have to win some of these men over, and drive some of the rest into retirement.

As Police Commissioner, Murphy was stuck with all patrolmen, all sergeants, all lieutenants, all captains. He was forbidden by law either to promote or demote any of them. He could not even order up a new Civil Service examination so as to provide a new list of qualified candidates for promotion. The Civil Service Commission, an independent city office, took care of this, and the input from the Police Department and from its commissioner was nil.

The Police Commissioner did have the power to turn patrolmen into detectives and back again overnight. He did have the power to promote or demote in all the ranks above captain. In actual fact, before Murphy, captains progressed only upward, and there had never been conscious effort to force a dull man to retire, which was what Murphy wanted to try soon. But he would have to go very, very slowly.

Similarly, with the exception of himself, there was very little precedent for jump promotions. A man was expected to progress upward, one rank at a time. To fill vacancies on top, the Police Commissioner was expected to choose from the rank directly below, whether anybody in that rank was qualified or not.

This was the command structure: The Police Commissioner was a civilian, and on the level directly below him stood seven deputy commissioners, all of whom were also technically civilians. These men outranked all uniformed members of the force. All had the power to suspend from duty, or to reinstate, any member of the uniformed force, from lowly patrolman to four-star chief inspector. Any deputy commissioner could have exerted command authority in any sort of police situation, though this was rarely done. But in theory, in keeping with civilian control of the police forces, these civilians were the ranking commanders of the New York City Police Department. In actual practice, each of them had one specific area of responsibility. Their titles largely explained their responsibility: Deputy Commissioner of Legal Matters, Deputy Commissioner of Departmental Trials, Deputy Commissioner of Administration, Deputy Commissioner of Community Affairs, Deputy Commissioner of Public Affairs, and the soon-to-be-appointed Deputy Commissioner for Organized Crime Control.

The senior man was the First Deputy Commissioner, who served as a kind of executive vice president. He was Acting Police Commissioner in the absence of the Police Commissioner, and under his command fell the several most sensitive units of the department: Intelligence, Public Morals Enforcement, Inspections Division, and Internal Corruptions Investigations. In all, the First Deputy Commissioner had direct command of about one thousand men, which was much more than most of the other deputy commissioners.

The highest-ranking uniformed cop was the Chief Inspector, who wore four stars. Patrolmen rarely saw such an awesome figure, and when they did they tended to stare. Traditionally, his authority within the Department had been equal to that of the Commissioner and sometimes exceeded it. A great many Chief Inspectors had gone on to become Commissioner.

Traditionally, the incumbent Chief Inspector always retired when the new Commissioner came in, meaning that Murphy, after only a few days in New York, had to make an appointment into which 32,000 policemen, plus a certain portion of the city at large, would read the entire message of his administration. A press conference was therefore called, and all waited to see whom Murphy would appoint.

On the level just below the Chief Inspector stood four so-called super chiefs. They wore three stars. These four men were equal to each other in rank and in pay, but the Chief of Detectives was usually considered foremost among them. Partly this was the detective mystique holding policemen and citizens enthralled as always, for the Chief of Detectives commanded only about 3200 men, 10 percent of the force, whereas the Chief of Patrol was in command of 17,000 precinct patrolmen. The Chief of Personnel, who reported directly to the Police Commissioner, held such high rank primarily so that he could move men about the city without any back talk, just as the fourth of these men, the Chief of Inspectional Services, had to have three stars so as to be able to command investigations into the activity of any policeman or commander on the force.

Below these men came 14 assistant chiefs, who wore two stars. Each bossed all of the uniformed forces in a particular borough, or all of the detective forces in a particular borough, or commanded other vast units: the Traffic Division, or Technical Services, or the Special Operations Division (this included aviation, harbor patrol, the mounted squadrons, the Stake-out Squad, etc.), or the Intelligence Division.

Murphy's choice as Chief Inspector, it was figured, would come from the level of three-star chiefs. But it didn't. He reached right past them and selected Michael J. Codd from the rank just below. If the super chiefs judged from this that Murphy wanted to get rid of all of them, they were right, and he soon began to do it.

Codd was 54 years old. He had first met Murphy back in 1948 when both were appointed acting sergeants and sent to the Police Academy for nine days of sergeant's training. It was the first of a number of Murphy appointments which would look backward toward those Police Academy days, as if the men whom Murphy remembered most fondly were those he had stood in classrooms with in 1948.

The Chief Inspector's job paid a base salary of $36,500 a year, $1,500 more than the First Deputy Commissioner earned. In addition, the Chief Inspector was entitled to overtime and other additional payments which civilians did not get, meaning that he earned more money than Murphy himself, whose salary was $41,000 a year. The Chief Inspector's pension was guaranteed by the City Charter and was superior by far to the pension of anybody else, and when all this was added to the apparent authority of the job and its obvious prestige, clearly no man could turn it down.

However, it was Codd's bad luck to be offered the job by Patrick Murphy. As he pinned the four-star shield on Codd, Murphy said, "I've always been impressed by his bearing, by his dignity, by his quiet, calm approach to the most pressing, trying, complex problems." For Codd, on the surface, was as unflappable as Murphy himself, and Murphy had told him so as he held out this plum of a job. But Murphy had also told him that Codd was being offered the job with certain stipulations. The authority and the responsibility of the Police Commissioner, Murphy said, could not be shared with anyone. Codd, if he took the job, would not be a sort of co-commissioner, he would be a sort of figurehead. There would be no vying for power. All major decisions would be made by Murphy. Codd would act as chief of field operations only—in fact, Murphy said, one of his plans was to change the proud title of the job from the traditional Chief Inspector to the more accurate (under Murphy) Chief of Field Operations.

Codd was born on Staten Island, one of ten children, and he once worked as a newsboy for the *Staten Island Advance*. He attended Blessed Sacrament Parochial School and St. Peter's High School, where his education ended. He always wanted to be a policeman—eventually, three of the seven Codd boys wound up on the New York Police Force. Codd himself started with two years as a state trooper. In 1941 he was appointed a probationary patrolman in New York, but a year later he was drafted. He became a military policeman, was promoted to second lieutenant, served in the China-Burma-India Theater, and attained the rank of major. Like Murphy himself, the war's end meant reverting from commissioned officer status to patrolman on the street. However, Codd stayed in the Army Reserve and he later retired with the rank of colonel.

Codd won three commendations for meritorious police

duty, each time capturing armed men. He worked his way up through the ranks at moderate speed, commanded two different precincts as a captain, was never a detective, and he had been the commander of all the patrol forces in Brooklyn North when appointed Chief Inspector.

Codd was a tall man with a ramrod back and a military bearing and almost white hair. Murphy wanted Codd as Chief Inspector because Codd would appear to the cops on the street as continuity with the past. He was one of them. He would provide an appearance of stability and of calm and of control, and if he pledged his troth to Murphy others might be influenced to do so too.

Murphy's meaning was clear to Codd. The job of Chief Inspector would crown Codd's career. He could later retire with the pension and prestige of all former Chief Inspectors, but he was never going to be the kind of Chief Inspector others had been. He was not going to command. Murphy was offering him a tarnished jewel, but Codd, after a moment, took it. It was, after all, the only jewel being offered him, and perhaps something could be worked out, or perhaps later on Murphy would change his mind, or perhaps . . .

Codd was very close to being the totally honorable man. He was loyal, and above all things he was correct. There was no craft in him.

Politically, Murphy had made a brilliant move. He had shared nothing.

With that out of the way, Murphy turned toward the First Deputy Commissioner's office. The incumbent there was John Walsh, 68 years old, who had held this powerful job for nine years under five different Police Commissioners. During most of that time Walsh had been the most feared man in the Department. Although there had been few enough corruption investigations, few enough indictments, few enough convictions, Walsh had been responsible for every one of them. Nonetheless, Murphy wanted his own man in that office, someone younger, with far more vigor, on whose devotion he could count totally, someone with whom, again he would not have to share power. A large order, but Murphy had just such a man in mind. All he had to do first was nudge old John Walsh out of the chair. Walsh had been a policeman 40 years and he did not want to go, but Murphy's eyes could turn icy; and after holding out for nearly a month, Walsh agreed to retire. The same day Murphy announced William H. T. Smith as the new First Deputy Commissioner.

Smith had known Patrick Murphy, and also Mike Codd, since the day on which all three had been assigned to the Police Academy for sergeant's training in 1948. Sergeant Smith's primary interest that year was singing in the police glee club—he was a somewhat stout tenor with a ringing high C. In those days the glee club was serious stuff, and although gifted singers like Smith were invariably assigned to precinct patrol, they did very little patrolling. There were too many rehearsals, too many concerts. That was a different and quieter time, and it was reasoned that men like Smith could prevent more felonies with song than with nightsticks. Gifted athletes didn't do much patrolling then either. New York's finest could draw a crowd in Town Hall or Madison Square Garden anytime, and the city still loved its cops.

When the Police Academy course ended, Sergeant Patrick Murphy went back into Emergency Service, Sergeant Michael Codd went on patrol in Little Italy and Chinatown, and Sergeant Smith went back to hitting high notes in Queens.

Smith had joined the Police Department in September 1941, but he served in the Army Air Corps as a B-29 navigator during the war. Again the Army officer returned to foot patrol as an ordinary cop. Smith had already attended two colleges on an aimless basis when in 1956, as a 40-year-old lieutenant, he won a four-year scholarship to Pace College. This necessitated a transfer to the Police Academy so that he could work days and go to school at night, and it was there that he ran into Pat Murphy again. For most of five years they saw each other every day, and what Smith once termed a "warm friendship" began to develop. There used to be a kind of canteen there where all the instructors ate lunch together, and Smith remembers sitting around the table with various fellow instructors, gossiping, making jokes. "But whenever Pat Murphy came over and sat down with us, the jokes and the gossip stopped immediately. The appearance of Pat meant an immediate upgrading of the level of conversation. Pat never had time for small talk."

Murphy probably learned to know Smith intimately during this period, for Smith was a loud, open kind of man, inclined to declare himself bluntly on most subjects. But Smith came to know Murphy hardly at all.

One night, many years later, I stood at a bar with Smith. When both of us had had a few drinks Smith admitted that he didn't really know Murphy well.

"Our wives know each other well," Smith said. "Our wives are really close with one another."

"Did you ever see him display any strong emotion?"

"No." Then he added, "If Pat ever lets his hair down, it will be with me." Then he added, "Maybe he has let his hair down once or twice in the past. Not often."

Smith at this time was 54 years old. One day I heard him extolling Murphy to a reporter. "Some guys are smart. Some guys are brilliant. But this guy Murphy is a—is a—is an intellect."

When Pat Murphy went to Syracuse as chief in 1963, he invited Bill Smith, a newly promoted captain, to go with him as First Deputy Chief, and when Murphy left Syracuse after 18 months, Smith succeeded him there as chief. When Murphy moved on to Washington, Smith soon followed, taking a job as director of the office of investigation of the Department of Housing and Urban Development. It was a police job. His division was responsible for the integrity of the 14,000-man federal agency. He lived with his wife and three daughters in a handsome ranch-style house in Arlington, Virginia, and he found time to sing in the choruses of several productions put on by an amateur group in Arlington. He sang in *La Bohème*, in *The Bartered Bride*, in *The Merry Widow*, and also at Sunday Mass at St. Agnes Church where he led the congregation in hymns.

Sometimes, when he was on his way to work in Washington, his small daughter, Julia, would sing out of the upstairs window, "Where are you going, Daddy?" Smith was likely to sing his answer in a dramatic tenor voice that rattled the windows all over the street: "None of your business." However, he was no show business personality. Although from now on he would be second in command of the New York Police Department, he almost never stepped forward as spokesman for the Department; and when obliged several times to appear on television, he seemed ill at ease, stiff, daunted by even the most bland questions. He liked to bowl, and he was a good deal more relaxed in a bowling alley than in public.

He seemed a tougher and rougher man than Murphy, a bare-knuckle fighter, and these qualities Murphy valued. The top man could not afford to make enemies; let the executive officer do the dirty work. Smith would soon acquire a reputation as Murphy's hatchet man. People would even call him ruthless.

Smith had been earning $35,000 in Washington, and he was collecting his New York captain's pension as well. That pension would be suspended (as was Murphy's) if he returned to the New York City payroll, meaning that the job of First Deputy Commissioner would cost Smith a pay cut of almost $10,000 a year. But he never hesitated.

"I owe Pat so much," he told me once. "I would just have to go with him anyplace he wanted me."

Smith's college degree was in business administration, and while Chief of Police in Syracuse he had earned his master's degree in public administration at Syracuse University. Like Murphy, Smith considered gun battles and dramatic arrests a highly exaggerated and overdramatized part of police work, really of minor importance. Like Murphy, he believed that the future of the Police Department lay in reforming its management techniques, in restructuring its upper echelon.

Even more so than Murphy, Smith seemed to believe that every cop on the street had his hand out, that every cop who was offered graft would take it, that police corruption was much worse than anybody else had admitted.

Murphy wanted to change all of the super chiefs, and a good many of the assistant chiefs, but for the moment he would stop with the appointments of Smith and Codd. Murphy commanded 32,000 men. He could make any of them hop, but not all at once. He would get rid of the super chiefs one at a time, allowing months to elapse between the "retirements" of each one. He would send them out with kind words, then would pull the shades down over his eyes, so that no one should guess what might happen next.

He had a number of schemes which he would make public with equal care, one at a time, when the time was right. He wanted to downgrade the detective bureau and break up the detective mystique. He wanted to force authority downward from headquarters to the precincts, making each captain responsible for crime in his own neighborhood. He wanted to reorganize a great many functions of the Department.

For instance, there were a number of small units concerned with intelligence gathering, and one of Murphy's first moves was to group them together into the new Intelligence Division under the command of Assistant Chief Arthur Grubert. Grubert was another loyal type Murphy could count on, for he was the son of a retired detective, his father-in-law had been a cop, his brother-in-law was a captain, one of his sons was also a cop, and two sons were agents of the FBI. This was not untypical. A great many high-ranking officers were surrounded within the Police Department by members of their own families, so that to sack any one of them would send traumatic ripples to the outermost precincts in the city.

Many months later Murphy distributed an extraordinary private memorandum in which he said he was astonished and appalled by the corruption and the lack of discipline he found as he took command. In some ways, he said, the Department had been almost out of control. In his more than 20 years as a policeman in New York, he wrote, he was "not lacking a realistic understanding of the facts of NYPD life." Cops were sleeping in their radio cars during the early morning tours all over the city. Commanders had a shocking ignorance about crime conditions in their own precincts. Patrol time was being wasted and poorly directed. The memo blamed crime on such factors as poverty and unemployment, meaning that captains could not be held totally accountable for crime in their precincts.

"But we cannot take the position that we can have no impact," he wrote. "We damn well can have much more of an impact than we had when I became police commissioner."

One day just after he took command, Murphy called together 144 officers above the rank of captain, and told them, "Indications of corruption must be exposed and expunged. This is your responsibility. I will hold each of you accountable for the misdeeds of your subordinates. With bold leadership you can—and you must—create a climate in which dishonesty is unthinkable. Let the word go out to every precinct station house, to every detective squad room, to every command and every man on every post: We will not tolerate dishonesty in any form. . . . I expect borough and division commanders to make frequent visits to station houses. I expect you to personally address the outgoing platoons and make sure that every member of the force of every rank gets the message: Corruption in any form is odious and repugnant to this administration. State your position to your men, eyeball to eyeball. Your declaration of contempt for dishonesty—in person—will have far greater impact than an order read across the desk by the platoon commander. The rank you have achieved is evidence of your success in a very proud profession. I will hold each of you personally accountable for any misconduct within the ranks at any level of your command. It will be my policy to increase significantly your authority with a view of achieving greater effectiveness and efficiency. In return, you can expect to be held to greater accountability for your exercise of direction and control. The law provides that each of you serves above the rank of captain at my pleasure. It is my responsibility to remove from high rank any one among you who cannot, or will not, meet the high standards of the executive level. Gentlemen, let me assure you that I take my responsibility seriously. . . ."

The new super chiefs presumably would have to come from among the 14 two-star chiefs and the 22 deputy chiefs, and Murphy looked over this group, and was not thrilled. A very few of them were excellent men. The rest had attained rank by waiting in line for 25 to 30 years. It was not necessary in the Police Department to have performed distinguished acts in order to get promoted to high rank. For the most part, all it took was a friend at headquarters and the keeping shut of one's mouth. One avoided decisions wherever possible—a decision could turn out to have been the wrong one. Chiefs were often men who shouted at subordinates but spoke obsequiously to men with more stars, especially commissioners. If Murphy wanted imagination, decisiveness, flair, he was not going to find much of it in the one- and two-star ranks. Partly this was because none of those men was really convinced that imagination, decisiveness, and flair were what he wanted. He could talk all he wished about forcing authority downward, about demanding responsibility and accountability from commanders, but in the past, other men had spoken this way but had nonetheless wanted to make all the decisions themselves. What they had really demanded from their subordinates was subservience and reverence. Murphy would have to prove that he was different. They were not convinced as yet.

And so Murphy waited three months to sack Chief of Patrol Henry Taylor, and to bring in Sydney Cooper, the two-star patrol commander of the Bronx. Cooper was a lawyer, and one of the few top-ranking cops who had taken Serpico's charges seriously. It was Cooper who had ordered the investigation which had resulted in the substantiation of many of Serpico's charges. Cooper too had taken sergeant's training with Sergeant Pat Murphy in 1948.

Murphy then waited three months more before bringing in Albert Seedman, still another from the 1948 sergeant's class, as the new Chief of Detectives. Six months gone by already.

Murphy wanted to change a number of the deputy commissioners too, and here at least he could reach outside the Department if he chose to, but he moved them in slowly too. He first spoke to me in February, but would come to no decision until May; and it was September, 11 months after he had taken office, before he had chosen William McCarthy, the last of them, as Deputy Commissioner of Organized Crime Control. The last of the incumbent super chiefs was not supplanted by a Murphy man until well after that, although a good number of the two-star chiefs had been "retired" in the interim.

This was the way Murphy did things. He was very crafty and very slow, and this seemed to earn him more resentment than he had bargained for. Instead of a quick purge followed by calmness and jokes, headquarters was in the grip of fear for a year. There seemed to be heads rolling in the corridors every few days, and Murphy began to seem a relentless and ruthless presence in the lives of the high ranks. The result was also not what Murphy bargained for. Fear—and inaction—adhered to the top brass like green mold. Murphy kept telling his commanders that he was forcing authority downward, but as they saw it he was merely waiting for them to make a decisive move, any sort of move, so as to have grounds for forcing them to retire.

The huge staff of the Police Commissioner's office could be a liability too. Most of the armed male secretaries in there had held their jobs so long, under so many indulgent commissioners, that they held the rank of first grade detectives. This made them among the highest paid clerk-typists in the world. It also meant that they were experts at reading all signs and portents. A number of them had the authority to sign Murphy's name to correspondence; there were so many "official" Patrick V. Murphy signatures on documents leaving that office that few subordinate commanders could recognize the real one. So it was impossible for the Police Commissioner to keep any decision, any confidential memo, a secret very long. These men knew what was going on the instant Murphy did, the rumors spread all over the headquarters building an instant after that, and these rumors had proved so accurate over the decades that, as each new one moved down the hall, no one questioned it. The Police Department was ruled almost as much by rumor as by fact.

Murphy gave a great many speeches, a great many interviews. He said he wanted everything upgraded, from fresh paint jobs for the older station houses, to computerization and new business forms to cut down on the time lost booking prisoners. "We still have bound books—the blotter and the arrest record—in which the lieutenant writes things out by hand," Murphy complained. But again he moved very very cautiously. In a few experimental precincts the blotter disappeared but in scores of others it stayed. In some precincts Murphy sent the desk lieutenant out into the street as the leader of the cars on patrol. This was something of a new concept, and it frightened nobody; but it was new, and the lieutenants on the whole therefore didn't like it. Next

Murphy installed his first Neighborhood Police Team in Brooklyn. A black sergeant was given 16 men and told that he was in command of a certain sector 24 hours a day. There were 800 or more sectors in the city and this was just one of them.

Presently Murphy gave orders that plainclothesmen assigned to gambling enforcement would be limited to two years in that role. If plainclothes was the greatest corruption hazard in the Police Department, and there was no question about it, then no man should be subjected to such temptation any longer than that, Murphy said. Commanders didn't rush to implement this decision, for they needed time to survey their men, to find out who had been where for what length of time. But eventually plainclothesmen began to dribble back into uniform, and they were furious. They had hoped to be promoted to detective but now they were being sent back into the bag. The bag, to a cop, was his handsome blue uniform. Later on Murphy would pronounce the same edict with respect to narcotics plainclothesmen and the cries of outrage would mount again. Objectively, Murphy's decision was sound. But the men had been promised detective assignments under the last commissioner, or so they thought, and this was proof once again of betrayal by headquarters. The sole purpose of headquarters, as they saw it, was to screw cops.

Their disappointment ascended like a symphony, but Murphy didn't seem to hear it, or if he did he gave no sign. They were only cops, and his control over them was absolute. Murphy dealt in concepts, not in individual pain, and day by day he moved on cautiously, always cautiously, never striking in the same area twice. A less cautious man might have got all the unpleasantness over with all at once and then started to build the new department—or perhaps, by acting fast, generated a mutiny.

And then the mutiny came anyway. A state Court of Appeals decision sent back to State Supreme Court for jury trial the police parity pay case. The cops thought the city owed them each $2700 in back pay. The contract was complicated. It took skilled lawyers to interpret all the various clauses. But the Patrolmen's Benevolent Association had taken the case to State Supreme Court and won, and then to the Appellate Division, which upheld the lower court. Two victories to zero. But the city went to the Court of Appeals, which now had ordered the jury trial. Perhaps now the cops would never get their money, and a good many of them had already borrowed against that windfall and spent it in advance.

The mutiny was spontaneous. It began virtually simultaneously in precincts all over the city. About 80 percent of the cops who should have been on patrol sat in the station houses or in their cars and refused to go out onto the street. It was winter. Murphy was on vacation in Florida. He and his wife had just gotten there, and it was almost two years since they had gone off alone together. But Murphy flew back at once. Murphy got very little sleep over the next six days. All superior officers were ordered to work 12-hour days, and the 3200 detectives went back into uniform on patrol. This was a pitifully small force, but Murphy stationed all these men in extremely visible places. There was no crime wave. The temperature during this whole job action hovered around 10 or 15 degrees, and in such weather criminals do not frolic any more than ordinary people do. "Jack Frost is the best cop," any cop will tell you, and rain is an excellent cop too.

As the strike continued, Murphy's number one job, as he saw it, was to take the emotional sting out of the situation as much as possible. And so he waited six days before taking a hard line. Delegates to the PBA would vote at a meeting on the sixth day. "I decided the critical issue was this meeting," Murphy said later. "Whichever way it went, at 4 P.M. that day, I knew I had to take strong control and leave no doubt about that." The PBA meeting, Murphy felt, would give the leadership a chance to convince the men to go back to work.

The city itself was of course appalled by this job action, this strike. For six days everybody hated every cop, and the cops themselves seemed shocked at the furious reaction of their fellow citizens.

At last, news of the vote—that the men would go back to work—came into headquarters. "That's great," said Murphy calmly. He had never been anything but calm during the six days, even though the situation was critical. This was the number one crisis in his career to date, and he was fully aware that, should he prove unable to solve it, his career might be destroyed.

Once the vote was known, Murphy changed the policy that had existed for 30 years that he knew of, and probably for half a century before that: "I gave authority down to the level of lieutenant to suspend any man on the spot who would not go out on patrol. No one, I was pleased to see, had to be suspended."

When he told me this, I said to him, "You mean you waited until what you considered the exact key moment before applying any pressure at all, and then applied maximum pressure all at once?"

"Yes."

"And it worked?"

"Yes," answered Murphy.

Did I detect a note of quiet pride in his voice?

At 4 P.M. the men went back to work. Murphy watched the reports come in from precinct after precinct, waiting past supper time to be sure. Then, having eaten and even slept at his desk during most of six days, he at last had himself driven home. He made no elated statements to his wife. He showed no elation, no emotion of any kind. He put the smallest kids to bed. While his wife cooked his dinner, he took her bike, and his beagle on a long leash, and for half an hour this apparently colorless man pedaled alone in the dark, cold night through the empty streets of Staten Island.

I have thought about that scene many times since, and wondered what it meant. Did he feel no triumph? Was he such a closed man, so essentially solitary that he felt triumph but was not able to share it, even with his wife? Was he so proud of himself he needed no applause but his own? The Department might have broken like a dropped light bulb, but he had caught it before it struck the floor.

Or perhaps he was already thinking ahead. The real saviors of the department had been the 3200 detectives who manned the radio cars. Although Murphy still wanted to diminish the Bureau's stature, he would have to move more slowly now than ever. Meanwhile, the patrolmen had lost so much prestige, so much of the city's former affection, that he could do what he wanted with them now. They would hardly dare protest. But at the same time he knew that the Knapp Commission was coming, the corruption scandals were coming. How could the Force suffer that on top of this? He would somehow have to build back some of their self-esteem. Not too much.

He pedaled back home to partake of his victory feast. Alone with his wife at the kitchen table, he dined on pork chops, washed down not with champagne but with a glass of sweetish Portuguese rosé.

A few days later Serpico was shot.

Would this winter never end?

Book Two / **SPRING**

1 / The Black Liberation Army: Front View

Along the Hudson River, between Riverside Drive and the West Side Highway, there is a strip of lawn two miles long or more. It is planted with pink dogwood, Japanese dwarf cherry trees, and flowering crab apples, and for one week each spring it is gorgeous, for all of those colorful trees are in bloom at once. As the sun went down that night the entire strip of lawn seemed in flames. Then the light softened, and the trees were turned into a row of gigantic pink puff balls extending from 72nd Street all the way up past the house where District Attorney Frank Hogan lived, at 404 Riverside Drive, between 112th and 113th Streets. The date was May 19. The time was 9:15 P.M.

There had been a police radio car watching Hogan's house around the clock for many months, for Hogan had brought 13 Black Panthers to trial on 156 charges, among them that they had conspired to bomb department stores and police stations and to murder policemen; during the course of that trial, the longest and most expensive in New York State history, the house of the presiding judge, John M. Murtagh, had been fire-bombed. On May 13 the trial had finally come to an end, with the jury, after deliberating only a few minutes, returning verdicts of not guilty on all charges for all defendants. Crushed and humiliated by this verdict, Mr. Hogan supposed that his police guard would now be removed, for there seemed no need for it anymore; but he did nothing to call it off, and nobody in the Police Department did, either. Whoever had ordered it in the first place had forgotten about it. This often happened. There were a dozen or more cops standing in doorways all over the city that night. They had been ordered there for some temporary specific reason, and two or three or five years later they were still there on guard.

So nobody had thought to remove Hogan's guard. At about nine o'clock the radio car stationed in front of his door was relieved and its occupants sped away in search of a bite to eat somewhere. The relief car contained patrolmen Thomas Curry and Nicholas Binetti, both 39 years old, and they had been on duty only about 15 minutes when a car came past them going the wrong way down the one-way street. They sped after it, and six blocks later, at 106th Street, pulled alongside. The driver of the pursued car scrunched down in his seat and the man on the passenger side reached across him and stuck a .45-caliber submachine gun out the window. The police car was only a few feet away. Some of the bullets stitched a nearly complete circle around the radio car's door handle. The police windshield shattered. Glass flew in all directions. Bullets smashed into Curry's face, neck, and chest. Binetti was shot in the neck, stomach, and arms. The radio car crashed and stopped. The assailants' car sped off into the night.

Shattered glass littered the sidewalk under the statue of a long-dead Civil War officer on a horse. The Civil War officer peered stoically out over the Hudson while detectives on hands and knees pawed through the glass looking for bullet fragments—or any evidence at all. A police tow truck dragged away the ruined radio car. At the Police Academy it was examined scientifically.

Curry and Binetti were rushed to St. Luke's Hospital. Teams of doctors worked on them. It was incredible that they were still alive. Mayor Lindsay arrived. Commissioner Murphy rushed in wearing a tuxedo. When the press had had time to gather, the Mayor said gravely, "I sure hope these fellows pull through." And he launched into a speech in favor of stronger gun laws.

There was no motive, no clues, no witnesses, and of course no pursuit.

Two nights later, in Harlem, another radio car team answered a call in a housing development where the old Polo Grounds baseball stadium used to stand—a woman had been cut in a knife fight. But she refused aid, and after a few minutes the two patrolmen, Waverly Jones, 34, a black man, and Joseph Piagentini, 28, white, strolled back through the warm spring night toward their car. They had to pass two black youths lounging against the fender of a parked car, and as they did so the boys fell into step behind them, whipped out guns, and opened fire. Jones went down and died instantly, shot three times in the spine, and once in the back of the head. Piagentini went down too, and the youths turned both of them over, yanked out their service revolvers, and then continued shooting. Piagentini was being shot repeatedly with his own gun. He had his arms up and was trying to brush away the bullets as if they were insects, but they kept socking into him. He was shot altogether 13 times before the two black youths ran off, carrying their own guns and the two cops' guns. Patrolman Piagentini died in the back seat of the radio car rushing him to Harlem Hospital.

This time there were a number of witnesses, and they later described how, before the shootings, the black youths, who were apparently waiting for someone, had moved from the car's fender to the hedge and back again, nervously plucking off leaves and sucking on them and then spitting them out, for 15 minutes or more, until at last the patrolmen reappeared. But the descriptions which the witnesses gave were vague and led nowhere.

Once again there was no motive, no apparent clues, and no pursuit.

At about 8:30 that same night, two hours before the double assassination, a package had been delivered to *The New York Times* containing a license plate, a live .45-caliber cartridge, and a message. By now the police had been given a license plate number in the machine-gunning of Patrolmen Curry and Binetti which was possibly the number of the getaway car, and it was this plate that was delivered to *The Times*. The companion license plate was delivered to radio station WLIB in Harlem at about the same time.

Here is the message that accompanied the plate delivered to *The New York Times*.

May 19th 1971.
All power to the people.
Here are the license plates sort after by the fascist state pig police. We send them in order to exhibit the potential power of oppressed peoples to acquire revolutionary justice.
The armed goons of this racist government will again meet the guns of oppressed Third World Peoples as long as they occupy our community and murder our brothers and sisters in the name of American law and order; just as the fascist Marines and Army occupy

Vietnam in the name of democracy and murder Vietnamese people in the name of American imperialism are confronted with the guns of the Vietnamese Liberation Army, the domestic armed forces of racism and oppression will be confronted with the guns of the Black Liberation Army, who will mete out in the tradition of Malcolm and all true revolutionaries real justice. We are revolutionary justice. All power to the people.

The day after Jones and Piagentini were murdered, a second letter arrived from this so-called Black Liberation Army. It took credit for the double assassination too; and laboratory tests proved that it was typed on the same machine as the letter claiming credit for the machinegunning of Curry and Binetti.

Latent fingerprints had been found on the wrapping of the *Times* package. They belonged to Richard Moore, 26, a known Black Panther who had disappeared last winter in the course of his trial, and to Eddie Josephs, 18, also a Panther.

It was something to go on, not very much. The cops had been looking for Moore since February and hadn't found him. He was believed to be in Algeria, together with others of the Black Panther leadership who had fled the country while being sought by the police for crimes.

But on the afternoon of June 2, a black man named Augustus Qualls was strolling around at Trinity Avenue and 163rd Street in the Bronx when a maroon Buick Riviera pulled up alongside of him. The driver of the car was Richard Moore, whom Qualls had known for 15 years. Moore introduced his passenger as "Bennie." Bennie later proved to be Eddie Josephs, who was also known by his African name, Jamal. Moore had an African name, Dharuba, and he used other names from time to time as well; and one of the problems that the police had when trying to track down these black extremists was that they were known by so many different names—a different name for each circle into which they moved—so that the track the police tried to follow never led easily from one circle into another.

Moore invited Qualls to step into the car, which he did; and as they aimlessly circled the block, Moore remarked that he needed money. Did Qualls know of any numbers runners or dope pushers they could stick up? Qualls later admitted to the police that he was no Black Panther, he was a professional stickup man and a dope addict. He told Moore he would look around, and after agreeing to meet that night, they parted.

That night they again drove aimlessly around. Qualls suggested that they hit an Argentine dope pusher who worked on the corner of 116th Street and Lenox Avenue. Moore rejected this idea; that area was too hot. Curry and Binetti had been machine-gunned exactly two weeks before, and the Jones-Piagentini murders were only 12 days old. In Harlem the police dragnets were everywhere. Qualls asked what kind of guns they had and was told that Moore had a .357 Magnum and Josephs a .45-caliber pistol. In addition there was a grease gun in a duffel bag on the floor of the car.

That was Wednesday night.

Qualls met them again Thursday night and again Friday night and they continued to drive around looking for a good place to stick up.

Saturday night came. A Panther named Irving Mason was strolling down Broadway near 148th Street at about 7 P.M. when he was approached from the rear by Eddie Josephs, whom he knew as Jamal, and whom he did not immediately recognize because Jamal had tinted his hair red.

"Where you been?" asked Mason.

"Don't you worry about that," said Josephs. Josephs then said that he would need Mason's help that night. Mason was to meet him on this same corner at 2:30 A.M. But Mason complained that the cops were everywhere since the shootings. He had a wife and child and meant to lie low for a while.

"We know where you're living," said Josephs. "We know you've got a wife and family."

Mason decided he had better meet Josephs at 2:30 A.M. as requested.

So Mason went home, sat around his apartment until about 9 P.M., then took his wife and son over to his mother-in-law's. His wife worked for the telephone company at night; he walked her as far as the subway and kissed her good-bye. Back home, he set his alarm clock, and when it went off in the middle of the night he dressed and walked to the corner of 148th Street and Broadway and waited.

About 20 minutes later a Buick Riviera pulled up and Mason stepped into the back. Inside the car were Josephs, Richard Moore, whom Mason knew as Dharuba, and another black man, unknown to Mason, who was Augustus Qualls. As they drove across to the Bronx, Josephs informed Mason that he was about to help the other three rip off a social club. Once in the Bronx, Moore pulled into the curb and turned off the engine, and the four black men sat there making small talk.

An hour passed. It was now 4 A.M. Moore turned the key in the ignition, and they drove up in front of the Triple O Club. Moore ordered Mason to stand on the corner as a lookout. Then he, Josephs, and Qualls left the car, carrying what appeared to be an Army-type duffel bag. Mason stood on the corner.

Presently the sound of shots split the night air. Mason ran into the building and up the stairs and opened the door of the social club, and was flabbergasted to find all of the customers lined up against the wall stark naked. Josephs had a shotgun in one hand and a handgun in the other. So did Qualls. Moore was out of sight for the moment. Josephs ordered Mason to get back downstairs to his post.

Mason went halfway down the stairs and just stood there. The robbery was taking far too long. Mason went to the door and peered out. The streets were full of cops. He ran upstairs again to report this fact to Moore, who now coolly ordered all the customers to put their clothes on and walk out of the building. This done, the four stickup men attempted to stroll out among them, but they were grabbed by the police at the door. The cops also collected the two shotguns, a .45-caliber Colt, a .357 Smith and Wesson Magnum, a 9mm. Browning automatic, and a .45-caliber submachine gun. On the floor of the Buick Riviera was a U.S. Army hand grenade.

The submachine gun was rushed to the Police Academy for ballistics tests, for it was the same type of gun that had cut down Curry and Binetti.

Normally ballistics tests were conducted by firing a shot into a box that was about a foot square and filled with cotton wool. The cotton wool surrendered an undamaged slug with the barrel markings cut plainly into it. A revolver could not be fired fast enough for the barrel to heat up, and so every bullet out of the same barrel would bear the same markings. But with a machine gun, if 20 or more shots were ripped off nonstop, as had been the case in the attack on Curry and Binetti, the barrel would get so hot that markings on the first bullet might bear little resemblance to the markings on the 20th. So in order to check the bullets that had been dug out of Curry and Binetti against bullets from this machine gun, 20 shots had to be ripped off rapid-fire, and this could not be done into a wad of cotton inside a foot-square box. So ballistics men rushed the gun down to the Police Academy swimming pool and emptied the magazine into the water. Then a swimmer went down to the bottom and retrieved all the bullets.

In this way it was proved that the machine gun which had stuck up the Bronx social club was the same gun that had riddled Curry, Binetti, and their radio car 18 days before.

The police attempted to interrogate Moore and Josephs, and so did the FBI later on; but the two knew the law, they knew their rights, and they would give no information of any kind. In the old days it might have been possible to "extract" a confession from either or both of them. Unspoken rules had existed. To get blood on one's uniform was frowned upon. Blood on the uniform showed a lack of expertise. There were cops in those days who laid out newspapers to keep their cars clean when transporting a suspect from the scene of the crime to the station house, for they would have "interrogated" him on the sidewalk, and possibly en route as well. Some cops liked to carry a certain kind of slapjack, to give suspects concussions with. The main thing was that the suspect didn't wear a turban in court. This special slapjack could turn his brains to jelly and never leave a mark. One of the Police Department's ace interrogators, scarcely a decade before, had been a light heavyweight boxing champion. The inspector or the chief heading up the investigation would announce, "I want this case broken," and then he would go home. He never gave any order, but it was an order nonetheless: Bring in the guys who break heads. This was considered a "scientif-

ic" investigation. While it was going on, calls would sometimes come in from across the street complaining about the
noise from the victim. And there was a famous case in
Brooklyn where the suspect was believed to have expired
on the squad room floor. The detectives called up the
borough commander.

"I think we killed him, Chief. What should we do?"

The borough commander, a two-star chief, explained
that they should get a body bag, some chains, and some
cinder blocks, and drop the suspect into Gravesend Bay.
But this particular suspect revived, and after leaving the
station house, checked into a hospital for two weeks.

This is the way it was, not very long ago. There were
cops still serving who had seen it done, and some of them
had done it themselves. But in New York in 1971 officially
sanctioned brutality was a thing of the past. There cannot
have been many suspects in the history of the Police Department as hated by cops as Moore and Josephs, but nobody laid a finger on them.

However, Mason and Qualls were willing enough to talk,
and a week later a call came in from an anonymous female
who stated, "The four men you are holding are not the
ones who shot the cops. They may know who did it. They
did not do it, neither the Riverside Drive shooting nor the
Harlem shooting. They were at my girlfriend's house, 757
Beck Street, Bronx. Her last name is Josephs. She is the
common-law wife of Eddie Josephs. They did nothing until
the social club. I don't want to see the innocent accused. I
will call again."

Detectives rushed to the Bronx address, found Pauline
Josephs, and quickly determined that it was she who had
made the call herself. Pauline was 22 years old and stood
only four feet nine inches tall. She worked as a receptionist
at $125 a week for a doctor, and she had a daughter named
Brenda Josephs—father, Eddie Jospehs. Eddie had disappeared during the trial of the Panther 21. Pauline hadn't
seen him between January 1971 and May 13, the day the
Panther 21 were acquitted, when he came to her house and
knocked on the door. She said that when she saw him she
couldn't believe her eyes and she began crying.

"Are you glad to see me?" asked Eddie Josephs, patting
her stomach. "I knocked you up, didn't I?"

"Yes," Pauline admitted. "How did you know?"

Eddie said, "I have ways of knowing things."

Now Irving Mason and his "revolutionary wife," Ila Barnes, came out of the interior of the house and welcomed Eddie home.

"But where have you been?" asked Pauline.

"Mind your own business," explained Eddie Josephs. "I'm back."

And so Eddie Josephs, 18 years old, moved in with Pauline and lived with her from that day until he was busted three weeks later. There were nine other Panthers, including Richard Moore, living in the same apartment at one time or another. Patricia Green, Moore's "revolutionary wife," lived with him there, but only on weekends. One night, Joanne Chesimard, brought in Robert Vickers, who was bleeding badly. He had been shot in the shoulder in the shoot-out with two cops in Harlem.

Mark Holder came by occasionally but then went into hiding because he knew the identity of the Panthers who had killed Robert Webb, also a Panther, on March 8.

Police interrogators listened to this recital with mounting excitement, all the time trying to display no emotion at all. Pauline was held as a cooperative witness by the District Attorney's office, and she was interviewed by apparently bored detectives taking notes. But as always happened when subjects began to blab extraordinarily detailed information, the room quickly filled up with detectives, with commanders, with additional district attorneys. To Pauline it must have been the most satisfactory audience of her life.

Later she was stashed in Room 653 at the Commodore Hotel, where she was interviewed many times. Pauline declared that she did not know any present Black Panther members, and yet every name she mentioned was a Panther, and nearly every member of the extremist wing of the party had apparently lived in her apartment at one time or another. Furthermore, every detail she supplied checked out. She said that Robert Vickers gave to Eddie Josephs the gun he had used in his shoot-out with two cops in a Harlem hallway on April 19. Vickers had remarked that Kimu and Harold Russell were his partners in the shoot-out. Well, there was such a shoot-out. The two cops and Kimu were badly wounded, and the 20-year-old Russell lived. All this happened essentially as Pauline had described it. Vickers had got away. The cops hadn't known who he was or that he was wounded, but they knew now. Pauline began talking of the murder of Sam Napier, a Black Panther, two days before the Vickers shoot-out. She named Michael Dennis Hill, Richard Moore, Eddie Josephs (her common-law husband), Andrew Jackson, Irving Mason, Mark Holder, and Frank Fields as the killers. She said they had gone out to Queens in a rented U-Haul truck to kill Napier.

Napier, 32, had been the circulation manager of the party newspaper, *The Black Panther*. He was loyal to the Huey Newton faction of the Panther Party. The seven men who had driven out to Queens in the truck were of the Eldridge Cleaver faction. Besides, the proceeds from the newspaper were in that office, and Sam Napier was alleged to have held back more than his share of a previous robbery.

Napier's body was found by firemen inside the blazing Panther office in Queens at about 5 P.M. His mouth had been plastered with adhesive tape, his hands bound behind his back with venetian blind cord, and he had been doused in gasoline, shot nine times with rifles and pistols, and then set on fire.

It was Pauline who had bought the adhesive tape at Sherman's Drug Store, she said. The men had left her house with several rifles and guns, with the tape she had bought, with the venetian blind cord, and with several bottles, one of them labeled "Apple Wine," which she and the other girls had previously filled with gasoline.

The four girls, Pauline, Marie Cookie Williams, Ila Barnes, and Patricia Green, had waited in Pauline's apartment. By 5:30 the men were back. They put the radio on to hear the news and bragged of how they had burned the building and killed Sam.

Knowing now where to look, detectives canvassed Bronx U-Haul yards and found the one where Frank Fields had rented the van on the day of the murder. In Pauline's apartment was found a length of venetian blind cord which, lab tests proved, matched the scorched cord recovered from the bound hands of Sam Napier.

Now Pauline began to talk of how black extremists on the lam managed to get from Harlem to Algeria with such ease. The leaders of this extremist wing were apparently Moore, Jackson, and Joanne Chesimard. They were the contacts in New York for wanted blacks from any part of the country. Joanne would make up phony identifications. From New York the subjects would be sent by train to Canada, where they would contact the Canadian Liberation Front to obtain passage to Paris. From Paris they went to Algeria. Pauline was vague. She had no experience in passports or other such documents and could not supply other details.

Pauline had a friend who was a theatrical makeup man, and Moore and Eddie Josephs kept asking her to find this person who might help them change their physical appearance. Ten days went by, during which Pauline was unable to find her friend. So Ila Barnes went to Sherman's Drug Store where she bought hair dye. That night Eddie Josephs and Richard Moore became two red-headed black men. Josephs thought this so successful that he began to discuss the possibility of using the dye to darken his skin.

Gradually the police interrogation zeroed in on the machine-gunning of Curry and Binetti on the night of May 19. Pauline insisted that Eddie Josephs, her common-law husband, had nothing to do with this crime, because when Moore got back to the house he and Eddie got into a fight.

"You knowed I wanted to go with you," shouted Eddie. "We gonna off some pigs, I wanna be there."

As far as Pauline knew, the machine-gunning was carried out by only two persons: Moore, who was driving the car, and a man named Mark D., also known as Joe. Pauline had never met this Mark D. Moore and Josephs talked about him frequently, but always called him Joe. Occasionally Moore would refer to Mark D., and Eddie Josephs would ask, "Who's that?"

Moore would say, "You know. Joe."

About 45 minutes after the machine-gunning occurred, Pauline had gone downstairs to help Michael Dennis Hill, Richard Moore, and Frank Fields clean out a dark-blue Maverick sedan. She saw a machine gun in the car and empty bullet casings all over the floor. Moore said to Hill, "You handled the grease real good, but not good enough; you didn't kill them." They all went upstairs where Hill, Moore, Fields, and Eddie Josephs discussed the possibility of going to the hospital to finish off Patrolmen Curry and Binetti. Finally they decided against this, for the eleven o'clock news came on, there were scenes of the hospital, and it was swarming with policemen.

Detective novels were one thing, real-life crime solving was something else. Crimes were solved by informants, not deduction, and detectives would search for weeks and months to find an inside informant who knew as much as Pauline Josephs knew. All they had to do now was keep her talking, then go out and verify the details of what she said.

A cousin of Andrew Jackson was located. The cousin had been to Pauline Josephs' apartment several times and there had met numerous male and female Panthers. Jackson had declared that he and his crowd had split from the original Panther Party and were "into a heavier thing." The cousin understood that this meant stickups. Jackson said that he had plenty of money, but the heat was on, and he had decided to take a vacation to the Virgin Islands to visit his pregnant girlfriend, Jule Henley. One day in the apartment Jackson showed his cousin a grease gun and talked casually about a possible raid on this apartment by the police or the FBI. He brandished the gun. It would be used to grease any pigs who tried to get in that door. The cousin and Jackson then got stoned on grass, the cousin said. Later on they went to a second apartment where Frank Fields displayed some hand grenades.

The detectives went back to the Commodore Hotel to talk to Pauline Josephs again. This time Pauline described Richard Moore writing the two "Black Liberation Army" letters to *The New York Times* and to WLIB. She said Patricia Green had typed these letters out on a portable Smith Corona electric typewriter (it was later found by detectives), and Ila Barnes had been the one who delivered the letter and the package.

What about the murders of Patrolmen Jones and Piagentini in Harlem? That night, Pauline replied, Jackson, Ila Barnes, Eddie Josephs, Richard Moore, and herself all were eating pepper steaks and drinking Boone's Farm Apple Wine at her house, when Irving Mason rushed into the room saying, "Hey, man, two brothers just offed two pigs in Harlem." They all rushed to the TV and watched the eleven o'clock news: views of the bloody pavement, of the distraught Commissioner Murphy, of the policemen and reporters swarming around the hospital where the two bodies had been taken.

Eddie Josephs spoke up. "Mason, find those bloods who iced those pigs."

"I'll try," said Mason.

But did Pauline know anything more about the double murder?

No.

Lineups were formed. Moore, Josephs, Mason, and Qualls stood among black detectives. The witnesses from the Polo Grounds housing project recognized no one as a shooter of Piagentini and Jones. The witnesses were shown photos of Jackson, Fields, Hill, and the rest.

No.

The FBI was asked to interview Jule Henley, Andrew Jackson's girlfriend, in the Virgin Islands, and did so; and dozens of other interviews and interrogations were carried out as well. But not one of these provided a single serious lead into the assassination of Patrolmen Piagentini and Jones.

One terrible crime, the machine-gunning, had been solved, though Curry and Binetti had been crippled for life. Curry was disfigured and would never walk or talk normally again. Binetti had one paralyzed arm.

A great deal of information had been acquired about the band of black outlaws who called themselves a liberation army. This would prove of immense value later, for the war against the cops was still on and there were more assassinations and attempted assassinations coming.

2 / Guns

Jones and Piagentini were the sixth and seventh policemen murdered so far that year. There would be three more. In hot July, a patrolman named Robert Denton would come out of a bodega in the Brownsville section of Brooklyn in the middle of the night and a man with a butcher knife, for no reason at all, would suddenly lash out and slice Denton's throat open, nearly cutting off his head. This would be the only one of the ten not killed by guns. The identities of approximately 18 men involved in these murders became known to the police. All were black. The city's politicians refrained from pointing this out, and so did Commissioner Murphy. But the fact remained that approximately 65 percent of the city's arrested murderers, muggers, armed robbers, proved to be black men; about 15 percent were of Hispanic origin; and about 20 percent were white. The overall racial breakdown of the city went approximately this way: whites, 63 percent; blacks, 20 percent; Hispanics, 17 percent.

So the dangerous precincts, any cop would tell you, were the black precincts. Most of the violent crime in the city took place there, and of course most of the victims were black too. In the Sixth Division, which meant the three Harlem precincts, the homicide rate in 1971 was 96.4 per 100,000 residents, and in the worst Harlem precinct, the 28th, it was nearly 200 per 100,000 residents. This meant, someone calculated, that one out of every 500 persons strolling the streets of central Harlem that year could expect to be slaughtered before the year was out. There were altogether 1466 criminal homicides reported in New York in 1971. More than half of the corpses, 784, were black. The rest of the racial breakdown of the victims went this way: 370 white, 306 Hispanic, 6 miscellaneous. So the violence in the black precincts was out of all proportion to the population of the city, though perfectly in tune with the poverty of those precincts, and with the misery, the hopelessness, and the drugs.

Weekends were when cops on patrol were busiest. Saturday led the list in murders with 284. Sunday came next with 231, then Friday with 229, and Tuesday last with 154. More people were murdered between midnight and 1 A.M. than any other time, 110 bodies having turned up at that hour; 109 homicides took place between 9 and 10 P.M.; and 104 between 11 and midnight. Summer was the worst season. On hot summer nights, tempers ran short and violence erupted regularly. The cops could count on a lot of killings in July, August, and September every year. But in 1971, December would lead all those other months, 174 murders to September's runner-up 147. December was a warm muggy month, the country was in a recession. In the ghettos there were often no jobs, and so no Christmas tree, and the Christmas present for many was death.

Overall, the murder rate in New York was up 31.2 percent over 1970. This did not make New York the worst city in the world in murder, for eight out of the ten largest American cities surpassed New York easily, some of them spectacularly. But the New York rate of murder was spectacular enough, and month after month as the crime statistics were released, the newspapers headlined the sensational increase in homicides. This infuriated Commissioner Murphy. He wanted the headlines to focus on decreases in other categories of crime. He wanted mention of murder toned down. When the Planning Division's statistics came into his office each month, he would scrawl messages in the margin to the effect that in, say, 68 percent of the murders in which the circumstances were determined the victim and the murderer were acquainted. He had done the mathematics himself, at the bottom of the page, complete with long division: Make the newspapers take note of this fact.

In truth, 522 of the murders, more than 35 percent of the score, were as a result of fights—and fighters know each other—often in bars while drinking, often with neighbors in hallways; and 132 times that year a family dispute ended with a dead body on the floor—and family members know each other. Other common-law relationships or boy-girl relationships were terminated fatally 78 times. Murphy's point was that the police couldn't prevent people who know each other from also murdering each other, but that only 229 innocent citizens got murdered while being robbed, and only 109 during the commission of other felonies: 338 out of the overall 1466. Of course in almost 400 cases the cops found only the body and didn't know what caused it to be there. Anyway, 1195 victims were males. Only 271 were females. Usually the cops zeroed in pretty quickly on the murderer; they would make 1144 arrests for murder before the year was out.

The use of guns in homicides, like the number of homicides themselves, kept going up year by year. In 1971, 695 of these victims would be shot to death. Ten years previously the total had been 98. So guns were now the favorite instrument of death, accounting for 47.4 percent of the

corpses. Knives, ice picks, and the rest came next, 35.9 percent. Then came physical force, usually meaning fists, or
fingers clamped around the throat. Blunt instruments accounted for relatively few homicides, only 45; such killers
used everything from clubs to chairs, and there was one
murder by toilet tank cover.

So cops knew all about violent death. Although few of
them ever had or ever would fire their guns in the line of
duty, all of them had coped numerous times with corpses.
To bundle a slashed or shot, still-warm body into a body
bag was bad enough. But too many of these crimes were
not neat at all. There were "floaters" recovered after a
quantity of time in one of the rivers who were inflated like
balloons; they would split apart the moment the cops tried
to lift them on board, spilling maggots out all over the
cops' shiny black shoes. There was the odor to warn that
behind the locked door of furnished rooms somebody had
been dead for days. Before the year was out, detectives
would break into a flat in Greenwich Village, to find a man
lying dead. He had been stabbed, but they couldn't tell that
at first, for the murderer had closed him up in there with
his dog. It was a big dog, it had no food, and between the
day of the murder and the day detectives broke down the
door, man's best friend had partially eaten his master. It
was not a pretty thing to look at.

There were burglars who would defecate beside the safes
they looted—why, no cop ever knew. Usually, the first
time a cop saw this, he was afraid to mention it on the
grounds that no one would believe him.

There were the tenement lobbies in which drunks would
urinate between the sections of the radiator; when the heat
came up, you wouldn't believe it. And these were the buildings cops were called to enter all the time. One day a janitor came upon a drunk urinating in his hallway, so he went
down and got a shotgun, and the guy was still at it, so the
janitor put the shotgun up real close and pulled the trigger.
In that hallway for the next three hours, while the torn-
apart body lay there and the blood clotted, while the stench
rose each time the heat rose, the cops coped with the homicide: the police photographers took their photos, the ballistics men recovered pellets and plotted their angles, the de-

tectives interviewed tenants, the responding radio car team wrote out its report.

A cop was as intimately connected to both life and death as a racing driver. There were the same peaks of excitement with long hours of boredom in between, and the same possibility of an instantaneous, brutal end.

Life and death.

Later that year, within three hours of a single tour, a patrolman named Thomas Courson would both deliver his first baby and kill his first gunman.

Reporters found Courson at the station house. He said, "That one tour epitomizes this whole job. Within three hours you can watch a life come into the world and then watch one go out."

Life and death. Violence. Violence was never far from any cop's life. One of them was in an elevator on his way to visit the widow of one of his closest friends, who had been killed trying to stop a holdup. Suddenly the man in the elevator beside him whipped out a knife and demanded the off-duty cop's money. A moment after the cop killed him, the elevator door opened. The cop stumbled to the apartment of the widow he had come to console and announced, "I've got to use your phone. I've just killed a guy."

Violence. The Police Academy taught recruits how to deliver babies, and it also taught them about the use of "deadly physical force": defined under the penal law as "physical force which, under the circumstances in which it is used, is readily capable of causing death or other serious physical injury." New York for many years had had possibly the tightest procedure in the country concerning the use of force by its police officers. And Patrick Murphy claimed some credit for this from the time when he was training officer at the Police Academy under Mike Murphy. At that time Pat Murphy helped develop a special study course called "The Moral Aspects of the Use of Firearms." Pat Murphy then and now liked to stress the tremendous moral implications of the use of the gun. "Because policemen must use their guns on occasions," Murphy told the recruits then, and now sometimes told the city, "it is very important that they be as good at using them as possible, that they be very accurate and self-confident. A wild shot can kill a person in a crowded city like this."

Murphy's successors at the Police Academy were still teaching his course. Although the training of most law officers across America amounted to a few weeks or less, and in many of the smaller communities to no training at all, before they were equipped with gun and badge—they were expected to pick up all they needed to know on the job and the street—police recruit training in the seventies in New York lasted six months, 910 hours in all. Of this total, 398 hours went to academic instruction in Police Academy classrooms, and another 105 hours to college-level education courses at John Jay College. Field training experience accounted for 140 hours, physical training for 180 hours, firearms training for 56 hours, water safety instruction for 24 hours, and administrative/security duty for the final 14 hours.

The largest portion of the classroom work, 119 hours in all, involved the study of law: constitutional law, New York State criminal law, traffic law, criminal procedures, children and the law, civil rights law. But there were also courses in human behavior, human relations, family crises, street problems and behavior. The physical training portion of the curriculum included, of course, a good deal of calisthenics, but the rest of it was practical. Recruits were taught self-defense through use of the nightstick, how to search and frisk suspects, unarmed defense, and first aid.

But firearms training came very early and was very intensive: seven straight days. The course started with seven hours of indoctrination in the nomenclature and operation of the revolver, the ballistics of it, safety precautions, how to clean the gun afterwards, plus a hundred rounds of firing at targets in the basement of the Police Academy. The second session was another seven hours in the same Police Academy range: review of safety precautions, review of combat firing, dry firing practice. Then came target practice again, first at 15 yards then at 25. This was followed by a lecture on judgment in the use of force, and finally by pointers on the safeguarding of firearms. Most cops from then on would own two guns, and although one was on their person by law at all times, in fact, in their own homes most would put their guns away somewhere. There were cops who would handcuff their guns to waterpipes in their basements. Others kept them in strongboxes, others unloaded them and buried them under clothes on a shelf, and still others made a practice of leaving their guns fully loaded in the open so their kids could get used to the idea.

Each day during the firearms course recruits were taught:

1. You may shoot only to defend yourself or another from deadly physical force or to arrest a person who has committed a felony involving deadly physical force or is attempting to escape by use of deadly weapon. You can't shoot a man stealing a parked car, for instance.

2. You may shoot to prevent the crimes of kidnapping, robbery, rape, forcible sodomy, or arson of a premises. Do not shoot unless it is necessary to prevent the commission of such crime.

3. Do not shoot from or at a moving vehicle unless necessary and it is safe to do so.

4. Do not fire warning shots unless circumstances permit the use of deadly force. Such practice endangers the lives of bystanders and may prompt the suspect to return the gunfire.

5. Do not shoot on mere suspicion. An officer should know with virtual certainty that the suspect committed an offense for which the use of deadly physical force is permissible.

And so for seven straight days the recruits listened to these lectures and fired scores of rounds of ammunition at targets. They fired by daylight. They fired in dim light, and they fired in the virtual absence of light.

After the sixth session, if the recruit had attained a 70 percent score in slow fire, and a 180 out of a possible 300 score for slow, timed, and rapid fire combined, he was rated qualified, and was thereupon armed and permitted to carry his service revolver. Other recruits went back to the clinic for more training. The seventh day of this course pointed out to the recruits something which up to now they had only suspected: A policeman firing in an actual gun battle does not enjoy the ideal shooting conditions accorded to recruits on the range. Now the instructors tried to explain to the young cops about terror. The closest that terror could be approximated in a classroom situation was to make the recruits jog from the classroom to the range, and then make them shoot before they could calm down. The jogging gave them the increased heart beat, the heavy breathing, the muscle tremors, and the other physiological reactions that combat would bring on. But it still wasn't terror and none of these young men knew how they would react if they ever came face-to-face with a gunman who was shooting.

A study had been done on gun fights the year before. There had been 634 incidents in all, in which 659 cops had fired a total of 1643 shots, including 183 warning shots. The majority of these cops had been confronted by more than one criminal. The score: seven cops shot dead, 242 injured; 19 cops had had their guns taken away from them and had been assaulted with their own guns. As for the criminals, 50 were shot and killed, and 212 wounded. This study showed that almost all gun fights took place within seven yards, and many times the criminal and the cop were close enough almost to touch each other. Almost never did a cop have a chance to cock his gun, stand in profile, and take careful aim at his target. He had time only to yank his gun out of its holster, point it in the general direction of his adversary, and pull on the trigger as hard and as fast and as often as he could. The vast majority of the reported incidents occurred not only at night but in very poor light, sometimes only by the light of the moon or the stars or a street light halfway down the block. Most shoot-outs with cops happened on Friday and Saturday nights, and August and September were the leading months, except for April. Perhaps the coming of spring led a number of young bloods to think that they could win a shoot-out with the police. Shoot-outs occurred in ghetto precincts with far greater frequency than anywhere else, and they took place outdoors, especially on the street itself, by a two to one margin over apartments, stairs and hallways, subway stations, and the like. Only four captains and eight lieutenants got involved in shoot-outs during that year, only 38 sergeants. All the rest, over 600 of them, were patrolmen or detectives. The average shoot-out involved 1.62 adversaries, and it was all over in under two seconds. Of the

1643 shots fired by cops, 436 hit the target. There were only 75 "gun fights" worthy of the name, in which multiple shots were exchanged between cops and criminals.

The result of this study was that Police Academy techniques had just undergone abrupt change. The Police Academy range got very much dimmer and the targets were moved up very much closer to the recruits. Shooting at multiple targets simultaneously was introduced. The combat position remained unchanged. Cops were taught to crouch, to hold their guns at arm's length with both hands, and to shoot rapid-fire without aiming. They were to point the gun like a flashlight. They were taught to fire quickly. If it was all to be over in under two seconds, then it was speed that counted, more than accuracy. The recruits were taught to reload without looking, for if a cop had to reload in the dark his eyes wouldn't help him find the holes in the chamber. The lectures that went with these instructions were often light-hearted: "Most perpetrators are right-handed, and they are not trained. Therefore, when they fire at you, their guns will jump slightly to your right, and their bullets will tend to pass over your right shoulder. Therefore, before you go into your combat crouch, take half a step to the left. Of course you may run into a left-handed shooter who has been trained, and in that case you will get an inspector's funeral."

Young cops usually found such comments amusing. There would be inspectors' funerals for a number of them in future years, but nobody was thinking of that now.

The Police Department required that all cops qualify with their guns twice a year. This was a formal order, and there was no getting out of it. It bound all cops, even 50-year-old chiefs. Although the brass could phone for an appointment, drive up in front with their chauffeurs, sign in, blast away, and be out in an hour (the cop-chauffeur often was able to get in and out in an hour too), for the average cop, training took all day. He signed in. His guns were checked out and sometimes repaired for him, he listened to lectures, fired 50 rounds, listened to lectures, fired 50 more rounds, and so forth. He fired standing, he fired prone, he fired fast and slow, close-in and long-range, and with each of his guns; and it was always mid-afternoon before he was allowed to sign out and go home.

The summer shooting cycle took place at the Department's outdoor range at Rodman's Neck, near Orchard Beach, in the North Bronx. A dirt road led in there, and one soon came upon a group of low huts and buildings reminiscent of a temporary army post from World War II. Behind the range area, which was more than 150 fire lanes wide, rose mounds of garbage, for this area was also one of the principal dumping grounds for the city's Sanitation Department. The garbage had been bulldozed into neat piles and covered with dirt, and these artificial hills served as the backstop for police bullets. Not just revolver bullets either. It was here that the rifles, the machine guns, the shotguns, the tear gas grenades, all of the ferocious competence of the Police Department, were tested. Even .38-caliber revolver bullets cost a nickel apiece, and the Department's bill for ammunition alone—ten million bullets—ran to over $500,000 per year.

In addition to the two formal training cycles each year, cops were urged to practice regularly. There were shooting ranges in the basements of many of the station houses, and 50 free bullets per month were offered to any cop who wanted to fire them. But the instructors in all the ranges had found that those men who were already good shots practiced constantly, whereas the poor shots never practiced at all.

A number of cops had become cops just because they loved guns, or in order to be able to carry guns; but this did not seem to be the case with most of them, and a great number turned out to be inept shooters. Shortly after Jones and Piagentini were murdered, a radio car on the East Side was ordered to respond to a Chinese laundry, where a robbery was supposed to be in progress. The driver of this radio car decided to get his revolver out while still some blocks away. Did he expect to fire through the windshield, or what? Before the gun came clear of the holster, it went off, and the bullet went through both his partner's legs and into the side of the door.

There was a story making the rounds of a cop whose kid's baseball went down into a sewer. The cop raised the sewer lid by prying it up with the barrel of his gun, which bent.

There were stories about cops who cocked their guns either in the heat of action or accidentally, and then didn't know how to uncock the gun without its going off. This was a tricky matter. In recruit training, cops were taught to put their left thumb between the hammer and the bullet, to let the hammer down lightly upon their thumbnail and then, withdrawing their thumb, let the hammer down lightly the rest of the way. Otherwise, it was difficult to uncock a gun without a bullet exploding out of the chamber. But there were stories about cops who had forgotten this technique or who had never learned it. And guns caught on pants or belts or holsters, and became cocked somewhat easily. One cop to whom this happened decided to solve his problem by firing his gun into his toilet, with the inevitable results. Another carried his gun around in his holster with the hammer taped back; it wasn't going to go off under *any* circumstances. Still another cop, a captain, trying the thumbnail trick on his accidentally cocked gun, had sent a bullet up through the ceiling into the office above. His first fear was that some cop was lying dead up there. This proved groundless. Next he was certain that his career would be ruined if word got out, and he was frantically trying to plaster the hole in the ceiling before anybody noticed it.

Cops carried guns every day of their lives, and learned to feel naked without that weight on their hips. But on the whole, few enough were in love with guns, and very, very few ever used one in combat. Those who had done so were listened to in some awe by the others, principally because no one could know what it was like in combat except those who had been there. A cop owed it to himself to collect all data available on the subject.

That very summer a man would walk into the room on the second floor of the Federal Court House, just down the street from Police Headquarters, grab a cleaning woman, put a gun to her head, and demand to see a bankruptcy referee named Roy Babitt. His call brought instead 125 city policemen and U.S. marshals, many of them wearing helmets and bulletproof vests, and packing shotguns, rifles, and tear gas canisters. But the cleaning woman was the first concern, and so a blond, 30-year-old detective named Richard Condon, and a patrolman, John Mulligan of Emergency Service, went to the door of the barricaded office. Mulli-

gan was dressed in a judge's robes. Condon, wore ordinary
civilian clothes. Mulligan was able to persuade the madman
that Condon was a lawyer, whereupon Condon offered to
replace the cleaning woman as hostage if she be permitted
to leave. The madman agreed to this, and presently he and
Condon faced each other across a desk. The madman's gun
was pointed right at Condon's chest. After talking soothingly for a while, Condon bent down to scratch his ankle.
He had a snub-nosed revolver there, and now as the gunman's attention was diverted, Condon tried to yank it out.

But it caught on his sock.

"What are you doing there?" demanded the madman.
His gun described a small circle in the middle of Condon's
chest.

"Nothing," said Condon.

A moment later, Condon bent to scratch his ankle again.
This time he came up with his revolver, and emptied five
shots at the madman, who was only a few feet away.

Later Condon mused, "On the range I've never shot anything less than 'excellent.' But I squeezed off five shots at
that guy from less than five feet away, and I only hit him
once." He added, "When the hammer of my gun caught in
my sock, I thought I was a dead man."

Condon's dying target was placed on a stretcher and
rushed out of the Court House—but on the wrong side of
the building. The ambulance was on the other side. The
stretcher was run around the corner after the ambulance,
which itself was circling the block. Meanwhile the American Civil Liberties Union was writing a formal complaint
to Police Commissioner Murphy demanding that Condon
be disciplined, because he had presented himself to the
gunman as a lawyer.

Cops, listening to Condon's story, noted the part about
the stretcher chasing the ambulance around the block, an
odd touch, and the part about the lawyer—if you were a
cop, lawyers could not be trusted. But mostly when they
listened to Condon they were thinking about missing the
perpetrator four times out of five from a distance of five
feet—Condon, a guy who always shot "excellent" on the
range.

The police service revolver was a .38-caliber Colt or
Smith and Wesson with a four-inch barrel. Most cops had

as a second gun a .38-caliber Colt or Smith and Wesson with a two-inch barrel. This was always referred to as the off-duty gun. A certain number carried 9 mm. Browning automatics as a second gun, or else a .25-caliber automatic that could be concealed in one's pocket.

The Emergency Service trucks carried shotguns and snipers' rifles as standard gear. The shotguns could also fire tear gas projectiles if necessary, and the snipers' rifles had such a tiny bore that most cops, when they first saw one, couldn't believe it. These rifles fired a bullet smaller than a .22 but with such velocity that if it touched its target anywhere, he went down. In addition the bullet would disintegrate on contact with so much as a leaf, or so it was claimed. Thus there was no risk of killing some citizen a mile away. These rifles were fitted with snipers' scopes, and it was possible (for I did this myself at the police range one day) to put the cross hairs on the chest of an old man sitting on a park bench across the river, said old man being invisible to the naked eye. Of course it was terrifically difficult—impossible for me—to hold the rifle steady enough to keep the cross hairs fixed on the target at such a range, but the Police Department had men who could do it. It was the job of these Emergency Service patrolmen on the one hand to give oxygen to derelicts suffering spasms on the sidewalk, or to deliver babies if they got there in time; and on the other hand to be ready to use these awesome shotguns and snipers' rifles, and occasionally the same cop would perform both functions within a single day. When Commissioner Murphy was a patrolman, and then a sergeant, working in Emergency Service, the trucks carried the same gear as now, that is, both the emergency lifesaving gear, and these weapons of death. But Murphy, however often he may have used the one, never used the other at all. "We never had to," he said, when I asked him. "There were whole years in those days when not a single policeman would be killed." During those same years it was never necessary to take those guns out of their cases in the trucks.

A cop always tried to get his man without having to use guns, because if you took a shot at him, this usually meant that he would get off a shot or two at you at the same time, which could be unpleasant. Whenever possible, if a murderer or armed robber, a sniper or madman, were holed up on a rooftop or in some apartment somewhere, the cops would try to talk him out through the door onto the street. There were well-known routines for doing this. The Police Department arsenal included machine guns, though these could only be deployed under the signature of a captain or above, but said machine guns might be exposed in great numbers more or less in the open, where a barricaded perpetrator could see them. Next some cop would get on a bullhorn, claiming to be captain so and so. "Shotguns ready on the right," he would shout. "Machine guns get into position on the left. Get ready to storm the place." The next voice on the bullhorn might be softer, pleading. "This is Father Gleason speaking. Your soul is in jeopardy. This is no way to die."

If the perpetrator failed to give up at that point, they went in after him.

Killing was never taken lightly. If a cop killed somebody, he was immediately withdrawn from his unit and assigned to division or borough headquarters upon the orders of Chief Codd himself. The theory was that no cop could kill without being upset by it. You didn't want him answering the same type of run the next day or the day after. You knew that the killing had some effect on him. You wanted him to have a month or so to get over it, before going back into his radio car.

Any time a cop fired his gun on or off duty a report had to be made, and these reports were very detailed. His gun was taken to the Police Academy and tested by ballistics. Any bullets he had put into somebody would be dug out of the person, fragments of meat still attached, each bullet in its separate envelope, stinking after a day or two out of all proportion to its size, though not its potency; and these bullets would be compared to those fired by his gun in the test. After that, the Firearms Section copied down all details and added them to its statistics for the year. Where was the cop standing? where was the perpetrator standing? how many shots fired? what was the lighting? where did the bullets go? All policemen who killed a citizen went before a grand jury. Usually this was just a formality, but each time a policeman killed a citizen, even though in the commission of some terrible crime, a grand jury would rule on whether or not he was justified in using "deadly physical force."

The policeman tended to see himself as isolated from the public that he served. He was surrounded by a sea of hostility, and because he could do nothing about this hostility, and because he hated it, he often gave hostility back. I once tried to describe to Sergeant Durk the hostility that the journalist felt when demanding interviews in which to pose hard questions. Durk, the career policeman, replied, "Don't talk to me about hostility, pal. You don't know what hostility is."

Presumably each cop wanted to be considered a normal member of society, a man among men, but this was denied them by their role. They saw themselves as separated from other men by their shields and their guns—principally by their guns—and so to each of them this gun became something precious—precious not as a weapon but as a symbol. The gun was the real badge of their office, and the shield they referred to as "the tin." If in fact it was this gun that made other men hostile, then each policeman would try to believe that this same gun made him something special. The gun more than the shield made him the man who kept the peace. It was because of the gun, not the shield, that he would go into a dark building after a dangerous criminal.

All of this was a good deal more subtle than it may sound. Not only had most cops not fired their guns on duty, but most New Yorkers had never in their lives seen a uniformed policeman with a gun drawn. Cops were under orders to leave that gun holstered unless absolutely necessary. The public was not to be uselessly alarmed. A reaction from the public, whether of aversion or admiration or possibly of violence, was not to be provoked or even to be risked.

The off-duty gun was almost always worn concealed. In August heatwaves individual off-duty cops would stand packed into sweltering subway cars unable to remove their sports jackets—lest the gun show. Or if they wore sport shirts, the shirttails had always to hang outside the belt, however sloppy this might look or feel, again to conceal that off-duty gun. A belly holster had been developed. It fitted around the middle like an abdominal support, under the shirt, so that the gun rode snuggled into rolls of whatever flab the cop had developed, showing dim outlines or none at all. One left the shirt buttons open under the tie so as to be able to get at the thing if needed. But the belly holster was hot too, and also constricting, and was favored by very few. There was also the ankle holster—a two-inch wide, felt-lined leather band with holster attached which was laced like a brace around the lower shin. The gun was solidly anchored to the leg, out of sight in hot weather or cold, and made no giveaway bulge under that year's bell-bottom fashion, but it felt funny when walking.

Often cops used their guns to identify themselves to one another. At headquarters downtown, hundreds of cops worked in civilian clothes, meaning in shirtsleeves, and so did hundreds of civilian clerks. The cops were supposed to wear their shields showing, but few did, and the civilians were supposed to wear their ID cards clamped to their shirt pockets, but few did. So the only way to tell the cops from the civilians was by the presence or absence of the gun in the belt. One or two cops would lock their guns in a desk drawer as soon as they came to work in the morning, for carrying that extra weight and bulge around all day was a nuisance, but such men were very rare. The gun was the price of admission to the police world, and no cop wanted to be mistaken for a clerk or, worse, for some tourist in there on a visit.

Similarly, inside station houses, cops in plainclothes would often hook their thumbs in their belts, just to sweep their coats back enough to display their belts to other cops they didn't know. It was a way of saying, "I'm a cop, too."

So in the vast majority of cases the gun wasn't for firing, and it wasn't for show either, but every cop knew it was there on his person, and it was precious to him. Nearly all cops, once they retired, would keep one or all of their guns, and very few would ever go out of their houses unarmed. One detective who retired about this time, Stanley Perlmutter, even was lobbying to get a bill through the legislature in Albany that would concede to retired policemen the power to make arrests in any sort of an emergency situation.

"We all still have our guns," Perlmutter said. "We see things other citizens don't see, because we've been trained to see them. We want to take action, and we can't."

If indicted, or arrested, or sometimes if even accused of a serious crime, a policeman would be suspended from duty, and the first act of his commanding officer would be to remove from his person his shield and his gun, and this was often more traumatic to him than the outcome of his eventual trial. In addition, certain cops who had been judged somewhat unstable by the Police Medical Board, had been stripped of their guns, though not their shields, and assigned work as clerks or messenger boys, often in the basement offices at headquarters, and this was known in derision as the Rubber Gun Squad, or the Bow and Arrow Squad; and it was in many respects the ultimate disgrace that a policeman could experience. Every man in the Police Department was aware of the gun mystique, though probably few had ever thought out all its implications. One day someone walked into the police garage on Broome Street and drove away in the car assigned to Deputy Commissioner Louis Stutman. This had never happened before, and Commissioner Murphy laughed to hear of a thief that brazen. "People will say that Murphy's getting more diabolical every day," joked the Commissioner. "Look how subtly he's getting rid of Stutman; he gives him the word by stealing his car." And then, somewhat more seriously, "To take a man's wheels away is the last thing you do before you take away his gun."

The bravery of cops always seemed to me quite extraordinary. I do not think that each cop took his bravery from his gun—after all, the criminals always had guns too—but rather that he took from it a sense of responsibility. That gun was his honor, and it dragged him into danger like a locomotive pulling a train. Cops knew terror just like anybody. One day in a face-to-face shoot-out, a cop emptied his service revolver into an armed criminal. Then he reloaded his gun and kept on firing into the body, momentarily gripped by a terror he could not control. Cases such as this had occurred before, and surely they would occur again, and there had been and would always be citizens and newsmen who would equate this overkill to police brutality, such persons never having experienced the terror of a shoot-out. The fact is that cops were brave even when outnumbered, brave even when unarmed, brave gratuitously, only because they were or had been cops.

That year a detective named Thomas Young shot a stick-up man who had just robbed a taxi cab and wounded its driver in Harlem. Young was not only off duty at the time, but that was the day that his retirement from the Police Department took effect. One Dominick Papa intervened in a Queens liquor store holdup and was killed. He was a retired lieutenant, and he was 72 years old at the time.

In the Bronx, a Lieutenant Jack Kaminsky, 42 years old, heard a woman scream, and saw a man racing down the street away from her. Kaminsky chased the man, who, as Kaminsky overtook him, turned and began lashing at Kaminsky with a huge knife. Kaminsky grabbed the guy, disarmed him, and held him until two patrolmen, also drawn by the woman's screams, ran up. Kaminsky then presented them with the prisoner, the knife, and the cash and jewelry stolen from the woman. Kaminsky had just been indicted for perjury, growing out of charges that he regularly accepted bribes. He carried no shield, no gun, at the time. Once a cop always a cop.

That day—or one just like it—a sergeant who worked for me, Edward Powers, remarked, "There's no shortage of volunteers when there's a shoot-out. Every cop will volunteer for that."

I never heard of a cop accused of cowardice.

The ninth cop killed in 1971 would be Kenneth Nugent, aged 40, father of eight. He had been in shoot-outs before, the most recent of them two months previously in the darkened basement of a supermarket in Queens. He lived way, way out in Long Island in the same suburb as so many other cops, and he was driving to work on August 20 to do a midnight to 8 A.M. tour. Since he was a bit early, he decided to stop at a candy store in Queens to buy some cigarettes. He walked directly into three armed junkies who were holding up the place. They were young and black and desperate, and the odds were three to one. But Nugent drew his off-duty gun and announced himself. The three men turned and started shooting. Nugent shot one of them dead. Almost simultaneously a bullet struck him in the center of the forehead, and parted his brain. He was rushed to Long Island Jewish Hospital, and out of my office rushed my Night Duty Sergeant, Jack O'Grady, one of his best friends.

The press congregated of course. The shooting of a cop, if it happened early enough in the evening, always made a

big story the next day. It was O'Grady's job to relay information to the press, but instead he spent his time that night
trying to console Nugent's wife, who had also been rushed
to the hospital, and he and I were criticized for this later.
The press can be arrogant and unfeeling, and there were
those who wanted to know why O'Grady wasn't doing his
job. But the murder of a policeman always strikes personally many, many other cops. Nugent had no chance, and
soon died; and a few days later, a great many of us, about
5000 in all, drawn from police departments all over the
metropolitan area but especially from New York City, and
including almost the entire complement of the 103rd Precinct, Nugent's precinct, attended his funeral. The 103rd
Precinct, emptied of its own cops that day, was patrolled
principally by cops from the Special Events Squad, an elite
unit used to police the city's riots, demonstrations, World
Series baseball games, and political rallies, and used also to
patrol the home precinct of a slain cop on the day of his
funeral.

Always the funeral of a cop drew hordes of other cops,
all wearing black bands around their shields. They gathered
in the street outside the church in orderly ranks, filling it
for blocks in both directions. In front of these ranks, directly in front of the church doors, stood all of the important chiefs: the Chief of Detectives, the Chief of Patrol,
the Chief of Inspectional Services, the Chief of Intelligence, and many of the chiefs commanding boroughs as
well, most of them in civilian clothes; and in either that
row or the one behind it, also in civilian clothes, stood all
the political cops: the sergeant who headed the Sergeants'
Benevolent Association, the detective who headed the Detectives' Endowment Association, the lieutenant who headed the Lieutenants' Benevolent Association, and probably a
number of political cops and high-ranking chiefs from
other police departments also. In the row in front of all
these men stood the deputy commissioners, and in front of
the deputy commissioners stood the Chief Inspector, the
Police Commissioner, and the Mayor.

The sun was very hot that morning and coming straight
down, and the wait as always seemed interminable—no funeral ever started on time. But presently came scores if not
hundreds of people hurrying down the sidewalk toward the

church, filling up the lawn and trampling the bushes on either side of the church doors. These were people who had waited outside the funeral home until the coffin was brought out of there and now had hurried to the church. The ranks of cops and officials in front of the church door now stood straight and stopped talking, for here came the procession around the corner and down the street toward them, moving very, very slowly, led by a barely moving radio car from the 103rd Precinct, Nugent's precinct, dome light mournfully turning. Next came two cops on motorcycles, the motorcycles creeping ahead so slowly that the leather-booted drivers could barely keep them upright. Then came a gap, followed by two black-suited chaplains walking almost infinitely slowly, and the hearse, barely moving, just behind them.

The Police Academy lieutenant moved the hearse into place some distance past the church doors, and the television cameramen, cumbersome gear clamped onto their shoulders, sprinted up to get shots of the casket.

Meanwhile the limousines pulled up in front of the church, one behind the other, until all were stopped. Policemen now came forward and stood by each door to open it. So the family stepped out and stood waiting, while six cops—always the same cops at every funeral that year, a permanent detail—lifted the casket out of the hearse and onto their shoulders. At that, 5000 policemen in the street snapped their hands up in salute, rigidly holding this salute until the casket had been carried inside the church. The family then walked indoors behind it, and although all police funerals were sad, this was one of the saddest, for Nugent's wife looked as drab as drab, cried out, as drab as a pretty 39-year-old blonde woman can be when left with eight children and a murdered husband. The children all were there, all blond, all looking alike, but the heads all at different altitudes, a step upward through Nugent's small sons, coming at last to his oldest daughter, who held in her two hands his service cap and on top of that a bouquet of flowers.

After the family had moved into the church, the Mayor and the Police Commissioner led the rest of us in, as many as the church would hold, meaning that for each funeral thousands of policemen waited outside in the street while the funeral Mass was sung. The funeral service was almost always a Catholic Mass. In my time I never went to a Jewish funeral, and to only one Protestant one, although at each Mass the Jewish Chaplain, Rabbi Alvin Kass, and always several of the Protestant chaplains were in attendance inside the altar rail. The Catholic funerals always lasted a long time, and Nugent's was no exception, for when it came time to distribute communion, the aisles filled up with bare-headed young Catholic cops, all in uniform, caps under their arms, guns flapping. The Mayor, who was not Catholic, remained in his seat, but the Police Commisioner and the Chief Inspector invariably led the way to the altar rail.

At last that day's funeral Mass ended and we all marched outside again and waited in place in the same ranks as before. The family came out and stood on the sidewalk, Nugent's teen-age blonde daughter still holding his hat with the bouquet of flowers on it, and then the pallbearers came with the casket on their shoulders. At this moment the thousands of cops in the street saluted once again and a bugler somewhere nearby played taps. Mrs. Nugent did not cry. She looked as though she had no tears left. But many of the rest of us cried.

When the coffin had been slid into the hearse, and the family had stepped into the limousines, the radio car from the 103rd Precinct, its dome light mournfully turning once again, led the slow way to the cemetery, followed by the two motorcycle cops rolling very slowly, with many corrections to the handlebars, followed by the hearse, and the flower car, and the limousines of the family. When the hearse was out of sight at last, the order was given, and we all broke ranks. The Mayor and the Police Commissioner were rushed to a nearby lot where they boarded the police helicopter for an express trip back to the city. Many of the other cops repaired to the parking lot of a nearby shopping center where a canteen had been set up by the PBA, and where sandwiches and beer were dispensed free to all the thousands of cops who had come all the way out here on Long Island—once again—to attend the funeral.

This, with variations, was the funeral all of us attended many times that year and also the next. It was called an inspector's funeral, but it wasn't really; it was a slain cop's funeral. Inspectors held bulletproof jobs, and although certain of them had died in office, this was always of natural causes; and no one went to their funerals but their families, and perhaps a representative of the Mayor and/or the Police Commissioner.

Seven days after Nugent was killed, his partner, Huey Curtin, who had ridden beside him in the same radio car for ten years, formally applied to the Chief Inspector for permission to turn in his own shield, and henceforth to wear Nugent's. His previous shield, Curtin said, had no history. It meant nothing to anyone. But shield Number 16022, Nugent's shield, did.

"For ten years we spent eight hours together every day in the radio car," Curtin told a reporter. "It was like a marriage. In the Department you know very quickly whether you can make it with someone or not, and we did. I guess we'd have lasted forever." Patrolman Curtin received his former partner's shield on a Friday and that weekend he took some of his eight children over to Nugent's house to show it to Mrs. Nugent and her eight children. They sat in the kitchen, a dozen people, all of them kids except for Mrs. Nugent and Huey Curtin. Patrolman Curtin later said, "In the radio car you talk about schools, about your kids, your home, the job, and you talk about life. You get around to talking about just about everything."

"My husband and Ken Nugent were closer than he and I are," said Hugh Curtin's wife. "Once I told Huey, 'I think you talk to Kenny more than to me. When you're home you watch TV and the kids are always around.' But he and Kenny lived together. They had a perfect relationship. They knew what each other was thinking."

The love of cop for cop was a very real thing, though few of them would have been willing to put it in such "sissy" terms. But it took no imagination at all for any cop to put himself in Nugent's place, dead, or in Curtin's place, bereft of his partner of ten years. The world was hostile, the city was hostile, a cop had no one he could depend on or turn to except another cop. And so a signal 10:13 on the police radio, Assist Patrolman, brought an avalanche of radio cars, every cop within earshot or radio range rushing to the defense of whichever of his fellows was in danger. Similarly, off-duty cops knew that they could break minor regulations, particularly traffic regulations, with impunity anywhere in the world. A New York cop caught for speeding in Los Angeles, would merely show the "tin" and the California cop would pat him on the shoulder and let him go. He knew he would. He also knew he would do the same for that California cop in New York.

The cop was the guy with the gun. The cop was the guy who enforced society's laws. The burglar didn't want to be caught any more than the illegally parked motorist, and both of them would hate the cop who did the job. The cop had no one who loved him except his family and other cops, and he knew it, and he arranged his life accordingly. There were corrupt cops, and there were honest cops who knew who the corrupt ones were and did nothing; and if asked, an honest cop would say, "I'm not gonna turn in another cop."

But this year a man was Commissioner who spoke openly of police corruption, and a commission had been formed headed by Whitman Knapp that was dedicated to exposing police corruption in all of its ramifications, a commission which planned to use honest cops to entrap corrupt ones, which was willing to destroy any cop, corrupt or not, who got in its way.

The murderers of Patrolman Nugent were soon caught, indicted, and convicted. The murderers of all patrolmen almost invariably were identified at once and caught soon after. Organized crime almost never shot at police officers, and it was years since any cop had been gunned down by a Mafia figure. Organized crime was too smart to get involved in the type of investigation that followed a cop killing. A great many solvable crimes in the city were never solved, because not enough men were assigned to the case, or because those assigned were lazy or hardly cared or got sidetracked.

But when a cop got killed, no other cop got lazy, no other cop got sidetracked. Detectives worked on the case night and day, and so did every other cop in that precinct and many other cops throughout the city. Cops were all ears as far as murdered patrolmen were concerned; they heard details all over the city and followed leads on their own time and fed all this into the detectives who had the case. In effect, the citizen who murdered his wife's lover was sought by a team of detectives, two men. But he who killed a cop was sought by 32,000. Such odds were considered too poor by organized crime. They often bought cops, or tried to, never slew them, and there was no threat to cops' lives from the Mafia.

However, now in the 1970s violence abounded, guns abounded, and young hoodlums who didn't know better shot cops by accident, and the Black Liberation Army, which also didn't know better, shot them on purpose. These days virtually any encounter between a cop and a citizen, especially at night, could end in gunfire, could end in the cop's murder; two cops had been machine-gunned over a traffic ticket, and this was irrational; the general hatred of cops was irrational, but it was also true. Even the madman who had virtually sliced off Patrolman Denton's head, though later certified as a lunatic, was not a lunatic in a vacuum—he was a lunatic in a society which had been taught to hate cops, and to call them pigs.

After the machine-gunning of Patrolmen Binetti and Curry, Commissioner Murphy made an impassioned declaration, one of the few of passion that he was to make that year, and also one of the few of which cops approved. Murphy said, "No citizen can be secure while our peace forces are subject to murderous attack in the street. No offer can be expected to perform his duty at the high level which the public properly expects of him if he must be continually apprehensive that even his most routine activities will bring him face-to-face with senseless and unprovoked gunfire. This deadly violence is wholly indiscriminate. Any policeman, at any time, has become a target for a killer, and this is plainly intolerable. Any person who commits an armed assault on a police officer will be hunted with every resource available to this Department. We will not conduct business as usual while a would-be cop killer is loose. I call upon all citizens to consider clearly what effect impassioned rhetoric condemning all policemen may have on the desperate or deranged. A climate of hostility that equates policemen with animals unquestionably in my view encourages the possibility of lethal violence against the men who are sworn to provide safety and justice for all our citizens and who, with very few exceptions, live up to this duty."

Someone once asked Murphy, "How does it make you feel, Commissioner, to hear cops called pigs?"

Murphy replied, "In my family we weren't allowed to call police officers cops."

But they called themselves cops. These were the men—separated from the public by their guns, turned inward toward each other by the basic human desire to be loved—whom Murphy was trying to rule. Could Murphy, who refused to carry a gun, who apparently did not need to be loved—at least by cops—could Murphy understand them? And if not, could he rule them? The odds, after all, were 32,000 to 1.

3 / New Ideas

The ultimate brotherhood: to hunt down the killer of one of us. On the night that Patrolmen Jones and Piagentini fell assassinated to the sidewalk, off-duty cops from precincts all over the city flocked into the 32nd Precinct station house in Harlem. Their shields hung safety-pinned to their outer garments, and most carried two guns. A good many were crying. These cops had been exposed to violence and gore and degradation in all forms for many years, but real tears ran down faces that night. Cops had been killed before plenty of times, but never assassinated before. That was the difference. None of them was safe. And the city wasn't safe either.

Probably not one of them was aware that ten cops (which was to be 1971's final score) had also been murdered in 1930. This fact appeared in none of the recruiting brochures. In 1930 there had been 17,710 police officers, somewhat more than half the present complement, although the population of the city was virtually the same as now. But ten cops were murdered out of that much smaller force, and the tears and the heartache must have been as great then as now, if not greater. One cop that year, chasing a high-backed sedan on a motorcycle, was literally blasted out of the saddle.

No one remembered his name. No one could describe his funeral.

Most times, one learns nothing whatever from history.

The Black Liberation Army sounded like something new, partly because no cop alive today could remember when the country and the city swarmed with anarchists, bomb throwers, irrational killers. But what was this Black Liberation Army if not a collection of anarchists—modern anarchists, black anarchists, but anarchists nonetheless—haters of the established order?

Even this year's corruption investigations were nothing new. The Lexow Committee, named for State Senator Clarence Lexow, had investigated the Police Department from February to December in 1894. That committee took testimony from a captain who claimed to have paid $15,000 for his precinct, repaying the loan later with graft; and from a brothel owner who claimed to pay $50 a week plus $100 at Christmas and $500 every time the police hierarchy underwent a shake-up, in order to stay in business. Five years later, Commissioner Theodore Roosevelt himself had started a vigorous but brief effort at reform. In 1913 came another scandal and another investigatory commission, this one led by one Henry J. Curran. The charges and the testimony sounded much the same as the charges and testimony that had been offered in 1894, and which would soon be offered in 1971. And don't forget the Seabury investigation, which began in 1930, and which was conducted among and in spite of all those police funerals. That year a vice squad detective was unable to explain his income of $90,000 over three years, and a midtown lieutenant was caught with a bank balance of $230,000.

The corruption investigations came along every 20 years or so. No generation of cops had escaped one of them, and certain police careers, including now Patrick V. Murphy's, inevitably were sandwiched in between two of them. In 1949 Sergeant Murphy had watched the Gross scandal break. Gross was a Brooklyn bookmaker who claimed to pay a million dollars a year for police protection. By the time that investigation ended, over a hundred policemen had suddenly retired, or else been indicted, or both, and three cops committed suicide. That year, as always in good times and bad, all those police guns invariably resulted in a number of cops blowing out their own brains.

The Police Department was a living, breathing organism.

It had its hands and its feet, its eyes and its ears, its head, but it had no memory; and it never had had a memory. A year ago was ancient history. The Police Department always in the past had been like a football team. It no more studied its own history than a football team did, for why bother? Yesterday's plays don't work, old-fashioned formations would draw laughs today; and so what difference did it make who had been in the backfield on the 1930 team, or who the opponents were that year? For everyone, from Commissioner Murphy on down, this year was the only year that counted. To Murphy, the threat this year was Knapp. To cops, the threat this year was Murphy.

The Department's lack of memory extended in all directions. For instance, no one ever called the Police Commissioner "Pat." Murphy was addressed as Commissioner—by everyone, even by his old friend and former protégé First Deputy Commissioner Smith. It was as if none of his colleagues had ever known him as Patrolman Pat Murphy, or Sergeant Pat Murphy, or Lieutenant Pat Murphy, or had ever in their lives considered themselves his equal. Murphy himself commented on this to me one day, as if he were astonished himself. Though why should he be—he had known the Department longer than I had.

"They wouldn't consider calling me Pat, not one of them," Murphy said.

All superior officers were treated by their subordinates as if they had never held any other rank. All two- and three-star chiefs invariably addressed Chief Inspector Codd as "Chief." I never heard anyone call him Mike, even though all had been at least his equal until a few months before, and two had outranked him. Only we deputy commissioners called him Mike, but then we were one rank above. It was a rare thing to hear any superior, even a captain, addressed by his first name by anyone who was even one rank beneath him.

Only the patrolmen were not bemused by rank. Though they quivered in its presence, they cut it into raw meat as soon as its back was turned, for who could reduce a patrolman? Murphy could command the instant obedience of his chiefs and inspectors—none would question even his most farfetched idea, not even in a bar after work, for the man's career could end if some bigmouth ran back to Murphy with the news. But the patrolmen criticized Murphy openly to each other. They called him the "Little Tin God," and the "Little Boy Scout," and other such names, and it was normal to apply to him whatever doses of obscenities they cared to. Almost none of them were personally aware of investigatory commissions in the past, and so to each of them this year's was the first ever to question the integrity and devotion of cops, and Murphy was the first commissioner ever to embrace such a commission. His kisses had gone to an outsider, not to his own, and there was a terrific emotional reaction in the ranks: they found his conduct revolting.

Murphy knew this, and that spring he was still moving very slowly. He was like a circus performer on a bicycle on a tightwire, crossing a deep gorge with a pyramid of people on his back. If he could once get to the other side he could perform glorious acts, but if he fell he would dash out everybody's brains.

His role was so incredibly complicated that a different man, less cool, less detached, might have got tangled up in his own passions from the start and perhaps made a botch of it already. Murphy, who saw the need for 50 reforms, had to put them in one at a time, and not necessarily in the best order, without alienating any more of his subordinates than he absolutely had to, and without stiffening the resistance of the cops. At the same time, he was obliged to steer the Department past the State Investigation Commission that spring, knowing that the far more awesome Knapp hearings awaited him in the fall. The machine-gunning of Patrolmen Binetti and Curry, and the assassinations of Patrolmen Jones and Piagentini, further complicated his job. Those murderous acts seemed to show every cop in the city how much he was hated, and from his Commissioner in this time of grief he wanted love, and Murphy couldn't give it to him—partly because Murphy didn't feel it, mostly because the need for reform was so great.

One by one, the earliest of the reforms were put in place. Each precinct commander had been ordered to select one sergeant—and there was no way of ordering him to select a sergeant of talent—to serve in the new role of Precinct Planning Sergeant. This was the first most sergeants had ever heard about planning of any kind, for in the past, police planning meant rushing out into the street and coping with whatever happened. But now these sergeants were supposed to study probabilities and patterns, and to nail up street maps of their precincts on the wall, and to mark down with colored pins when and where each crime of each type occurred each month. In other words, they were being taught how to relate the avalanche of statistics that poured into the Police Department every day, to the facts of crime in their own streets. Every Tuesday for ten straight weeks the Planning Sergeants turned up at the Police Academy, and the instruction never got much more sophisticated than pin maps, but it didn't have to. It now became possible for the best of these sergeants to plot with some accuracy when and where certain crimes would occur in their own precincts. The first pins to stud the street maps on the walls were red ones, representing armed robbery. All crime was skyrocketing, but armed robbery was the one New Yorkers most feared, and it was also a crime where clever police work could have some effect, because usually it happened on the street, or else inside a store or a hallway, close enough to open air for a cop either to prevent the robbery from happening, or to grab the stickup man immediately afterwards.

So the Planning Sergeants that spring concentrated on robbery patterns first, throwing in burglaries and the rest as soon as they became somewhat sure of themselves.

Toward the end of spring, shortly after Patrolmen Jones and Piagentini were murdered, Commissioner Murphy felt sufficiently encouraged by the results to invite Mayor Lindsay to a briefing at the 5th Precinct in Chinatown.

Murphy arrived first, and was introduced to the Planning Sergeant in question, William Riordan, a white-haired paunchy man who had joined the Police Department the same year Murphy did and who had relatives in the same village in Ireland where Murphy's forebears had come from. The two men spent five minutes telling each other how Irish they were, and Murphy seemed to enjoy this just as much as Sergeant Riordan did. They had been in the Police Academy together but had not known each other there. Now, 24 years later, one of them had advanced to the top of the Department, and the other had advanced one rank.

At last the Mayor arrived, looking as detached and

preoccupied as an absentminded professor. Mayor Lindsay regularly attended police briefings; he sat there hour after hour over the months, dutifully nodding his head as things were told to him, and he always seemed to try very hard to think up incisive questions for whoever was giving the briefing, but he usually failed, as he did today. Either he had too many other cares, or else he was rather dumb; and cops, who hated Lindsay, leaned toward the latter explanation.

During the next hour the enthusiastic Riordan told how he had begun plunging his colored pins into the map, had seen which corners led which other corners in which types of crimes, and how he began to send patrolmen out to specific spots at specific hours. His precinct comprised almost 25 miles of streets, and it was one of the oldest in the city. Its station house was built 90 years previously, and was the most dilapidated in the city.

In addition to Chinatown, the precinct's jurisdiction included Little Italy, famous for Mafia hoodlums, and the Bowery, famous for its alcoholic derelicts. In the old days the cops used to lock these derelicts up regularly, and after each arrest they'd come out of jail healthy. Then somebody said that the police were violating the civil rights of the drunks, so the procedure was changed. Today the police no longer arrested derelicts, and so they died quickly, especially in winter, which caused one cop to remark, "We used to be civil rights violators, now we're murderers."

Sergeant Riordan had soon seen that the upper end of the Bowery was top-heavy with pins. He began to assign plainclothes cops up there, and pretty soon the forest of pins thinned out on his map. He became so cocky—and he told this to the Mayor that day—that one night he invited Captain William Gundersen, his commanding officer, to go up there with him and watch a holdup he predicted would occur. It did occur. Two knife-wielding stickup men were immediately seized by pre-positioned cops in plainclothes. Captain Gundersen was incredulous.

Sergeant Riordan had gone on to predict two other robberies. One was on Livingston Street and another on Hester Street, and again pre-positioned plainclothesmen made the arrests.

The Bowery soon became the safest street in town for a derelict to take a snooze on. Cops began to dress up as bums and to lounge against the wall, and they arrested so many thugs who preyed upon the sleeping drunks that pretty soon there were almost no thugs left. Some were in jail. Others had been chased into neighboring precincts. The bums, according to natural law, might then have been expected to multiply, but they did not, for their principal enemy was not crime, but alcohol and the weather.

"I would say, sir," said Sergeant Riordan to Mayor Lindsay, "that two out of every three robberies on the Bowery are now being cleared by arrests. Before we put in the Planning Sergeant," added Riordan modestly, "we had solved only two of the last 23 robberies on the Bowery."

"Thanks, Sarge," said the Mayor, and shook hands with everybody and left.

Though the Planning Sergeant idea apparently worked, no massive bragging could be done by Murphy or anyone else, for, city-wide, crimes of violence were still increasing. Statistics compiled as of next July 1 would show robberies up 14 percent over the year before. Murphy could count this a triumph if he wanted—robberies had gone up 62 percent during that same half year the year before—but no one else in the city was likely to consider a 14 percent increase a triumph of any kind. Sometimes at press conferences Murphy would advance the current statistics, then try to claim a modest improvement. None of the newsmen ever laughed outright, but it was clear to Murphy that no one was very impressed.

A second scheme was also in operation. Beginning slowly, as always, Murphy had ordered each precinct to assign one man in civilian clothes as an "anti-crime" patrolman. Presently this was expanded from a single man to two-man teams, and after that Murphy allowed each precinct commander to assign up to five percent of his complement to these plainclothes anti-crime patrols. The cops who got these jobs loved them. They could dress up as bums, or women, or cripples, or district attorneys, and they loved the surprised look on the faces of the criminals they grabbed. Most often the criminals refused to believe it, and many protested all the way to the station house that such arrests were just not fair.

When cops bragged, they bragged about how many collars—arrests—they made, and these anti-crime patrolmen were making far more collars than anybody else, principally because the criminals had no idea that they had been spotted and followed since long before they even began to commit their crimes. Anti-crime work wasn't even particularly dangerous. Most often the cops had their guns out and in the thugs' backs before the thugs even comprehended what had happened. The only real danger, since some of these cops looked so disreputable, was getting shot by some guy in uniform who just happened to be passing by.

The anti-crime patrols were so successful that later in the year a special 200-man squad of anti-crime patrolmen would be formed. The intention was that all or part of it could be injected in massive doses into high-crime areas, could clean up that precinct, and then be yanked out and stuck in another. The detective division also decided to dress a squad in outlandish garb and do the same thing. Soon there were so many anti-crime cops acting in disguises throughout the city that the danger from the uniformed forces became acute. A precinct commander in Harlem equipped his anti-crime squad with orange ski caps, which they would carry in their pockets until such time as they moved in to make an arrest. At that point, on went the orange hats and out came the guns. Every uniformed patrolman in Harlem knew that those orange hats meant cop, and no incidents occurred there. On a city-wide basis, a decision was made that anti-crime plainclothes cops would carry colored headbands which they would don when moving in to make an arrest, different-colored bands for each day.

But one day a black detective had his gun in a stickup man's back, and a traffic patrolman ran in and shot him dead.

Eventually, with five percent of the force wearing civilian disguises on duty, some of them playing defenseless old women with shopping bags, it became clear that this idea too was a stunning success. These few men, this five percent of the Force was making 32 percent of all felony arrests. But still the crime statistics kept going up.

"I've always tried to avoid a cynical attitude," Murphy said. "There's always something which can be done."

The journalists were often around him.

"We all tend to see police work in terms of the chase, the arrest," Murphy said. "But most of a policeman's time is spent dealing with human problems. The policeman is a peace keeper, he's not just a crook catcher. Our police work is people work."

He explained his visits to the station houses by saying, "It's very important in a large bureaucracy to find out what's making the men tick. You learn so much that's never going to reach you otherwise."

Still, patrolmen weren't used to talking to the Police Commissioner, and some refused to talk to him out of bravado, and some simply got tongue-tied. Captains and lieutenants rarely told him what he needed to know—this came under the heading of bad tidings, and one of the first things any cop learned was that no boss liked to hear bad news; they may say they want to hear it, but they really don't. The precinct visits evidently came to seem empty exercises to Murphy. Soon he quit making them.

Nonetheless, that spring, on the whole, must have been a good time for Murphy. The massive acceleration in the crime rate, which had begun under Commissioner Leary, seemed to have been choked off to some extent. The Mayor seemed pleased with him, and the city as well, though how can one ever be sure? His only fear was that the Knapp Commission would bury him, bury his reforms, bury what cops call "the job."

The State Investigation Commission inquiry had come and gone. A number of lawyers, cops, and former cops testified, and some accused themselves of corrupt and criminal practices. But the major witnesses were never solidly identified. A member of the Department's Narcotics Division, identified only as Patrolman X, testified via a hi-fi loudspeaker system from the next room. A second witness, identified only as a former policeman and addressed by the Commission's chief counsel as "Mr. Witness," testified that he and his partner had attempted to bribe an assistant district attorney on behalf of a drug dealer. A second former cop, identified as "Mr. T," claimed that he had forced a man that he had arrested for possession of narcotics to sell a hundred bags of heroin for him on the street.

The words of the mystery witnesses seemed as vaporous

as their identities. They had all the morning-after clout of a ghost imagined the night before, though the hearings went on for three weeks.

The Commission's chief counsel, Joseph Fisch, then announced that the Police Department had had "no appreciable effect on the flow of heroin in New York City and that one reason for this was police corruption."

Whereupon Commissioner Murphy denounced the Commission: "I think it is a false assumption to say that corruption on any level is significantly contributing to the flow of narcotics."

"How deep are the police in heroin traffic?" asked one headline, but nothing whatever had been proven.

The State Investigation Committee, despite its ponderous title and its ponderous hearings, had little or no political muscle. The prestige of nobody important was tied to it, and Murphy was in no way obliged to genuflect in its presence. One week after it ended, it was forgotten. It had stung like a mosquito. The Police Commissioner had smacked it dead.

Whereas the Knapp Commission, which was coming on fast, would hug the city like a grizzly bear, and Murphy seemed to know this in advance.

Already last January, two Knapp Commission investigators had stumbled upon eight cops committing grand larceny. In the middle of the night, while wandering around Greenwich Village glancing into after-hours bars, the two agents accidentally came upon the warehouse of the Great Plains Packing Company, Inc., 449 West 13th Street. To their astonishment they watched the eight uniformed patrolmen exiting from the plant with stolen meat slung over their shoulders. The meat was being dumped into 6th Precinct radio cars. Without identifying themselves, the investigators phoned this information into the precinct station house. They waited and nothing happened, so they telephoned again. They had taken down the numbers and license plates of the radio cars and given this information to the precinct operator, but no investigation was begun until shortly before 7 A.M., when the Commission agents at last were able to telephone through to higher command levels.

The packing plant from which the meat was stolen

turned out to be owned by James Reardon, formerly a plainclothes cop, who had been an associate of Harry Gross more than 22 years before, at the time of the last, most recent corruption investigation of the Police Department. Reardon had been convicted of perjury in 1952 and sent to jail for three and a half years.

That the Knapp Commission, then in its infancy, had chanced upon this incident was pure accident, but the result of Knapp's good luck was that, three quarters of a year in advance of the Commission hearings, an aura of fear began to accrue to his name.

Murphy made no immediate move after the scandal came to light. It was as if he suddenly felt clumsy, like a heavyweight fighter standing in the ring with an opponent he suddenly suspects he can't beat. Oh, it was easy enough to suspend the eight patrolmen who had looted the warehouse, but what about the precinct's duty lieutenant that night? What about the duty sergeants and the patrolman who had taken the information over the telephone? Most of all, what about the commanding officer of the precinct who had been home asleep at that hour? Was he responsible for the conduct of eight of his patrolmen out of 250? Murphy had declared many times that he would hold superior officers responsible for patterns of corruption in the ranks beneath them. Was this a pattern or an isolated act? Should he make an example of the fellow or not?

Nearly three months passed before Murphy made the decision to sack the captain commanding this particular precinct—the first time in the history of the Police Department that a commander legitimately in bed had lost his job. The reasoning was best expressed by First Deputy Commissioner Smith, here making his first solid appearance as Murphy's hard-liner, or Murphy's hatchet man, as he would later be called. "Do you realize how bad the corruption must be in that precinct?" Smith kept asking—he was still injecting the same rhetorical question four months later, his voice rising on a righteous, incredulous note—"for those eight guys to dump stolen meat into their own radio cars, without making any effort to hide what they were doing, apparently without any fear whatever of getting caught? Why, the whole precinct has to be rotten . . ."

So the precinct captain was fired. Murphy could not reduce the man from his Civil Service rank, or force him to resign. All he could do was move him from his present coveted desk to another, not coveted desk, elsewhere.

So it was spring, and the two contestants were already in the ring. Knapp was moving fast, landing blows. The Police Department was standing there taking it on the chin. There are some fighters who, though they remain standing 15 rounds, never recover from the sucker punch inflicted by their opponent at the opening bell. Would Murphy recover in time, or had Knapp's chance haymaker already won the bout? And if Murphy was already the loser, what of all the reforms that the Police Department so desperately needed, and which Murphy, the man of ambition, desired to leave as his legacy to the city, to the Department, and to the future?

Book Three / **SUMMER**

1 / The Bottle Club

Serpico still walked the streets of the city with his dog and his cane. His hair and his beard were shaggier and more unkempt than ever. His eyes glowed fierce as coals. He still carried his guns in a sack over his shoulder. Fragments of the bullet were still lodged near his brain, but in his pocket rode a shiny gold shield. Serpico was a detective at last.

He was bitter about the way it was done.

At this time he was testifying in departmental trials against the policemen whom he had first accused of corruption three and four years before. That was a long time ago, he had since been shot in the head, and on the witness stand it was easy enough for defense lawyers to confuse him. Eighteen different policemen stood accused, but a number of these cases now began to fall through, because Serpico on the stand could not remember his own past testimony, or else contradicted it.

Some days when he was scheduled to testify he did not show up at all. Once, in the midst of cross-examination, he suddenly claimed that he was ill and demanded to be excused. "I have to state in all fairness to the people of the City of New York that I cannot continue along these lines in my present condition, because it would only be hurtful to myself," he said. "I couldn't give a proper answer without due deliberation, which is causing pressure in my head and giving me pain." Another time he complained that the Police Department had put him on the stand without giving him an opportunity to go over his notes and other documents. Often he told friends that the Police Department was using him again, exploiting him, that everyone Frank Serpico had ever known had exploited him.

A great deal of work had gone into these trials. Their chief architect was Chief Sydney Cooper, who had been the Borough Commander in the Bronx under Commissioner Leary and who had been brought to headquarters by Murphy as the three-star chief of personnel. Cooper was 51 years old, a big hulking man with a bald head and a beefy, prominent nose. He was probably the fiercest character and certainly the fiercest worker in the entire Police Department hierarchy. Sydney Cooper literally worked nights, Saturdays, and Sundays. His wife rarely saw him. He had been a corruption fighter all his life, even in the years when this was unpopular; Sydney Cooper didn't change his personality for anyone, least of all for Patrick Murphy. Cooper was a lawyer and his quick, hard wit was as spontaneous, and as cutting, as it was unexpected. He often convulsed entire executive conferences with his remarks. But the men who worked for him invariably feared him, and a great many hated him. He was a shouter who demanded obedience and loyalty from his subordinates, and he got it not through kindness but by the force of his rage. People would rather do what he said than be exposed to his voice.

For all of that, Cooper could be warm when he wanted to be, and he was a con man at heart. It was he who had taken Serpico's accusations and substantiated them, and prepared all these trials, and it was Cooper personally who listened to Serpico's complaints either in person or on the phone, and who coaxed him day after day onto the witness stand. It was also Cooper who suffered both personally and professionally each time one of the trials fell apart because the prosecution's and Cooper's chief witness, Serpico, disintegrated on the stand.

A cover article on Frank Serpico entitled "Portrait of an Honest Cop" appeared in *New York* magazine, written by myself. A few days later, in the midst of one of the trials, Serpico was profiled in *The New York Times* as that day's "Man in the News." The *Times* called him: "A hated, hunted man within his own Department," and pointed out that he had long done the work of a detective without the pay or title, and was a "lonely crusader against police corruption."

All this to the Police Commissioner, who read every word of police news every day, constituted extreme pressure to promote Serpico. If he didn't, the public might doubt his own sincerity on corruption. Cooper now added additional pressure: the gold shield might turn Serpico into a happier and more docile witness. Murphy still didn't want to promote Serpico alone, to single out as hero a man hated by patrolmen throughout the city; the Police Commissioner didn't need to rub that hatred off on himself. But suppose Murphy was to designate, say, five new detectives, patrolmen who had taken part in his. Murphy's, fight against corruption? Serpico and four others. Who else was there to give the gold shield to at this time?

Cooper suggested Terry Gibbons, the policewoman who had done much of the leg work and interviewing which had backed up Serpico's charges, and at length three other patrolmen were found and thrown into the stew. Whereupon Murphy convoked the press and at a single ceremony distributed five gold shields.

Serpico, who had waited 11 years for this day, got the headlines nonetheless, and everyone seemed happy except Serpico himself. He had been used again, this time by the Police Commissioner for the Police Commissioner's own purposes, and Serpico muttered about this each time a friend asked to see the new shield. He still intended to retire on three quarters disability pay, he said. The shield meant nothing to him except that this pension would now be somewhat higher.

Chief Cooper joked, "You don't think we gave you that shield so we'd be sure of losing you, do you, Frank? We need you. You're what this job is all about, Frank. Why, I read in the paper that you were an honest cop. By the way, Frank, you're due on the stand tomorrow at 10 A.M. I hope you'll be there on time."

And a day or two later Murphy summoned me from home to say he wanted me as his Deputy Commissioner, Public Affairs. No, he hadn't read the Serpico piece yet. Would I take the job? If so, how soon could I start?

I judged that he thought his anti-corruption campaign would have additional credibility with me on his team.

And so I moved into Police Headquarters.

Murphy wanted nothing to do with Durk either. Murphy was certainly not going to ally himself with subordinates who were presumably hated by other cops, and who were furthermore independent enough to criticize their Police Commissioner publicly if it suited them. He considered Durk and Serpico, from his point of view, profoundly unreliable.

Durk had won another grant and was on his second leave of absence, giving speeches in colleges and to police departments and civic groups from one side of America to the other, even in such outposts as Montana. Murphy knew that sooner or later the Durk problem would return to plague him, but for the moment Durk was out of sight. The apostle to the college boys was wowing them elsewhere.

Murphy had met with Durk. To Murphy, a meeting with Durk meant that Durk talked—and Durk talked endlessly. Murphy found him articulate, but not coherent. Never mind that other police departments—Los Angeles, Dallas, Cleveland—found him coherent enough and were anxious to hear him. To Murphy, Durk's sentences never led anywhere. His ideas were unconnected. Each time Durk left his office Murphy felt as if both his ears had been chewed off. Durk had a dozen, or perhaps it was a thousand, ideas for the improvement of the police service, but in these conversations with Murphy he showed no notion of how a single one of his ideas was to be implemented. He also had no concept of what the police bureaucracy was, nor how it worked, nor what Murphy thought possible within it and what impossible. He was the implacable presence in Murphy's life. His ideas and sentences poured forth. Murphy would schedule an interview with Durk to last half an hour, but they always lasted longer, and Murphy found it almost impossible to uproot Druk from his office once Durk's monologue started. It was Murphy's habit to cut short interviews by glancing ostentatiously at the clock above his door. This was usually followed by the remark, "Well, I'm running a little late." Not one of Murphy's subordinates failed to take the hint. Each time Murphy glanced at the clock and said, "Well, I'm running a little late," subordinates jumped to their feet and scurried out. Except Durk.

Here was this sergeant on whom no hint seemed to have any effect. Durk just sat there and talked, nervous, ill at ease, knowing he was not getting through to his listener, his eyes all the while accusing Murphy of lack of—of what? Courage? Lack of honesty? Lack of interest? The latter was certainly true. Murphy saw Durk not as an ally but as a foe, and Murphy most of the time was convinced that he could defeat Durk any day he chose. After all, Durk was a sergeant. Murphy knew all about sergeants. One did not negotiate with sergeants, one gave them orders.

Durk did not know, and, because my loyalty was now to Murphy I did not tell him for many months, that in virtually all high level conferences his name was brought up. For Murphy apparently brooded constantly about the oncoming Knapp Commission, and Durk was part of this brooding. No conference with any of the rest of us, on whatever subject, was immune from a discussion of the Knapp Commission. Knapp had released an interim report: Corruption was not restricted to "a few rotten apples"; the climate of the Department was inhospitable to attempts to uncover corruption and protective of those who were corrupt. It was easier for a rookie to become corrupt than to remain honest, Knapp said, Durk's point indeed. The interim report identified some nine prime corruption areas: narcotics, gambling, prostitution, liquor, hotels, construction, tow trucks, sabbath law payoffs, plus a number of miscellaneous areas where policemen were "tipped" with some regularity.

This interim report had also praised Murphy as "possibly a great Commissioner," a line Murphy often pointed out to us in passing during executive conferences. But what he wanted to know each time was, "What are we doing concerning these findings and what new approaches can we make? Should I meet with Whitman Knapp and Michael Armstrong?"

The conversation, speculation, and conferences went on week after week, and in every single one the names of Durk and Serpico, particularly Durk, appeared. What would Durk's role be in the Commission hearings? Would Durk come out in favor of Commissioner Murphy or against him? What were Durk's ultimate aims? Was he running for public office? Did he want to be a deputy commissioner? (Murphy could not promote Durk to lieutenant, but he could make a deputy commissioner out of him, if he chose.) When did Durk's leave of absence run out? Did Durk want to stay a cop or not? If so, he was vulnerable. Ultimately a sergeant would do what he was told. If Durk hoped to be made a deputy commissioner, so as to help change the Department from the top, then he was also vulnerable. But if he meant to leave the Department, and blab on the outside, then he was dangerous. Was there any possible way to discredit him before this occurred?

It was amazing that a simple sergeant could so upset the timing and the thinking of the massive bureaucracy that was the New York City Police Department.

Serpico's name arose during these discussions too, but less frequently and with far less impact. Chief Cooper, among others, was willing to discount the importance of Serpico in the eventual Knapp hearings. Serpico was unable even to withstand an hour or two in the witness box at the Departmental trials. He gave the impression of paranoia and instability. He was much less of a threat to Commissioner Murphy and the Police Department than Durk was.

What about the third member of the trinity, Commissioner Murphy then wanted to know? What about St. Paul?

Inspector Paul Delise at this time commanded the Tenth Division in Brooklyn. He had recently submitted a three-page report of steps taken in his own command relative to corruption and corruption-hazard conditions.

"The personal involvement technique rather than the traditional paper curtain procedural method has been the only approach used by this writer in fighting corruption," Delise wrote in his report. He then gave examples. An anonymous call had tipped off the existence of an illegal cabaret. Delise, the 51-year-old inspector, though he lived in far-off Westchester County, had personally sat outside the place during a number of nights and had discovered that the allegations were true. So he went in there with the commanding officer of the precinct in which these flagrant violations existed, and "summary" action was taken.

It had come to Delise's attention that a patrolman on sick report was "involved intimately with female not his wife." Delise suspended the cop and preferred charges against him.

Delise personally directed the removal of two vending machines from a station house after having discovered that no authorization had been obtained by the precinct commander.

Delise personally directed investigations into the issuance of gun permits by his precinct captains, gun permits being another source of payoffs.

Delise preferred charges against a patrolman who was selling fireworks illegally in a grocery store he owned, which he shouldn't have owned.

While on vacation, Delise had assisted in the investigation of a cop alleged to be involved in the sale of guns.

There used to be a high-ranking cop who hated gamblers, call him Chief Boyle, who had become known as Death-on-Bookies Boyle. Boyle was a department legend. One day Chief Boyle and two patrolmen screeched to a stop in front of a certain candy store in which an important bookie was known to hang out. Boyle lunged into the candy store, grabbed a man, and began beating him nearly to death. One of the patrolmen jumped on Boyle's back screaming, "Chief, Chief!"

Turning from the victim, Boyle snarled, "I hate bookies."

"But Chief," the cop cried, "that's the guy who owns the candy store. The bookie's over here."

Inspector Delise was by no means Death-on-Bookies Boyle, but, like Durk and Serpico, he was a crusader himself, and on the subject of gamblers he was implacable. He personally went over the U.F. 47 reports of his plainclothes personnel relative to a gambling operation which had disappeared, and then he personally went out and found its new location. After personally lurking nearby during several days of surveillance, Delise effected the arrest (on Belmont Stakes Day) of two horse room clerks, one of them a KG, and seized $3409 in bills, plus "sizable" gambling bets and paraphernalia. Considering this operation "notorious and flagrant," Delise then began an investigation into possible laxity, or even corruption, by plainclothes and precinct personnel. His report pointed out that this operation was part of the Colombo gambling network. Delise added that he was personally conducting an investigation of the entire Colombo organization within his jurisdiction.

"Should I promote Paul Delise?" Murphy regularly asked us.

But most of his high-ranking subordinates were against promoting Delise; and Cooper, the only one who knew Durk, Serpico, and Delise personally, one day declared that Delise, Serpico, and Durk were all alike—all talk—but ask them what they had done to prefer specific charges in specific instances, and the answer invariably was, Very little.

Nonetheless, Murphy decided to promote Delise to Deputy Chief. Delise was on vacation in Cape Cod with no telephone. Murphy ordered his chief secretary, Deputy Inspector Bill Devine, to telephone the Massachusetts State Police. "Talk to them as policeman to policeman," Murphy said. "Have them drive by his house and tell him to phone in at once."

Delise was ordered to report to the Police Academy the following day, wearing his uniform. He was not told why. The promotion process within the Police Department was always kept secret. The good news was withheld from the promotee. Apparently, in the past, a man who knew he was going to be promoted would often try to buy an assignment to go with his new rank; that is, a precinct or division or borough where the graft was good. And so it had been decided years and years ago that no one would be told of his promotion until, at the earliest, the night before. That way, though he might covet some assignment, and have the desire and the money to buy it, he wouldn't have time to do so. He wouldn't even have time to get his uniform pressed. One didn't buy assignments anymore, but the rule remained, and men getting promoted still didn't have time to get their uniforms pressed.

And so Delise was promoted with fanfare, and Serpico was promoted almost tentatively—two of the Department's best-known corruption fighters promoted by its corruption-fighting Commissioner—and with these acts and certain others, Murphy sought to build his credibility in advance of the Knapp Commission hearings. In addition to top-level conferences, there came a barrage of memos. These he wrote at home in longhand on lined, yellow legal pads, being either unwilling or unable to dictate, and his secretaries would type up these memos in the morning and send them on. A number came to me.

How, he asked, could we place some of the blame for corruption on the Civil Service philosophy and system, for the Police Commissioner had no authority or even input into the promotion of sergeants, lieutenants, and captains. In addition, there were not enough supervisors. The Department's ratio was 1 sergeant to 14 patrolmen—and no man according to modern management thinking was able to manage 14 people without help. But in actual practice the ratio was often 1 to 20 or 25, and it was the unsupervised cops who fell most easily into corruption.

Another time the Police Commissioner wanted me to

think up ways to lay the blame on the so-called respectable businessmen who bribed underpaid policemen for permission to violate laws and regulations. And could not blame be laid on society, which failed to provide the salaries necessary to attract the college graduates that were necessary, not just desirable? How much blame could be laid to the disrespect for the police among many "liberal" segments of society? "During my Washington experience I repeatedly saw the attitudes of such people turn around after two rides in a police car," Murphy told me one day.

He was looking around for possible allies before additional Knapp reports began to appear. What about Governor Rockefeller? "I've sung his praises many times relative to his strengthening of law enforcement." Could Rockefeller be enlisted to support Patrick V. Murphy, Police Commissioner of the City of New York? In July Murphy went to Washington to testify before the Senate Foreign Relations Committee about narcotics, and came back elated. "Congressmen Scheuer and Rangel were glowing in their praise of me."

Could Scheuer and Rangel be enlisted to support Murphy against the Knapp Commission, the Police Commissioner wanted to know?

As the Knapp hearings came closer, Murphy focused on Durk again. "What can Durk be expected to say about me?"

Durk was saying nothing publicly at this time, but privately (for we still met occasionally) Durk's one overriding question was, "What is Murphy doing to motivate cops?"

The answer, as Durk saw it, was, Nothing.

Then Durk added, "Murphy says the right things, but as a New York cop he kept his mouth shut for 20 years."

Durk was under no illusions about the failure of his interviews with the Police Commissioner: "If he'd just stop looking at that goddam clock once in a while and listen to what I'm trying to tell him—"

Durk could not believe that his passion, his torrent of words, did not work on Murphy. His passion was real and it had swayed nearly everybody else so far. But Murphy was a cool—perhaps even cold—man. From his subordinates he wanted measured arguments presented in a low voice. He was immune to passion, he distrusted it, he shut it off, as he had long since shut off Durk.

Durk kept hoping to be offered a job as deputy commissioner or at least Special Assistant to the Police Commissioner.

But Murphy had no intention of offering Durk any job at all, I realized. Murphy had taken a dislike to Durk. Murphy was again asking, Is there not some way to discredit Sergeant Durk?

As summer started, the Police Commissioner had held office nine months. He had made a number of hard statements about reorganizing the command structure, and especially about rooting out corruption, but he had backed this up with very little muscle. His hard line on corruption, following the silence of his predecessor during almost five years, sounded new enough, and it focused the minds and fears of the city on the dismaying notion that cops could not be trusted. But what was Murphy changing? Which mass of cops was being arrested? The command structure stayed much the same; a few more Murphy men had now replaced a few more Leary men—but this always happened when commissioners changed, and was not particularly significant.

The patrolmen hated Murphy's constant talk of corruption, for they saw themselves as despised enough, and shot at enough, already. They also saw Murphy as riding to glory on scare headlines, inflating his own importance at their expense. They wanted him to stop.

But he couldn't stop.

He had to act, and act soon. His deeds had to catch up with his conversation. "When the day comes that I can do nothing more to stop police corruption," Murphy told me one day as we rode back to headquarters in his car, "that's the day that I'll quit and take an easier job." An *easier* job. The word impressed me. To a dedicated man there were few "better" jobs, but dozens of "easier" ones that paid more. "You can tell anybody who wants to hear it that I'm an absolute fanatic on the subject of corruption."

He had decided, it was clear from the conferences, memos, directives, that the way to win was to beat Whitman Knapp to every punch if possible, to dilute the impact of Knapp as totally as he could. Let Knapp expose corruption hazards that Murphy had already corrected. Let

Knapp indict corrupt policemen whom Murphy had already put in jail. Let Knapp recommend changes in the Department that Murphy had already put into effect. Let the city applaud Murphy only.

The investigation of an alleged bottle club at 554 West 146th Street in Manhattan came to the Police Commissioner's attention. It seemed clear that this club was paying plainclothesmen in order to go on operating, and always in the past in such cases, charges would have been preferred from headquarters against the plainclothesmen and sergeants in question. This matter had been bucked up to Murphy, and now he bucked it back down again. The two-star chief in charge of Manhattan North, Ferdinand Catalano, was virtually ordered to prefer charges not only against patrolmen and possibly sergeants, but also against the inspector in command of Catalano's Fifth Division, the deputy inspector commanding Catalano's Fifth Division plainclothesmen, and the captain commanding Catalano's 30th Precinct.

Catalano at length prepared such a report and signed it, though clearly he did so with excruciating reluctance. Catalano did not want to be the villain. Why couldn't headquarters play the villain as always in the past? Catalano had been asked to ruin the careers and possibly the lives of three high-ranking officers who worked for him, and whom he knew well. He didn't want to do it. But he did do it, because he had no choice, and he was publicly praised for this by Murphy, though he would pay for his reluctance—he would lose his command—before Christmas came.

An ordinary bottle club—hundreds operated illegally all over the city—had become a cause célèbre. This case Murphy considered of supreme importance, possibly the most important step he had yet made. He had forced a field commander to cashier his own men. Murphy was delighted. No longer could field commanders let subordinates weep on their shoulders. No longer could they say, "I'm on your side, but those guys in headquarters are bastards." Murphy had forced his own get-tough policy down onto his field commanders, onto Chief Catalano anyway, and from now on they would be obliged to buy it if they meant to go on commanding.

The Fifth Division included all of Manhattan Island

north of 86th Street between Eighth Avenue and the Hudson River, and its commander, Inspector Casimir Kruszewski, was charged with "failing to properly supervise his staff to assure a thorough and adequate investigation of complaints alleging violations of law relating to Alcoholic Beverage Control at 554 West 146th Street."

Deputy Inspector Daniel O'Connell was charged with failing to note that his plainclothesmen were not able to locate this club.

It was charged that Captain William Lakeman, in whose precinct this club was located, could not find it.

Kruszewski, O'Connell, and Lakeman were not charged with corruption, but with faulty supervision. However, this distinction was difficult for their families and friends—not to mention the city at large—to perceive, and their reputations seemed ruined. Of the three, Murphy apparently knew only O'Connell, whom he had always liked. Even so, Murphy chose to accord no sympathy.

"I'm willing to believe that Danny O'Connell never took a dishonest dollar in his life," Murphy remarked to me. "Dan O'Connell's an honest man. But if he's going to hold supervisory rank, he's going to be held accountable for the conduct of his subordinates. Responsibility and accountability have to be forced downward."

Catalano's Manhattan North was divided into three police divisions, one of which Murphy had now thrown into convulsions. Reaching into the Internal Affairs Division, Murphy chose Deputy Inspector William Bonacum, the second highest ranking (after Chief McGovern himself) corruption investigator, promoted him to full inspector, and put him in charge of the Fifth Division.

Bonacum was 48, a big man, lantern-jawed, phlegmatic. He had just graduated from John Jay College of Criminal Justice at the top of his class, a college graduate at last at nearly 50, and, as valedictorian at graduation exercises, had made an hour-long address which put large numbers of his fellow graduates and their families to sleep. Bonacum had looked down at this, set his jaw, and gone on talking.

Bonacum, who had never been a field commander before, was about to get an education in gambling enforcement. He was also soon to come into conflict with Sergeant Durk.

The Sixth Division, which included the three Harlem precincts, was no doubt the most corrupt in the city, if only because Harlem was the headquarters of all the black gambling operations. Murphy now withdrew the commander there, Deputy Chief Walter Kendall, 57, and in his place installed Inspector Donald Cawley, who was only 41, who also had never commanded in the field in his life, who had spent the last ten years overseeing corruption investigations as a staff officer in the First Deputy Commissioner's office, and who last but not least was the protégé of Murphy's protégé, First Deputy Commissioner Smith. Young (by police-command standards) Cawley went up to Harlem and promptly sent back a report to the effect that every plainclothesman in his division was on the take (though how could he have known so fast?); he wanted them all changed. The Police Commissioner seemed to enjoy such talk as this, and Cawley seemed to rise instantly in his estimation. Within two months, Cawley would be jump-promoted to three-star Chief of Patrol. Cawley was another recent college graduate, having got his degree from John Jay the previous winter.

Meantime, Murphy and Smith asked each other: "What does Cawley's report tell us about Walter Kendall?" If the Sixth Division was so corrupt, should Kendall be held accountable or not? Kendall was put in command of the Inspections Division, and was presently promoted to two-star Chief and later was made the three-star Chief of Personnel.

A good deal of any shifting of Police Department personnel was the merest shuffling of cards—the same cards over and over again, as Murphy well knew. Since it was impossible according to Civil Service law to bring in new blood, one was forced to promote, or to shift around, what was already there, good or bad; and at the top levels, such shifts could sometimes be based on no more than whim or caprice, the liking or disliking of the cut of a man's uniform, and whether or not he displayed proper reverence for those who outranked him. Reverence was very important. High-ranking officers were rarely cunning enough, or sophisticated enough to play a tune on the strengths and weaknesses of their superiors. Rather they were men who stuck to the percentages. Almost all of them, when in the presence of a man of superior rank, were to a greater or lesser degree obsequious. They agreed with all his opinions, prasied all his decisions, and addressed him either by rank or as "Boss." Fifty-year-old career policemen with stars on their shoulders treated me this way, and each time it happened I was astonished.

Summer had just started, and Murphy had revamped the Fifth and Sixth Divisions, the two most potentially explosive divisions in the city. Next he sacked John McCahey, the deputy chief who headed the Narcotics Division. He lacked fire, and also the Narcotics Division was widely believed to be rife with corruption. So McCahey was out, reassigned to the Chief Inspector's office, where he sat with nothing to do, never smiling, until such time as he put in his papers and retired. No charges were ever preferred against McCahey. Meanwhile, Kruszewski, O'Connell, and Lakeman had loudly claimed that Murphy was unjust. No corruption or collusion could be proven against them. That they were ignorant of that bottle club did not make them derelict. They had merely been forced by the system to sign thousands of reports, as the Police Commissioner himself did, without knowing personally what was in them.

Headquarters gossip held that Murphy's number one object was to show force. To prove how tough he was. Obviously it was essential that he prove this. He was a small, mild-seeming man, and no one was going to believe it until blood flowed. But why wrong McCahey, a good man, and why had he chosen these dubious charges against Kruszewski, O'Connell, and Lakeman? These charges would not stand up (and months later in court they would in fact be reversed), and when all were returned to duty exonerated, the Police Commissioner would look foolish. Murphy did not seem to care for this reasoning, or else he knew better. He had won the battle of now, and this could not be lost months later. Exoneration would be a different battle, a footnote. He could lose it and no one applauding today would notice.

One day Commissioner Murphy called in Chief of Personnel Cooper and Chief of Inspectional Services McGovern, and informed them that they were switching jobs. McGovern would take over Personnel, and from now on the number one corruption fighter in the Department would be Sydney Cooper. McGovern, Leary's man, was the one Murphy wanted to get rid of, and soon would. Cooper was the one Murphy believed in. But Personnel was a better job. The three-star Chief of Personnel commanded more men, and he also reported directly to the Police Commissioner, whereas the three-star Chief of Inspectional Services was a subordinate of the First Deputy.

As Murphy saw it, he was strengthening his own image and position by sticking the fiercely honest, highly educated Cooper in the most sensitive job in the Department. But as Cooper saw it, Cooper was being demoted. In the corridors of power the gossips would see him as humiliated, and so that's the way he felt. Tough as he was, Syd Cooper was crushed. His long face now put a damper on top-level conferences, and for a time there were no more jokes.

But the summer had just started.

2 / The Shake-up

How should a business executive move to take total control of his organization? Should he act decisively, fast? Or carefully, slow? Should he attempt to seduce the organization, hands caressing it in various sensitive places? Or should he clamp his fingers around its throat? Moved by belief in the product, and by fervor to leave their mark on the organization, most chief executive officers in these modern times seemed to opt for the fingers-on-the-windpipe technique. The throat was easier to find than the sensitive places, force was quicker than seduction, and it lasted longer, or so the newest management textbooks seemed to suggest; and also it was so much more satisfying. To act tough often gave a pleasant feeling. Often it made one feel very much a man.

That summer the Police Commissioner went for the throat of his 32,000-man bureaucracy.

An extraordinary confidential memo went to the executive corps—those 500-odd men who served in the ranks of captain and above. Murphy was dissatisfied with progress in reducing corruption. His predecessors had attempted to control corruption almost exclusively with a relatively small headquarters unit or units, which caught only a rela-

tively small number of corrupt cops. That system did not
work. Murphy had discarded it. Murphy's current system
placed responsibility in field commanders. They had been,
and would continue to be, held accountable to an ever-
increasing degree for corruption in their commands.

Such a system could work, Murphy wrote. He was determined to make it work. Commanders who failed to act vigorously against corruption would be removed for the advancement of those who would.

All that Murphy knew about accomplishing major
change in large police departments in the United States
convinced him that the key was change in higher ranks.
New thinking in people in the top positions. It was questionable whether high-ranking officers, after more than 25
years of service, could adjust to his basic policy changes.
But change must and would occur at the executive level,
his memo went on. It was unhealthy for leadership to become stagnant. Opportunities for advancement would be
made available for the many young captains. The highest-
ranking officers tended to remain in service far beyond the
average, a heavy lid on the aspirations of promising young
captains. This would end.

Murphy's responsibility, he wrote, was to the city and to
the Department. He could not permit friendship or respect
for individuals to deter his obligation to place in top positions those most determined to accomplish long-overdue
changes. Murphy would take even "the most personally
painful steps" of removing any executive who failed to act.

In one corner of the Police Commissioner's office stood
a stainless steel easel on which reposed two charts Murphy
had ordered drawn. One listed those 19 chiefs wearing two
stars and above. The second was for the 22 deputy chiefs.
Beside each name ran a kind of barometer which changed
color as it extended out toward the edge of the chart. Each
color represented a different rank in which each man had
served, and the length of that particular color showed how
long he had served in that rank. Each barometer began
with the officer's date of birth, moved to the date he was
sworn in, and continued to the present. At a glance Murphy could now tell who were his oldest chiefs, and his
youngest, who had risen most rapidly in the Department,
who had held present rank longest. Often Murphy would

stand before these graphs, studying them. He was about to force a number of the older chiefs to retire, but it was not clear to him yet which ones.

Meantime, he wanted to know how rich they all were, and so he summoned every single officer above captain to the Police Academy one morning to find out. All of them were to appear in uniform, including even detective chiefs who hadn't worn uniforms for years. After speaking a few brief words from the stage, Murphy ordered distributed a new confidential memo, and the three-page financial questionnaire that accompanied it. The memo pointed out that all above captain served in their high rank at the Police Commissioner's pleasure. Murphy could revoke any or all such designations. They were to fill out the attached confidential financial report, such information being necessary and appropriate if Murphy was to determine accurately whether the high rank of each of them was to be continued. In Murphy's judgment, a superior officer's financial status was relevant to the public trust he held. Therefore every officer was to fill out and return this form in a sealed envelope marked confidential within one week.

Murphy left the hall. The commanders began muttering to each other.

The questionnaire asked the police brass, men tough cops in the street were afraid of, to list all "current residences—any premises where you spend more than ten nights a year or for which you pay the rent." They were to list all income from all sources during each of the last four years, plus all indebtedness of self, spouse, or dependents. They were to show all amounts on deposit in banks, all cash on hand or held other than in bank deposits, current value of bonds, stocks, or other securities, the cash value of insurance policies, and the current market value of all real estate owned. In addition they were to list the value of automobiles, boats, and airplanes owned; the value of jewelry, furs, stamp or coin collections, antiques, and art treasures; and the value of all other personal property, such as furniture, cameras, etc. Lastly they were asked if they or their dependents paid rent on any other premises where they did not live personally. Had they or their dependents ever given gifts valued at more than five hundred dollars? Had they or their dependents ever made a loan greater than five hundred dollars? Did they or their dependents have a financial interest in a business or enterprise, whether or not a partnership or other formal relationship had been established?

And so the executive corps was being forced to disclose intimate information. This had never happened before, and symbolically it said that the Police Commissioner owned them. They had been ordered by the biggest kid in the school to turn their pockets inside out, and they were neither big enough nor brave enough to tell the bully no.

Within the next week every single commander would sign and return the questionnaire.

Previously the Knapp Commission had sent similar questionnaires to 125 commanders. This was denounced by the Captains' Endowment Association, and the questionnaires in question were ignored by almost everybody. On the subject of financial questionnaires the Police Commissioner now led Knapp by a score of 1 to 0.

Murphy continued to study the graphs in his office. A confidential memo on the subject of superannuation was sent around to a few top people. Basically this plan would limit an officer to two years in each rank above captain. A man not promoted within two years would be considered passed over, and would be "encouraged" to retire. Perhaps some day, the Police Commissioner noted, it would be possible to *force* such men to retire. In addition, age limits and length-of-service limits would be established for each rank, and if an officer exceeded both the age limit for his rank and the length-of-service limit for his rank, and had also failed to attain a promotion within two years, then he would be demoted to the rank of captain. Murphy wanted this plan to go into effect January 1, 1972.

Still the graphs stood on the easel in the corner of Murphy's office, and entering there I sometimes found him staring at them. The shakeup of the top ranks was coming ever closer.

The Chief of Patrol at this time was Elmer Cone, one of the last holdovers appointed by Leary. Cone was a big florid man, heavy of figure though not stout, and despite his rough New York accent, he was an educated man and a lawyer. As Chief of Patrol he supervised the 17,000 cops who rode radio cars. The Police Department was everything to Cone. He was another of those who put in very long hours. Whatever the crisis, big or small, whatever the hour of day or night, Elmer Cone could be found on duty.

Now Murphy said to me, "Elmer Cone is going to retire."

We were in the Police Commissioner's car and had slowed to a stop at a midtown corner. As I looked out the window, there stood Cone in uniform, a three-star chief to startle every pedestrian who walked by him, for most New Yorkers had never seen a cop of such rank, and people stared as if he were the star of a TV comedy hour. They noted only his costume, not his stricken face. Murphy and I had just driven uptown to join several other ranking police officials, one of them Cone, for a conference in a restaurant with a number of the leaders of the black community.

Murphy said, "He said he wanted to talk to me, and I see he's waiting for me now."

Cone had obviously been pacing the street corner for some time. He was biting his lower lip and he looked as if he had been crying, although to me at the time this seemed inconceivable. Murphy said, "After I talk to him, I suggest that you go talk to him, and then you should figure out how the announcement is to be made."

Presently, in a private room at the restaurant, the conference between the police leaders and the black leaders got under way. Cone was being treated by the black leaders, and also by the other police officials present, with the deference due to the second-ranking commander of the uniformed forces, and he looked to me to be trying desperately to act normally. In between long silences he would attempt his usual rough, jovial manner.

I could see the strain he was under, and presently I took him aside and suggested that the two of us ride back to headquarters. This was done. Cone and I then sat in his office. He was red-eyed, his voice sometimes husky. If he hadn't been doing the job, he said, then he should be forced to retire; but he had been doing the job, or at least he thought he had been, to the best of his ability. He had never done a dishonorable act, but now, forced out in the midst of Murphy's corruption campaign, he would be considered corrupt. There was no other way people *could* think, and his name was destroyed.

I told him I saw no reason why he could not retire with honor. He had been a policeman over three decades, and had reached exalted rank. He had nothing to be ashamed of.

Murphy had said to me, "Cone is a hard worker, he'll work all night for you, but the times have passed him by. He thinks of police work on a day-to-day basis. He doesn't have any notion of modern management techniques. He never thinks in terms of programs."

I had then asked Murphy if he wanted Cone to leave in disgrace.

"Oh, no," the Police Commissioner replied. "You can quote me as saying all the best things about him, about his integrity and his dedication and his energy."

Cone during his long career had seen countless others of high rank forced to retire. He must have known that one day it would happen to himself. But now it was clear that he was unable to cope emotionally with his present status. He was like a man who had been in a car crash. Try as he might, he couldn't reconstruct the events leading up to the catastrophe. His one desire, which was to stay a cop, was not allowed him. He, who at present had authority over 17,000 men, tomorrow would be a nobody. He could no longer walk into headquarters without people feeling sorry for "poor old Elmer." He would no longer be part of the vast police brotherhood. The cop at the reception desk at headquarters would outrank him. He would not be able to cross a police line at a street disturbance.

Most of all, Cone was certain that his departure would be seen as evidence of corruption. He had not yet completed his financial questionnaire. He must do that at once and hand it in, he said.

Invariably, the first act of any cop in Cone's position was to visit the pension bureau on the second floor of headquarters, for he would want to know how much money he would have coming to him. So the pension bureau was the one place watched above all others by the hallway politicians. No one went in or out without being seen. Men watched the door like hawks, and it was sufficient for an officer to enter there for word to circulate through the corridors of headquarters.

"Cone's out."

"Cone put his papers in."

The next rumor after that would be, "I hear Murphy fired him."

The subject of the rumors was always aware of them at once. Sometimes he overheard conversations about himself in the men's room, or through open doors. He could make all the denials he wanted, and never stop the rumor. Those close to him would drop by to ask if it was true. No bluff worked. The confident grin fooled nobody.

This was one of the primary causes of a man's humiliation. There was no way to silence those rumors. How long could a man deny them, how long manage to grin, when everyone knew they were true?

Cone asked if there was anything I could do to help him retire with honor. A little honor, anyway.

Yes, there was, and we began to construct the scenario of his departure. First of all, he would stay away from the pension bureau, and he would resign on the following Sunday. There could be no comment in the halls that day as he walked out, because the halls would be empty, and he would have walked out the previous Friday night. There would be no press conference. His resignation would be announced in a press release, kept rigidly secret until 4 P.M. Sunday afternoon, and then handed without comment to the press. His phone number was not listed. Nonetheless, certain reporters might have it. There he was to leave home before the news broke and go on vacation somewhere with his wife.

Cone appeared to cheer up. Perhaps there was a chance that he could escape with honor, although this hardly mitigated his current feeling of humiliation. Finally we worked out that with his terminal leave, his accrued vacation, and the days off owed him, his official retirement date could be pushed forward into the next year, so as to fall exactly on his 60th birthday. He could claim in the press release that he had resigned of his own free will to take effect on his 60th birthday, and this would be backed by the kind words that the Police Commissioner would say about him.

"Still, no one will believe that I wasn't forced out."

And so Elmer Cone, three-star Chief of Patrol, 59 years of age, somewhat cheered up, but no less humiliated and miserable, took his leave of the Police Department. His pension would total over $20,000 a year. If he so chose, he would never have to work again. I suggested he could now take a long vacation. He might once again practice law. He nodded his head. He would give both ideas much thought. But all he really wanted to do was stay a cop. Once he went out that door he would never come back. There were dozens or hundreds of other Elmer Cones out there living on their cushy pensions, but not one of them, with very rare exceptions, ever came through that door again.

The Monday morning headlines were for Elmer Cone. But the Monday working day started with the funeral of the last of the ten cops killed that year.

The press conference at which Cone's successor would be named was scheduled to take place after the funeral— two ceremonies in one day, one of them lugubrious. We all stood outside the church in the far reaches of Brooklyn, and today most of the thousands of cops in ranks in the street were detectives in civilian clothes, for the body in the coffin belonged to Joseph Morabito, 29, a detective sergeant working out of the Narcotics Division. Morabito had been found dead the previous Wednesday, lying in his Volkswagen, which was parked on the verge of a section of the Belt Parkway. He had been shot twice, once in each side of the head, and both his guns were missing and so was his wallet. He had been found shortly after midnight, but he'd already been dead a long time by then; and one chief remembered driving by the parked car on his way to work that morning, and then passing it again on his way home, at which time he wondered why an apparently abandoned car had not been stripped by automotive ghouls long ago.

The reason it hadn't been stripped was that Morabito was lying dead in it, the shock of their lives for any spare-part thieves who circled in. Morabito lay with his head toward the passenger door, face up, part of his skull blown away. Both his index fingers pointed nearly straight and they were separated from his other fingers, which suggested that he might have committed suicide. However, the Medical Examiner ruled murder, and it was announced as murder. Chief Sydney Cooper, who responded to the scene in the middle of the night, was convinced it was murder too, just from looking at it. It was just too messy. Could Morabito have lain down across the front seats of that

Volkswagen, despite all the hardware in the middle, and shot himself simultaneously in both sides of the head, one bullet going through the floor into the grass? This didn't seem too likely, although there had been cases in the past where cops killed themselves with simultaneous shots into either ear.

The detectives bagged Morabito's hands—the dead man's hands were wrapped inside of plastic bags—and back at the morgue a prima residue test was done on these hands. If he had used the guns himself, in theory, tests would show the presence of certain chemicals on his palms and fingers. However, such tests, like most so-called scientific tests conducted by police labs not only in New York but everywhere, were not really conclusive, whatever America's television audience of millions supposed.

A fingerprint turned up on the car, and this was later attributed to a certain junkie who had been one of Morabito's informants. Perhaps the junkie lured Morabito to the verge of the Belt Parkway and there murdered him. Or perhaps two people murdered him, one sitting in the passenger seat beside him, the other pointing a gun in the window. Or perhaps he murdered himself, and the junkie showed up later and decided to steal the guns and wallet. Or perhaps several people were involved, one murderer, one junkie to steal the guns, someone else to steal the wallet. The parked car, after all, would have attracted numerous honest citizens whose intentions were only to steal parts from the car.

The mystery deepened, and it never did become clear, not that day nor ever. Morabito was two months from his college degree in psychology. He was devout and would never have killed himself, friends attested. Morabito at least once had wept in front of his commanding officer as he begged to be taken off Narcotics. He was not known to have dated girls recently, he had no wife, but he did have a twin brother. In fact, one of his brothers drove up to the scene after midnight, looking, he said, for his brother, who hadn't come home or phoned since morning; and detectives asked themselves how he got there, who told him, why was he there?

And so that day we all attended a funeral that was disturbing rather than sad because we didn't know what had happened, and most of us were convinced we would never know. The funeral was mostly a formality that we had to get through in order to proceed to the real business of the day.

Life belonged to the living, and in a police sense former Chief of Patrol Elmer Cone was as dead as former Narcotics detective Morabito. The new Chief of Patrol was Inspector Donald Cawley, 41 years old, lifted by the Police Commissioner over 72 officers who outranked him. Cawley, who had been commander of the Sixth Division in Harlem for precisely two months, had never commanded anything else in his career. The Police Commissioner introduced him as "a foe of crime and corruption," and declared that there was a "generation-and-a-half gap in the Police Department. We have men in their fifties with more than 30 years in the Department, and although they are fine, upstanding men, many of them are finding change difficult. The key to change is in the higher ranks."

Cawley had been the youngest inspector in the Department, and his promotion was the most dramatic since 1954, 17 years previously, when, in the wake of the Gross scandals, an obscure inspector named Stephen P. Kennedy was jumped to the position of Chief Inspector.

There was not much to any résumé of Cawley's career. He once held a job mixing sodas at the local Schrafft's Restaurant, where he met the brown-haired waitress who was to become his wife. Her father was a patrolman. Young Cawley entered Brooklyn Polytechnic Institute, intending to become an engineer, but money and desire ran out after one year. He got married at 20, passed the Police Department examination, and worked eight years on patrol before being promoted to sergeant. Two years later he was assigned to the Gambling Inspection and Review Board, and there he met a young captain named Patrick V. Murphy. However, Cawley's immediate superior was the then Lieutenant, now First Deputy Commissioner William H. T. Smith: "He was terrific. He said all the right things about corruption and management. And the longer I knew him, the better opinion of him I had." Cawley had spent the next ten years working out of the First Deputy Commissioner's office, part of the time beside Lieutenant Smith; and although most officers were immediately transferred to a different command upon promotion, Cawley survived in that one office for ten years despite promotions to Lieutenant, to Captain, to Deputy Inspector, and to Inspector.

Cawley was a big man, six feet two, about 200 pounds, and he had an open, frank face. Though extremely nervous under the lights, his answers were candid and engaging.

The press conference was a success, the demise of Sergeant Morabito and Chief Cone were at no time remembered. When the press conference was over, Cawley turned and shook hands with First Deputy Commissioner Smith, saying, "Thanks, Commissioner Bill."

"Murphy asked for three recommendations for Chief of Patrol," Smith told me. "I don't know who else he asked, or what other recommendations he got, but I know what I told him. First choice: Don Cawley. Second choice: Don Cawley. Third choice: Don Cawley." Smith spoke about the financial questionnaires. By now he had looked through a number of them: "You'd be surprised how many of our sterling heroes have made very wise investments over the years. To read those questionnaires you'd think they were all financial geniuses. I know I didn't make any wise investments over the years. I know Don Cawley didn't make any wise investments over the years."

Leaving the press conference, the new Chief of Patrol dutifully shook hands with other members of the police hierarchy, making a special point about calling each of us (with the exception of the Police Commissioner, the First Deputy, and the Chief Inspector) by our first names.

The hallway gossips had at first been struck dumb by the appointment of Cawley. However, presently they recovered. Murphy could not get away with such an appointment. He had just given Cawley a 10,000-dollar raise in pay. Cawley had gone from no stars to three overnight, over men who had been waiting in line for years, and he had no experience. Two months in command of the Sixth Division in Harlem wasn't enough. Murphy had made a terrible mistake. He couldn't get away with this.

But of course the Police Commissioner had already got away with it, and he had no intention of stopping there. This would be the most explosive week of his reign.

The Police Commissioner, Chief Cooper, and I had ridden back from Morabito's funeral in Cooper's car, trying to decide what to do about "cooping"—sleeping on duty at night. On August 23, exactly a week before, Cooper had been up all night raiding precinct station houses throughout the city. He and a handful of men checked about 20 of them between midnight and dawn. For in the night, when the streets were empty and the radio was quiet, cops tended to drive off into the backs of parking lots or gas stations or school yards, there to park and snooze.

As we drove out of the melancholy crowds that milled about the church, Cooper began to describe what he had found. He had it all down on a chart, complete with the times that he had raided various precincts. He had hit the 4th Precinct station house in Manhattan at 4:55 A.M. At that hour there were supposed to be two cars on patrol, but Cooper had found two sleeping cops parked in one of them. The precinct commander there had had the job only three months. A lieutenant had been in charge at that hour. He and the two sleeping cops would come up on charges. Was the captain in or out?

At 5:38 A.M. Cooper had hit the Central Park Precinct station house. Among the weeds behind this building a patrolman had been growing marijuana—and had been caught at it—only a few weeks before, to the great embarrassment of the Police Commissioner and everybody else. Now in the night Cooper had to beat on the locked door there to wake up whatever cops were asleep inside. He found the sergeant asleep and not on patrol. There were supposed to be two sector cars on patrol at that hour. One of them Cooper eventually found many streets away, not even parked in the confines of its own precinct, the two patrolmen asleep inside. Cooper wanted to bring up the lieutenant, the sergeant, and three patrolmen on charges. What about the precinct captain? Was he responsible for this? Did he stay or go, and did the subject of marijuana enter into whatever judgment was to be made?

In the 122nd Precinct in Staten Island, Cooper had found the sergeant and his chauffeur in the coop. At the 43rd Precinct in the Bronx, Cooper found doors to the roof and into the back alley not locked. The lieutenant there would go up on charges of failing to supervise his station house. In the 107th Precinct in Queens, the desk was abandoned, one car was in the coop, the duty officer was in the coop, and the security officer was in the coop. In the

111th Precinct in Queens, Cooper came upon a radio car whose crew had evidently changed the numbers of their plates, perhaps to cut down on chances of getting caught at some little game they were playing. The sergeant would go up on charges for failing to inspect a radio motor patrol car, and the crew for changing the numbers.

And so it went. Cooper described banging on doors in the middle of the night, and also the expressions on the faces of the sergeants or patrolmen or detectives, some of whom stood there in their underwear, when they realized that Sydney Cooper himself had just burst in on them out of the dark.

Well, cooping was corruption too. What did the Police Commissioner intend to do about it?

The patrolman who was Cooper's chauffeur drove calmly through the streets of the city. I watched the back of his head, and no longer wondered where all the rumors came from that filled the corridors of police headquarters. One tended to treat one's chauffeur as if he were deaf, but very likely he wasn't.

So the following morning there was another press conference at which the Police Commissioner sacked six precinct captains for failure to supervise their men. For decades the tradition of the Department had been to concentrate discipline on the patrolmen. Now suddenly the commanders were being hit. It was Murphy's hope that the patrolmen throughout the city would be somewhat pleased—he was going after the bosses, not only after them. But one of my own chauffeurs, a patrolman, expressed what I supposed was the reaction of the entire force. He saw nothing wrong with being in the coop in the middle of the night. "You're not sound asleep," he said. "You're only dozing. If your number comes over that radio, you hear it."

Murphy did not sack the commander of the 73rd Precinct in Brooklyn. That was Brownsville, a black precinct and a high-crime precinct with nine cars on patrol all night. The commander was Deputy Inspector John Wilson, a black man. Cooper and his men had closed in on a vacant lot there, having been tipped off by David Burnham of *The New York Times* that cars cooped there every night.

It was against regulations for any officer to keep whiskey on police premises, but Wilson kept a bottle locked in his drawer; and when ranking police officials visited the 73rd Precinct, at whatever hour of day or night, he always offered a glass of Scotch. He had even offered a glass to the Police Commissioner a week or so before, prior to a community ceremony that began at ten o'clock in the morning.

Cooper's men, closing in in the middle of the night, had peeked around the corner into the vacant lot and spotted two 73rd Precinct cars there. So they lurked in the dark ness for about two hours, but nothing more happened, so they rushed in, and of course there were not two cars in there, there were four. They hadn't seen the other two. As they were getting the details from these cooped cops, in came a fifth car to coop.

However, there were only eight black men in the Department who had obtained the Civil Service rank of captain, seven of whom were Deputy Inspectors or higher, and Wilson to Murphy was a valuable man. Wilson was a good officer, he commanded one of the toughest precincts in the city, and he was black, and Murphy could not afford to humiliate him. Therefore Wilson was not immediately removed. In the back of Chief Cooper's car, Murphy kept saying, "Let's think about it. We're not obliged to act right away. Burnham may hit us with this or he may not."

Many heads rolled the next day, but not Wilson's. Burnham must have assumed that his vacant lot in the 73rd Precinct, during the night of the inspections at least, had been vacant of radio cars. The six other captains sacked seemed to satisfy Burnham, whereupon he quit the scene of battle, leaving victory to the Police Commissioner.

One of my subordinates once asked the Police Commissioner what his ultimate goals were, what his overall program was based on. Murphy replied, "My program is based on yesterday's headlines."

The next day Murphy called still another press conference, the third in three days, at which he announced that he had demoted two high-ranking officers, accepted the retirements of two others, and had appointed the former commissioner of the Nassau County Police, seventh biggest police department in the country, as his special assistant. Five more shells lobbed into the midst of his own bivouacking army.

The new special assistant was Frank Looney, 54 years

old, a heavy, scholarly man, who, when he spoke of himself at the press conference, used the editorial "we": "We are pleased to accept—" It would be Looney's job to run the Criminal Justice Bureau, a new agency that would watch what happened when cops came up against the rest of the criminal justice system—especially the district attorneys and courts—which cases were prosecuted, which dropped, which won, which lost. This was a new role for the police, and possibly an important one, but Looney was chosen principally because he was a vice-president of the International Association of Chiefs of Police.

There were approximately 40,000 separate police departments in the United States at this time, and the IACP was the professional organization that represented many of them. The chiefs of most of these departments were small-minded small-towners, who had little use for Commissioner Murphy's relative liberalism, his stand on gun control, his new ideas, his sophistication, his wide experience, and his quest for national police stature. Looney could well serve as the doorway toward wider acceptance within the IACP for Murphy.

"I may need him," Murphy told me, "if I want to go up against J. Edgar Hoover." It was often said that Murphy was after Hoover's job, and perhaps he was; but it also seemed clear that he saw room at the top of the police profession in America for more than one man. The pinnacle was perhaps broader than anybody thought. There was perhaps room up there, in addition to Hoover, for Patrick V. Murphy.

The press conference passed on to the important business of the day. The two-star patrol commander of Queens, Gordon Dale, was retiring. The two-star Chief of Integrity Control, Lawrence T. Flood, was being demoted one star. Inspector David Fallek, commander of the Fourth Division, was retiring. Inspector James Mooney, commander of the Seventeenth Division in Queens, was being demoted.

Why these particular men?

For the past several weeks the Police Commissioner had announced that he was "fed up." He had promised a shake-up of the hierarchy. At executive conferences he had begun to say, "I don't want to, but if I have to, I'll spill blood to get the changes I want."

These conferences were held in the fourth-floor conference room around a gigantic table. The Police Commissioner sat at the head. Also present were all the deputy commissioners, the Chief Inspector, the four three-star chiefs, the 14 two-star chiefs, and certain other high commanders as well.

Most of these people had stared blankly at the Police Commissioner as he promised bloodshed. The words did not ring in the air, they sort of lay there on the table. The Police Commissioner's eyes sought out no individual. There was nothing personal in anything he said. No individual in the room felt threatened. The Police Commissioner's words, if they had any meaning at all, must be aimed at someone else. Around the table there was no reaction. None at all.

These executive conferences had been held at the rate of one a month, and each month only five or six of the many individuals around that table ever offered an opinion, or entered a discussion, or spoke a word. In the Police Department, silence was not golden; it was merely the safest posture.

But there had also been other conferences restricted to the Police Commissioner, the Chief Inspector, the First Deputy Commissioner and one or two others, and at these Murphy said he had decided to force an unspecified number of high-ranking officers to retire. That would show that he meant business. Who would these high-ranking officers be?

Well, Chief Dale could go. He was 58, he had been a policeman for 31 years, and furthermore the Police Commissioner had been embarrassed by an event in Dale's borough scarcely three weeks before—the FBI had filed an affidavit in federal court to the effect that a certain gambler had been distributing regular payoffs to 32 policemen in Queens. The recent realignment of the divisions there had required the gambler to double the roster of cops being paid off, according to the affidavit. Why had Dale known nothing about this FBI investigation? Why hadn't he been conducting such an investigation on his own?

Chief Inspector Codd was ordered to inform Chief Dale that he would either retire, or be demoted.

Who else?

Two months before, Murphy had appointed Assistant Chief Lawrence T. Flood to a new job, working full time on integrity control. At 62, Flood was the oldest man on active duty (the mandatory retirement age was 63) and he had already put in nearly 34 years of service. Flood was a rough-talking florid-faced man. As a policeman he had held nearly every job: he had been a plainclothes supervisor, he had been a detective, he had commanded precincts—one of the few headquarters brass ever to have commanded a precinct. In addition he had been a hero. As a 36-year-old patrolman he had caught three holdup men running from the scene of an armed robbery, and one of these was later convicted of the murder of two detectives. As an inspector in charge of gambling investigations, Flood had led the raid which uncovered the largest policy bank in the history of New York City. Only the year before, while in command of Brooklyn South detectives, Chief Flood's men had identified and caught the killers of two cops.

Flood was known to be absolutely incorruptible.

Flood was known as Mr. Cop.

But Chief Inspector Codd was ordered to call in Chief Flood and tell him to retire, or be demoted.

Who else?

Two division commanders should probably be dumped, Murphy said. Which two?

Inspector David Fallek, Commander of the Fourth Division on the upper East Side, had refused to testify before a city commission investigating bribery the winter before. After much pressure he at last did testify, but it seemed clear that his heart wasn't in the right place.

Who else?

One of the division commanders in Queens should go, to show that accountability and responsibility extends all the way up through the ranks. Chief Dale, the borough commander there, was about to be fired, and a number of the patrolmen, sergeants, and lieutenants whom the FBI affidavit had named were now under investigation. A victim at some middle rank now seemed essential, and after some conversation the Police Commissioner settled upon Inspector James Mooney, 50, 25 years a cop, the current commander of the Seventeenth Division.

Chief Dale, after being informed by Chief Inspector

Codd that his career was over, was sent along to see me. When he came through my door his face was empty and drained, and he looked exactly like Chief Cone the week before. Dale wanted it known that he had filled out Murphy's financial questionnaire. This had nothing to do with his integrity. His integrity had never been questioned. He stood there before me, a stricken man. They had broken his sword. They had ripped his buttons off.

Next, Chief Inspector Codd summoned two-star Chief Larry Flood, Mr. Cop.

When he heard the news, Flood exploded. He rushed out of Codd's office, up the stairs, and barged into the outer offices of the Police Commissioner. A number of Murphy's secretaries, a deputy inspector, a lieutenant, jumped to their feet to hold back the enraged Flood. His fists were clenched and his face was red.

"You can't go in there, Chief," the deputy inspector cried, barring the way. Much later, Flood was admitted to the Police Commissioner's presence. He had calmed down by then.

Flood said that he found Murphy's conduct incredible. Two months previously Murphy had called a press conference and presented Flood as one of his principal anti-corruption aides. Now this.

Murphy pointed out that Flood had since shown no evidence of accepting the additional authority. He had shown no desire to accuse fellow officers of either corruption, or incompetence, or outright dereliction of duty. Murphy was asking Flood to retire for the good of the Department, to take his liberal pension, and to go off into honorable old age.

Flood began to get angry. He said to Murphy that he could not retire. It was out of the question. He was the only officer still on active duty who fitted into a former pension category. After eight more months of duty, plus vacation and terminal leave, he would complete 35 years on the Force and be able to retire on full pay. He was presently earning about $29,000 a year. That would also be his pension if he could last out eight more months. Were he to quit tomorrow, his yearly pension would drop to between $21,000 and $22,000 a year. The eight months, to Chief

Flood, would be worth approximately $8,000 a year for as long as he lived.

Murphy had not known this.

"So I can't retire," said Chief Flood. He was asking that Murphy let him hold his two-star rank only a short time more, and he believed he deserved it after 34 years' service. He was getting angry again. Flood was a choleric individual, and Murphy knew this, and there was always the possibility that Flood would start swinging.

So the soft, calm voice of Patrick V. Murphy went into action. The Police Commissioner had never intended to humiliate Flood, only to force him to retire, and one of his options now was to back off a step, allow Flood to continue in rank a short time longer, and be satisfied to have chopped the heads off only three men, rather than four. If Murphy retained Flood under these circumstances, the news would certainly get around, but Flood was so popular that this would surely redound to the Police Commissioner's credit: Patrick Murphy had a heart after all. Furthermore, there were plenty of other chiefs and inspectors ripe for the axe, and even one or two almost that old. Flood's head could be replaced in the basket.

Apparently Murphy never considered this option and, shortly, former Assistant Chief Lawrence T. Flood left the Police Commissioner's office still fuming, but a beaten man. The soft, quiet voice of Patrick Murphy had triumphed again.

One hour later there was a meeting in Murphy's office, and as we came in he was so pleased with himself he was practically chortling.

"You should have seen Flood come in here," he remarked. "But I said to him, 'Now, Larry, calm down, Larry, take it easy. Now, Larry, you're not gonna do anything stupid. There's no point to that, Larry, you have too much to lose. Now, Larry, I'll tell you what you're going to do. You're going to take your demotion, Larry, and in eight months' time you're going to retire with a full pension.'"

At the press conference, Murphy was asked why he had given Flood the challenging integrity assignment only two months before. Murphy said calmly, "I made a mistake. I have made a lot of mistakes, and I'll probably make a lot more. It was a very challenging assignment, and my action today reflects my dissatisfaction with what was achieved during the time Chief Flood had this job."

And so from the outside, the hero of the day seemed to be Murphy. He had bitten the bullet. He had made the hard decisions. However, within the Police Department and especially within the upper echelons, there was shock. Deputy Chief Eli Lazarus, president of the Captains' Endowment Association, called Murphy's action "devastating, a psychological uprooting beyond the memory of any of us."

The next day, Murphy went to the Police Academy and promoted men to fill the voids. The heads were emptied out of the basket and the blood mopped up, and a week allowed to pass before Murphy announced the retirement of Deputy Commissioner Theresa Melchionne, 56, the highest-ranking woman in the Department.

"Her departure is our loss," the Commissioner told the press. "She brought imagination and considerable talent to many demanding assignments over the years." Theresa didn't want to go either, and tearfully implored Mayor Lindsay to intervene with the Police Commissioner. Mr. Lindsay declined to do so. Executive clemency was not granted. The execution went forward on schedule, neat and almost painless. That void too was filled almost instantly. Her slot, marked Deputy Commissioner for Youth, was eliminated, and a new sign went up on the door: Deputy Commissioner for Organized Crime Control. The man selected for the office was William P. McCarthy, 55, who had retired from the New York Police Department seven years previously, after 24 years of service, with the rank of Deputy Chief. In the interim, Bill McCarthy had moved to Florida and had had a variety of jobs; as a police management consultant, a teacher, and even as a golf pro.

Now it would be his job to structure a new office, and if that office was to have any weight within the Department he would have to steal vast numbers of men from other commanders. A new political power struggle was promised by the appearance of McCarthy, but for the moment the upper echelons of the Department appeared in such a state

of numbness that McCarthy's arrival was scarcely remarked upon.

3 / Rape

The two uniformed patrolmen, forcing their way in the
second-floor window, saw first the girl's bare knees. Apparently she was lying on the floor beyond the bed and,
above the level of the mattress, only her knees showed. The
bed was so new it had never been slept in, and the mattress
was still encased in transparent plastic. The mattress had
slid part-way off the bed and rested on top of her face.

It had been a lovely summer evening, the city just beginning to cool down. A routine run: Some guy's girlfriend
hadn't answered the phone all day. All that the cops had
expected to do was prove her apartment empty. Instead,
this.

The two cops stared. The unmoving knees were all they
could see, or needed to see. Someone was home after all.

The two patrolmen came on into the room.

The edge of the mattress rested on the panty hose stuffed
into her mouth. Her arms were above her head under the
bed, and her bra and sweater were tangled around her elbows. Her underarms were shaven smooth, and she had
lovely big breasts. She was lying, knees spread, as if eager
to receive a man; and perhaps her lover would come out of
the bathroom, surprised to find them there, but he didn't.

Around her neck she wore a blue rope, thick as a gun
barrel but furry, like knitting wool, and knotted tight. The
leg of the panty hose was knotted around her neck too, in
some places intertwined with the rope, throttling her twice.
The color was gone from the rest of her flesh, but that part
of her face that the two cops could see was gorged red. Her
hair was dark brown with hints of auburn. Her skin was
flawless, except for some pink and purplish bruises on her
thighs. She had very pale, rather small aureoles. She probably had had an exciting figure, though no one would ever
know again how her bosom looked when she stood up. The
orifice between her legs gaped, as if her lover had just with-

drawn—to a girl for whom eternity had started, one second ago or four hours ago were the same, and it had not had time to close.

She looked to be about 23 years old.

The detectives came, first two of them, then many more. As they entered at the front door they could look straight down the corridor into the bedroom at her, though men moved back and forth, blocking the view. Their first glimpse of her, from a distance, was of shins, inner thighs, and pubic hair; and this seemed incomprehensible. Why was she lying there naked when there were so many men in her room, all clothed?

Each new detective entering the bedroom stared wordlessly down. An arm's length from her right hip, against the wall, lay a used sanitary napkin. She could not move to hide it, and no one else did.

In the living room, the two uniformed cops were writing their report, listing the names of all the detectives who were now filling the apartment: men from the precinct squad, from District homicide, technicians from Latent Fingerprints, the police photographer who began to set up his tripod.

Chief of Detectives Seedman, a middle-aged, burly man, came through the door chomping on a cigar. He looked down at the stuff knotted around her throat.

The mattress was slid back onto the bed, uncovering her face.

There was a smear of blood on the plastic mattress cover, and a bit more blood smeared on the floor. That was easier to look at than her beautiful face.

A few coins lay scattered on the floor. When the murderer had stripped her, perhaps the coins fell out of her pants pockets. What else had the murderer found as her pants came clear? That she was having her period. Did this stop him? No.

Her eyes were closed. Her mouth was open and still stuffed with the panty hose, and when this was removed it was seen that there was blood on her teeth. Her cheeks were blotchy and red, and her face was as contorted as if she were in the last stages of sexual excitement. Her hands were above her hair with her fingers curled, for the murderer, while raping her, had entwined his fingers in hers above her head.

She was as lovely a girl as any of them had ever seen. Raping such a girl was perhaps understandable. It was the killing that was not. Any man in his right mind might love to make love to such a girl, but why did some pervert have to kill her?

She had fought him. The bruises on her legs, her bloody mouth, attested to that. Had she screamed? Or had his first act been to cut off her air?

Teeth marks formed a complete circle around the nipple of her left breast. Grateful as any lover, the murderer had sucked in a mouthful and at some moment nearly bitten it off. When? At the instant of orgasm? At the instant of death? Perhaps they were simultaneous, his and hers, and he bit down.

Chief Seedman muttered to the photographer, "I want a close-up of that breast." A dozen men contemplated a girl's left breast.

The reporters were clamoring for news outside. They wanted to ogle the naked girl too. Jealously, the cops kept her for themselves. No one entered here but cops. The crime scene was the one exclusive club left in America. Admission to crime scenes was by shield only.

Hours passed. The girl still lay there, surprised in the attitude of love. Men stepped back and forth over her. She had become just another piece of furniture in the room. She was in the way.

Detectives were going through her closets and drawers, through her jewelry and underwear. In the living room the men from Latent were dusting the opened can of Coke she would never drink, and the box of Bohack groceries whose contents she would never place on shelves. In the bedroom the photographer laid a six-inch ruler next to the teeth marks, and fired away. The invasion of her privacy was total but would get worse.

At last the stretcher came into the room, and the girl was lifted onto it. She was stiff. The attendant put his hands on her knees, and leaned, straightening out her long slim legs. So much time had passed that the detectives had grown used to her there on the floor. But on the stretcher they gazed down on her again. Jaws hardened, eyes narrowed.

If they had seen such a girl in the street yesterday they might have stared harder than now. Yesterday, they could not have hoped ever to see such a girl nude.

The rope, intertwined with the stocking, remained knotted around her throat. Instinctively one wanted to cut it, as if to hear her sudden intake of breath. But no one touched it.

On the stretcher her legs were still parted, and between them she still gaped, a promise of voluptuous pleasure; and some of the detectives were reminded of their own wives years ago.

But this girl's pose was not related to that.

The soles of her feet were filthy. She must have walked around barefoot a lot.

The four canvas corners were folded over her, and the belts drawn tight. She was clothed again, all of her. As she left her apartment, the press closed in around her. She moved toward the street in the crowd.

At the morgue the belts were undone, the canvas thrown back, and bright lights revealed her to the attendants who lifted her onto a drawer and slid her, feet first, into the refrigerated wall. Her dirty feet went into the wall; her bruised legs, her bitten breast, the knotted rope choking her to death, the bra and sweater tangled around her elbows, her curled girlish fingers, all disappeared in that order.

The next day she was laid on a slab under lights and photographed in color from all directions, including from the soles of her feet straight up toward her crotch. Later she was moved into a room containing a row of tables, all taken but one, which was hers. There were corpses in various stages of dissection on top of each, and an assistant medical examiner, moving to her side, began her autopsy, dictating to a stenographer as he did so.

"Body is that of a well-nourished, well-developed 23-year-old white female . . ." the report began. It described the color of her nipples and the color of her pubic hair and other incidentals, then got down to business. Death was apparently due to the rope ". . . which I now cut."

The girl had worn her snug necklace most of yesterday. She had worn it all night in the drawer, and now she wore it a few seconds longer, for it proved more difficult to cut than the assistant medical examiner had imagined.

At last it parted.

The assistant medical examiner paused a moment to look at her face, as if wondering how she liked the sudden relief of pressure. Then he went on with the autopsy, dictating all the while.

Examining her vagina, the assistant medical examiner noted the number, extent, and location of various small tears in the membranes, and the quantity of semen deposited therein. His scalpel cut deep. She gave up the last of her girlish secrets. The assistant medical examiner noted the quality and quantity of urine in her bladder, and the contents of her intestines. He weighed her liver and noted the condition of her ovaries, though what for?

A mold was made of her bitten left breast and set aside to harden, after which the breast was lopped off and placed in preservative.

Breast surgery was successful. It would be the undertaker's job not only to powder her blotchy face and to hide the deep, discolored groove around her throat, but also to pad the dress she would be buried in.

When his report was concluded and typed up, the assistant medical examiner signed it. A copy was rushed up to the detectives who had the case, and it went into the girl's file.

By now the detectives—there were about a dozen working on the case at first—knew that the girl had been a stewardess. She had just signed a lease on the apartment, was having furniture delivered piece by piece, and she was working on the apartment every other day between flights. She had gone to a Catholic high school, and she still phoned her mother several times each day. She was a lovely girl whom male passengers invariably tried to pick up on flights, and when this happened she would get snippy and brush them off.

There were young men who knew her, and some claimed to have been in love with her; but when her apartment was ready, moving in with her would not be one man, but two other stewardesses.

The detectives had to know everything about the girl if they were to have any hope of drawing a picture of her murderer.

They knew a lot about him. He had left three partial

fingerprints—not enough to match him to any other set of fingerprints on file, assuming he was in the file at all, but enough to prove, if they could find the right man, that he had been in the room with the girl that day.

They knew his blood type, for he had left dried saliva all over the girl's breast, and this had been analyzed at the morgue and determined to be from a man with type O blood.

They knew what kind of bite marks his teeth made, and in later weeks a number of suspects would be sent down to the medical examiner's office, where one of the dentists would have them bite down into dental putty. From this, molds of grinning teeth were made and pressed against the dead girl's former breast, biting it again.

The truckmen who had delivered the brand-new bed were checked out. There had been letters in a pile near the front door, though the lock to the mailbox downstairs was broken, so perhaps the letter carrier had brought the letters to her door. The letter carrier was checked out. The superintendent might have been asked upstairs to help put the new beds together. The superintendent was checked out. A handyman was missing for some days, so he could have been the one. Detectives ran him down. He too was checked out, and didn't fit.

All current and former boyfriends were checked out. Every delivery man and repairman known to have been in the building recently was checked out.

Some of these men bit down into the dentist's putty, and some agreed to take polygraph tests from the Police Department's polygraph examiner, and all passed.

It had to be someone she knew, or why had she opened the door to him? Or was it someone who had followed her in off the street? Or a burglar already in the apartment?

All the tenants of the building were interviewed, and many in the neighboring buildings. None had heard screams. None had seen suspicious persons.

Many, after these interviews, went out and bought new locks and even burglar alarm systems for their doors.

The strangulation rope was taken on a tour of rope dealers: Do you sell rope like this? Dealers hefted it, called it a most unusual rope, possibly a maritime rope. Maritime rope merchants were canvassed, and a limited few were found—less than a handful—who had once carried this rope. None carried it now. Could it have belonged to a sailor?

The stocking that had been intertwined with the rope had contained a 25-cent coin near the girl's adam's apple, knotted in there in such a way as to bring pressure against her windpipe. The murderer had been able at will to open or close this pressure. Detectives speculated that the girl, forced to submit to rape, might have lain passively under the rapist. However, when he screwed the stocking tight against her windpipe, her face would have got red, and she would have thrashed around in her fight for breath, perfect counterfeits of passion, delighting the murderer. Whenever he wanted to believe her responding to him sexually, his hand would twist the quarter up against her windpipe. She would thrash, his own orgasm would come closer. He might have kept her alive a long time like that, alternately passive and thrashing—and then kept her thrashing until his own orgasm came, after which he would screw down one final time, simulating hers, until her thrashing stopped altogether and she lay beneath him as if enjoying the delicious languor that follows love.

A coin knotted inside a garrote was a common enough torture method in the Orient, detectives learned, and they began to speculate that the murder was a veteran of Vietnam. But how many veterans of Vietnam must there be walking the streets of New York?

Detectives pored through unusual occurrence reports on present and past rape cases, searching for details that matched their own. Nothing.

They requested to be notified of every sex crime taking place in the city, and one or another detective would rush to each likely scene, searching for some similarity to the rape murder of the stewardess. They never found any such similarity.

Gradually there were fewer and fewer leads to check out, and the number of men assigned to the case dwindled. After a year there would be only two left, and they had no hope of solving the case unless a suspect was captured committing another crime just like it. They would then check such a man out—prints, bite, blood type. They would have him at last.

From time to time they would get the horrible photos out, and as they stared at them, the old emotions welled up. How young, how exposed, how vulnerable she looked. How beautiful. One detective said one day, "She was a nice girl. She didn't deserve an end like this."

Probably the case would never be solved. The lovely young girl was in her coffin under the earth. She had become a statistic. She had been one of 2415 rape victims who came to the attention of the police in 1971; there were no doubt, many other girls and women who went home, took a bath, and said nothing to anyone. Even those rape cases the police did learn about were reported, on the average, two and a half days later.

She was one of only 41 homicide victims of sex criminals.

She represented as thorough and as competent a job of investigation as the Police Department had ever done. The detective work was flawless, and it had led nowhere. She was a file five inches thick in the office of Fourth District Homicide, nothing more. The murderer was still out there somewhere, strolling around.

4 / The Cops' Summer Camp

The time had come, Murphy felt, to try to win points with patrolmen on the street. Having concentrated totally on his executives, having forced them even to show what they had in their wallets, having rid himself of one deputy commissioner, three chiefs, two inspectors, and six precinct captains—all either gone, or humiliated, or both—the Police Commissioner perhaps expected a bit of applause from ordinary cops. But this had not happened. Newsmen who had strolled into the affected precincts, reported hearing charges like "gestapo" and "Nazi tactics" hurled at Murphy, bombshells that would never explode. The removed commanders had all been fine men, all of them unfairly punished. The troops were angry, spokesmen maintained. These spokesmen generally were unwilling to give reporters their names.

And in the halls of headquarters, no one cheered the way

the Police Commissioner had treated Larry Flood. Mr. Cop was still there, walking the halls, going to work every day and going home every night for eight more months, with a cheery hello for everybody. No self-pity showed on his face or in his voice. He did not slink about.

Shortly after this, a *New York Times* reporter, Martin Arnold, interviewed captains, lieutenants, sergeants, and patrolmen—several dozen men in all. His conclusion: Policemen of all ranks had become so apprehensive about being caught taking payoffs, that "nearly all forms of corruption appeared to have decreased noticeably." In black area precinct houses, according to Arnold, "for the most part the residents are treated with more courtesy and understanding, even when they enter to complain about a patrolman. In a Brooklyn precinct, where several months ago a visitor noted that the desk sergeants were dressed in baggy, unpressed uniforms, all now appear in crisp, freshly clean uniforms—just in case 'one of the Commissioner's men,' if not the Commissioner, drops by."

According to Arnold, whenever a radio car team was investigating an incident, another car was sure to arrive in about 15 minutes, this one containing the sergeant, come to check on his men. Arnold quoted one sergeant as saying, "The men hate Murphy. But right now a cop would lock up his partner—with all the pressure that's on him."

Over and over again, cops of whatever rank complained to Arnold that their wives and kids were being ridiculed by neighbors because of all the police corruption charges. A detective explained that cases were not solved with brain work but by tips from the public. The detective wanted to know, "Who's going to help us if they believe we're all dishonest?"

Apprised of all this, the Police Commissioner shook his head and remarked, "All the talking I did about corruption for eight or nine months did little to shake up the top commanders until there was bloodshed."

Privately and publicly both, Murphy defended his tactics: "I have always said that the vast majority of the men were honest, and I have always referred to the others as traitors. That there is a certain damage to all their reputations I don't deny, but we're going to come out of all this stronger than ever."

But there must be ways to show the cops on the street that he was on their side at heart, and Murphy now was actively looking around for some of them. Paul Canick, Deputy Commissioner of Administration, had arranged with the city's budget office to make money available for the washing of radio cars by gas station attendants, rather than by cops themselves out in back of station houses, and a memo to this effect went forward to the Police Commissioner, who sent it back having scrawled in the margin, "Great! This, hopefully, will be very popular with the men. We should exploit it as a demonstration of PC's interest in problems at the ptlm level."

But perhaps the vast majority of cops, though they no longer had to wash their own cars, would fail to connect their slightly enhanced dignity to the Police Commissioner personally. What else could he do?

He had agreed to speak before 1200 cops and guests attending the 77th annual convention of the Patrolmen's Benevolent Association at the PBA's summer resort camp in the Catskill Mountains, and it worried him. He would have to face vacationing cops on their own turf. The cops would be wearing sport shirts, and some of them would be drunk. Suppose they hooted him down? Suppose they started to throw rolls at him? Anything was possible. Suppose he were forced to return to New York with his speech unspoken? The camp was at Tannersville, New York—about three hours from the city by car, in the midst of densely wooded mountains. The camp was built halfway up a mountain. Below ran a fast-moving stream. It was green and cool and dark under the trees. The camp existed so as to offer police families a low-cost summer vacation area. It consisted of a vast, rambling hotel, below which were ranged several rows of motel-type buildings, each with a concrete veranda outside, facing out over the valley.

Summer was nearly over and there would be no wives nor kids there today, just cops.

We rode up there: Chief Sydney Cooper; Robert J. Eliasberg, the PBA's principal lawyer; and First Deputy Commissioner Bill Smith, in Smith's car, one of Smith's chauffeurs driving. The Police Commissioner was flown up by helicopter. The honored guests—there were about 60 of us who would sit on the dais in two rows—were first treated to a reception thrown by our patrolmen hosts. Hard liquor flowed.

After about an hour, we were formed into rows outside and marched downhill toward the main hotel and into the dining hall. Luncheon started with canned fruit cocktail. Instead of wine or beer, there was a bottle of Scotch in front of every second or third plate. Most bottles would be empty before the luncheon ended, and some before it started.

Below the dais sat over a thousand men, most representing their various precincts and units as delegates to this convention. They were clowning around, drinking, making plenty of noise. Presently the luncheon program got underway, starting with the "Star Spangled Banner," with the great tenor voice of First Deputy Commissioner Smith ringing out over the hall, overriding a thousand other voices at the final B flat. Then came the invocation from one of the police chaplains, and then Patrolman President Kiernan moved to the lectern and began to introduce each of the 60 dais guests. Some of these guests were former PBA officials, some were PBA officials from other cities, and a number were politicians of various minor ranks.

Kiernan was a big man with a big belly and a big voice. He knew the mood of his audience exactly, and tried to exploit it in his introduction of each dignitary. If the cops hated Murphy and Syd Cooper and Bill Smith, they did not hate Chief Inspector Codd, whom they saw as a link with the traditional Police Department of the past. Therefore, Kiernan introduced the Chief Inspector, a man with all the presence and dignity of the late General MacArthur, as "straight-as-an-arrow Mike Codd," and as the applause rang out, men began to stand—a thousand or more hard-drinking cops rising to their feet, giving Codd a standing ovation.

Kiernan moved down the dais introducing guests, approaching the Police Commissioner, and it seemed to me I could feel the tension build. What sort of a greeting would Murphy receive? It was Syd Cooper, whose career was devoted to catching crooked cops, who broke this tension. As Kiernan introduced him, the boos and the jeers nearly shook the building down. Cooper rose slowly, a broad grin on his beefy face, withdrew his pipe from his pocket, and mimed an old-fashioned camera man cranking his film. Cooper, grinning, pretended to take movies of all the booing cops, presumably to use as evidence in court, and after about five seconds the boos and jeers turned to hearty, genuine laughter, after which Cooper, too, got a standing ovation.

There was no tension left as Kiernan's introduction fell upon the Police Commissioner, who rose to his feet and sat down again, amid very mild applause. It was all over before the few boos and jeers were even noticed. Later came a number of speeches leading toward the Police Commissioner's keynote address. Introducing Murphy this time, Kiernan said into the microphone, "These people on the dais are our guests in our house, and I ask you to treat them as you would treat a guest in your own home."

And so the Police Commissioner of the City of New York moved to the microphone.

Kiernan had been relaxed among his own men. He was about 50, six feet three, 230 pounds. The small, mild Murphy could not match him in size or volume or ease.

The Police Commissioner's speech now began with the recounting of what was apparently a police anecdote from another city. A husky truck driver had parked his rig outside a diner and ordered scrambled eggs, bacon, and coffee. There was a roar of motorcycles pulling to a stop outside, and three tough-looking hoodlums in leather jackets entered the diner. They stood over the truck driver's table. One of them lifted the bacon off the truck driver's plate and ate it. The second grabbed a handful of scrambled eggs and gobbled it down, the third lifted the truck driver's coffee cup and drained it. For a moment the truck driver regarded them gravely, then he got up, paid his check, and left the diner. At this the three toughs swaggered over to the cash desk and one of them said to the girl, "Did you see that truck driver? He wasn't much of a man, was he?"

"No, he wasn't much of a man," said the girl. "And he wasn't much of a truck driver either. Because when he left here he just ran over three motorcycles."

This did not sound like a bad joke to me; it was skillfully told, and Murphy had even made it sound originally like the report of some curious crime. As Murphy had started to speak, there had been some hooting and some heckling from the far reaches of the room, which the Police Commissioner had ignored.

When the punch line came, although there was some laughter among those of us on the dais, there was almost none below him in the hall.

Nonetheless, the Police Commissioner grinned confidently down on his men. He noted that they had applauded Chief Cooper with "mixed feelings," a remark at which no one so much as snickered. As everyone knew, Cooper had formerly been Bronx borough commander, and so, still grinning, Murphy added, "When you have a good thing, it's not fair to keep him in the Bronx; the whole city ought to enjoy him."

No one snickered at this line either.

For the last hour these delegates had been applauding nearly every cretinous remark by every speaker. But Murphy now began to talk about their bravery and their devotion to duty, and they sat on their hands. He spoke of "the Police Department that I love and cherish and respect so much," and still nobody clapped.

He had decided on a number of points which he intended to make. He was not backing off from his position on corruption, or from his position on the accountability of superior officers. But he also wanted to assure them that they had his support: "I intend to go on being critical of some judges and some prosecutors, but I'm tired of the bum rap that the Police Department has been getting. This must be corrected. As long as I am Commissioner I will work to correct it."

No one clapped.

From time to time he interposed a short joke or humorous remark, at which no one laughed.

He said that the following day he would make a speech before the Chamber of Commerce in New York, where he would make plain that it was just as wrong for someone to offer a cop a bribe as it was for a cop to accept it. This would be the start of a new campaign against bribery of policemen. From now on they were to arrest every single person of whatever age or sex or rank in life who offered them a bribe of whatever kind.

There was still no applause, but the heckling had stopped. Finally a few of them even chuckled at one or an-

other remark. He spoke without notes, although in his hand
he held a card numbering the five points he had come there
to make, which card I had given him earlier. However, he
had made only three of these points when he put the card
in his pocket, thanked the men for their attention, and sat
down.

The strain, during the 10 or 15 minutes he had spoken,
had been palpable. The room had felt it, we on the dais had
felt it, and it was clear looking at his profile that Murphy
had felt it. He had managed a masterful political performance to survive even that long on his feet, and he knew it.
He was like a cop who, threatened by a man with a gun,
had slowly, methodically walked toward the gun until at
last he took it away from the man and laid it on the table.

Presently the luncheon broke up. The Police Commissioner, "running late" as usual, meant to start back to New
York at once, shaking hands all the way to his helicopter;
but there was a good deal of political work to do before the
rest of us could leave, and First Deputy Smith, Chief Cooper, and I now began to do it. The men had spilled down
onto the concrete verandas of the so-called villas, where
many of them sat drinking, staring out over the wooded
valley, while from inside their rooms their record players
sent music blaring out over the valley. For a time, the loudest music was the "Marine's Hymn."

> *From the halls of Montezuma*
> *To the shores of Tripoli—*

The martial tune seemed to fill all the valley with noise.

Other villas served as headquarters for the various line
organizations, and Smith, Cooper, and I now began to visit
each one. Outside the Emerald Society villa we were treated to Irish jigs by a bagpipe band in kilts, the bagpipers and
drummers passing in review before us, led by a cop in a kilt
carrying a broom for a baton. There was drink and food in
every villa. The Shomrim Society cops offered us kosher
sausages, and at the Greek Society villa a cop wearing a
white dress and a kind of fez began kissing the First Deputy Commissioner. A few of the bravest cops began calling
Cooper "Syd," though in the streets of New York City they

would have trembled to see him glance their way.

And so Smith, Cooper, and I mended the Police Commissioner's political fences as best we could; and now in the midst of the bagpipe bands, and the kissing Greeks, and the kosher sausages, there came the batting of rotors overhead, and the police helicopter swept into view above the trees. A great many heads turned upward. It seemed obvious to me that Murphy had ordered his pilot to fly directly over the festivities so that every cop in that valley, looking up, should see him there, suspended in the sky; should note the word Police (which was interchangeable with the word Murphy this year) emblazoned in great letters on the helicopter's sides. Everyone should realize who it was who dominated the Police Department, and thus dominated their lives.

Let's see them heckle him now.

Presently, having had food and drink at eight or ten different villas, Smith, Cooper, and I made our way back up the hill toward our car, passing the empty swimming pool with its cracked sides, and the tennis court on which two cops were batting a ball back and forth across two park benches which, with a two-by-four strung between them, served as net.

Climbing the hill, we were joined by some reporters. They had been living near here several days, covering the convention of PBA delegates. Their job was scary, they suggested, and they always hurried away each night as soon as it got dark, "because these guys are drinking so hard, and they all have guns."

Suddenly one of the reporters said, "I hear that the killers of Piagentini and Jones have been caught by the police in San Francisco."

Smith, not wanting to lie, said that he wasn't sure, he hadn't been fully briefed. But once inside his car he began cursing. Tomorrow the news would be in the papers, no doubt; and in San Francisco City Jail Tony Bottom, suspected assassin, would do no more bragging to the man who had been planted in the adjacent cell. Some drunken detective with a loud mouth, a delegate to this convention, had blabbed secret information to the reporters.

As Smith's chauffeur steered down the road in front of the villas, five or six cops, including the Greek in his dress, lay down in front of the car, waving bottles at us. We had to stop and coax them to clear the road before we could go on.

We talked about cops much of the way back to the city in the car—who would ever understand cops? Chief Cooper had been a cop 30 years, and he still didn't understand cops, he said. He began to tell of some crazy Texan holed up in a brothel in midtown New York, armed with guns, firing shots out into the street. Two detectives volunteered to go in there after him. They kicked their way in a back window, and dodged the shots, and captured the madman without bloodshed; and they were immediately put up for the Police Department's Medal of Honor, the highest decoration.

But a few days later the madam of that brothel showed up at Internal Affairs Division headquarters, claiming that the two detectives had returned to her place. Either she'd pay them $500, or they'd close her down.

The madam tossed a reel of tape down onto the desk. She had recorded the shakedown attempt.

Later there was a departmental trial, and the two detectives were dismissed.

But how do you explain that? Cooper wanted to know. How do you explain that the two detectives were brave enough to go in there after the Texan in the first place? And then how do you explain them selling off their Medals of Honor for $500? How could anybody ever understand cops?

The following day, with his speech to the Chamber of Commerce, Murphy's anti-bribery campaign went into effect. "There are two sides to the crime of bribery," the Police Commissioner told the Chamber of Commerce. "There are those who accept bribes and those who offer them, and the two are equally guilty. From now on we will vigorously pursue and arrest all those men and women of this city who either occasionally or as a matter of course would attempt to corrupt a policeman. No longer will the officer's response to a bribe attempt be, You can get into trouble talking like that. Instead it will be, You are under arrest for bribery." That same day Murphy sent a teletype message out to the Force: "You have the opportunity and the obligation to defend your dignity as the law directs.

Whatever the person, whatever the occasion, every person who offers you a bribe is to be arrested."

The Legal Division was ordered to print up a bulletin on the subject of bribery: what it was, how the law read, what actions a policeman was obliged to take. Cooper's Internal Affairs Division prepared a memo to all commands. He had ordered a special round-the-clock phone number to receive reports on attempted bribes. Electronic recording equipment, special dyes with which to mark money, and other such paraphernalia were now to be available in all five boroughs. Techniques for arresting bribers were outlined.

In addition, Murphy sent a two-page letter to the five district attorneys of the city urging them to give bribery cases the "special attention I believe they deserve . . . I earnestly request that you share my view that an attempt to bribe a police officer is an insidious attempt to subvert the rule of law itself. Such attempts should be regarded as separate and serious offenses to be dealt with severely."

In the past, the average cop usually would rather forget an attempted bribe, especially cases involving small amounts, as, for instance, bribe offers from motorists. A bribery arrest was legally tricky, and the district attorneys had the habit of dismissing such cases almost at once. They were hard, almost impossible, to prosecute. Normally it would be the cop's word against the citizen's word. Although in traffic violations the courts traditionally, since the dawn of the automobile, accorded preeminent weight to the word of the cop, so that the accused violator stood automatically convicted—nonetheless, in all other cases in American jurisprudence, juries almost always would take the citizen's word against the unsubstantiated word of a police officer. So the district attorneys liked to steer clear of bribery cases. Bribery cases sent their conviction statistics way down.

The Police Commissioner meant to have a try at changing all that.

5 / The Black Liberation Army: Side View

About halfway through the investigation into the assassinations of Patrolmen Jones and Piagentini, Chief of Detectives Albert Seedman added up the score so far. He found that detectives working on that case had arrested more than 40 people in connection with other crimes, mostly gun charges and possession of narcotics, but that a number of police shootings going as far back as 1968 had also been solved, as had the machine-gunning of Patrolmen Curry and Binetti, and the Sam Napier murder.

These were proud achievements for any squad of detectives, except this one. They wanted the men who had shot Jones and Piagentini in the back, as did Seedman, but after nearly three months there was not one single, solid lead. So much time had now passed that many detectives thought it was hopeless. They had so far penetrated the obtuse structure of every black extremist cell that they had come across. But they still had not a hint to the identity of the murderers who at point-blank range, had sent bullets crashing through the summer shirts of two young cops.

Then on August 28, on the other side of the continent, Sergeant George Kowalski, of the San Francisco Police Department, was driving his radio car west on 16th Street approaching Folsom Street when he was stopped by a red light. Now a car came across the intersection, and as it approached Sergeant Kowalski's car it swerved directly in front of his bumper and stopped, broadside, about a car length away. In the front seat were two young Negroes. To Kowalski's astonishment, the passenger leaned out the window with both hands, and aimed a submachine gun at him. The machine gun's muzzle was about 20 feet in front of Kowalski's face. Kowalski dove for the floor. But nothing happened; so after a moment, Kowalski glanced above the window, noting that the other vehicle was now moving slowly forward, with the passenger still leaning out pointing the submachine gun at the radio car.

But still nothing happened. Presumably the submachine gun had jammed. Now the suspect vehicle accelerated, racing across the opposite crosswalk at a high rate of speed.

The chase began. Sergeant Kowalski was driving with one hand and broadcasting a call for help with the other. Ahead of him, hanging out the window with a handgun, the suspect passenger pulled off either two or three shots. Sergeant Kowalski saw the muzzle blast and drove into the noise.

It was one minute after midnight. It was Friday night. The streets were brightly lighted, not crowded. Two blocks from the original intersection, the escaping vehicle veered right into 14th Street. An instant later Sergeant Kowalski, broadcasting the new direction, careened around the same corner in close pursuit. He saw the gun pointed back at him fire. Two more shots. The suspect vehicle turned right, then left, then left again, with Sergeant Kowalski radioing each change. Sergeant Kowalski's right rear tire blew out, perhaps hit by a bullet. While Sergeant Kowalski fought the skid, foot heavy on the brake, a second radio car appeared ahead—nearly every radio car in that part of the city was converging on those streets by now. Trying to get through the intersection ahead of this second radio car, the escaping car crashed into a light-blue Ford.

The two cops in the second radio car jumped to the street, guns ready. Patrolman Rames had a shotgun. Patrolman Gurneri had his service revolver out. The passenger of the crashed car jumped into the street and pulled off one round at the two cops. Both returned fire. Apparently hit, the suspect ducked back into the passenger side of the car. Now Sergeant Kowalski, wobbling along on one flat tire, reached the scene, and jumped out. The two other cops were nearing the crashed car, whose driver was hunched over in the seat, not moving. The passenger was similarly hunched over, with his feet partially out of the car. Kowalski saw a gun in the right hand of the passenger, who was now raising himself up from the front seat. Kowalski fired one shot in through the window, and the suspect passenger fell to the seat and lay still.

That was the end of the chase, and the shoot-out, half a minute of excitement, no more.

As all cops knew, chases and shoot-outs lasted only a few seconds each, but the work that came afterward lasted hours, if not weeks. The contents of the car had to be inventoried, beginning with one .45-caliber submachine gun with 29 live rounds in its magazine. A second magazine with 29 live rounds lay on the floor in the rear of the car. On the floor in front lay one Smith and Wesson .38 police special with five expended shells and one live round. A Colt .45 automatic taken from the passenger suspect was found to contain one magazine with six live rounds, and one spent cartridge. There was one flare gun with flares. A magazine loaded with seven live rounds, fitting the .45-caliber automatic, was found in the pocket of the driver. Both inert suspects were searched before the ambulance arrived. The driver suspect wore a leather pouch belted around his waist. It contained 59 rounds of .45-caliber ammunition. In the pockets of the passenger suspect were two plastic bags, one of which contained 13 and the other 15 live .38-caliber shells. There were six .38-caliber rounds loose in his pocket.

The clothing of the two suspects also had to be inventoried. Removed from the driver in this order were one blue shirt, one bluejeans held up by a black belt, tennis shoes, underclothing, and socks. The passenger wore bluejeans held up with a black belt, plus a green jacket.

Meanwhile, Sergeant Kowalski had hurried back along the route of the chase, eventually finding two witnesses who had observed the suspect car driving at a high rate of speed with the radio after it, and who had heard gunshots. Kowalski also found a parked car that had been struck by a bullet just below the windshield wiper, cracking the windshield glass.

Who were these two black men, and why were they so heavily armed?

Where did the guns come from?

Where did the car come from?

From the hospital where he lay heavily guarded, the man who had tried to machine-gun Sergeant Kowalski, and who still claimed that his name was either Harold Stevens or Robert Johnson, but whose real name was Albert Washington, wrote a letter to a woman. The letter began:

All power to the people.

I am improving and my spirit is strong. I know how you worry and haven't heard nothing must be a drag.

What is there to say? Where there is struggle there is sacrifice and even in defeat, there is victory. Having taken the cause of the people, it brings us that much closer to each other and makes us more human by trying to break the chains that bind our people. Historically our people have taken abuse after abuse yet we remain passive. So we come to this point in time when Malcolm said we must talk in the tongue of our oppressor. Our children must be taught that man's inherent right is to be free from all kinds of oppression and exploitation. When that day comes mankind will come to a better world. 'There's a new world coming.' So it's in the songs that you hear and the talk on the lips. Tomorrow I will be discharged from the hospital and probably taken to jail. I guess you could come see me there. Life with me hasn't been too beautiful for you but then, when millions of people have to eke out an existence, why should we even think of beauty? You have brought some of the happiest moments into my life and if it be written there will be more. I said it before and I say it again the future of our people depends on our youth for they are tomorrow's soldiers. May our people never stop struggling until they are free so for now that's about it. Take care of yourself. With revolutionary love—

There were a number of postscripts: "You know what ran through my mind when I got hit?" the letter asked, and added poetry.

> _If I fall rose in hand_
> _You'd be free and I a man_
> _For slave of natural death who dies_
> _Can balance out two dead fles_
>
> _Rather to live with the shame_
> _Of a bullet lodged within my brain_
> _If we were not to reach our goal_
> _May bleeding cancer torment my soul_

Last night George and Jonathan Jackson's mother was on TV and it brought tears to my eyes. How many more black women will suffer the loss of a son, brother or husband? Probably plenty more, and we still have 350 years of pain and suffering and death. Be strong and help others to be strong.

By now both suspects had been identified positively by fingerprints. The man who had tried to machine-gun Sergeant Kowalski, and whose true name was Albert Washington was 30 years old, five feet ten, 175 pounds, dark-complexioned. Born in New York, Washington had a long history of assault and other anti-social activity. At age 15 he had been admitted to Rockland Hospital, where he remained for three years before being transferred to Creedmore Hospital, from which he escaped in June of 1965. He was arrested for armed robbery in Denver and entered the Colorado State Penitentiary on March 28, 1967, where he stayed three years before being transferred to the Colorado State Hospital in Pueblo. The various medical diagnoses of Washington over the years ranged from neurosis to schizophrenia. He had an eleventh grade education, was known to read extensively in the works of Eldridge Cleaver, Mao Tse-tung, and Malcolm X. It was Washington's belief that the white world was against the black world and that he should do something about it. Using the alias Lawrence Williams, Washington was arrested in New York on June 29, 1971, six weeks after the assassinations of Jones and Piagentini and two months before he tried to machine-gun Sergeant Kowalski, in connection with the armed robbery of a Beneficial Loan company. At the time of his arrest he was in the company of Ronald Carter, a New York City Panther member, and Robert Jackson, brother of Andrew Jackson, also a well-known Panther.

Washington had written articles for *The Black Panther*, the official newspaper of the party, and he had also contributed so-called "revolutionary" poems. The title of one was "In the Black Colony." He called another "Where It's At," and he signed this one Albert Washington: Denver County Dungeon.

Albert Washington had once lived in the housing project in Harlem where Patrolmen Jones and Piagentini had been assassinated.

The driver of the car, whose California driver's license

identified him as James Jeffrey Williams, was Anthony Bottom, six feet one, 170 pounds, also dark-complexioned, with a wide nose and long sideburns. Born in Oakland, California, Bottom was six weeks short of his twentieth birthday. Bottom during 1968 had been arrested four times as a juvenile. Earlier in 1971 he had been arrested on a traffic warrant. Bottom had been employed by the Department of Human Resources of the State of California in San Francisco but had not been to work since April 12. Ironically, his employment there was officially terminated by the department precisely on May 21, the day that Patrolmen Jones and Piagentini were assassinated in Harlem.

The .38-caliber Smith and Wesson revolver found on the floor of the suspect car bore Serial No. C-177598.

It was Patrolman Jones' gun.

This word was telephoned to Chief Seedman in New York, who, hearing it, took in a deep breath. After he had hung up, he sat staring at the wall for several minutes.

The .45-caliber automatic found on the person of Bottom was tested by ballistics men and the bullets it fired matched the slugs dug out of Patrolman Jones. So the pedigree of that gun had to be traced back to the point of origin, and so did the pedigree of the car in which the two suspects had been riding. Tracing the car was a job for the San Francisco Police, and tracing the various guns, since they led immediately out of state, was a job for the FBI. Back in New York, Seedman at last knew approximately what he was looking for, and therefore where to look. Presently, very quietly, he flooded the south Bronx with detectives.

Meanwhile, back in San Francisco an effort was made to interrogate Bottom and Washington on the day after the shoot-out, and again on the day after that. Both refused to answer questions. However, both boasted that they were members and soldiers of the Black Liberation Army.

The car they had been driving was a 1965 two-door black Oldsmobile. This vehicle turned out to be registered to Eugene and Lenora Padilla. It was summer, these people were on vacation, and it took a while to find them. When at last they were run down, Padilla was able to prove that he had sold his car to a local Chrysler-Plymouth agency, and that he himself was a law-abiding citizen.

Which Chrysler-Plymouth agency?

Detectives rushed there and found that the car had been turned over to a wholesale dealer. Which wholesale dealer? At last the dealer was found. His records showed that he had sold the car for $500 to a young black man who claimed that his name was Samuel Lee Penegard.

Who was Samuel Lee Penegard?

Detectives rushed to the address that Penegard had given the dealer: 955 Pierce Street, Apartment 1. There was no one there. However, the San Francisco Police knew the address well, for a Black Panther named Richard Kenneth O'Neill had lived there, and this man had been charged with shooting a special police officer in San Francisco months before. The California Motor Vehicle Bureau was now searched for a driver's license in the name of this Penegard, and one turned up. Penegard was 22 years old, black hair, brown eyes, six feet tall, 165 pounds. His application for his driver's license carried his photo, and an inked fingerprint.

Contrary to popular belief, it was almost impossible to identify any suspect on less than a complete set of ten prints. But in the case of Penegard the FBI also had a photo and description to go on, and so the single print on Penegard's driver's license application was identified as the right thumbprint of Herman Bell. Herman Bell's card was now matched against the latent print developed on the Mustang against which the murderers of Jones and Piagentini had lounged during the time when they were nervously waiting for the two cops to reappear in the street— and it checked.

Herman Bell, it was discovered, had once played quarterback for San Jose City College. Bottom had been a student there for a short time too.

The deeper detectives probed, the more horrifying the conspiracy appeared.

The trail of certain of the guns led back to Salt Lake City, where, the previous January, two black girls had entered Wolf's Sporting Goods Store and bought a .45-caliber pistol and a 9 mm. automatic for two black men. One of these girls, Nancy Monroe, was a friend of Bottom's sister Stephanie. Nancy Monroe, when found, pleaded that she had been duped into making the purchases of the guns at

Wolf's Sporting Goods Store. The two men with her had been Francisco Torres and Albert Washington, she said. Washington and Torres had told her that they had come to Salt Lake City to purchase weapons, and that they belonged to the Eldridge Cleaver faction of the Black Panther Party.

Who was Francisco Torres? An investigation into the pedigree of this man was now begun.

Three months later, Nancy Monroe had purchased additional guns at Duke's Sporting Goods in Salt Lake City. The money was given to her by Albert Washington, whom she knew as W, and he waited in the car outside while she went in to buy him a .38 automatic and a 9 mm. automatic. She used her birth certificate and her University of Utah ID card to buy the guns.

All these guns were purchased legally according to Utah law. A car in which certain of the suspects and certain of the girls rode had even been stopped by the police for going through a red light, and the guns were found and confiscated. The driver and the passengers were released on bond, however, and later the girls went back to the police station, and demanded their guns back. The police had no choice but to comply. To some extent the fates of Patrolmen Jones and Piagentini were sealed at the moment that the desk officer passed those guns back across the desk to the young black girls from the University of Utah.

In New York, information on Francisco Torres was beginning to turn up.

Not one word had so far been made public about recovery of the gun of Patrolman Jones. Bottom was confined in the San Francisco City Jail, and ten days after the attempted machine-gunning of Sergeant Kowalski, a 21-year-old black street cleaner, serving a nine-month sentence for receiving stolen property, went into the cell next to Bottom. Back in New York it was Chief Seedman's hope that news of the recovery of Jones' gun could be kept on ice indefinitely, for Bottom and the street cleaner had become friends, and Bottom had begun to blab. Presumably, the moment Bottom knew he had been connected to the Harlem assassinations, his mouth would close and stay closed. In the meantime, Bottom and the street cleaner often talked in one of the cells or in the corridor, and the street cleaner later signed statements as to what those conversations had covered, and he agreed to testify in court against Bottom.

In these jail house conversations Bottom claimed to be a revolutionary. He remarked that he was in jail because of a shoot-out with the San Francisco Police, and that the gun used in this shoot-out had also been used in the killing of a New York City policeman. Did you kill the pig in New York? asked the street cleaner. Bottom answered yes. Bottom now began to take credit for other attacks on policemen. He had accompanied the black demolition expert who blew up the Paris station house in San Francisco. He had been involved in a police shooting in the Haight area of San Francisco, and he had cased the Ingleside Station before this station house was shot up. According to the street cleaner, Bottom claimed that Washington had accompanied him on all his shoot-outs with the police; their organization consisted of five individuals, Bottom claimed one day, but on another day he claimed it consisted of seven.

Knowing better what they were looking for and where, San Francisco detectives were able to lean on certain "confidential" informants. A good detective in San Francisco or New York or anywhere else would have a number of informants that he considered "confidential," and the names of these people never appeared in police reports. Most such confidential sources were underworld characters. Detectives usually hid the identities of their confidential informants, even from their own superiors.

San Francisco detectives now found one such individual who claimed he had known Bottom for two years, and Washington for 16 years. During those 16 years he thought Washington's name was Johnson. Once again the police were having to cope with the impenetrability of these black extremist cells.

This particular confidential informant confirmed that Bottom had claimed that he had killed a New York police officer, that two other men had been involved in this murder, that Bottom and Washington were both part of the Black Liberation Army, and that there was more to the plot than now showed. This Black Liberation Army was also responsible for the shoot-up of the Ingleside Station, including the murder of the desk sergeant there on the day following the attempted murder of Sergeant Kowalski. The

Ingleside shoot-up was conducted by a group that called itself the Jackson Salty Five, after George Jackson.

Another confidential source was found. He not only confirmed the original information on the shoot-up of the Ingleside Police Station, but he described how, several days previously, Bottom, with an unknown black girl and an unknown Negro male called "Blood," had entered the Ingleside Station to make a false police report concerning an imaginary stolen bicycle. During this visit, Bottom and the others had carefully noted the layout of the interior of the station house, and especially the traffic pattern: the cops going in and out of the watch room. The plan later decided upon was to force open the door to this room and plant a bomb in the center of the building. Four persons were to have entered the station house, three with guns and the fourth a demolition expert. Shotguns and a Browning automatic rifle had been selected as the weapons to be used. Outside, two cars would wait along Ocean Avenue, drivers behind the wheel, engines running. As soon as shots were fired, the drivers were to drive around onto the shoulder of the freeway, which the shooters would reach by diving through a cut in the fence which had been made earlier that same afternnon.

Three individuals did enter the station house and murder Sergeant John V. Young, 45, while two remained outside in cars. A woman clerk was wounded in the shooting. After the fusillade of shots, the three men ran out of the station house, dove through the fence, and got into two cars parked on the freeway, and from there drove to an unknown address in San Mateo.

The actual killer of Sergeant Young was said to be the individual known as "Blood." He had walked up to the glass partition, poked a suddenly revealed shotgun through the hole in the glass, and virtually blown the unsuspecting Sergeant Young apart.

This same confidential source explained that the shoot-up of the Ingleside Station was supposed to be part three of a four-day plan. On Thursday night a bazooka round was supposed to have been fired into the Mission station house, and it was supposed to have had some kind of delayed fire mechanism so that it would explode inside the building. But the projectile was found to be a dud and so part one of the four-part plan was canceled. Part two was the attack Friday night on Sergeant Kowalski. Part three was the attack on Saturday on the Ingleside Station and the murder of Sergeant Young. Part four was to be the assassination on Sunday of two uniformed cops, names unknown. However, it was specified that these were to be a black cop and a white cop working as a team out of the Southeast station of San Francisco. This attack was canceled, possibly because by then Bottom and Washington were in custody.

And so the assassination of Patrolmen Jones and Piagentini, which had baffled so many New York cops for so long, was unraveling fast in San Francisco. Bottom and Washington were in jail, and Herman Bell and Francisco Torres had been identified and implicated.

Where was Bell? Where was Torres? It was one thing to identify a suspect, and another, especially with people like this, to find them. They were people without jobs, and without possessions, apart from their artillery. They had no fixed addresses. They didn't even have fixed names. By now it was known that Torres had resided in San Francisco under the name of James Holmes until the summer of 1971, and after that under the name of Charles Wilson. Such men could live under the surface for months at a time. There was no way to find them. The chances were, as every cop realized, that not one would turn up until caught or shot in the commission of some other terrible crime.

At 10:10 A.M. on September 20, three weeks after the attempted machine-gunning of Sergeant Kowalski, three young Negroes, two of them armed with shotguns, the third with a handgun, stepped into the Bernal Heights Branch of the Bank of America in San Francisco. They scooped up $15,000 out of two cash drawers, found an off-duty cop working as a teller, and relieved him of his gun; and this cop was wounded when one of the gunmen began shooting for no apparent reason in the bank vault. As the three men fled from the bank, it was noted that a fourth Negro male had stood on the corner as a lookout, and that a fifth was the driver of the getaway car.

The FBI grabbed the bank surveillance cameras and developed the films. Easily identified as one of the gunmen was Francisco Torres, who had got away again.

Two detectives from the 32nd Squad, the home precinct

of Jones and Piagentini, had been in San Francisco for 15 days running down leads there and reporting to Chief Seedman in New York nearly every day. It was time to conduct a lineup. On the day following the bank robbery a party of eight flew out of New York to San Francisco: the Assistant District Attorney in charge of the case, four black witnesses, two more detectives, and a black policewoman named Olga Forde, who would later be promoted to detective for her work on the case.

One of the witnesses was Clarence Lee, an 18-year-old Brooklyn youth, who had been visiting in Harlem on the evening of the assassination. After Jones and Piagentini had crashed to the pavement, after the final bullet had pounded down into the squirming Piagentini, while the noise of the shots still hung in the air, the terrified Lee had watched one of the gunmen sprint right at him. The killer paused long enough to say, "Be cool, we don't want you." Then the killer turned the corner and was gone.

During the intervening four months, Lee had been held as a material witness, at first in Civil Jail and then in Howard Johnson's Motor Lodge on West 51st Street, guarded around the clock. Lee was hostile to the detectives who questioned him, and about as afraid of the police as he had been of the killers. But of all the eyewitnesses to the assassinations, he had had the best look at one of the killers, and on his shoulders now rode the chief hopes of those New York cops who still mourned Jones and Piagentini.

The lineup took place on September 23, four months and two days after the assassinations, in the sixth-floor auditorium of the Hall of Justice in San Francisco. Cops stood guard at the elevators and turned back people attempting to get off at the sixth floor. The lineup was conducted by New York Assistant District Attorney Roderick C. Lankler.

In the audience stood a six foot high green metallic panel, with a two foot square one-way mirror set into the middle of it. Curtains came back along the sides, forming a kind of cubicle. The witnesses were totally invisible to the eight men on stage—the two suspects plus six men culled from the city jail.

One by one the witnesses were brought into the auditorium behind that screen, to review the men on stage. Bottom was positively identified by one witness as one of the killers of Patrolmen Jones and Piagentini; and a second witness said he much resembled one of the killers. Neither of these witnesses was Clarence Lee, who failed to recognize anybody. When apprised by telephone, Chief Seedman back in New York shook his head in disgust.

"Do you realize how much it cost the City of New York to guard that guy for four months?" asked Seedman. "That kid never lived so high in his life. We made a gentleman out of that guy."

None of the witnesses identified Albert Washington.

Back in New York, Seedman now knew that the murder conspiracy involved five men, and he had all the names: Tony Bottom, Herman Bell, Francisco and Gabriel Torres, and Albert Washington. Three young women had been found and had separately given testimony, and credit for making them talk went almost exclusively, Seedman was to state later, to Policewoman Olga Forde.

One of these women, call her witness A, was being held in protective custody at the Westchester Hotel in the Bronx. She was 28 years old, unemployed. She had been arrested previously for narcotics possession and for prostitution. She admitted that she earned her living as a prostitute, and that she had five children, all residing in the South on a plantation with her mother, who was a domestic there. Two of these children, she stated, were by George Washington, one by Henry Davis, one by "some Irish boy," and one by a man she knew as Michael Williams. Michael Williams was Tony Bottom.

Miss A had lived on Fox Street in the Bronx, and on the day of the murders she was awakened in the middle of the night by the noise of her boyfriend, Bottom, moving about her room, stuffing his things into a suitcase. She had known Bottom about four years, and had had a child by him, but believed that his name was Michael Williams. She was also acquainted with Michael Williams' half-brother, Reggie Williams—this was Albert Washington. Reggie she thought a vicious individual.

In the night, this dialogue took place, according to Miss A—

"Baby, I've got to go, because Reggie just shot some cops."

"How I gonna find you?"

But, she attested, she was high on pills taken before going to bed, she did not remember what Bottom answered, or even if he answered, and she had fallen asleep again before he left the room.

Two weeks later, she met Bottom at a condemned building on Simpson Street in the Bronx, where he and Washington were hiding.

"The cops been asking you questions about me?"

"No."

"You're lying."

"Yes, but I haven't told them anything."

Bottom said he believed her, and then he told her that Reggie (that is, Washington) had killed the two cops on Friday, May 21. He had been there himself at the time of the killings.

"Where is Reggie?"

"Mind your own business."

For about two weeks, Miss A brought food every day to the abandoned building on Simpson Street. Bottom always waited alone, until one day Reggie was there too. Reggie accused her of talking to the cops, but Bottom calmed him down, insisting that she would never do so.

The next day when she came with food, no one was there. She found a note that read, "Baby I'm sorry." It was signed, Mike.

During the time she was bringing food to Bottom, she was being interrogated regularly, first by New York detectives, then by the FBI, but she never admitted to any of her interrogators that she knew where Bottom was hiding out.

The two young black women who were witnesses B and C were in their apartment when the five men came back on the night of the assassinations. The men were Tony Bottom, Albert Washington, Herman Bell, Francisco Torres, and his brother, Gabriel Torres. According to witnesses B and C, the five men were as excited as if they were drunk or high on drugs, and the dialogue went this way.

"Man, we really offed them pigs."

"Yeah, but one of the pigs was a brother."

"You just have to live with it."

"A pig is a pig."

"Fuck all the motherfuckers."

"That white cop sure didn't want to die. Did you see him trying to get up, saying, 'Don't kill me, don't kill me'?"

Witness C, in bed in the dark with one of the five men that night, heard him recount how the two cops had been murdered. According to witness C, the shooters were Tony Bottom and Herman Bell. Washington and the Torres brothers had waited as a back-up team. If the cops had strolled back to their car from the back of the building, the shooting would have been done by the back-up team, or if the ambush out front had failed, the back-up team would have rushed forward with more guns firing.

Patrolmen Jones and Piagentini had never had any chance at all.

The killers had taken the cops' guns to keep as trophies.

The investigation was quietly pushed a few steps further. Two weeks later, New York detectives raided a flat at 893 Crotona Park North in the Bronx in the middle of the night, and there grabbed Francisco Torres, Gabriel Torres, and three other persons.

Four of the five killers were now in custody. Where was Herman Bell?

And how many more men like this still roamed the country looking for cops to kill?

6 / Political Crime

The Police Commissioner stayed aloof from crime. He was not interested in crime and apparently never had been.

That summer there were the banal purse snatches, muggings, armed robberies, occurring by the tens of thousands. And there were the rare crimes. Murphy never got involved in either type. Perhaps he knew better than to tie his prestige to the solution of any one of them, or perhaps he had a deep psychological aversion to crime. What man of honor could understand how a criminal's mind worked? Perhaps to Murphy crime seemed dirty.

From time to time there was pressure from the Mayor regarding specific crime, and to this Murphy did respond. That summer midtown was overrun by prostitutes, and the Mayor's office was bombarded by complaints. Men walking with their wives were solicited by girls who would bump them, grab their arms, perhaps insult the wife. A foreign diplomat went upstairs with a prostitute and was robbed and shot.

The Mayor telephoned his order to the Police Commissioner: Weed those girls out of the theater district.

Ideas were thought up by one commander or another, and certain of these Murphy approved, and a campaign against prostitutes was begun. Additional cops in uniform were sent into the area carrying Polaroid cameras. They couldn't arrest the girls without an overt solicitation, and which girl was stupid enough to solicit a uniformed policeman? But ostentatiously, the cops would photograph the girls, hoping that this alone would scare some off, the amateurs and part-timers at least; and this campaign did have some effect.

These cops also arrested 389 girls for loitering, but every single case was dismissed in court. Meanwhile, the pimps drove around the area in flashy automobiles with custom-made body work, oak paneled interiors, and headlights big as apple baskets. The cops were ordered to slap traffic tickets on these cars, which soon became known as Pimpmobiles, at the slightest provocation.

"Massage parlors" had sprung up everywhere, and were still another problem. These were out-and-out brothels, but the girls were wise enough to offer only a massage until the customer was stark naked: They would not touch him until his clothes, his badge and gun if any, all reposed in a pile in the corner. In order to have the grounds for making an arrest, a policeman would have to submit to a massage first. A cop could not be ordered to undergo such a massage; and if he did undergo it, any arrest he made would be thrown out of court on grounds of entrapment.

Next, policewomen were sent out in civilian clothes to lean against walls swinging their handbags, and each time a John came by to solicit such a girl, he got arrested.

Most Johns turned out to be well-heeled, well-known out-of-town businessmen, and an attempt was always made to publicize such arrests, so as to terrorize other visiting businessmen in search of excitement which didn't exist in their own towns—indeed, the proliferation of such men was part of the reason why so many girls and massage parlors infested those streets, and why the girls were so brazen. The policewomen who were used for the job, although volunteers, turned out to be a good deal less hardened than anyone had suspected. They found the job degrading rather than funny, and few would talk about it. One, coming back to the station house with her first arrest, was asked in what terms her prisoner had solicited her.

"Oh, Chief," the girl protested, "I couldn't repeat such language in front of you."

"Why not?"

"It's too—too—I just couldn't."

"But you're gonna have to tell the judge in court."

"I know, Chief, but that's different."

Cops were people who knew the worst about life, but on the subject of sex, or even explicit language, a good many of them were prudes. In my presence two detectives who worked on the Jones-Piagentini assassination were shocked one night to hear a third detective use the word "scumbag" in front of his wife and daughters, though the word meant only fourflusher within the Police Department, and outside it meant nothing at all. What about using explicit sexual language in the bedroom with your own wife? I asked them.

The first two detectives, shocked, were unwilling to believe that any decent man would use such language in front of a wife he loved and respected. These were homicide detectives who had been catching murderers and rapists for most of the last 20 years.

To them, as to many cops, a whore was a whore, and a respectable woman was a respectable woman; and with respectable women the proprieties were to be rigidly observed.

There were store fronts advertising live sex shows inside. One day driving in midtown with Chief Cawley, the new young Chief of Patrol, Chief of Detectives Seedman said, "See that place? My chauffeur went in there, he paid five bucks, and they took him into a dark room and he watched this couple screwing. There was a mattress on the floor, and this couple was on top of it, screwing, and a bunch of men were standing around in their overcoats watching it. Why don't you clean that place up?"

The new Chief of Patrol said, "Are you kidding me?

You mean to say that really goes on here?"

The Chief of Detectives answered, "Detectives get information from such people. They want to be known as good guys to such people. Detectives want the Patrol Force to arrest the whores, bookies, porno operators, and so forth. They don't want to do it. So take care of it, Don, you're Chief of Patrol."

The drive to clean up midtown became known as "the Mayor's task force on prostitution." Murphy did ask for reports on this, and he also got involved in the murder of a *New York Times* truck driver. A black man, walking past the *Times* building, had words with the truck driver, who jumped down and began to beat the black man to a pulp. The black man then pulled out a gun and shot the truck driver dead, afterwards running off into the night with other truck drivers chasing him, and presently a cop grabbed him. Immediately, the truck drivers went on strike, shut down *The New York Times,* and the papers did not get delivered that day.

Again the Mayor telephoned the Police Commissioner. *Times* officials were pressing the Mayor for extra cops there. Otherwise the truck drivers wouldn't go back to work. Each newspaperless day would cost the *Times* a fortune. The weight of the most important paper in America was on the Mayor. The Police Commissioner had to do something.

Again Murphy responded. It became his job to get the *Times'* unions to agree to put the paper out that night. So he had himself driven up to the *Times* Building, where a conference was held around an enormous table in the publisher's 14th-floor conference room. Present were half a dozen of the newspaper's top executives including Arthur Ochs Sulzberger, the publisher; all of the presidents of the approximately ten unions involved in publishing *The New York Times;* and approximately ten high-ranking police officials.

As the meeting opened, each of the union leaders seemed to feel the need to make a speech about the absence of proper police protection around *The New York Times* Building in the middle of the night, so we had ten such speeches. All these leaders wanted a return to the days when Sanford Garelik had been Chief Inspector. According to the union leaders, Garelik had ordered two uniformed policemen to patrol either end of 43rd Street and two to patrol the middle, making six men on one block. It was unlikely that Garelik had ever given any such order, but Murphy ignored this point and began to talk to the union leaders in his quiet, mild way, explaining that this unhappy event would have been no more than a fistfight except for the fact that one of the men was carrying an illegal gun.

He explained that his new anti-crime patrols, cops in civilian clothes, were now flooding this area. The very fact that they were not in uniform was what made them so successful. Therefore union leaders should not suppose that 43rd Street was abandoned each night, just because there might be no uniformed policemen in sight.

Around the table the union men now began shouting. They wanted cops in uniform on their street. They wanted no more blood baths like last night. They wanted at least six uniformed men to stand around the clock on that one block. They wanted a cop on a horse as well. Otherwise they would not order their men back to work, for they could not risk the lives of their men on such a dangerous street as 43rd Street. They seemed all to be making speeches to each other, presumably hoping word would get back to the working men about how hard each of them had come down on the Police Commissioner, how each of them was the single man who had forced the Police Commissioner to capitulate.

Murphy now began to explain quietly that he could not afford to put seven men on one street, that the *Times* Building was half a block from Times Square, one of the most crowded and heavily patrolled areas in the world, one of the most brightly lit. Seven cops didn't really mean seven cops, he explained, for there were three shifts a day, so that meant 21 men; and when you added vacations and days off and sick leave, the six men that the union leaders were demanding turned into 30 men or more, and the Police Commissioner didn't have that many men; there were too many other streets in the city which also needed to be patrolled. He went back to his anti-crime patrols, who were taking bad men off the street all the time, off 43rd Street too. The union leaders said they didn't care about anti-crime patrols and they didn't care about the other streets in the city, they just wanted 43rd Street to be safe. They wanted six men plus one on a horse. Otherwise *The New York Times* would never be published again.

The *Times* officials sat there, somewhat numb. It was up to Murphy.

The union leaders all had strong New York accents, so strong that it was almost impossible to believe that these accents were not affectations. The Police Commissioner himself spoke quietly and correctly, without the accent of New York or anyplace else.

Now Murphy began to negotiate with them, still quietly. He would put two men in front of the *Times* Building tonight, and one mounted patrolman, and he would order his commanders to study the situation further.

For a time, the loudest of the union leaders tried to argue for more, but got nowhere, and gradually the leaders agreed to order their men back to work that night. But now one of them shouted at Murphy still again: "I want to know what you're going to do for my men."

For the first time, Murphy's voice was raised. "I just told you what I was going to do," he shouted. "There are going to be two men in uniform on the street tonight and one mounted patrolman. That's all I know at this time, and when I know any more I'll tell you. All right?"

That was the first and only time I ever heard the Police Commissioner raise his voice to anyone.

The contrast was so shocking that all of the union leaders fell silent, and the conference broke up at once. As the Police Commissioner filed out of the room I said to him, "You were beautiful."

He turned, grinning, and said, "I thought that fellow deserved to be put down, didn't you?"

But apart from these and similar instances, the Police Commissioner would have nothing to do with crime. Although in speeches and interviews Murphy had referred to the assassinations of Patrolmen Jones and Piagentini as "the most terrible crime, the most important case probably during my administration," this did not mean that he was burning to know what the eventual solution would be. The day came when Chief of Detectives Seedman and I stood outside the Police Commissioner's office, waiting to be admitted to his presence.

Seedman said, "I know something you don't know."

"Like what?"

"There was a shoot-out in San Francisco. Two guys are in custody there. One of them had Jones' gun. And that's not all. We found women here. These bastards were living with them, and after the shooting they came back and got their clothes and went to hide out, and they brought them food every day. There were five guys in on it."

There was a series of light bulbs above one of the doorways in the Police Commissioner's outer office. If the red bulb was lit, as it was at this moment, this meant that the Police Commissioner was on the phone on his private wire. As we waited for this light to go off, Seedman added, "I don't know whether he's interested or not, but I thought I should go in there and tell him what we've got."

"My God, of course you should tell him."

When Seedman and I entered Theodore Roosevelt's old office, the Police Commissioner in his shirtsleeves rose and came toward us. He was sucking on a Lifesaver. He sucked Lifesavers all day, and had a selection of various flavors in the drawer of his desk.

"Yeah, Al?" he asked.

Seedman seemed unexpectedly nervous, like a man who had barged into his superior's office on a matter of very little importance.

"I know you're busy, Commissioner. I hate to bother you, but I thought you might like to know what we got."

"Yeah, Al?"

The Chief of Detectives briefly outlined what he had just told me: Jones' gun had been found in San Francisco. I waited for the Police Commissioner to ask excitedly for details, for the "most important case of his administration" had been broken. But he asked nothing.

Instead Murphy looked up at the clock above the door and said, "Well, Al, I'm running a little late."

Seedman nodded and turned to leave. Murphy patted him on the shoulder and said, "Al, I know you'll do all that needs to be done."

So Seedman and I left the Police Commissioner standing

there sucking on his Lifesaver, and went and put in a call
to the Chief of Police of San Francisco.

7 / The Joe Colombo Rally

Whatever else might be said of Cristoforo Colombo, he
was without any question the first Italian to visit the new
world. Therefore it was fitting that the second annual
Italian-American Unity Day rally should take place at the
foot of his statue in vast Columbus Circle, traffic having
been diverted. These Unity Day rallies, like the Italian-
American Civil Rights League which was their parent, had
been forced into existence by the will of one man, Joseph
Anthony Colombo Sr., 47 years old, 1164 83rd Street,
Brooklyn, known to the New York Police Department
under numbers B-415516 and KG-4717, the most celebrated and most recognizable Mafia chieftain the city had ever
had.

An hour before the rally was to begin that hot summer
morning, Joe Colombo stood in shirtsleeves at the feet of
Cristoforo Colombo, and waited for the arrival of the
quarter of a million people he had predicted would attend.

The two Colombos were separated by 500 years and several dozen feet in altitude, and around them waited 1500
patrolmen and 250 superior officers, for there had been rumors there would be trouble.

Citizens milled about, most of them trying to get close
enough to catch a look at Joe.

A young black woman waved and called, "Hi, Joe."

Colombo, who was perhaps contemplating his kinship
with the statue, turned to face the black girl, and he waved.
Beside the girl stood a black man with a movie camera, and
Colombo, having approached a few feet closer, obligingly
posed.

Colombo then turned away, for celebrities must be strict
with their admirers, distributing their smiles like coins to
beggars, one at a time.

An instant later, three bullets smashed into the back of
Colombo's head. The black man had somehow exchanged

his movie camera for a 7.65 mm. Menta, a black German automatic which somewhat resembled a Luger, had advanced to within two feet of Joe Colombo and opened fire. One bullet lodged high in Colombo's neck. Another plowed through into the left side of his jaw. The third penetrated three or four inches deep into the middle of Colombo's brain. The force of the shots sent Colombo stumbling forward. There was a police barricade which he seemed to be trying to reach, but before he got there he crashed to his face in the street.

About 15 people tackled the gunman. The ball carrier went down under the entire team. On top of him were three patrolmen, a police captain, a deputy chief inspector, and citizens too numerous to count, one of whom pressed a .38-caliber Smith and Wesson revolver to the gunman's back and pulled the trigger three times. Within a few seconds it was all over. It had taken very little longer than it takes to read this line:

Crack, Crack, Crack. And then: Crack, Crack, Crack.

Colombo was born in Brooklyn on June 16, 1923, the son of Anthony Colombo, a Sicilian-born immigrant. Anthony found work in the Profaci mob, but his employment was terminated in 1938, owing to his having been garroted to death. Young Joe was then 14 years old and attending New Utrecht High School in Brooklyn. After two years of high school, Joe had had enough of books. He spent three years in the Coast Guard, then had enough of that too. Claiming to suffer from psychoneurosis, he received a medical discharge in 1945. For the next ten years he worked intermittently as a longshoreman, then for six years he sold meat for a company controlled by the brother of a Mafia leader. He then went to work for Anthony Cantalupo, a Brooklyn real estate broker. This was Colombo's job of record at the time he was gunned down, and it paid him either $35,000 or $20,000 a year, depending on which informant was giving out the news. Colombo did not appear to work very hard for so much money, but, as Cantalupo later explained to the Joint Legislative Committee on Crime, "Colombo has the sincerest group of clients—they don't cheat him out of his commission." It was the opinion of the committee that Colombo's real job was running his gang, but Cantalupo said he personally found Colombo "a perfect gentleman."

As a young man, Colombo had piled up a string of not very impressive arrests, 13 in all, most on charges such as running a crap game, consorting with known gamblers or criminals, vagrancy, disorderly conduct. Convicted only three times, he paid two gambling fines, and served one 30-day sentence for contempt.

As a big-time hoodlum, Colombo was a flop. Later, after Colombo had became famous, a New Jersey Mafia chief named Simone DeCavalcante described Colombo as a "bust-out guy all his life," in a telephone conversation wiretapped by the FBI. A bust-out guy, in Mafia language, was a petty gambler. The police always spoke of the early Joe Colombo as a gofor, meaning that the most complicated job the mob would trust him with was to go for coffee.

However, Colombo was not yet 40 years old when, about 1963, he came to power as head of one of New York's five Mafia families, the youngest Mafia leader in the country. Fittingly, the mob he took over had once been Profaci's, the mob his pop had served faithfully until his last breath.

How did Colombo's rise come about?

Within the Police Department, and other law enforcement agencies, there were keen students of the power struggles within the Mafia hierarchy. It was the opinion of these men that around 1962, one Joseph Bonanno, leader of one of New York's five families, decided to try to take over the other four. The surest way to do this, in Bonanno's opinion, was to knock off Carlo Gambino, leader of the Gambino family; Thomas Luchese, leader of the Luchese family; and Stephano Magaddino, leader of the Magaddino family.

The contract for assassinating these gentlemen was given to Giuseppe Magliocco, leader of the Profaci family, Joe Profaci having recently died of cancer. Magliocco farmed the assignment out to Joe Colombo, then newly appointed as a captain in his family. This appears to have been the first big assignment Colombo had ever been given, and he knew it. He must have seen Mafia leadership as his for the asking, provided he made no mistakes, which he didn't—he went straight to Carlo Gambino with the plot. Gambino, the "Boss of Bosses," was then 62 years old and at the height of his powers.

Bonanno was kidnapped, terrified, and forced to retire to Arizona. Magliocco died shortly thereafter, whereupon Carlo Gambino assigned Joe Colombo, formerly a bust-out guy, formerly a gofor, to the leadership of the family once owned by Profaci.

According to the intelligence files of the Police Department and the FBI, Colombo's new stature greatly disappointed various other high-ranking Mafia gentlemen. They felt he had neither the character nor the experience to rate as a Mafia don. He wasn't tough enough and he wasn't respected at all.

The rackets he inherited included numbers and sports gambling rings, teams of hijackers and loan sharks, and a network of fences who dealt in stolen goods. Colombo was also believed to direct the narcotics traffic in the black communities of the city, and presently he took it upon himself to act as mediator between black gangsters and organized crime syndicates in disputes over territory and rackets. Colombo also had interests in at least twenty legitimate businesses, including an undertaking parlor, for which, according to the irreverent, he also sometimes provided the clients.

Formerly only a few detectives even knew who Colombo was, but now he began to get big-league attention. By the time he was shot he was under federal indictment for income tax evasion, had been convicted of perjury in his application for a real estate broker's license, was implicated in a jewel robbery in Nassau County, was under indictment for contempt in Brooklyn, and he had also been arrested by the FBI two months before and charged with operating a multimillion-dollar gambing empire in Brooklyn, Manhattan, and Nassau County.

In 1970 Joe's son, Joe Jr., had gone on trial on charges of conspiracy to melt silver coins down into silver ingots, which were worth more. Joe Jr. was 23 years old, and Joe Sr., outraged, decided he would personally and almost single-handedly take on the FBI. That spring he began leading pickets around the FBI Building at 69th Street and Third Avenue. When TV cameras rushed to watch, Joe began accusing the FBI of harassing himself, his son, and others, purely because they were Italian. Night after night he went on TV and denounced the FBI. It was almost hysterically funny. Almost. What a country.

Joe Jr. was acquitted when the government's chief witness recanted his testimony.

Joe Sr. forthwith formed the Italian-American Civil Rights League, installing one Natale Marcone, a 57-year-old former union organizer, as president, and Joe's oldest son, Anthony, 26, a five-feet-five inch, 230 pounder, as vice president. The League opened an office on the 17th floor of a skyscraper on Madison Avenue at 59th Street, and it opened numerous store-front chapters in Little Italy, Brooklyn, and elsewhere, to which new members flocked. Colomobo had struck a nerve. Americans of Italian extraction seemed to feel hard done by everywhere, and thousands upon thousands with no links to crime at all paid $10 each in dues and joined the League. Colombo began opening chapters in other cities. Why not?

Possibly to the astonishment even of Colombo, the money was pouring in. It was also vanishing, no outsider knew where. The League had a summer camp called Unity One in upstate New York which was to open to two to three hundred kids, who would receive free vacations. The League also collected clothing for poor Puerto Ricans. This, plus Joe Colombo's press conferences and TV appearances, was all the activity to which the League could point despite all the money it had collected.

A concert at the Felt Forum in New York raised half a million dollars. Four months later there was a testimonial dinner in honor of Joe Sr. in Huntington, Long Island, at which the keynote speaker credited him with "restoring dignity, pride, and recognition to every Italian"—and which raised over $100,000.

Colombo appeared on television at the slightest provocation. Talk show hosts were delighted to have him—imagine, a real live gangster.

The rest of the Mafia hierarchy was at first appalled by Colombo, and after that, alarmed.

There existed a crisis of leadership within the Mafia. Many of the tough old hoods had died, and it was hard to replace them. They weren't making that kind of man anymore, and the newly appointed top hoods were likely to be old and sick or young and stupid, or else someone like Joe Colombo. Meanwhile, Congress had passed new and harder laws, and there were new federal-city-state task forces operating against organized crime. This was an outright drive to destroy the Mafia, all the leaders knew it, and here came Joe Colombo striding the sidewalks in front of the FBI Building, goading the enemy into action.

What to do?

The Godfather was being filmed at this time. Joe Colombo forced the producer to remove all references therein to the Mafia, or Cosa Nostra, or Italians, threatening to have his League boycott the film if this was not done. Next, references to Mafia, Cosa Nostra, and Italians disappeared from a television series called "The FBI." Various elected officials, always on the alert for something to be afraid of, decided it would be wise to drop all references to the Mafia, Cosa Nostra, and Italians as well. There even was a meatball commercial on TV which Joe Colombo declared was offensive to Italians, and it was promptly canceled by its sponsor, Alka-Seltzer. The commerical went, "Mamma mia, thatsa soma spicy meatball." Alka-Seltzer, the commercial had promised, would mute the gastric acidity of such a meatball. Instead, Joe Colombo muted Alka-Seltzer.

Colombo was at the peak of his fame. He had even appeared at a joint news conference to announce that his league had joined forces with the extremist Jewish Defense League, headed by the firebrand rabbi, Meir Kahane, to fight federal harassment of both organizations, particularly harassment by the FBI.

Colombo was a smash hit to everybody but the men, especially Carlo Gambino, who had put him where he was. Every time Colombo's face appeared on the front page of a newspaper or filled the television screen during a prime-time show, Gambino and the other old guys in the Mafia hit the ceiling.

In addition there now began to be grumbling about Gambino's leadership. Old Carlo was now 72 and suffering from heart trouble, and his judgment was probably shot too—he was the one responsible for Joe Colombo.

Colombo ignored all this. The take from the Italian-American Civil Rights League was stupendous. In addition to legitimate membership dues, Colombo's men were in the habit of walking into small businesses and "suggesting" that their owners make a "contribution." The contribution should of course be more than ten dollars. It was the opinion of the Police Department at this time that the League had taken in millions of dollars, and that Colombo had skimmed almost all of it, having thoughtlessly declined to give a share to Gambino or anybody else.

The first Unity Day rally the year before had drawn about 50,000 people, and for the second, Colombo had promised five times that many.

But there was one important difference this year: Crazy Joe Gallo, who hated Colombo, had just got out of jail. He wanted his old mob back, and he wanted a share of Colombo's territory.

A decade before there had been a brief, bloody war between the Colombo and Gallo factions of the Profaci family. The *Daily News* once claimed that this war resulted in about 20 corpses, most of them employees of Gallo, though the police had discounted a few dead hoodlums as being unrelated to either faction. In truth, it was hard for the police to keep track of what went on within these mobs as it was hard for the police to keep track of the personnel and movements of the various black extremist factions. The public expected the police to have it all down in a ledger somewhere, separate columns for each item, but men outside the law kept no neat ledgers themselves. They operated according to different rules, or perhaps according to no rules, which is why they were outside, not inside; and very often it was impossible to fathom what they were doing, or why. They were not always reasonable men, they did not always operate rationally. Crazy Joe's gang at one point kept a lion as a watchdog.

The Gallo-Colombo war ended when Joe Gallo went to prison for extortion—he had been in the habit of asking merchants to turn over half their businesses to him. If the merchant asked for time to think over Gallo's proposition, Gallo would reply, "Sure, take three months in the hospital on me." And so he had been sentenced to seven and a half to 14 years, and he had been paroled four months before Colombo was shot, after serving nine years.

As the date of the second Unity Day rally neared, Gambino let it be known that this rally was unpopular with him, and certain Gallo goons—some said accompanied at times by Gallo himself—toured South Brooklyn, ordering merchants not to close on Unity Day, as Colombo had "requested."

Colombo had been warned of possible trouble at the rally, and it was against the wishes of his immediate family that he attended it. He was perhaps encouraged by the knowledge that no Mafia don had been assassinated since Albert Anastasia was riddled with bullets while sitting under a hot towel in a hotel barber's chair in 1957.

Columbus Circle looked festive enough when Joe got there. Forty-foot-long red, white, and green (the colors of Italy) plastic streamers stretched from Columbus' statue to the lamp posts, to trees. Plastic straw hats and golfing caps in the Italian colors were on hand by the tens of thousands. There were shopping bags and pennants in the same colors, and buttons were being stuck onto everybody's shirtfronts by League workers. The crowd was somewhat sparse, and there were unauthorized peddlers around hawking food and drinks, so Colombo called over the top cop on hand, Assistant Chief Arthur Morgan, and began arguing about those peddlers. Barry Gotterher, aide to the Mayor, was there listening in—Mayor Lindsay wanted no trouble with Italians when the next election came up. Colombo wanted the peddlers driven off. Chief Morgan pointed out that they had a legal right to be there. The annoyed Colombo walked away behind Chief Morgan. Colombo had ordered up 200,000 sandwiches for this rally, and 400,000 orange and grape drinks, and perhaps the last thought he ever had was that, because of the peddlers and the sparse crowd, the League workers were going to be eating this stuff in the clubhouses for a long time to come.

Colombo then smiled at the black girl who had called to him, turned away, and, an instant later, felt the first of three bullets plow into the back of his head.

The assassin started to go down under a mass of men. Chief Thomas Reid saw a hand with a gun and grabbed it and pushed it down. He saw that arm was already held by other hands, and that there was someone on the assassin's back. On the ground the gun hand was still waving, and Captain George Manning went for the gun also. Then the second set of three shots exploded. Looking down, Captain

Manning saw blood coming out of the assassin's mouth. There was a big hole in the assassin's left side, and wet blood coming from there too. According to Chief Reid, there were at least 25 people on top of the assassin at this time, and he himself was near the bottom. He had to fight his way up off the ground.

There had been six private ambulances standing nearby, in case anybody got sunstroke. Colombo was run off toward one. The assassin was already dead. The medical examiner later reported that the bullets had penetrated the assassin's heart and lungs and that he had died instantly.

A number of patrolmen had rushed in to form a circle around the bodies, and once Colombo, and then the assassin, had been rushed out through this circle, the patrolmen stood there guarding an area of pavement on which lay two little pools of blood, an empty camera case, a brown attaché case, three guns, a pair of horn-rimmed spectacles, and a comb. One of the guns was the automatic that had been clutched in the assassin's hand. Later it was found to contain three spent shells and two live rounds. The second gun proved to be the .38-caliber Smith and Wesson Chief that had killed the assassin. It also contained three spent shells and two live ones. The third gun had come flying through the air and landed at the feet of Sergeant Edward Powers, who worked for me.

People were screaming and rushing in all directions. There were shouts of "They got Colombo!" Someone rushed to the bandstand and ordered the musicians to play, so in a moment music rang out. A man, later identified as Anthony Seccafico, attempted to reach the attaché case inside the ring of cops. A patrolman stopped him.

"That's Joe's bag," he said.

The attaché case was opened. Inside was a .38-caliber Colt pistol and scores of Unity Day buttons. Seccafico was handcuffed and hustled from the scene.

Certain of Colombo's relatives stood weeping. One woman was shouting, "It's only in the arm. I heard he was only shot in the arm."

The camera case, the attaché case and the guns were removed, and barriers were placed around the two puddles of blood, the horn-rimmed spectacles, and the comb, and at noon the rally got underway. The Reverend Louis Gigante, chaplain of the League (and brother of Vincent Gigante, who was once tried and acquitted of the attempted assassination of Mafia boss Frank Costello in the lobby of a Central Park West apartment house), strode out onto the platform and announced that he had just come from "anointing Joey Colombo. I lost a great friend," said Father Gigante, who believed Colombo to be dead. Then he added, "This day must go on. Joe told me he's not the League, we're the League." He then asked the crowd to pray to St. Jude for Joey's soul, and he led the Lord's Prayer.

After that, to the rostrum came a number of politicians. Congressman Mario Biaggi announced that "your founder was shot by the same type of revolutionary that executed those two police officers." Anthony Imperiale, a former city councilman from Newark, said, "A disgrace happened here today." He urged all people of Italian extraction not to forget that "the blood of the Roman gladiators" flowed in their veins and that they had to fight for "your place in the sun."

Presently it was announced from the stage that "the most beautiful body in the world" was about to appear. The program had promised Sophia Loren, and now a crowd which may have totaled 10,000 people, or perhaps much less, seemed to sigh in unison, "It's Sophia Loren!" But it wasn't, it was a weight lifter named Pete Caputo, recently named Mr. America. Caputo stepped forward and showed off his swollen biceps.

A number of black men in the crowd had been set upon and beaten up, and a number of patrolmen were hurt rescuing them. By two o'clock in the afternoon many patrolmen were wearing riot helmets. There were bulletins about the condition of Joe Colombo in Roosevelt Hospital, and speeches followed speeches. The highest-ranking city official present was Comptroller Abraham Beame, who declared that he was a Jew who sympathized with Italians: "It's time to put a halt to the slur that stigmatizes Italian-Americans."

The rally petered out at 3 P.M. with the League's president, Natale Marcone, standing beneath the statue of Columbus, exhorting the mob: "Go home but never forget, be proud to be an Italian all the time!"

Meanwhile, Colombo had been rushed into the emergency room at Roosevelt Hospital, blood still leaking out of the back of his head, clotted blood caked on his face. His sons strode beside the stretcher, their clothes, too, marked with blood.

Doctors came forward.

"Do everything you can for him. I'll pay anything," pleaded Joe Jr.

The emergency room was crowded with Colombo's sons, friends, rally leaders, and with cops. On the table Colombo had stopped breathing, and doctors were rushing about amid the noise and confusion. A tube was rammed down Colombo's throat, and the plastic bulb at the other end, which a man began rhythmically squeezing, forced air into Colombo's lungs.

Colombo began breathing again. He was stripped naked, covered by a sheet, and wheeled to an elevator, with a bottle swinging on a pole above his head. His skull underwent multiple X rays. When these were ready, Dr. Evron Hanson, the neurosurgeon who was about to operate on the Mafia don, held them up to the light. He was surrounded by half a dozen medical students, and with his pinky he calmly pointed out to his students details within Colombo's ravaged brain.

Surgery lasted five hours. The bullet in the center of Colombo's brain was removed. The bullet in his neck was removed. The bullet embedded inside the left side of his jaw was, for the time being, left there. Eight pints of blood went into Colombo.

Dr. Hanson, exiting, rated Colombo's chances at less than 50-50.

Colombo's wife, Lucille, and three of his four sons—Anthony, Joseph and Vincent—stayed at the hospital all night, sitting up in a second-floor lounge. Vincent kept repeating, "He's going to be all right, Ma. He's going to be all right, Ma." Rabbi Kahane visited the hospital twice within the first 24 hours, staying a total of five hours. Mr. Imperiale made a visit, and so did Mr. Gotterher, representing Mayor Lindsay.

Outside the hospital a prayer vigil began. About 25 men, four women and two children marched round and round in a slow oval, reciting the Hail Mary and the Lord's Prayer. They had been instructed by Father Gigante to direct their prayers to St. Joseph, patron saint of Joseph Colombo, and to St. Jude, patron saint of the impossible, and now they were chanting, "St. Jude, help Joe Colombo; St. Joseph, protect him." They were carrying a five foot wide, green map of the United States, its outlines drawn in white and red carnations, with a large gold Roman numeral I planted in the center. The I symbolized Italian-American unity. This map had stood on the stage below which Joe Colombo had been shot. The vigil marchers also carried burning candles, which the summer breeze kept snuffing out.

Inside the hospital, the body of the assassin lay almost totally forgotten and ignored.

All the next day and the next the vigil continued outside. The marchers grew in number; now there were 50, now 75. Statues of St. Jude and St. Joseph were carried by the marchers—the pageant got richer all the time. Press photographers kept clicking off shots, and a beefy captain of the League, arms crowded with muscles and tattoos, threatened to smash all cameras and all reporters' faces as well. Sammy Davis Jr., a black man, a Jew, and a famous entertainer, not necessarily in that order—a man having no known links to Italians or to crime—drove up in a Cadillac and made his way through the marchers into the hospital to Colombo's bedside, but left without singing a song. A short-haired blonde woman arrived outside, carrying a crooked driftwood cane which she claimed had considerable religious significance.

Ten days later Colombo was operated on again. A plastic catheter was inserted into one of the holes in his skull and slid up behind and above his right ear. The other end of this tube was attached to a vein in the lower part of Colombo's face. In this way a blockage of blood and bone fragments at the base of the cerebellum was bypassed.

After a month, Colombo was still alive. His son Anthony claimed that Colombo's reflexes were good and that he was breathing unaided for a couples of hours each day. He denied that his father was being kept alive only by machines, but admitted that Joe Colombo could neither talk nor move. "But he makes responses in other ways," insisted Anthony, refusing to elaborate. Police speculated that a struggle for control of Joe's mob was then in progress, and that a live Joe Colombo, even though in effect a vegetable, was still a force to be reckoned with. If for no other reason, Joe Colombo would be kept alive as long as humanly possible.

Two months after the shooting, Colombo was removed to Anthony's home in Brooklyn. More than a year after the shooting, Joe Colombo would still be counted as alive. He was moved from place to place, was even hospitalized again for a short period, and police surveillance on him was relaxed. He was understood by detectives to be fed through a hole in his stomach, and when he was moved, to be first packed in ice.

8 / The Colombo Investigation

Immediately after Joe Colombo was gunned down, the dilapidated old 18th Precinct station house on West 54th Street became the command post of the investigation. Detective commanders took over offices on the second floor, and more than fifty detectives from all over the city were called in. They sat on the stairways waiting to be used.

In one of the offices the worldly goods found on the assassin were laid out on the desk top: wallet, cards, photos, money, the automatic, the camera case. Detectives picked through the cards and came up with a number of addresses at which the assasin perhaps had lived, and a number of names under which he had probably lived.

His name appeared to be Jerome Johnson, or else it was Jerome Addison, or perhaps Addison Rand, or Jerome Rand. He was 24 years old. His papers gave his address as 88 Throop Avenue, New Brunswick, New Jersey. But perhaps he also lived at 176 Elizabeth Street, a few blocks from police headquarters; and he had recently lived, or perhaps was still living, at the Chelsea Hotel on 23rd Street, if not at 101 West 23rd Street, or in the Hotel Christopher in Greenwich Village.

Two by two, detectives were dispatched to all these addresses with the exception of New Brunswick. A phone call was made to the chief of police there by his brother, a New York police lieutenant, and New Brunswick detectives drove to Throop Avenue, found the assassin's mother, and sent her to New York to identify the body. Then they began questioning the neighbors. Later they phoned their reports to New York.

Meanwhile, other detectives were sent out to bring in Carlo Gambino, Joey Gallo, and various other hoodlums, and these persons were interviewed at the West 54th Street station house. This was a formality only. Nobody expected an intelligent word out of any of them, but the public demanded that its police department at least lean on them. And cops liked to do it. Gallo was a cheap thug, but Gambino was one of the richest old guys in the world, a veritable tycoon, and it was nice both to command his presence and to stand in the same room with him and flex one's muscles, so to speak.

There had been a photographers' stand near the scene of the shooting, and some cameras had been rolling before the shooting, and some after, though none during, it turned out later; and all this film—or at least as much of it as the police could grab—was confiscated on the spot, and was rushed to be developed, with detectives now waiting for it out in the halls.

Detectives had been dispatched to take the fingerprints of the dead man, and these cards were rushed downtown to the Criminal Investigation Bureau. Presently the dead gunman was identified as Jerome Johnson, and it was found that his previous arrest record was substantial. He had been arrested in New York a year ago for assault and attempted rape, and also only 25 days ago for possession of dangerous drugs; and he had been arrested five times in Los Angeles between 1966 and 1969 on a variety of charges, including rape and burglary. He had been convicted once or twice but each time got off with a small fine or a suspended sentence. He was very good-looking, and apparently well-spoken. Judges tended to like him—and to let him go. He had also been arrested three times by campus police at Rutgers University on charges of entering dormitories illegally. Girls' dormitories.

Other detectives were checking ownership of the four guns found at the scene, and still others were working by telephone to trace the camera case which apparently had belonged to Johnson and which, according to its attached label, had been rented at a shop in Boston.

And of course all the cops who had been on top of Johnson, or who had recovered any of the material at the scene, were being interviewed by detectives one by one.

A call had gone out to bring in all those detectives, most of whom worked out of Brooklyn, who were familiar with the workings of the Colombo mob, the Gallo mob, the Gambino mob, the Persico mob, and all of the other off-shoots of organized crime that might be responsible for the shooting of Joe Colombo. So these men filled the halls too.

Inside the station house, the noise, the coming and going, the excitement, the waiting, the assembling of all this information looked, to any outsider, like pure confusion, if not pandemonium. But by four o'clock in the afternoon, less than five hours after the hit, enough information had been put together for Chief Seedman to call a news conference.

In the muster room downstairs waited about a hundred journalists, together with lights, cameras, and microphones belonging to every television station in the New York area and some from abroad. The writing press surrounded Seedman as he came down the stairs. As the floodlights burned down on him, as people crowded ever closer, sweat began to pop out on his brow, and he looked like a man on trial. Speaking slowly, deliberately, he outlined what little the police already knew.

The press wanted to know the reaction of Gambino.

"Mr. Gambino tells me that he knows nothing about this case. In fact," said Chief Seedman without cracking a smile, "he said he was grief-stricken to hear about it."

The press conference lasted 45 minutes. The room got hotter and hotter. The press did not want to let Seedman go. This was a circus, they were in the front row, and the audience for what they would report would be enormous.

But Chief Seedman waded out through the mob. People were still clamoring for answers Seedman did not yet have, and perhaps would never have. He went back upstairs. More information had been assembled in his absence, and still more would come in during the night, and all the next day, and he wanted to know what it was.

Tuesday afternoon Seedman held a second conference, at which he displayed a cardboard box filled with what he called "the worldly goods" of Jerome Johnson: a curved Indian sword, a black cane, a serape, a golden maroon cape, a riding crop, a book titled *Fragments of a Faith For-*

gotten, which was about the origins of Christianity, and a box of cartridges which fit the automatic that had sent three bullets crashing into the head of Joe Colombo. There were also several sheafs of blank checks overprinted with the name Bark Book Distributors, Inc.

Johnson had had other belongings which were not in the box: a collection of pornographic photos showing a white woman having sexual intercourse with a black donkey, and also the same woman committing sodomy with that same black donkey, or perhaps another. All these goods had come out of one of Johnson's last known residences, a store at 176 Elizabeth Street in Little Italy. Also on the premises when detectives broke in there was a small and unfed monkey.

Upstairs before the press conference, the detectives stared at those pornographic photos, making jokes. At one point, Seedman had tossed me the photos, saying with a grin, "Do you think we should show the press this?"

Then he asked, "What do you think we should do about that monkey?" Answering his own question, he said, "Well, we could give it to the zoo. Or we could have it stuffed and send it to Carlo Gambino."

Seedman had been a detective for most of 30 years, much of it in Brooklyn. Some years ago he had even been among the raiders who hit Joey Gallo's headquarters on President Street there. This was during the Colombo-Gallo war. The Gallo mob was getting thinned out so fast that the survivors and their lion had taken to the mattresses on President Street. Except for the mattresses on the floor, the thugs, the lion and the guns, the rooms were empty.

Seedman and some other detectives had gone in and cleaned the mobsters out of there.

Two things about Seedman: Nothing these people could do could surprise him. And he could see the humor in all of it, however grim it might appear to outsiders.

The shooting of Joe Colombo was now about 28 hours old, and the world—that is, the press—was already beginning to doubt that Jerome Johnson had ever been the trigger man. Were Johnson's fingerprints on the gun? the press wanted to know. Seedman refused to answer this question. There were in fact no fingerprints on the gun. There were almost never any fingerprints on any gun. For the most part, there were no surfaces on any gun which would hold human fingerprint, something Seedman knew but which the world disbelieved, having seen too many movies. Seedman was wise in the ways of crime, wise in the ways of detective work, and also wise in dealing with the press; and he was not going to get caught in any argument over fingerprints.

Instead he announced that the police were examining three possibilities—

1. Johnson was a free-lance nut who shot Joe Colombo just for the hell of it.
2. Johnson was an agent of black revolutionaries and had shot Colombo because Colombo was responsible for the narcotics traffic in Harlem and in the black community.
3. Johnson had been hired to kill Joe Colombo by one of the other Mafia bosses in this city.

"But how do you know that it was Johnson who shot Colombo?"

"Because the gun was in his hand, and because we have witnesses who saw him do it."

"Were his fingerprints on the gun?"

"I have no comment on that question."

"How do you know it wasn't a cop who killed Johnson?"

"Because we have the gun that killed Johnson; it's been tested by ballistics and it is not a police gun. We have traced this gun back to the last several owners."

"Who was the last owner?"

In actual fact, the last registered owner had been a policeman in North Carolina, and he had reported that gun stolen nine years before. "No comment on that question," said Chief Seedman, for he didn't want the press imagining that the Southern cop was involved in this case.

There were already two links between Jerome Johnson and organized crime, one of them the sheafs of checks belonging to Bark Book. According to the State Investigation Commission Hearings the year before, Bark Book specialized in pornography and was owned by one Joseph Brocchini, known and identified as a member of the Luchese crime family. The address on the Bark checks was 110 West 24th Street, but sometimes prior to the shooting,

Bark had moved out, and the Club Orgy, a live nude sex show, had moved in. It was presumed that the Club Orgy was run by organized crime too, but this was impossible to check now, for the building had since burned down, possibly not accidentally.

A second link between Johnson and the Mafia was a phone number: 242-8938. Johnson had given this number to friends, but when detectives called there, the telephone company switched them to 486-9415, which, it turned out, was the number of the Italian-American Civil Rights League. Checking back, detectives found that Johnson had switched his number first to one answering service then to a second, had stiffed both on their bills, and finally had had his number assigned to the Italian-American Civil Rights League. Why?

Every day Seedman sat in a dingy office on the second floor of the 18th Precinct station house while detectives came and went. Listening to them, he would often nod without saying anything, or else he would make the detective flip back through his notebook and go through the facts again. Each day for four days, Seedman held a news conference and told the city and the world some of what his detectives had discovered during the last 24 hours:

—That Johnson had rented a 16 mm. movie camera in Boston three days before the shooting, paying for it with a rubber check.

—That those bodyguards of Joe Colombo known to the police were nowhere near him when Jerome Johnson suddenly stepped forward shooting.

—That all film confiscated at the rally had been developed and was being studied by detectives. One picture, showing Johnson within three or four feet of Colombo, photographing him, Seedman released to the press.

—That Johnson preyed upon girls. Most were white girls. The detectives had run down a number, one of whom stated that Johnson had forced his way into her apartment and raped her. Seedman then told the press with a straight face, "After raping her, Johnson then moved in with her and lived with her for three or four months, during which he continued to rape her whenever he felt like it." This woman, and a number of others with whom Johnson had lived, were prostitutes. During his rare minutes alone, Seedman brooded. "This is such an odd case," he said once.

Seedman knew he would get no information from Mafia figures. The only way to solve the Joe Colombo hit was via Jerome Johnson. And unfortunately, Johnson had traveled widely. Furthermore, he had had a habit of recording names, addresses, and telephone numbers of even casual acquaintances in address books. This meant that every city in which Johnson had moved, plus every single name, address, and telephone number in Johnson's various address books, had to be checked out by detectives.

During the next few days Seedman sent detectives into five states: New York, New Jersey, Connecticut, Massachusetts, and Pennsylvania. Leads were followed into the major cities of five other states: into Los Angeles, Denver, New Orleans, St. Louis, Detroit, and into North Carolina. One detective, who had been working around the clock on the case, had a heart attack.

But gradually the character of Johnson became clear. Detectives learned that he was always armed, often showed his gun, and sometimes threatened people with it; that he had certificates from the National Rifle Association attesting to what a good shot he was; that he was a small-time narcotics dealer, but was not on drugs himself, for the only drug in his system when he was killed was nicotine; that he was a collector of pornography; that he spoke beautifully, for a tape had been found on which he read poetry while apparently attempting to seduce a girl; that he was trying to become a pimp; that he never held a job; that he had no money; that he was a dreamer, going after one big score; that he had been intimate with more than five girls in the last few months, four of them white girls.

But it still wasn't clear whether the shooting of Joe Colombo was a mob hit, or a political act by a black revolutionary, or a kind of solo lark by Johnson.

Colombo was shot on Monday. On Friday afternoon my phone rang. It was Chief Seedman. He wanted to set up a conference with the Chief Inspector and the Police Commissioner in an hour. He was in Brooklyn, on his way in.

The Police Commissioner was gone for the day and the weekend, but Chief Inspector Codd and I were waiting when Seedman came through the door.

Seedman said, "It was a mob hit!"

We waited.

Seedman said, "According to my information, the contract was let by Gambino himself. The price was $40,000. Furthermore, Colombo is supposed to be the first in a series of hits. Next on the list are Mrs. Colombo and the two oldest sons. It's to be a reign of terror, the object of which is to destroy both the League and the Colombo mob completely."

Seedman had just come from interviewing a man who, by chance, had overhead these details being worked out two weeks before. Seedman did not identify his informant, except to say that he was a legitimate businessman who overheard people talking. He had not heard Johnson's name, merely that Colombo was to be killed by a black man at the rally. The real reason that Colombo was to be killed was that he had skimmed so much money out of the League without giving any to anybody else.

So Codd, Seedman, and I talked. What would be the result if we released this information to the press? Would it prevent other murders? Would it accelerate other murders? What would be the result if we kept this information quiet? Maybe it wasn't even true.

The major question was, How much confidence did Seedman place in his informant?

A good detective built a career on informants, knew who to believe and who not to believe, knew when to trust his instincts. A good detective was like an artist; he had hunches and feelings and he followed where they led him. Something sounded right, or it sounded wrong. One judged the look in a man's eyes, and the sound of his voice, and whether or not what he said made sense.

For five days Seedman had brooded. To Seedman, the Colombo shooting had felt like a mob hit from the moment it happened. He had studied the films over and over again. All four known bodyguards were well away from Colombo at the moment of the shooting. Then, instants after the shooting, Johnson went down under a mass of people, one of whom stuck a gun in his back and pulled the trigger three times. To Seedman, the Johnson killing was planned too. The killer of Johnson must have had his untraceable gun in Johnson's back almost before Johnson finished shooting Colombo. Then, having pulled his trigger three times, the killer opened his hand and dropped the gun on the ground. It all happened so fast that there wasn't a single witness. The gun was in his hand two or three seconds, no more.

Whose reflexes were good enough to perform such a feat without forethought, without foreknowledge? The answer, to Seedman, was nobody.

At least two or three of those mob guys had been on top of Johnson. None ever came forward. And then there was the evidence of Johnson himself. It was simply not possible to believe such a man a black revolutionary. Black revolutionaries traveled in groups, committed stickups, espoused ideologies. Black revolutionaries were men like Richard Moore and Eddie Josephs, Panthers now in custody and implicated in the machine-gunning of Patrolmen Curry and Binetti; or like the still unknown men who had gunned down Patrolmen Jones and Piagentini; whereas Johnson was a con man and maybe a sexual pervert as well, and the only cause he was dedicated to was getting his rocks off.

To Seedman, the conclusion was inescapable: Colombo had been set up. And Johnson, the dreamer hoping for one big score, was a hired gun. Johnson had been so naïve to think the mob would let him get away afterward.

Johnson had participated in group sex for money, and was bisexual. His primary object appeared always to be to exploit girls, either sexually or financially. At times he represented himself as a professor, particularly at Rutgers, using this "stature" as a way to connect with girl students. On occasion he hired limousines for the day, driving up in front of some new acquaintances he was trying to impress.

He did not consciously avoid black people, but nearly all of his contacts were white, and almost all of his lovers, male or female, were white.

When unable to move himself into some woman's apartment, he would stay in cheap hotels. Detectives never found any place where he had worked, and so assumed he never had worked anywhere, but they came upon an enormous number of unpaid bills and bad checks. He paid for some of his purchases with the rubber checks, and others with stolen credit cards.

Such a man, Seedman had brooded, could not be a black revolutionary. It was not possible. On the other hand,

Johnson did not sound crazy either. He had lived on his wits too long and too successfully to be crazy.

As motive for the shooting of Joe Colombo, that left only—

To Chief Inspector Codd and me, Seedman said, "I believe every word my informant told me."

I said, "If we tell the press that we know it's a mob hit, and if we announce that we have the list of those who are to be hit next—we don't need to say who is on that list—it seems to me that all their plans will get canceled immediately. They won't dare make a move until they find out how much we know, and how we found out, and where their leak is. I say we should tell the press what we know."

Codd and Seedman both agreed.

The Chief Inspector now phoned Commissioner Murphy at home. After outlining Seedman's information, Codd said, "Al and Bob think we should go with a press conference, right away." He hadn't said, "Al and Bob and I," I noticed.

Codd and Murphy talked for a few minutes, then Codd hung up.

"The boss says that if you feel confident of your information, Al, then we should definitely go ahead."

All right. Then who should do the job?

Codd had repeatedly shown himself reluctant to conduct press conferences. Though the highest-ranking member of the force, he had not conducted one. He had never sought the limelight, and he was not at ease in public. He was content to sit at Murphy's side at press conferences, his stature evident to all, but the spotlight on Murphy.

Murphy hadn't offered to drive back to headquarters to conduct the press conference himself. Perhaps he had promised an outing to his kids. Perhaps he didn't want to involve himself in the Colombo case, in the event that we were about to act on wrong information.

Crime wasn't Murphy's kind of thing anyway.

Seedman suggested that I conduct the press conference. There would be certain advantages. I could not be tricked or forced into giving away the identity of Seedman's informant, since neither Codd nor I had asked who he was.

I could refuse to answer certain questions more gracefully than Seedman could, since it would be assumed merely that I had been insufficiently briefed, whereas it was Seedman's case, and he was supposed to know everything.

Seedman may even have been observed in the company of his informant earlier. If he now pronounced dramatic new developments in the Colombo investigations, this might in itself give away the informant.

It was also true, though this was not mentioned, that Seedman had already conducted four press conferences that week. Murphy might be getting restive about all the attention currently going to Al Seedman. This was called professional jealousy, and perhaps Murphy was not above experiencing same. To see Al on TV a fifth time in one week might annoy the boss.

Perhaps Codd too was afraid to appear to usurp the Police Commissioner's chair.

In the Police Department, the name of the important game was not murder, but holding station in the steady currents that moved along the corridors of power.

And so it was decided that the stunning news which the Police Department was about to divulge would be divulged by yours truly, which seemed safe enough. Being relatively new in the job, I could not easily be accused of unsurping the chair of anyone.

That day, detectives had found the camera that Johnson had been carrying. Someone had picked it up at the scene and stolen it, but then had come forward to give it back. There was no film in the camera when it was handed to detectives.

Suppose I went before a press conference, holding this camera? The camera—physical evidence—would add weight to the proceedings. We decided that I should refuse to answer questions about film. Seedman had said, "Let those mob guys think there was film in it. Let them wonder what that film showed. Let them wonder what we know and what we don't know."

And so I stepped before a jammed press conference, waved Johnson's movie camera in front of the cameras, and then read a short announcement: Joe Colombo had been gunned down on orders of "certain segments of the Italian-American community." This was Codd's phrase, though I accepted it, and it was a mistake, for it won me a number of angry letters from honest Italian-Americans. I should have said "orders of the Mafia," but during the past year Joe Colombo in his campaign to stamp out real or imagined slurs against Italians had brainwashed all of us, and the word Mafia had virtually disappeared from the police vocabulary.

9 / Mob Hit

And so the Police Department, meaning Chief Codd, Chief Seedman, and I, with the consent of Commissioner Murphy at home with his kids, called the Joe Colombo hit a mob hit. The bizarre aspects of the case had made it front page news all of the past week; today's announcement would make it front page news every time it was mentioned, until the day came that the case was either solved, or abandoned; and we all knew that. The Police Department, traditionally shrouded in mystery, was for once showing part of its face to the crowd. Though our object in so doing was to avert further bloodshed, unparalleled pressure would now be placed upon Chief Seedman and his detectives to come up with proof. And we knew that too.

Unlike a mystery novel, a case like this was not conducted by a single man, and it did not conclude with the dramatic disclosure of the solution of the case. It was instead conducted by a multitude of detectives flung out from a central command post into a multitude of different directions. Day by day each came back with a single detail or perhaps many, a single fact or perhaps many. These were assembled by Seedman and his chief commanders at first, and then later on, after the investigation had settled down, by Sergeant John Weber, whom Seedman had placed in charge of the investigation, and who reported to Seedman, briefing him whenever enough information had been amassed to make a briefing worthwhile. There would be no dramatic solution. The case was already solved. The object was to collect enough evidence to go before a grand jury and win indictments against (1) the man who had killed Jerome Johnson, and (2) the man or men who had assigned the contract to hit Colombo to Jerome Johnson.

Weber, though only a sergeant, was college-educated

(Gettysburg and Fordham), and he had been a detective nearly 20 years already. He was 45, a big stolid, stubborn man, who seldom spoke. Seedman had met him years before and had run into him a number of times since, notably during a curious homicide on the Lower East Side the year before. A youth went through a window on Grand Street, tied up an old lady, and stole her jewelry. When the police came, the old lady was apparently unharmed, but dead in her chair. The Medical Examiner ruled she had died of fear. Weber had been appalled by this crime—so-called hard-bitten homicide detectives were often shocked and angered by the crimes they were sent to investigate. As always, men from Latent came to dust for prints, only to find Weber's own men working with a test kit, also trying to find prints.

Whatever the popular notion about fingerprints, they were always extremely difficult to find, for upon exposure to air, prints would "aviate"; that is evaporate and disappear, with greater or lesser speed depending on the surface on which they lay; and it took a great deal of skill, patience, and time to bring them up. One didn't find millions of sets of prints at a crime scene; one found very few, and on exposed surfaces one found almost none, and it was likely to take hours of work to make any that might be there show themselves.

The Latent guys were likely to look at certain surfaces and not even try for prints there, or else perhaps try but give up too easily. With Weber's own crew on hand, with Weber standing over them, they would be forced to try harder. They would hate the competition, and hate Weber, but they would do the work. As a result, prints were found on the *outside* of the window, which was unusual, almost incredible. And when the murderer was caught in the commission of another crime a month later by uniformed cops, he was instantly related by his prints to the frightened-to-death old lady.

Weber rushed to take over that case too, a piece of the old lady's jewelry was found in the prisoner's possesion, and in due course the man was tried and convicted of murder, the first time in 90 years that death by fear had resulted in a murder conviction. It was Weber who had overseen the painstaking work that had gone into both the investigation and the conviction, and Seedman had noted this and been impressed.

Now, as Colombo lay with three bullet holes in the back of his head, Seedman thought of Weber as ideally suited to head the investigation. Weber was tenacious. He would get his teeth into this, and never let go.

But Weber was also his own man. The first thing he did upon taking over the case was to ignore completely the information given by Seedman's confidential informant, and also the official Police Department conception of the case as presented during my press conference. For Weber, this was no mob hit until his investigation proved it so.

At this time Weber held in his hand an anonymous letter saying that Johnson was in fact a professional killer, who had been used in black radical campus activities throughout the country, working always for a fee. In addition, immediately after the shooting of Joe Colombo, the press had received a message signed by a so-called Black Revolutionary Assault Team. This message had taken credit for the Colombo hit after the fact, as it had previously taken credit after the fact for placing a bomb in the consulate of Rhodesia. But now, two days after the shooting of Joe Colombo, a bomb had exploded in the Bronx apartment of a notorious drug dealer. Within seconds the news media had been notified that the Black Revolutionary Assault Team was responsible for this bomb also, and this time there was no doubt about it. No one except those who planted the bomb could have known so soon that any such bomb had exploded.

That the Black Revolutionary Assault Team was at the root of the Colombo hit seemed to Weber extremely probable, and he pushed his squad of detectives very hard along this line. If to Seedman the key to the hit was the personality of Jerome Johnson, to Weber the key was the black woman who had called out to Joe Colombo instants before the shooting. It was she who must have exchanged the black automatic for Johnson's camera. She would also know where he had come from and where he was going. Immediately after the shooting, witnesses had described her hurdling the barricades and running off; and Weber had spent hours watching the confiscated films of the rally, sitting in the dark, showing it over and over again, and what he was looking for mostly was the face of that black girl.

In the midst of the Catskill Mountains, not far from the PBA summer camp at Tannersville, there existed a "Republic for New Africa" training camp. Supposedly this camp was used for the rehabilitation of ex-convicts, but in actual fact the Intelligence Division of the New York Police Department believed it a front for subversive groups, especially Black Panthers. When another confidential informant came forward to describe a 1968 tan Volkswagen, New Jersey license plate URM 666, which had left the camp on the morning of the shooting carrying a number of black persons, Weber phoned New Jersey Motor Vehicle authorities and presently learned that the car was registered to Patricia Daly of 100 Memorial Park, New Brunswick, New Jersey, an address frequented by Johnson.

To Weber, this seemed to indicate strongly that this was no mob hit at all, but a black radical hit, for Pat Daly was a 37-year-old avowed revolutionary. She had a light complexion, sharp white facial features, and an Afro hairdo and was very pretty. She had been involved either as a student or a teacher at a number of universities in Ohio, New York City, New York State, and even at Guadalajara, Mexico, and her last known place of employment was Rutgers University—where Johnson had been arrested three times trying to break into the girls' dormitory. Weber now dug up people who had known Pat Daly, including her ex-husband, and these persons described her as a dedicated revolutionary moved by a hatred of the white race.

Weber phoned the New York State Police for further information about the camp in the Catskill Mountains. He found that it was financed by the Federal Government, but that much of what went on there was target practice and firearms training.

Further informants were found who knew Pat Daly and her associates, and it was reported that during the time that Colombo was picketing the FBI, these people, watching television, had remarked that men such as Colombo should be assassinated. There were further incriminating details. One of Pat Daly's closest associates was a white playwright who had once been stabbed by Jerome Johnson during a lovers' quarrel.

One of the confidential informants was a black New

York Housing Authority patrolman who had known all these people, even Johnson. Cops always tended to believe other cops.

For weeks, Weber pushed the investigation along this line. Pat Daly could not be found. Was she the black woman who had accompanied Jerome Johnson to the rally? If so, she was the person who had put a gun in his hand. This would make Jerome Johnson an agent of black revolutionaries. If so, you could forget about any idea of a mob hit. Colombo was not shot because of a mob contract after all.

Every week or ten days, Weber would brief Chief Seedman and me, the three of us, and certain other detectives sitting around the conference table in Seedman's office. Seedman would nod at each of Weber's disclosures. It seemed to me that the prestige of the Police Department depended upon proving that Jerome Johnson was indeed acting under contract to Carlo Gambino and/or Joey Gallo, and each time Weber strode stolidly out of the office I would remark to Seedman, "But why don't you tell him to push a little harder along the other line. He's not doing anything to connect Johnson to the mob. All he's doing is trying to connect this thing to black revolutionaries."

Seedman would look at me over his cigar, and sometimes peer at me through smoke. Usually he said nothing. Once he said, "You can't order a man to conduct an investigation in a certain way. You have to let him conduct the investigation his own way, follow his own instincts, develop his own hunches and leads. Don't worry. Weber will hit enough stone walls, and he'll come back to the line of investigation that both of us want him to follow."

Eventually Pat Daly was located living under an assumed name in Atlanta, the newest headquarters of various black radical groups, including the Panthers. Weber came to Seedman for money for airline tickets. He wanted to send two uniformed patrolmen to see if they recognized Pat Daly as the black woman who had accompanied Johnson. The two uniformed cops would be accompanied by Weber and Ray Condon, a detective working on the investigation. Weber and Condon would stop to brief Justice Department agents on the way back. Seedman nodded, and instructed one of his secretaries to get money out of his safe—Seedman kept a thousand dollars of Police Department money in his safe at all times, principally for the purpose of buying information and/or airline tickets as the need arose.

Seedman handed the money across the desk to Weber.

In Atlanta, Pat Daly was "discreetly observed" by the two cops, who could not identify her one way or the other.

Meanwhile, Weber, who was far too smart to go down one road exclusively, had collected other information with his left hand, so to speak, much of it from confidential informants in Brooklyn.

Two and a half weeks prior to the Colombo hit, one informant had overheard Joe Gallo, Rosario Musico, who was Gallo's chauffeur, and an unknown male discussing the forthcoming rally. Gallo had stated that the rally wouldn't get off the ground. He had a surprise waiting for Colombo at the rally.

Two weeks prior to the Colombo hit, Colombo was sitting with his entourage in Monti's Bar in Brooklyn when, according to two different informants, Gambino suddenly walked in. Witnesses were treated to the spectacle of TV star Joe Colombo, the famous gangster, who a day or two later (June 16) would celebrate his 48th birthday, getting his face slapped by the 71-year-old Mafia tycoon. Gambino, backed by his own entourage, shouted that Colombo was to "cut the crap," or words to that effect, and at the conclusion of this speech the old man slapped the younger man's face and strode angrily out of the bar. Joe Colombo, one cheek burning, sat staring silently at the table top.

Five days prior to the Colombo hit, another confidential informant had seen Jerome Johnson at a location in Brooklyn with three male whites, all apparently of Italian extraction. Johnson had driven up with these men in a dark-green late-model Chrysler. Johnson had approached the informant, pulled a roll of bills out of his pocket, peeled off $20, and repaid a loan he had made some days previously. The informant, who had never expected to see his $20 again, was startled. He watched Johnson get back into the Chrysler with the three whites and drive away.

Weber and his detectives had studied the films so long and hard that by now they were able to piece together fragments into an almost coherent sequence. Individual frames showed a person backing out of the crowd on Johnson after Johnson had been shot. This man was matched by his clothes (for he was wearing a blue shirt) to other footage where he was identifiable as Philip Rossillo, known as Chubby Rossillo, a heretofore minor Brooklyn hoodlum who worked for Colombo. It was Rossillo who had been carrying Colombo's attaché case, which attaché case he had later dropped to the pavement. Why had he dropped it?

And why was Rossillo backing hurriedly out of the mob on top of the mortally wounded Johnson?

To Weber, and Seedman as well, Rossillo became the Number One suspect in the shooting of Jerome Johnson.

Further confidential information was developed. Two weeks prior to the shooting, Rossillo had turned up at a certain location and there asked for Gallo. Told that no one by that name was present, he returned to his car and waited. A second unknown male had waited with him in the car. Presently a second car drove up, bearing two occupants, Joe Gallo and Rosario Musico. Rossillo got out of his own car and into Gallo's, and both cars left the area.

Detectives went over the photos and film footage again and again. As a bodyguard of Colombo, Rossillo had both motive and opportunity, and in Brooklyn during the days immediately following the rally, Rossillo both acted the part of hero, and was treated as such by his fellow hoodlums.

And what about the dropped attaché case? Rossillo must have known that Joe Colombo's attaché case contained a gun. The boss's attaché case had been entrusted to him, Philip Rossillo. One did not drop the boss's attaché case for no good reason. But one possibly dropped it in order to pull a gun of one's own.

Seedman was being pressured by the press for an estimated date on which he would go to the grand jury for indictments. If he knew so damn much, then when would the indictments come down?

Of the quarter million arrests being made by the police that year, most were summary arrests effected by some cop in the street. But in an elaborate case such as this one, summary arrests were extremely rare, because fine legal points were involved. A stickup man caught during a robbery would be arrested summarily, and the assistant district attorney assigned would take over the case at that point. Additional evidence needed, if any, would be gathered later. Witnesses would be rounded up later. The assistant DA would worry about his courtroom tactics later. The stickup man would probably plead guilty to reduced charges anyway, and there would never be any trial.

But in the Colombo hit (or any similar important crime involving a long investigation), the assistant district attorney assigned was consulted on every point from the first day. He was the one who would have to present the case to a jury (such cases would go all the way to trial), and so he was the man who decided when or if an arrest should be made, when or if certain evidence would stand up in court; and in addition he usually reinterrogated all informants and witnesses himself, after detectives had brought them in.

The District Attorney of New York County was Frank Hogan, who was served by about 145 assistant district attorneys. These men were broken down into various specialties, each under a bureau chief. Thus the chief of Hogan's homicide bureau was 42-year-old John Keenan, and in homicide cases, Keenan was in charge. To the Colombo hit, Keenan had assigned one of his young prosecutors, Steve Sawyer. Accordingly, the detectives' information on Chubby Rossillo had been presented to both Sawyer and Keenan, and it was their belief that, although an indictment of Rossillo might in fact be voted by a grand jury, there was not enough evidence to convict him. High-priced mob lawyers would exploit every technicality, and the jury, which distrusted cops and detectives anyway, would acquit him or perhaps call the Johnson homicide justifiable. Better to wait for detectives to find additional hard evidence. A jury trial, Keenan explained, meant getting 12 persons to agree unanimously on guilt. In our times, and especially in this liberal city, it was virtually impossible to get 12 persons to agree, unless a criminal was caught in the act, smoking gun still in his hand.

Seedman, who never argued with district attorneys, nodded his head and ordered the investigation to continue.

Meanwhile, various of Colombo's hoodlums were at the hospital every day, and one day federal agents searched certain Colombo cars, found a number of illegal guns, and arrests were made. Stopped and searched was Rossillo, who was clean. One hoodlum blurted out, "What are you bothering us for? Why don't you go after the Gallos, because they're the ones who shot Joe Colombo."

I said to Seedman, "We could have arrested those guys anytime we wanted. Why didn't we? Why do we let the Feds do it? The people of this city are wondering what we are doing. We would have proven that we were doing something, that we were on the ball."

Seedman blew out some cigar smoke and said, "Don't worry, we'll break this case yet. You should be pleased that that hoodlum laid the blame on the Gallos. It backs up what we said. This was a mob hit."

Anthony Colombo reacted with a press conference. More than 50 reporters and photographers jammed a room 10 feet wide by 20 feet long. Roly-poly Anthony had trouble waddling through such a crowd, but made it to the microphones and announced that his father was "getting better," and had had no bodyguards on rally day or any other day. According to Anthony, there was no Mafia, only attempts to malign Italians. Certainly Carlo Gambino had had nothing to do with the hit, Gambino being a "very dear and a close friend of my father's and is a real gentleman, and also the godfather of my six-year-old sister. I don't have to say any more than that." Johnson had acted as a lone "deranged psychopath, the same kind that killed John Kennedy, Martin Luther King, and Bobby Kennedy. My father was the head of the League, he was a possible political leader, he was open to assassination." Father Gigante stepped forward to add that Johnson had perhaps been hired by the CIA, the FBI, or other "so-called legitimate forces." Added Anthony. "Think about it."

Meanwhile, most of Weber's energies were being forced down what both Seedman and I hoped and believed was a false trail.

Some weeks passed. Seedman was quietly having other work done. Presently on his desk lay about ten thick scrapbooks. They contained the names, records, and photos of every black criminal with whom Joey Gallo had ever served in any of the several prisons in which he had done time. These scrapbooks contained information even on other blacks friendly with the blacks with whom Gallo had been friendly, for it was Seedman's guess (and this proved correct) that the contact with Johnson had been made via some black man whom Gallo had met in prison. The wardens and other officials at Attica, Auburn, and Greenhaven had at Seedman's request done an awful lot of work.

Quietly, on his own, Seedman was pursuing his own view of this odd case. To Seedman, all of the evidence piled up so far only corroborated what he had thought all along. There even had been a series of simultaneous raids on after-hours joints in Greenwich Village, most of them catering to the homosexual trade. One of these was Christopher's End, 180 Christopher Street, also the address of the Christopher Hotel, Jerome Johnson's last known address. The proprietor of Christopher's End was one Michael Umbers, who had been arrested several times and had served one five-year stretch in jail. But the actual owner had been identified as Paul DiBella, a soldier in the Gambino family. Were Umbers and DiBella the link between Jerome Johnson and the contract to hit Colombo?

But the weekly briefings from Weber went on, and the mere sergeant sat across the table from the Chief of Detectives and said, "I see it as black revolutionaries." The Chief of Detectives blew out cigar smoke and said nothing.

More weeks passed. At length a detective who was not even working on this case came forward to announce that one of his confidential informants, who had always proven reliable in the past, had been in the Boston area three days before the shooting.

In the bar of a certain motel in Roxbury, a suburb of Boston, this informant had observed Jerome Johnson, whom he had known previously, with a black female named Terry Johnson, who was also known to the informant, and a male white known to the informant as a Mafia hoodlum working in the Boston area. Also present were a number of other black and white individuals unknown to the informant. The motel in question was known by Boston Police to be frequented by members of the Angulo Mafia family of Boston, and also by the Patriarca Mafia family of Rhode Island.

The informant had asked the purpose of the meeting. He was told that a contract was being set up to hit Colombo. He was further told that Terry Johnson, the black female accompanying Jerome Johnson, was the link between John-son and the contract, for Terry Johnson's husband, Arthur, had served time at Greenhaven Prison with Joey Gallo. Arthur, who was still in prison, was a direct representative of Joseph Gallo, and it was Gallo who had ordered the contract on Colombo's life.

Which gave Weber a new black female to investigate, who was perhaps the one who had accompanied Jerome Johnson to the rally.

Weber was a dour man. One seldom knew what he was thinking, and never what he was feeling. To Weber, a good detective revealed nothing until the case was ready for the grand jury. To Weber, a good detective was a man who could keep his mouth shut. To Weber, a good detective operated without emotion of any kind.

For weeks Weber had pursued Pat Daly tenaciously. Now, with equal tenacity, he set about uncovering facts that would bolster this tale of a Boston motel meeting. One of the names and phone numbers in Jerome Johnson's possession, although apparently not in Johnson's handwriting, seemed to prove that Johnson had had contact with one Charles Belardinelli, who lived in an apartment building owned by the Longwood Realty Corporation—a business owned by the Angulo family. Belardinelli's toll telephone calls were now examined, a number had gone to New Jersey and to New York, and Weber sent his detectives out to check the destination of each one.

Chief Seedman knew that the FBI was conducting its own investigation of the case, so he arranged a meeting between Weber and the FBI's agent in charge. This agent stated that FBI informants also named Joey Gallo as responsible for the Colombo hit; that Gallo, who may or may not have acted on orders from Carlo Gambino, had used black radicals to arrange the job for him and that he was presently unworried. No connection could ever be made between him and the shooting.

According to Police Department regulations, each detective was required to submit a form as he concluded each assigned job in an investigation. This form was numbered DD 5. Now in November, four and a half months after the hit, more than 500 of these DD 5's had been submitted.

Some represented an hour's work by a single detective,

some a week's work by a pair of detectives. In all, they represented more than 2000 man-days of work, and there were citizens who rejected the expenditure of such time and money merely to solve the shooting of two men whom society was well rid of. To this Seedman replied quietly, "Don't you think it might be a good thing to throw some of these top hoodlums in jail?"

Weber still had ten detectives working full time on the case. Weber had contacted local authorities in approximately ten other states and Canada, asking their detectives to check out one or another point for him. In addition he sought cooperation from the New York and New Jersey State police; the Alcohol, Tobacco and Firearms Unit of the Treasury Department; the FBI; and even the Royal Canadian Mounted Police.

Chief Seedman professed to be certain that the case would break, and asked only a little more patience. He was pleased to think of himself as the first chief of detectives who would ever bring such a case into court—the hit of a Mafia chieftain exposed. But Weber was elated too. As he saw it, he had discovered an alliance between organized crime and black revolutionaries. If he could bring the case a little further he believed there would be an outbreak of violence among all concerned, and the incipient alliance would be destroyed, together with a good many black and white mobsters. Furthermore, so much information would be brought in regarding the leaders and the inner workings of the various groups that he would force them to go low profile for months, if not years.

Weber's investigation went on, and presently he had enough evidence to request a wiretap on a certain Mafia telephone. The laws governing court-ordered wiretaps were so strict that a case had to be proven to a judge's satisfaction (meaning proven almost conclusively) before any judge would sign one, and some judges would almost never sign one; it was a waste of energy even to ask such a judge. This meant that Weber spent a number of days at Criminal Court waiting for the best judge to sit.

At length Weber presented his evidence and his request.

The judge signed the order, the tap went in on the wire of a Mafia figure who, it happened, was not an Italian but a Jew, and whose specialty was hijacking.

To stimulate conversation on this wire, Seedman accorded an interview to *The New York Times* in which he declared that the police knew the identity of the man who had killed Jerome Johnson. Seedman was confident the case would be solved, he said.

Discussing this wiretap a day or two later, Seedman laughed and said, "Every time he picks up his phone he hollers into it, 'You fuckin' cops!' After that, he dials his number. Even though he thinks his phone is tapped, he says things on it."

Enough additional evidence was gathered to request two more wiretaps. And get them.

Detectives monitoring the three tapped lines were hearing things nearly every day, including rumblings, three months before the event occurred, that a contract was out on the life of Joey Gallo.

10 / Seedman

The Detective Division (usually referred to by cops as "The Bureau"), which Albert Seedman commanded, numbered at this time about 3200 men, the largest municipal detective force in the country, and bigger than most entire police departments. The basic detective unit, until Seedman changed it, was the precinct detective squad. There were as few as 14 detectives working out of second-floor offices in the station houses in slow precincts, and as many as 30 in high-crime precincts, and these precinct squads were assigned to investigate all crimes within their jurisdiction: a murder today, a burglary tomorrow, a rape on Thursday. Each squad was commanded by a lieutenant, and the precinct squad lieutenants in each of the 16 police divisions were subordinate to their detective district commanders, the word "district" being the detective equivalent of "division." The next higher supervisors were the borough detective commanders working out of borough headquarters. Over them all stood Seedman, who was responsible only to the Chief Inspector and the Police Commissioner.

Also reporting directly to Seedman were a great number

of specialized detective squads: the Auto Squad, the Forgery Squad, the Narcotics Division, the Missing Persons Unit, the Pickpocket and Confidence Squad, the Safe, Loft and Truck Squad, etc. Each of these specialized squads was assigned to cope not with individual crimes, but with patterns and with major crime rings. That is, the Precinct Detective Squad would start work only after a specific crime had occurred; it was the job of the specialized squads to develop informants and information and in many cases know which crimes were about to occur, and thus to be on the scene waiting when the criminals appeared. For instance, about this time the Safe, Loft and Truck Squad, knowing in advance that a certain truck was to be hijacked, painted an identifying number on the truck's roof, trailed it through the streets of New York by helicopter, and actually had reporters on hand in trailing cars when the truck was finally stopped and its occupants arrested at gunpoint.

The sizes of the specialized squads varied greatly. There were to be in 1971 nearly 100,000 cars stolen on the streets of New York, about 300 a day every day. This was grand larceny on a grand scale, and it was the job of the Auto Squad to cope with it, though the tools assigned were minimal. The commanding officer was Lieutenant Arthur Deutsch, a brash, hard-driving crew-cut man in his late thirties who had already shot two stickup men and killed one murderer in previous assignments, and who liked to organize auto raids and lead them himself. However, assigned to Deutsch were only three sergeants, two first grade detectives, 11 second grade detectives, 10 third grade detectives, and a total of 29 patrolmen. The odds favored the auto thieves, for Deutsch had only 56 men to cover the entire city. Seedman allocated detectives like money in a budget. It was a question of priorities; since car thieves didn't kill or maim anyone, few detectives were sent after them, despite the staggering number of cars disappearing every day.

Some other squads were even smaller than the Auto Squad, and one squad, the Narcotics Division, was huge—about 800 men, plus six girls who worked as undercover buyers in the streets. The head of the Narcotics Division was not a lieutenant but a one-star chief. The Narcotics Division was the largest single unit under Seedman's command.

Not all of the men assigned to the Detective Division were detectives—almost all of the specialized units were liberally dosed with patrolmen hoping to get the gold shield soon. Similarly, not all detectives were under Seedman's command, for about 340 of them worked for the Intelligence Division, and about a hundred worked in Internal Affairs, investigating other cops.

In theory, most detectives had got their gold shields because they had shown special zeal or aptitude while patrolmen. In the past, any act of remarkable heroism, any particularly brilliant arrest, would be rewarded at least by assignment to the Bureau as a patrolman, and some such cops were handed the gold shield on the spot, a sort of battlefield commission. But most men were detectives because they had had a "rabbi" or a "hook"—meaning that they had had influence with someone important. Now in Seedman's time, so-called "Career Path Guidelines" had been formulated. To get a gold shield, a cop had first to work two years in a high-crime precinct, followed by two years in either Narcotics or plainclothes. He would also be interviewed by and judged by an examining board. In theory now, the "hook" was dead.

Seedman worked out of a suite of offices on the second floor of police headquarters. He had a staff of about 20, all detectives. A captain sat in the anteroom to Seedman's personal office and served as his executive secretary. This captain controlled which individuals, which phone calls—and to some extent which cases—got through to the Chief of Detectives.

Seedman's personal office was a vast high-ceilinged room with two big windows looking out onto Centre Street. In one corner was a safe which contained both confidential files and emergency money. A number of filing cabinets stood along one wall. There was a conference table at which Seedman was regularly briefed by subordinates conducting major investigations. And there were usually a number of easels standing around bearing diagrams and charts of crime scenes. All that summer, on a small table against one wall stood piles of blowups of the individual frames of the confiscated movies of the Colombo hit.

On Seedman's desk, which stood two thirds of the way into the room, were three telephones, two of them with multiple buttons, and always a great number of papers requiring his signature.

At this time Seedman was 53 years old. He stood five feet ten, and had once been a slim young man. But age had thickened him everywhere, and though he weighed only 185 pounds today, he was often described as stocky. His curly hair was gray and lightly oiled. He had a rough accent and he tended to growl his words without removing his cigar. He looked tough, and when he gave orders he sounded tough. He wore suits cut in the latest style, meaning that year, wide lapels and bell-bottom trousers. He wore ties with big knots and monogrammed shirts. His cuffs were usually visible below his sleeves, and on these the name "Al" was invariably embroidered in script. He could easily have passed as a fight manager or promoter.

Seedman wore a great deal of jewelry. He had a number of watches, some of them incrusted with diamonds, and he also wore rings on both hands, sometimes changing them from day to day. His cuff links changed from day to day too. Some were miniature Chief of Detectives shields and other were in gold or precious stones. He never carried the Chief of Detectives shield which he had been issued. Instead he carried one which had been exquisitely handcrafted out of solid gold, and which virtually glowed in the dark.

He owned a number of .38-caliber revolvers, including a smoothly polished model without a hammer, and it too seemed to be not an ordinary firearm but a work of jewelry. Obliged like all cops to be armed at all times, Seedman sometimes wore this gun or another in a suede holster, but he had also had certain of his suits made with pistol-shaped pockets sewn into the lining above his appendix. Seedman was the only high-ranking policeman that I knew of who wore jewelry, or monogrammed shirts either; he was one of the few to wear a suede holster and carry a hammerless revolver, and he was a Jew, and it sometimes seemed amazing that such a man had ever risen to the top of what was basically an Irish Catholic police department.

Seedman was one of the most educated of cops, his Bronx accent notwithstanding. Although a number of the high-ranking officers had obtained college degrees as a means of advancing their careers, Seedman's Bachelor of Administration from City College had come in 1941, and at the normal age, 22. Later Seedman earned a Master's degree in Public Administration from City University, and he was at present a candidate for a doctorate in Public Administration at N.Y.U.

As Chief of Detectives, Seedman no longer mixed with the sordid types ordinary detectives mixed with. He knew a great many rich people, he played golf with some of them and handball with others, and they were quick to see to it that he got discounts on a great many luxuries. Through one of these friends he was able to buy a tuxedo for a small price—$45 I think; it was hanging in the back of his police car one day, and he showed it to me. Another lent him a house for a week in Florida.

Seedman knew jewelry. He knew exactly which expensive jeweled watch would please his wife on her birthday, and he bought it for her, something not many men would have dared; and he showed me this too, stating matter-of-factly that he had good taste in jewelry. He knew restaurant owners socially, and when he entered one of their places he could be sure of the best table, and the best service, and also of an eventual bill which perhaps would not reflect the drinks or wine that his party had ordered, and this would soon get him into a great deal of trouble.

Seedman believed in the good life. He kept a small refrigerator in the corner of his office and he stocked Chivas Regal whiskey. He liked to be waited on by detectives. Sometimes after work he would order a detective in from his outer office to pour out whiskey for himself and whatever other police officials were present. Sometimes, after tasting his own glass, Seedman would hand it back growling, "You dummy, didn't you ever hear about ice? You know what that is in the corner? That's a refrigerator. Put some ice in this."

Seedman often growled "You dummy, you," at detectives, but they didn't appear to mind, possibly because there seemed to be affection in his voice rather than venom. Seedman liked detectives, he understood all about them, and they seemed to sense this. He rode them hard, they obeyed his orders or got fired, but he was never gratuitously mean, and he humiliated no detective publicly. Furthermore, Seedman was not nearly as tough as he pretended to be and they knew this or sensed it. Perhaps the major reason he assigned Weber to the Colombo investigation was because Weber, whom he liked, had been ill with heart trouble and was terribly worried about himself. To Seedman, a complex case such as this was possibly the exact therapy Weber needed. "I wanted him to be able to forget his own problems," Seedman admitted later, "He was an extremely capable guy, and he needed that case."

Seedman was born August 9, 1918, the son of a cab driver. He was a quiet, studious, rather timid boy, who nursed a secret ambition to become an FBI agent, which was why, when he went to City College, he studied accounting—either accounting or law degrees were mandatory for FBI agents then. When he got out of college in 1941, Seedman did work briefly as an accountant, and he also worked briefly as a Transit Authority patrolman before switching to the Police Department. There were, then as now, a number of law enforcement agencies within New York City: the Transit Authority Police, the Housing Authority Police, the Port Authority Police, and some of these agencies were substantial, numbering up to 3000 men or more.

But when one spoke of the New York Police, one meant the Police Department police, the best in the world, or so the propaganda went, and so that is where Seedman began to make a career for himself. Asked what made him want to be a cop, he always tended to give a laugh and a silly answer such as, "I liked being a stairwell monitor in school." He was a difficult man when reporters asked him direct questions. Like other detectives, he tended to turn questions over and over in his mouth like chewing gum, tasting their implications, before speaking some sort of evasive answer. In Seedman's case the evasive answers were almost invariably amusing, and so people tended not to notice.

During World War II Seedman served as an enlisted man with the allied military government, much of the time in France. He learned to speak, and still spoke, quite competent French, and he spent those years helping to organize order out of chaos, to find food for whole cities to eat. He also, during those years, was quite a ladies' man, or perhaps these were just funny stories he told in later life. He once recounted spending the night with a girl in Paris; and when he woke up in the morning she was in the bathroom, and he checked to see if his wallet was still in his pants. It was, but there was no money in it. He hunted all over the room looking for his money, and finally found it in the girl's purse under the bed, together with a loaded gun. Seedman recaptured his money and, according to the story he later told, pocketed the bullets from the gun. When the girl came back, Seedman was about to leave the room. "Oh, by the way," he told her, "you shouldn't have stolen my money like that."

The girl lunged for her handbag, pointed her gun at Seedman, and demanded the money. Seedman stared down the barrel of the gun he knew to be empty and said blithely, "If you want to commit a murder just over a little money, go ahead."

Then he turned and walked out of the room.

This was typical of the stories Seedman told about himself. It was highly imaginative, highly amusing, and possibly even true.

Seedman came back to New York just in time to walk a beat all one winter in the Bronx; and as the next winter approached, he said to himself, "I can't stand another winter on the sidewalk." So he went to a former general for whom he had worked in the army, who was now a politician, and he asked this man to get him a gold shield. Almost immediately another local politician was murdered—this was on election day, 1946—and because many new detectives were needed to cope with this crime, Seedman was made a detective the next day and assigned to guard the murdered man's brother. Seedman had become a detective thanks to what cops called a "hook," and this was nothing to be ashamed of. In those days, and also for many years to come, this was virtually the only way to become a detective. However, once he became Chief of Detectives, Seedman, with the blessings of Commissioner Murphy, put an end to hooks.

As a young detective, Seedman had his gun out only a very few times, and he was never in any sort of shoot-out, which is not to say that he was never in danger.

Seedman won all together five citations, but most of the stories he liked to tell about himself were anything but heroic. One time he arrested a criminal who, unknown to Seedman, had already been shot by a cop. Seedman noted that blood was leaking down below the man's pants leg over his sock. "You know what that is, don't you?" asked the criminal.

"Sure," said Seedman, imagining that this must be some kind of new treatment for venereal disease.

Another time, Seedman was investigating the murder of a grandmother—the other detectives were certain the old lady had been raped as well. Seedman said, "Are you crazy? No one would rape a woman that old. Somebody killed her for her money." Eventually Seedman found that in fact her son-in-law had killed the old lady for her money. Seedman would learn later that plenty of grandmothers got raped and killed by sex perverts, but at this time he didn't know this, and his own insistence on robbery as the motive did solve that case.

And so Seedman progressed from a young detective to an old one. He learned that the best way to make a dangerous arrest was to come crashing in through the doors and windows at 5 A.M.

"Get up and get dressed," Seedman ordered one such criminal. The criminal's young and beautiful wife lay wide-eyed beside him in bed. The criminal slid out of bed and stood up. He wore nothing except a limp condom.

"How's that for life's most embarrassing moment?" asked Seedman in later years.

Seedman learned all there was to learn about sex and crime, none of it titillating. One time he muttered broodingly, "If you're interested in seeing dead naked bodies, become a detective. There's no other way." Other detectives were much moved by the luscious young stewardess, dead.

Seedman said, "Aah, I've seen a hundred dead girls."

Another time he said, "Many a time I sent a detective down on a dead girl, inches away from her pussy, trying to find a different colored hair, a red hair, a black hair, a blond hair, any pubic hair caught in there that wasn't hers. Then at least we know what we're looking for. Get down and shine a flashlight on it."

Seedman liked to say that he'd always been a detective, but this wasn't strictly true. He was four years a sergeant on patrol, two years a precinct desk lieutenant in Queens, and four years in the Police Academy. Other than that, Seedman was in fact a detective all his career, and even when on patrol, he noticed details other cops didn't see, and brooded thoughts that occurred to him only.

By the time he was made Chief of Detectives, he had looked down on at least 2000 murdered bodies, and he had watched impassively while other victims, still breathing, were rushed off to hospitals. When Joe Colombo, shot three times in the head, was given up for dead by everyone else, Seedman remarked, "He may pull through." Asked why, Seedman could give no answer except, "I've seen at least two hundred guys shot in the head, and you get a feel for it."

Shortly after the stewardess was raped and murdered, a witness described the girl and a young man trying to cash a check earlier that afternoon. A composite drawing of her companion was put together. The detectives wanted this released to the press as the suspected killer. Seedman let the drawing lie on his desk several days.

The detective in charge called. "When are we going to give out the drawing?"

"We're not going to give it out at all," said Seedman. "That isn't the guy who did it. Look, she was having her period and the killer raped her anyway. He nearly bit off her breast. The evidence is that he raped her after she was dead. Does that sound like some young guy she'd cash a check with?"

Within a few days, the check cashing incident proved a false lead, and the composite drawing was destroyed.

At the Police Academy in the mid-fifties, Lieutenant Seedman, as director of recruit training, was charged with the administration of an academic program involving some 2000 recruits at a time plus 30 instructors. He was running a good-size college, and he reported to Patrick Murphy. The two men never mixed socially except for occasional department functions. Seedman and a number of other lieutenants were studying for the captain's exam and Acting Captain Pat Murphy was invited to join their study group. But Murphy rarely showed up, for he was too busy working. Eventually Murphy failed the test that Seedman and the others passed, and reverted to lieutenant. Some days after work, Seedman would stop for a drink with other officers, none of them Murphy. "Murphy only knew one road in the entire city, and that was the road from wherever he was stationed to home. He never palled around with the guys, and his only friend seemed to be his brother John."

When his Police Academy assignment ended, Lieutenant Seedman went back into Narcotics, commanding a squad of about 20 detectives. In those days the Narcotics Division numbered not 800 men, but under 150. After promotion to captain just before Christmas in 1959—Murphy did not make captain until more than two years later—Seedman served in a variety of detective staff functions. His rise was fairly rapid: Deputy Inspector in 1963, Inspector a year later, Deputy Chief two years after that. Patrick Murphy he rarely saw, and presently Murphy retired and went to work in Washington. Seedman got his second star in June of 1969, and with it command of Manhattan South detectives. He was now the second-ranking detective commander.

After Patrick Murphy was appointed Commissioner, while Murphy was still in Detroit, Murphy's brother John came to see Seedman. John had been asked by Pat to interview a number of top commanders. Who did Seedman think should be named Chief Inspector?

Seedman's first choice, he told John Murphy, would be Mike Codd. His second choice would be Al Seedman.

Memos began to reach Seedman from Murphy in Detroit. Seedman was given to understand that if he were not named Chief Inspector, he was Murphy's choice as Chief of Detectives.

Seedman was almost never without a cigar, and sometimes, especially when he was on the phone, teeth clenched on the cigar, rings flashing on both hands, he looked like a man who belonged not in police headquarters but in the garment industry, another tough and dirty business. He looked like a man ordering truckloads of suits, hiring and firing employees at the same time.

Indeed, a highly successful business executive is exactly what he was. He had an astonishing memory. He knew every detail of his business, including the names and skills of all of his key employees, and of a good many minor ones as well, not to mention those of a vast array of present and past criminals—his clientele, so to speak. He had been named Chief of Detectives by Murphy because of his known skills as an administrator, and that's what most of his time and thought went into, and it was as if he kept up with detective work on the side, as a hobby. As with all businesses today, his own was caught in what might be called a profit squeeze. The amount of crime was increasing at a staggering rate, while the number of detectives remained stuck. Somehow the 3200 detectives had to be made to produce more. They had to be organized better and supervised better. More had to be done with less, and the name of the game was management.

Under Seedman the entire detective division was about to be reorganized. As Seedman saw it, the old precinct detective squads were obsolete. Criminals no longer worked in only one precinct or in only one geographical area, or even in only a single category of crime. Criminals now roamed the city hitting targets of opportunity, a mugging today, a burglary tomorrow, and the precinct squads could no longer fight them effectively.

Similarly, in the old days it was sufficient for a few top commanders to comprehend city-wide patterns, and they kept all the major crimes in their heads. In the old days, good detective commanders used to be able to remember the facts of all murders each year, and where each investigation stood, but there were only a couple of hundred murders then, whereas this year there would be over 1400, and next year probably more than that, and where was the detective commander who could keep 1400 murders in his head?

No, there would have to be teams of coordinators in each crime category, and the precinct squads to which so much detective romance was attached would have to go, and if the romance disappeared with them, another casualty of modern times, that might be unfortunate, but it could not be helped.

So starting on the first day of the next year, the detectives would be regrouped by specialties, and they would work not in single precincts but throughout entire districts. Each district would have its own Homicide-Assault Squad,

Burglary-Larceny Squad, Robbery Squad, and so forth. Each detective would become a specialist on a single type of crime. Theoretically, this would give each more experience, more expertise, more speed.

At the same time, patrolmen responding to the scene of a crime would be made to handle much of the paper work detectives had been saddled with previously, and in certain specific instances they were to do all of the work themselves, freeing detectives for major crime investigations.

This was the first major reorganization within the Police Department in fifty years or more; the problems were staggering, and each of them Seedman either solved himself, or else he approved the solution suggested by one or another of his staff.

The reorganization would give Seedman the excuse to eliminate much detective featherbedding as well. Formerly, detectives rotated tours much like patrolmen. The result was regular turns at all-night duty, during which, traditionally, detectives caught up on their sleep at full pay; for on the one hand few new crimes requiring detectives occurred at 4 A.M., and witnesses to old crimes were asleep; and on the other hand there were dormitories in many of the precincts, and most nights there were detectives asleep in them in their underwear. Night tours for detectives didn't make sense, Seedman ruled, and he ordered them eliminated.

But how could the proud and pampered detective force be made to acquiesce in such radical change, for a whole way of life was being uprooted?

Let every detective choose his own crime specialty, Seedman ruled, accepting the avalanche of paper work this entailed in order to reap his detectives' cooperation.

On featherbedding he refused to bargain at all, though he met often—and each time calmed—Jim Kelly, the detective who was president of the Detectives' Endowment Association. The amazing result was that no serious protest, no anger, no recrimination ever occurred.

"When can Detective Specialization go in?" Commissioner Murphy had asked.

"January first."

"You'll never make it," said Murphy.

"We'll make it," growled Seedman, and in fact specialization was to go into effect precisely on schedule.

Even Seedman's target date had been chosen with care—the three-day New Year's weekend, when crimes would be relatively light, so that the truckloads of typewriters, filing cabinets, and other gear could be moved from outlying precincts to central ones without disrupting investigations in progress.

Seedman was careful in a great many ways, big and small. As a captain in 1962, standing with a man named Anthony Dellernia, who with his partner had murdered two detectives but who now refused to pose for photographers, Seedman had grabbed the guy's hair and jerked his head back, exposing the murderer's face to the world. The resulting photo was highly dramatic, for the much younger Seedman had a cigar clenched between his teeth, and the caption might have read: Justice Triumphant. However, the New York Civil Liberties Union demanded that Seedman be reprimanded for abusing the prisoner and, although no action was ever taken, Seedman had never since allowed himself to be photographed with a cigar in his mouth.

This was only a detail. To Seedman, details were important.

Seedman, who as Chief of Detectives earned $29,000 a year, was a careful man with money. Every three months that year, the city's banks, to stimulate deposits, offered gifts such as radios or kitchen mixers to anyone who opened an account in the amount of $100 or more. So every three months Seedman sent his chauffeurs around to banks to open new accounts in Seedman's name, and to come back to headquarters with the giveaway premium. Later, when Murphy demanded that all his commanders list all of their bank accounts, Seedman was in the position of having to note down a great many.

But on the subject of banks, Seedman was also careful to note that a great many stickups occurred just after the vaults opened at 9 A.M. So he ordered his commanders to assign idle detectives to watch banks for one hour—commanders were to spread their detectives around as far as they would go. Particularly, every detective due to testify when court opened at 10 A.M. was to watch some bank during the preceding hour—these were guys who otherwise would spend that hour having coffee, Seedman thought. There were many more banks in the city than detectives, but presently one stickup did occur in a watched bank, and the detective staked out there got his man.

Seedman was careful also to observe all of the social amenities of the Police Department. He attended all of the line organizations' functions without exception. Although he was a three-star chief, and bossed some 3200 men, he was careful never to call his superiors—that is, Chief Inspector Codd, the seven deputy commissioners, and Commissioner Murphy, by their first names, though he had known some of them 25 years. He called Codd "Chief." He called the rest of us "Commissioner."

And Seedman was careful when it came to divorce. At this time, age 53, Seedman had just married for the second time. In the basically Irish Catholic Police Department divorce and remarriage were major steps, and Seedman knew this, and he had thought about it carefully for a long time. He had a son 28 years old, and another 23, and his daughter Marilyn was 19. He and his wife, the former Sylvia Alabaster, had drifted apart, and presently Seedman had begun to date a divorcée, Henny Josephs, who had been born in Germany and raised in France. More than a year had gone by. Seedman wanted to get married and he had about decided on a Mexican divorce; he had had the papers for this divorce for a long time but done nothing about it because, he told me one night at dinner, "You know how the Department is, you know what the morality of the Department is, and I was afraid that if I got divorced it would hurt my career. With me, my career came first. Then finally just before the possibility of getting divorced in Mexico expired because of changes in the law, I went down there and I got divorced. When I came back, I went in to see Pat Murphy and I told him I was divorced, and he said, 'Are you taking care of your ex-wife?' I told him I was. 'Any scandal involved?' asked Murphy. I told him there was none. 'Fine,' said Murphy, and he hasn't spoken of the matter since."

Like all cops, Seedman was entitled to 28 working days' vacation per year, five and a half weeks, and to these were added however much overtime he put in—since crimes happened nights and Sundays too, he put in plenty. As a result Seedman was able to take a week off at regular intervals and he usually went off somewhere with his wife—once one of his rich friends got him a cut rate on a Caribbean cruise. Learning that Seedman was away again, Murphy shook his head and remarked, "Al's off on another honeymoon, eh. I guess he must really like that new wife of his."

But this was the only criticism of the divorced Seedman, if that's what it was, I ever heard voiced.

Like other business executives of his stature, Seedman was driven by chauffeurs everywhere he went. The black unmarked Plymouth assigned him was a lesser car than Commissioner Murphy's or Chief Inspector Codd's—they had air-conditioned Mercurys—and First Deputy Smith had a two-year-old Chrysler that was also air-conditioned. The rest of us had Plymouth Furies, and were not entitled to air-conditioning. Seedman had had air-conditioning installed at once, paying for it himself. He lived an hour out on Long Island and liked either to sleep or do paper work during the two long trips each day, and in summer only the air-conditioning made this possible.

He always rode in the front seat. It was the notion of police commanders (and Seedman accepted this) that the highest-ranking officer rode in front next to the driver; everybody in the back was a mere passenger. One of the few who regularly rode in the back of his own car, perhaps because he felt himself more a business executive than a cop, was Commissioner Murphy.

Seedman's alternate chauffeurs lived near his own unpretentious suburban house, and if an important crime occurred in the middle of the night, whichever one had the duty was routed from bed to drive the Chief of Detectives back into the city, where he would stride from his car to the scene with a cigar in his mouth and his hands in his pockets. He would stare down at the body, making no comment—to him it was nothing but a question mark.

Like other business executives of his stature, Seedman carried an attaché case. In it were three packs of .38-caliber bullets, a pair of handcuffs, a sap, and a magnifying glass on a tripod. It also contained confidential reports on important cases, for Seedman did his homework religiously. No matter how complex an investigation, he wanted to know everything about it—he even had memorized all the names and aliases of the Mafia figures and the Black Liberation Army figures. He knew the calibers of the murder guns, how many bullets were dug out of the body and the wall. He could pick up a discussion of such cases at no matter what stage he entered a room. Detectives who worked on only one of these cases at a time sometimes couldn't do this, and he could do it on many cases at once.

Furthermore, he was the only top commander who bothered to keep on top of investigations. Murphy knew only what he was told in briefings, and he rarely asked questions. First Deputy Smith, Chief Inspector Codd and the others rarely even asked to be briefed. In my time none of them ever appeared at a crime scene, except Murphy once —he was in the neighborhood of a bank robbery and so stopped in. After standing around for 15 minutes looking embarrassed, nodding his head when briefed by Seedman, but asking no questions, he went away.

Murphy had never been a detective at any stage in his career. Certain detectives, pointing this out, claimed that the Police Commissioner had once wanted to be a detective (didn't everybody?) but had failed, and so had had it in for the Detective Division ever since. It was known that among Murphy's long-range plans was the downgrading of the Detective Division. He even wanted to drop the word detective, and start calling them investigators. Often in his speeches he pointed out that the patrol force was the backbone of the department, not the detectives. The patrol force was where his loyalty lay. It was also true that the patrol force had the most votes. At any rate, he saw no reason to be at the scene.

Whereas Seedman showed up at all major crime scenes, even in the dead of night; and one day in an interview for a *New York Times* article about Seedman, Murphy seemed to explain this away. After praising Seedman's ability as an administrator, Murphy added, "Of course when you've been a detective as long as Al has, I guess you can't stay away from crime scenes. I guess he feels he has to keep his hand in, has to be where the action is."

First Deputy Smith once said, "Seedman shouldn't be at crime scenes. He's supposed to be in his office administering the Detective Division."

I said, "But he's got the experience, he sees things his detectives don't see—"

"He should have a lieutenant doing that."

Well, there was always jealousy within the Department toward the Bureau, and toward whoever happened to command it. Especially now with television. Seedman had been interviewed on television a lot.

Seedman himself once said, "When you get a case that you know is going to get a lot of attention, then I want to see it handled properly. I want to see that the right detective catches the case, and that he goes off in the right direction. Maybe I can tell him what he should look for."

Seedman was the only one who seemed to think it important to solve the big crimes. And so he went to them, and once he was on the scene, the TV reporters invariably grabbed him for interviews. Month after month they also asked for progress reports on the Colombo case. One day after Seedman on camera had promised still again to break the case, First Deputy Smith remarked: "Why doesn't he keep his big mouth shut for a change?"

Seedman ignored this and continued to go to crime scenes. As a detective, he had two things going for him: memory and intuition. Put together, this meant the ability to come up with ideas, and ideas were rare in any line of work. In Seedman's presence one day someone had referred to the top police commanders as "the cream of the crop."

"That's not true," Seedman had corrected. "The cream of the crop were the guys who became doctors and lawyers. The police commanders are perhaps the cream of those guys who became cops."

Seedman judged that the other commanders knew nothing about detective work, whereas he did.

On a winter day a cop was shot. Arrested some blocks away, the suspect had no gun. Seedman ordered his detectives to trace the route back from where the man was caught to where the cop was shot. "Then I want you to get flame throwers from the army and melt every snow bank along the route until you come to the one he must have thrown his gun into as he was running away." The gun was found.

On a summer morning, a Brink's money delivery to the Municipal Credit Union on the third floor of the Municipal Building, across from City Hall, was intercepted by two armed gunmen. The gunmen opened fire at once, and so did the Brink's guards. Despite the fact that this gun fight took place at point-blank range, no one was seriously wounded. However, the gunmen grabbed the money, raced downstairs, leaped into a getaway car, and disappeared across the Brooklyn Bridge. Seedman appeared on the scene almost at once. Someone asked, "How could trained guards empty their guns at such short range, and miss their targets?"

Seedman mused, "At a time like that you gotta be a psychopath for your arm not to shake." Then he added somberly, "That's why so many cops get killed. Because the guys who shoot cops are psychopaths."

Four tentative license plate numbers were given to Seedman. The make and model of the getaway car was also known. Seedman said, "You'll find that it's a stolen car, and that they abandoned it in one of those deserted streets just on the other side of the river under the bridge. I want every radio car in that precinct to go through the streets until they find the getaway car."

The getaway car was found with blood in it, residents of that area were canvassed by detectives, and the license number of the second car into which the gunmen had transferred themselves and their loot was now known.

The owner of this second car could not be found. Seedman reasoned that his wife, assuming that she was not legally his wife, could be thrown in front of a grand jury and made to testify as to where he might be. Seedman sent detectives scouring through marriage records, trying to prove either that the man and his wife were never married, or that their marriage was invalid. When this failed, Seedman issued a national alarm, and the man was soon in custody and indicted.

In Brooklyn a bank was robbed. By the time Seedman

reached the scene, it swarmed with detectives and FBI agents. Seedman himself began to interrogate bank personnel. Their accounts seemed to indicate that the robbers had known who the head teller was, though presumably they had never seen him before. After interrogating the head teller, Seedman stood against the opposite wall. Every once in a while the head teller would look up, catch Seedman's eyes boring into him, and glance nervously away. Seedman called over the detective commander who would head the investigation. "I want you to proceed with the investigation in the normal way except for one thing. You see that head teller?"

As the head teller looked up this time, both Chief Seedman and the other detective were staring at him. Again he glanced quickly and nervously away.

Seedman continued, "I don't want you to go near that guy for two days. I don't want him questioned, I don't want him tailed, I don't want any of our guys to say a word to him. I want him to think he got away with it. At the end of two days I want you to really bust his chops. I want him to see a detective every time he turns around. I want detectives to follow him into the bathroom."

On the fifth day, the head teller confessed to having masterminded the bank robbery.

One night a sniper fired shots from the roof of Hunter College into the living-room window of the Russian Consulate. It was after midnight before Seedman reached the scene. The fingerprint technicians, photographers, and detectives had already done their work and gone. Nonetheless, Seedman insisted on mounting to the roof, where he stared off across the parapet toward the window of the distant Russian Consulate. Asked why he had bothered, he answered, "I wanted to see what it looked like to the shooter." This case too was broken within a few days.

A girl driving west on the Belt Parkway in Brooklyn at 50 miles an hour suddenly went off the road and crashed. The medical examiner found a tiny bullet hole just above her left ear. The detectives suddenly had a murder on their hands. She was dead of a rifle shot from the direction of the ocean. A group had been seen on the beach just prior to the shooting. They were photographers and fashion

models, and one of their props was a rifle. This was reported by two patrolmen in a radio car, and the cops were good
—they had noted down the license numbers.

Seedman ordered men to track down this group, which
was done, and the rifle turned out to be nothing but a prop.
The barrel was plugged. All that work had led nowhere.
The case, Seedman said later, was driving him nuts. How
far away might the bullet have come from? Because he had
done similar research in a similar case some years previously, and because he had spoken to the medical examiner
about the depth that the bullet had penetrated into the girl's
skull, he came to the conclusion that the bullet might have
been fired from beyond the limits of the beach. Now he
called in the police helicopter, and went up into the air to
study the possibilities. The pilot flew back and forth, while
Seedman brooded, at length coming to the conclusion that
the bullet had to have been fired from the water. There was
no other reasonable possibility. Therefore, it had been fired
by some guy in a boat, who could have had no idea that his
bullet would meet that girl's head at that specific spot and
moment in time. Therefore the guy was firing at seagulls,
or tin cans.

Back on the ground, Seedman called his detectives together. "I want you to canvass every house and apartment
on that beach. I want you to find a guy who owns a boat
and a rifle. When you find him you'll have the guy who
killed that girl."

The detectives protested vigorously. "But Chief," one
said, "you're asking us to canvass hundreds and hundreds
of addresses. How do we know where to start?"

Seedman spread a street map out on the desk, rammed
his finger down on a specific corner. "Start right here," he
said forcefully. He had no better idea than his detectives
where to start, but he knew they needed specific directions
from him, and so that's what he gave them.

On that specific street corner, within ten minutes, the detectives found the man who had inadvertently killed the
girl, found his rifle, too, and took him into custody.

The detectives were terrifically impressed with Seedman.
"But Chief, how did you know that was the corner?"

Seedman answered, "That's why I'm a chief and you're
only a detective."

Book Four / AUTUMN

In order to give his top aides some notion of where he might be at any given hour, it was the Police Commissioner's habit to send around his coming schedules each week. These usually arrived Friday afternoon. They blocked out his time for the week following.

The schedule for the week beginning September 20 read this way.

MONDAY: 1000 hours—fourth-floor conference room with First Deputy Commissioner et al, re: patrol sergeants' function. 1430 hours—Police Commissioner's office with Deputy Commissioner Administration. 1500 hours—Police Commissioner's office with First Deputy Commissioner et al, re: entrance into the Detective Bureau.

TUESDAY: 0900 hours—WCBS studio, taping "Ask the Commissioner." 1445 hours—fourth-floor conference room with First Deputy Commissioner et al, re: identification of patrol work performance. 1600 hours—Police Commissioner's office with First Deputy Commissioner et al, re: corruption. 1800 hours—reception with Mrs. Murphy, 55 East 72nd Street (meet new British Consul General).

WEDNESDAY: 1000 hours—executive conference. 1100 hours—Police Commissioner's office with Captain Schimmel [Gertrude Schimmel was the highest-ranking policewoman]. 1430 hours—Mr. Weinstein's office, 2 Lafayette Street, Room 1512, re: peddling in lower Manhattan, with Captain Farrell and Lieutenant McPortland. 1645 hours— the "David Frost Show," 240 West 44th Street.

THURSDAY: 1030 hours—Police Commissioner's office with Chief Inspector et al, re: auto thefts and recoveries. 1100 hours—Police Commissioner's office with Dr. Scribner, Board of Education, with the Chief Inspector and Captain Protter. 1530 hours—Police Commissioner's office, taping with reporters from WLIB. 1615 hours—Police Commissioner's office, taping for WGBH/TV, Boston.

FRIDAY: 1200 hours, Police Commissioner departs for International Association of Chiefs of Police Convention,

Anaheim, California, returning NYC 10/3/71.

On those days when he had no luncheon date scheduled, the Police Commissioner would send one of his secretaries for a half pint of milk and a sandwich—usually tuna fish or chicken salad on white bread—and he would eat this hurriedly, sometimes while also conducting a conference. This particular week, however, he had luncheons scheduled every day except Friday. On Monday he lunched with Nat Goldstein, *New York Times* circulation director, at Sardi's. On Tuesday he made a luncheon speech to the Lotus Club on East 66th Street. Wednesday's lunch was with Sergeant Harold Melnick, president of the Sergeants' Benevolent Association. On Thursday, lunch took place in the sixth-floor office of Dorothy Schiff, editor and publisher of the *New York Post*. A number of top editors were present, and these people grilled the Police Commissioner throughout the two-hour lunch. Murphy lunched regularly—that is, at the rate of about one luncheon per week—with newspaper, magazine, and TV editors.

Virtually all the Police Commissioner's paper work—and he went home with two to three inches of papers to read every night—was done nights, weekends, or early in the morning. It was impossible for him to get paper work done in the office. In between meetings blocked out in advance, there were numerous others called on an impromptu basis. Top commanders brought urgent problems to him either between regularly scheduled appointments, or perhaps during one of them, for often Murphy would step out of his own office to meet, say, the Chief Inspector or the Chief of Detectives in an anteroom.

Murphy budgeted his time rigidly, and almost never conducted a meeting through to a conclusion. He liked to call major conferences for the fourth-floor conference room. There, eight or ten or more top commanders, yellow legal pads and pencils ready, would await the arrival of the Police Commissioner, who almost always came late. No meeting started without him. Eventually he would arrive, start the meeting, toss ideas around, get his subordinates discussing a problem, and then look at his watch and say still again, "I'm running late. Please go on with the discussion and see what you come up with." A nod all around the table, and he was gone. Sometimes one or another of his

top aides left with him, and the remainder of the conference was something like a wedding reception after the
bride and groom had left, or a football rally after the team
had been bundled off to bed by its coach. Desultory conversation ensued for some time longer, then the meeting
broke up.

The Police Commissioner was capable of walking out
even on meetings in his own office. He would budget 30
minutes for a meeting he knew would take an hour or
more, and he would conduct this while popping Lifesavers
into his mouth, occasionally cracking his fingernails, and at
the end of 30 minutes he would put his hat on, signal his
secretary to send the chauffeur for his car, and go downstairs in his private elevator, leaving the rest of us to carry
on as best we could. In the course of these conferences,
Murphy would sometimes say, "Why don't you see if you
can take care of that, Mike?" Or Bill, or Phil, or Bob, or
whoever. This was the closest he ever came to giving a
direct order. His wish was the command of all of us, and
there was no need to give a direct order. The Police Commissioner very rarely—almost never—put orders in writing. There was no reason for not doing so. This was simply
a whim of Murphy's. Or perhaps it was an ingrown police
habit—What you don't put in writing can't haunt you later.

In addition to the conferences—and I understood that
no previous commissioner had ever held conferences on
anything like Murphy's scale—there came a barrage of
memos, two, three, four, per day. If his orders were never
committed to writing, his ideas always were. A great many
of these, though they seemed sound enough to me, were
never followed through on, not by Murphy and not by anyone. He was like a man sticking a note in a milk bottle
which he then tossed into the current. If it found a destination, fine. If not, he would send out another later.

About this time, a memo came through suggesting that
the rank designations be changed. There were at present
four ranks containing the word chief, and five containing
the word inspector. It was Murphy's idea that the rank
Deputy Chief Inspector should be shortened to Deputy
Chief. Assistant Chief Inspector should be shortened to
Chief. The four three-star ranks would remain unchanged,
and the Chief Inspector should become Chief of Field

Operations. The memo asked for our thoughts.

I sent a memo back and assumed everyone did, but heard no further word on this subject for six months or so, at which time I asked Murphy what had happened to the idea. He replied, "Oh it's still out there somewhere floating around." Shortly afterwards a second memo on the subject, basically unchanged from the first, arrived. But nothing seemed to come of it this time either.

Murphy's memos covered every variety of subject and a great many were brilliant.

He suggested studies be made relative to the guarding of prisoners in hospitals, for he had been horrified to learn when he took over the Police Department that more than 215 patrolmen performed no other duty than the guarding of prisoners in hospitals. This was enough men to staff an entire precinct. His memo read, "It is obvious on its face that a paralyzed prisoner need not be guarded. Aside from gaining cooperation from district attorneys and courts, should we seek revision of charter or other provisions to eliminate the requirement for guarding if a doctor certifies a medical condition which makes the possibility of escape remote? Criminal Justice Bureau should pursue this vigorously. Deputy Commissioner Public Affairs and Special Counsel should be prepared to have us go public on this should we seek revision of charter or other provisions to attorneys. Every reasonable effort should be made to obtain cooperation before resorting to this."

Because he met regularly with the heads of the various line organizations, Murphy was aware that his "accountability" doctrine was causing confusion, worry, and fear. So he sent a three-page memo to all 3700 superior officers: "I want to correct what appears to be an unfortunate misunderstanding of one of the most important policies of this department.

"When I speak of accountability I do not mean that a commander is automatically and personally responsible, like an insurer, for every incident of misconduct or inefficiency that takes place within his command. That standard would be unrealistic and unfair. No officer who has been demoted or reassigned has been held to such a standard, and no one will be." Superior officers would be held accountable, he now explained, only when the acts in question were "so serious, repeated, or widespread that he either knew or by reasonable diligence should have known of them, or that the conditions would not have developed or persisted if he had demonstrated a level of leadership and supervision commensurate with his assignment."

Sergeant Melnick, who was also chairman of the Superior Officers' Council, described this memo as "more human." "I think it's great," Sergeant Melnick said. "He's saying what I've been saying all along—go after the guy who's really accountable, not just the guy who's sitting two floors up, innocent, when something bad happens downstairs. I only wish he had said it in the beginning. Instead, he made all those blanket statements. He made a lot of guys feel tainted."

Before Murphy even reached his office each morning, his schedule for the day, blocked out by his appointments secretary the previous week, was jammed full. He rarely made phone calls during the day, and he accepted calls only from the Mayor or Whitman Knapp, or from one or two other important persons. He would schedule interviews with almost any journalist, provided his secretary could fit it in, but rarely would take a call from a journalist. By ten o'clock in the morning each day, his schedule probably was running half an hour late, meaning that people were waiting in line in his anteroom.

If he were summoned downtown by the Mayor, then the entire day's schedule would have to be canceled or rearranged; and all too regularly he would have to cancel an entire morning in order to attend a police funeral. Many chores, such as visiting a wounded cop in the hospital, he accomplished by stopping off either on his way to the office or on his way home.

He was rarely alone in his car. Either a reporter rode with him, interviewing him all the way, or else one of his immediate subordinates rode with him. At times two or more of us rode in that car, each with a list of points to be covered, and Murphy listened to each of us in turn. Once I got to his car only to find Chief Inspector Codd already installed in the back seat. That meant Codd's turn came first. We reached our destination just as Codd finished, and so my turn had to wait until the ride back.

Occasionally the Police Commissioner's car would be

stuck in traffic. Perhaps he was scheduled to dedicate a new station house ten minutes ago. There were times when he radioed ahead that they should start without him, and other times when he gave his estimated time of arrival and asked them to wait. When returning to his office, he almost always asked his chauffeur to pass the microphone into the back seat as soon as we were within ten blocks of headquarters, at which time the dialogue would go something like this—

"Car 200 to Room 200. K."

"Room 200. K."

"This is Car 200. We're about five minutes out. K."

"Room 200, 10-4."

"Car 200, 10-4."

The word "K" was the Police Department equivalent of a period at the end of a sentence. The signal 10-4 was the acknowledgment closing out all conversations. Car 200 was the Police Commissioner's car and Room 200 was the number over the door of the Police Commissioner's office. All of our cars had call numbers, and in most cases these had nothing to do with anything. My car was Number 9. The Chief of Detectives rode car Number 4, and so forth.

The point was that the Police Commissioner normally gave his secretaries five minutes' warning of his imminent arrival so that the next scheduled appointment could be on his feet at the door, ready to enter the office from one side of the room as the Police Commissioner himself entered from the other.

Murphy wasted no time at all. Not ever. There was never any small talk. The amenities, such as a handshake, were of course observed, but they were crisp and businesslike. Only two or three times over the many months I was deputy commissioner did Murphy call me in there for no apparent reason. What ensued was not exactly small talk. It was almost like a friendly chat. It was, of course, of extremely short duration, but there seemed to be warmth and almost affection flowing from Murphy during those few seconds or minutes, which invariably ended with "Thanks, Bob, appreciate it." I always left the office feeling absurdly gratified, knowing that a few minutes small talk was Murphy's way of informing me that he was pleased with me.

Whatever impression he may have given on TV, to me

the essential Murphy exuded charisma. That is, he exuded power, and he also exuded the enjoyment of using his power. He was in command of the Police Department and the impotent mutterings in the hallways were just that—impotent mutterings. He was the man responsible for the excitement. He was the author of the new ideas. He was the man who made things happen. Although his lengthy typed memos were signed—by one or another of his secretaries—Patrick V. Murphy, brief scrawled messages would also arrive from him, and these handwritten notes were signed "M." A single letter, the royal seal.

The next examination for sergeant was about to be scheduled. Murphy sent around a memo suggesting that we explore with the city personnel director the possibilities of overcoming the extreme weight given to the written exam. "Mayor Lindsay is consistently troubled at our promotion ceremonies by the small number of blacks and Puerto Ricans advancing in rank. I share his concern.

"It is absurd that a man's prior performance on the job is meaningless in the promotion process. One result of this long-standing practice is the burden we carry in the persons of many captains, as well as lieutenants and sergeants, who cannot, or will not, function as effective managers or supervisors. Incidentally, we must find a way of forcing their retirements when they are eligible for pension.

"I'd like to explore the options available to us in building a performance evaluation component into future promotion exams.

"The recent federal court decision re: exams for school principals should be exploited in some way to help destroy the Civil Service—Delehantyitis which has come close to destroying the New York City Police Department [the Delehanty school tutored cops for promotion exams].

"Chief of Personnel: Please take responsibility for pursuing this."

At the same time the Police Commissioner asked that plans be drawn up requiring at least one year of college for each new policeman within a year or two, and a college degree for all promotions and for all new patrolmen within the next eight to ten years.

It now came to Murphy's attention that a 31-year-old black detective, John J. Grimes, had recently been forced to resign in order to accept a three-year scholarship to Harvard Law School. Police Department regulations had limited leaves of absence without pay to one year. Detective Grimes, having started law school, had made a number of requests for a three-year leave, and had been supported by District Attorney Thomas Mackell. It was "a most unusual circumstance which I thought deserved a favorable response—that is, a black member of a law enforcement agency receiving a scholarship to the most prestigious law school in the country," Mackell wrote Commissioner Leary. Leary passed this problem on to the then First Deputy Commissioner John Walsh, who ruled: "A legal education, while valuable and particularly so to a concerned individual, is not a priority study in our view."

Murphy now overruled this year-old decision, and ordered Detective Grimes reinstated at once, simultaneously according him the leave of absence he needed, and announcing also that henceforth any cop who wanted a leave of absence of any duration in order to attend college or graduate school, could have it. Traditionally, the Police Department, almost without realizing it, had been a foe of formal education—only three percent of the men on duty had any sort of college degree. Murphy knew of the Department's antipathy personally, because when he was a young cop he had found it impossible to schedule his tours so as to take regular college courses—he had lacked only one year for a degree at the time. Nor was this antipathy to education confined to New York. When he was Commissioner in Detroit, Murphy had instituted a program requiring some college education for police promotion. But no sooner had he left town than his successor scrapped the program.

But in New York now it was possible to believe that things were different. In New York one day Patrick Murphy walked in and slew all the know-nothings.

Murphy, who had been Police Commissioner now a few days under a year, had been on TV and in the headlines so often that he was known everywhere. He had begun to be mentioned as a candidate for mayor, and there were those who thought that he should be president, pointing out that his low-keyed, mild manner, which at first had seemed dull, by now seemed extremely honest and full of a certain deep strength. In addition, his talents as an administrator seemed extraordinary. He had organized men and ideas and time in a way that they had never been seen in a cop before. The Police Department had been like a gigantic gray battleship stuck in the mud for decades. Murphy had got it floating again, and under power again too.

One day I asked what he thought of all of the talk. Would he consider running for mayor?

He said he didn't think so, he was really too old (51) to start that career now. "Besides," he said, "I don't think I would be any good at making the kinds of deals that you have to make in the political world."

And so Murphy flew to Anaheim, California, for the Chiefs of Police convention, where his new fame had preceded him. At the last minute he was invited to make one of the keynote addresses. The inbred, insular Chiefs of Police there gathered, most from small towns, perhaps only wanted to bask in Murphy's reflected glory. Perhaps they were no more receptive to his strange new ideas than in the past. But at least this time they were listening. Some months later, meeting with Murphy in Delaware, a group of them would even vote for a motion favoring stronger gun control laws.

At Anaheim people stopped Murphy in the hallways, elevators, and even the streets of the town, and some of these people were chiefs of police but most were ordinary citizens who had seen him on television. First Deputy Commissioner Smith, who accompanied Murphy, later reported that only once was he able to talk to Murphy alone—one day they sat on the edge of the swimming pool and talked for an hour or more. "The rest of the time there were people all over Murphy the whole time," said Smith.

In Murphy's absence headquarters was a dull place to be. There were no top-level meetings, no press conferences, no ideas floating around. No business went forward for ten days. Out in the precincts, routine crime was handled in a routine way.

At last Murphy was back, and I was glad to see him but he greeted me matter-of-factly, and began immediately to talk business. As I left him I encountered Phil Lacovara, a young lawyer whom Murphy depended upon for legal advice. I said to Lacovara, "Murphy is not a demonstrative man, is he?"

Lacovara said: "You mean he didn't kiss you on the lips either?"

The Knapp Commission public hearings were exactly two weeks away and closing fast. Murphy appeared cautious but unworried. All of his programs were in place.

Elsewhere in the Police Department the mood was less confident. No one quite knew what evidence, what witnesses Knapp would put forth. First Deputy Smith had had detectives trying to find out for weeks, but Knapp was playing a tight hand, and no one could get a look at his cards. It was known that his investigators had caught a midtown patrolman named William Phillips committing some kind of corruption and had enlisted Phillips as an undercover agent. Phillips had been sent out wearing wires, closely tailed by Knapp agents who would record incriminating conversations between Phillips and other cops who would talk openly in front of Phillips, knowing him to be a crook too. Although the Police Commissioner had met with Knapp and with Michael Armstrong, Knapp's chief counsel, and although Murphy had moved Phillips from place to place at Knapp's request, the Police Commissioner had never been told what the results had been.

In fact Knapp and Armstrong seemed to play games at the Police Commissioner's expense. Murphy had appeared on a number of talk shows on national TV, once sharing the 90 minute "David Frost Show" with a number of police heroes, including Detectives Eddie Egan and Sonny Grosso, who nearly a decade before had broken a million-dollar narcotics smuggling ring. This had resulted in a book called *The French Connection,* and now the movie of the same name was about to open.

Later Armstrong remarked to Murphy, "We've been looking into the activities of those two guys. When I saw you appearing on TV with them, I couldn't believe my eyes."

Was this a veiled threat, or an empty one? Was Armstrong trying to scare him?

Similarly, two Brooklyn anti-crime patrolmen, David Greenberg and Robert Hantz, who because of their flamboyance and effectiveness had become known as Batman and Robin, turned in a man who tried to bribe them. This happened on a Saturday night, and on Sunday Murphy called me at home. He was considering promoting Batman and Robin to detective the next day. What did I think? Would I talk it over with the Chief Inspector?

But the Knapp Commission was interested in the "activities" of Batman and Robin also, which Codd knew though Murphy didn't, and Codd's reply when I called him was, "Let's put that one on the back burner for a while."

In the last few days before Knapp's public hearings opened, Murphy made a number of forceful public appearances. There was a press conference to announce that he had hired six civilian management specialists, one a Chicago lawyer, one a mathematics professor, another a computer technologist. There was too much inbreeding in the Police Department, Murphy declared, and not enough civilian expertise.

Next came a press conference in which Murphy announced that in the 18 days since his speech to the Chamber of Commerce, 45 arrests had been made for attempted bribery of police officers, as against eight such arrests in the 17 days preceding the speech.

Murphy thought he had found in bribery an exquisite battleground, one where Knapp could not even find him, much less fight him. Not only would the city applaud his stand but so would the cops. On the subject of bribery, Murphy could have it both ways.

But he had picked the wrong day. Dennis Dillon, a Justice Department lawyer who headed the Southern District Strike Force against organized crime, had just declared that his investigators in Brooklyn and Staten Island had found payoffs of up to $25,000 to teams of narcotics detectives. Dillon called police corruption "widespread."

And so Murphy sat behind microphones under bright lights, sweat visible on his scalp, and was bombarded by questions not about bribery arrests (which he wanted) but about "widespread" narcotics corruption (which he wasn't ready for). Murphy hadn't even heard the charges yet.

Bitter about the publicity and the headlines from Dillon's unsubstantiated charges, Murphy tentatively decided to call another press conference at which to refute Dillon, but first he wanted the rest of us to meet. He wanted to know exactly what evidence Dillon might have. This meeting was attended by Arthur Grubert, Chief of Intelligence; Syd Cooper, Chief of Inspectional Services; George Heubsch, Chief of the Public Morals Division; by First Deputy Smith and myself, and by Richard Condon, an intelligence lieutenant who had evidently done most of the legwork running down Dillon's charges.

The most vulnerable areas, then as always, were the plainclothes divisions working in gambling enforcement. These were the responsibility of Huebsch, and so all waited to hear what he would say. It was his opinion that Dillon had a few cases in Brooklyn, nothing in Staten Island.

What did Knapp have? Smith wanted to know.

"The Knapp Commission has done what the district attorneys never would let us do," Condon said. "They've turned guys around."

The phrase, to turn a man, or to turn a guy around, or to make a man roll over, all meant the same: to promise a crook immunity from prosecution if he would work for the prosecution. To work for the prosecution these days normally meant to go out wearing electronic devices, so as to record fellow crooks making damaging statements which later could be used as evidence in court.

Because the district attorneys would not allow the Police Department to use this tactic, the fight against corruption within the Department had never shown great success in the past. Now Knapp would come on and reap all the credit, the Police Department would be damaged as well, and all because the rules had been changed to favor Knapp.

And with this doleful warning, the meeting broke up.

The next morning the press conference was jammed. The Police Commissioner read a short speech that attempted to take at least some of the sting out of the upcoming Knapp Commission's hearings. Murphy admitted that there would be a number of indictments, perhaps as many as 20, growing out of the Knapp Commission investigations. "But what is so vitally important is that the people of this city always keep in mind there are far more honest policemen out doing their job than dishonest ones." Even if there were a thousand crooked cops, Murphy declared, "and I do not concede this figure for a moment," that still only added up to three percent of the force, a percentage which surely compared favorably to the number of crooked doctors, lawyers, judges, or members of any other profession.

Murphy declared that he was "angry about some of the recent statements" that used the expression "widespread corruption." He never mentioned Mr. Dillon by name. It was not fair for any official to claim "widespread" corruption without naming names or citing figures. "The 30,000 men of the New York Police Department deserve better than wild statements that are not supported," Murphy said.

Murphy's speech seemed to go over beautifully with most of those in attendance, including Chief Eli Lazarus, head of the Captains' Endowment Association. At last Murphy seemed to have swung over onto the side of his men. Chief Lazarus was chortling and grinning, rubbing his hands together. As Murphy moved away from the microphones, Lazarus leaned over until he was practically kissing the Police Commissioner, as he told Murphy how great the speech was.

However, one of the reporters present was David Burnham of *The New York Times*. Burnham had seemed to grow more and more outraged as the press conference unfolded. Toward the end he leaned forward to ask one question only of the Police Commissioner. He seemed barely able to control himself, though his voice was more or less normal, it wasn't choked, he wasn't shouting. He wanted to know if, when the police caught two or three criminals in a certain borough, did this mean that there were only two or three criminals out there? Was Murphy trying to claim that since only a few corrupt cops had been implicated in Mr. Dillon's investigation that there were only a few out there?

Murphy avoided Burnham's question. "I'm not satisfied that Mr. Dillon's statement was an accurate statement in all respects."

Burnham was a smoldering personality. He would nurse his wounds quietly, go back to the office and release all his venom via his typewriter. However, as he filed out of the room out of the crowd, he put his face very close to mine, and his cheeks were quivering as he said, "All that press conference was—was—was bullshit, and you can tell Pat that for me."

Murphy summoned Lacovara and me to his office and said, "Thank you, thank both of you."

Any sort of appreciation from Murphy, since it was so rare, always gratified his subordinates inordinately.

Looking back, it is clear that Murphy that day should have become aware that he was surrounded by fanatics, by David Burnham, and David Durk, and Michael Armstrong, and Whitman Knapp, and that these people intended to claw him to death if they could, and that blood was about to be shed. But Murphy seemed so calm, so sure of himself, that I personally wrote off the Knapp Commission as a serious threat in advance. Whatever might be coming in the next few days, Patrick Murphy would cope with it. The Police Commissioner of the City of New York was Patrick Murphy, and not anybody else, and we were lucky that this was the case.

Monday of the next week was the Columbus Day holiday. On Tuesday Murphy lunched with the editors of the *Daily News* in their dining room at the top of the *News* Building. On Wednesday he officiated at the promotions of five chiefs, six inspectors, seven deputy inspectors and 30 lieutenants, and later he drove up to the 40th Precinct in the Bronx to officiate at an award presentation to a hero cop. On Thursday morning he drove from home directly to the WCBS studios on 52nd Street, there to tape answers to questions sent in by listeners as part of the station's continuing "Ask the Commissioner" series. He lunched with the editors of *New York* magazine. On Friday, three days before the Knapp Commission hearings were to begin, Murphy came in early, moved through his regularly scheduled appointments, had lunch, canceled his late appointments, and went home early to be with his kids.

It was a quiet day. Nothing was happening. I met with the Chief of Detectives for a briefing on the current important cases, and afterward we chatted. Almost always Seedman had funny stories to tell, and today was no exception. He had been driving down the East Side Drive, heading for headquarters, running a little late, and he had told his chauffeur to step on it. They were exceeding the speed limit by 5 to 10 miles per hour, when suddenly a motorcycle policeman pulled alongside, waving them over. The police plate was lying between them on the seat of the car, and so Seedman pressed this plate up against the glass. The plate bore one word, POLICE in capital letters, these plates were official, and Seedman assumed that the motorcycle cop would now drop back out of sight. Instead the guy shook his head violently, and motioned the car to pull over.

Seedman got out of the car, walked up to the motorcycle cop, and showed his Chief of Detectives shield.

"I showed you the police plate," Seedman said, "so why did you pull us over?"

"How did I know who you were? Everybody and his brother has those police plates," said the cop.

Seedman said, "Now that you know who I am, are you going to give me a summons?"

"No," said the motorcycle cop. "But can I ask your chauffeur to write down his name and shield number on a piece of paper and give it to me?"

Seedman said, "No you can't, but you can write down your own name and shield number on a piece of paper, and give it to me."

When he got back to headquarterters, Seedman had sent for Fred Kowsky, Chief of the Traffic Division, and handed him the motorcycle cop's name and shield number, saying, "Freddy, take care of this guy for me, will you please."

It was such a quiet Friday afternoon that presently I asked my chauffeur to bring the car around in front, and I had him drive me home. About six o'clock my duty sergeant called to say that the Chief Inspector was trying to get in touch with me, and I was given a number at which to call him. I made several attempts at this number but got no answer, but I was not unduly concerned. If Chief Codd wanted to reach me, he would reach me.

About two hours after that the phone rang again, and this time the duty sergeant said, "Murphy just flopped Seedman."

"What?"

"Seedman is out as Chief of Detectives."

"What?"

"It's got something to do with corruption."

Behind the wheel of the radio car parked in the middle of the night on 65th Street near the corner of Amsterdam Avenue sat one bored cop.

"Can you believe it?" he remarked to his partner on the seat beside him, "A Friday night in this town being this dead?"

The young cop's name was Ralph Mannetta. He was born May 7, 1945, so at this moment he was 26 years old.

Tonight it was Mannetta's job to patrol Sector B, 20th Precinct, which he had been doing since midnight. Sector B was seven blocks long, running from 59th to 66th Streets, extending in width from West End Avenue to Amsterdam Avenue. It was a single ice cube out of the tray that was the 20th Precinct, and the precinct was a single ice cube out of the bigger tray that was Manhattan Island.

Sector B, 20th Precinct, included some empty lots, some parking garages, some brownstones and apartment buildings, and one enormous housing project, whose roadways and parking lots had to be patrolled. The back of the Lincoln Center theater complex scraped one side of Sector B, and early in the tour Mannetta drove past hordes of exiting theatergoers. Later, the last stragglers moved into his sector to their cars, and then out again.

That was hours ago, and since then, nothing. The radio sounded like it was broken, nothing.

The cop, Ralph Mannetta, continued to steer up one street, and down another. He and his partner, Paul Dellacona, peered into the doorways, into whatever dim hallways were visible, and sometimes there were loiterers whom their glance sent scurrying. Sometimes Mannetta turned into the one-way streets against the nonexistent traffic, perhaps to glide slowly up on some malefactor or other, some crime in progress, from an unexpected direction. But tonight he saw no malefactor anywhere; no crime in progress seemed to exist.

Now it was between two thirty and three o'clock in the morning. The streets were empty. The lights had gone off in most of the buildings.

The radio was so silent that the two cops had fiddled with the dials from time to time to make it squawk.

The cop, Mannetta, had no idea that anything was about to happen to him. His gun was in his holster, half tucked under his thigh. He was so used to its weight and bulk that he was not aware that again tonight he was virtually sitting on it. There were six bullets in the chamber, and 12 more, by regulation, in his belt.

The ceiling light was on. A moment ago, at an all-night diner, Mannetta had pulled to a stop. He got out, stretched, and bought coffee in cardboard containers for himself and his partner, while Paul stayed with the car. Then he forced himself to climb back into the car. The radio car's front seat was half caved in, and springs prodded them both, though the car looked new from the outside. But it had rolled 24 hours a day, seven days a week, since it was put in service, and would continue to do so for as long as it lasted. The front seat, deformed by ten or more different drivers each week, was always the first casualty. It had ceded to various cops' weight in various directions and by now conformed to the spread of none of them.

Mannetta, who had parked, had the still closed cardboard container of coffee in his left hand, and with his right he reached into the back seat for tomorrow morning's *New York Times,* which he had bought as he came on duty and tossed back there. He unfolded the paper across the steering wheel. His heart beat was normal, his hands steady.

Mannetta smoothed the newspaper across the steering wheel, took his first sip of the coffee he would never finish, and began to scan the headlines. There was not much there to interest a 26-year-old patrolman. The lead headline read: Japan Agrees to Restrict Flow of Textiles into U.S. Below that: Water Vapor Has Been Found on the Moon. Also: Harvard Economist Wins the Nobel Prize. In the left hand corner: Murphy Removes Detective Chief Pending Inquiry.

Mannetta began to read this story, although he had never seen either Commissioner Murphy or Chief of Detectives Seedman, and did not expect to. To him they were august personages, and their names were part of his life, but not their faces, and certainly not their careers.

History stretched away from the young cop in both directions. He sat alone on a pinnacle that was moving. He was not at the moment aware of this idea, or of anything else except for his paper and his coffee.

He had been a cop four years. He had never fired a revolver in his life until, at the Police Academy, they thrust one into his hand. Although a number of his classmates there perforated bulls-eyes with regularity, he himself was only an average shooter. Since leaving the Academy it had never been necessary for him to fire his service revolver either in warning or at a suspect.

He was 5 feet 11 inches tall, smooth-cheeked, with a set of beautiful white teeth such as movie actors pay dentists $10,000 for. He grew up in an Italian neighborhood in Brooklyn and considered himself a tough kid. As a teenager he hung out in poolrooms and knew guys who worked for the Franzese mob. After high school he tried many jobs. Once he worked as a ticket agent in a bus terminal, and another time for a stock broker. Between jobs he shot pool. Pool and the football Jets were his passions.

His wife Marie was virtually the only girlfriend he ever had. At 16 she gave him a signet ring which he still wore. Her father owned a small soda factory; his truck delivered soda to the local pool hall, among other places, and the truck driver kept telling the girl's father that Mannetta was no good—he was always in the pool room. The father tried to break up the romance, but failed. After Mannetta applied for the Police Department he and Marie got married. They were both 21. Mannetta said he chose the Police Department because it represented security. He was always one to think ahead. For instance, each spring he would try to sign up fellow patrolmen for a bus ride to the Jets—Giants August exhibition game in the Yale Bowl. It would only cost $7.50, everything included, he would tell them. But he could never get enough fellow cops to part with that much money that far in advance, and the bus ride always fell through.

At this moment, sipping coffee in his radio car, Mannetta owned a pleasant mortgaged house in a distant Long Island suburb. He and Marie had two small sons. He didn't want to be a patrolman all his life. He wanted to make a big success of some kind. He was an aggressive cop. He made a lot of arrests, worked a lot of overtime. If a number of cops responded to a dispute, Mannetta was usually the one to take charge, to push to the front, interrogate the complainant, listen to the defendant, and then—very quickly—to decide whether to make an arrest or not.

Mannetta wanted to be noticed by the bosses, and in fact had been. The 20th Precinct had a complement of about 250 men and the commanding officer, Captain Dave Pascal didn't know half of them, but he knew Mannetta and often joked with him.

"Jesus, it's quiet," Mannetta said to his partner.

By this time on an average Friday night they should have done at least four jobs, maybe even six or seven; there should have been maybe a family fight, or a prowler run, or an aided case of some kind, or a brawl in a bar, or all of these things.

But tonight, nothing.

At this moment the radio spoke: "Signal 10-85, patrolman holding three, Amsterdam Avenue at 85th Street, which car responding?"

Probably some citizen had telephoned 911, the police emergency number, and given information. This information may or may not be accurate, it may or may not be complete. It could be a false alarm. It could be the response of a citizen awakened by noise downstairs, or peering out the window in the middle of the night at a scene across the street he could not measure and did not comprehend.

The request did not originate via police radio; Mannetta would have heard it.

The police operator sitting in the bustling and brightly lighted radio room on the fourth floor of the otherwise dark and nearly empty headquarters building, at 240 Centre Street, far downtown, had interpreted the citizen's phone call as a 10-85, and had so transmitted it on the frequency used by 20th Precinct radio cars.

The signal 10-85 was a request for additional men. It indicated no urgency. The event, whatever it was, was apparently over.

In this case, Mannetta understood that a cop had arrested three persons and needed another car to get them to the station house. Normally on such a dull night, such a call would draw cars from all over the precinct. A bored-enough cop would respond to anything.

And in fact, this began to happen even now.

When the radio spoke again, Mannetta recognized the voice of his friend Sal Rosato. Rosato's sector was the adjoining one, and Rosato, who in a moment would be shot, calmly announced he would respond to the scene.

Mannetta and Dellacona, his partner of six months, eyed each other. They were not needed uptown, and they had just started on their coffee. The job was more than 20 blocks away. Without a word spoken, they decided to sit where they were.

Suddenly the radio blurted, "Sector car responding to that 10-85 please be advised it's a possible 10-30, robbery in progress. Proceed with caution."

So a second phone call, slightly less vague than the first, must have gone in to headquarters.

Mannetta flung his coffee out the window. So did his partner. Their radio car began speeding uptown, siren wailing, dome light turning. Mannetta had no idea what he was driving toward. He was reasonably certain that other cars, many of them now, were converging on that same corner. Sirens were approaching it from all directions. Dome lights whirled, spilling red and white light onto the walls of the many buildings rushing by.

It could still be a false alarm. Probably that's what it was.

Mannetta's radio car sped uptown on Amsterdam Avenue. He had to slow at each intersection, not wanting to crash into some citizen, or perhaps another radio car, and his engine was so worn that its pickup each time was sluggish.

He kept one eye on the street signs flashing by.

He had reached 72nd Street when a panicky voice that Mannetta didn't recognize, not Central, some other cop, came on the radio. "We have a cop shot. Signal 10-13. Signal 10-13."

"It's Sal who's been shot," muttered Mannetta. "I know it is. Sal's been shot."

Mannetta knew that in the sector adjacent to Rosato's there was a car with two rookies in it. The voice must belong to one of these newcomers.

Within a few seconds, the 10-85 had become a possible 10-30, and then a certain 10-13. Mannetta rammed his accelerator into the floor.

Now the radio filled up with the babble of other voices; and the noise of sirens.

"What is the exact location, Central?" Mannetta could barely make out the words because of the sirens, his own and that of the cop transmitting.

"Shots fired confirmed. Cars responding, proceed with caution."

"How many perpetrators, Central?"

But Central did not know. "Report of a patrolman shot. Signal 10-13. Proceed with caution."

As Mannetta neared 85th Street, he heard more shots fired. There was an empty radio car, dome light flashing, blocking the entrance to 85th Street, and now a second radio car backed out of the street and sped away. A wounded cop, or perhaps a dead one, was being rushed to a hospital. There was no other possible explanation.

On the radio, a voice cried: "They're running along 85th Street toward Columbus Avenue."

This was hard information, if it was accurate.

Mannetta decided to block 85th Street at Columbus Avenue. He raced across 86th, turned down Columbus Avenue, jammed on the brakes; and as he and his partner leaped from the car, they heard another fusillade of shots. Mannetta's gun was out. He had no idea what had happened, or was about to happen.

Another radio car was on the street, two, three. One had its back window shot out.

The first person Mannetta spied was his friend Sal being hurried to a radio car. Sal's face was white, and his mouth hung open. He appeared unable to speak. He recognized no one. His hand was clutched to his middle. Blood ran down his hand and his coat. He was pushed into the car, the siren came on, and that car too sped toward Roosevelt Hospital.

The glass doors of the apartment building close to the corner had been shot out. The pavement was covered with glass, and with fragments of brick and plaster, and with empty bullet casings.

A cop named Mohrmann cried, "They just ran in there.

I think three of them. They got everything. They got carbines, shotguns, automatics. They got everything. I wouldn't be surprised if they got hand grenades."

"What happened?"

"They blasted Gary Hunt. He had holes all over him."

Mannetta knew Hunt to be a 21-year-old rookie just out of recruit training.

"Is he dead?"

"I don't know."

Hunt possibly killed, Sal apparently gut shot. Three heavily armed men to go in that building after.

"What happened?"

"They stuck up the Red Carpet Lounge. Hunt was the first car. He drives up thinking it's something else, and they come out shooting. He went down. Then more radio cars came. They ran down this street to here, stopping to fire every time they saw a radio car. We chased them on foot. Everybody was shooting. Sal got hit."

Mannetta supposed that, seeing so many radio cars converging on the two corners, the street now encircled, the gunmen had run into the nearest building. Perhaps they planned to escape over the rooftops. Perhaps they knew this building, would barricade themselves, and shoot it out.

Half a dozen or more cops now congregated outside the building. Glass grated under foot. They were all patrolmen. No one was entitled by rank to take command.

A man ran up in civilian clothes. His automatic hung in his fist against his leg. No one knew him. Perhaps he was a detective, or an off-duty cop from some other part of the city. One by one the cops eyed him. He was with them. Without challenging him, they opened ranks and he was admitted.

The eight men now entered the building over the glass. They moved forward along the hallway, close to the walls.

The hallway was empty. The gunmen must have gone up the stairs, how high no one knew. There were two staircases which mounted apparently to the roof. No one knew how high the building was, or if it gave onto other rooftops —most of the buildings on this street seemed to be low brownstones.

Mannetta supposed no one had checked the elevator. He

was so uptight that, as he pushed the button, he also cocked his gun. It was three o'clock in the morning and no one was supposed to be in that elevator. As the doors slid open, he was pressed to the wall, ready to blast anything inside that elevator that moved.

But there was nothing.

Mannetta was so relieved he took no precautions as he let the hammer drop back onto the loaded chamber. Most times, handled this way, the gun would fire. Explosive relief. This time it did not.

The board inside the elevator showed that the building was 13 stories high. If the gunmen expected to escape over rooftops, they picked the wrong building. This one was surrounded by air.

Meaning that they were still up there somewhere, and he was one of those who must root them out.

The search began.

Some men went up one staircase, some up the other. At each landing, cops gingerly pushed open the steel door onto the hallway. Gun barrels and noses protruded into the dim light.

Each hallway was only about 30 feet long—10 yards for a first down, no more. Five apartments gave off each floor, but there were nine doors to check out: the elevator door, a service closet, and the two steel doors which concealed the front and back stairways. On each hallway these two stairway doors nearly faced each other, only four feet apart across the hall.

Tension increased. The gunmen were somewhere just above and cornered. The cops approached the sky, and the gunmen were between them and it, getting nearer. Each cop was stretched nearly to his limit in the foyer, but now it got worse. They had been taught in the Police Academy not to cock their guns in combat, lest they blow away each other, or some citizen. But one by one, the guns cocked. Mannetta could hear them click.

Each floor was a conquest. Once Mannetta pushed open his door onto a landing, and simultaneously, across the four-foot hall, the other stairway door opened too. The two cops eyed each other, gun muzzles nearly touching. First the two muzzles drooped, then the two pairs of eyes. It was a miracle that they hadn't shot each other, and they knew it.

On nearly every floor apartment doors flew open. Faces peered out.

"Say, officer, what's going on here?"

"Close that door."

"But you woke my wife out of a sound sleep—"

"Close the fucking door."

Mannetta had lost his partner. He could not say how or where, but Paul was gone, and at his side was someone else.

Close to the roof, there was a commotion. As Mannetta came out onto the penthouse floor hallway, having found no one during his 13-floor ascent, he saw a black man in handcuffs being hustled toward the elevators.

Cops and prisoner disappeared. Seven cops and the un-known guy in civilian clothes had started up the stairwells. Two had just gone down with the prisoner; there should have been six cops left, including the detective, or whatever he was.

But this wasn't the case. On the penthouse landing stood Ralph Mannetta, and another cop he didn't know, with whom he had just climbed 13 flights.

For the first time Mannetta noticed the guy's insignia— he was from the 23rd Precinct across Central Park, on the other side of the island.

He must have answered the 10-13. A cop in trouble.

They stared at each other. They had never seen each other before. Perhaps the same thought ran through both their heads: If you want to do it by the book, then you no-tify headquarters that the stickup men have run into the building, you surround the building, covering all possible exits, and after that you wait till the emergency service guys get here with the shotguns and the bulletproof vests. Hoping meanwhile that the perpetrators—that was the word cops thought in—don't kill anyone, or take hostages.

The two cops never even asked each other's names.

Without a word, Mannetta in the lead, they mounted the last flight of stairs to the roof.

At such a time, what flowed through a man's brain was not his whole life, but the years of technique. They had been trained never to do certain things:

For instance, one never walked in front of a car with a suspect in it.

For instance, one never ran up 13 flights and out onto a roof, out of breath, heart already pounding, hand shaking. Never.

The staircase came up onto a cramped landing ending in a steel door out onto the roof. Mannetta tested it. It was not locked.

He knew there was someone out there, probably two of them. They were armed, cornered, desperate. They had already shot two cops. He searched his mind for other knowledge which might help him. There was none. He had no idea what the roof looked like. He had no idea how much cover there would be out there, or how much light. He himself would be framed in the doorway. They could blast him right away, perhaps throw a hand grenade at him. Would he be able to see them at all? How much light was there down on the street? He couldn't remember. Was there a moon? Any stars? What kind of guns did they have? In an ambush any gun was good enough, though certain ones would kill him quicker.

They must be scared too. But they had positioned themselves. They knew the door he would have to come out of.

He knew that they were out there, and that they had already shot two cops.

Mannetta did not want to go out onto that roof.

From inside he gave the door a violent kick, flattening himself against the wall as he did so.

The door flew open, slammed backwards against the wall, and sprang shut again.

Mannetta was instructed in the Police Academy to kick doors open like that, should the occasion ever arise. The suspect was tense too, and if the sudden noise and movement caused him to start shooting, at least you knew where he was.

But nothing happened.

Mannetta was so tight that he kicked the door open a second time, and then still again. There was no response from outside.

The third time, the other cop caught the door before it

shut, holding it open at a 90° angle. Then Ralph Mannetta, husband of Marie, age 26, father of Ken, four, and Scott, three, fan of the football Jets, stepped onto the roof.

He was pressed flat against the wall beside the doorway. At his back was the housing for the stairwell and elevator gear. The half-open steel door protected his left flank. But it also hid most of the left side of the roof.

It was very dark. Out of this darkness, any second, he expected to hear and feel the shotgun blast that would kill him.

The rooftop seemed to be the size of a large living room, and it was as cluttered with furnishings, but was no place to relax.

Mannetta's doorway stood about 15 feet in front of the low wall that rimmed the rooftop, and eight feet from the side wall. In front of Mannetta, like a huge rolled-up rug, ran some sort of ventilator conduit behind which a man or men could be hiding. It was so high and thick that it was meant to be crossed by means of a small wrought-iron bridge.

Mannetta expected a face and gun—or two faces and two guns—to jump up from behind that conduit. Any second it would happen. He could do nothing about that yet. He must check out his right flank first.

Inching swiftly to the edge of the wall at his back, Mannetta peered around the corner there. More ventilator conduits. The conduits used up most of the thin space between the wall of the housing, and the wall of the roof. On that side Mannetta could see no one.

All this Mannetta saw and decided within seconds.

"This side is clear," he called out.

Four feet in front of him, bisecting the open part of the roof, ran the major conduit. He could cross this via the wrought-iron footbridge, but it would frame him, exposing him front and back for a second or more. He would have to hurdle it, perhaps leaping right into the muzzle blast, a duck shot out of the air. He wanted to jump back inside the door. A hundred other cops would be here in a while. Let them do it.

Mannetta hurdled the conduit.

At this moment the other cop stepped out onto the roof,

and the door swung shut behind him.

While still in the air Mannetta saw that the other side of the conduit was empty.

Perhaps it was the noise of the slamming door that caused Mannetta to spin around, facing back toward his partner.

Close beside the now closed door was a kind of brick-and mortar lean-to nine feet high. Perhaps it contained tools, or ventilator machinery. Its narrow roof extended about three feet out from the wall, a ledge as long as the body of a man.

On this ledge, which previously had been locked from view by the half-open door, lay a man with a gun. The gun, a revolver like his own, seemed to Mannetta as huge as a cannon.

"Look out," cried Mannetta, and in that instant, for the first time that night, he had all the facts and details that he needed to know, every one. On that single instant in time, his life, and the gunman's life, and the night itself focused in.

Then the instant was over. It was all in the past. It could never be reproduced. It was gone. Mannetta had ripped off three shots. He heard them sock home. He heard the sharp intake of breath that was the audible terror of the other cop, whose name Mannetta still didn't know, as those shots flew directly over his head.

In the next instant there was silence again. Nothing happened. Nothing at all.

Then the man rolled sideways off the roof. Below him the huge conduit made an abrupt turn into the lean-to. He smacked down onto the conduit, still rolling. He rolled off it onto some pipes that thrust up out of the tar paper.

There were audible thunks each time. The man struck the tar paper and lay still. The sheriff had won the shoot-out. The desperado lay at his feet.

Back to back, guns ready, eyes straining in the dark, the two cops examined the rest of that portion of the roof.

Nothing.

The stickup man lay at Mannetta's feet.

Mannetta supposed him dead. Leaning down, Mannetta recovered a .357 Magnum. On the lean-to roof lay a carbine with a fully loaded banana clip.

Now came a commotion on the other side of the elevator housing. Cops stepped onto the roof from the other stairwell. Voices informed Mannetta that another suspect had been captured in the penthouse apartment below. So three gunmen had run into the building, but all were now in custody.

The door opened once more, and an Emergency Service patrolman lumbered onto the roof. He wore a bulletproof vest complete with helmet and steel mask, and he carried a shutgun. He looked to Mannetta like the Tin Woodman.

"You're too late," mumbled Mannetta, looking down at the man he had shot. "It's all over."

Voices babbled.

"Who is he?"

"Who knows?"

"Or cares."

With flashlights the cops made a careful search of the rooftop. They were looking principally for discarded guns. They found none.

The body in Mannetta's flashlight beam stirred.

"The bastard's still alive."

Mannetta searched him, removing a bandolier containing 24 bullets, and another loaded banana clip.

On a borrowed walkie-talkie Mannetta tried to raise headquarters. This man must be taken down off the roof and removed to a hospital. Mannetta kept shouting, "Twenty Boy to Central," into the walkie-talkie, but no answer came back.

Presently Mannetta slung the gunman over his shoulder. The gunman was Mannetta's prisoner, and no one else wanted to carry him down. Mannetta's felt the man's weight on him. He felt the tar-paper bubbles crushing underfoot. He could hear the blood drip. Going down the stairs from the roof, the drip was louder, the spots spread beside his shoes, and he was careful not to step in them and slip. Someone had immobilized the elevator. He half dragged, half carried the gunman down 13 flights.

In the street Mannetta saw a number of radio cars, but no ambulance. The sidewalk had been roped off and hung with placards declaring it a crime scene, but beyond the rope waited two dozen angry black people, who began screaming obscenities. As Mannetta ducked under the rope with his burden, hands began to rake at him. Mannetta understood that these were the patrons of the Red Carpet Lounge. Less than 20 minutes ago they had been forced to lie on the floor there. Though the gunmen had addressed their victims as "brothers," they had robbed them of their money and jewelry nonetheless. Two "brothers" had been pistol-whipped by the gunmen as well.

Now these two dozen men and women tried to tear loose Mannetta's prisoner. Fists punched at the handcuffed, bleeding, unconscious gunman. They would kill him if they could. Cops rushed to Mannetta's aide. An alley was formed to the nearest radio car. The door was opened, and Mannetta threw the wounded man in on the back seat.

He got in the front. "Roosevelt Hospital," he ordered.

But this car too was from somewhere across the city. Like all cops, this radio car team knew the locations of hospitals in its own precinct, but not here, and Mannetta had to explain where Roosevelt was.

Dawn was breaking before Mannetta left the hospital. He had learned that Patrolman Hunt, shot in three places, had been operated on and would survive, that his friend Sal, who had been led to the radio car with blood dripping down his hand and coat, had been shot in the hand, not the gut, and was okay.

The sun was up as Mannetta came out into the street. The gunman was still upstairs on an operating table, one slug in his stomach, another in his leg. Mannetta's principal emotion at this moment was hunger. He didn't care whether the gunman lived or died. Forensic personnel had responded to the hospital to roll the man's limp fingers onto fingerprint cards. In a few hours his identity would be known with certainty, although Mannetta did not see what significance this could have. A stickup man was a stickup man.

Mannetta had not eaten since 5 P.M. the night before. He was ravenously hungry.

At 68th Street, reporters swarmed around the station house doors. Mannetta was hurried past them inside, a prisoner himself. The place was crowded with inspectors,

chiefs, assistant district attorneys, FBI agents, men Mannetta had never seen before.

A detective whispered to him, "Do you know who you
shot?"

"No."

"They say it's H. Rap Brown. Don't say I told you."

Mannetta was so hungry he could scarcely think.

The brass surrounded Mannetta, interrogating him.
What did he see? hear? do?

"Who was up on the roof with you?"

"Some cop from some other precinct. I think he was
from the Two-three."

"What was his name?"

"I don't know."

Later he learned it: Patrolman Mario Toppi.

The interrogation continued. What were the distances?
the elapsed time? How many shots were fired in all?

"Can I get something to eat?"

"Plenty of time for that later."

The interrogation was endless. He told his story to one
group, and as it moved off satisfied, he was immediately
surrounded by another.

"I sure could use something to eat."

He learned that two loaded shotguns, one carbine, one
.38 special, one .357 Magnum, a 9 mm. Luger and over
3000 rounds of ammunition had been seized from the prisoners. A fourth gunman was arrested in the street by detectives.

The guy in civilian clothes, it turned out, was a New
York State Treasury agent who had been drinking in Don-
ohue's bar when the shooting started. It was he who had arrested one of the gunmen in the stairwell opposite Mannetta's. He had made his statement and gone home. Because
he wasn't a cop, the brass couldn't hold him. But the eight
cops involved—this included Hunt's partner and Sal's
partner—were all being held incommunicado until their
statements were taken down and checked out.

It had become mid-morning. Mannetta was sleepy. He
was trying to remember who H. Rap Brown might be. A
black militant of some kind. A fugitive. One of the FBI's
ten most wanted men. Principally Mannetta concentrated

on how hungry he was. He could think of almost nothing else.

The decision was now made to take Mannetta back onto the rooftop, to describe his actions for the investigators and the police photographer.

As Mannetta stepped out onto the roof this time, he was almost overcome by the sudden onrush of terror. In sunlight he saw how close everything was.

Blood rushed to his face, and as suddenly drained away. He swallowed hard.

The roof was tiny. There was cover enough there for any number of perpetrators, cover he didn't even perceive in the dark. The roof of the lean-to on which Rap Brown had lain loomed almost directly over the head of whoever stepped out the door onto the tar paper. Bullets could have struck Mannetta in the top of the skull; he would now be lying dead in a stained uniform in an impromptu morgue, while out front the Mayor made a speech to newsmen.

If the other cop hadn't held the steel door half open . . . if the gunman had been on one knee instead of prone . . .

By now the blood would be dry on the uniform of the slain cop, himself.

The iron footbridge, Mannetta saw, crossed the conduit within 10 feet of the man's gun muzzle. If Mannetta had crossed by the bridge, instead of hurdling it . . .

"Can I get something to eat now?"

At 11 A.M. they at last brought him something to eat.

"Can I go home?"

They told him that there would be a press conference at the station house this afternoon. The Police Commissioner was coming and would want to congratulate him. Had he not noticed the mobs of newsmen and TV crews out front? This was a controversial case. It was the most important case of the year. He would have to stay where he was.

Mannetta waited. For an instant last night he was in command. Now he was a subordinate again. He was a patrolman and could be ordered around by almost anyone.

Afternoon came. Commissioner Murphy shook his hand, but scarcely seemed to see him, his mind no doubt on weightier matters. Murphy, Mannetta, the other seven cops, the other police brass, all filed out of the precinct commander's office into the big room, which was packed. The blinding lights came on, newscasters shouted orders to their technicians.

Murphy read: "H. Rap Brown has been missing 17 months, since May of 1970, at which time a car exploded in which friends of his were riding, in Bel Air, Maryland. He was affiliated with The Student Nonviolent Coordinating Committee. He was wanted for one trial in Maryland and for another in Louisiana at that time. The Maryland charges were arson and inciting to riot, and failure to appear for trial. The Louisiana charge was assult on a federal officer.

"The bodies in the car were fragmented, and some believed that Brown was killed in that blast.

"H. Rap Brown was captured on the roof of 102 West 85th Street. Patrolman Ralph Mannetta, who made the arrest, is here to tell you about it."

Mannetta, shocked that he had to speak, stepped behind the forest of microphones, and mumbled three or four sentences. "I stepped out onto the roof. I turned and saw the perpetrator pointing a gun at me, so I fired."

After two dozen words the hero could think of nothing more to say.

A television reporter, seeking to impress his millions of viewers, asked in dramatic tones, each work sounding separate, heavy with import, "Patrolman, did you shoot Rap Brown?"

Mannetta stared at the floor. He licked his lips. Then he managed to look the man in the eye. Sounding almost ashamed, he answered, "Yes, sir."

3 / The Fate of the Chief of Detectives

At approximately 11:30 that morning Chief Seedman had received a phone call from Julius Impellezzeri, one of the Knapp Commission lawyers. Impellezzeri had had some important points he wanted to discuss. How soon could the Chief of Detectives receive him? Seedman had said come right over, and Impellezzeri did.

Seedman had had visits from the Knapp Commission before. So had a number of people in the police hierarchy.

This time Impellezzeri got right down to business. Some months ago the Knapp Commission had begun investigating what was apparently common practice by many of the major midtown hotels: the granting of free meals, and in some cases free lodging, to police personnel. Impellezzeri now was in possession of a list of policemen who had apparently accepted free meals at the Hilton, the Americana and the Plaza. The highest-ranking name on this list was Chief of Detectives Albert Seedman. What did Seedman have to say about the appearance of his name on this damning list?

"You got me," said the Chief of Detectives. "I guess I better put my papers in."

This response, Impellezzeri later said, proved that Seedman was aware both of the gravity of the charge and that the Knapp Commission had him cold. His only choice, therefore, was to retire.

To Seedman, his remark was a joke. If making it was a mistake, then the mistake was this: He had shown irreverence for people who took themselves very, very seriously.

Impellezzeri had an $84 dinner check from the Hilton signed in Chief Seedman's name. The check was dated March 6. This was more than seven months ago, when Seedman was not yet Chief of Detectives. Seedman wondered why the Knapp Commission was bringing this dinner up now, three days in advance of the public hearings, and this is exactly what Commissioner Murphy and the rest of the police hierarchy were going to wonder also, a few hours later.

Seedman explained that he had done some consulting work for the Hilton, and as a result had been offered dinner there. Come any night, the man had said. Bring friends if you like. On March 6 he had appeared with his wife and another couple, had asked for the bill, and was told there was no bill. So he left a big tip and walked out.

Impellezzeri wanted to know the nature of the consulting work. Seedman said he had been asked to take a security reading on the hotel, and he did this and was able to offer them some advice.

Impellezzeri nodded, and went back to the Knapp Commission offices.

At first Seedman decided that Impellezzeri's visit was of no importance, but as the afternoon wore on he began to brood about it, and he decided to speak to Commissioner Murphy. However, Murphy was at first too busy to see him, and when Seedman reappeared in Murphy's outer office he found that the Police Commissioner had already left for home for the day. After brooding a bit longer, Seedman went downstairs and into Chief Inspector Codd's office. People were coming and going. Seedman waited for the office to clear out so he could talk to Codd in private. However, Codd's phone now rang. It was First Deputy Commissioner Smith summoning Codd to Smith's office on the third floor.

Codd said, "You wanted to see me, Al?"

Seedman said, "I'll wait till you get back."

Codd said, "I don't know what it is. It shouldn't be more than a few minutes."

Seedman sat in Codd's office, waiting.

Impellezzeri had returned to the Knapp Commission offices, where he went into conference with Michael Armstrong and Whitman Knapp. Presently they prepared a page-and-a-half memo to Commissioner Murphy about their investigation into free meals offered to cops by the midtown hotels. Attached to this memo was a Xerox copy of the $84 check signed in the name of, but not by, Chief Seedman.

The memo reached Commissioner Murphy about three o'clock, and he called in First Deputy Commissioner Bill Smith. Murphy's office was on the second floor at the northern end of the headquarters building. Smith's was directly above it, connected by a private staircase and also by a three-passenger bird-cage elevator. Murphy handed Smith the Knapp memo, told him to get together with the Chief Inspector and decide what should be done. Murphy then, inexplicably went home.

About two hours passed before Smith got around to working on the memo. At that point he summoned the Chief Inspector. Also present in Smith's office was Phil Lacovara, Special Counsel to the Police Commissioner.

These three men, presently to be joined by the brand-new Deputy Commissioner for Organized Crime Control, William McCarthy, now met to decide the fate of Chief of Detectives Al Seedman.

Lacovara, who had recently turned 28 years old, had six children, and his wife was pregnant with their seventh. He was a small young man, shorter than Murphy, and he stood out among the Police Commissioner's other close advisers, all of whom were six-footers or better, all of whom were in their forties or fifties, and all of whom (except for myself) had been professional policemen all their lives. Lacovara's appearance was scholarly. He wore rimless glasses, and vests, and his short figure was already somewhat ample. His black hair was worn long, and he wore a mustache. He had graduated first in his class at Xavier High School, a New York City Military Academy; he earned his college degree from Georgetown in three years, graduating magna cum laude, then led his class at Columbia Law School for each of three years, graduating summa cum laude and winning the John Ordronaux Prize as outstanding graduate. Before long he had a job as assistant to Thurgood Marshall, then the Solicitor General of the United States, now a Supreme Court Justice, exactly the type of juicy job every law graduate hoped for but that only the brightest got.

Lacovara had been recruited by the Mayor's Talent Search office, an office within the city's budget bureau. It collected résumés on thousands of people. Shortly after Murphy became Commissioner, he had informed this office that he was looking for an executive assistant, someone with a civilian background, and probably a lawyer, for Murphy was the first Police Commissioner in 20 years who was not a lawyer himself. The Talent Search office had sent over a batch of résumés, one of them Lacovara's, and later Lacovara had met with Murphy twice. The second time, Murphy hired him. Lacovara had asked only that his title be changed from executive assistant to something more in keeping with his legal background. Lacovara suggested "Special Counsel to the Police Commissioner," and Murphy agreed. Lacovara had completed his duties with the Wall Street law firm for which he then worked, and had moved into a cubbyhole office in police headquarters the previous February 15—approximately three weeks before Albert Seedman was named Chief of Detectives.

Lacovara, who had a sort of professional mind, had begun by interviewing various cops, for he knew nothing about the police. He interviewed Chief Inspector Codd, Chief of Personnel Cooper, the Police Commissioner's chauffeurs, and also many of the cops who worked as clerks in the Police Commissioner's outer office; and within three weeks he was able to begin writing detailed and quite astute memos to the Police Commissioner on the problems facing the Police Department, and on the directions in which the Police Department ought to be heading. Murphy was most impressed.

Lacovara always spoke in slow, measured cadences. There was no hint of passion in his voice ever. His arguments were carefully marshaled so that anyone could see exactly what he was driving at. On the whole, all of the top cops—and this included most of the deputy commissioners—were men of strong feelings, and therefore strong opinions. Murphy, who apparently distrusted emotion of any kind, virtually refused to listen to any argument put forward emotionally. Lacovara's arguments, on the other hand, were always cool, detached, and more and more Murphy warmed to them and to him.

At the beginning, Murphy had urged that Lacovara go out into the precincts, ride in radio cars, find out what police work was like. Lacovara had still never found time to ride in a radio car, had still never been to a crime scene; but he had recently read a great many books on police theory, and his influence on the Police Commissioner, much to the annoyance of many of Murphy's other top subordinates, was by now out of all proportion to his age and experience.

At this moment in the First Deputy Commissioner's office, Lacovara, who could talk rings around the First Deputy or Chief Inspector Codd or any several other top cops, began to outline the issues in the Seedman case.

The Knapp Commission admitted having had all this hotel information since June—four months or more already. Why had they come forward with it now, three days before hearings were to begin? The timing was "awkward," to say the least.

What else did they have on Seedman? Was this the tip of the iceberg? Was Seedman perhaps guilty of accepting other payoffs? Was it possible Knapp had such evidence? Was Knapp hoping Murphy would do nothing, so that the Commission could thoroughly embarrass Murphy next week when further evidence against Seedman was brought out at the hearings?

There was a moment's silence. First Deputy Smith did not trust people who wore jewelry, and he had never liked Seedman anyway, but he did not say so now.

Chief Inspector Codd said, "Al Seedman is an honest man."

Lacovara pointed out that the one free meal at the Hilton, to which Seedman had admitted, even in itself was a potentially serious charge. The acceptance of a bribe by a police officer was a Class A misdemeanor, punishable by a year in jail.

Exactly what offense had Seedman committed? Had he violated the law, and did this violation justify his dismissal from the Police Department? Was it merely a violation of Department rules? Was it even less than that—merely bad judgment?

First Deputy Commissioner Smith said, "We need some more input." Smith believed in group discussions and consensus decisions. He did not send for Chief Cooper, he did not send for me. He did call in Deputy Commissioner McCarthy, whose office was adjacent to his own.

Although McCarthy, during his previous 24-year police career, had risen to the rank of Deputy Chief, in his new role as Deputy Commissioner for Organized Crime Control he had been on the job exactly 12 days. He had been playing golf in Florida when the unexpected phone call came from Murphy, inviting him back to New York to take over a new and still unstructured office.

McCarthy did not know what the job would amount to, and he guessed that Murphy didn't either. McCarthy supposed that he would command a staff of about 15 men, and that he would oversee, coordinate, and administrate—but not command—other existing units. He considered Murphy's offer for three days, then called back. McCarthy's New York pension, which would be suspended if he went back into the Department, amounted to approximately

$10,000 per year. He didn't have to make very much more to live well on such a pension in Florida, and he could play golf, which he loved, every day.

Nonetheless, he accepted Murphy's offer. He would join Patrick Murphy's crusade against inefficiency and corruption. McCarthy, something of an idealist himself, was going to help drive the rascals out.

He also had no intention of quietly accepting the big rank, the big title, and the command of nobody. During the afternoon of his first day on the job, meeting with Commissioner Smith, myself, and some others, he had pointed out that his office should logically command all plainclothesmen, and also the entire Narcotics Division. He was asking, that first day, for command of 1200 men. About 400 of these would be stripped from Commissioner Smith, and the other 800 would come from Seedman's Detective Division.

Smith did not want to give up any of his men, but it was the opinion of a number of others attending this conference, including myself, that McCarthy's job was meaningless if he had no troops, and that in truth he was the logical commander of the plainclothes divisions. After all, the plainclothesmen worked principally in the area of gambling, and gambling was the life blood of organized crime. About an hour later McCarthy had left Smith's office in command of the 400 plainclothesmen and also of the narcotics administrative division—a group of under two dozen men. For the time being the Narcotics Division stayed with Seedman.

But Smith's command had decreased by 400 within an hour, and McCarthy had become a force to be reckoned with within the Police Department. Furthermore, it was clear that McCarthy would keep after the Narcotics Division until he got it.

McCarthy had been a B-24 bomber pilot over Europe during World War II. He had flown 32 combat missions, and won the Distinguished Flying Cross, the Air Medal, and other decorations. Mustered out a captain, he returned to the streets of New York as a patrolman, accepting a 50 percent decrease in pay and a decrease in prestige which was even greater. He first met Patrick Murphy in 1949, when both worked in Emergency Service. Then came the Korean War, and McCarthy was recalled for active duty. Eventually he was to retire from the Air Force as a lieutenant colonel.

He had got his college degree magna cum laude, and in the mid-fifties, as McCarthy saw it, the brains of the Police Department worked at the Police Academy. So he wrangled an assignment for himself there. He was a lieutenant, Pat Murphy was a lieutenant, Bill Smith was a lieutenant, Al Seedman was a lieutenant—they all knew each other there, and sometimes they talked about how they would run the Department if they could ever get to be Police Commissioner.

McCarthy was in charge of firearms training. In those days there was no outdoor range, and very few indoor ranges. Each cop was obliged to fire off only 10 practice shots three times a year. Apart from that, he had to pay for his own ammunition. The level of firearms skill within the Police Department was deplorable. McCarthy now began to structure a new firearms training program—and in 1971 this was still in use—and he also forced into existence the outdoor range at Rodman's Neck.

Most cops, one of them Seedman, saw corruption around them and considered some of it serious and some of it not. "There's a great difference," Seedman used to say, "between taking a free cup of coffee, and taking bribes to give perjured testimony in court. They're not the same and they shouldn't be treated the same."

McCarthy agreed that "resolving the ethical problems is the hardest job a patrolman has to do. But one thing I was sure of as a cop: If the result of my action was of any tangible benefit or reward to me, this could not be done. If our policemen are not honest and efficient, then democracy goes down the drain. But the principal reason I never took anything was that I would have felt so damn humiliated. I would have lost that part of my self-esteem that I valued so much."

McCarthy, though acquainted with Seedman during these Police Academy years, rarely saw him. Murphy he knew somewhat better, though never in the personal or social sense—"I remember that when my mother died, he came to the funeral home." In fact, the two men would not meet socially for the first time until almost a year after McCarthy returned as Deputy Commissioner, when one night he and his wife would be invited to the Police Commissioner's house for dinner.

After leaving the Police Academy, McCarthy took over the job of untangling midtown New York's monumental traffic jam. There was only one thing to do, eliminate the illegally parked cars. So McCarthy ordered his cops to tag every illegally parked car they found—absolutely every one, no exceptions.

When he remembered this in later years, he often laughed. "I was merciless. I tagged the Cardinal's car, I tagged judges, I tagged the cars belonging to the *Daily News*—the *Daily News* thought everybody should be tagged but them."

The outcry was stupendous, and for a time Inspector McCarthy was transferred to a temporary "emergency" assignment elsewhere. But presently he was promoted to Deputy Chief and returned to command of the Traffic Division.

"They can't buy me with one star," he said to himself, and again his men began slapping tickets on every car in sight. One dignitary complained personally to McCarthy, "I was only double-parked for one minute and he tagged me." McCarthy said, "Only one minute, eh? That's a very efficient cop. I wish all my men were as efficient as he is."

Some 13 years after they had worked together at the Police Academy, Patrick Murphy had remembered Bill McCarthy and brought him back to New York, and this "merciless" former traffic cop was one of the men who now sat in judgment on the Chief of Detectives. McCarthy said later, "I saw that the Seedman case involved an ethical problem, and on the subject of ethics I tend to rigidity."

McCarthy had entered Smith's office and been briefed on the discussion so far.

McCarthy said, "Obviously there's got to be an investigation into Seedman's conduct."

Nobody could deny this. All were agreed also that the investigation should be conducted by Syd Cooper personally and that it should start at once, and a call was put in ordering Cooper to headquarters from his office in the 84th Precinct, just across the Brooklyn Bridge.

While waiting for Cooper, the discussion continued. No longer was the subject a single $84 meal for which Chief Seedman had provided a more or less reasonable explanation. The subject now was the possible felony of bribery, the possible Class A misdemeanor of accepting gratuities. The evidence had been officially presented by a bona fide New York City law enforcement agency. This would not be an easy decision for the Police Commissioner, but he must be straight and objective. A violation—a possible crime—had been committed by a person who was part of his official family. The Police Commissioner was awaiting advice from this group.

Lacovara said, "It's a hard decision for us to come to, and it's hard advice to give, but we're public officials too. Knapp will not hesitate to bring this all out if we try to minimize it." Lacovara then pointed out, in the words of Justice Frankfurter, that "not only must justice be done, but justice must appear to be done," and that obviously Chief Seedman could not be left as Chief of Detectives where it would seem that he was conducting an investigation into his own conduct, or at least was in a position to influence the outcome of such an investigation.

That was the first decision: Seedman was out as Chief of Detectives. According to Smith, it was now the opinion of McCarthy and Lacovara that Seedman be suspended at once, that his gun and shield be taken away from him, pending results of the investigation. On the other side of the table, Chief Inspector Codd was clearly suffering. He admitted that something had to be done, but not that. You couldn't take the man's gun away. Seedman would be disgraced and would never recover, even though he might be exonerated by the investigation in a matter of days. The next suggestion was that Seedman be reassigned to Codd's office, and that Assistant Chief John Kinsella, the second-ranking detective commander, be moved into Seedman's office as Commanding Officer, Detective Division. Apparently Codd thought even this too strong. Seedman still would be humiliated, and the investigation possibly would turn up no wrongdoing of any kind. But when Smith now accepted this advice, Codd said no more on the subject. Codd had risen high in two services—to four-star rank in the Police Department, and to colonel in the army, and in neither world did one argue with the decisions of one's superior.

Smith telephoned the Police Commissioner at home. The conversation lasted ten minutes or more, during part of which Lacovara spoke on an extension. Smith outlined the issues, the possibilities, and the consensus of the four men present in his office. Then he presented the alternatives, including removing Seedman's gun and shield, and there was some discussion back and forth between Murphy and Smith and Lacovara. Presently Murphy agreed that the consensus decision was the best one, especially given the "awkward" timing of the Knapp Commission memo; for above all, the consensus decision seemed to protect the Police Commissioner from whatever tricks Armstrong and Knapp might have up their sleeves.

No one had suggested that the "charge" against Seedman was perhaps not significant. No one had seriously suggested a quiet investigation over the weekend before taking action of any kind. No one had thought to call up Knapp or Armstrong and have it out over the phone: What's the point? Speak up, what else have you got? Are you asking us to do something with that memo, or are you playing games?

Instead, instant fear had set in, as irreversible as rigor mortis.

Murphy chose to begin the traumatic hearings by allowing Knapp to terrorize him.

It was about 6:30 when Chief Inspector Codd reentered his own office where the unsuspecting Seedman still waited for him. Codd was badly shaken, but too correct to admit to Seedman that he disagreed with the decision that had been made. Cooper then came through the door, and his interrogation of Seedman began. This interrogation lasted about 30 minutes. Like Impellezzeri, Cooper asked Seedman if there were any other free meals elsewhere which would turn up in the next few days. Was there anything else that the Knapp Commission might have on Seedman?

All three of these men were upset. Seedman saw himself disgraced, and his 30-year career in ruins. Codd saw himself involved in a decision which he believed unjust. Cooper, after interrogating Seedman, considered the decision unjust too, for he believed what Seedman had just told him —after all, if Seedman lied now, Cooper would find out, and Seedman would be in worse trouble. Therefore Seedman had not lied, and the case against him was extremely flimsy.

Cooper was a Jew too. This was neither here nor there perhaps, though at the very least it must have made Cooper uneasy. But Cooper saw this as still another high-level decision which he had not been invited in on. Murphy was using him not as an adviser, which he thought he had earned by now, but strictly and solely as a detective, a snoop. This offended Cooper, as did the injustice done Seedman, and in addition Cooper now would be up most of the night checking with the hotels on the Seedman case.

Presently Cooper departed.

Cooper said, "Let's go get a drink, Al."

They drove uptown in Codd's car. Seedman had ordered his own car to follow. They went into a bar on Third Avenue and had several drinks.

Later they stood on the sidewalk. Codd shook hands with Seedman, then patted him on the back, got into his car, and drove away. Bulletins were being flashed on radio and TV news broadcasts. Unbelievable news: Chief of Detectives Seedman, the best-known cop in New York apart from Murphy himself, had been relieved of his command. The official Police Department announcement was only two paragraphs long: Seedman had been relieved over one $84 dinner at a midtown hotel. Commentators found this explanation incredible. Obviously, before Murphy would act this drastically he would need more important evidence than one meal. A major scandal was no doubt in the making. What else was Seedman guilty of?

I telephoned Codd. He was upset and defensive. I told him I thought a mistake had been made. If this single $84 meal was the whole story, then to relieve Seedman of his command was overreaction of the worst kind. I said, "Perhaps there's more to this than I know about. Perhaps Seedman's the worst crook that ever lived."

Codd said with feeling, "Al Seedman is an honest man."

I said, "Then how could the four of you possibly have come to this decision?"

Codd, suffering, but unwilling out of loyalty to Murphy to say what he felt, said, "You better call the Boss and talk to him."

I phoned Murphy and told him I thought a mistake had been made. We talked for about 20 minutes, during which he tried to justify his decision. The main question to the Police Commissioner was, What did the Knapp Commission have? Why confront him with this late on a Friday afternoon, three days before the hearings started? What had they expected his reaction would be? What other evidence did they have? Obviously Knapp was trying to damage him in some way. Why were they doing this?

Again I asked, Was there more about Seedman than I knew?

"Absolutely not," said Murphy. I then told him that the public was going to find the charge against Chief Seedman ridiculous, and the Police Commissioner's decision overreaction, if not panic. I told him that Murphy was the man of stature in this city, not Knapp, but by reacting so hurriedly in this case, he had abdicated his role. He had given the Knapp Commission power over him, and power over the Police Department. He had shown them they could push him around. We lived in an expense account society. Everybody accepted free meals every day, including himself. He had possibly ruined Seedman as an effective Chief of Detectives, and he had possibly ruined Seedman's life also, and there was no evidence nor even a substantial charge to support such drastic results. Murphy, on the other end of the phone, began to go away from me, and presently I could hear his other phone ring in the background.

He said, "I have to answer the other phone. Talk it over again with the Chief Inspector."

So I talked to Codd again, and later, just before midnight, we had a third conversation. I also talked to Seedman, who came onto the phone in a voice so small I could hardly hear him. It was the voice of a man who had been crushed, and who still couldn't understand how or why. He said, "If only Murphy had talked to me himself. Why wouldn't he at least call me himself?"

Seedman had a favorite chair in his living room, and now he sat up in it staring at the opposite wall for the rest of the night. A detective named David Frisher had come over, and he sat up all night with his chief. On the opposite side of the room sat Henny Seedman, and for hour after hour no one spoke. Occasionally Henny would walk behind Seedman's chair and put her hands against his cheeks. Occasionally Seedman put a hand over hers, but he said nothing. About eight o'clock in the morning the door bell rang. It was another detective, come to see if he could be of help. And from then on the phone rang with detectives offering to do what they could, and to ask if there was any way they could help their chief.

About 4 A.M. my phone had rung again. It was my duty sergeant. A cop had been shot in the 20th Precinct.

Only three headquarters offices were manned all night: mine, the Chief of Detectives', and Command and Patrol. Whenever a cop was shot, these offices notified various ranking officials, and each of us, groggy with sleep, was obliged to decide whether or not the case seemed serious enough to warrant our getting dressed and racing to the scene in a radio car.

This first call was followed in the next half hour by two others. A second cop had been shot. The third call informed me that both cops were apparently not seriously wounded.

I tried to go back to sleep but couldn't. I lay there worrying about Chief Seedman and also about Commissioner Murphy. As I saw it, Murphy's prestige was in jeopardy. Some way had to be found to salvage both Chief Seedman and Murphy's prestige.

Saturday morning a call from Lacovara woke me up. I explained my point of view, and Lacovara explained his. His voice was quite mellifluous, and his arguments were calm, measured, and absolutely unassailable. They included every important fact, except for human feelings, human prejudices, and the commonly observed rules of the world we all currently lived in. Lacovara could not be budged. Next I telephoned Codd and Smith, but neither answered. I called my duty sergeant, ordering him to reach out for Codd and Smith by radio.

Smith called. He was as defensive as Murphy had been

the night before. "Don't blame me," he said. "I was the one who held out for the compromise decision. Lacovara and McCarthy wanted to take his gun and shield away."

Smith's other phone now began ringing. He came back on the line to tell me it was Chief Cooper, whose investigation so far had verified every word Seedman had said. No sooner had Smith hung up to continue his conversation with Cooper than my phone rang again, and it was Codd, who mentioned that he was at the 20th Precinct; one of the stickup men caught last night and at present lying in Roosevelt Hospital was H. Rap Brown.

My phone rang still another time, and it was Seedman. He sounded better than the night before, though still low. He asked if I thought he ought to call up Murphy's house and ask to speak to the Police Commissioner.

I said, "You know him better than I do. You've known him 15 years or more."

Seedman said, "I knew him so little in all that time, that I don't know whether I ought to call him or not."

How did I know what to tell him? The whole situation looked incredible. It seemed to me that everyone recognized now that a mistake had been made, but that no one knew what to do next, and even that all were looking to me for some kind of solution. I called Codd back and told him we would have a press conference at the 20th Precinct to celebrate the arrest of H. Rap Brown, and that I would get there as fast as I could. I was in the country for the weekend, and one of my chauffeurs, Patrolman Tom Burke, came to get me. We were halfway to New York when there was a call on the radio. From a phone booth I called my office, and was told to call Cooper. So I called Cooper. He was furious. He was furious because he had not been consulted at the start, and furious because he had been up until three in the morning running down facts at a number of midtown hotels. He said that as near as he could tell, the Knapp Commission had nothing on Seedman. They had this one free meal. They also had a list of about 60 cops who had been taking free meals at the Hilton and elsewhere, 20 of them captains and above, 20 lieutenants, the rest patrolmen and detectives. A number of the names occurred repeatedly: Assistant Chief Arthur Morgan and Deputy Chief Arthur Savitt. Also on the list were Patrolmen P. Murphy, Patrolman S. Cooper, and Patrolman W. Knapp. Obviously the hotels didn't care who they gave free meals to, anybody with a uniform could walk in and sign any name he chose, and some of the wags among our noble troops had signed Syd's own name among others.

Cooper then suggested that I offer Murphy this idea: Seedman should announce to the press that he had asked to be removed while the investigation was effected. Cooper felt certain Seedman would agree to this, if Murphy would.

Back in my car I told Tom Burke to put on the light and the siren, and we blew everybody off the road the rest of the way into the 20th Precinct. The reporters and television crews were packed ten deep outside the door; they surrounded me as soon as I got out of the car, and I had to wade inside through them. Chief Kinsella, the new commanding officer of the Detective Division, was there, and I asked him to brief me on the Rap Brown arrest. Was it as sensational as it appeared to be? I then met with Codd alone in the precinct captain's office. I told him I thought Murphy should seize this opportunity to conduct the press conference here, ostensibly to praise those cops who had done this heroic deed in the middle of the night. It was a fabulous bit of routine bravery, and here was the Police Commissioner's chance to associate himself with it, and at the same time to soften the Seedman thing, to prepare the terrain for the reinstatement of Seedman in a day or two.

Codd said he thought I should be the one to call Murphy.

So I called him, and he was listening, and he was suffering, and it seemed to me he was going away from me the whole time. He said he still didn't know why Knapp and Armstrong had thrown this thing at him late on a Friday afternoon on the eve of the hearings. If he came to the press conference, the reporters would ask him questions he couldn't answer. He felt so terrible personally that he didn't think he could face it.

He said, "Couldn't it wait until next week?"

I said, "Of course it can wait."

After a pause Murphy said, "But you mean it wouldn't be fair to Al?"

I said, "There's an awful lot of Christianity involved here."

Murphy said, "I just don't think I can do it. I feel so terrible about all this."

I understood that he didn't think he could bring off a press conference, and so I said, "Let me hang up, give you time to think about it without being pressured by me. You know how I feel and how strongly I feel."

Murphy said, "All right, I'll think about it, and if you don't hear from me, it will mean I've decided against it."

Codd, Kinsella, and I now decided that we should start this press conference in an hour, if only to announce the splendid arrests of last night, and that Chief Codd should conduct it, for I didn't believe Murphy would show up. Perhaps Codd could say something to soften the climate around Chief of Detectives Seedman, I suggested. Chief Cawley came in at this point, and stood listening to our discussion. We didn't say five words to him. I think we were all waiting for Murphy to call back and say he was on his way in, but the phone didn't ring; and so presently we decided to go out and have a sandwich, and we invited Chief Cawley to accompany us. On the stoop of the station house I told the press that there would be a press conference in precisely one hour, and then Kinsella, Cawley, Codd, and I walked out onto the street, the four of us walking up toward Columbus Avenue with reporters running alongside, asking questions.

"Which one is Chief Kinsella?"

The photographers were snapping pictures of us. Kinsella had snow-white hair and was almost 60 years old.

"Which one is the new Chief of Detectives?"

"Can I get your photo, Chief?"

As the four of us reached the corner, the press dropping back now, a car screeched to a stop and out jumped Chris Borgen, a reporter from WCBS-TV. Borgen managed to separate Kinsella and me from Cawley and Codd, who walked on ahead.

Borgen was angry. "You tell Murf this: that he owes it to the public and to Chief Seedman to qualify this; and tell him that if he doesn't do it, I'm going to ask some very hard questions. I'm going to give the date of the game and the number of the box, a 20-dollar ticket that Murf sat in and didn't pay for. Tell him that."

Borgen was unique among the reporters assigned to

cover the Police Department. Ten years before, he had closed out six years as a narcotics detective. He was apparently as brave and devoted a cop as had ever lived. He worked principally under cover. His number one role was that of Pepe the Pimp. The Police Department listed Borgen under another name. He had been born on the Caribbean island of Martinique. He spoke not only beautiful English, but French and Spanish as well; and three times during his police career he had agreed to spend time in jail in hopes of acquiring information and evidence there. Once he stayed in jail for six months, and afterward was rewarded by promotion from third grade to second grade detective.

All of us respected him more than any of the other reporters, for he was very good on TV, but also he still loved and understood cops.

"It's a bum rap," Chris said now. "The whole business is no fucking good." I judged he was using profanity because it was the only way he could think of to express how upset he was.

Cawley and Codd, who were well ahead of us and waiting on the corner, hadn't heard this, and as we walked up, Codd's chauffeur and mine were standing there. We sent the two chauffeurs for sandwiches and then walked on to my apartment, which was only a few blocks ahead.

In the elevator I said, "And now the whole complexion of the game has changed still again in the last five minutes." And I told Cawley and Codd what Chris Borgen had threatened.

Upstairs in my flat, we waited for the sandwiches. The other men all refused anything to drink.

Cawley suggested, "We could offer the P.C. this as an out: that one cup of coffee is not a crime, but multiple cups of coffee begins to be a crime, or is; and it's the same with free meals."

This was followed by silence.

None of us really believed that Borgen, who loved the Police Department, would attack it or Murphy. Nonetheless, I thought that Codd should call up Murphy and tell him what the situation was. Codd suggested that I call Murphy. But presently Codd dialed the number himself. One of Murphy's teen-age sons came on, reporting that the

Police Commissioner was not home. So Codd hung up.

The chauffeurs now came to the door with our sandwiches.

After we had eaten, we walked back to the precinct. Borgen was outside, still upset. "You know the press is very much against all this," he said. "They say it's a bad rap. Look at today's *Post*. Look at the *Daily News*. This is overreaction by Murphy. This was panic, and it shows."

We had promised the reporters that the press conference would start at 2:30. Although it was slightly past this now, I thought it was worth trying to talk to Murphy one last time. But one of his sons came on the line and said, "He's gone for a haircut."

I said, "Well, if you can reach out for him in the next five minutes, ask him to call me."

As Codd, Kinsella, and I walked out of the captain's office toward the big room where the reporters had set up their cameras and lights, a patrolman came running along the hall.

"Commissioner Murphy wants to talk to Commissioner Daley."

I told Murphy what Borgen had said. Then I added, "There's no point in me saying anything more, you know how I feel."

There was a long silence.

I was remembering how our previous conversation had ended. Murphy had said that he didn't think he could come. Would I try to understand? I had replied, "Look, I'm on your side, whatever you decide."

He had said, "I know you are. Thank you."

But now the pause ended. Murphy said, "You think I should come up there for the press conference. All right, I'll be up there as soon as I can."

In the room crowded with reporters, I stood under the blinding lights and announced, "Commissioner Murphy's on his way here; the press conference will be delayed until he gets here."

Returning to the captain's office, I sent a patrolman for some paper—in the Police Department they doled out paper one sheet at a time, and there was none beside the captain's typewriter. When the paper came, I began to type out a statement for Murphy to make about the fantastic arrests of the night before. Precinct Captain Dave Pascal, Chief Codd, and Chief Kinsella were dictating the facts over my shoulder. Once this was finished, we all stood out on the front stoop waiting for Murphy to arrive.

When his car pulled up and he stepped onto the sidewalk, he looked refreshed and relaxed and fine. I had supposed that he would have spent all his time in the car working on a statement about Seedman, but as he entered the station house he had nothing. I handed him the statement on the holdup and the arrests, and he nodded politely and took it. Then we filed into the other room and stood behind the microphones under the blinding lights, surrounded by eight of the patrolmen involved in the arrests. Murphy read my statement, and afterward introduced Ralph Mannetta, and asked Mannetta to describe how he had captured Rap Brown. Mannetta could face an armed stickup man on a rooftop in the night, but in front of the television cameras he went quickly to pieces, which was absolutely charming.

Then the line of questioning that Murphy had dreaded began.

What about Chief Seedman?

Murphy declared that if the investigation proved no wrongdoing on Seedman's part—and there was no proof of any wrongdoing at this time—of course Chief Seedman would be reinstated as Chief of Detectives. "We hope to clean this up in the next couple of days. It came to our attention only late yesterday afternoon, and the decision that we made had to be made very quickly, on the basis of what evidence was available to us at that time."

When it was over and we had filed back into Captain Pascal's office, we were all pleased. Murphy had faced the press and the TV cameras. He had placed the Seedman case in perspective. He had allowed himself room to reinstate Seedman. He had at least half convinced the press that his decision yesterday had been made after due deliberation, rather than out of sudden panic.

Now Murphy drew me over into the corner and explained again how terrible he had felt, how unfair it was for the Knapp Commission to throw this Seedman thing at him without warning, forcing him into a corner when he didn't expect it. There was a lot of touching at this point. I had patted Murphy on the back after the press conference and now he touched me on the arm. As we were leaving the building Codd patted me on the shoulder. Chief Cawley shook hands with me and also with Codd.

We were all in this together.

"So long. See you Monday."

In the street the TV crews were loading gear into their cars.

On Monday I was confident that the Seedman case would be resolved, having seriously damaged no one. Seedman would resume command of the detectives. Murphy would resume all his old stature.

On Monday the Knapp Commission burst like a sewer pipe over the dress blue uniform of the Police Department.

4 / Corruption

Xaviera Hollander was born in Holland about 1940, or perhaps even prior to that. In 1971, a minimum of 31 years later, this made her precisely 28 years old.

Indonesia at that time was the Dutch East Indies, Xaviera's father was "that rare human being, an intellectual, raconteur, lover of the arts, bon vivant, and a truly generous-spirited man." A doctor, he owned a hospital of his own, and two palatial homes, and he bossed many servants. You can read these and many other true facts in an absolutely true book called *The Happy Hooker*, which Xaviera wrote at the age of 28, or whatever she was, with the aid principally of Robin Moore, who here enters our story for the first time.

Xaviera's Dutch-Jewish doctor father spent three years in a concentration camp conducted by the Japanese, while Xaviera herself, who was either not yet born or a babe in arms, was incarcerated with her mother elsewhere by the anti-Semitic Japanese. Xaviera's crime, presumably, was that she would one day become one of the most famous prostitutes in the world. After the war, the family returned to Holland, where Xaviera received a "fine European education" and learned to speak (so she said) seven languages fluently. Between infancy, whenever that was, and the year 1969, Xaviera never went to jail once.

She lost her virginity, if that's the correct word, to her first girl at the age of 15, her first boy at the age of 17, and her first dog some years after that. By her own admission she grew into a big-busted, nymphomaniacal, bisexual, multilingual Dutch secretary, performed professionally only in the latter line of work, and once won a thousand-dollar prize as the best secretary in Holland.

But Holland began to bore her, so she went to South Africa to live with her stepsister. After seducing her brother-in-law, and also the couple's German shepherd, she flew to New York and began to live with a Dutch boy-friend there. This cad kept promising to marry her but never did, and eventually he abandoned pretty young Xaviera. Xaviera, who now found herself in desperate need of "warmth and reassurance," began picking up men in bars. Eventually, without being asked (so she said), one of them gave her $100. At that moment she began to realize that she was an extraordinarily talented person. The next gift was $150.

These two momentous nights, which were to have such extraordinary repercussions on the New York Police Department, took place in the spring of 1969, two and a half years before the start of Whitman Knapp's public hearings.

Xaviera was taking dictation in a consulate by day, and hooking by night. When she got fired from the consulate, she went to work for a certain ambassador to the United Nations, and soon seduced the ambassador (so she said). She was still holding down a job and hooking on the side. Her little black book became swollen with names. She was at her typewriter eight hours a day, and on her back every other minute, very little of it sleeping. She appeared to have got by on two or three hours sleep a night.

Presently she signed on with a high-class bordello. She was apparently brilliant at her job. She could satisfy men in face-to-face encounters, and she could satisfy whole rooms full of men with various exhibitions that she liked to put on. Still, when she began handing out her cards to Madam's clients, Madam was obliged to let her go.

Xaviera Hollander went into business for herself.

Xaviera's success was immediate and even extraordinary. A good many of her satisfied customers were dignitaries attached to the United Nations—they spent their days deciding the fate of the world and their nights relaxing at Xaviera's.

Xaviera was busted a number of times and spent many hours of revulsion jammed into holding pens with common street walkers. Xaviera had been arrested as part of an organized raid by a team of plainclothesmen and detectives, whereas the common whores sharing her fate that morning had been captured in the doorways of flea-bag hotels by ordinary uniformed cops. Life simply was not just, and Xaviera was aware of injustices that ordinary citizens never noticed.

Each time she was arrested, she went to lawyers. Xaviera's main worry was that she would be convicted of a crime involving moral turpitude, and deported. Each time she was arrested she had somehow to get the charge reduced to loitering, or disorderly conduct. A prostitution conviction would be fatal. The golden goose would be on the next flight to Holland.

Arrested again in March 1971, Xaviera asked her lawyer, Irwin Germaise, for help. Germaise sent Patrolman William Phillips to her door. Phillips showed his shield and I.D. card and identified himself as a man who could end her police problems once and for all. All it would cost her was a little money. Patrolman Phillips suggested that he meet with Xaviera's "boyfriend," to arrange the technicalities and the amount of regular payoffs.

A man named Teddy Ratnoff, 33, had wormed his way into Xaviera's life. Ratnoff was short, portly, bald, he wore thick glasses, and he had wet lips. He was a genius at electronic listening devices.

How Ratnoff came to enter Xaviera's life was never clear. Ratnoff later said that he had "gained her confidence." He told her he was a free-lance agent for the New York Legislative Committee on Crime, that he was interested in judicial acts of indiscretion, or information about courts and politicians—he had no interest whatsoever in prostitution, and she had nothing to fear from him. He wanted to bug her place to get evidence against certain of her customers, particularly those who were highly placed politically. No one ever mentioned blackmail. Absolutely not.

Xaviera later said that Ratnoff had been introduced to

her by Robin Moore. Robin Moore had not only written *The French Connection*—and there would be Knapp Commission and police interest in this within a few weeks too—but also a book about Vietnam called *The Green Berets*. Moore turned out a variety of books under a variety of names, often using co-authors, and when he brought Ratnoff into the Happy Hooker's brothel, if in fact this is what happened, he told her he was writing a book about her. Ratnoff would install some bugs so that juicy conversations between customers and call girls could be recorded during intimate activities. These recordings would be used to give the book "authenticity."

Ratnoff later said that Moore was indeed writing a book, but that it was about Ratnoff, not Xaviera.

In any case, by the time Patrolman Phillips first knocked on the door, Ratnoff was already there. Xaviera detested Ratnoff. She considered him slimy, but she enjoyed listening to the recordings afterward, and she claimed she never realized that he had also installed a television camera behind the ceiling mirror in her bedroom. One day the wires, or the frequencies, or something got crossed, and Xaviera and a customer unexpectedly became the uncovered undercover stars of a live broadcast on one of New York's UHF TV stations. This particular station catered to a Spanish-speaking audience, which that night received a real treat.

Ratnoff had in fact worked for the Joint Committee on Crime, and he had also worked for William Lambert, an investigative reporter for *Life* magazine. He had a reputation for being able to plant really sophisticated bugging devices in various incredible places. The Knapp Commission needed such devices. Michael Armstrong asked around and was led to Teddy Ratnoff, who supplied them. However, Ratnoff's real contribution to the Knapp Commission was Patrolman Phillips, in person. The Commission, which had not yet even begun to audition actors, had suddenly found a star of great magnitude. Without Phillips, Knapp would have produced just another dull play, or maybe no play at all. The voluptuous vehicle would have fallen flat. But with Phillips as star, a smash hit was suddenly possible.

Later Ratnoff's apartment would be raided by District Attorney Hogan's men, and all Ratnoff's tapes scooped up; soon after that, Ratnoff would be indicted for grand larceny, conspiracy, bribery, and 36 counts of illegal bugging; whereupon Armstrong would piously insist that Ratnoff had never been on the Knapp Commission payroll, and that "95 percent" of the $5000 paid him had been for supplying electronic devices only. If true, this meant that Ratnoff had accepted the considerable risk of entrapping Phillips purely out of the goodness of his heart.

Ratnoff met with Phillips several times. Always Teddy was wired from his toes to his teeth, while Knapp Commission agents planted nearby recorded their conversations. In the course of these meetings, Phillips agreed to guarantee police protection for Xaviera and her girls. Knowing that Xaviera had paid $10,000 for certain address books she had bought from another madam, Phillips wanted $10,000 to take care of her. He claimed he could fix the precinct cops, the division cops, and the borough cops.

If she dealt with Phillips, she was clear. If she didn't deal with Phillips, she would get deported. The cops, Phillips said, knew all about her, for her fingerprints had turned up her immigration records.

Ratnoff began beating the price down, all the time asking leading questions. One day he asked Phillips what those decorations were on his chest. Phillips said, "I killed three fucks up here."

Teddy Ratnoff said, "Killed three fucks, yeah."

Phillips said, "Oh yeah, I blow them up like they're fucking nothing."

But Phillips slowly became suspicious of Teddy Ratnoff. First of all, Ratnoff was always immaculately dressed, and never opened or removed his coat. Secondly, Ratnoff was always carrying a briefcase, which he waved around, as if aiming it toward people or things. Thirdly, Teddy was asking far too many questions, and he kept asking them, and once he even asked that the name of a crooked judge be repeated. One day, as soon as Teddy entered Lawyer Germaise's office, Phillips grabbed Teddy from behind, and felt the wires.

The dialogue as recorded live by the Knapp Commission, went this way:

PHILLIPS: "What do you got there? You wired?"

TEDDY: "You're crazy."

GERMAISE: "What is that?"

TEDDY: "It's a transmitter."

GERMAISE: "What is that?"

TEDDY: "It's a paging system."

PHILLIPS: "Yeah. Take it off."

TEDDY: "Pick up the phone, I'll show you it's a page. It's a paging system."

PHILLIPS: "Take it off."

TEDDY: "It's a paging system."

GERMAISE: "What do you page?"

PHILLIPS: "Well, how come you're so shaky now?"

GERMAISE: "What do you page?"

TEDDY: "It's a paging system."

GERMAISE: "What do you page?"

TEDDY: "Huh?"

GERMAISE: "What do you page?"

Teddy, terrified, stalled. If they would just allow him to use the phone, he would have himself paged on the contraption they had just discovered on his person. Phillips kept trying to disconnect it. Teddy kept turning it back on, explaining that it was a beeper, a miniature walkie-talkie. Phillips, who had been a detective, had been a plainclothesman, knew an electronic listening device when he saw it, but for a number of minutes the frantic Teddy bluffed him nonetheless. Phillips was still asking Teddy to prove that it was a paging beeper when there was a commotion in the outer office, and Teddy's back-up team burst in on them.

The Knapp Commission's tape ended this way:

GERMAISE: "Who are you, sir?"

ANSWER: "We're with the Knapp Commission."

Phillips was rushed downtown and introduced to Michael Armstrong. Armstrong told him that he would cooperate with the Knapp Commission, or he would go to jail. Phillips never hesitated.

"I'll cooperate," he said.

It was as if Armstrong were about to found a museum

and had discovered an attic stuffed with a hundred lost Rembrandts.

For Phillips, by his own admission, was the crookedest crooked cop then living, perhaps the crookedest cop of all time anywhere. He knew names, dates, places, and the amounts of payoffs. He threw back the covers on the dirty bed.

Phillips was also a brave man, as his many citations attested. He was a crook by instinct, and the higher the risk, the more he loved it. He had flair. He also seemed to love, for a time, working on the side of the good guys, possibly because, according to his curious code, his new role was as crooked as any of his old ones; after all, he was still betraying people who trusted him, in this case other cops.

Phillips knew personally other cops who had accepted payoffs. Wearing wires, he repeatedly met with a number of them, and these incriminating conversations were recorded. He soon led Michael Armstrong to Patrolman Edward Droge Jr. Several dozen witnesses would testify in the nine days of Knapp Commission hearings, but the three principal ones would be Phillips, Droge and Waverly Logan, a black man, formerly a cop in Harlem, who had been arrested for accepting a $100 narcotics bribe, and who had been dismissed by the Police Department four months previously. Among the numerous other witnesses would be narcotics informants, Knapp Commission agents, members of the State Investigation Commission, professional gamblers, tow truck operators. These people would round out the picture which the Knapp Commission was attempting to present: that corruption within the Police Department was not a question of a few rotten apples, but rather a long, sordid story of a rotten barrel. But the star witness was Phillips. He was 40 years old, with an honest, open face. On the stand his voice was good, his accent was good, his choice of words was good. As he began to pronounce his litany of sins he showed no nervousness, and no remorse. He wore an expensive suit that day, and a different expensive suit the next day.

He was absolutely convincing.

Phillips' father had been a cop too. Somewhere during Phillips' testimony, a gray-haired patrolman said, "Thank God Billy's dad is dead."

Meanwhile. the slippery Teddy Ratnoff fled the country. The lawyer. Irwin Germaise. also fled. landing in Israel.

Back at 155 East 55th Street, the Happy Hooker went hooking happily along.

5 / Deliberations

The Phillips revelations were just starting as deliberations began again into the fate of Chief of Detectives Albert Seedman. At about 10:15 there came a message from the Police Commissioner: He was in his office if I wanted to come down. I stared at the curiously tentative message, then signaled that I wasn't ready. I would see him later. Cooper called. He had by now been investigating Seedman all weekend and had come up with no more than the one meal. Cooper thought Seedman should be reinstated at once. He knew there were those who felt that the status should remain quo until the Knapp hearings ended—suppose Knapp and Armstrong had something more on Seedman, and were waiting and hoping for Murphy to reinstate him. But Cooper felt that if two weeks were allowed to go by before Seedman was reinstated, then all of Seedman's stature and authority would have evaporated. There would be nothing left of the man. To Cooper, Seedman should be reinstated at once, or never. I next won the agreement of Lacovara. For all his youth, Lacovara displayed an acute sensitivity to each and every wind of power that blew through the halls of headquarters. He seemed to feel now that sentiment was swinging toward Seedman, and away from the consensus decision that had exiled Seedman last Friday.

Next I summoned Chief of Intelligence Grubert. If it was going to come to a vote. I wanted plenty. Grubert wore only two stars, and he had not been involved in the decision on Seedman at all. In truth, he stood a step below the level of power, but he was a steady, calm, reasonable man and his vote could be useful. To my surprise, he said that if he had been Police Commissioner last Friday, he would have done exactly what Murphy did. Grubert had been made a detective on the same day as Seedman in

1946. He had known Al all that time, he said, and never known personally of anything Seedman had done that was crooked. But there was always the possibility . . .

Grubert thought that nothing further should be done on Seedman until he had contacted John Malone, head of the New York office of the FBI. Two of Grubert's sons were FBI agents, and Grubert had the best connections with the FBI of any of the police brass, with the possible exception of Seedman himself. However, Malone would be out of town until the end of the week. Grubert saw no sense in trying to clear Seedman on any level lower than Malone. Could we wait to decide on Seedman for four more days?

I said to Grubert, "Suppose Murphy does reinstate Seedman, and a week from now the Knapp Commission comes out with proof that Seedman accepted a $50,000 bribe on something. Or supposing Murphy doesn't reinstate Seedman and a week from now the Knapp Commission comes out with proof of that $50,000 bribe. Does it make any difference to Murphy either way?"

Grubert said, "Absolutely not. It would be a terrible thing for Murphy either way." Then Grubert added, "Furthermore, supposing Murphy doesn't reinstate Seedman, and he puts John Kinsella in as Chief of Detectives, and next week the Knapp Commission comes out with proof than Kinsella took $50,000. Same thing."

Everyone was absolutely terrified of the Knapp Commission.

Grubert left my office saying, "You look at something like this, you see Seedman there, and you say to yourself, 'There but for the grace of God goes—' "

Much later Seedman said of Grubert, "He's the type of guy who, to cover himself, would say he agreed with what Murphy did. He's also the type of guy that if his brother did something wrong, and he believed that his brother did something wrong, he'd arrest his brother."

Chief Inspector Codd was in a meeting in Deputy Commissioner Canick's office. I pulled him out of there and said to him in the hall, "I have to speak to you about Seedman."

He said, "Let's have lunch together."

So at noon I went into his office. He hung his uniform

coat behind his door. Unpinning his shield from its breast, he slipped this into his pocket, put a sports coat on over his police pants and gun, and we went out to Paolucci's on Mulberry Street. Like many other ranking officers who sometimes liked to have a drink before lunch, Chief Inspector Codd invariably went to lunch wearing a sports coat. Cops weren't allowed to drink in uniform.

Codd now listened to my reports of my conversations with Lacovara, Cooper, and Grubert. At the end he said, "Let's go back and talk with the Boss."

As we came into headquarters, Lacovara was in the lobby, so the three of us went up to see the Police Commissioner. Codd spoke first. Then Lacovara spoke. Both told Murphy that they believed the thing to do was to reinstate Seedman.

Murphy said, "Alright, that's the thing to do."

I said, "When shall we do it? Immediately or tomorrow?"

Murphy said, "It's already 3:15. I guess we should do it tomorrow."

I said, "Well, we can do it today if you want to."

He said, "Do you realize that it's already 3:15?"

"Alright then, tomorrow," I said. "Shall we keep this a secret from Seedman, or shall somebody tell him, so he can get a good night's sleep?"

Murphy said, "Well, go check with Cooper one last time to make sure he still hasn't got anything on Seedman, and if that's the case Mike should hint to him so that he'll be able to sleep tonight."

Cooper was in a meeting in First Deputy Commissioner Smith's office. Peering through the glass in Smith's door, I saw about 15 men grouped around the table. I sent one of Smith's lieutenants in to get Cooper out for me.

"Commissioner Daley would like to see Chief Cooper."

All eyes followed Cooper out of the room. This kind of thing often happened at high-level police meetings, and it was always impressive. Conversation in the meeting would be killed dead. Fifteen pairs of eyes would follow the summoned individual to the door: What's so important that this guy's being taken out? So much of police business was secret that the possibilities were endless.

In the anteroom outside, Cooper said that he had not yet talked to Whitney North Seymour, who was the Federal attorney for the Southern District, about Seedman, nor had he yet talked to the FBI. He would call them both in an hour when he got out of this meeting.

That hour passed, and there was no call from Cooper. I went looking for him and found him in another meeting in the Police Commissioner's office. I went in there.

Murphy said to me, "Tell Mike Codd to tell Seedman that things are okay."

In the hallway a bit later I said to Cooper, "Did you ever speak to Seymour or the FBI?"

Cooper said, "No, we decided on an administrative decision."

I glanced at him, wondering what this meant.

Back in my own office I phoned Chief Inspector Codd. "It's on for tomorrow, Mike. Tell the party in question so that he sleeps well."

In the morning it was my job to write the statement that Murphy would read at the noon press conference. I did this, and then took it up to the First Deputy. After reading the statement, which ran to three pages, Smith said, "We better have Cooper in on this."

One of Smith's secretaries summoned Cooper from across the river, and presently he came in the door with a pipe in his hand and a grin on his big beefy face. Cooper read the statement, and then Smith read it again, and they began to go over it line by line. Smith, who seemed reluctant to pass on it, ordered Deputy Commissioner McCarthy called in. McCarthy began to read the statement. Now all three of them began to argue about certain words. I had written that the Knapp Commission had sent over a "confidential memo containing terribly serious allegations."

"But were they allegations?" asked Smith.

"Were they terribly serious?" asked McCarthy.

They began to discuss the meanings of the words until finally I cried, "Yes of course they were allegations. Of course they were terribly serious. That's what those words mean. Now let's go on to the next paragraph."

And so they did.

I saw that the true problem was that Smith and McCarthy were reluctant to exonerate Seedman.

Smith now sent a secretary for the page in the penal law which covered bribery and gratuities of public servants, and we each had a turn at reading this. Section 200.35 read, "A public servant is guilty of receiving unlawful gratuities when he solicits, accepts, or agrees to accept any benefits for having engaged in official conduct which he was required or authorized to perform, and for which he was not entitled to any special or additional compensation. Receiving unlawful gratuities is a Class A misdemeanor."

Smith said, "That's what Seedman did. He accepted an unlawful gratuity. He's guilty of a Class A misdemeanor. A Class A misdemeanor is punishable by one year in jail."

Now they all started to go back the other way. And the hard line was becoming even harder.

I said, "It wasn't a gratuity at all. He had dinner on somebody's expense account. We live in an expense account world. It happens a million times a day. When was the last time you had dinner on somebody's expense account?"

"This was no ordinary dinner. This one cost $84."

"What's $84 got to do with it?"

"What did they have, caviar and champagne?"

"Eighty-four dollars for four people is not particularly expensive these days. Have you eaten in a first-class New York restaurant recently? That's about what it would cost anywhere."

"Well I never spent $84 on dinner in my life. A man spends that much on you, he expects favors. We're not talking about a free cup of coffee, we're talking about a payoff of some kind."

Since this line of argument was getting us nowhere, we began to go over the penal law word by word. Seedman was in no sense "required" to give security advice to the hotel. Strictly speaking, he was not even specifically "authorized" to do so. He did not work in that area of the city, he had no official dealings with that hotel at all, was in no position to give favorable police treatment to that hotel. It was strictly a personal arrangement between Seedman and the friend or acquaintance on the hotel staff who had asked his advice, and afterwards accorded him an expense account dinner.

However, no one was interested in this kind of reasoning

either, so I pointed out that the Police Commissioner had already decided to reinstate Seedman, that Seedman had so been told, and that a press conference was on for a few minutes from now, and I picked up the papers and walked out of there.

Press conferences were held in the board room at the top of the stairs on the second floor of police headquarters. This was the same room which at other times was used for Departmental trials. That is, it was the same room in which Seedman might have stood trial, charged with accepting gratuities or even with bribery, and as a result might have been dismissed from the Police Department after 30 years' service. Instead, today this room was jammed by the press, cooked by the blinding lights, and the platform in the rear was crowded with cameras standing on their long thin stalks, like birds. The reporters knew they had been summoned for a decision on Seedman, one way or the other. As soon as Murphy came through the side door with Seedman just behind him, they knew the answer, the buzz went up, and the cameras started turning. Murphy, Seedman, Codd, several others, and myself now sat down, and Murphy began to read my statement:

—It seemed to me that the allegations against Chief Seedman were potentially so serious that a full inquiry had to be made.

—For the last five days Chief Cooper and his staff conducted virtually a round-the-clock inquiry into this and other possible allegations against Chief Seedman. They were checking to find out if there was a pattern of any kind, numerous or regular appearances by Chief Seedman as the guest of the Hilton management or any other management. There is no such pattern. This is an isolated instance. They sought to learn if there were any favors, real or implied, connected with this one isolated instance. There are no favors real or implied.

—One of the hotel executives is a former policeman. Another hotel executive told Chief Cooper that Chief Seedman was "my direct guest." Chief Cooper also checked other midtown hotels, and although he found nothing damaging in any way to Chief Seedman, he did find that virtually all of them are treating city, state or federal law enforcement officers to free meals, and even free lodging. Anyone in uniform, in fact—even mailmen.

—A number of hotels told Chief Cooper they intended to go right on doing it. I wish they would stop doing it totally and at once. These are the people, our fellow citizens, yours and mine, who tempt policemen and, if it is to their advantage, corrupt them if they can. Chief Cooper's investigations into these hotels continue.

—Our inquiry into Chief Seedman's conduct is now completed. There is no serious wrongdoing here. There is no indication that Chief Seedman is other than an honest man. I am returning him today to his own office as Chief of Detectives.

In a brief meeting before the press conference started I had said to Seedman, "Perhaps it would be helpful if you claimed that in Murphy's place you would have done the same thing Murphy did."

Seedman said, "Yes of course that's what I'll say, but in his place I wouldn't have done anything of the kind."

Now, questioned by the press, Seedman said, "Commissioner Murphy had no choice but to act as he did. If I had been Police Commissioner I would have done exactly the same thing."

A journalist asked "Chief Seedman, how do you feel right this minute?"

Seedman had tears in his eyes as he answered. He said, "I feel like the only man in the history of the Police Department who was appointed Chief of Detectives twice."

That afternoon the Police Commissioner called and talked my ear off for several minutes about nothing in particular, which was unusual to say the least.

The next morning Commissioner McCarthy came in to see me. He said, "I can't get in to see the P. C. I've been trying for a week. There's something I simply must talk to him about. Can you get me in to see him?"

Later in the day I told Murphy that McCarthy wanted to see him, but couldn't get past his secretary. I don't know whether Murphy ever received him that day or not.

McCarthy's star was to rise very high in the months to follow, but for the moment the star on high was mine.

6 / Phillips

At the Knapp Commission hearings Patrolman Phillips spoke for three days, most of the time on live television.

He told how plainclothesmen extorted regular amounts of money from gamblers. He told how much went to each plainclothesman in each different part of the city. He explained that each plainclothesman received a single share, but the bosses got a share and a half and a certain inspector, who commanded a division, was earning $1500 a month from gamblers.

He told of a narcotics arrest involving two or three kilos of heroin and $137,000 in cash. The three cops turned in $57,000 and walked out of the station house with $80,000 in cash in a shopping bag.

He talked of extorting money from shopkeepers at Christmas time: "Each detective at Christmas time was given a list of between 10 and 15 establishments to go to pick up money: bars and grills, hotels, and other business establishments. The money was all brought in, it was divided equally among all the detectives in the squad. The lieutenant and sergeant had their own Christmas list. They did not participate in ours."

Phillips told of arresting a Mafia figure. "We brought him into the 17th Detective Squad, and we brought all the witnesses in to identify him. We knew no one would identify this individual because they were afraid. And we had him behind an X-ray mirror. We paraded about five witnesses in front of the X-ray mirrors, and as each one went by we told him that he was identified. I received a telephone call that someone wanted to see me outside the precinct. I went outside the precinct and he asked me if I had their friend upstairs.

"I said, 'Yes, I did. And he has been identified.' They said, 'What can we do in this case?' I said, 'The case is worth about $5000.' We agreed on a price of $3000, which would be paid the next morning. I went with my partner and myself and they gave us $3000. The case was closed because no identification was made on the individual. I went back to the detective squad and had a conversation with the squad commander, and I told him we had made $1000, and I gave him $200. He said, 'That was pretty good work.' "

There was more, much more. Phillips had driven around the city in a Triumph sports car with British plates on it. He would park this car wherever he wished and go in and make his collections. "It's never too late to do business," he told the Knapp Commission panel. Money could be extorted at any time between the arrest of a suspect and the trial in court.

Although Phillips had never finished high school, and had been able to join the Police Department only after attaining a high school equivalency diploma, he never lost his composure on the stand. He licked his lips lightly from time to time or took a sip of ice water, and he answered Armstrong's questions in an orderly, earnest way. It was as if the two of them were reading parts from a play which they had rehearsed many times. Phillips came across like an executive explaining the intricacies of his business.

He described payoffs to precinct personnel in the Sixth Division—Harlem. Pickups for the precinct captain were usually made by a "bag" man who sometimes continued the practice after the replacement of a corrupt captain by an honest one.

Sergeants were paid between $10 and $20 per month per gambling operation in their precinct. Radio car patrolmen got between $10 and $30 per month per gambling operations in their sector. Foot patrolmen got $10 per month per gambling operation on their post.

Phillips was followed onto the stand by Droge, who claimed that of the approximately 200 men assigned to his Brooklyn precinct, he had known about 75 personally. Of these, he knew of only two who didn't take bribes. The others, he said, were earning betwen $60 and $100 per month extra. He told how he himself had "flaked" a teen-age heroin dealer. To flake, in police jargon, meant to plant evidence on. He told how he had taken $200 from the girlfriend of a cocaine dealer, and in return he let the dealer go. He described a shirt factory which burglars frequently broke into. "Every time we received a call that there was a break-in in this particular factory, cars would zoom down there and cops would be walking out with shirts under their coats, stuffed in their pants."

After Droge came former Patrolman Waverly Logan, who described how, while he was in training at the Police Academy, the other recruits had openly discussed corruption. Instructors ignored jokes about corruption which were made openly by the students.

After graduation, Logan was assigned to the 73rd Precinct in Brooklyn—Brownsville. He found that on late tours men did not patrol on foot because it was considered too dangerous. Instead, they hid in the station house cellar, went to a girlfriend's house, or went home. He found that 6-packs of beer could be had free just by walking into a bodega, picking up the merchandise, and walking out again. Supermarket owners would pay radio cars $5 to drive them to the bank with their receipts. Cars responding to stores that had been broken into invariably would be stuffed full of stolen merchandise before they left the scene.

Presently Logan had been transferred to the Preventive Enforcement Patrol Squad in Harlem. This was a new idea in patrol. Men from the neighborhood would patrol their own neighborhoods. But, Logan said, nearly every member of the PEP Squad was on the take. Logan himself now began to extort money and narcotics from people he arrested. Once he and a partner arrested a man with $1000. They vouchered $200 as evidence, and split the rest of the money. The flaking of suspects was common. Any valuable belongings that a suspect might have in his pockets, or his car, or even his apartment, the arresting officers invariably would steal. One day he and his partner and a PEP Squad lieutenant raided the apartment of an important narcotics dealer. The dealer and another man were caught with illegal guns. Patrolman Logan found $2800 in a dresser drawer. This money, plus $200 which was found on a card table, was placed in a bag. In the station house the lieutenant gave $800 to the family of one of the arrested suspects, and split up the rest, giving $500 each to Logan and his partner.

Was it true? Was every cop in the city a crook? Was the

city in more danger from cops than from criminals? Should you call a cop when in trouble, or did calling a cop merely multiply your troubles? Was the cop the guy who put his body between you and the criminal's gun, or was he the guy who would ransack your wallet or your apartment if he could?

In headquarters, and also in every station house in the city, there was consternation. Yes, there had been and still were crooked cops. Phillips, Droge, and Logan were proof of that. But most cops were in no position to make a score. Many served in jobs which offered no contact with the public whatever, others were not brave enough to take such risks, and still others were scrupulously honest. As tales of corruption followed from the witness stand, all of these men—the vast majority of the police force—suffered.

Murphy had to do something. The men wanted and needed support from him. In addition, the city could not be allowed to think that it was being "protected" by an army rivaling in size and rapaciousness that of Attila the Hun.

On the fourth day of the hearings—and on the third day of testimony by Phillips—the Police Commissioner went before a press conference.

The day before, two stickup men had invaded an employment agency on the 20th floor of 341 Madison Avenue. All the employees were tied up and made to lie on the floor. However, one secretary had been on the phone to a girlfriend as the stickup men entered with guns drawn, and she had gasped, "We're being robbed," before slamming the receiver down. This information was transmitted to the police as a burglary, and by the time it reached two cops in a radio car, it was a "past burglary." The two cops got off the elevator nonchalantly, guns in their holsters, had only a second to notice all the employees on the floor, before one of the gunmen opened fire. Within a few seconds this stickup was all over, one of the gunmen lay dead, and the building was infiltrated by police, who soon caught the accomplice.

Routine police action.

Now during this news conference, Commissioner Murphy introduced the two young men, Francis Heitmann and James Morein. He said he was recommending them for promotion to the Detective Division.

The reporters began to question Heitmann about Patrolman Phillips.

"I personally love the Police Department," said Heitmann, "and that is all I have to say."

Patrolman Morein said, "I'd rather not say what I think of Patrolman Phillips."

Commissioner Murphy now called Phillips a "rogue cop," and described him as "squirming to get off the hook." Murphy then released the text of a message which he had just recorded, and which was to go out over the police radio into every radio car in the city once during each of the next three tours. This message read—

"For the last several days the honor of us all has been under attack. I want to assure you today that I believe in you, that I have confidence in your basic integrity, and that my pride in your courage is without limits.

"Only last night two of you again displayed that courage, which is so routine to members of the New York City Police Department, in a shoot-out on Madison Avenue. To me, incidents such as this again prove how much the average police officer wants to do a 100 percent job.

"There is no reason to be ashamed because one or another traitor to the uniform that you wear so proudly seeks to justify his own dishonesty by pretending that none of you is honest. That is not true. There are bad policemen. I ask you to help me rid this Department of them. The dishonest cop is not our brother.

"Don't be discouraged—24,000 times a day the people of New York call 911 and demand your help, and they get it. A thousand times each hour you justify their faith in you, and mine."

I had prepared this statement earlier that morning, and gone over it with the Police Commissioner in his office. It was lying on my desk when Commissioner McCarthy came in about 11:30. After reading the message, McCarthy said that it wasn't good, it was wrong, it was terrible. Phillips was absolutely right; most cops were crooked. You mustn't attack Phillips or the Knapp Commission and you mustn't praise cops on the grounds of their courage. Courage excused nothing. What he wanted was a hard-line statement by Murphy that would defend the Knapp Commission, and impress on all cops the notion that every single one of them who was guilty would get caught and nailed. He then suggested a few minor changes in the phrasing, which I made. Then he approved the statement and went away, leaving me puzzled completely.

The Knapp Commission moved relentlessly into its second week of hearings. Two addict informants, wired for sound, found 11 Harlem policemen willing to furnish them with narcotics in return for cigarettes, whiskey, stereo equipment, power tools and a mini-bike, all of which they had stolen in burglaries so as to get the money to buy heroin.

The chairman of the State Investigation Committee Commission, Paul J. Curran, testified that 68¼ pounds of narcotics seized in police raids disappeared between the station house and the laboratory.

A tow-truck operator testified that police harassed him because he wouldn't pay kickbacks. Two captains visited his bosses to get him fired. One of these captains, whom he did not name, was now an inspector, he said.

Meanwhile, in the halls of headquarters, and presumably wherever cops talked to each other, the conversation was still about Phillips. He was still a patrolman in good standing. He was still being paid the same salary they were. He was still carrying a shield and a gun. In high-level conferences we often discussed Phillips too, but all agreed that Murphy should do nothing about Phillips until the hearings ended.

And apparently they would end without ever having called Durk and Serpico—who had started the whole thing—to the stand. Durk was outraged. The blame was being dumped square on the heads of patrolmen again. What about the higher-ups? Durk also had all those telephone lines coming into his house, and now he began to call everybody. Then, by accident, he appeared on a radio program with Councilman Matthew Troy, the Queens Democratic leader, who listened to his story. On the next-to-last day of the hearing, Troy demanded that Durk and Serpico testify before the Knapp Commission.

Troy's telegram to Knapp read, "Because of serious charges made by Sergeant David Durk that Jay Kriegel and Arnold Fraiman, now a Supreme Court judge, deliberately covered up concrete acts of corruption to protect Mayor

Lindsay's image, which facts were presented by Sergeant Durk and Frank Serpico. I demand that your Commission subpoena these two police officers to testify. If they are not called by you, it will give credence to a strong rumor that your Commission is in business solely to protect the administration from being connected with the corruption probe."

The next day Knapp capitulated. Additional public hearings would be held two months later, during which Durk, Serpico, Kriegel, Fraiman, and others would be invited to testify.

Meaning that neither Murphy nor the Police Department was out of this yet. Would these hearings never end?

7 / Backing Down

What to do about Phillips and Droge?

The question had been discussed months before, but no decision had been reached.

Murphy had had no idea their revelations would be so juicy. Even Knapp was surprised at what a brilliant witness Phillips had turned out to be. Day by day Knapp had rearranged his schedule of witnesses so as to keep Phillips on the stand. He and Droge were the only active cops who had testified to their own corruption.

Now the question of what to do with them was urgent. Cops could talk of very little else. They wanted to see Phillips destroyed. They wanted to believe that Phillips had never existed. Droge too.

So Murphy knew he must suspend Phillips and Droge. Any other course would surprise the citizenry, and demoralize all other cops.

The Commission hearings had ended the previous Friday afternoon. Monday morning Murphy asked me to prepare a statement suspending Phillips and Droge. He also asked that I check with District Attorney Hogan's office and with Federal Attorney Seymour. The head of Hogan's racket squad, Alfred Scotti, said, "Go ahead and suspend them," but Seymour had certain reservations. To remove their guns and shields would increase the problem of protecting them; it would militate against other cops' being turned around; they would be less available, or unavailable, for all the investigations that now would follow. However, Seymour indicated that he could live with Murphy's decision either way.

No one checked with Whitman Knapp.

By noon Murphy had read over my statement, nodded his head, and sent for Syd Cooper. He told Cooper to have somebody remove the guns and shields from these men, and then he went down the hall, stepped before a press conference, and read the statement.

"During the last two weeks, two members of this Department publicly acknowledged the commission of criminal acts and official misconduct. Not wanting to prejudice the course of the public hearings then in progress, I withheld taking action until now.

"Today I am suspending from duty Patrolman William Phillips and Patrolman Edward F. Droge."

When the press conference ended, grinning headquarters cops were shaking hands with each other in the halls.

But as Murphy was returning to his office, one of his lieutenants hurried up to him, saying, "Whitman Knapp's on the phone, and he said he's going to sit on the phone until you talk to him."

Murphy went into his office to take the call.

A few minutes later, Bill Smith and I entered the office.

In a quiet voice, Murphy said, "Knapp just hung up on me."

Murphy looked at me, and he looked away, and he began pacing the room. Knapp was furious at him for suspending the two corrupt cops, he explained.

Murphy began nibbling at his fingernails. "Now Knapp may blast me."

None of us knew what Knapp had promised Phillips and Droge in order to get them to testify. Only a district attorney could promise immunity from criminal prosecution, and only the Police Commissioner could promise immunity from prosecution on Departmental charges. Murphy had promised nothing. So far as any of us knew, neither had the district attorneys, nor the federal attorneys. But obviously also, Knapp had promised Phillips and Droge something. Perhaps he had promised even that he would persuade the Police Commissioner to let them go on carrying guns and shields, still cops in good standing. But Phillips and Droge had used those guns and shields to rob and shake down fellow citizens. Could such power be left in their hands one day longer?

The Police Commissioner said, "But Knapp may blast me."

In addition, Phillips had served more than 14 years. In a few more months he would be eligible for what was called a "vested interest" pension—three quarters of half pay for the rest of his life. Unless he were suspended at once, the city would be forced to reward him with a pension for 14 years as a corrupt cop.

Murphy stared at the phone he had just hung up. "Now Knapp's going to blast me."

An extraordinary—for Murphy—24 hours had begun.

The Police Department wore the body politic on its back like a lead suit. Political pressure was constant. Some was serious, some comical, most was somewhere in between, but it was always there.

One day at a press conference, the young Chief of Patrol, Don Cawley, announced the formation of his new 200-man anti-crime squad. About 25 cops stood behind Cawley, each wearing a different disguise. The next morning, photos appeared in the centerfold of the *Daily News*. Prominent were two young cops dressed in black suits and wearing Roman collars.

The chancery office attacked at once. An important monsignor got through to Murphy by telephone and read him off about dressing cops as priests. Murphy politely put the monsignor on to me. The monsignor was representing the cardinal, I was told. How could we do such a thing as to dress cops as priests? Now parishioners would suspect all priests of being cops. Since this line of reasoning seemed a bit farfetched to me, I attempted to calm the monsignor with a joke. These two cops weren't masquerading as priests, I told him. One was pretending to be a Lutheran minister, while the other one was an Episcopalian. The monsignor didn't laugh. "Episcopalians are called priests, too," he said.

I put him on to Don Cawley. A day or two later, Chief Cawley spent most of a morning trying to cope with a three-priest delegation from the chancery office. Eventually Cawley put them onto Monsignor Joseph Dunne, the number one police chaplain, who possibly would be able to talk to them on more equal terms. Oh yes, each of us in turn had promised that never again would we dress policemen up in clerical garb.

Pressure from the Mayor was frequent. One day, meeting with Murphy for a ceremony in a precinct station house, Lindsay remarked that he had had a letter from Congressman Rangle. Rangle had named three street corners in Harlem where his constituents said narcotics were being openly peddled. Lindsay had sent this letter on to Murphy, had Murphy seen it yet? Murphy said he hadn't. Lindsay said, "Well, you better put a tracer on the letter, or at least write a letter to Rangle saying that the matter is being looked into and that you'll get back to him."

One day the Mayor called me up.

"Hello, Bob, how are you feeling?"

"Fine, Mr. Mayor, and you?"

After a pause, Lindsay said, "There's a very important man here from WABC radio and he wants to talk to you, and I'll put him on." WABC radio broadcasted music aimed at teen-age girls. My own girls listened to it all the time.

An individual from this station, whose name I didn't catch (the Mayor obviously hadn't caught his name either), now explained that his station had six million listeners. The station wanted to encourage all these listeners to buy whistles. Then whenever one of the listeners saw a crime, or heard another whistle, this listener would blow her own whistle so as to attract the police. Whole neighborhoods would blow until the police came.

This idea seemed so excellent to this man that he asked me to arrange a high-level meeting with the Police Commissioner, the Chief Inspector, Chief Cawley, myself, the Mayor, everybody.

In the background I could hear Lindsay's voice. Then a great many people laughed. Then Lindsay's voice said something more, after which there was another roar of laughter.

I said into the phone, "How many people are in Lindsay's office with you?"

He said, "About 25."

"It sounds like he's funnier than Bob Hope."

"Oh yes, he's very funny." The telephone voice in my ear began to speak enthusiastically of equipping everybody with whistles. I thought I could hear several million whistles screeching inside my skull. It was a harrowing prospect.

I said, "How does the Mayor feel about this idea?"

He said, "Oh, the Mayor is all for it!"

I suggested he check with the Mayor. I would lay the meeting on for any day the Mayor promised to be there.

Lindsay was an expert at slipping a guy like this onto somebody.

In the garment district, parked trucks were getting looted with great regularity. The merchants got onto Lindsay, and Lindsay got onto the Police Commissioner. If Lindsay wanted something done, a wise Police Commissioner did it, and so presently Murphy approved a plan whereby 11 men and one sergeant were assigned to clean up 35th Street. Hopefully after that job was completed, they would clean up 36th Street, and then 37th. The Police Commissioner so informed the Mayor, who presumably informed the merchants. Chief Inspector Codd had advised against putting any more men on that street, and so had Chief Seedman.

"It won't work," Seedman had said. "The thing the Mayor doesn't realize is that these trucks never move. They're used as rent-free warehouses. Eventually one truck gets emptied and another truck pulls up. The first truck pulls out and is immediately replaced. The thieves know that the trucks are there more or less permanently, and that they're full. The cops on one side of the street can't see what's happening on the other side because it's wall-to-wall trucks."

The new squad went to work on 35th Street, but the merchants informed Lindsay that they were not satisfied. The Mayor called Murphy and suggested more men. Though the talk in headquarters was that no more men would be forthcoming, the Police Commissioner presently capitulated, and another 12 men went to work in that same area. They had to be stripped from some other place of course, but Murphy chose to give in to the Mayor's wishes.

Later in the year Lindsay would ask that the police complement in the two midtown precincts be doubled. The tax base of the city was built upon midtown business, and upon the tourism which the theaters brought into New York— but now people were becoming afraid to venture into the streets there after dark.

Pressured by Lindsay, Murphy would send an extra 500 men into the two midtown precincts. Neither would ever be considered high-crime precincts as compared, say, to the 28th Precinct in Harlem, which would lead the city in murders for the year, and which had less than 300 men assigned, and for which, no matter how hard business leaders there pleaded, no additional men could ever be found.

Pressure such as this was common from Lindsay, but in private Murphy often stated that Lindsay was the best mayor he ever worked for—and he had worked in three other cities. Often in New York in the past, the mayor would "suggest" that the police commissioner promote so-and-so, or grant someone else some coveted assignment. Lindsay never did this once, Murphy said.

Nearly everyone tried to lay off political pressures on subordinates, and of course I did too. One day a Miss Fran Lee called. I switched her to Sergeant Powers of my staff, who wrote the following report.

> From: Sergeant Edward P. Powers, Shield Number 2411
> To: Deputy Commissioner, Public Affairs
> Subject: THREATENED SHIT-IN ON CITY HALL STEPS.
> 1. Telephone message received this date from Miss Fran Lee, 15 West 81 Street, N.Y.C. tel. 873-5507, who identified herself as the editor of a paper called "Children Before Dogs." She has recently headed the "Mothers March Against Dog Dung" and complains that at 81 Street and 5th Avenue, 92 Street and Central Park West, and on the East River Drive from 49 to 52 Streets one stands in shit up to knee.
> 2. Miss Lee further states that while appearing on

the David Susskind show some dissidents threw shit at her to which she retaliated by waving her "Scoop the Poop" shovel under Mr. Susskind's nose.

3.   Miss Lee is an expert in the disease of tocicara; a disease which stems from dog shit and causes infectious worms to emerge from the ground and sicken children.

4.   To dramatize her complaints Miss Lee proposes to bring many babies with shitty diapers to the steps of City Hall and there to dump the contents of these diapers.

5.   Chief Inspector's office has been notified of dog excrement sites.

Edward P. Powers
Sgt. #2411

One day a reporter from the *New York Post* phoned. He had an extremely serious problem to report, he said. It had the gravest possible implications for the Police Department. He was tense, and so I became tense too.

The story was this. A couple had come into a bar the week before and occupied three stools, for they had a dog with them. They seated the dog on the third stool and ordered three martinis. The third glass was placed in front of the dog, and the dog lapped it dry. Another round of martinis was ordered. The couple kept drinking down dry martinis, matched each time by the dog. The dog kept lapping up dry martinis until it fell off the stool, twitched on the floor, and died.

I said to the reporter, "Did you call up to report the murder of the dog?"

He said gravely, "There's more to the story than that."

It seems that another individual had witnessed all this from a stool further along the bar, and when the dog died this man jumped up and telephoned the precinct. He wanted a radio car sent at once, and he wanted to press charges against the couple for having bought martinis for the dog.

The precinct telephone operator hung up on him.

The guy went out into the street, but the first three radio car he tried to flag down wouldn't stop. The fourth one stopped, but then radioed to all the other radio cars not to stop at that bar again that night until the guy had gone home. The outraged witness then went to the station house to depose a civilian complaint against the Police Department.

The *Post* reporter said: "There's been no sign of that civilian complaint since."

"Are you asking me to find out what happened to it?"

"Some cop destroyed it; that's what happened to it."

The reporter said, "The witness tells me that one of his hobbies is recognizing accents. He said he would recognize anywhere the accent of one of those patrolmen who responded to the bar but refused to take action. That same accent has called him up three times, offering to sell him cemetery lots in a nonexistent cemetery."

There was rather a long silence.

The reporter said, "I want to know what the Police Department is doing about this case."

I said, "I see."

"In addition to what was done to the poor dog, this is rather a serious case of police corruption."

I told the reporter that there were so many people getting murdered these days, and our work load was so heavy, that I didn't see how the police could throw out a dragnet for the murderers of this dog a week after its demise. This failed to move the reporter. I said hopefully, "Do you suppose the dog enjoyed those martinis?"

The reporter said, "Are you going to do anything about this?"

I said, "I really don't see how I can," and I hung up.

But what happened during the hours immediately after the Police Commissioner suspended Patrolmen Phillips and Droge was not amusing in the least.

Murphy's home phone rang all that evening. Knapp called, as did other members of his commission. These people were outraged, and some were not far from hysteria. As Murphy understood it, they were ready to denounce Murphy, denounce Lindsay. They wanted Phillips and Droge given back their guns, shields, and salaries. They saw Murphy's move as a repudiation of their commission. It was also apparent that they saw themselves as knights in shining armor. They were the ones engaged in saving the city and perhaps the world, and no one was going to thwart them now. Murphy was informed that the district attorneys and the federal attorneys stood behind Knapp's demands.

In the morning the Police Commissioner was summoned to the Mayor's office. He arrived accompanied by Lacovara and by First Deputy Commissioner Smith. Deputy Mayor Dick Aurelio, Corporation Counsel Lee Rankin, Hank Ruth, who headed the Mayor's Criminal Justice Coordinating Council, and Jay Kriegel, who was the Mayor's liaison with the Police Department, all were present.

It was election day. One of the items on the off-year ballot was a referendum on a Transportation Bond Issue. The men assembled discussed whether or not this referendum would pass.

But presently Lindsay began to discuss Knapp. This latest unpleasant development. This tension. This possible public confrontation. This suspension situation.

Clearly Knapp had been on the phone with Lindsay too. Lindsay had heard many of the same threats Murphy had heard.

The Police Commissioner stated that he didn't see how he could fully reinstate Phillips and Droge, that returning their shields and guns seemed out of the question.

Rankin now suggested that Murphy could continue to pay the salary of the two corrupt cops, if Murphy so chose. There was precedent for this. Some years ago, something like it had been done in the Sanitation Department.

Lacovara got out a yellow pad and began to scribble a statement that the Police Commissioner could make, as he returned Phillips and Droge to the Police Department payroll. The situation was being resolved nicely. Not a single voice had been raised.

As Lacovara wrote, there were suggestions from all corners of the room, and he tried to work in the best phrases of everybody. When he had finished and read the statement back, and no further suggestions were forthcoming, it was suggested that he telephone Whitman Knapp and read the statement to him. Lacovara did this. Then he read it to Michael Armstrong. Around him, the Mayor's office was silent.

Knapp told Lacovara that he appreciated the effort that

everybody was making, and he especially appreciated their letting him know that the new statement would be given to the press forthwith.

Knapp's heroes, who were not the Police Department's heroes, were back on salary.

About an hour later, Lacovara's draft had been typed up, and he came into my suite of offices and ordered Lieutenant Paul Murphy, Commanding Officer of the Public Information Division, to release the statement to the press at once. Paul Murphy read it and was shocked and appalled. Paul Murphy was 43 years old and had been a cop 21 years. He had killed two men in the line of duty and won the Combat Cross, the Police Department's second highest decoration. He was not only a college graduate but had earned two Master's degrees, and was studying for a Ph.D. in theology.

As the door closed behind Lacovara, the office personnel crowded around Paul Murphy to read the statement. All were stunned. Like most cops throughout the city, they wanted to see Phillips and Droge in front of a firing squad. Instead, the Police Commissioner was rewarding them with full pay.

Lieutenant Murphy put in a frantic call to me in my car.

"You've got to do something, Commissioner."

I told him to hold the statement, I'd be right back.

But when I had the statement in my hands, I found that the Police Commissioner was not in the building. He had gone home. I was immediately received by First Deputy Commissioner Smith. I told him I was against this statement. It weakened the Police Commissioner's stature. It was all too clear that he had backed down to the Knapp Commission.

Smith said, "You don't know what's been going on for the last 24 hours."

Smith's phone rang, and his secretary announced Whitman Knapp. As Smith picked up the phone, I could have sworn that his hand was shaking, and when he spoke his voice was not steady either.

Knapp wanted to know when the statement was going out. Why hadn't it been released yet?

Smith assured Knapp that it was in the works, and hung up.

I told Smith that it was not fitting for the Police Commissioner to back down to Whitman Knapp. And what about police morale? Every cop in the city would be outraged.

Smith said, "Well, it's got to be done."

The phone rang. It was Whitman Knapp again. Less than ten minutes had passed since his first call. He again wanted to know how soon he could count on that statement going out.

After Smith had hung up this time, I called the Police Commissioner at home.

I told him I thought restoring the pay of the two corrupt cops was a mistake. "Does it have to be done?"

After a moment's pause, Murphy said, "Yes, I'm afraid it has to be done."

I said, "Alright."

Murphy now began to talk in that fatherly way he had, trying to convince me that this was a good and proper decision. "You don't know how it was last night. It was unbelievable."

I said, "Can I at least change the statement so as to make you look bigger and stronger?"

He said, "No, I'm afraid it has to go out without a comma changed. It's all been agreed upon by Knapp."

The statement said that in restoring the pay of Patrolmen Phillips and Droge, the Police Commissioner was acceding to requests by the Knapp Commission, and by various district and federal attorneys who would need the cooperation of the two corrupt cops in order to construct cases against many other corrupt cops.

As I came through the door into my own office, the phone rang, and I heard someone call, "Whitman Knapp calling Lieutenant Murphy."

This call I intercepted. When I had identified myself, Knapp giggled nervously. "I just wanted to ask Lieutenant Murphy how soon that statement was going out. I understood he was holding it up for some reason."

"No, I was the one holding it up. We're just sending it out now."

The next morning the Police Commissioner phoned. "How do you think it went?"

There had not been much criticism in the press, although

certain of the reporters had remarked privately that the Police Commissioner had come off "weak." How he had come off with patrolmen in the street was perhaps another story. They were cynical about police commissioners to begin with, and this one had just "rewarded" two corrupt cops with the same wages honest ones earned. How could cops believe in Murphy personally, or in the sincerity of his anti-corruption campaign now? And if they didn't believe, how far would they follow where he led?

Murphy might be able to win them back later, and he might not.

"It was unbelievable last night," repeated the Police Commissioner, and he began to explain why he felt he had done the right thing. He didn't want to polarize the city at this point. Surely Knapp would be dropping out of sight slowly now. He guessed he had saved a good many votes for Lindsay, for Knapp would surely have tried to sink Lindsay otherwise. He said he had always believed that the muscle behind the Knapp Commission was Michael Armstrong, but now he believed it was Knapp himself.

The next morning the September crime statistics came in. Murder was up 70 percent. Rape was up 42 percent. Crime as a whole was way up for the month. In addition ten corrupt policemen were that day indicted.

A feeling of hopelessness pervaded many of us.

I entered the Police Commissioner's office carrying a speech which he was to deliver that evening. As he glanced over it he crossed out a certain paragraph, saying, "That's one Knapp wouldn't like."

He had wanted to promote the two Brooklyn cops known as Batman and Robin to detective, and we set a tentative date for this now.

"Did you know that the Knapp Commission tried to bribe them?" he asked. "Do we dare say that when we promote them? Why don't you have Syd Cooper check with Knapp to see if they'd mind if we said that—that Knapp sent Patrolman Droge out to bribe them and they turned in Droge and the Knapp agents as well. Have Syd clear it with Knapp."

Suddenly everything had to be cleared with Whitman Knapp.

"If Knapp and Armstrong start to scream, well, alright,

we won't mention it," Murphy said. "And that means they owe us one."

8 / The French Connection

In between the first disastrous Knapp Commission hearings starring Phillips, and the second disastrous Knapp Commission hearings, which would star Durk, fell the unfortunate case of Detective First Grade Eddie Egan.

Egan, who was then 41 years old, had earned six Police Department citations. All but two involved narcotics surveillances and arrests; the two others involved armed robbery arrests.

Egan was promoted to detective after only 19 months in uniform, and within four years of becoming a patrolman he had been promoted to first grade detective and was earning lieutenant's pay, a record never approached by anyone. He spent most of 12 years in the Narcotics Division, and he was flamboyant. To make surveillances, he would stand on a street corner tending a hot dog wagon, and at Christmastime he would dress up in a Santa Claus suit and stand on the sidewalk ringing a bell.

He had friends in the press whom he invited to photograph him in these costumes, and he received a great deal of publicity. So did his partner, Sonny Grosso. Still, the two detectives were small-fry then, and they were also heroes—in the Police Department it was possible to be both at once. But one night the two of them, drinking in a nightclub after midnight, chanced to spy a little man throwing money around, a little man who shouldn't have had that kind of money in his pockets. They tailed him home in the wee hours of the morning, and watched him open up his newsstand. This was all Egan needed. No proprietor of a newsstand had any right to fling money around nightclubs. Something was fishy.

This was the case that became known as *The French Connection*. The book, which was written by Mr. Robin Moore (again), was published in 1968, approximately six years after the event.

Almost immediately, Egan later remarked, he could feel the jealousy all around him. He and Grosso were bounced out of the Narcotics Division and separated. Grosso was assigned to Harlem, and Egan now went to work in the 81st Squad in Brooklyn. He was still a Detective First Grade, but it was different. Egan now spent his days capturing petty addicts instead of major smugglers, confiscating one bag of heroin, or one marijuana cigarette, or one hypodermic syringe, after which he was faced by the morass of paper work which then—and to some extent still —was strangling the Detective Division. All contraband had to be sealed and transported to the lab, and from there to the property clerk.

Egan was no intellectual. He also was no innocent. He knew very well that no junkie would be sentenced to jail for one bag, or one needle. The courts were far too lenient. Meanwhile, Egan, who had great street sense, couldn't spell. Reports and forms didn't so much baffle him as they infuriated him. And he didn't want to waste time at the lab either. He wanted to be out on the street busting heads. He liked to dispense justice himself. This was how a detective perhaps gained information that would lead him to some sort of major criminal or important crime. Egan liked to terrorize his slice of Bedford-Stuyvesant. They called him Mister Egan there.

On misdemeanor cases Egan began to skip some of the paper work. He didn't always go to the lab or turn up in court.

Chief Seedman once remarked that all aggressive detectives eventually got into trouble. This didn't mean that they beat up a prominent lawyer they mistook for a petty thief. It didn't mean that any of those they arrested were related to the District Attorney.

It did mean that they would abuse some criminal who was also a registered federal informant, which criminal would then begin to inform on them to other agencies.

New York City teamed with federal law enforcement agencies. All of them, though not the Police Department, had a great deal of money to spread among criminals who were potential informants. Now, in 1968, some of these criminal informants began to name Eddie Egan as a crooked cop.

Presently, balanced against his six commendations, there were eight active investigations into the conduct and character of Detective First Grade Eddie Egan.

The first allegation, coming from an unnamed federal source, was received in April of 1968, one month after Egan began to operate in the 81st Precinct in Brooklyn. In those days allegations of corruption were pursued with less zeal than now, and three years went by before Egan was brought in to answer, if he could, this allegation. Investigations, once commenced, developed their own momentum. Egan was questioned once a month for three months, and nothing happened.

Then somebody dug up another allegation. This too had come from "federal sources," regarding an incident alleged to have occurred sometime in 1968. But Egan's answers were either totally satisfactory, or else they merely obfuscated everything, for this case was not pursued.

The French Connection had reached the screen. It was in no sense a portrayal of the life of Eddie Egan. The hero, in fact, was known as Popeye Doyle—everyone now began to call Egan Popeye also, although his original nickname had been Bullets. Bullets Egan was known to other detectives as a gun nut, and one once described him as the only detective he'd ever seen who wore a gun belt with 68 bullets in it.

In the film, Eddie Egan was portrayed as a tough, even brutal cop, who stomped on the civil rights of suspects. In the denouement, the Egan character clumsily rubs out a federal narcotics agent, without shedding a tear.

The French Connection was the hit of the season. It won a number of Academy Awards, and became one of the biggest moneymaking films of all time.

Now Egan was seen often on TV. Usually Eddie walked on stage dressed like a truck driver who had just climbed down from his rig, and he spoke rough New Yorkese out of the side of his mouth. This was no act. This was Eddie Egan in person.

Egan had played a small role in *The French Connection* (Grosso had played an even smaller one). Egan played it very well indeed, and he was an authentic tough guy whom Hollywood moguls liked to be seen with. Certain of them had even thought of buying him for a mascot, their own personal detective. Eddie Egan would come very cheap, for he knew nothing about money. For a few thousand dollars a year he would sign any contract, and such a contract was being offered to him now.

The P.B.A. retained its own law firm. Its head lawyer was Robert J. Eliasberg, and any time any cop was in trouble he headed straight for Eliasberg's office. When Egan was first questioned by the Internal Affairs Division early in 1971, he had immediately contacted Eliasberg and was assigned a staff lawyer. By August, having now been questioned for the fourth time that year, Egan informed Eliasberg that he wanted to retire and sign a contract as an actor. Eliasberg told him to hold off until after Eliasberg had had a chance to meet with Syd Cooper and ask the hard question, Why are you harassing Eddie Egan?

So Egan had still not signed his film contract. However, he and Grosso did file a request for a leave of absence in order to promote their film. Whenever such a request came, a routine investigation was made before granting it. In this case, the four interrogations of Egan so far that year were quickly turned up. Also turned up was a new allegation, this one from the Brooklyn District Attorney, to the effect that after arresting 14 persons for possession of stolen government checks, Detective Egan had failed to cooperate with the District Attorney's office, had failed to appear in court, and as a result the case was dismissed.

Meanwhile, the Chief Inspector's Investigation and Evaluation Division had begun to look into the affairs of Sonny Grosso. Grosso had been thrown down a flight of stairs while trying to make an arrest in Harlem the previous May. He had broken his knee and been on sick report for 105 days. Once while on sick report he was seen at a filming location—a cop on sick report was not allowed to leave his house. Accorded permission at one point to work as an actor, he apparently arranged similar employment for three other detectives through the Silvia Fay Agency. The Chief Inspector's investigators suspected that these detectives were being used not as actors but to control crowds and maintain order at filming locations. If true, this meant in effect that they were hiring out their guns. A cop might moonlight with permission, but he was never allowed to hire out his gun. This was possibly a serious violation by Grosso.

Nothing had been proven against either detective, but inside the Police Department suspicion was enough. The eventual denial of their requests for leaves of absence ran to two and a half pages and was stamped "disapproved," and signed by Patrick Murphy.

Suddenly Egan and Grosso were standing in all the spotlights at once, and there were men—moved in some cases by jealousy, in other cases by pure righteousness—who were out to get both of them. Grosso proved impossible to get. No one could prove him guilty of any serious wrongdoing, and in certain meetings on this subject Grosso was always referred to not as possibly innocent, but as "cute." "Cute" in police jargon usually meant that a superior could find no ground on which to nail a subordinate whom he wanted to nail.

But Egan, whom some of his admirers called Super Cop, but who could just as easily have been known as Sloppy Cop, was not cute at all.

Eliasberg, as P.B.A. lawyer, some months previously had arranged a meeting with Cooper. Cooper had been newly switched to command the Internal Affairs Division, and Eliasberg wanted Cooper's agreement on certain ground rules. To go after real corruption had the approval of everybody. But hardly any cop or detective on the force, it seemed, was able to keep absolutely accurate memo books and other records, and if investigators put in a lot of time looking for corruption but failed to find it, they were often loath to let a guy get off scot-free. So they would hurt him with whatever paper violations they could find.

Eliasberg pointed out that the line organizations were against this policy. Cooper agreed that he was against it too, and it would not be done under his command.

Egan had already passed through the four earliest interrogations with apparent success. But he still wanted to retire, and Eliasberg so advised Cooper, suggesting that Cooper look into the Egan case as soon as possible. Cooper replied that he needed time to familiarize himself with his new unit. He was very busy. He would get to the Egan case when he could.

Two months later, Eliasberg finally succeeded in getting

a second appointment with Cooper.

Eliasberg sat there next to Cooper's desk while Cooper took telephone calls, or was questioned by his staff, or fired questions back, or ran from room to room to check on other problems. Obviously Syd Cooper had little time to spare for Detective Egan, so Eliasberg left, and the next day he advised Egan to file his application for retirement.

But as soon as papers were filed, everyone suddenly had all the time in the world to study the Egan case.

Six days later charges were served against Egan. There were six different counts:

    1. During the year 1969, respondent did fail to maintain his memo book in a manner prescribed by the rules and procedures of this department.

    2. Having been directed to see Assistant DA of King's County, on seven occasions during 1969 did fail to do so and did fail to notify the Assistant DA that he would not appear.

    3. On five occasions did make entry in memo book regarding his attendance in court when in fact he was not performing that type of duty at the time specified.

    4. On 11 occasions during 1969 did make entries in memo book that he was scheduled to appear in court, when in fact there was no case scheduled.

    5. During 1968 did make four phone calls to Brooklyn Criminal Court that he was unable to appear due to other police business when in fact no other necessity existed.

    6. On 18 occasions, did fail to submit his court appearance form to his commanding officer.

These were charges designed only to slow Egan down, not to stop him, while Cooper's investigators tried to bring up a howitzer.

Next came a second set of charges, eight specifications, all having to do with evidence in criminal cases not having been safeguarded. Then came a third set of charges, six specifications, also having to do with the safeguarding of evidence.

In court later, a number of these charges would prove beyond the three-year statute of limitations and would be dropped. But all of them, both those that would be dropped and those to which Egan would plead guilty, involved derisory amounts of narcotics evidence: in one case a single hypodermic needle, in another a single pill alleged to be Doriden, in a third a piece of metal foil alleged to contain cocaine. All of this missing evidence lumped together amounted to less than a single handful—and suddenly Egan walked through the door of the Internal Affairs Division and dumped it all out on the desk. He had vouchered it after arresting the suspect. He simply had never delivered it to the Property Clerk, but had thrown it in his locker, where it had lain in some cases for years.

Suddenly there was no real case against Detective First Grade Eddie Egan, but a good deal of pride had been invested by now, and so the case went forward, like an empty trailer truck rolling driverless downhill. By November 12, Chief Cooper had prepared a two-and-a-half-page confidential memo to the Police Commissioner, marked "Charges and specifications pending against Detective Edward Egan, Shield 373, 81st Squad."

On the day that Egan had dumped the missing narcotics out on the desk, he had also dumped two guns that he couldn't account for. Now, in addition, he was charged with possession of guns that he hadn't registered with his commanding officer. The most serious charge against him was that he had failed to appear in court to testify against those 14 persons arrested for possession of stolen checks. Egan soon proved that this was not accurate. As a matter of fact, Egan claimed, the Assistant District Attorney had blown that case, for he never could get all the witnesses there on time. Once the case was dismissed, Detective Egan got mad, went before the grand jury, testified for three hours, won an indictment, testified in court—and got convictions on the leader and several henchmen, who were still in jail at that moment.

Cooper's memo to the Police Commissioner pointed out that *The French Connection* was currently playing in a Broadway theater, had received favorable notices, and that Egan had not only worked as an actor in this film, but had also reportedly signed a movie contract for other pictures. "As a result," Cooper wrote, "Detective Egan has developed an image which projects the 'ideal' for young, impressionable patrolmen." Cooper said his investigation showed an entirely different picture of Detective Egan, that of a flamboyant cop who disregarded Departmental regulations, and who conformed only casually with the rules regarding evidence.

Egan, Cooper wrote, concentrated on quantity rather than quality in his pursuit of arrests. As Cooper saw it, the contrast between the "image" and actuality was so great that it ought to be exposed. Disciplinary action against Egan would no doubt result in much publicity, but the Department should take the opportunity to demonstrate that the qualities exhibited by Egan were not exemplary; he was not a "good cop," but the opposite. Cooper recommended that Egan be flopped to patrolman, and the charges against him expedited.

Immediately after receiving this memo, the Police Commissioner sent it with a handwritten note to First Deputy Smith. Note the December 2 (the date of Egan's retirement) deadline for trying and perhaps dismissing Egan, Murphy wrote. This was a glaring example of the Department's failure to establish responsibility for the total performance of subordinates. Nothing deserved higher priority than to develop a workable system of reports, controls and supervision which would permit commanders to bring charges against superiors who failed to control subordinates such as Egan. As Murphy saw it, Egan deserved to be dealt with as harshly as possible, but so did his superiors.

At this point the Egan case became public property, and it was therefore necessary to disclose the evidence against him. The press received this evidence with derision. And apparently so did most of the city.

It was going to prove impossible to take the hero of *The French Connection* and slide him soundlessly out of the Police Department on charges such as failure to deliver one marijuana cigarette to the property clerk. A week before his trial was to start, I talked to the Police Commissioner about it. Murphy hated bad language and never used it himself, but now I informed the Police Commissioner that public opinion at this point considered the charges against Detective Egan to be chickenshit, pure and simple.

Sometimes Murphy had a way of recoiling at such words, but this time he did not. I had done some investigating. The TV newsman Chris Borgen had served with

Egan, and knew Egan, and had told me that he would lay his life on the line for Eddie Egan as an honest man. Borgen had said, "He's crazy, he's a fanatic, in some ways he's stupid. He nearly blew that French Connection case because he's got four left feet and he fell all over them while tailing a guy. But honest he is. He just has no use for the dumb regulations, and no time for them. He nearly broke up Grosso's family because he kept on calling up at three o'clock in the morning saying, 'Sonny, we got to meet an informant,' and Grosso would go with him. He's a completely gung-ho cop. He loves being a cop. All he cares about is the Police Department."

Murphy said, "Yes, the same goes for Batman and Robin. They're fanatics too. You only have to talk with them for 15 minutes to realize it."

Clearly Murphy was against fanatics. In a 32,000-man department, it was possible to argue that all types were needed, including fanatics. But Murphy thought otherwise and showed no sign of changing his mind. Surely this was why he had no time for Durk or Serpico. Murphy simply could not personally understand fanatics.

"I've looked into the Egan case thoroughly," I informed the Police Commissioner. "I'm told, and I believe it, that Egan is so broken up that he can't even be talked to. As soon as anyone tries to say something to him, he bursts into tears."

Present during this conference were Chief Inspector Codd and Deputy Inspector Joe Priess.

Only a few minutes before, Murphy had given the order flopping Egan back to patrolman, even though the trial had not yet begun.

I hadn't known this. I said, "Can't you at least wait until the trial is held?"

Murphy said, "Well, that's not necessary in order to flop him back to patrolman."

Codd said, "Detective rank is a mark of special trust by the Police Commissioner. If there is no special trust, then the Police Commissioner is in his rights to flop the man back to patrolman without trial."

I said, "This is all very true. But the public doesn't know this. They'll say that you prejudged him before trial. They'll claim that you consider him guilty until proven innocent. They'll say that your conduct is unjust and also un-American. We can't afford just to ignore the public all the time. We keep on doing it, and it's wrong."

For a moment this stopped Murphy. He said to Inspector Priess, "How far along is this?"

Priess said, "I just made one phone call. At this stage it's a phone order. And of course I'm such a numbskull that I don't know what I'm doing and obviously I did it wrong. You can get out of it that way."

I said to the Police Commissioner, "The public considers Egan one of our heroes. He is not just any detective. We've just been through those traumatic Knapp Commission hearings, and we can't afford to lose the sympathy of the public still again."

Presently Murphy said, "Alright, let me think about it, and then I'll make my decision."

The next morning as I started up the steps into headquarters, I had the misfortune to run into Eddie Egan, who immediately began to protest his innocence. He looked like a man who hadn't slept in days, and I could well believe the stories that when anyone asked him about this he started to cry. Lawyer Eliasberg, who was with him, said, "Eddie's been flopped back to uniform."

I said, "Is it official, because I spoke to the Police Commissioner last night, and perhaps he has countermanded that order?"

However, I soon learned that it was indeed official now. Murphy had not countermanded anything. Detective Eddie Egan was now a patrolman.

I went in to see Murphy. I said, "I still feel that it was wrong to flop him back to patrolman. This is the guy who made the two biggest heroin hauls in the history of the Department, and now we do this to him. There is no missing evidence. The man to be blamed for his shoddy bookkeeping is his supervisor, not him. What he did was a common practice among the detectives."

I said, "It's true that Codd, Cooper, and Seedman all advised you to flop him back to patrolman. But they are only one voice."

His face took on a thoughtful expression. Presently he volunteered that if Egan would withdraw his application for retirement, perhaps something could be arranged.

There would be enough time then to investigate all the charges thoroughly. Murphy himself would certainly have to see the case differently, perhaps revise his thinking.

The Police Commissioner asked me to talk to Egan about possibly withdrawing his request for retirement.

So I arranged to lunch with Eliasberg, who said that the movie company would move Egan out to the West Coast two weeks from now. Eggan would not want to withdraw his retirement application.

I could see how this would be received at headquarters: Ah ha, further proof of guilt.

I went to see Chief Seedman, who was holding himself as aloof from the case as possible.

When pressed, Seedman admitted that he hadn't read the charges himself, he had merely accepted Cooper's word for the fact that they were grave. According to Seedman, Cooper and certain others seemed to be against Egan principally because he was flamboyant and in the movies. Then Seedman said, "Of course, I've been through this kind of thing myself. I know how Egan must be feeling. If you had come to me last week, perhaps I could have done something."

Originally Seedman had thought that an appropriate punishment for Egan would be to drop him from first grade to second grade detective, reducing his salary by about $2200 a year. But Chief Inspector Codd had got together with Cooper and Cawley, and the three of them then recommended most strongly that Seedman bust Egan back to uniform. Seedman apparently felt this pressure was too much to buck. He too had recommeded flopping Egan all the way back.

Eight days before his retirement with full pension rights was to take effect, the trial of former Detective First Grade Edward Egan began in the board room on the second floor of police headquarters. Egan, who was dressed in civilian clothes, wore his unaccustomed patrolman's shield on his sports coat. He was represented by Mr. Eliasberg and also by Frank Natoli, a second P.B.A. lawyer. The prosecutor was Sergeant Edward Smith, one of the police lawyers assigned to the legal division. Judge and jury was Louis Stutman, Deputy Commissioner for Trials.

In the audience, which sometimes numbered 30 people

or more, were five character witnesses for Patrolman Egan, including William Friedkin, director of the movie *The French Connection.* Also present all day was Roy Scheider, the actor who had played the role of Sonny Grosso in the same film. The actor did not testify. It would be Commissioner Stutman's job to listen to the witnesses, to decide on the guilt or innocence of the defendant on each of the charges and specifications, and afterwards to recommend a course of action to the Police Commissioner.

In an ordinary year, hundreds of Departmental trials took place, and after each one Commissioner Stutman submitted his recommendations to the Police Commissioner, who normally stamped these papers "approved" after giving them only a cursory reading, or perhaps not even that. Most times, in other words, Stutman was the final judge. The Police Commissioner's participation in Departmental trials was a formality only.

However, the Egan case had reached the public print. Murphy and Stutman had already consulted. Murphy had asked, "This is not a breaking charge, is it, Lou?"

Stutman had replied, "No, it's not. If I find him guilty on every charge, still I don't see how I could recommend more that a 30-day rip."

But that was already several weeks ago. Even in the last several hours it was possible to feel that the mood inside the police hierarchy had hardened against Patrolman Egan.

And so the trial began.

Egan's career was sketched. The French Connection case in 1962 had involved the arrest of nine persons, with 112 pounds of heroin seized,—heroin later valued at 32 million dollars. Five years later Egan had seized 20 million dollars worth of heroin. In 1969 he had served on a legislative committee which conducted hearings to consider changes in narcotics laws. He had also lectured to detectives at the Police Academy.

Now the character witnesses came forward. The first was Edward Carey, who had retired as a deputy chief to become Police Commissioner of New Rochelle. Carey had been Commanding Officer of Narcotics when Egan was assigned there. Carey said that Egan's work was excellent, that he put in long hours, that his integrity was of the highest degree, and that he was a gung-ho detective.

The second character witness was Captain Francis O'Connor who as a lieutenant had commanded the 81st Squad when Egan was assigned there. O'Connor had found Egan to be trustworthy, dedicated, and an outstanding detective, with a capacity to clean up street conditions. He rated Egan as one of his top men.

Lawyer Natoli had asked Carey to explain how and why Egan had been promoted to second grade detective after only two year's service. Carey said he had told the men to decide among themselves. Who was the best detective? Who deserved the second grade money? It went to a vote and Egan won. Two years later, there was an opening for one first grade detective, and Carey again put this to the vote of the squad. Who's the best detective? Who deserves the money? Again Egan won.

Most of the charges against Egan concerned keeping contraband in his locker, rather than making the long trip to the Property Clerk every time he either seized such evidence or needed it in court. Under Murphy this whole procedure had just been redesigned. To avoid the loss of so much detective time it was now permitted to safeguard such evidence in the station houses.

In otherwords, Egan was being tried for violations which no longer existed.

But technically Egan was guilty, he knew he was guilty, his lawyers knew he was guilty, and all were aware that Stutman would be obliged to find him guilty on most counts. That was not the point. The point was that Egan stood eight days away from his pension, and about two weeks away from a blossoming movie career and he was willing to suffer any sort of rip that Sutman might recommend. What Egan could not afford would be the disgrace of being dismissed from the Police Department. If this happened there would of course be no pension. In addition, there would very likely be no movie career either.

Meanwhile, in the conference room outside the Police Commissioner's office a conference was underway on the subject of Christmas gratuities. As Patrolman Phillips had testified, and as every cop of whatever rank knew, it had long been the custom of policemen—not all of them surely, but a great many of them—to solicit "gifts" during the holiday season.

These "gifts" took many forms. A foot patrolman might walk into a liquor store on his post, and the owner might present him with a bottle of Scotch without even being asked. Or the same patrolman might pluck a bottle of Scotch from the shelf and offer to pay for it but be told by the owner to accept it as a Christmas present. Or he might walk into the same liquor store and demand either one bottle of Scotch, or a case of Scotch, or even money; and this was in fact extortion, and a crime. Nonetheless, it had been done.

The practice of soliciting at Christmastime was by now so time-honored that lists of "gift givers existed nearly everywhere. Precinct patrol forces had them, detective squads had them, and even units which never met the public at all, the fingerprint section or the photo lab, had them. In the past, the most lucrative job in the entire Police Department was said to have been the captaincy of the 14th Precinct, for this precinct contained Macy's, Gimbels and other major department stores, and its captain, if energetic, was said to have been able to clean up $5000 in "gifts" every Christmas.

As the Egan trial continued in the board room, those of us in the conference room tried to decide what to do about Christmas "gifts."

A four-page memo lay in front of each of us. This had been dictated by Syd Cooper beginning at 7:30 that morning, and the meeting now began with Cooper reading his memo aloud.

This would be the first Christmas season to test the effectiveness of Commissioner Murphy's anti-corruption campaign.

In the past, various approaches had been tried to stop the soliciting of Christmas gifts. The only thing all past programs had in common was their ineffectiveness.

The prevailing attitude was that Christmas "gifts" were a fringe benefit. They went with the shield and the gun. Cooper noted that this attitude was shared not only by certain captains who raced their men to the most lucrative spots, but also by honest cops who would refuse gifts themselves but who also would refuse to denounce participants to higher authority.

In the past, form letters had been sent out to various

business leaders asking their cooperation, but these did no good. As Cooper put it, businessmen believed that the Christmas gifts were by far the cheapest way of buying goodwill from large numbers of policemen. Where else could one buy an entire precinct for as little as 75 cents a day, Cooper asked. For ten cents a day extra, a businessman could buy the precinct detective squad as well.

The newspapers, far from denouncing the existence of these Christmas lists, willingly contributed. District attorneys more or less refused to prosecute the few cops who, in the past, had been nailed. Special units had stood by special telephone numbers to respond to complaints, but few calls ever came in. Roving patrols of corruption unit investigators had been tried, and that didn't work. Certain commanders had been sent out to visit businesses requesting that they refrain from giving Christmas gifts to policemen and that they report any solicitation. This also failed. Units were sent out to stop radio cars and search them on the spot, for surely their trunks would be filled with loot. But this didn't work very often. Radio cars were seen cruising through business districts with off-duty cops making their Christmas stops, and these were sometimes tailed by the corruption units, but it took a lot of time and there were very few cops captured.

Cooper looked at us above his glasses, and apologized for having recited such a long list of tactics that did not work. This year they might work. Perhaps a climate now existed where the community would be fearful of offering and the policemen fearful of taking. Cooper said, "We might even progress to a point where our personnel will feel that it is actually wrong."

Cooper now suggested special techniques for this year. Since Murphy's bribery speech about two months before, 178 persons had been arrested for attempting to bribe cops. We could publicize that fact. We could publicize our corruption unit's special telephone number too. Again Cooper peered at us over his glasses. "Up to now, that number is noteworthy principally by the fact that those charged with publicizing it cannot remember it."

As Cooper saw it, no techniques and programs would have any effect unless we were able to nab cops very early and make immediate examples out of them. This would be possible only with the cooperation of the local commanders for they would be able to provide us with active targets. However, Cooper pointed out, the most knowledgeable commanders should probably be those who had been the most active shoppers themselves in the past.

There were smiles all around the table, and even a smattering of applause. Cooper took several bows, grinning, then said, "When you dictate at seven in the morning, that's the kind of thing that comes out, you can't be responsible for it."

Now we began to decide on tactics for this year.

Commissioner McCarthy thought we should make the suppression of Christmas lists the responsibility of each precinct commander. Traps should be laid for these commanders. A deliberate attempt should be made to catch 30 or 40 cops from a single precinct; the cops should be arrested, and the commanding officer sacked.

Chief Cottell suggested that Christmas parties be forbidden—not only parties in the station house itself—and these were rare enough because of the rule against liquor on police premises—but also parties in any hotel or anywhere else nearby. In order to have a Christmas party, cops or detectives would have to get permission, and afterwards show receipts proving that everything had been paid for.

I said, "How soon do we have to decide?"

Chief McGovern answered, "The cops are out there in the streets shopping right now."

"Christmas is still a month and a day away," I said.

Cooper said, "We should announce all this the day after Thanksgiving."

I said, "The Police Commissioner leaves today on a trip, and won't be back until December 6."

Cooper said, "If we wait till he gets back, it will be too late."

First Deputy Commissioner Smith suggested that we attempt to turn every patrolman into a potential informant. We should try to get them to inform their precinct commanders as to which cops were out there soliciting gifts.

"Knapp's right," Smith suddenly cried, "they're all out there doing it, every single one of them."

Commissioner Neco began to give legal advice on still

another idea, the attempt to prove conspiracy to commit bribery. Maybe we could catch and arrest the president of one of the big banks. I suggested that the liquor stores were the worst offenders, because they corrupted cops in the greatest numbers. Smith said, "That's not true. It's big business. It's things like *The New York Times.*"

Seedman at these meetings generally kept his mouth shut.

Smith said, "What about the detectives, Al?"

Cooper began to describe past Christmas parties thrown by detective squads: lavish suites, ever-flowing fountains of drinks and never diminishing mounds of canapés.

Smith needled Seedman. "Aren't you sorry that you weren't Chief of Detectives five years ago, Al?"

Seedman said with a grin, "What I'm really sorry about is that I missed Prohibition."

Finally the meeting ended. As usual, nothing much had been decided. Commissioner Neco had agreed to prepare a memo on the legal implications of gift-giving to members of the force. It was my job to decide what part the Police Commissioner should take in this campaign, and when and how any announcements by him were to be made. Cooper was to devise whatever methods seemed useful in order to catch individual cops in the act, and to terrorize the personnel of entire precincts if he could.

Meanwhile, Egan was on trial almost for his life.

I took Cooper and McCarthy to one side, wanting to talk about Egan. The only private place seemed to be the Police Commissioner's office, for his doors stood open, meaning he was out—they were always closed by secretaries the moment he reentered his office. The doors served as a signal to the rest of us. We could tell at a glance whether the Police Commissioner was in or out.

We stood between Theodore Roosevelt's old desk and the portrait of him as Police Commissioner over the fireplace.

I said, "Syd, what do you have on Egan? You don't have anything on him, and he is a hero and we all look bad. We look like we're persecuting him because he got into the movies."

It was my intention to ask both Cooper and McCarthy to join with me in advising the Police Commissioner to make a very careful ruling when the trial ended tonight. But Murphy suddenly entered his office by the back door and, in effect, caught us there. I therefore explained to the Police Commissioner what we were discussing.

Cooper said, "Every agency we go to on Egan says the guy is no good. The District Attorney of Brooklyn. The Federal Attorney for the Southern District."

I said, "But they have nothing specific on him, right? It's all rumors, right? The rules of the game are that if you don't have anything on him you have to let him go. As far as the public is concerned, Egan is a hero, one of the very few police heroes. The Knapp Commission hearings hurt us all. We can't afford now to hurt ourselves over one detective. Enough people hate the police already. We don't need to be hated even worse because of Eddie Egan."

Cooper said, "I'm going to call Phillips and see what Phillips has on Egan. Phillips will know whether or not Egan is a wrong guy."

First Durk, then David Burnham, and now Phillips were turning the Department upside down, and they were not even present while doing so; and I doubted that they had any awareness of the impact they had made. The first two were at least honorable men, but Phillips was a self-confessed extortionist, perjurer, and criminal. To consult with Phillips on the Egan question seemed to me preposterous.

Murphy had stood a little way off, listening. I regretted that he had returned so unexpectedly, for this made twice already today that he had heard about Egan from me, and he did not like to be badgered. Several hours earlier I had been advised by lawyer Eliasberg that a separate attempt to strip Egan of his pension rights was also underway.

According to Civil Service regulations, no cop was eligible for pension unless he had put in five years of uninterrupted service. However, Egan had taken a two-and-a-half-month leave of absence in order to work in the movie. Although this leave had been requested by the movie company via the Mayor's office and been approved by all up and down the line, it was now being charged that it constituted a break in Egan's uninterrupted service. Therefore he was not eligible for pension.

Apprised of this by Eliasberg, I had gone immediately in search of Deputy Commissioner Canick, and had found him with his coat on, standing with the Police Commissioner beside Murphy's car. Canick was a direct, perceptive man.

Canick said, "I'm certainly not about to let crap like that go through. Don't worry about it."

Murphy had listened to this exchange with a similar bemused expression.

Still, by now he would feel he was being badgered.

He was leaving the city the next day. He and his wife would spend part of a week with relatives in Florida. From there Murphy would fly to Dallas, where for three days he would serve as chairman of the Law Enforcement Council of the National Commission on Crime and Delinquency. Then he would go on to Louisville to conduct a seminar at the Southern Police Institute.

I now reminded him that the decision in the Egan case had to be made by December 1, on which date Egan's retirement would take effect, and that since he was leaving the city tomorrow, this meant he should make his decision today.

Murphy nodded, but said nothing.

I began to worry that Murphy would walk away from this, allowing Bill Smith, Acting Police Commissioner in his absence, to decide.

I looked in on the trial for a time. Egan's lawyer was making an oration. His client had committed no crime. No corruption was charged. These were bookkeeping mistakes only. Egan sat there scarcely listening. He wore his gun in an ankle holster, which must have caused his calf to itch, for occasionally he raised his pant leg slightly and scratched himself.

Late in the afternoon Murphy and I drove downtown to meet with District Attorney Hogan, who was about to announce indictments of the five killers of Patrolmen Jones and Piagentini. Many of the detectives involved in the case also were present, and those I talked to were concerned about Egan. Did I think Murphy would bounce him out of the Department?

So in the car returning to headquarters, I thought it worth trying to talk to Murphy once again. First I showed him the six-page statement that Eliasberg had prepared, outlining the petty nature of the charges against Egan, and the chronology of all the interrogations. This statement ended by noting that Commissioner Murphy had made great efforts to change police procedures, a monumental task. In the past, new rules and procedures had been added without eliminating old ones. If Murphy could succeed in streamlining police work to induce greater productivity, he would also succeed in eliminating the causes that produced these charges against former Detective Egan.

Murphy dutifully glanced through this statement, but I could see by his face that he had already listened to all he could take of the Egan case. Handing the statement back, he said, "Egan must have paid Eliasberg a lot of money for this."

"The P.B.A. pays Eliasberg. He gets no more nor less whether he defends Egan or not."

I then told Murphy how former chief Carey had described Egan getting second-grade money and then first-grade money by vote of the squad.

Murphy said, "Oh, Chief Carey's on Egan's side? Well, that should sink Egan."

I was unable to decipher this cryptic remark.

Murphy began to stare out the car window.

As I reached the second floor of headquarters, the trial was just ending. People spilled out into the hall, one of them Eliasberg, who asked, "What's going to happen?"

I said: "I don't know, let me talk to Commissioner Stutman."

Stutman and I walked down toward Murphy's office. There was a spy hole in one of Murphy's doors, to allow his secretaries to peer in at a meeting without disturbing it. Perhaps the meeting was breaking up. Perhaps the visitor had left by the back door. Perhaps the Police Commissioner was free for his next appointment.

But commanders also peered in, trying to judge how long they might have to wait for their own audience with the King, and sometimes what they saw was someone else winning a smile from him. Even the spy hole seemed part of Murphy's power.

Stutman and I in turn peered in through this spy hole. Murphy was sitting at his desk, leaning back in his chair with his hands behind his head, and he was smiling. In the chair beside his desk sat Lacovara. They were chatting amiably.

Stutman and I waited for Lacovara to come out. Stutman felt that Murphy would want to know at once what Stutman's recommendations were. "I'll probably give Egan a 20-day rip on each of the two sets of charges," Stutman said.

"But will the Police Commissioner approve your recommendation, or will he decide on something harsher?"

Stutman said, "I'll ask him."

Presently Lacovara came out. Murphy's head appeared beyond the door. He saw Stutman and me standing up now, and he ducked back inside. We saw Deputy Inspector Devine, his chief secretary, go into his office and then come out again. Devine said, "Commissioner Stutman, are you waiting to see the P.C., because he's not going to be able to see you. He's got a few phone calls to make and then he's got to get to the Mayor's office."

Stutman said to me, "I'll call him at home. I know he'll want to talk to me before he leaves the city."

But in fact Murphy chose not to take Stutman's call, and no conversation between them took place before Murphy left. Stutman's official report was dated five days later, and it was eight pages long. The final paragraph read, "I recommend that the respondent be fined 20 days' pay on Case No. 45797 and 20 days' pay on Case No 45830."

In the absence of the Police Commissioner, this report was submitted to Acting Police Commissioner William H. T. Smith.

Smith's decision came down seven hours before Egan's retirement was to take effect. Smith noted that certain charges had been dropped because of the statute of limitations. And he took issue with this finding, claiming that Egan's conduct constituted "continuing violations for which an officer remains liable until three years after he complies with the relevant rules and procedures of this Department." That is, Egan, who had seized evidence more than three years ago, was required to safeguard that evidence and deliver it to the property clerk on that date, and remained, Smith added, "Subject to discipline indefinitely if he fails to correct his continuing violation."

Nonetheless, Civil Service regulations prevented Commissioner Smith from reversing Commissioner Stutman's finding on these specifications, and now Smith took up the question of penalty. He found that the seriousness of the charges against Patrolman Egan could not be minimized. They involved a pattern of misconduct rising to the level of establishing that Patrolman Egan should not be a police officer. Although Egan claimed to have made 5000 arrests during his career, Smith noted that police work was not merely making arrests, and that making large numbers of arrests was not necessarily a demonstration of effectiveness. The arrest was merely the beginning of the process ending in trial, conviction, and sentence, and that honest and dedicated police involvement was necessary throughout. The record established that Patrolman Egan had regularly failed to live up to such standards.

Smith wrote, "Accordingly, by virtue of the authority vested in me by Section 432 of the City Charter and by Section 434A-14.0 of the Administrative Code, I hereby order that Patrolman Edward Eagan be DISMISSED from the Police Department on each set of charges before me."

Before handing down his decision, Smith had conferred with the Police Commissioner in Dallas by telephone. Smith had told Murphy how he intended to rule. Murphy, who had walked away from the case eight days before, chose not to overrule Smith's decision.

The French Connection was still packing them in, and the newspapers would not let the case lie, neither in New York nor across the country.

As soon as the Police Commissioner returned to New York the name of Egan was often raised. Murphy, Smith, Lacovara, Cooper, repeatedly sought to congratulate themselves on the decision that had been made, whereas I continued in dissent.

"What are you sticking up for that guy for?" Smith asked.

I explained that there would be other cases like it, and I saw no reason for us to hurt ourselves by such questionable actions and decisions as had just been made. We had to win back the trust and confidence of the people, and this was no way to do it. Smith pointed out that Egan had not been hurt in any way. Sure he had lost his pension, but he had no doubt made a fortune on *The French Connection,* and with the money he was going to earn from now on as an actor he had no worries.

By this time I had taken the trouble to delve into Egan's finances, and Smith's appraisal could not have been more wrong. Before undertaking to write their story as *The French Connection,* Robin Moore had signed Egan and Grosso to contracts that were so strict, and so favorable to Moore, that Egan's total take to date from the book, the sale of the book to the movies, his role as actor in the movie, his promotion tours in behalf of the movie—his total take so far—was $3900. Egan had a new lawyer now, Frank Miller, who attested to these figures in a signed letter to me. I called Robin Moore, who was evasive at first, but then confessed that the expenses on the book had been "very high," but that he couldn't believe that Egan had received only $3900 to date. Surely Egan had received more than that. But even if he hadn't, the movie was such a success that perhaps eventually Egan and Grosso would make real money out of it. Moore had sold the book to the movies, and with it his contracts with Egan and Grosso, for $85,000.

As for the "lucrative" contract which Egan signed, it now developed that no one had yet signed it for Hollywood; for the moment Egan was merely out of a job. On the day he turned in his guns and shield, his bank balance was $89.79. He was in arrears in his rent, and his only remaining "valuable" possession was a seven-year-old car.

The Police Commissioner, and also Bill Smith, showed surprise to learn this. But they didn't really believe me. Smith began to insist that Egan was really a wrong guy, far worse than any of us had suspected. "We're starting to get things in from Miami on this guy." Lacovara mentioned the name of a former federal attorney who had told Lacovara, "We tried to get that guy for years but couldn't get him. I'm glad to see that you got him at last." One day I came upon Smith, Chief Inspector Codd, and Chief Cooper whispering in a hallway. As I walked up the whispering stopped. It took no great brilliance to realize that all of them were annoyed with me for my part in the defense of Egan. They were annoyed at Stutman, too. I had just overheard Smith saying, "We got to act just as harshly on Litsky when he comes up, but Stutman won't recommend it." Litsky was a captain accused of minor violations.

Discussing the Egan case a *Daily News* reporter said, "I found out something about Smith I didn't know. He's ruthless. He wouldn't give a cop an even break."

I had received a letter from Andrew Wilson, who had served in the police hierarchy in Detroit when Murphy was there and whom I knew Murphy liked. This letter enclosed a clipping from the *Detroit Free Press* about Egan. Wilson had noted, "This is how it looks in the hinterland. It looks awful." I had sent this letter on to Murphy, and when I entered his office the next morning, Lacovara was standing beside his desk holding the letter. Lacovara flashed it at me so that I would know he had it, and then said, "Commissioner, I had lunch yesterday with members of the Bar Association, and I want you to know that they thought you had done incomparably the wisest thing in dismissing Egan from the Police Department. They realize that it was unpopular, but they thought it had to be done and that you did it brilliantly."

Murphy looked pleased.

Without meeting my eyes, he noted that he had been denounced by Detective Kelly, head of the Detectives' Endowment Association, but that, reading between the lines, he felt that Kelly supported him. Kelly had denounced the Police Commissioner merely as a formality.

Kelly's statement had read in part, "Detectives all over the city are incensed at the treatment accorded Eddie Egan. When our morale is at its lowest ebb, our own administration shot down one of our best detectives."

A week after the decision, I met with Commissioner Stutman and Commissioner Neco. We knew Egan planned to appeal this decision in court, and now Neco said, "The court is going to measure Smith's decision against Egan's 16 years of service, and this decision isn't going to hold up. The court is going to reverse it." Stutman concurred.

The only lawyer among us who believed that the courts would sustain Smith was the 28-year-old Lacovara.

A few months later the decision would in fact be re-versed in court, and Egan reinstated as a policeman with his pension rights restored. Lacovara would again advise the Police Commissioner that the correct decision had been made in the Egan case, but that unfortunately the case had come before one of the dumbest judges on the bench: "He's so dumb that when he walks, his knuckles trail on the ground." Lacovara talked about appealing the decision, but in fact no appeal would ever be made. Of course Egan chose not to return to active duty.

It was during the final hours of the Egan case that the Police Commissioner began to speak to me of Walter Arm, who had held my job during the years when Steve Kennedy was Police Commissioner. According to Murphy, Arm had managed to project Kennedy as a man of great character and toughness. Murphy too wanted to be projected as tough. Perhaps I should talk to Arm, and find out how he did it. I explained to Murphy that I believed in toughness too, and thought that tough decisions by him were manda-tory. However, I thought it might be possible in the future to pick our targets with a bit more care.

Presently I sent the following memo to the Police Com-missioner, with copies to Smith, Codd, Cooper, Seedman, and Cawley.

We have just taken something of a drubbing image-wise in the case of a certain detective. Regardless of the merits of the case, and whether or not the ultimate decision was correct, the mass of public opinion as re-flected in the media—and the media is neither more or less than reflected public opinion—this public opinion is convinced that the detective was basically in the right, and that our action was capricious and spiteful.

This man was only a detective, and of no interest personally to any one of us.

On the whole we hurt ourselves more than we need-ed to. And if he ever wins a reversal in civil court—which certain of our own lawyers believe he will—we will be hurt again at each stage of the proceedings.

If it is true that we can't have an effective police de-partment without the cooperation and respect of our fellow citizens, then we ought to think of everything

we do in terms of its effect on that cooperation and respect. It takes an awful lot of solved bank robberies to
undo in people's minds our apparent injustice to one
of their heroes—one of their *few* police heroes, by the
way.

9 / Second Knapp

The second of Sergeant David Durk's year-long leaves of
absence was coming to an end. Although he was willing
enough to stay on leave a short time longer—he was studying for his Ph.D. exams at N.Y.U.—no word went out
from the Police Commissioner to accord him such an extension. Durk himself seemed to have abandoned hope at a
fairly early date. Instead, he was asking for one of two
jobs. Preferably, he wanted Murphy to appoint him Deputy
Commissioner—it was never clear which deputy commis-
sionership he was eyeing. But he had been offered similar
rank in other cities—St. Louis was one—and thought he
had earned it here too.

If Durk were not to be Deputy Commissioner, then he
would accept a civilian line, which would have to be created for him: Special Assistant to the Police Commissioner.
Had not Murphy previously created just such a job for
young and inexperienced Lacovara? Why should he not
create such a job and title for Sergeant David Durk?

When Durk wanted something he lobbied fiercely. He
telephoned everybody. Murphy accorded him an audience,
but once in Murphy's office and on stage, Durk repeatedly
ignored his exit cue.

"Well, Dave, I'm running a bit late—"

"And furthermore," said Sergeant Durk.

"Yeah, well, Dave—"

There had followed a number of meetings between Durk
and Lacovara, for Lacovara by now was serving as Murphy's *éminence grise*. Lacovara was only too willing to lift
any drudgery from the Police Commissioner's tired brow.
Murphy had no intention of awarding Durk a deputy com-
missionership, and Lacovara had no intention of recommending that Murphy hire Durk on Lacovara's own level.

Week after week Lacovara made vague promises to Durk, and the problem was put off.

Although Murphy had ceased suggesting that an attempt be made to discredit Durk, he never failed to point out that not only Whitman Knapp, but also various of the district attorneys and federal attorneys were all sick and tired of the endless phone calls from Durk, of the pressure from Durk to launch and complete this or that incredibly complicated investigation at once. Lacovara would say, "The Mayor's office advises us not to have anything to do with Durk, because Durk has denounced Jay Kreigel again."

The days of Durk's leave dwindled like water running out of a bathtub. Murphy saw that Durk was caught in the whirlpool. Time would suck Durk back into the Police Department. Murphy didn't have to do a thing. Eventually, in place of his earlier demands to be made a deputy commissioner or at least a special assistant to the Police Commissioner, Durk asked only that he be named a detective sergeant on special assignment. This meant that he would collect lieutenant's pay.

And to this, Murphy, not wanting it to seem that Durk had gone totally unrewarded, agreed. The problem had resolved itself just as Murphy had always known it would.

Only it hadn't.

Soon the Knapp Commission hearings were upon us again. This time they took place in the great hall of the New York Chamber of Commerce at 65 Liberty Street. This was a vast room under a high red and gold-leaf ceiling. On the red velvet walls hung over 200 portraits of formerly famous New Yorkers: Thomas Edison, DeWitt Clinton, Commodore Vanderbilt, John D. Rockefeller. Knapp and the other commissioners sat on a kind of oak throne, four chairs behind a judge's desk. In front of a table crammed with microphones, well below the level of the commissioners sat former commissioner Howard Leary, a big baldish man. He spoke with a Philadelphia accent, an obvious outsider again. Though he had bossed the New York Police Department for four and a half years, that accent must have given him away every day. He seemed a mild man. and it proved impossible for Michael Armstrong to force him to answer any questions in any meaningful way. Leary claimed that although Serpico had made his allegations in the spring of 1967, he, the Police Commissioner, was not told about them until the fall of that year. He said he was at a "total loss to rationalize" why none of the officials who had heard the charges had come to him with them.

Armstrong asked why there had been a steady reduction in the number of men assigned to anti-corruption units during Leary's tenure. Leary denied any such specific policy. "It's always difficult to recruit people for this work," he explained.

It was useless questioning such a man. It was useless questioning nearly all of the hierarchical figures who appeared before the commission during this second series. All were experts at providing answers which merely blurred the question.

When Justice Fraiman testified, Mr. Armstrong said, "It is difficult to understand why this information was just dropped."

Justice Fraiman replied, "It was not the only error in my three years in the Department of Investigation."

Jay Kriegel, the Mayor's aide, seemed to contradict some of his own previous sworn testimony. There was a flurry of talk about indicting Kriegel for perjury, but no one really believed this would be done, and it wasn't.

Former First Deputy Commissioner John Walsh testified. He had become a policeman in 1930. He was old now and completely bald. Yes, Inspector Behan had told him of Serpico's charges. Yes, he had expected Behan to arrange a meeting for him with Serpico. "When it was not arranged, the incident left my mind."

From the thronelike platform, Whitman Knapp snapped, "The ball was dropped in April. From April to October nothing was done."

"I assumed everything was going alright," Mr. Walsh replied.

"Why the hell did you wait six months before checking with Behan?" Mr. Knapp asked.

Old John Walsh, formerly the most feared man in the Police Department, gave no answer.

Serpico, his bushy hair neatly trimmed, his beard neatly trimmed also, wearing a business suit, appearing totally in control of himself, explained how he had come forward with allegations of corruption, and how all these many years had elapsed before anything was done. Finally, at the invitation of Whitman Knapp, Serpico read a statement. "Through my appearance here today I hope that police officers in the future will not experience the same frustration and anxiety that I was subjected to for the past five years at the hands of my superiors because of my attempt to report corruption. I was made to feel that I had burdened them with an unwanted task. The problem is that the atmosphere does not yet exist in which an honest police officer can act without fear of ridicule or reprisal from fellow officers.

"We create an atmosphere in which the dishonest officer appears the honest one and not the other way around.

"Police corruption cannot exist unless it is at least tolerated at higher levels in the department."

But the star of the show was Detective Sergeant David Durk, who in response to questions from Michael Armstrong again described the tortuous journey he had made, leading Serpico by the hand, ending at last before these microphones and this commission. At the end of his testimony, Durk too was asked if he cared to make a statement.

What Durk then read was not a statement, but a passionate plea to the Knapp Commission and to the public from a man who said, "I'm a cop, and I intend to go on being a cop.

"Being a cop means serving, helping others.

"If it's not too corny, to be a cop is to help an old lady walk the street safely, to help a 12-year-old girl reach her next birthday without being gang-raped, to help a storekeeper earn a living without keeping a shotgun under his cash register, to help a boy grow up without needles in his arm.

"Being a cop is a vocation or it is nothing at all. And that is what I saw being destroyed by corruption in the New York Police Department—destroyed for me and for thousands of others like me. We wanted to believe in the rule of law; we wanted to believe in the system of responsibility."

Durk said his message was "harsh, brutal and impolite—but it is the truth."

He had seen too many policemen give in to corruption,

so that "they weren't cops anymore . . . they were on the way to not being men anymore.

"Once I arrested a landlord's agent who offered to pay me if I would lock up a tenant who was organizing other tenants. As I put the cuffs on the agent and led him away, a crowd of people assembled and began yelling 'Viva la Policía." Of course it was not just me or even the police that they were cheering. They were cheering because they had glimpsed with that one arrest the possibility of a system of justice that could work to protect them too. They were cheering because if that agent could get arrested then that meant that they had rights, they were citizens, and maybe one day life would really be different for their children.

"For me, that moment is what police work is all about. But there have been far too few moments like it, far too many times when I looked into the faces of the city and saw not hope and trust, but resentment and hate and fear. Far too many of my fellow officers have seen only hate. Far too many have seen their dreams of service and justice frustrated and abandoned by a corrupt system and superiors and politicians who just didn't care enough.

"It took five years of Frank Serpico's life and five years of mine to help bring this commission about. It has taken the lives and dedication of thousands of others to preserve as much of a police force as we have. It has taken months of effort by all of you to help show this city the truth.

"What I ask of you now is to help make us clean again, to help give us some leadership we can look to, to make it possible for all the men on the force to walk at ease with their better nature and with their fellow citizens, and perhaps one day on a warm summer night to hear again the shout, 'Viva la Policía.' "

Durk's voice broke as he finished. He half choked, half sobbed "Viva la Policía!" into the thicket of microphones before him, then got up and strode from the great hall.

The nonplussed Chairman Knapp announced that there would be "a temporary adjournment," as many of those in the room applauded the seat where Detective Sergeant Durk had sat.

It was nearly Christmas. The Police Commissioner had sent an edict out into the precincts that there were to be no

Christmas parties and especially no liquor on police property this holiday season. Nonetheless, Murphy sent an invitation to all deputy commissioners, to the Chief Inspector, to all super chiefs, and to other high-ranking headquarters personnel, inviting them to a party in the conference room outside his office.

A table had been pushed against the wall, and on it were bowls of potato chips and pretzels and other hors d'oeuvres. On the floor stood a waxed basket of ice with cans of beer shoved down into it, and on another table stood a row of whiskey bottles ranged like trophies against the wall. It was noon. Being reluctant to be the first to drink liquor on police premises that Christmas, I opened a beer which I didn't really want, which was perhaps silly of me. Before long, the room filled up, and there was a drink in nearly every hand.

At the Police Commissioner's Christmas repast a certain amount of business was conducted. I brought up Durk's name and Durk's moving speech several times, but nobody bit. That Durk should suddenly start crying on TV seemed to have impressed much of the city, but in the halls of headquarters it was scarcely noticed. Once I mentioned that Durk had received a great number of congratulatory letters, many from cops, but this was received with skepticism. Had I actually seen these letters myself, or what?

As a matter of fact, I had.

Deputy Chief Mike Lonergan stood in the corner, beaming, accepting congratulations, and when Murphy appeared, Lonergan walked over and said, "Thanks, Boss."

This was the first I realized that the Police Commissioner had presented Lonergan with an extra star, plus command of Manhattan North as a Christmas present.

I said, "What's happened to Chief Catalano?"

Murphy said, "Catalano has been reassigned to the Chief Inspector's office."

Chief Cawley made a joke to the effect that they were looking for a man with Catalano's qualifications in Singapore.

Somebody else said, "I don't care where he goes, as long as he gets the message."

Catalano had been Commander of Manhattan North

last June, when Murphy had forced him to bring charges against his own men in the Fifth Division. Catalano's reluctance had been plain, and he was paying for it now.

There were a number of jokes about him.

As in the army, once you were out, they closed ranks behind you and no one dared say a word in your behalf.

Cawley said, "We've killed Santa Claus," and he began to tell of a relative of Jay Kriegel, who owned a liquor store, and who usually gave out $500 to cops at Christmas. No cop had come by this year to collect the money. Another of the Mayor's aides, Carleton Irish, was having a party in the Bronx with cars double-parked, and he went out and talked to the cops. Later he went out to the sergeant's car and said, "Look I realize you can't come in for a drink, but I'll give you a bottle. You and your partner can drink it in the car."

The sergeant said, "Are you crazy?" and rolled up the window and drove away.

According to Cawley, the feedback on our Christmas program was a success.

I stood chatting with the Police Commissioner.

Two days previously he had made a speech to the Bar Association, written by me, which criticized the courts: "The court system must accept the giant share of the blame for the continual rise in crime. . . . We the police pour arrested criminals into the wide end of the criminal justice funnel, and they choke it up until they spill over the top. . . . Imagine each criminal as a rubber ball and the court system as a wall. We throw the ball against the wall and he bounces right back into the street again and commits another crime. The court system is not dealing with these criminals. . . ."

This morning the *Times* editorial had applauded Murphy for this speech, as had a column on the Op Ed page by Tom Wicker.

"Did you see the *Times?*" Murphy asked.

In addition, because I had argued the importance of showing solidarity with his men who had been through so much this year, Murphy had just granted Christmas amnesty to all cops facing minor disciplinary charges.

Now I stood with him sipping a beer. Deputy Commissioner Ben Ward came over.

"The amnesty was a good idea," he said to Murphy. "I recommended it last year."

Murphy said, "Well, it was Bob who put it through this year."

Since the Police Commissioner was so pleased with me, I felt I could afford to pour myself a real drink.

I stood sipping whiskey on police premises, though this was forbidden to every cop in the city this year.

Book Five / **WINTER**

1 / The World's Greatest Jewel Robbery

In the wee hours of the night after the first day of the New Year, there came a rapping on the locked door on the 61st Street side of the Hotel Pierre, one of the most elegant hotels in the world. An unarmed security guard named Thomas Grady peered out through the glass. He saw two well-dressed men who called out that they had reservations. Behind them, carrying suitcases, stood an individual who looked to be their chauffeur—in any case he wore a chauffeur's cap—and parked outside at the curb was a limousine.

So the guard opened the door. Why not?

But as the men came inside under the lights, feet soundless on the plush carpet, the guard saw to his astonishment that one wore a rubber nose. He also saw a hand with a gun in it. He was an old man who had been dozing in a chair beside the door. Security guard? His job was to turn the key in the door if anybody knocked, not this.

"Turn around. Don't look at us. Now move."

The old man did.

The three gunmen, presently joined by a fourth and possibly even a fifth accomplice, now proceeded to round up 18 hotel employees on duty at that hour. This was the Hotel Pierre, after all, and even in the pre-dawn hours of the night after New Year's Eve it was possible that some guest would suddenly call down for a sandwich, or a bottle of champagne.

Most of the captives were surprised from the rear and ordered not to turn around. All were herded into the executive offices and forced to lie on soft red carpet in the light of crystal lamps. The bandits had come equipped with 14 sets of handcuffs, and with several rolls of three-inch-wide adhesive tape. The captives were handcuffed, and when the handcuffs began to run short, certain were handcuffed to each other. The bandits then tore strips of tape off the rolls, and pasted these blindfolds to the eyebrows and noses of everybody.

The Pierre Hotel was 42 stories high. It fronted on Fifth

Avenue and overlooked Central Park. About 440 of its 700 units were cooperative apartments of from one to eight rooms. The biggest apartments were said to have sold for as high as half a million dollars each, and maintenance charges on certain of them were said to cost $68,000 dollars per year.

The remaining 260 units were rented to transients: millionaires, socialites, movie stars, and even famous politicians—President Nixon had stayed there in the past.

It was ten minutes to four when the bandits came through that door.

In the cashier's office in the wall were about 200 safe deposit boxes, the doors of which measured about two and a half inches by five inches. All these doors were about half an inch thick. It would have taken dynamite to blast through each door. However, the hinges were exterior ones, little knurled knobs, and the bandits simply took hammers and chisels, and knocked the hinges off each door. Working from a map furnished by a terrified clerk, they opened about 50 boxes, some of which were no doubt empty. But a good many were stuffed with ropes of diamonds and with ruby brooches. Great handfuls of this stuff were dumped into the bandits' suitcases.

The elevator buzzer was ringing and ringing.

A 25-year-old Brazilian lawyer named Helio Fraga was stopping at the Pierre after a honeymoon in Europe with his bride Silvia. Silvia's mother was also on hand, chaperoned honeymoons being not unusual among the South American upper classes. When this threesome had returned to the hotel shortly after 3 A.M., Fraga's bride had got off at the 20th floor and gone to their room. Fraga had continued up to the 37th floor with his mother-in-law, and bid her goodnight at her door. He had been standing in the hallway with his finger on the elevator button for a long time now.

Suddenly the elevator opened. Inside stood a surly individual dressed in the jacket to the uniform of a Pierre Hotel elevator operator. This man reported that the regular operator had had a heart attack. Fraga stepped onto the elevator, but the man in the jacket was unable to make it descend, and suddenly he whipped out a gun, marched Fraga back to his mother-in-law's room, and from there phoned downstairs to his accomplices. He ordered another elevator sent up to get him.

The second elevator arrived. Fraga, his mother-in-law, and the two bandits descended to the 20th floor, where Fraga's bride was routed out of her room. The three new captives were brought down and forced to lie on the floor in the executive offices. With that the bandits' moment of panic was over.

Now the noise of hammers striking chisels, of knurled hinges breaking off the boxes, and of jewelry cascading down into the suitcase continued unabated for two hours. For two hours no other guests attempted to enter the lobby. No phones rang. No one summoned the elevator. The Hotel Pierre slept.

Soon it was quarter to six in the morning. In a 19th Precinct radio car rode Patrolmen Frank Lorello and William Casey. Their radio spoke. A Wells Fargo alarm at the Hotel Pierre had just gone off, signaling a possible robbery in progress.

The patrolmen discovered 21 people lying on the floor. The bandits were gone—clearly they had tripped the Wells Fargo alarm as they were leaving the building. The cops rushed out onto the sidewalk, but there were no witnesses around. It was cold and dark, and the streets were empty. The two cops radioed for an emergency service unit to cut the handcuffs off the victims. They also radioed for detectives. Those few who were on duty at that hour—the six-man Night Watch working out of Manhattan North headquarters—arrived quickly and immediately called for lab technicians. Presently the Hotel Pierre swarmed with cops, for this was apparently the most successful jewel robbery in the history of the city. The earliest estimate of the loot was one million dollars, and before long it began to appear that the true figure was four times that. The bandits had gone out through the revolving door, climbed back into their limousine and disappeared. It was up to the detectives to find them, and to recapture the loot, and what was so hard about that? They were out there somewhere, if not in this country then in another. They had stepped out the door into the world.

The size of the detectives' job was staggering. The routine tasks alone would take dozens of men many days.

Each of the captives was interrogated and fingerprinted. Checks were run on all this personnel—perhaps one had fingered the job. Photos of all known jewel thieves and hotel thieves were brought in, and the captives were asked to pick out a familiar face.

No familiar faces were noted. Hardly anybody had got a look at the robbers.

Who were the owners of the looted safe deposit drawers? Detectives rode the elevator up, and banged on doors. What was in your box?

A number of these people were so rich they had no idea. A number of others were not in the hotel, nor even in the country, and the hotel executives were obliged to place calls to Palm Springs and Palm Beach, to the French Riviera, to Rome, to Greece, and to other such points. Hotel Pierre executives had prided themselves on being so professionally self-effacing as to be almost invisible. To inform wealthy patrons of a robbery of this magnitude at the Hotel Pierre was, for such men, an extremely distasteful task.

Every limousine company in the city had to be checked out. Men from Latent dusted surfaces all over the lobby and the offices of the hotel. Sets of elimination prints had to be taken from everybody who had legitimate access to these areas, including police personnel. A technician found a used-up roll of tape—and then a print inside it—and hopes rose. However, a few minutes later this print was found to match those of one of the cops standing guard.

What about the wealthy guests themselves? It was not inconceivable that one or another was less wealthy than it appeared, and had engineered a robbery of his or her own jewels so as to collect insurance. It was one thing to check out the pedigree of a Puerto Rican elevator operator and quite another to check out secretly an oil millionaire's wife. If he or she found out, there would be trouble; you could count on it.

One of the biggest losers appeared to be a woman who was supposed to be red-eyed with grief at her loss. However, by Monday afternoon she was able to receive a delegation of detectives and myself in her apartment. The detectives sat around a coffee table on which reposed photos of her fabulous jewels. Some were missing. Some she thought might be in a safe deposit box elsewhere. One piece originally reported missing had turned up in the pocket of her bathrobe. She was a woman somewhere over 40, with very white skin and an opulent bosom. Although it was the middle of the afternoon, she was wearing an extremely low-cut dress, and repeatedly leaned over detectives in order to point out this or that feature in a photo, each time practically brushing the detective's head with her bosom. The detectives couldn't take their eyes off that bosom.

Who was this woman? Where was her husband? Where had her money come from? What nationality was she? She had a slight accent. The newspapers had reported that she was probably Swiss, or Belgian, assuming that she was not either German or Dutch.

One of her necklaces had been a double rope of diamonds, about 158 of them I estimated from the photo, from which had hung five tear-drop-shaped emeralds, each about an inch long, each also surrounded by diamonds. The piece was said to be worth over half a million dollars, and the central emerald was insured, she said, but that's all. Far from being red-eyed with grief, she seemed excited by the attention she was suddenly getting.

She liked to move from Raffles to the Côte Basque to the Metropolitan Opera, and she often went to dinner parties at the homes of friends. The place card in front of her sometimes read The Princess. She was not a princess.

One of the bandits had been heard to say, "Which safe deposit box belongs to The Princess?"

Perhaps the bandits had picked up the trail of this lady and her fantastic emerald necklace at a party; perhaps one or another of the bandits had worked as a waiter there, gazing down past her bosom at her jewels, meaning that all servants at many parties had to be checked out too. What a headache.

And what about the lady herself?

The detectives felt they couldn't interrogate her. She might panic and bolt the country.

The Police Department's intelligence files had nothing on her, nor on any of her frequent associates. But this meant only that she was not a member of organized crime or of any political extremist group, and had never instituted a law suit against the Police Department. Police intelligence files were in no way related to the morgue files of newspapers. Publications started a dossier the first time a person's name appeared in print, and new clippings were added with each mention after that. There would be considerable files on the lady at *Time, Newsweek, The New York Times* and the *Daily News,* but access was traditionally denied to the police as an invasion of freedom of the press.

Some of these files contained confidential information on the lady which had never been published: how she had first appeared inside the Horse Set about ten years before, how she had been girlfriend to a number of extremely rich boyfriends. A short time ago she had apparently come into real money—no one seemed to know how—and had commissioned an estate by the architect Edward Durrell Stone. She was said to love this house so much that she had sworn no one would ever live in it except her. Once she was dead, it was to be blown up.

Through contacts I was able to satisfy the detectives' curiosity without alerting or alarming the lady.

The Hotel Pierre robbery was pretty racy stuff. It made headlines day after day. There was no shocked or outraged public to deal with. Instead, the public was amused, even titillated by each new development. Possibly not a soul in the city felt sorry for The Princess or any of the other "victims," and to many spectators this seemed an almost benign crime. All that seemed lacking was proof that the robbers intended to endow a research hospital, or a home for delinquent boys. Once this proof came in, the applause could commence.

Unfortunately, however, the rape of the Hotel Pierre had been a callous, cold-blooded crime, perpetrated by vicious men. It was not the kind of thing which, in the movies, would be engineered and carried out by some portly, bungling actor such as Peter Ustinov; and it did not seem likely that the criminals would be brought to justice in time for the next popcorn break. In the movies, a woman like The Princess would no doubt prove to have been involved. But this was not the movies, and therefore these differences now occurred.

(1) The Princess was checked out because everybody was checked out. The FBI went through the names of Pierre guests of the past three months. The New York Police Department, which liked to think of itself as more efficient than the FBI—though aware that a deluded public thought otherwise—checked through past guests for a period of one year. The information on The Princess—and on everybody else—was dropped into a basket, and presently there were rows of baskets filled to the top. A good detective performed such leg work, believing in his heart that it would lead nowhere, while waiting for an informant to show up to tell him where the swag could be found, and when and where the criminals could be nailed. The good detective was principally a collector of evidence that could be presented to a grand jury. Therefore stories about the Horse Set and the idle rich didn't much interest him. The good detective didn't even care particularly which jewels were real and which paste. The good detective didn't care where a lady came from or what feats she might have performed to earn those jewels. He only cared that she not leave town; not because he believed she was somehow implicated in the robbery, but because he wanted her there to identify jewelry—and possibly faces—if a break in the case came. The best detective work in the world was without value without eventual testimony by the victims. As a matter of fact, work on the Pierre case was held up for days because a number of victims refused to come back to New York even to make depositions as to what was missing. If detectives tended to hate the filthy rich, this was the principal reason—such people repeatedly failed to cooperate in investigations.

(2) Reporters had laid siege to the lobby of the Hotel Pierre. Those self-effacing executives who managed the hotel were furious. They wanted the publicity to stop, the robbery never to have happened. The hotel's chief of security had been John Keeney, formerly a second grade detective in the New York Police Department. It was Keeney who had disclosed most of the details out of which the first lurid reports were composed. It was Keeney's notion that his job as security chief—and also the hotel's very real devotion to security—should be defended in the public press.

So Keeney talked and appeared on television, but on the third day when reporters asked for him, he had "gone home for the day." Mr. Keeney was shortly thereafter encountered in the street. Asked what he was doing these days, he was obliged to reply that he was now a free-lance security consultant. In his absence the hotel lawyer, John Sherry, and the hotel manager, one James Bennett, "requested" that reporters and police clear the lobby. All of us were herded down halls, under smiling cherubs and crystal chandeliers, and into a secluded room where our numbers would no longer remind the guests that they had been the victims of the biggest jewel robbery in New York City's history. Glancing at the name plate above the door, I learned that we had just been exiled to the Sapphire Room.

(3) So much hoopla surrounded the robbery and the ensuing investigation, that the Police Department began to receive complaints; in a city full of muggers and murderers, was it not outrageous for us to spend such manpower and devotion to recover the jewelry of such people? The reply to this was obvious. We wanted to clear the case up quickly in order to go on to something else; this was not isolated hotel robbery—there had been a number with identical MO's: safe deposit boxes smashed open, fake noses, and adhesive tape—meaning that the police were dealing with a ring of hotel thieves and it was important to smash this ring; and lastly, it was purest chance that no one was hurt during the robbery of the Hotel Pierre. There were no benign criminals in the world. A criminal was a criminal, and in the course of one crime was likely to commit any violence that he thought urgent. These people menaced the city every bit as much as the muggers and murderers.

Captain Richard Nicastro one day remarked wearily, "There weren't any of those guys virgins. We have their photos and their prints in our files somewhere. All we have to do is find them."

A special phone number had been established, and the calls kept coming. Every one was checked out. One day three detectives put in a total of 16 hours checking a call which proved useless. One man had been standing in a bar. The man next to him withdrew money, and out flopped a rubber nose. The two stared down at the rubber nose on the floor, then the guy picked it up, rammed it into his pocket, and left the bar.

There must have been a dozen calls referring to rubber noses. Every person in the city who owned a rubber nose became a suspect.

A man came forward who claimed to have seen the bandits leaving in their limousine. But when checked, he proved to be an addict. Should the police believe him or not? He was interviewed and reinterviewed.

At the Hotel Pierre life went on. One elderly guest complained about the detectives. "Do they have to stand around like that?" Another passed out envelopes to employees, each containing a $10 bill. "This is one of your lowest days," she told them, "and I would like to buck you up."

Cops accompanied by owners of the looted boxes visited Cartier's, Tiffany's, Harry Winston's, Van Cleef and Arpels. The detectives wanted pictures of every stolen brooch or necklace.

Life went on normally at the hotel. The hotel lawyer, John Sherry, remarked, "Our guests continue to believe in us."

"Brilliant" though the Pierre case was, an almost perfect crime, it broke on the sixth day, like a chandelier from a Pierre ceiling crashing to the floor. Sudden refuse.

Later it was announced to press and public only that the FBI had received a "tip" from an informant, which it had passed on to the Police Department.

I myself was not told what had happened, or why or how; and even as the prisoners were being brought into the 19th Precinct station house in handcuffs, I was still struggling to find out. At eight o'clock at night—after having been on top of the case since three that afternoon—I still didn't know. Each superior officer I questioned pretended not to know either, and finally I cornered Captain Nicastro, head of the Major Crime Squad and demanded he tell me, but he wouldn't, referring me to Chief Kinsella, Acting Chief of Detectives, for Chief Seedman was on vacation.

Kinsella drew me aside and quietly explained all. After that, he begged me to say nothing to anyone. To disclose details would possibly result in the murder of the informant; it would possibly result in no further cooperation from the FBI, and the Bureau had really been surprisingly generous on this case.

And so press and public were told nothing. I spoke of the case to no one. Anyone who sought information was turned away. The Pierre case was closed, and the secret of how it was solved would be kept possibly forever.

Presently I summoned Captain Nicastro to headquarters and informed him that if ever again he withheld information from me, he would find himself in serious trouble. He explained that secrecy had seemed so critical and so vital that he himself had not wanted to be the man to disseminate the facts even to a deputy commissioner.

I told him I understood his feelings, but I would not accept them.

He apologized profusely, and I let him go.

A few weeks later he was promoted to Deputy Inspector, and he thanked me for the promotion, for the publicity that had come to him in connection with the Pierre case had surely helped, he said.

Nicastro, like everyone else within the ranks, had no idea how promotions were made. A day or two before, I had sat beside the Police Commissioner in his car. Murphy had a list of names submitted to him by commanders. There were eight openings for deputy inspector, and 12 names on the list, one of them Nicastro's. Murphy stared at the list for 15 minutes as we drove along, drawing checks next to names, then erasing them, then drawing them again. It was a kind of guessing game. Who came recommended by whom? Finally the check beside Nicastro's name stayed. Murphy had heard of him or read of him, but not of some of the others. Captain Bracey got promoted because he was black and had the 32nd Precinct in Harlem; Captain Clark got promoted ("made" in Police Department jargon) because he was recommended by the First Deputy; Captain Voelker because he had had some publicity as head of the city-wide Anti-crime Squad.

I watched Murphy erase tentative check marks beside names he could not quite attach to faces.

I said nothing at all.

Nicastro, thanking me for his promotion, was jubilant.

Possibly he was pleased also that I had kept secret the Hotel Pierre solution.

But for reasons which will become clear, I believe it is time the tale was told.

New York detectives kept a string of informants on an informal basis. From time to time detectives paid informants Department money for specific information. But many detectives handed out their own money to informants in order to keep the guy "friendly." This didn't involve a great deal of money. The goodwill of a criminal informant in New York City could be had for five or ten dollars a month, enough for a single fix or perhaps two.

But within the Federal Bureau of Investigation, the cultivation of informants had been carried to higher levels. Whenever a special agent developed an informant, the man was photographed, fingerprinted, and some sort of a financial deal was worked out with him. Perhaps he received regular amounts. Perhaps he was paid only on delivery of specific information. Shortly after the relationship between special agent and informant was established, the informant was brought in again and introduced to at least one other agent. This way, if the first agent should be killed, or leave the Bureau, the valuable informant would not be lost.

On the question of money, the Bureau, like all of the other federal law enforcement agencies, had access to almost unlimited funds. Payments were concealed in various corners of the FBI budget, and no outsider ever knew how much an individual informant was paid for a big case such as this one. However, the Hotel Pierre "tip" which the Bureau had now received was of such importance that Chief of Intelligence Grubert later guessed the informant's fee as approximately $25,000.

The robbers had sped away from the Hotel Pierre in their limousine, then split up. Having been up all night they now went to bed—what could be more normal? But like actors after a particularly brilliant and taxing performance, certain of them had trouble sleeping, for the applause (their own) still rang in their ears.

They slept most of Sunday, and on Monday made their

first efforts to dispose of the loot. As perfectly conceived and executed as was the robbery itself, apparently no plan at all had been made for afterward. To the police, later, this seemed inconceivable—proof again that crime and criminals follow no rules.

But on Monday morning, like clothing merchants with a glut of yesterday's suits upon the rack, the robbers attempted to attract buyers into the store. It was not learned how many potential buyers were contacted, but among the first of these was a professional informant—that is, a professional criminal—on the regular payroll of the FBI. This informant now had to decide which profit to take. He could involve himself in the Pierre crime, but risk jail if caught. Or he could earn as much, perhaps more, by selling his information to the FBI. He would have to pay tax on it, and the robbers might kill him if they found out. Judging that the safer money was the FBI money, the informant arranged a meeting for noon the next day at the Cattleman restaurant between himself, his FBI contact man (who would pose as a fence) and the man who had just phoned him claiming to be exclusive agent for the Pierre jewelry, one Bert Stern, 45 years old. The informant was told to bring money; a small transaction would take place at lunch to prove good faith on both sides: to prove that Stern had the jewels and that the informant could raise the money.

With other FBI agents watching from another table, this meeting took place on Tuesday as planned. The informant was shown securities stolen from the Pierre, and he purchased them for $700. It was later theorized that the robbers, though in possession of $4 million worth of jewelry, were otherwise broke and needed cash to pay their hotel bills.

When Stern left the restaurant he strolled calmly across town, entered the coffee shop in the Manhattan Hotel, still closely tailed by the FBI surveillance team, and there he was seen in conversation with two unknown men.

In a television play or movie the audience would have been privileged to watch the crime committed, and now, observing the three men, would have recognized each for whatever role he had played in the robbery scene. But the FBI surveillance team had unfortunately not been present at the robbery scene, and now could only observe three men. They had not been close enough to Stern in the Cat-tleman restaurant even to know for certain if he was who he claimed to be, and/or had access to the Pierre jewels. As for the two other men with Stern, perhaps they were old school chums or relatives. Perhaps the conversation under-way concerned sports or politics.

There were only two FBI agents to tail three men as this meeting broke up. The decision was made to let Stern go. Apparently the office knew his name and therefore he could be found again. But who were the other two guys? One agent followed one of them, who sauntered along the sidewalks staring in shop windows. If the agent had stuck with him, he would have seen him return to the Hotel Manhattan and ask for a key—it would have been an easy matter to discover his name and room number. The FBI would have known where to find him later. But the suspect was not at ease. He kept looking around. Any moment he would make the tail. The FBI agent decided to withdraw. Meanwhile, the second suspect had walked to an illegally parked white Ford Galaxie with Jersey plates, thrown a black satchel in the back, and driven away. The second FBI agent watched the car until it disappeared in traffic.

Both agents then went back to the FBI Building, where they met with the informant, with the informant's FBI con-tact (call him Agent Jones), and with special agent Robert Hartman, who was about to become co-director of the Pierre case investigation.

The securities purchased by Agent Jones were scruti-nized. Contact had indeed been made with the jewels from the Pierre Hotel.

A meeting was now arranged to inform the Police De-partment's ranking detective commander, John Kinsella, and also Captain Nicastro, head of Seedman's Major Crime Squad.

This was followed by still another meeting at the office of the Manhattan District Attorney, for the FBI had no ju-risdiction in this case. It would have to be prosecuted —assuming arrests were eventually made—in Manhattan Criminal Court. Therefore Assistant District Attorney Richard Lowe was assigned to the case at this stage. Lowe was to be kept abreast of all developments, and no arrests were to be made without Lowe's authorization.

Although the FBI had no jurisdiction, it was their informant who had made the connection. To protect this informant, and also for the glory, they wanted in. Consequently, a special squad was set up that consisted of 20 two-man teams. Each consisted of one FBI agent and one city detective, an arrangement which had never been tried before. The squad would be under the joint command of special agent Hartman, and of Detective Lieutenant Edward O'Connor, commander of the Fourth District Robbery Squad, within whose territory the crime had occurred.

O'Connor was a big, heavy man, 53 years old, with thinning gray hair. He was married, with five children, and he lived in Queens. As a young man, O'Connor had served nearly six years as a state trooper. At first he had worked in traffic control on Long Island, but after the war he was transferred to the state police barracks near Binghamton, and there, far upstate, he lived with other troopers while his wife and kids lived in New York City. Like all troopers he got one night a week off—from 5 P.M. till 10 A.M. the next morning—during which he would drive home. He also got four days off a month. He couldn't continue this sort of life, so he took the test for the New York City Police Department and came out near the top of the list.

Within five years he was a detective. He had worked in high-crime areas—four years in the 28th Squad in Harlem, other years in Bedford-Stuyvesant and the South Bronx.

When the Mafia don, Albert Anastasia, was murdered in a barber's chair in 1957, Second Grade Detective O'Connor had caught the case. He worked on it 18 months. It was such a defiant type of crime that 75 detectives were assigned at the beginning; and although this number dwindled steadily, O'Connor stayed with it until the end. No successful prosecution resulted, but O'Connor later remarked, "We got so close, that if they could have bought back those bullets, they would have paid any price." Fourteen years were to pass before the next hit was ordered on a Mafia don—Joe Colombo—and O'Connor took modest credit for having forced the Mafia underground for so long.

When detective specialization went into effect on January 1, a few hours before the Hotel Pierre robbery, O'Connor was given command of Fourth District Robbery.

January 1 was a Saturday. O'Connor was to remember it later as "a beautiful, quiet day." He came to work at 8 A.M., and calmly put in ten hours structuring his new office.

Sunday was to be more of the same, the entire city sleeping off the New Year's Eve binge, but O'Connor's phone woke him up at 6:45 A.M. He dressed and drove straight to the Pierre, planning to grab breakfast as soon as he learned what had happened. It was five o'clock in the afternoon before he at last took time out to eat "breakfast," and from there he worked straight through until 1 A.M.

His first job was to call in eight detectives—he named the ones he wanted. When they got there, O'Connor dismissed the six who had been on duty all night. Interrogations of the captives lasted for hours. It was O'Connor's order that each be interrogated separately. The first day's interrogations provided him with the scenario of the robbery which was of course useful, but with only two other clues: (1) that one of the robbers had demanded to know which box belonged to "The Princess," and (2) that one of the robbers had been addressed by one of the other robbers as "Bobby."

By 8 A.M. the next morning, Monday, O'Connor knew that the three South American guests had checked out and flown back to Rio. Only a few of the witnesses, almost all of whom had been accosted from behind by a single robber, had caught even a glimpse of a face, but the three Brazilians had descended in an elevator face to face with two of them. But suddenly the Brazilians were gone. They had chosen to go home. It was an American problem and a New York problem. They wanted nothing to do with it. They were gone. There was no way O'Connor could hold them. Besides, they had not asked his permission. They were simply gone, and O'Connor was deeply offended, both morally and professionally. The way O'Connor saw it, it was the duty of every citizen in the world to make that world a better place if he could. O'Connor knew that his own code was more stringent than most. Certainly it was more stringent than that of his three best witnesses.

Toward the end of Tuesday, the third day, O'Connor was summoned to the FBI Building on 69th Street and informed that contact had been made between an agent for the jewel thieves and an informant for the FBI. O'Connor was informed that he would be joint commander of a joint investigation.

He had his misgivings, for he had "cooperated" with the FBI before, and almost always the cooperation was one-sided. Too many investigations had consisted of the Police Department sharing all its secrets, and the FBI sharing nothing. Whenever a joint investigation was successful, the FBI usually succeeded in hogging all of the glory. The co-operation between FBI agents and detectives on the street was sometimes excellent, for both believed in the existence of real evil, and fought it every working day. Other times, even street-level cooperation was poor. FBI agents were at least college graduates, and a good many had advanced de-grees in law or accounting, whereas most detectives had high school educations. Agents wore button-down collars and ties to every investigation, whereas detectives often ap-peared in windbreakers. It was always easy to tell the dif-ference between detectives and FBI agents at crime scenes —the FBI guys were the ones with the short sideburns. Mr. Hoover refused to let his men adapt to the fashions of the times, and since they got paid at least $5000 per year more than detectives, they could certainly afford plenty of hair-cuts.

That is, FBI agents often had a snooty opinion of their own abilities, and certainly the public did.

On command levels the cooperation between the FBI under Hoover and the Police Department was usually poor. There was jealousy on both sides. The FBI was empowered to conduct investigations out of the city and into other states, and usually withheld the results of such investi-gations from the Police Department, which had a real need for the information.

Often the FBI was loath to undertake joint investigations at all. In Mafia cases, there were usually two separate inves-tigations, two sets of dossiers and conclusions, and often enough, no arrest.

Hoover seemed determined to keep the FBI separate. The FBI did not share.

And so O'Connor was unhappy with the arrangements which now confronted him. Later he was to declare with astonishment that cooperation was perfect. He was to urge much more of the same. Working together, the police and FBI would be able to break cases heretofore considered insoluble. With a pooling of men, informants, intelligence, and equipment, the fight against crime could enter a golden age.

When the Tuesday night conference at FBI headquarters got down to specifics, O'Connor mentioned that one of the Pierre robbers had been called "Bobby." An FBI agent remarked that there had been someone known only as Bobby involved in the Sophia Loren jewel robbery also. So the FBI files were got out. Although some of Miss Loren's jewelry was recovered, and some arrests made, no Bobby had ever been identified. Suspicion had also fallen upon an otherwise unknown character called Sammy the Greek.

Was Sammy the Greek involved here too? The FBI had never had solid evidence against him and did not know his name. His trail had led to an apartment on West 45th Street, and no further.

In jewel robberies, then as now, one did not move up close until in possession of solid facts. Otherwise the jewelry simply disappeared to no purpose.

As of that night, the investigation had one individual, Bert Stern, positively identified, and it was probable that the two individuals Stern had met with in the coffee shop at the Manhattan Hotel were also involved.

(No one knew it yet, but the FBI surveillance team that afternoon had actually watched Stern in conversation with "Bobby" and with Sammy the Greek. It was Bobby who was staying at the Manhattan, and Sammy who had driven off in the white Ford Galaxie. The investigation was closer than it knew.)

The first job was to find that car. The plate number gave up an address in Jersey, which was discreetly checked out. Apparently law-abiding people lived there. For the moment, that line of investigation was stopped.

One place to look for the car was at the exits of all bridges and tunnels entering from New Jersey. Detectives were placed there early the next day, Wednesday. For hours they watched streams of cars enter the city.

The second place to look was in the neighborhood of the Manhattan Hotel. O'Connor flooded the area. There were surveillance teams on foot and in cars. Teams checked out the parking garages and lots. Surveillance cars crisscrossed the island, some moving north and south, some east and west. Others were parked near the hotel.

All were equipped with a special radio frequency provided by the FBI. The New York detectives had never been able to get any special frequencies for themselves, no matter how heavy a case. Whatever else J. Edgar Hoover might be, he was a magician at getting money and equipment for his men. Detectives did not regard agents with awe, but rather with wistfulness. If only we had the gear—and the informants—they had.

At last the white Ford Galaxie entered the surveillance grid and was spotted. There were three men in it. The man later identified as Sammy the Greek was driving. As this car cruised near the Manhattan Hotel an unmarked car dropped in behind, and O'Connor and Hartman were notified by radio. But the drive was so aimless and lasted so long that O'Connor and Hartman began to believe that the suspects had made the tail. The tail was immediately withdrawn and nothing further was done that day. They would wait for Stern to make contact with the informant again.

Nonetheless, perhaps something had been learned. The Manhattan Hotel seemed to be headquarters for this gang. The chances were that one or more of them lived in a room there. But which room, out of hundreds, and under which name? The only useful name that had yet come to light was Stern, and now Assistant District Attorney Lowe began the onerous job of obtaining a court-ordered wiretap on Stern's home phone in Queens. Affidavit upon affidavit had to be drawn up, each supported by evidence. The draft of these affidavits had to be approved by District Attorney Hogan, and then Lowe had to go before a judge to obtain the order. In a country which took its freedoms seriously, obtaining a court-ordered wiretap took much more than a solid day's work.

While awaiting the order that would permit the wiretap, the decision was made not to go near that Manhattan Hotel. Once the tap was in, Stern might phone the hotel. This would give up a room number.

Stern was the key. They would wait for the wiretap on

Stern, or for Stern to contact the informant again.

On Thursday nothing happened. By Friday morning everybody was jittery. They still didn't have the wiretap, and where was the informant?

Suddenly the phone rang.

Agent Hartman, Lieutenant O'Connor and Captain Nicastro took the call at one desk among about 50 in a vast room in the FBI Building. All around them other agents busy with other cases came and went. The noise and the movement made for a kind of privacy of its own.

Stern had called the informant, who had called his FBI contact (Agent Jones), who had now phoned in. Jones reported that a meeting was on for 2 P.M. that afternoon at a different hotel, the Summit. The informant would rent a room there—amazingly, Stern had let the informant make all the arrangements. On hand would be members of the gang, a crooked jeweler who would serve as appraiser, and many, possibly all, of the jewels.

Jones was given instructions: Rent not one room, but two. The FBI would pay for both, thus having legal right of entry. In the second adjacent room would be stationed agents and detectives.

O'Connor, Nicastro, and Hartman conferred. All agreed that arrests would be made today. They felt too close to losing the case completely. This afternoon a sale was to be made. Some of the jewelry would be on hand. That would be evidence enough.

Nobody informed Assistant District Attorney Lowe.

The day's first contact had been made about 10 A.M. Long before 2 P.M. detectives and FBI agents were in position in the hotel. The meeting was to take place in Room 1544. In the room next door waited two FBI agents and two detectives. Through the wall they could hear men enter Room 1544.

In the lobby Stern met with the informant and Agent Jones, and they strolled into the bar, where Stern produced and showed a single enormous stone. This was a sample of what waited upstairs, he said. Agent Jones said that the stone looked good to him, and he would step into that phone booth over there and phone his people to bring the money. He did step into the phone booth, and he phoned upstairs to the other agents and detectives. Stern, meanwhile, said he would look into Room 1544 to make sure all was ready.

Presently Stern came down again, and the three men strolled up the street, entered the Cork & Bottle and ordered drinks.

Back in the vast noisy room at FBI headquarters, Lieutenant O'Connor took the call from the Summit. A detective had been listening at the door in the corridor. Inside Room 1544 were two men talking about jewelry.

O'Connor ordered, "Take them."

A second call came in from the surveillance team outside the Cork & Bottle.

O'Connor ordered, "Don't make a move while they're in there. I'll be right over."

He got there, and Stern, the informant, and Agent Jones strolled out onto the sidewalk.

O'Connor ordered all three arrested, and hustled off to FBI headquarters, where Stern was dragged into a room and the other two released.

Meanwhile four men had burst into Room 1544. On the television set, and under a hat on a rack, lay a quarter of a million dollars worth of jewelry.

There was no resistance. Taken into custody were Dominick Paulino, 46 years old, 5 feet 4 inches tall; and Benjamin Fradkin, 65 years old, a jeweler.

So three men were now in custody, plus less than 10 percent of the stolen jewelry. Missing were at least two, and possibly four, bandits, not to mention the bulk of the loot. In order to safeguard whatever security was left, the prisoner had been brought not to the 19th Precinct police station but to the FBI Building. The mood there was disappointment. Had the arrests been made too soon? Was it possible that none of the three men in custody had even taken part personally in the robbery?

In Paulino's coat was found a bill from the Manhattan Hotel. There was a room number on it: Room 1553. The bill was made out to R. Comfort and D. Paulino.

O'Connor sent four detectives hurrying over there. They got a chambermaid with a passkey, and showed their shields. Increasingly nervous with each step, she accompanied them to the door of 1553, and even inserted her key in the lock. When she saw the detectives' guns she screamed. They pushed her out of the way and burst in the door. On the bed watching TV, shoes off, glancing up now with surprise, lay Robert Comfort, 39 years old, 5 feet 10 inches tall. In Comfort's possession as he was arrested was a small amount of Pierre jewelry. They stripped him to the skin but found no more.

When the detectives reached the FBI Building leading Comfort in handcuffs, O'Connor was delighted. "It looks like we found Bobby," he said.

He, Hartman and Nicastro were by now feeling somewhat better. Still, Fradkin was a jeweler, and Stern was possibly nothing but a fence. Paulino's role was not clear. That meant that Comfort was the only one of the stickup men in custody.

Although later the suspects refused to make statements of any kind, the supposedly hardened Comfort had blabbed his head off to the detectives as they arrested him. Comfort even boasted that Sammy was the ringleader. They'd never get Sammy, and they'd never get the rest of the jewels.

So the decision was made to go after Sammy the Greek. No one knew what he looked like. No one knew his name.

The only lead was the old stale one developed during the Sophia Loren robbery 15 months before: Sammy frequented an apartment on West 45th Street.

Two FBI agents and two detectives, one of them George Bermudez, were sent to that address. Bermudez was a rough-looking, rough-talking man with many years as a narcotics detective behind him.

The four men found the apartment teeming with girls. The girls said they worked as topless dancers. Sammy the Greek had loaned them the apartment. They didn't know what his last name might be. The girls were extremely hospitable. The afternoon began to slip away. Food and drink were served. Always the detectives and agents—especially Bermudez—kept bringing the conversation back to Sammy the Greek. Night fell. By now the three girls had equipped Bermudez with five or six aliases for Sammy the Greek. One girl had visited Sammy's apartment somewhere in the Bronx. She didn't know the address, but it was a big apartment building on a hill. It was near a highway and a fire station. She was sure she'd recognize it. Presently a car containing two detectives and two FBI agents, guided by a fully dressed professional topless dancer, began cruising the streets of the Bronx. It was after midnight before the girl said, "That's it, that's where Sammy lives."

The startling break in the "brilliant" Pierre robbery—four suspects in custody, quantities of jewelry recovered—had been announced on every radio and TV broadcast of the last several hours. The morning papers were already on the street and one clarion headline read: BAG FOUR IN PIERRE CAPER. If Sammy the Greek was still home it would be a miracle. And even if he was still there, on what grounds could he be arrested? There were laws against illegal search and seizure. There was no hard evidence of any kind linking Sammy to the Pierre robbery.

The rest of us who had taken part in the day's momentous events were home in bed. From 3:30 in the afternoon, when it had become known that the case was breaking, I had been in constant contact with the Police Commissioner. With four prisoners ready for booking and a quarter of a million dollars worth of jewelry sealed into plastic evidence pouches, the Police Department could claim its part in a sensational triumph. Unless the FBI tried to grab all the glory.

If both the FBI and the Police Department claimed credit, the public would no doubt believe the FBI. The public believed that the FBI was infallible, incorruptible, even omnipotent. Whereas the Police Department had just come through the Knapp Commission hearings.

Whichever claim was accompanied by possession of those prisoners was the one that would be believed.

It seemed absolutely vital to get the prisoners back from the FBI at once.

The Police Commissioner ordered me to FBI headquarters to get the prisoners back. Then he called to say that he had just spoken to John Malone, Special Agent in Charge of the New York FBI office. Malone had proven surprisingly docile. He was perfectly willing to give the prisoners back. His only concern was to protect the anonymity of the FBI informant who had unlocked the case.

About 7 P.M. the prisoners began to trickle in to the 19th Precinct station house, each manacled to a detective.

After that came the jewels, already sealed in the evidence envelopes. The Police Commissioner arrived.

Although it was known that there were other Pierre bandits still out there, the decision was made to go public with the case as it then stood. The secret could not be kept long anyway, the city had a right to know, and besides, the Police Department needed the glory. None of us knew that even then George Bermudez was closing in on the house of Sammy the Greek.

In the lobby of 946 Anderson Avenue in the Bronx, Detective Bermudez was running his finger down names in the building directory. Sammy the Greek could be named Carpenter, or Nelo or Malo, or perhaps Fisher—Bermudez's finger stopped on the name Fisher. Although Bermudez had no name for Sammy, and therefore no photo, the girl had described him, and Bermudez, accompanied by Agent Ed Holiday of the FBI, now rapped on the superintendent's door and asked if this man Fisher resembled the description, and if not, did anybody else in the building resemble the description?

It was 1:30 in the morning when Bermudez telephoned O'Connor. We may have found Sammy the Greek, Bermudez said, but even if we have, we have no probable cause for arresting him. O'Connor could only answer: I hope some sort of probable cause turns up. Suddenly, with the announcement that here came Sammy the Greek past the superintendent's door, Bermudez hung up.

The super said, "That's Fisher."

Fisher was carrying two parcels. It was the middle of the night. There shouldn't have been strange men in the lobby of his building. A few minutes before, he had turned on his television set for the first time that night—and learned of the break in the Pierre case.

Seeing the strange men, Fisher seemed to hesitate, then he went out onto the sidewalk where he attempted to stuff one of his two shopping bags into a garbage pail against the wall there. Carrying the other, he walked away into the darkness.

Agent Holiday was running down the block toward the car in which sat the topless dancer and the second FBI Agent-Detective team. Holiday wanted to get the girl to identify Fisher as Sammy the Greek. Fisher dropped his second shopping bag beside a parked car, and began to run back the way he had come. But he ran right into Georgie Bermudez, who had only a second to decide if such conduct—running, dropping a shopping bag on the street—constituted probable cause for an arrest. George grabbed him.

"The game is up, Sammy."

"My name is Fisher."

"Look, we know who you are, Sammy. The game is up. We got Bobby Comfort. Come on, let's go inside."

"I don't live here."

"I know you live here, Sammy, so cut it out. The game is up."

As they were walking upstairs, Sammy asked, "How did you find me?"

But Bermudez declined to answer.

On the street the two discarded bags were searched. One was stuffed with papers—letters, press clippings and the like—which perhaps would prove incriminating when examined. The other contained hammer, crowbar, and chisel —burglar's tools. Later, Bermudez was to say, "Why didn't he just leave those tools in his apartment? Nobody would have noticed. In an apartment they're only tools. They become burglar's tools when you carry them on the street or attempt to get rid of them."

Upstairs Bermudez found three rings, some of them with jewels pried out of the settings, and Sammy's passport in his real name, Sorecho Nelo. On the bed lay two full suitcases, one already closed and locked. Sammy had been on his way out of the city and country. Ten minutes more and he would have been gone. On the wall were newspaper photos of Anne McDonnell Ford, Maria Callas, Sophia Loren, and other rich women wearing jewelry, some of them past victims of Sammy, some of them perhaps future ones. Nelo was 40 years old, and there were so many arrests like this one on his record that it was clear that he made his living by sticking up hotels. Bermudez was up all night processing him, and at ten o'clock in the morning, still on his feet, Bermudez and two other detectives stood among the men who had stuck up the Hotel Pierre in a series of lineups conducted by Assistant District Attorney Lowe.

Lowe was furious. He had arrived at the 19th Precinct

station house the night before, as the prisoners did. When he left there at 4 A.M., he was convinced that there was no prosecutable case against any of the defendants. Most of the evidence would be suppressed in court on technicalities, and all five men would be released. Since very little of the loot had been recovered, all five could be expected to live happily ever after on their profits.

For Lowe had been informed that the FBI had no intention of producing in court either their informant, or Agent Jones, the informant's contact man who had actually met with Stern. If no informant existed, then how did detectives justify breaking into Room 1544 in the Summit Hotel? If they couldn't justify the arrests in the Summit, how could they justify the arrest of Comfort in the Manhattan Hotel? And without these arrests justified, on what grounds did they arrest Sorecho Nelo? To Lowe it seemed highly unlikely that any judge would admit the evidence found in Nelo's room, once he had already thrown out the four previous arrests.

Lowe, 30 years old and unmarried, had been an assistant district attorney on Frank Hogan's staff almost five years. He earned only about $15,000 a year. Like all of Hogan's assistants, he considered himself shamefully underpaid. But his respect for Hogan personally, in this age of non-heroes, was total. Lowe once said, "Mr. Hogan is a man who goes out of his way to protect the rights of the very people his office is prosecuting. I never respected any man more than Mr. Hogan except my father." Each time Lowe asked for a raise, he was told there was simply no money there. He kept claiming that he would quit and go into private practice, but so far he had not.

Lowe was the son of a detective, Chink Lowe, who had put in 25 years in the Police Department. Three times Chink Lowe was shot. The last time he was hit five times and the next morning lay full-length, covered with blood, across the front pages of the *Daily News* and the *Daily Mirror*. His 14-year-old son Dick was in YMCA summer camp. Another boy came running across the grass with the morning tabloid in his hand, crying, "Hey Lefty, isn't this your father?"—recognizing Chink Lowe because the weekend before, Chink had driven up to the camp with a carload of fruit for all the boys. Dick Lowe stared at a photo of his father lying in a hospital with tubes up his nose. The newspapers said there were two bullets in him that could not be removed.

Chink Lowe recovered but was invalided out of the Police Department on three quarters pay. He was the father of four girls and twin boys, one of whom, Bobby, grew up to be a policeman. The other was Dick, who came out of Evander Childs High School in the Bronx wanting to go to college, found that there was no money, and so went to work. For two years Dick Lowe sometimes held two jobs at once. During one stretch he worked from nine to five as a stock boy at Saks Fifth Avenue, and from 10 P.M. to 6 A.M. in the Sealkap paper cup factory. Night after night he fell asleep over the paper cups, but at the age of 20 he had enough money to go off to the University of Wisconsin. During summer vacations he worked at small jobs in Mr. Hogan's office, and after law school, partly because he was the son of a cop, he was taken on as an assistant at $6750.

Lowe was tall, thin and, like many lawyers, beautifully spoken. He was a black man with an Afro haircut.

Once any case passed into the hands of the District Attorney, most policemen and police officials tended to forget it, even though many knew from painful experience that often such cases were just beginning.

But Lowe had left the 19th Precinct station house in the middle of the night, half angry, half despairing, having ordered a lineup in his own office the following morning. Detectives had to be sent out to find and bring in 18 witnesses —they managed to find only 15. Other detectives had to bring the prisoners in. The suspects had to stand in lineups with other men who resembled them, and in New York this was almost always done by using detectives. However, none of the detectives who had brought the witnesses down could be used to pose as suspects.

This left George Burmudez and two other detectives sitting on a bench in a brightly lighted room along with Paulino, Stern, and Comfort. Bermudez by now had been up for nearly two days, he hadn't shaved in that time, and he looked like a hoodlum. But he sat placidly on a bench for some four hours facing a wall in which was set a one-way glass the size of a chess board. Each of the six men wore a number around his neck.

In a darkened room on the other side of the one-way glass stood Lowe, and an assistant district attorney named Kevin McKay, myself, and lawyers representing the suspects, while each witness entered in turn.

Missing of course were the three South Americans. Lowe would telephone them in Rio a number of times, but he knew from that first day that he would never persuade them to come back to identify a suspect or testify. He would have to make do with what he had.

And today he knew he didn't have very much: 15 witnesses, most of whom had been accosted from behind by only one robber. All of the witnesses were men: old and hapless so-called "security" guards; Puerto Ricans who spoke little or no English; black menials who had worked in the most posh hotel in the country but lived in tenements in Harlem and the South Bronx.

Most of these men were frightened. They feared for their jobs, and also for their lives. A positive identification of one of the suspects could cost them either or both.

But without positive identifications, Lowe had no case. Positive identifications were essential.

And so the lineups began. The witnesses were kept in a single small office. Some sat staring at the floor. Some paced and smoked. One by one, each entered the dark room. To each Lowe explained what was about to happen: "The men on the other side of this window cannot see you. Each will walk up to this window. Do not attempt to make any identification until you have looked at all of them. Do not speak or make any sign until I speak to you."

A telephone intercom connected the two rooms. Lowe picked up the phone.

"Start the lineup," said Lowe.

The man wearing number 1, a detective, rose and approached the window. After staring at the window for a moment, he put on a pair of dark-rimmed glasses. Then he turned in profile. Then, still standing in profile, he removed the glasses. After a moment he turned, strode back to the bench, and handed the glasses to man number 2, who was also a detective. This process was repeated until all six men had passed in front of the window. Number 3 was little Paulino. There was no difference between his demeanor and that of the two detectives who had preceded him. Man number 4 was a detective. Man number 5 was Stern, and man number 6 was Comfort. Each time, after Comfort had returned to the bench and sat down, Lowe would ask softly: "Do you recognize anyone in that room? Are you sure? Would you like to look at any of them again?"

Each of the witnesses to each of Lowe's questions responded, "No, sir."

"Thank you," said Lowe.

One by one, Lowe used up his witnesses. His face showed no expression. He was operating on almost no sleep and his mood was glum.

In the office formerly crowded with 15 witnesses, a single man was left. His name was Elijah Weathersby, a middle-aged black cleaning man. It was Weathersby who, almost a week before, had told Lieutenant O'Connor's interrogators that he had got a good look at at least two of the stickup men, he would recognize them anywhere. And so now Lowe had kept Weathersby, presumably his strongest witness, but also his most reluctant, for last.

Lowe and Weathersby were alone in the office. Weathersby, his eyes fixed to the floor, said that he did not want to identify anybody, that if all the jewelry in the world had been robbed from all the rich people in the world, this meant nothing to him. He was a black man. He had no use for the police. He was scared.

Lowe told Weathersby, "You've got to help a brother. There are only a few of us on Hogan's staff, and if people like you let us down, we'll never get ahead here or anywhere. You're our best witness, and this is my first big case."

This last, strictly speaking, was not true. Lowe by now was an experienced prosecutor who, the year before, had brought some 20 cases to trial and lost only two by acquittal.

Weathersby said, "I don't blame you for having this type of job, even though you have to prosecute a lot of the brothers."

"That's all the more reason to help me. Here's a chance to get back at whitey. These guys are nothing but a bunch of white hoods."

Lowe said again, "You've got to help a brother."

Weathersby stared at the floor.

Weathersby stood in the dark peering through the one-way glass. Lowe watched his face. Stolidly Weathersby watched all six suspects pass in front of him and sit again side by side on the bench.

In the darkened room, the tension and the silence were palpable. At last Lowe spoke. "Do you see anybody in that room you recognize?"

A moment longer Weathersby stared through into the brightly lighted room. Then he thrust the five fingers of one hand toward Lowe's face. An instant later, the first finger of his left hand was added to the other five—six fingers in all.

Lowe's face broke into a broad grin. "Are you telling me that you recognize numbers 5 and 6.?"

"That's right," said Elijah Weathersby.

The darkened room seemed to fill up with Lowe's contented sigh. Then Lowe said, "Thank you, sir. Now if you'll just go through into this other room—"

Weathersby had identified Comfort and Stern. Later he would say to Lowe, "The reason that I recognized Comfort was because I had seen him only a week before at the Cotillion Ball. He was wearing a tuxedo and pretending to be drunk, but he wasn't drunk. I remember asking myself, 'Why is that man pretending he's drunk?' I went to get the security people, but when I got back he was gone."

The detectives who had spent four hours in the small bright room often chatting with the perpetrators of the "most brilliant" jewel robbery in New York City's history now stepped out into the hall. Detective Georgie Bermudez said, "I never expected this kind of clientele. What a bunch of assholes."

Bermudez now looked in on Sorecho Nelo and discovered an astonishing scene. Nelo, who was about to take his turn in the lineup before the same 15 witnesses, was a little man, about 5 feet 7 inches tall, and he was stone bald. Only one of the robbers had been that short—the chauffeur. However, the chauffeur was later described as having a full head of hair. Therefore, Nelo had worn a wig for the robbery. When arrested, Nelo had been wearing a wig. Knowing he would be ordered to clamp it on his bald pate for the lineup, Nelo had quickly torn the wig in two. Detectives had been guarding the two pieces ever since. With an amused smile, Bermudez now watched two detectives attempting with thick, clumsy fingers to pin the wig together again, using the enormous safety pins attached to the backs of their shields.

Eventually the second lineup took place, and Nelo was identified by one witness, who said he would feel more certain if he could hear Nelo speak. Nelo was asked to say, "Don't turn around. Don't look at me. Put your hands down."

He read these lines with little enthusiasm. Hearing the voice, the witness cried out, "Un-fucking-believable. That's him. I'd know that voice anywhere."

No witnesses identified either the 65-year-old jeweler, Fradkin, or the 5-feet 4-inches tall Paulino.

For many days afterward, Lowe contemplated his case. He had no so-called scientific evidence at all, no fingerprints, no ballistics tests, no material in possession that could be linked via microscopic examination or any other examination to the robbery. Nelo's burglar's tools may or may not have been used. No one would ever know. No detailed plan of the crime had been found. No independent witness could testify to hearing the crime planned. The jewelry that had been recovered could not be introduced in evidence because, barring testimony by either the informant or FBI Agent Jones, or both, this jewelry had been recovered as the result of illegal search and seizure. No, all Lowe had were his few positive identifications by witnesses. And what jury was going to believe that out of 21 witnesses only four or five could identify only one robber each. It would sound to the jury not like positive identification, but like conflicting testimony.

Lowe still didn't know how many men were involved in the actual robbery and neither did anybody else. It could have been six or four or seven or five. Repeatedly shown to witnesses were photos of other known jewel thieves, among them, one Terry Bloom. One witness identified Bloom, who had another case pending. Ostensibly to talk about this other case, Bloom was asked to come down to Lowe's office—where he was arrested. The witness thereupon picked Bloom out of a lineup. But Bloom had an alibi. He could prove to have been in California for all except 22 hours surrounding the robbery. Bloom was held for a while, and then his case was dismissed.

Photos of a jewel thief named Carpenter were identified by witnesses. Carpenter could not be found.

Meanwhile, the investigation into other jewel robberies continued. Securities were recovered that had been stolen (along with jewels and money) from the Hotel Drake last Christmas Day. Evidence pointed to Nelo and Comfort as the perpetrators of that robbery. The Regency Hotel had been stuck up while Elizabeth Taylor, Richard Burton, and 500 other guests slept. The bandits had handcuffed 15 employees and two guests, clapped tape over their eyes and mouths, and fled with 19 safe deposit boxes and a small safe. Value of the loot totaled over $100,000. The stolen car used had been found. In it were safe deposit boxes from the hotel. Inside one box were some used Band-aids—the bandits had worked with their fingertips taped. From the back of one of these used Band-aids, detectives had lifted a single print, which now was shown to match the hand of Robert Comfort. Even this was not legally sufficient evidence to charge Comfort with that crime. He could always claim in court that somebody went to his house, stole some of his Band-aids, and planted them in those stolen safe deposit boxes in that stolen car. In court it would not be possible to charge that the Band-aid fingerprint should be considered conclusive precisely because Comfort was a jewel thief and hotel stickup man by profession. Never-mind that someone called Bobby also had stuck up and terrified Sophia Loren while her baby slept in the next room; this was inadmissible evidence in any prosecution against Comfort. As for Sammy the Greek/Nelo, witnesses from the Sophia Loren robbery, now that Nelo was in custody, had been asked to pick him out of a lineup. One witness put him at the scene that night, but the main witness, Sophia Loren, refused to return to New York to attempt an identification, and this case too had to be dropped.

Detectives had evidence linking Nelo to a West Side murder approximately a year and a half ago.

Two days after Nelo's arrest, the FBI recovered three quarters of a million dollars worth of Pierre jewelry in Detroit. No arrests were made, and no information was given to the public. But in fact, Nelo, having arranged to dispose of the jewels in Detroit, had entrusted his package to a professional criminal—who also happened to be on the payroll of the FBI. For a fee, this informant handed the jewels over.

That is, twice the Pierre robbers had attempted to dispose of their loot and both times had hit men on the FBI payroll. How many criminal informants was the FBI paying, anyway? Who could one trust?

So Nelo was in somewhat more trouble than any of the others, although only for the Pierre robbery. None of the defendants were in trouble proportionate to the public menace that they constituted. Assistant District Attorney Lowe wanted to prosecute all of them on the stiffest charge possible. For Nelo and Comfort this meant armed robbery, maximum jail term, 25 years. But this was simply not going to be possible unless Lowe could get the testimony of the FBI informant and/or Jones. Lowe went back to the FBI and was flatly refused.

So Lowe went to Frank Hogan.

Hogan had been District Attorney of New York County for 30 years, having won eight straight elections. Much of the time he ran unopposed, such an incorruptible and dedicated public figure that other potential candidates tended to consider him unbeatable.

Trial date had been set, and a jury empaneled. Judge Andrew Tyler had begun listening to pre-trial motions by defense lawyers to suppress most of the evidence. Then he had met separately with Lowe, and with the defense attorneys. Lowe later accused Tyler of playing poker with justice. Tyler seemed not to want to have to decide on the delicate legal questions posed here. He had told Lowe that he probably would have to grant the defense motions for suppression. He had told the defense that he would probably have to rule in favor of the prosecution.

He had suggested to both sides that they settle their case without a trial.

Lowe said to Hogan, "The FBI has got to let us use their agent to testify, or most of our evidence will be suppressed."

Lowe wanted Hogan to argue with the FBI. "Stern was arrested in the company of the informant and Agent

Jones," Lowe said. "He can have no doubt who sold him out, and if he knows, the others know. Why won't the FBI let us have Jones?"

The outraged Hogan confronted the federal attorney's office. He wanted the FBI ordered to produce Agent Jones. Hogan could not threaten to subpoena the informant, for no one knew who he was except the FBI. There were consultations in New York after that and other consultations between New York and Washington. The decision was relayed to Hogan by Robert Morvillo, an assistant federal attorney for the Southern District. If Agent Jones testified, Morvillo said, this would risk compromising the informant, and the informant was engaged in a number of other important cases.

The angry Hogan pointed out that there could not possibly be a bigger case than the Pierre jewel robbery. At least three other jewel robberies had been perpetrated by some or most of the defendants in the Pierre case. More than $2 million worth of Pierre jewelry was still out there somewhere. If, as a result of Agent Jones' testimony, the informant was blown, then that was just too bad. Informants were uncovered all the time in order to win convictions in specific major cases. The FBI owed it to the City of New York to take this risk now so as to convict Nelo, Comfort, and the others.

Federal Attorney Morvillo said flatly that Special Agent Jones would not be available to testify. If Hogan tried to subpoena him, the subpoena would be fought all the way to the Attorney General. Case closed.

In a soft, angry voice Hogan said, "Will you put that in writing?"

"Yes," said Morvillo, and he did so.

Hogan chose to make none of this public. Assistant District Attorney Lowe was ordered to accept pleas of guilty on the stiffest charges he could manage. The men who had stuck up the Hotel Pierre would never come to trial.

Presently Lowe worked out the following deal. For Comfort and Nelo, he accepted pleas of guilty to second degree burglary, entering a dwelling with a dangerous weapon, a Class C felony carrying a maximum prison term of seven years. For Stern he accepted a plea of guilty to criminal possession of stolen property, which carried a maximum prison term of four years.

Over Lowe's protests, all of the defendants were then granted release on bail to await sentencing. Lowe demanded $500,000 cash bail; this would prevent them from reaching the $2 million worth of missing jewels still out there. Judge Tyler released Nelo and Stern in $50,000 bond, $5000 cash bail; Comfort in $30,000 bond, $3000 cash bail."

Six months after pleading guilty, nearly a year after the robbery and their arrests, they were at last sentenced. But Judge Tyler, over Lowe's protest, ordered the execution of this sentence stayed to allow them the Christmas holidays with their families, if any. Nelo, who had now been out on the street for 11 of the 12 months since his arrest, was shot three times on the sidewalk at Broadway and 79th Street on New Year's Eve. Hit in the jaw, abdomen and leg, he refused to tell who shot him or why, or to cooperate with the police in any way. Released from the hospital six days later, he was not scheduled to go off to jail for another 18 days.

Only Comfort had begun serving his sentence. Stern was granted an additional stay by Judge Tyler, after Stern's doctor testified that the Pierre case, plus thoughts of jail, had caused Stern's entire family—wife, son, daughter and Stern himself—deep psychological problems. Prosecution of Paulino and Fradkin was still pending.

Lieutenant O'Connor accepted the notion that the FBI should protect their informant at all costs, that otherwise his life would have been in danger, and that a human life was well worth the fortune in jewelry still missing. O'Connor expected to see Nelo and Comfort out of jail and back on the street in approximately two and a half years—one third of their term—and to find evidence of their handiwork not long after that. Something just like the Hotel Pierre case would have to be broken all over again.

As for Commissioner Murphy, he had lost interest in the case once the first arrests had been announced. I never heard him ask about it after that.

2 / Gambling

That winter, in theory at least, the New York Police Department dropped out of the gambling enforcement business. The decision was made by Murphy at the risk of being dismissed by the Mayor or Governor for malfeasance. He was saying in effect that he, the Police Commissioner of the City of New York, henceforth would refuse to enforce certain laws validly enacted by the New York State legislature.

And so Murphy put his career on the line.

For decades the primary purpose of the police had been to suppress gambling—or so it must have seemed to every cop, each one, all of them.

Gambling was on every cop's mind 24 hours a day, like sex on the mind of an adolescent boy. There were cops like Serpico who crawled across rooftops munching on grapefruit halves, making observations of gambling operations across courtyards. And there were the gambler-corrupted cops, against some of whom Serpico testified.

In between were cops who used bookmakers and policy operators as informants, allowing gambling operations to continue provided information against hard criminals stayed good. I knew of one otherwise honest cop who, being about to receive a civilian complaint for slugging a prisoner, had gone to the bookmaker in his sector and said, "You wanna do business here? Then get those people off my back. I don't care how you do it. They hang that complaint on me, I'm locking you up."

Corrupt cops on pads often earned more from gamblers than from the Police Department, but such cops were probably nowhere near as numerous as corruption probes such as the Knapp Commission always claimed. For professional gamblers went to extraordinary lengths to protect their operations. They set up elaborate alarm systems, they encased their doors in steel, they developed intricate codes. Would professional gamblers have been that insecure if they could buy off every cop?

Especially in the black enclaves, the citizens wanted their

gambling, and would pay any price to have it. If the price was corrupting the entire police force, then they would pay that price. They had always bought protection in the past, and meant to go on buying it. A study made by the New York State Joint Legislative Committee on Crime indicated that numbers banks alone grossed over $200 million dollars a year in New York City; five percent of earnings were set aside for legal fees and bribes. Bookmakers were believed to take in five to six times that amount in bets on horse races and sporting events.

In an interview with Nicholas Gage of *The New York Times* the Police Commissioner conceded that he would favor legislation which would legalize numbers and sports gambling. "It would cut off organized crime from a chief source of revenue," Murphy said, "and it would eliminate a main cause of police corruption."

Decades of enforcement of the gambling laws showed abject failure by every conceivable measure of the stick, as could be seen by certain gambling events of the very recent past.

JULY: Investigation into allegations of "stand-in" arrests at 1409 Fifth Avenue. An anonymous letter had been received by the Police Department alleging a policy operation in a glazier's store at that address. It claimed that six persons were paid $100 each to take "stand-in" or "accommodation" arrests, and that a lot of cops were being paid off too. The glazier's store was placed under observation. A policy operation was being conducted in a flagrant manner, alright, so a plainclothesman entered, placed a wager, and when it was accepted, arrested five persons. Investigation now showed that during the previous nine months there had been 20 gambling arrests effected at that address. However, an analysis of the criminal records of these 20 prisoners revealed that 11 had previous narcotics arrests. They were not gamblers, they were junkies. These 11 persons were then questioned, and 10 stated that they had agreed to get arrested on one or more occasions as stand-ins for gamblers running this policy operation, and they were paid a $100 fee each time.

That is, plainclothesmen assigned to that sector had to come up with prisoners from time to time, and the gamblers in question were always happy to provide same.

Presently, in addition to the five gamblers under arrest, six cops were involved in the investigation.

OCTOBER: The long, lurid recitation of Patrolman Phillips before the Knapp Commission was followed by indictments of more than 20 policemen on charges either of having protected gamblers, or of having given perjured testimony about the protection of gamblers.

NOVEMBER: Inspector William Bonacum, the 48-year-old John Jay College valedictorian who now commanded the Fifth Division, a hotbed of gambling, appeared on the Dick Cavett Show, where he produced some startling statistics. He noted that a sampling had been taken of 1225 convictions for gambling offenses in 1970 and that the cases—all of them convictions—were disposed of in the following manner. Fined under $100—457 gamblers. Fined from $100 to $300—665 gamblers. Fined from $300 to $500—74 gamblers. Fined over $500—10 gamblers. Only 19 of these convicted gamblers had done any time in jail at all, only three for more than 90 days.

The next morning, when *The New York Times* quoted Bonacum, Murphy summoned Lacovara and myself. The Police Commissioner pointed to the newspaper in some distress. "Wouldn't you think he'd know better than to say things like that?" The Police Commissioner expected telephone calls from one or more district attorneys lambasting him. One of his subordinates—and not a very high subordinate at that—had in effect criticized the DA's prosecution of gambling cases.

Lacovara said, "No. I saw the program. Bonacum came out fine."

"Oh. He did?" said the Police Commissioner. During the brief silence that ensued, the Police Commissioner began to look pleased.

The echoes from the Knapp Commission hearings had not yet died away, and Murphy was defensive about nearly every subject, as if he had been shouted at so much lately that he couldn't face any more of the same.

Five days later, Inspector Bonacum sat down and wrote a five-page single-spaced memorandum. Subject: Recommendation for Revision of the Department Gambling Enforcement Policy.

Bonacum's hour-long valedictory address at college may

have sounded pedantic and stolid, but this memo was a cry from the heart.

Seven days previously, after two undercover cops had made bets and after a search warrant had been obtained, Bonacum's plainclothesman had arrested one Samuel Jarmark and two others inside a grocery store that was a "hard core" gambling location at 518 West 159th Street. A total of 414 policy slips containing about 5000 bets were recovered. Jarmark and the two others were charged with violating Sections 225.10 and 225.20 of the penal law. A felony affidavit was drawn up. But when the case came before the judge, charges against Jarmark and one of the others were dismissed, and the remaining defendant was allowed to plead guilty to a misdemeanor, possession of gambling records, and he was fined $150. When the arresting officer protested, the assistant district attorney said, "We're lucky we got this plea."

In his memo, Bonacum noted, "This case is just one more indication that the present policies of the district attorney's office and of the courts relative to gambling enforcement are inconsistent with this department's efforts to suppress gambling." Jarmark had a history of 34 gambling arrests dating from 1942. He had been arrested five times in 1970 and five times already in 1971. He had at least 11 convictions on his record. The greatest fine ever levied against him was $500. His grocery store contained a minute amount of old merchandise on dusty shelves, as obvious a front as one could ask for. Bonacum called Jarmark a policy operator who "continues to operate unaffected by 29 years of enforcement effort."

In the four and a half months since Bonacum had taken command of the Fifth Division, his plainclothesmen had made 104 felony-gambling arrests. Not one of the arrested gamblers had yet been indicted, not one had yet gone to jail. Bonacum wrote, "The undersigned is beginning to feel like a charlatan when he exhorts and encourages youthful plainclothesmen on to greater efforts. Greater efforts for what? To have the results of their efforts given away for fines that amount to no more than walking-around money for the persons involved in gambling."

Recently Bonacum had reviewed the arrest records of

seven KG's operating within his division. The seven men had been arrested between 50 and 150 times each. None had ever been sentenced to any meaningful time in jail. The fines extracted from gamblers were of no significance. Two years before, Bonacum noted, an assistant district attorney had prepared a study showing that the cost of gambling arrests and prosecutions was 40 times greater than the fines collected.

Bonacum then cited another study which estimated the annual gross income from policy operations at about $237 million per year. From this sum the courts had extracted less than 1/200th in fines.

What Bonacum was asking was that gambling enforcement manpower be greatly reduced throughout the Police Department. Bonacum saw five salutary effects from such a policy: (1) The Department could concentrate its efforts on reducing crimes of violence; (2) With greatly reduced work loads in the courts, the Police Department could insist on trials for arrested gamblers instead of pleas, jail sentences instead of fines; (3) Young policemen would be removed from this area of frustration and corruption; (4) Community tension—after all, the people did want their gambling—would be reduced if these unpopular laws were less stringently enforced; and (5) Such a policy would draw public attention and perhaps encourage the legalization of gambling.

Next Bonacum noted the argument that enormous profits went from gambling into organized crime. However, it seemed obvious that enforcement was not reducing those profits by any appreciable amount. Bonacum noted, "If we can't be more effective, concede the profits, and move into more meaningful police work."

Signing his name, Bonacum deliberated a moment, then ordered this memo widely distributed through official channels, en route to the Police Commissioner. Eleven copies were mimeographed and scattered around.

The original went to Chief Ferdinand Catalano, commanding officer of Manhattan North, who two days later affixed his own endorsement. He disputed Bonacum only on the disenchantment of plainclothesmen, saying that this was not an absolute fact. Constant direction, supervision, and encouragement by high superiors would maintain high morale and performance for the period of the assignment, Catalano noted piously.

Six days later, a second endorsement was added by Chief of Patrol Donald Cawley. Cawley wanted the Department to embark upon a major educational and legislative campaign to extricate itself from attempting to enforce laws that the public did not want enforced. If the Department was to stay in the business of enforcing gambling laws because of legal necessity, Cawley wanted its commitment drastically reduced; men no longer needed in this fruitless undertaking would be transferred to high-crime precincts to cope with violent street crime.

Another four days passed before the third and final endorsement was added by Chief Inspector Codd, who noted that the analysis and recommendations of Bonacum summarized all that had been said before relative to enforcing unpopular laws. Codd recommended serious consideration to the thoughts set forth by Bonacum. The Department should aim at those who control and direct gambling operations. If such higher-ups were unable to operate, then gambling operations would dry up.

Bonacum's five-page memo (now grown to seven pages in length, counting the three official endorsements) went into the Police Commissioner's thick attaché case; and when he got to it more than two weeks later, he scrawled in the bottom margin, "This may be a good example of an opportunity to seek a meeting with the district attorneys and chief judges to obtain concurrence on the best use of available resources in the Police Department, district attorneys' offices, and courts to appropriately address the problem."

The Bonacum memo was now three days less than one month old, and that, perhaps, was the end of it. It had been approved by everyone, and the buck passed on. Murphy's endorsement had done little more than allow it to lie there somewhere in the pile. No specific action was ordered or suggested. Either Murphy had given the Bonacum memo only casual attention, or else he perceived the inevitable next step, but was afraid to take it.

The next step—to order his men to cease enforcing the street gambling laws—was radical surgery. It would be like cutting a vital organ out of the Police Department, perhaps the heart itself, who knew? And it would be a bold affront to the city and to its lawmakers. Even those who would favor the elimination of gambling laws could be expected to reject a Police Commissioner who, in effect, wrote out new laws with his own hand. If Murphy could decide not to enforce the gambling laws, who was to say he might not choose still other laws tomorrow, announce that they displeased him, and cease enforcing them to?

The Bonacum memo lay on all of our desks. The Police Commissioner had either to step forward, or stand still. He couldn't do both. That the district attorneys were not prosecuting gambling cases was all too clear; but they were elected officials for one thing, and for another they were engaged in an arcane trade beyond the comprehension of most citizens. Whereas the Police Commissioner worked under a fragile appointment in plain view of everybody, armchair detectives all. The city second-guessed every move he made.

For the moment it seemed clear that he intended to make no move at all. His one and only mandate was to enforce all laws on the book. Any other mandates were merely implied. In the crunch they were as vaporous as conversation and would not stand up.

I was one of those who believed Bonacum correct. I also saw Bonacum as a rather minor subordinate unable even to deliver his message in person. In the Police Department high-ranking subordinates believed in protecting their own flanks. They would approve Bonacum's memo, but in the presence of the Police Commissioner not one was likely to argue any specific action by him. If the Police Commissioner should ask their advice—and Murphy was temperamentally unable to ask advice on subjects such as this—they would couch their replies so as to cover both sides of the question and possibly the middle as well.

So I wrote the Police Commissioner the following memo:

December 9, 1971

MEMORANDUM FOR THE POLICE COMMISSIONER:

Relative to Inspector Bonacum's report on gambling enforcement, it is my feeling that nothing can be done about the gambling laws through normal channels for many, many years to come. It is also my strong feeling that up to 90% of the New York public would agree 100% with Inspector Bonacum's points.

I believe that your leadership would be accepted by the public in this matter. There are very few leaders in this city or country at this time, and your success so far is due to the fact that you are accepted as one. Therefore, I suggest that you assert your leadership in this matter as soon as possible. Either curtail gambling enforcement down to the level of virtual nonexistence, reassigning the forces to anti-crime patrol and announce this dramatically. Or else do so, and don't announce it. I am inclined to favor the second course. The word will, of course, leak out fairly soon, but the low-keyed approach would probably go down better with our fellow citizens, and when the press does come after you on the subject, you have all the statistics necessary to support your decision. At that point you state: "It is not that I unilaterally refuse to enforce a specific law; I merely decided to assign only ten men to such enforcement (or whatever the figure). That's how many it rates according to our priorities."

Again, why wait for a leaderless legislature to act? This would take years. Why not simply act with the power that the people think you have and act right now?

I have talked this over with members of my staff. All agree in principle. Some suggest that your decision be preceded by off-the-record meetings with important judges, bar associations, editors and publishers, all of whom presumably would be on your side. I am inclined to think such backing is not needed. Why take too long, and why water down your image as a dynamic leader?

Nearly a week passed. The Police Commissioner did not bring the matter up at all. I sent a second memo. There was always the possibility that I was urging him to make a highrisk decision I would not have dared make myself. I considered this, and rejected it. I could not really believe that if appropriate orders were given there would be any outcry at all. I was convinced that the response would be applause.

The second memorandum read as follows:

December 14, 1971

MEMORANDUM FOR THE POLICE COMMISSIONER:

We talked the other day about a program. My feeling is that you had one, a good one, but it got shot out from under you by Knapp. You can't afford to accentuate corruption any more without demoralizing both the city and the department.

I suggest that your speech next Monday start your new program. It should attack the current court system as being unable to cope with the arrests we make, offering some statistics.

The following Sunday you should go on Newsmakers on CBS. I have already sounded this show out and they are eager to have you. The date is December 26th. You should expand your feelings about courts and corrections.

On or about December 27th, you should give a specific order to Commissioner McCarthy, to the effect that a single patrolman in each precinct henceforth will be responsible for street gambling, and he will arrest only in response to a specific complaint. We then wait several days to let this leak out. If it doesn't leak, I will leak it to Federici of the News. He will write his story: Murphy no longer enforcing the gambling laws. He will not be able to interview you for this story. Perhaps he will be allowed to interview Bill Smith or Bill McCarthy, who won't tell him much.

We then wait a day or two for the pressure to build up, at which time, in response to pressure, you have a press conference, presenting the reasons why you have reduced the priority of gambling enforcement to the point where street gambling virtually isn't being enforced at all. Failure of DA's to prosecute, corruption hazards of gambling enforcement, cost of it, etc., as per the Bonacum memo.

Obviously this program must be kept flexible, and

perhaps it will be necessary to adjust it along the way.

It has virtues. It is bold, it is varied, it is statesman-like rather than parochial. You have roughly fourteen more years of public service in law enforcement ahead of you. It is up to you to lead the nation. Like it or not there is nobody else. Your focus must be the big focus, because you can't do anything about the rise in stickups anyway. Not only will you look good person-ally, but as a result the department you head will look good. For as long as you are Commissioner, your image and the department's image are inseparable.

This program puts you and the department back on offense. It is clear to anyone who thinks about it that we have been on defense solidly ever since three days before the Knapp Commission started. A man said to me this morning: "Murphy's really been showing a low profile lately, hasn't he?"

All right, let's show a high one. The time has come for one man to point and say follow me.

The speech attacking the courts went off on schedule, but as the days passed, Murphy still said nothing about gambling. Two days before Christmas he sent on to me a confidential memo to him from Deputy Commissioner Mc-Carthy. The FBI had apparently been conducting gambling investigationsl for some time. McCarthy had been making available to them any and all information. But now, colli-sions in the field had begun to develop. A number of cops, stumbling upon FBI agents, had imagined that the FBI was there investigating cops rather than gamblers. The reaction of the cops was to protect themselves at all costs, even to the point of blowing the investigation. McCarthy had con-tacted the New York office of the FBI and tried to work out some sort of joint activity, without success. H noted in the memo that effectiveness was going down as cops spent more time looking for the FBI than for gamblers. He ac-cused the FBI of leaving him in a vacuum as to their operations. He expected that very soon would appear an FBI press release announcing indictments against hundreds of gambling figures, and that this would stand implicitly, if not explicitly, as criticism of the Police Department.

And so gambling and gamblers were on all our minds.

But still the Police Commissioner gave no sign that he meant to take any action.

McCarthy's memo was dated December 10. Murphy initialed and dated it and sent it on to me. The date was December 23—so much paper piled up on his desk that memos now waited nearly two weeks before their turn came to be scrutinized. Very few people had immediate access to him: First Deputy Smith, Lacovara, the Chief Inspector, and myself. Other commanders might write what they thought to be urgent memos, but such memos went into the pile and then into the attaché case, and the Police Commissioner got to them when he could.

In general, a commander sent Murphy a memo and waited patiently for a response. He did not follow up with a request for an audience. He did nothing at all. The next move was Murphy's. Within the Police Department the feeling was widespread that one had a "right" to request an audience only with one's immediate superior. To request an audience with the Police Commissioner, or even to send him a second memo on the same subject, was presumptuous.

But now on December 29, in his office, I said, "What are you going to do about this gambling business? Are you willing to order the nonenforcement of the street gambling laws?"

He stared at me a moment.

I said, "You did exactly the same thing with regard to nonenforcement of the Sabbath laws about a year ago, and that worked out very well. If you were to order the nonenforcement of the street gambling laws, I think—"

The Police Commissioner interrupted me. In a mild, almost uninterested voice he said, "Why don't you go ahead with it?"

If Murphy thought this a momentous decision, it did not show on his face.

"Okay," I said. Somehow I had expected this decision to sound more dramatic than this. I suddenly understood the existence of 21-gun salutes and military marching bands. How else was a man to know that he had done something important?

From Murphy's office I went directly to McCarthy's.

McCarthy said, "So he's really going to go ahead with

it." McCarthy began to chuckle. "He's got a lot of nerve. He really does have a lot of nerve." After gathering McCarthy's suggestions as to how the order should read, and how it should be promulgated, I met with Chief of Patrol Don Cawley. Cawley wanted an order that would state in black and white that we were not, repeat *not* going to enforce the gambling laws anymore. I kept saying, "No, that's a negative order. We have to have a positive order. We can't use any negatives. Murphy will get arrested and indicted if we try it."

Next I met with Chief of Detectives Seedman, who almost exactly a year before had urged that enforcement of Sabbath laws be abandoned. This would reduce the corruption possibilities. Cops on patrol would be specifically ordered to stay away from grocery stores, autowash places, etc., on Sundays. Any police action would be taken only at the direction of a superior officer. A number of tentative drafts of such an order were later written, and one was mimeographed for distribution to all commands. But it was judged too risky. Murphy might be accused of defying the legislature. The order could be used as evidence against him. And so it was never promulgated. Instead it went out by word of mouth, down through the chain of command, and eventually into the newspapers. There was no public outcry at that time, and for the past year Sabbath law violations had been ignored by cops all over the city.

Seedman's advice now was to handle the nonenforcement of gambling laws in exactly the same way. Nothing formal. Nothing on paper. Send the order down by word of mouth.

But gambling enforcement, I felt, was a subject of such weight that a formal order of some kind was essential. The traditional importance of gambling in every cop's brain could not be overturned by word of mouth.

Before drafting the order, I talked to my own staff. Several of these men had been cops more than 20 years. The strongest opinions came from Sergeant Powers, who felt that although bookies now would not have to pay off cops anymore, they would go right on doing it just for goodwill. As for the cops themselves, they had been harassing the bookies for so long, that we would be changing their way of life. They were not going to believe it. The hardest job would be to convince the cop on the street that Murphy's order existed and that it meant what it said.

When I had finished with the draft, it read this way.

January 11, 1972

MEMORANDUM FOR: CHIEF OF PATROL
SUBJECT: ENFORCEMENT OF THE GAMBLING LAWS

1. Due to the size of this city and the tremendous number of violent crimes in the city and the attendant manpower priority of violent crime it would require an inordinate amount of manpower to also enforce completely all the gambling laws.

2. Accordingly, every effort shall be made to place gambling law enforcement in proper perspective in relation to the department's overall enforcement program.

3. In accordance with the Police Commissioner's directive to the Deputy Commissioner, Organized Crime Control, officers assigned to that command shall concentrate their gambling enforcement efforts as exclusively as is practicable on high-echelon crime figures who engage in gambling as a business, and whose profits help support the organized crime infrastructure.

4. Gambling enforcement by the patrol forces shall be concentrated insofar as practicable on:
a. Intelligence gathering.
b. Responding to those specific complaints that may be forwarded by the Organized Crime Control Bureau.
c. Responding to those street situations which in the judgment of the precinct commanding officer constitute a public nuisance requiring summary of police action. Arrests must be made pursuant to the direction of a superior officer.

5. Precinct commanders are directed to deploy their uninformed forces so as to give first priority to the prevention of violence, particularly street crime.

6. Commanding officers concerned, and in particular, patrol precinct commanders, shall thoroughly in-

struct members of their commands in the provisions of this order.

> S/Michael J. Codd
> Chief Inspector

In theory, step two would be for Cawley to call in his borough and division commanders and read them this order. Step three would be for me to leak the contents of this order to Bill Federici of the *Daily News*.

None of us knew what step four would be.

I met with Chief Cawley, who read through the draft and said, "This is really good."

After reading it, Commissioner McCarthy began to giggle. It was a nervous giggle, but he was very pleased too. He began to tell me how he had left the Department in 1964, figuring that nothing could be done to change the system, to eliminate corruption, to make the Police Department what it ought to be. He figured it was hopeless then, and here he was back in the Department. He had given up golf and fishing in Florida, and after three weeks in his new job he had hated being back, he didn't see how he could stand it another week. But now he thought there was a chance. He didn't feel any of us or all of us could change the world, but we could certainly make an exquisite Police Department. Cawley added that if only all of us were given another year, we would change this job so that no one would ever recognize it.

Next I showed the draft to First Deputy Commissioner Smith who, after reading it, began to giggle nervously just as McCarthy had.

All of us were agreed. This was an earth-shaking, shattering thing both for the Police Commissioner, who was, in effect, writing a new law on his own authority, and for cops in the street.

That afternoon I took the draft in to Murphy. But he waved it away without looking at it. He said simply, "Go ahead and put it out."

Chief Cawley called in all his borough commanders, read them the memo and told them they were not to enforce the gambling laws anymore. The following morning Cawley called in his 16 division commanders and did the same.

About noon I phoned Federici and asked him to meet me at a coffee shop across the street from the *Daily News* Building. I gave him a copy of the memo and told him about Cawley's meetings with the division and borough commanders.

Federici said, "Murphy's putting his job on the line. When this comes out the shit will hit the fan. For all you know, Murphy's finished. I agree with him and with you that it's a good idea, and the *News* will support you, but ..."

Leaving him I was somewhat shaken.

When Federici's story broke, what would the city's reaction be?

By eight o'clock that night the *Daily News* was on the street, and within a few minutes I received a mild query from *The New York Times* about our "momentous" decision. As a result of this phone call, *The New York Times* put an extra paragraph into an existing story on some other police subject, the whole thing being buried somewhere near the middle of the paper.

And that was the extent of public reaction to our "momentous" decision. There was no demand from the press for a single additional statement by the Police Commissioner on the subject of gambling. Even such applause as Murphy drew for his decision was mild, and the Police Commissioner was apparently disappointed. It was as if he had attacked a machine-gun nest single-handedly, but was not put in for a medal.

As a result, he now decided to attack a second machine-gun nest single-handedly. Perhaps he would get his medal that way.

And so on the day following, being scheduled to address a promotion ceremony for new captains at the Police Academy, Murphy called to say that in his speech he planned to attack the Civil Service system. Please arrange a good turnout to hear him do it.

Press turnout at the Police Academy was adequate, and Murphy attacked the Civil Service as promised, reading four or five paragraphs that he had written himself, the import of which was that the Civil Service system promoted and encouraged mediocrity, and the Police Department could not live with the system much longer.

The headlines that he got for this short speech were far bigger and blacker than those accorded his decision to stop enforcing the street gambling laws.

As far as the Police Commissioner was concerned, the gambling subject was closed. However, a small amount of additional work remained to be done. Two weeks were allowed to pass, at which time Chief Cawley formally promulgated the directive. Two weeks after that, Cawley sent forth another memo authorizing the removal of the KG mug shots which were currently cluttering up the bulletin boards in each station house. Instead, photos of known robbers were to be posted. Cawley then went into the 25th Precinct station house in Harlem, and in full view of assembled television cameras, personally tore KG mug shots off the bulletin boards there, and pinned up in their place photos of stickup men and murderers.

3 / Ambush

Patrolman James Liedy speaks: "They were waiting there for hours. One of the guys that did the shooting, they left without him. I figure they may have seen a radio car come around. It may have been my radio car. I don't know. He ran to 14th Street and got a cab. These guys were so lucky they got away. There were so many cops there so fast.

"We had a job at 13th Street and Avenue A five minutes before. Disorderly youths. It wasn't a phony job. If they wanted to call in a phony job they could have called in a 10-13 at Houston and First Street, right?

"So I was up there on 13th Street. There was nothing there. I was driving. When the job came over—it was a 10-13—I made a U turn. I stepped on the gas, and started going down. When I got halfway down I thought, I'm going to get there quick because there's no cars double-parked. The light was red. I was thinking I gotta slow up for the light, and then it turned green. Dominic and Danny came across 11th Street, against the one-way, and that's where the perpetrators were. But they were already gone.

"I was coming down. I made the right turn from Avenue B on 12th Street. I just got, like, 25 feet from 11th Street, and zoom. Dominic and Danny shoot right out. They park on the west side of the street. But now I see a group on the east side of the street, on the corner, right? Danny's out of his car, walking. He doesn't see it. He knows something happened, but he doesn't know what.

"But I saw guys there on the corner, and I went, zoom, right in against the curb on the wrong side of the street. I jumped out of the car. My partner jumped out of the car on the other side and ran around. My door was still open. I reached back inside and grabbed the phone and said, 'Two cops shot. Two cops shot.' Then I thought, they might still be here, and I had my gun out. You can't even hear me on the tape. You don't have to hear the tape. At 240 Centre Street down in the sub-sub basement or something they have the transcripts of the tape. It's all on paper, how the jobs come over, who responded to the jobs. I didn't even pick the job up. I didn't take the time to tell them I was going. I was so close. I was already there. I think it came over: 'shots fired,' when I got halfway there. I don't know. It's all on paper.

"What happened, evidently, was this girl was on the phone to 911. She was talking. Her husband must have been at the window looking down. You could hear him say, 'Somebody's firing shots.' Then you could hear him say, 'They're shooting a cop.' Then she says into the phone, 'Oh my God, they're shooting a cop.' Something like that it was.

"Then I pulled the car in at the curb, like this. I drew this so many times. I never heard the shots fired. The window was closed. It wasn't that cold that night. Rocco had his winter blouse on and Greg had his winter overcoat on, lying there on the sidewalk. I pulled in at the curb. "I could see the crowd there on the corner. I knew something had happened. I said, 'Oh, somebody got shot.'

"Like, I know these cops who are on this post. Like, when you go on a 10-30 you can almost tell if it's a real one. You say, Liedy's got that post, or Rocco and Greg have got that post. You know, there aren't that many footmen. You say, 'Geez, there's cops there,' and you know you got a 50-50 chance right away. Now these guys—I worked with Rocco once. I could see the guy was active, right? I knew that these guys who had that foot post were active guys. That Rocco Laurie, he'd break your back.

"So then I saw this group there, maybe four or five people. So then I went this way with the car. I went right against the curb. There were no cars there. I was halfway out of the car when I grabbed the phone and gave, 'Two cops shot.'

"I remember one kid there was a hippie. He had blood all over him. I saw the empty holsters lying out from their hips and I thought, Oh no, it's happened again. It's Jones and Piagentini all over again.

"Now I got my gun out, right? I picked up Foster. I couldn't pick him up. I picked him up a little, and I held him. I tossed my gun in on the floor of the car. Later on I couldn't remember what I did with it. I thought, Holy shit, I've lost my gun.

"I picked Greg up and held him and threw my gun on the floor of the car. Then I picked him up again and looked at his face and he's dead. Forget it. He was cold. One bullet came right out of his head. He had a split in his forehead, here. They said he got it from falling, but I don't think so. Then he had a hole in his hat. In the band. Did you see the photos from the morgue? He had three holes in his eyes. They told me there were brains all over the sidewalk, a quarter of an inch thick. I didn't know there were brains. I thought it was saliva. I never saw that. I knew he was dead. He was spread-eagled, Greg, on his stomach like he was sunbathing at the beach, lying on the side of his face, and the blood was coming out. So I picked him up and I just set him back down.

"They had Rocco in a sit-up position now. I looked at Rocco Laurie. He had a hole in his neck. He was all white, you know, like somebody who has a cardiac. I thought, he's dead too. But he don't look dead. I don't see any really bad wounds. Just that one wound in his neck. I mean, that's bad enough, but compared to Foster—

"I said, 'Get him in the car.'

"Now the cars were coming from all over. They're starting to block—I'm yelling, 'Get out of the way, get out of the way.'

"So they were putting him in. I guess Dominic. I heard Vetrano say, 'Okay, who saw it?' I thought, that's good, he's going to take care of that. I jumped in the seat. Danny jumped in the back seat. Danny had his head in his lap.

"We left. I had the siren full blast. You couldn't get by Tenth Street. It was all congested. Police cars. There was a bus there, I know that. I drove all the way up on the sidewalk. Danny Brennan is hitting me in the back shouting, 'Shut the siren off.'

"I was saying, 'I'm alright, I know what to do.'

"Danny has 12 or 13 years on the job. He was smart; a good cop. He was saying, 'Shut the siren off,' and I was saying, 'We gotta get there.' He was thinking that we couldn't hear the other sirens coming. Which was true. Because I'm going to take all the lights now. He wanted me to hear the other cars. There were cars coming from all over. Some of them were going 90 miles an hour.

"Finally Danny says to Grawzo, my partner, 'Shut the siren off.' And Grawzo reached over and shut it off. I wasn't taking my hands off the wheel. It was a new radio car. It was in pretty good shape. I was going as fast as it could go.

" Then when we got to 14th Street and Avenue A. As soon as we made that turn, Danny said, 'Okay, now turn your siren on.'

"When we went up First Avenue, those guys were down in the subway there. That's when they reloaded their guns. Who knows, they might have thought the sirens were for them. That we were going to go downstairs after them. They waited 20 minutes for a subway. But we didn't know they were there.

"Rocco never woke up. When we went up on the curb, Danny said, 'His eyes just opened and rolled back.'

"I don't think we even closed the back door of the radio car. His shoes were sticking out. He was in the hospital in three minutes after he was shot. You see, the precinct's so small, that 9th Precinct, only 14 blocks by eight, and we got 11 radio cars, 11 sectors. There had to be a radio car there right away. If it wasn't me, it would have been somebody else. There were Manhattan South cars in there. You got Narcotics working that area, you got Anti-crime. These guys were so lucky to get away. They gotta be good. They can't be just lucky.

"When we got to Bellevue, they were all waiting. Cops, doctors, nurses. There was a police barrier there. I think I hit it and knocked it down. I was going top speed. We got

him onto this table. Everybody was yelling, 'Get him on.'
He rolled off the other side and I guess the doctors or the
hospital cops grabbed him. I know I grabbed him. They
took him in and started taking off his clothes, and I came
back out, and somebody said, 'They're bringing in the other
guy.'

"And as I turned around, Foster was going by, looking
right at me, with no eyes. It was like, when I had picked
him up and set him back down, his head sunk into the
pavement. Not just the back of his head, his whole face,
everything. It was like a marshmallow. He was a big guy.
They were big. I didn't know Greg was that big. I didn't
know them personally real well. I was just getting to know
Rocco. Like, he didn't work with me. I drove him home
once. His wife was waiting for him on the other side of the
bridge. All the guys said to me, 'Will you give Rocco
Laurie a ride home?' I said, 'Christ, of course.' His wife
was waiting for him. He was a nice guy. He wanted to pay
me for the bridge. I said, 'No good.' He was well-known in
Staten Island. A good athlete. When I first saw him I said,
'So that's Rocco Laurie.' I'm a sports buff, and every time I
used to pick up the paper I used to see this kid. He was the
best on the eastern coast. He broke all the high school
records for the shot put. They didn't have a football team
there. He played baseball. I used to see his name go by on
his father's trucks.

"After they brought Greg Foster in past me, they had
me on the phone. Central, or this dispatcher or somebody.
Greg had lost his shield and been issued another one, but I
didn't know that. I had his hat, and I gave them the
number off that, and it didn't correspond. I was speaking to
this guy on the phone and he was giving me this 'calm
down' stuff, 'take it easy.' There was a nurse there; she
wanted to give me a shot. I don't know what I said. I'm
surprised I even went through with it, I'm surprised that I
did anything right. Later I said to myself, 'I didn't do this, I
wasn't there.'

"I never saw Foster's father. I would have went over and
consoled him. You know, 'Come with me. You belong
with me, not with anybody else here. You can cry on my
shoulder.' All the other guys there—the Police Commissioner was there, Codd was there, the Deputy Mayor was

there. They were just looking. I don't know. I guess they go through so much. They were probably shook up too. Like Murphy. He was all white. Codd was there, wearing this Russian hat. His father used to deliver ice to my grandfather's bar. The Mayor wasn't there. Later, all the guys were yelling. I said, 'Fucking Lindsay didn't put the bullets in them; if you don't like the guy, vote against him.'

"When I went in to see Foster, they were pounding on his chest. I knew he was dead. What could they do? They did that when JFK got shot too. I thought, let me get out of here before they open his chest. I've seen that already. They open a guy's chest that's been shot and take his heart out and massage it. I've seen that. I've taken a lot of people to Bellevue that have been shot. Three weeks ago Fred Schroeder and I—he's a good cop—dragged this guy out of a hallway, and he'd been shot, and we had him in the back seat and he was talking to us; and when we got to the hospital I said to Freddy, 'This guy may die.' Freddy says, 'Naw,' but sure enough he died, 17 years old.

"Thank God I didn't have to go to the morgue for Rocco and Greg. By the time they got me at home the next day, Grawzo had gone.

"They had cut the winter blouse lengthwise down the sleeves to get it off Rocco Laurie. That winter blouse, that's the finest-looking uniform there ever was. When I became a cop, they put me on the street. There was a sergeant. They took him out of a car to walk with us. There were about 15 of us. I wanted to stay out. He didn't want to stay out. And like, I stayed out all night. I was walking in that uniform and it felt, like, it really felt good. It didn't take me long to realize—I thought that you could walk up the street and everybody would say, 'Hello' and 'Hi.' It didn't take me long to find out that a lot of people don't like you. You didn't do anything. You're not doing anything. You're just a cop, and they just don't like you. During the Knapp Commission hearings when Phillips was testifying, a man came up on Second Avenue and spit at me.

"I was proud of that uniform. I really take care of all my uniforms. I always wear the best one to court. Then, if I get a midnight to 8 A.M. tour I wear my oldest uniform then, because it's dark and it doesn't show, and you can get blood on it.

"The only new friends I have are cops—except my wife has this girl friend and we see her and her husband. When he talks about his job, I'm bored. But whenever I talk about my job, everybody, like, is listening very attentively.

"I'm one of eight children. My great-grandfather had a bar. That bar has been in their families all their lives. I tended bar there. When I was 18 years old, a guy put a .45 to my head. I let him stick the place up and then I cried. Why did I become a cop? It's a good job. I was working on tugboats at the time. My date of appointment was June 7, 1968. I was almost 28 years old. I'm 31 now. Rocco Laurie was 23, and Greg Foster was only 22. The reason I was so old was I didn't have a high school diploma. I had to get an equivalency certificate. I never talk about my past, only about the future. Some reporter told me I have some extraordinary love for being a cop. Everybody does, don't you know that?

"In the 9th Precinct, I had a foot post, Third Avenue from Tenth to 14th, or sometimes 12th to 14th. You come to work with a bunch of guys. You meet on Staten Island, whoever's going in, whatever squads are working that day, four or five guys. We all get in the car, everybody throws 50 cents in, that's $2.50 for the driver. He pays the tolls. The next day if there's only three guys, he only gets $1.50.

"So that particular day we drove in, right? I went up and changed. When I came down I found out I was going to ride in a car, so I went up and changed again. I put the blouse on. I was glad I was riding. I was the recorder for the first four hours. We had sector Charley, Avenue A to C. It goes from First Street to Fourth Street. But you often get out of your sector in a busy house. Sector Edward, where they got killed, is the worst sector in the precinct, in the whole city. That corner—Narcotics is always pulling them in there, the girl Fitzgerald got killed there. It was always bad there. What I learned from other cops when I asked which was the busiest sector, like, they said Edward, then David, then Charley. Or maybe it's a tossup between Adam, which covers the project, and Charley.

"One of the first jobs I handled that night was a mugging in a hallway. It was a busy night. They mugged him just two minutes ago. So we said, 'Get in the car.' This particular guy, we drove him around. The perpetrators, they can go anywhere. A lot of times we get them though. You got a good chance. Many times the guys pick them out—'That's him.' But tonight we didn't find anybody. The muggers didn't get much. They never get much down there. The people are too poor. They wouldn't get much off me. My money clip is worth more than I ever had in it.

"About ten o'clock the most interesting thing came over. Because maybe these guys that shot them were there and had already picked out Rocco and Greg by then.

"I wanted to see Schroeder. We used to be partners, but I hadn't seen him in a long time. When we were turning out he said, 'Hey, you want to walk with me tomorrow night?' I told him, 'I'm not in the neighborhood police team.' He said, 'My partner's going bowling tomorrow night.' So I said, 'Okay, you set it up. You see your roll call man and set it up. I'll walk with you and we'll have some fun. We'll handle a few jobs together.'

"So now I wanted to see him, to see if I was going to work with him tomorrow night. Then I heard Schroeder pick up a job, a dispute in front of Tenth Street and B. Then Foster and Laurie said they would take it, because they're, like I said, active guys. They had the portable radios, and they were cutting each other off. The radios were faint. So I said to Grawzo, 'Come on, we'll take that job, we're right there.'

"So I got towards B, and I could see two guys standing there, and it was Foster and Laurie. They were shining flashlights on the building. It was dark. Then I saw Schroeder and Kenny walking up. So now you got six cops there, and if anybody's going to do any fucking shooting, they're crazy, right? Ten-ninety, that job was. Unfounded. A dispute. Nothing there but six cops. There was no such address. So we just chewed the fat a minute, and then left. I spoke to Freddy, because I really didn't know Foster and Laurie that well. I knew Rocco Laurie had made this fantastic drug arrest. He had a whole suitcase full of marijuana. He had made the buy with his own money. He was quiet, and I guess I was quiet. I kidded with him. He didn't want that collar, I said. I'd take that collar from him. He had made that buy with his paycheck. He didn't have any money to live on.

"I remember after he was killed, this colored guy came

in the station house and said how nice Rocco was. Rocco had locked him up, but he was so nice about it.

"We had a couple of jobs after that. But I keep thinking about Rocco and Greg shining the flashlights on the building numbers. Maybe those guys were going to shoot Rocco and Greg then, they had been there long enough by then; but all of a sudden there's six cops there.

"It wasn't long after they brought Foster into the hospital that a guy came out and said, 'Greg's dead.'

"I said, 'Yeah, I know.'

"Rocco wasn't dead yet. They told me he had 13 holes in him. I saw him naked but I didn't see that many holes. Danny had blood all over his jacket and I said, 'Where'd that blood come from?' He said, 'It was coming out of the back of his neck,' because he had his hand there. But the only hole I remember is the one in the side of the throat. Maybe that nurse was right that wanted to give me that shot. I had to be shook up. I walked in. I walked out. I only remember looking at Foster, because he was the worst. I knew he was dead. They were working on Rocco in the same room. They were opposite each other. Their feet were facing each other. When I came back in again, Rocco was gone. They had taken him up to the operating room. The next time I came in, Greg was gone. Into the next building, I guess, which is the morgue.

"When I first got out of the car, I threw my hat away. I threw it down on the ground, and then I kicked it. I was crying. I cried after that too. I called my wife up, because she watches the news. I said, 'Hey, something happened. I'm all right.' She was in bed sleeping. I said, 'Good, go back to sleep. I don't think I'll be home for a while,' and I hung up the phone.

"These guys from ballistics, they took all their clothes at the hospital and set them out on the floor. These guys are good. They can tell where the bullets went in by the holes in their clothes. They can tell how each guy was standing, and it will hold up in court. They had the clothes all spread out, and then they put them in these big bags and told us not to mix them up, and to take them back to the station house. That's a patrolman's job, I guess. When we got outside it was snowing, and the reporters were there snapping pictures of us with these bloody pillowcases. I'm glad they didn't use that in the paper. That stuff's no good for their families. I went to Rocco's wake. I thought I'd go to his first because it was close to the house, and then I'd go up to the Bronx. Rocco had an open casket. It was terrible. So I never went to Greg's. A bullet fell out of Greg's mouth when he was on the table, did you know that? Danny found it.

"When I got back to the station house there was guys there from all over the place. There were guys there I knew from the Bronx.

"All the guys in the station house, they were praying. They were praying for Rocco. Rocco was still alive then. They were down on their knees. I had done that before when Larry Stefane was killed. When I came in I had all their clothes. I had them in these two bloody pillowcases.

"Then we started back to Staten Island. I got home very late. It was snowing out. I was driving that night. All the guys waited for me, and we drove back across the bridge. The snow was coming down. It was very bad, very dangerous. I dropped them all off. I got out of my car in front of this rotten apartment I had on Grimes Hill Road, and it was cold. I was cold. Then I got in bed. And I could see those guys, and I could remember everything that they looked like when they were on the ground. And you know that you'll never forget that. It was maybe five o'clock in the morning, I touched my wife, and my wife woke up and said, 'Hello, how are you,' and I reached out and hugged her.

"Maybe I got an hour's sleep. I got up with her when she went to work. I thought about maybe getting transferred to Staten Island, but, I don't know, in the 9th Precinct you're more a cop. I don't want to go to Staten Island and get fat. I mean I guess the cops in Staten Island can get killed just as quick as they can in the 9th Precinct. But there's, like, there's more there for a guy. Most of the guys there are real good cops. You talk about the other precincts, but the 9th has got to be the worst, because it's so small. The Bronx is bad. The whole division is bad. I haven't been up there, but I know it's bad. But the 9th is a cesspool. Up in Harlem where everybody's black you might be more on your guard. But here the guy that will kill you might be white. It used to be worse when the hippies were down there, but the hippies all got mugged.

"When I got back from taking my wife to the ferry, the phone rang: You gotta come in. When I got in I was drawing maps for them and answering questions. About one o'clock I was tired. There are some beds there upstairs and I tried to go to sleep. Me and Danny. We were lying down there, and Danny said, 'I can't believe that those guys are dead.' We couldn't sleep. We just gave it up, both of us. Danny said, 'I can't believe this could happen.' Then I said, 'Danny, how many times do you think we maybe walked past guys with guns who were saying to themselves, should we kill 'em or not?'"

"The next night, Saturday night, everybody was saying, 'These fucking guys are still in the precinct.' I was out there on a foot post. Somebody called up and said three cops would be killed that night. The call came over to come back in to the station house. I took my gun out and walked down Second Avenue and back into the station house with my gun out.

"You talk about cops cooping at night. In the 9th nobody coops. Are you crazy? You don't even stop the car to drink coffee except on the busiest streets under the lights. Every time a car pulls alongside you, you eye the guy. He thinks you're waiting to catch him going through a red light, but you're waiting to see if he'll pull a gun and start shooting at you.

"Then a couple of weeks later they caught some of those guys, and this guy Carter was killed. You know those photos they make of guys on the slab in the morgue? Well, somebody got hold of the photo of Carter on the slab. He looked real good. He looked great in fact, and this guy pins the photo up on the wall in the squad room, and every cop that went in there after that would look up and salute it. But then one of the bosses made us take it down.

"Listen, I'm afraid if you write about me I'll come out looking foolish. You can put in about me walking down Second Avenue with my gun out. The guys will rib me for that, but I did it—we both did it that night. But I just hope you won't put anything in that will make me look foolish."

Patrolmen Foster and Laurie were shot at 10 minutes to 11 on the corner of 11th Street and Avenue B. At about 11 o'clock I was sitting in bed with the light on, reading, when the phone rang.

My duty sergeant said, "We have two cops shot in the 9th Precinct."

"Bad?"

"I don't know."

One or the other of my chauffeurs was on call 24 hours a day, but it would take time for him to get here with the car. I told my duty sergeant, "Send me a radio car from the 20th Precinct. I'll be outside in five minutes."

It was cold, and the air held a hint of snow. The radio car was waiting double-parked in the street. I got in beside the driver and saw that it was Ralph Mannetta. His partner, Paul Dellacona, was in the back. We went across through Central Park and down Second Avenue. Mannetta said, "I haven't seen you, Commissioner, since the night that Ralph Mannetta shot Rap Brown. I thought that the Detective Bureau would want to talk to Ralph Mannetta by now. Ralph Mannetta would certainly like to become a detective, if you know anybody."

It made me smile. I said, "I'll talk to Chief Seedman tonight, Ralph."

Mannetta was driving slowly, eyeballing the sidewalks on both sides, a good cop every moment he was on duty.

On the radio, units were being told to report to the 9th Precinct, or to Bellevue. Presently the dispatcher said, "One of the cops shot in the 9th Precinct D.O.A."

I said, "Step on it, Ralph. Let's get there."

When we pulled up in front of the 9th Precinct station house, Mannetta offered to wait, but the street was already jammed with cars. Besides, I had stripped the 20th Precinct of one of its cars, and so I told Mannetta to go on back. He said, "You won't forget, Commissioner—"

"No, Ralph. You can count on it."

I did give his name to Chief Seedman, and the following

week Mannetta was called down and interviewed. Presently he was informed that he was on the list and would be made a detective when his turn came. But later, after Seedman and I had both left the Department, leaving a certain animosity behind us, Mannetta was contacted again and informed that he was a patrolman and would remain one, and if he didn't like it he should study for the sergeant's exam.

The station house was beginning to fill up, but the mood was not yet the pain and grief that would take over an hour from now. Because as yet there was no focus. No one was sure exactly who had been shot, much less how and why. A few witnesses had been scooped up off the corner and brought in. They were waiting upstairs, but no one had interrogated them yet. No superior officer had yet reached the scene. I stepped behind the desk and asked for the UF10 cards belonging to the two cops. These gave their names, ages, and the serial numbers of their guns. If their service revolvers were taken, what about their second guns? I ordered their lockers opened, and their second guns were found intact. No one could tell me how they had been shot —had they interrupted a stickup, or what?

I hurried upstairs to a room that served as a kind of dormitory. The place was crowded with iron beds, on some of which lay mattresses without sheets. The three witnesses, all males, huddled in a corner, and I began questioning them. One was the owner of the Shrimp Boat Restaurant at 173 Avenue B. He said that moments before the shooting Patrolmen Foster and Laurie had stepped into his narrow store to ask about an illegally parked car across the street. Did he know who owned the vehicle?

The proprietor did not, and the two cops headed out the door to the street. He walked behind them and looked left. They turned right, moving up Avenue B. When they were scarcely ten feet away, the owner of the Shrimp Boat heard what sounded like "Pop . . . pop . . . pop . . . pop"—many shots, and he turned in time to see the two cops fall. Then a bullet smashed in right beside him. He dropped to the floor and didn't look up again for several minutes. As he lay there he heard many more shots.

The other two witnesses now explained how three black men had been walking downtown on Avenue B. They parted to let the cops through. As soon as the two cops had passed them. they whipped out guns. spun around, and opened fire, shooting the two cops repeatedly in the back. As the two cops lay on the pavement. the three men stood over them pumping in more bullets. When the shooting finally stopped. two of them reached down and ripped the guns out of the cops' holsters. Two of the killers ran west along 11th Street and disappeared, but the third began to do a jig in the street, and he fired a gun repeatedly into the air. Later I would talk to a young Puerto Rican who scarcely spoke English. He would describe how he rushed out of a bar, saw the man firing the gun, and grabbed him. But the man broke away and started to run, and the young Puerto Rican then ran to the side of the two fallen cops. An instant later the radio car containing Patrolmen Liedy and Grawzo screeched to a stop beside the bodies. The young Puerto Rican was covered with blood, and the cops thought he was the killer and grabbed him, and he yelled, "No, no, I help. I help."

They said to him, "Alright, if you want to help, help us get him into the car."

Once satisfied that these witnesses had furnished a rough but accurate scenario of the crime, I rushed downstairs and outside onto the street, and there cadged a ride to the crime scene with Detective Frank McCoy who had been my classmate through eight years of grade school at Good Shepherd, in the Inwood Section of Manhattan. One of the nice things about the Police Department, not only for me but for all of us, what that one was continually running into men who had once been schoolmates. A lot of us from Good Shepherd later wound up in the Police Department. One of the detectives on the Pierre case had been John Stein, from my brother's class, and one of the detectives on the Colombo case was Raymond Douglas. with whom I had once had a fight in the dust near the old World War I cannon that used to stand in the park in front of the school. The brotherhood that ran all through the Police Department was very deep, and caused by a number of things, but one of them was this, that it bound all of us up in the lives we had lived in this city.

McCoy parked his car near the Shrimp Boat. one of the seediest, dingiest restaurants I've ever seen. Patrolman Jim

Liedy once said of the 9th Precinct, "The restaurants around there you wouldn't eat in if you were starving to death." There was a traffic light on the southeast corner of Avenue B at 11th Street. The killers must have come across the street toward the two cops, and given each other some kind of signal as they did so.

The entire corner was roped off. Cops stood guard. Inside the roped area two puddles of blood stained the pavement. The bigger of the two was close to the curb and also in the street lamp on the corner. It was irregular in shape and thick and viscous, for it was blood mixed with brains. It looked like a congealed stew. It measured in length almost three feet, and at the widest part was about a foot across. Some distance away was a much smaller puddle which had welled out of the neck of Rocco Laurie.

Forensic personnel were already on hand, and they had drawn the outline of the two bodies in chalk on the sidewalk. I saw that Foster and Laurie had lain feet to feet in an open V, and I saw also that they had been shot repeatedly while down, for there were bullets impacted in the sidewalk, and each of the bullets was circled in white chalk also. McCoy and I and some others stepped carefully about, searching the sidewalk for other bullets, and for spent shell casings. We found several. Some of the bullets had splattered, and we could see that a number had copper jackets, meaning that they came from automatics.

Later, another witness would describe hearing one of the killers shout, "Shoot them in the balls," and ballistics would publish its grim report; that Patrolman Rocco Laurie was shot twice in the groin while down, one bullet piercing his penis; and that Patrolman Gregory Foster, a black man like his killers, had been deliberately shot three times in the eyes after he was already dead. They had turned his brain to soup and so much had run out onto the pavement that his skull at this moment must be empty.

The police photographer was calling, "Stand back, please. Would you mind stepping out of the way, sir?"

It had started to snow. The snow was coming down soundlessly, thick wet flakes, and I stood watching it cover evidence of the warped act which, only a few minutes before, had taken place on these few square feet of New York sidewalk.

McCoy and the others now stepped back inside the ropes and went on collecting bullets. Eventually we would learn that Laurie had been shot six times, three times in the back. All of the bullets had passed completely through him, each making entrance and exit wounds, and one of them rebounding up off the pavement to enter his body a second time. Foster had been shot eight times, three times in the back and once in the back of the head.

It was a crime of such savagery that it was almost incomprehensible.

In the street, I flagged down a radio car and ordered myself driven to Bellevue Hospital. The Police Commissioner and some others were already there, pacing a waiting room on the ground floor, and the press was already gathering outside. I began to interrogate cops. Who could inform me of facts I did not yet know? In this way I came upon Patrolman Liedy, a hulking, distraught figure, who once he began to talk could not stop. He had driven the mortally wounded Laurie here and now did not know where Laurie had gone, or what someone might be doing to him, or whether he was still alive. And so the two of us prowled the corridors of that hospital until we found the operating room behind whose door Patrolman Rocco Laurie, 23 years old, was spending the final minutes of his life. There was a small square window in the operating room door, and Liedy and I peered in at about eight doctors and four or five nurses, all working on Rocco Laurie, who lay naked on the table. They were working the length of his body, on both sides of it, and I could see his face and also the bullet hole in the side of his throat; and they had his chest area opened up and peeled back, and what looked like entrails lay on top of his chest. I supposed that they would shove all that back in later—neatly if they could save him, any old way if they could not. They were making incisions and causing more blood loss; I watched the knives rise and fall and the blood spurt. But they were working frantically. Even once in a while someone would rush out the swinging door and down the hall, and then come running back and rush inside again. A young man, perhaps an intern, came out and said, "So far he's holding his own. It doesn't look that bad."

Presently we went back downstairs again. The waiting room was crowded now. The Police Commissioner was there, Chief Inspector Codd, the Deputy Mayor, plus other commanders and the chauffeurs of all these people. I began to brief Murphy, who knew nothing of what had happened. It was clear to me already that this was exactly similar to the Jones and Piagentini assassination, and I so informed the Police Commissioner; but he was cautious and said that he would wait to learn more. Chief of Patrol Cawley, listening intently, remarked, "First of all, these guys were making drug purchases. They all wanted to be detectives, and they were spending their own money to make drug buys and lock people up."

By this time all of us had learned of Laurie's fantastic drug arrest—the suitcase full of marijuana.

Cawley was urging utmost caution in any statements by the Police Commissioner or by myself. He thought that tomorrow we might learn that Foster and Laurie were engaged in something criminal, and that they were shot because they had reneged on some sort of deal.

I kept insisting that Cawley was wrong, that we had an assassination on our hands, a double assassination if Laurie died.

Seedman came in the door. He was the last of the hierarchy to arrive, because he had had the longest distance to come; and now I briefed him too, and his face went dark, and he seemed to understand at once what had happened and why. He listened to Cawley urging caution, that perhaps Foster and Laurie were crooks, and he was filled with disgust for Cawley, but for the time being said nothing.

About two o'clock, with Laurie still on the operating table upstairs, blood pouring out of him almost as fast as it was poured in, the rest of us left the hospital. Outside the snow was coming down hard. The television lights came on, and microphones were thrust in front of the Police Commissioner. Murphy announced the death of Patrolman Gregory Foster and the wounding of Patrolman Rocco Laurie. An investigation was underway, he said. Murphy was suffering—it showed in his voice and was visible on his face—but he said no more. He, Seedman, and I climbed into his car, and during the ride to the 9th Precinct I went over the scenario of the crime once again. The street outside the station house was jammed with cars, we had difficulty getting close to the door, and inside it was jammed with cops. Very few were in uniform. The rest had rushed in when they heard the news, and they wore their shields pinned to their coats. We moved through them and upstairs into the detective squad room, and this now became the command post for the investigation. The Police Commissioner stood there with his hands in his pockets, looking glum. Chief Inspector Codd came in, and his first order was to clear some of the men out of the station house so that those who were working would have room to move and to breathe.

Chief of Detectives Seedman took off his coat, and began to direct the investigation. Cops and witnesses stepped forward one by one, and Seedman calmed each of them down and drew out of them any salient information. When he heard that one of the killers had done a jig of joy in the street and fired his gun into the air, Seedman mused, "Sounds like they might be coked up. Get some narco guys in here."

Seedman gave instructions, one after the other. He wanted pictures of every known criminal in the 9th Precinct. He wanted these pictures circulated to see if any witness recognized one. He said, "I want to know who Foster and Laurie arrested lately. I want to know where each of the guys the arrested is at this moment."

Meantime, out in the street, 9th Precinct cops were stopping every black man they saw. They brought in something like eight men whom they had stopped and taken guns from. None of these men proved to have anything to do with the assassination, and none of the arrests would stand up in court, for they were the results of illegal search and seizure.

Before long, a radio car came upon an empty Chrysler up near 14th Street, parked with its engine still running. One of the witnesses who was rushed up there said, "That's the car. That's the getaway car."

The car was towed into the Police Academy on 20th Street, where detectives began dusting it for fingerprints. Meanwhile other cops, guns drawn, went downstairs into

the 14th Street BMT station where on a bench on the
Brooklyn-bound side they found part of a box of bullets,
and on the floor empty bullet casings.

So the killers had headed from here out into Brooklyn.
The killers were black. That meant Bedford-Stuyvesant or
Brownsville.

Seedman flooded the streets of the 9th Precinct with detectives. They canvassed every block, door by door, apartment by apartment. Other detectives began checking the
cab companies and presently found the driver who had
picked up the killer, who, dancing a jig in the street, had
been left behind by his colleagues. The cabbie described
how he was delivering a fare, a woman, when a young
black man yanked open the back door and jumped in beside the young woman. The cabbie let her out a few blocks
further on, and dropped the man off at another building in
the 9th Precinct. He remembered the spot very well because the man had stiffed him on the fare.

Heavily armed detectives were sent to the address where
the cab driver had dropped the fare. They found nobody.

Seedman ordered detectives who had worked on the
Jones and Piagentini case down from the 32nd Precinct in
Harlem, for he wanted to throw them immediately onto this
one. The same gang, the same names would turn up here,
Seedman was sure of it. Furthermore, Seedman remembered the pattern of the San Francisco shooting—a four-
day extravaganza of cop killings had been planned there.
There was a chance that the same thing had been planned
here in New York, for now Seedman remembered that a
patrolman in Brooklyn had been stabbed in the chest three
nights before as he sat in his radio car. And at 2 A.M. last
night there was a second attack on a policeman—a cop
named Bauer had stopped a car for going through a red
light. As he strolled toward the car the men in it opened
fire. Two bullets from an automatic went right through
him. The car was stolen earlier that night from a garage in
the 20th Precinct. Black men had walked in there, stuck up
the garage attendant, and stolen the car. Mannetta had told
me about this as we were driving down to the 9th Precinct
tonight. Seedman was programming all these facts into his
brain: car stolen in the 20th Precinct in Manhattan, cop
shot in the 90th Precinct in Brooklyn, car abandoned in the

79th Precinct in Brooklyn. Tonight's bullets had been found on the Brooklyn-bound side of the 14th Street subway station.

So the killers were in Brooklyn at this moment, and Seedman was sure he would find here the same gang of thugs that the killers of Jones and Piagentini, all but one now in custody, had been mixed up with.

In fact, detectives now began to show mug shots to the cab driver—who promptly identified Herman Bell, already under indictment for shooting Jones and Piagentini, as the man who had jumped into his cab.

It was past 3 A.M. when I asked Seedman if he could have his driver run me home. Outside the snow was five inches deep.

Rocco Laurie was still alive. He did not die until 4:35 A.M.

After two hours or less of sleep on the couch in his office, Seedman went back to the 9th Precinct, and for the next several days he personally directed the investigation to the exclusion of almost all his other duties.

Early that morning I met with the Police Commissioner, for promotions were scheduled, and at noon he was due to make a speech attacking the nation's prisons as a total failure. We decided that Murphy would appear in both places.

At the first of them the press was waiting, and he made a speech without notes about violence and about killing and about two young policemen who were dead, and there were tears in his voice if not in his eyes, and I thought he might break down. This was the only time I ever saw him lose his composure in public.

After the promotion ceremony I drove to the 9th Precinct to meet Seedman. He was certain now that last night's attack was a planned assassination of police officers. He was waiting for fingerprints off the abandoned getaway car and also for fingerprints off the taxi cab. Members of the press kept wandering into that squad room where pictures of Herman Bell sat in a pile upon a desk, and I ordered a detective to get them out of sight. We weren't ready to reveal this information yet.

Fingerprints did begin to turn up that day, a single print here, another there, all of them useless until you know whose card to match them against, but this time Seedman knew. Ballistics had told him within hours of the savagery of the attack, and witnesses had each contributed details, until Seedman saw the whole brutal scene, and understood clearly enough who was responsible for it.

Although he ordered the backgrounds of both slain cops examined minutely, he knew instinctively that there could be nothing there to match that cloudburst of hatred on a street corner in the night. This crime was a wanton assault upon the uniforms that the two young cops had worn, not on them personally. Therefore, Seedman knew where to look for the self-appointed assassins. He, like Patrolman Liedy, said to himself, "It's them. It's got to be. It's the same guys who killed Jones and Piagentini."

Not the same fingers pulling the trigger. All but one of those men were in jail. But the same warped minds at work. The same band of black assassins.

He ordered photos sent over of every individual known to be a member of the most extreme wing of the Black Panther Party, and after that he had men searching through piles of photos to find any other face ever seen in company with these people. These photos were placed in piles in front of witnesses, and identifications began to be made. So many detectives had flooded the area of the ambush, and they had worked so assiduously all night long, that about nine witnesses were rounded up. As these persons identified faces, Seedman began to be able to put together a timetable of the crime, for it now appeared that the killers were loitering in that area for two to three hours waiting to get a clear shot at Foster and Laurie. The two cops had had a foot post on Avenue B from Fourth to 14th Streets. They had marched up and down that block on one side of the street or the other from 4 P.M. when their tour started, until they were murdered six hours and 50 minutes later. The killers had met all kinds of people while waiting. They had gone into a shop and bought some groceries, and one even left a satchel behind on the floor. He later came back to get this bag, but it was gone. Detectives found it later, with usable fingerprints inside. It contained parts of guns and black extremist literature.

A special phone number had been set up. It was manned night and day by bilingual detectives, and it was attached to a tape recorder which turned itself on automatically each time the phone rang. The detectives kept logs of the calls. And the calls kept coming, each caller identifying suspicious persons or suspicious activities which might or might not be connected to the crime. Each bit of information was checked out by detectives, and eventually more than 100 arrests were made, most having nothing to do with the Foster-Laurie assassinations, most for possession of weapons and/or drugs.

The command post for the investigation was a small office behind the squad room on the second floor of the 9th Precinct. There in the corner stood the tape recorder. At the end of the table nearest it sat whichever detective was manning the special number. The little room was crowded, for Seedman hardly left it, and detectives kept coming in to report to him. Chief Kinsella and other subordinate commanders were always there too, but the investigation was Seedman's. He was probably the only man in the world who carried in his head all the names and all of the details turned up during investigations of every other crime committed by these black extremists anywhere in the country. He was the only one capable of sorting out the new information as it came in, and deciding what was significant, and what was not. Mostly he was cheerful. But sometimes he would stare off at the wall and mutter curses. "Those sons of bitches. There isn't a cop in the country who's safe until we find them."

Seedman had briefed the Police Commissioner. He had briefed all of us. I argued that the public should be told all that had happened, for there was sympathy out there for the police which had never existed before, and we needed that sympathy. It was clear to me that we were confronted once again by the so-called Black Liberation Army, but the Police Commissioner urged caution. Perhaps it was some sort of private vendetta. I argued that it could not be, that hatred as unparalleled as this could have only one explanation. Chief Cawley argued that we should keep silent. He thought that to call this crime an assassination would turn the cops into haters of the public, particularly the black public. The cops would all want to be carrying shotguns. The Police Commissioner agreed with this. So did the Chief Inspector. I argued that they were wrong to behave this way; this was an assassination, you couldn't call it anything else. That day at the 9th Precinct, mobbed by television reporters, I described how I had held the blood-soaked uniforms in my hands, and put my fingers in the holes in the backs of the coats of Patrolmen Foster and Laurie, and I told how I had got blood all over my hands, for I wanted the public to know. This was not the accidental murder of a cop who happened to interrupt a crime. This was an outright assassination.

There—the word was out for the first time.

The second day, Saturday, I waited with Seedman and his detective commanders in the 9th Precinct all morning. A letter had just been received by the United Press International, and after notifying us by phone, the letter was sent over by messenger. It read, "This is from the George Jackson Squad of the Black Liberation Army about the pigs wiped out in lower Manhattan last night. No longer will black people tolerate Attica and oppression and exploitation and rape of our black community.

"This is the start of our spring offensive. There is more to come. We also dealt with the pigs in Brooklyn." The handwritten note ended with the phrase "We remember Attica." It was signed, "The George Jackson Squad of the B.L.A."

Seedman placed the letter inside a transparent plastic folder, and handed it to a detective. "I want 50 copies of this," he said. "After that, take it to the lab and see if there are any fingerprints on it."

The detective said: "Right, Chief. I'll run it through the machine 50 times."

Seedman said, "You dummy, you. You make one copy of that, and 50 copies of the copy."

Seedman doubted any fingerprints could be left on the letter now. The only prints on it would belong to the editors of the United Press International.

The press was outside clamoring for a press conference. Seedman decided we would tell them about this letter. Because the attacks in Brooklyn (one cop knifed in his radio car, another cop shot twice trying to question a traffic violator) had not been publicized, Seedman was willing to believe that whoever sent this letter actually had "dealt with the pigs in Brooklyn." We were dealing with homicidal revolutionaries, and the public ought to now this. Chief Kinsella, white-haired, nearly 60 years old, a dour man who rarely spoke, now began quietly urging that I serve as spokesman for every honest man who had ever worn a police uniform.

Kinsella had read most of the same reports Seedman had read. This was guerrilla warfare, and the targets were cops, all cops, not just cops in New York. This gang was as wide-ranging as it was murderous, and everywhere any member of it went, shoot-outs with policemen almost inevitably followed. Kinsella's point was that I could say all this, for I wasn't a career cop myself; people would believe me. Somebody had to say it, Kinsella thought. Somebody had to say it soon. Somebody had to stand up for cops.

Always in the past the white-haired old detective had been such a quiet, low-keyed kind of man, and now came this earnest, emotional plea. He was almost as old as my father, and resembled him in many ways, and I agreed with everything he said. At that moment the Mayor was in Florida campaigning for the Presidency. It was Mayor Lindsay's proudest boast, and almost his only one, that there had been no major racial disorders in New York during his tenure. They had been the fear of Lindsay, and of nearly every other elected official in the country. Racial tension stood like a box of dynamite balanced on the peaked roof of our times. The merest breeze could blow it off, and if it fell it would explode, setting fire to a neighborhood or the city, or the world. Violence, once it started, perhaps could not easily be stopped.

To date, not one word had been spoken publicly by anyone describing these cop killers as part of a nationwide conspiracy.

Knowing the risk of so describing them, I summoned the press inside the 9th Precinct station house.

Speaking into a dozen microphones, I said it was the job of the police not only to catch these cop killers, but also to educate the public about the threat to public order which such a conspiracy constituted. I said, "The public doesn't seem to be aware of the danger. The time is over when the Police Department should keep its mouth shut on this kind of thing. Nobody doubts that the killings of Patrolmen Foster and Laurie were committed by black extremists. Always in the past the police have been quiet about this conspiracy because of fear of accusations of racism. But it isn't the black community that is doing this, it is a few dozen black criminal thugs, and it just has to be said."

I spoke as passionlessly as I could under the circumstances.

Perhaps I should have waited for the Police Commissioner to make such statements, but I sensed that he wouldn't do it, and so I made them myself.

As nearly as I was later able to determine, not one word I spoke was used by the media either that night or the next day. It would all have to be done again, for obviously the editors had decided that my statements were too hot to handle. For the next few days reporters remained camped outside the 9th Precinct station house waiting for a break in the investigation. Each day there were attempts to interview me, and during the next several days I repeated what I had already said about the Black Liberation Army, but still nothing appeared in the public print.

Almost one week after the double assassination, Martin Arnold of *The New York Times* was accorded an interview by the Police Commissioner, who, in answer to direct questions by Arnold, admitted that small, unstructured and unconnected bands of black youths, fired up by the rhetoric of better-known militants, might be responsible for some police killings. Murphy was being cautious, and low-keyed, but the import of his remarks was the same as the import of mine, and the next day this story ran on the front page of *The New York Times,* and it included, at last, many of the remarks which I had been making all week. Why shouldn't his remarks be the same as mine? We were both briefed by the same men, by Seedman, and by Chief of Intelligence Arthur Grubert; though I, in addition, had by now studied police and FBI reports from other cities. On the following Sunday I went on a half-hour interview program on ABC television, and repeated much the same information, also showing the Black Panther newspaper which was called *Right On!* The January issue contained in its centerfold the mug shots of 11 dead cops, and this paragraph: "Victories for the people in New York alone saw the assassination of 14 pigs. Malcolm X's birthday was celebrated with the assassination of two pigs Piagentini and Jones. Numerous banks were ripped off and the people began to relate to the art of political consequence. The lesson is being taught to the oppressor that every time he strikes a blow against the people, he can expect retaliation." Elsewhere in that same issue was a drawing of a policeman in uniform as a rifle target, and under it this caption: "Power to the Shooters." Rap Brown's photo was on the cover, and on an inside page there was even a picture of me kneeling beside deactivated bombs which some maniac had planted in downtown banks, and the headline above that read: "Pig Technology."

It was not my point to discuss the centuries of injustice that had gone into the making of such hatred—the hatred needed to form such a party and publish such a newspaper, the hatred needed to slaughter two young men by shooting them repeatedly in the back. Nor was it my point to discuss freedom of the press and freedom of speech. My point was only to tell the country that such hatred existed, that no cop in uniform was safe; and also to tell the cops in this city that someone in authority, if only myself, realized what they were up against and was with them.

I knew there would be repercussions, and I waited for them. If the Mayor had not been in Florida running for President such repercussions would have come quicker and been more severe.

Those were emotional days. A black patrolman named Ulysses Williams wrote an editorial for Harlem's *Amsterdam News* which began, "There are those who call themselves your brothers. They stand on rhetorical platitudes and shout at the top of their voices that they are fighting for the rights of their black brothers. But how black are they? Black is not only a color as it applies to us. It's a state of mind that stands for courage. And most of all, pride. A pride that would not allow a black man to cravenly shoot down another man when his back is turned, and then condone the act by calling it justice. Especially another black man who has sworn to protect and stand between his people and harm. Cast them out for they are not of you, they have become infected with a poison that could kill us all."

And a white sergeant named Salvatore Mazzarulli from the 26th Precinct on the edge of Harlem wrote the following poem in honor of Patrolmen Foster and Laurie:

> *One was black and one was white*
> *Brothers nevertheless*
> *A camaraderie as deep as love*
> *Nurtured by nervous war*
>
> *One was black and one was white*
> *Service in justice cause*
> *Victims of misguided tools*
> *Felled by ignorance and hate*
> *One was black and one was white*
> *How foolish prejudice seems*
> *Embraced as one by God*
> *One was black and one was white*
> *Like two that last year made this route*
> *One was black and one was white*

Another sergeant, William Moriarity, editor of the police magazine *Spring 3100,* wrote that Foster and Laurie were killed because of their color, which was neither white nor black, but blue.

The funerals took place on the same day, the first at St. Patrick's Cathedral, with 5000 cops or more lined up outside, filling Fifth Avenue from curb to curb for many blocks in both directions. Even those of us who attended in civilian clothes wore our shields on our overcoats with black bands around them. The second funeral took place that afternoon in Staten Island, which seemed half a world away, a rural community though part of New York City too, the cops and the parked police cars filling the streets of an entire neighborhood. Seedman had detectives scattered through the crowds and standing on rooftops in both places, lest other homicidal madmen—or perhaps the same ones—attempt to disrupt the funerals. The wives this time were very young because both of the dead boys had been so young, and both girls collapsed before it was over. One began to wail plaintively and had to be carried from the church. But this came as no surprise to those of us who had attended many of these funerals. Older widows, even those with many children, usually were far better able to accept their loss than were these young ones who suddenly found themselves widows while still girls.

Approximately ten days after the terrible crime, I met with Chief Seedman. He said, "We know who did the shooting, and we know who else was there. There's about nine of them involved. We got prints inside the getaway car and prints inside the bag that one of them left at the scene. Ballistics has matched up one of the bullets with a bullet dug out of a patrolman back in 1968, same gun. These guys never throw guns away. And in addition, witnesses have identified them from photos. I want to broadcast an alarm for the four guys who did the actual shooting, and for five other people wanted for questioning. I want to hold a press conference and give it the widest possible publicity.

"I want you to do me a favor," Seedman said. "I want you to talk to the Police Commissioner for me. I want you to get him to agree to go ahead on this."

I met with Murphy. "In a case of this magnitude," I told him, "it should be your press conference, not Chief Seedman's."

Murphy agreed. The press conference would be scheduled for noon the next day. I so informed Chief Seedman, who ordered posters made up, one for each of the nine wanted fugitives, each to contain his name, his aliases, his photos, and the various crimes he was wanted for.

Such posters were prepared. So was an additional poster which bore no photos; instead the nine names were listed on the left side, and on the right were listed about 20 crimes in many cities. Lines in a variety of colors linked each of the named individuals to those crimes in which he had taken part. The purpose of this poster was to show how interlocking all of these crimes and all of these people were, to show without an question that these people did constitute a dreadful conspiracy.

All of the charts having been prepared, I had them carried into Murphy's office.

Suddenly Chief Seedman received a call from Assistant District Attorney John Keenan, who "suggested" that the press conference be canceled. A suggestion from Keenan, speaking on behalf of District Attorney Hogan, had always in the past seemed virtually a command. Seedman had discussed the press conference with Keenan the day before, and at that point Keenan had given his okay. But this morning Hogan had been apprised of what the Police Department meant to do, and he was against it.

Murphy's office had begun to fill up, for it was nearly 12 o'clock, and down the hall our board room was jammed by the press. In Murphy's office we talked about whether or not to cancel the press conference. Before this discussion ended Murphy and convoked almost every lawyer in the Police Department: Lacovara, Deputy Commissioner of Community Affairs Benjamin Ward, Deputy Commissioner for Legal Matters Luis Neco. Chief Inspector Codd and Chief Seedman were also present. The discussion ranged back and forth. Seedman admitted that the wanted alarm could go out without any press conference. District Attorney Hogan was not against the alarm, only against the publicity.

I began to argue that the Police Commissioner owed it to himself, to every cop in the city, and also to every cop in the country to give the widest possible dissemination to information about this conspiracy. Deputy Commissioner Ward argued that there was no conspiracy. Lacovara and Deputy Commissioner Neco pointed out that legally the Police Commissioner had the right not only to transmit the alarm but to hold the press conference. District Attorney Hogan did not hold veto power over him. Hogan's point was that a fair trial would be impossible once this kind of publicity had taken place, but Lacovara and Neco were satisfied that legally nothing could change the identification of the killers, which had already been made by witnesses. I then brought in the Fair Trial Free Press rules which had been handed down by Chief Judge Stanley Fuld two years before. They specifically stated that the Police Department, in order to aid the apprehension of wanted fugitives, had the right to disseminate their names and photos as widely as possible.

Twelve noon had come and gone. Down the hall the press would be getting fidgety. Inside Murphy's office Deputy Commissioner Ward kept maintaining that there was no conspiracy. There certainly was no conspiracy just because I said there was a conspiracy, Ward stated. But once we had agreed to hold back the tenth poster—the one charting the activities, crimes, and travels of the nine fugitives—then Ward joined with Neco and Lacovara in advising the Police Commissioner to go ahead with the press conference.

Next to be discussed was the advisability of phoning Hogan to ask, in effect, for permission. So much time had already been wasted, and we had come so close to abandoning the press conference altogether, that I was opposed not only to further delay, but to phoning Hogan at all. I was afraid that somehow Hogan would change the Police Commissioner's mind at the last moment. I considered that the revelations which the Police Department was about to make were the most important that it had made in my time, and perhaps ever. I urged the Police Commissioner not to telephone Hogan, saying, "If you're determined to go ahead with it, why call him at all? He may say don't. In that case, if you go ahead with it anyway, then you've made an enemy."

But all around me were the other voices, each recognizing the Police Department's traditional subservient role in the DA-Cop relationship. They urged Murphy to call Hogan, and, in effect, to abide by Hogan's decision.

The Police Commissioner now picked up his phone and asked to be put through to District Attorney Hogan.

We waited in silence until the phone beside Murphy's desk rang.

"Well, Mr. Hogan, all of my legal people here tell me that it's okay to us to go ahead with this press conference."

Murphy, the phone to his ear, stared at us.

He said into the phone, "We feel that the more publicity we give this, the more chance there is of having these men picked up somewhere in the country."

There was a long silence.

"Yes, Mr. Hogan," said the Police Commissioner.

"Yes, Mr. Hogan," said the Police Commissioner.

Murphy hung up. Then he said to us, "Well, he tells me thanks for calling him, and he knew that we were going to go ahead with it regardless of what he said. He also said that this isn't the way things used to be done here."

So we sent two detective hurrying down the hall, carrying the easel which bore the nine posters. After a brief wait, we trooped down the hall in our turn and the press conference began.

Previously Chief Seedman had written a one-page statement which he had thought to read himself. But the press conference had become Murphy's, and Seedman had handed over the statement, which Murphy now read as his own: "A few minutes ago the New York City Police Department transmitted an alarm for nine people. Four of these people are named as the murderers of Patrolmen Gregory Foster and Rocco Laurie, and the five others are sought for questioning in the same case.

"This group and a handful of others have been responsible for killings and assaults on policemen, both black and white; holdups and assaults against ordinary citizens and businessmen, both black and white. This small group has labeled itself the Black Liberation Army. There is no evidence to connect these people to others who have used similar names such as Black Liberation Party or Black Liberation Front, etc. This is a handful of people who have taken it upon themselves to assault and kill police officers and who finance their activities by committing holdups and other crimes.

"What is the Black Liberation Army? It is composed of this small group of militants who do not have an organizational base, and who would like to give some semblance of legitimacy to their homicidal acts. Certainly it does not represent the thinking of the black community, since as a matter of fact these assaults have brought blacks closer to their police than ever before in an effort to combat a common enemy.

"The main purpose of the alarms we transmitted this morning is to put accurate information into the hands of policemen across the country, and to seek their assistance in tracking down these enemies of society."

Murphy had read it in a mild, calm voice, but now I began to slip each poster in turn over the top of the easel as Seedman read the awful information inscribed thereon: "Wanted for murder, Herman Bell, male Negro 24, six feet tall, 185 pounds. Also known as Samuel Lee Penegard, Herman Jonas, Herman Homer Simpson. Wanted for homicide of Patrolman Piagentini and Patrolman Jones. Wanted for homicide of Patrolman Foster and Patrolman Laurie. Wanted for bank robbery—California.

"Wanted for murder, Andrew Jackson, male Negro 25, six feet two, 160 pounds. Also known as Harvey Mitchell,

Kenneth Haynes. Wanted for homicide of Patrolman Laurie and Patrolman Foster. Wanted for attempted murder of police officers by hand grenade, 104th Precinct. Wanted for murder and arson, 110th Precinct. Wanted for escape from De Kalb County Jail, Georgia. Wanted for possession of dangerous weapons in Atlanta, Georgia.

"Wanted for murder, Ronald Carter. Male Negro 28 years old. Five feet eleven, 160 pounds. Wanted for homicide of Patrolman Laurie and Patrolman Foster. Wanted for armed robbery and bail jumping, 34th Precinct. Wanted for armed robbery, New York City.

"Wanted for murder, Ronald Anderson, also known as Floyd Brown. Male Negro 20 years old. Five feet eleven, 176 pounds. Wanted for homicide of Patrolman Laurie and Patrolman Foster. Wanted for escape from De Kalb County Jail, Georgia. Wanted for possession of dangerous weapons, Atlanta, Georgia. Wanted on a warrant for felonious assault on a police officer 103rd Precinct."

The other five individuals were listed as wanted for questioning in connection with the murders of Foster and Laurie. One was Sam Cooper, who had escaped from the De Kalb County Jail with Jackson and Anderson. Another was Twyman Meyers, who was wanted for homicide and robbery in the 32nd Precinct and also for the attempted murder of cops there. The final wanted fugitive was a woman, Joanne Chesimard, 24 years old, five feet six inches, 115 pounds. She was wanted for bank robbery in Queens—the bank cameras had photographed her in the act, gun in her fist. Later she had been in a car with Andrew Jackson which was being pursued by a radio car. She and Jackson escaped by throwing a hand grenade which rolled under the radio car and blew it up, though without seriously injuring the cops inside.

Later on, detectives working on the Foster-Laurie case were to come to the conclusion that Joanne Chesimard was the soul of the gang, the mother hen who kept them together, kept them moving, kept them shooting. Her name had first come up in connection with the machine-gunning of the two cops outside Hogan's residence eight months before. So had Andrew Jackson's. Later Jackson had been indicted for the murder of the Black Panther Sam Napier, and was the only one of those defendants still at large. Bell was under secret indictment for the murders of Jones and Piagentini, and was the only one of those defendants still at large. Sam Cooper, though only 22 years old, a little guy who wore eyeglasses, had already been arrested 11 times.

It was clear to all of us that these people were outlaws even within the black community, and so considered themselves—time and again we had come upon close associates who had lived with them and even borne children by them without ever knowing their real names. Time and again we had come upon them living in abandoned buildings. We did not know how many there might be. Chief Grubert thought it was about 75. We had no evidence of any formal organization, but I for one was convinced that there had to be a formal organization. The crimes were too widespread, and they were too much all of a type.

Many months later, when Anderson was captured without a fight on the street outside the Brooklyn tenement where he had been holed up, detectives found sentry posts complete with rifles in each of the three windows. They also found—for the first time—evidence of the size of the conspiracy, a list of 400 names broken down into small cells and extending nationwide.

But for the moment there was no such proof. My own part in bringing even as much as we did know out into the open had been considerable, and now I waited for whatever the repercussions would be. The wait was a short one. About an hour and a half later I was summoned by the Police Commissioner.

I sat down beside his desk.

He said that he had been getting some feedback about me being on television all the time, and getting my name in the paper all the time. He was somewhat distant and somewhat cool, and then he leaned forward and said, "First of all, I guess I should say it's just wonderful what you've been doing. We've never had anything like this before."

But it was clear that this abrupt change of pace was just a searching around for praise to throw out at me to mitigate the criticism. Now he went back to my half-hour interview on ABC television two days before. He had heard criticism. There were many people in the Department who had been around for years, who held high-ranking positions. Was there any way we could get more exposure on TV and in the press for them?

I said, "We try, but nobody wants to talk to them."

I explained that there were three natural spokesmen: the Police Commissioner as head of everything, Seedman as head of investigations, and me for all other information.

We talked for half an hour. It was clear that criticism came from the Mayor's office and also from the district attorneys—Hogan's office was sure to blame me for today's press conference. Queens District Attorney Thomas J. Mackell would, within a few hours, criticize Murphy for it: "I don't want to get into a war with the police, but there has been a new approach to public relations in the Department that I am somewhat surprised at. I am concerned about pre-trial publicity." Mackell, who was about to try five men—but not Andrew Jackson—for the murder of Panther Sam Napier, suggested that Murphy had now made it impossible for him to get convictions. But Mackell was a former detective, and the Police Commissioner was in no way afraid of detectives. That night Murphy penned a denunciation of Mackell which, the next day, I toned down and released. "If, God forbid, a prosecutor was shot in the back by cold-blooded killers, should I avoid telling our citizens who to look for as his killers? If not, then why should I withhold this information when our brave policemen, who live every day with crime and violence, have been the victims?"

Now, in his office, less than two hours after the press conference, Murphy knew more criticism could be expected; he had already heard some from the Mayor, and it was all aimed either at me, or at him through me. He mentioned that he hadn't seen my interview on ABC television two days before. But I was certainly getting a lot of publicity for myself, and people were beginning to talk about that. He said, "Your name is in the paper nearly every day." I did not know what answer to make, except to remark that I had a high-exposure job.

Murphy said he felt sure that the DAs had been calling Lindsay. Also, he was under the impression that *The New York Times* seemed to be mad at me personally, and at us the Police Department.

I was trying hard to read between the lines.

I had spoken for 30 minutes with Tom Morgan, the Mayor's press secretary, at City Hall. I had known Morgan for years, for he used to be a free-lance journalist. He was a tall man with a mustache. It was his opinion that I had made a major error in going on that interview program. My job was to stay invisible, and the Police Department's job was to stay out of politics. I answered that the subject in question was not politics but assassination. Morgan answered that everything was politics. He then told me that most of the information that I had released to the press and public was wrong. For instance, he did not believe that one of the killers had done a jig in the street. I pointed out that I had interviewed the witnesses myself. Morgan said, "I still don't believe it. He probably shot himself in the foot or something." Morgan not only rejected any idea of a conspiracy of cop killers, but he insisted that even if true, the Police Department should keep silent about it. I saw that his main worry—and Lindsay's main worry too—was the possibility of race riots. Two dead cops was preferable to Harlem in flames. If Harlem exploded, Lindsay would never get to be President, that was certain, for he was campaigning on his ability to soothe the racial passions of his city.

Morgan pointed out that he was paid $40,000 dollars a year, $10,000 more than I was; that he held the rank of administrator; and that he was outranked in city government only by the Mayor, the Police Commissioner, and one or two others. As a matter of fact, his salary was only $1000 less than Murphy's.

I had informed Murphy about this meeting.

Now as we talked in his office, Murphy remarked that the Mayor's people were all uptight lately. Perhaps they had had bad news from Florida, or Wisconsin or somewhere. Suddenly Murphy seemed as close and as warm and friendly as ever. He did not instruct me to do anything, or not to do anything. But he asked at one point if I thought that the Mayor's people were jealous, because we had been getting far more publicity than they had.

I said, "Yes."

City Hall was always jealous about whose name got into the newspapers, and how many times. After mine had appeared once or twice, someone down there remarked, "What's Daley running for?" The answer then as now was nothing at all, but that's the way their minds worked. Police Commissioner Murphy had become at least the second best known man in the city, if not first best known, and possibly he was far more widely admired than our Presidential candidate. If I was getting blamed for this, then I could understand it, which was not to say that it pleased me.

I left him feeling a bit shaken, but feeling also a kind of mandate to go on with what I was doing. Perhaps there was jealousy on Murphy's part too, each time my name appeared in the paper; the idea occurred to me, but I discounted it. At that point I believed this little man to be one of the biggest men I had ever met.

But I had been warned.

About a month later Murphy would say to me, "Do you remember that unpleasantness a while back? I think you can forget about that. It seems to have blown over."

But it hadn't.

After leaving Murphy I went uptown to *The New York Times* and met with Abe Rosenthal, managing editor, and Arthur Gelb, metropolitan editor. I told them I was being sniped at through City Hall, that somebody had told Murphy *The New York Times* was mad at me personally. Rosenthal said that not only was *The New York Times* not mad at me, but he was afraid quite the opposite was true, that the Police Department and I personally seemed to be getting more and better publicity than we should have gotten, because "I was one of their boys." He said, "I thought we were favoring you because you had worked here, and now you're complaining. You're getting paranoid too. Now stop that." Rosenthal and Gelb started talking about City Hall: They were all paranoid there. Rosenthal said, "You're in the big leagues now and you have to expect that people are going to take pot shots at you." Both of them began to denounce Lindsay, and Lindsay's aides, especially Morgan. The meeting closed with Rosenthal announcing that he wanted an article done about me and my concept of my job, about my role and the Police Department's role, because it was obvious that I was doing something that had never been done before. I departed, thinking, That's exactly what I don't need, my name in the paper again.

Two days later at 5:25 in the morning *The New York Times* received an anonymous phone call. A male voice announced that a policeman would be killed at 8 A.M. this date, unless the Black Liberation Army received $100,000. An hour and a half later the *Times* received a second call: "At 8 a.m. a cop will be killed, call Commissioner Murphy."

At 8 A.M. a cop was driving south of Harlem, alone in a radio car, when a man flagged him down from the curb. He pulled over, and the man lunged in at him with a knife and began stabbing him in the thigh, even as the cop threw the upper part of his body toward the passenger seat. The cop managed to get his gun out as the knife came flailing down again and again. He emptied his gun in the direction of his assailant. Out of six shots from an arm's length away, only one struck the assailant. It killed him. The cop was hospitalized but would recover.

What sort of mad world were we living in?

That night Channel 7 received a phone call. The caller identified himself as Josh Smith of the Black Liberation Army. He announced, "No longer will the pig hatchet men plant their heels on our people." He stated that next to be killed would be Commissioner Murphy and Deputy Commissioner Daley. Shortly afterward my duty sergeant phoned to advise me of this threat. Did I want anything special done? I told him no, and went back to bed, but the phone rang again. A Detective Quill from Manhattan North advised me officially of the threat on my life. Would I like him to send a detective to stand guard on my apartment?

There had been threats before—all of us in the police hierarchy received them with some regularity—but this one seemed to hold more menace than most. In the press and on television I had been identified with the exposure of the Black Liberation Army as a threat to all cops. Presumably the Police Commissioner would be heavily guarded and hard to kill. But if these thugs measured their success by headlines, I would do as a target, and I should be easier.

I told Detective Quill, "No, no guard. I don't think it's anything to get upset about."

He said, "Good night, Commissioner."

I got back into bed. My wife said, "Who was that?"

I said, "It was nothing, a detective querying me about something."

The Police Commissioner would not have asked for a guard. A month or so ago, detectives monitoring a wiretap in connection with another crime, had heard the details of a plot to murder the Police Commissioner. For a couple of weeks detectives preceded him every place he went in the city. Nothing happened. Presently he called the guard off. He had always refused to have guards in front of his house. And he walked through the city unarmed, which was more than I could say.

A detective who sat outside my door all night would have to be paid by the city. If there was in fact a plot against me, probably his presence there would make only for two victims instead of one.

But I lay in the dark wondering if I'd done the right thing. I knew that radio cars in the precinct would be told to keep a sharp eye on my building, and henceforth my drivers and I would be more alert than ever in moving through the streets. But if someone really wanted to kill me, there wasn't much I or anyone else could do about it.

Early in the morning of February 16, 20 days after the assassination, I received a call from the *St. Louis Post-Dispatch*. The reporter stated that two cops had been shot in St. Louis the night before by four male Negroes in a car. Were the shooters perhaps the men we were looking for?

The reporter was fishing. He knew nothing. But he was a good reporter and he knew where to fish. I told him that this department had not been informed of that crime, which was true. After hanging up, I rushed into the Chief of Detectives' office. I ordered the captain there to phone the special squad investigating the double murder. It worked out of the 9th Precinct. The squad was to contact the St. Louis Police at once.

About ten minutes later the captain came into my office and said, "It's them. They had Laurie's gun."

One of them had been killed during the shoot-out in St. Louis, and for the rest of the morning we received a series of false identifications as to who he was. At length the victim was said to be Ronald Carter.

Chief Cooper telephoned. He said, "Congratulations. You were right all along.

I said, "What are you talking about?"

He said, "Some of us are too close to the fire to see the flames, and you must feel pretty good."

"Syd, you're putting me on."

"No, you've been vindicated. It was a plot to kill cops, just as you said."

It was proving virtually impossible to find out who was dead and who in custody. I spoke with the lieutenant in charge of St. Louis homicide. He said, "Yeah, your picture on Carter checked out real good." I understood this to mean that the St. Louis cops were checking a dead face against a photo. What kind of police department were they running there anyway? Who were the two other gunmen in custody.?

As soon as Seedman reached the office he arranged for four detectives and an assistant district attorney to fly out there at once.

I informed the Police Commissioner of what had happened, and of the import of the scant information we had. I said to Murphy, "What are we going to say about the conspiracy aspect of all this?"

Now Murphy too seemed convinced of the existence of a conspiracy. He said, "We ought to be very conservative, and slow to speak on that subject." Then he said forcefully, "But if Al has the goods, I see no reason why we should keep our mouths shut."

Late in the afternoon Chief Grubert called. He had been in contact with the FBI, who now positively identified the dead gunman from fingerprints as Ronald Carter. Also positively identified from fingerprints were Henry Brown, 25 years old; and Thomas McCreary, 27 years old, from Brooklyn.

Were either of these other two prisoners dead or dying? No one knew. All we knew was that two St. Louis cops had stopped a car with cardboard Michigan license plates; but as they approached the car in the night, one cop to either side, the inside of the car erupted into flame and noise and bullets. One cop went down hit six times, one bullet breaking both his legs. The other cop was not touched. One of the cops ripped off three shots, the other six. The car sped off, but only a block away found itself in a parking lot surrounded by a chain-link fence. There had been a police narco team in the area. These men heard the gunfire and now closed in on the car in the parking lot. There was more shooting. One of the gunmen climbed the fence and got away.

Chief Seedman and I put in a call to Colonel Eugene Kane, Chief of the St. Louis Police. Seedman was on one phone, I on the other. Kane didn't seem to know any details of the shoot-out. He kept saying, "Chief, we've safeguarded the scene real good; we'll meet your men at the airport."

It seemed clear that they wanted the New York Police to conduct the investigation.

Seedman asked, "Who can I talk to in your department that would know the most about black militants in your area?"

Colonel Kane named the captain who headed his intelligence division. "He's got two black men working for him. They are really crackerjack men."

St. Louis was about 50 percent black, and the schools were supposed to be 65 percent black, but the intelligence division of the St. Louis Police Department apparently amounted to two black detectives.

Seedman asked, "Who's conducting the investigation?"

"Lieutenant Jacobsmeyer. He's in charge of homicide. You should speak to him about the details."

I phoned Lieutenant Jacobsmeyer. He confirmed that the prisoner in custody who carried identification papers in the name of Ronald Brown, but who then claimed to be Henry Brown, was hospitalized.

I asked, "Is he seriously wounded?"

"He's got a broken wrist."

"What about the third guy? How badly wounded is he?"

"He's got a concussion."

"You mean he was shot in the head?"

"No, they weren't shot."

None of this made much sense. Was it a shoot-out or a car crash?

Lieutenant Jacobsmeyer said, "There was no car crash."

"Oh," I said.

Dense of me. The prisoners had had to be—as the euphemism had it—"subdued." When people take shots at cops, you can't expect cops to treat them gently. Deplore this if you like, but in a real world, don't expect anything different.

I asked about the fourth gunman. Near the scene, a citizen had heard noise on his roof. Cops had mounted to the roof and found much blood. They had trailed this blood spoor back to the getaway car in the parking lot, but had been unable to trail it any distance in the direction of the fugitive's flight. The site was surrounded by abandoned buildings. The cops were going through these buildings now with dogs, and perhaps the gunman lay already dead in the rubble somewhere. This was the hope both in St. Louis and New York, another fact to be deplored. As cops saw it, if the wounded gunman were dragged out of that rubble alive, society would heal the snake, clothe him in his rights, and perhaps a year or more from now refuse in court to believe that he had taken part in the ambush at all. Cops preferred him dead.

More facts became known. In the trunk of the getaway car were found one .44-caliber Magnum carbine, two .30-caliber carbines, one Remington 30.06 carbine, one Fabrigne Deguerne Belgian rifle with a telescopic sight, one Colt A&R automatic rifle. In the welter of that trunk were found also two boxes of .44-caliber Magnum ammunition, two boxes of 5.56 mm. ball ammunition, one clip containing 30 rounds, 24 rounds of rifle ammunition, and 90 rounds of banana clips. Four handguns were found at the scene: one 9 mm. Browning automatic with seven spent shells; one .357 Magnum Colt; one .38-caliber Colt with a four-inch barrel (a police gun) Serial No. D-30886; and the .38-caliber Smith and Wesson, Serial D-186239, which had belonged to Patrolman Rocco Laurie. When I asked Lieutenant Jacobsmeyer where this gun was found, he answered, "The fellow named Brown threw it into the bushes when he was apprehended, and then he led us to where it was, and we found it."

I gathered he had led cops to the gun out of fear, but I did not ask how this fear had been applied.

Found in the pocket of the slain Ronald Carter were keys and a rental ticket for a U-Haul truck. Radio cars fanned out and by next morning had found this truck abandoned. In it were mattresses, clothes, a table, material from which plastic explosives could be made, and a suitcase containing black extremist literature. This literature was concerned with urban guerrilla warfare, and some of it mentioned the name "Black Liberation Army."

This truck was found to have been rented in Cleveland at 4:15 in the morning of the day before the shoot-out. Cleveland was 500 miles away, meaning that the van had been on the road during all the intervening time. It had been rented by a black female, 5 feet 4 inches tall, 115 pounds, who had produced a false New York State driver's license. Renting the van in Cleveland, the black woman had given a Cleveland address which proved to be nonexistent.

It took Seedman and me most of the day to find out even this much. Late in the afternoon, Seedman got Chief Inspector Codd on the line and said, "I want to go out to St. Louis. We can't trust the police out there to conduct the kind of investigation we want conducted. They sound like a bunch of hicks. Can I go, Chief?"

Codd gave permission, and Seedman arranged to be on a late plane to St. Louis. He was taking out with him a ballistics expert carrying envelopes containing every bullet shot into a cop in New York since 1968. There were ten guns out there. How many of them could be linked to assaults on cops?

It was ten o'clock at night before I was able to reach the Police Commissioner, who had been making a speech at a dinner. I told him Seedman was on a plane to St. Louis.

I then began to inform Murphy of the details from St. Louis, the blood on the roof—but he interrupted me. He said he would see me in the morning, and he hung up.

In the morning Seedman called. Ballistics had checked out the bullets. Ronald Carter had been killed by a bullet from the gun of Patrolman Laurie.

The fourth gunman had got away. There was no sign of him.

Seedman said that the St. Louis detectives had not performed even some of the most basic jobs of such an investigation—they hadn't even canvassed all the buildings surrounding the shoot-out and surrounding the abandoned van, to see if anybody had seen or heard anything, or knew anything. He was convinced that the St. Louis cops had been waiting for him to walk in there and take over the investigation, which he had now done. Although of course he had no authority and/or jurisdiction in St. Louis, he was now giving orders, and they were being obeyed.

One of the prisoners, Thomas McCreary, had had in his possession identification papers in the name of Joe Earl Bell of Windsor, North Carolina. Detectives went to Brooklyn to interview McCreary's mother. She stated that her son was never any good. She had known him to be a militant and a former member of the Black Panther Party. She stated that he quit the Panthers because they were not militant enough. She thought that he carried a Luger on his person.

A Mrs. Thelma Spivey was interviewed in Brooklyn. She stated that the defendant in St. Louis was Henry Brown, her nephew, and that he was using his brother's identification, but the real Ronald Brown was presently in jail. She stated that she had seen Henry in New York three weeks ago, about the time of the Foster-Laurie killings.

McCreary had requested that notification be made to one Deborah Green in Brooklyn. Miss Green was known previously as an active member of the Panthers. She was interviewed by one of Seedman's detectives and was thoroughly uncooperative. She proved to be in possession of a gun but produced a permit for it.

Her brother, Robert Green, lived close by the scene of the shoot-out in St. Louis. Is that where they had been headed?

By telephone from St. Louis Seedman said, "So now we have two new faces in this conspiracy. Two guys with no prior criminal records." Two new cities too, St. Louis and Cleveland. By the time Seedman called, Chief of Intelligence Grubert was sitting in my office. We were preparing a statement for Grubert to make relative to the Black Liberation Army conspiracy.

Three months ago, Sam Cooper, Ronald Anderson, and Andrew Jackson had been arrested in Georgia during the holdup of a supermarket. A month and five days later, all three escaped from the De Kalb County Jail by knocking a hole in the wall. But during his imprisonment, Cooper—small, wearing eyeglasses, possessing an arrest record going back to 1962, at which time Cooper was only 12 years old

—had done a lot of talking to interrogators. He said that he and about eight others had left New York last summer, driving to Atlanta in a panel truck. Five of the men and two of the women in the truck were wanted for a bank robbery in Queens a few days before. Cooper said the group left New York because it had become "too hot."

In Atlanta the group had moved into a house at 679 Fayetteville Road. Later they rented another one on East-lake Terrace. They took daily physical exercise, and kept to themselves.

After they were caught, Atlanta detectives tied Jackson, Anderson, and Cooper to a number of robberies in the area, including a bank stickup.

New York detectives were sent down to interrogate them. Seedman wanted them extradited to New York, but a cop had been killed in Atlanta on November 3, and there was some evidence linking this group to that murder.

While the three men were still in jail in Atlanta, a sheriff's deputy in North Carolina was critically wounded when he stopped and approached a Chevrolet for a routine inspection. Two men ran from the scene but were later captured. Later that same day another car ran through a nearby roadblock and the two men in it were eventually caught. All four of these prisoners were later identified as having come from the house on Fayetteville Road in Atlanta.

The Atlanta Police obtained a search warrant for the two houses. Both had been hurriedly abandoned. Inside one was a bomb made of a bottle of nitroglycerin, and a shoe box containing a stick of dynamite, and also a one-pound block of TNT. In addition, as one detective described it, the house contained "any kind of ID card you could want to see." These ranged from credit cards to a letter certifying one of the men as a security guard at the United Nations.

Part of this group had headed north, and at least four of them were now in custody in North Carolina. Another unit, which included Frank Fields, who was wanted for killing Sam Napier in Queens, headed for Florida, where Fields was killed in a shoot-out with the FBI.

In my office, Chief Grubert prepared his public statement on the Black Liberation Army. Grubert planned to say, "These individuals form and dissolve and reform in small groups or cells. A great many of these people who have been identified in connection with attacks on policemen, were themselves Panthers. Others were in jail with Panthers in Colorado or Georgia or here in New York. They appear to recruit new members in jail. They are obliged to commit bank robberies and stickups to fund themselves. It appears that their contact in each new city is with the most extreme members of the Black Panther Party. They keep to themselves, use false names, and evidence shows that they are not known by the general black community."

But prior to the press conference, Grubert, Chief Inspector Codd, the Police Commissioner, and I met in Murphy's office. Codd and Murphy read Grubert's statement, then Codd said, "I think it's wrong to give the Black Panthers any publicity whatsoever."

I argued that it was the duty of the Police Department to speak, that it was absolutely mandatory that it take on this new role in our times; to inform the public of what was happening and why. There had not been a single successful prosecution of any Panther anywhere in the country to date, and this was the fault of the police departments of America, which had been both unwilling and unable to try to convince the public of what was happening. Juries found charges of guerrilla warfare incredible and voted acquittal in every case.

Codd said, "We'll just cause new funds to flow into them."

Murphy looked from one of us to the other. He said: "That's certainly right, Mike. We always have to consider whether we'd do more harm than good in describing any of these things." Then he said to Grubert, "Arthur, how do you feel about it? Why don't you just go ahead and read what you have there?"

But Grubert either failed to see that Codd had been overruled, or else he chose not to risk offending Codd. When his turn came to address the press conference a few minutes later, instead of reading his statement, Grubert paraphrased it, never mentioning the Black Panther Party.

Chief of Intelligence Grubert then accepted questions from the floor.

"Chief, who are these people? Are they Panthers?"

Grubert looked sideways at Chief Inspector Codd, then answered, "Some of them are Panthers."

"Chief, are you suggesting that they are deliberately entrapping policemen into ambushes by using cardboard license plates, and running down one-way streets?"

Someone else asked, "Why do they keep those guns? Are they keeping them as trophies?"

Grubert, rightly, avoided inflammatory answers to both questions.

But the important thing was that the hard questions were being asked for the first time.

When Seedman phoned again from St. Louis he was satisfied that the wounded gunman who escaped had been Twyman Meyers, and that the truck had been tailing the car. When the car got into the shoot-out, the truck just drove away. The driver of the truck, Seedman said, apparently was Joanne Chesimard. Those in the truck drove it as far as they dared, collected a few things, and beat it.

In St. Louis Seedman sat in the hospital room of Henry Brown for hours, apparently making idle conversation.

Seedman said, "What's all this talk about icing a pig? Roast a pig I can see. But what would anybody want to ice a pig for?"

"Ice means kill. That's our talk."

"Okay, but still, what would anybody want to kill a pig for?"

"Pig is cop. That's the way we say. Ice a pig. Off a pig. That means kill a cop."

"Oh, I didn't know that."

This went on all Thursday afternoon, and again on Friday morning when Seedman suddenly accused Brown of having turned Patrolman Laurie's gun on Ronald Carter on purpose.

The shocked Brown said, "Just because he was shot with that gun, how do you know I shot him? How do you know I had Laurie's gun?"

Seedman said, "You dummy. You cocksucker. Didn't you ever hear of the science of fingerprinting?" Brown sat in stunned silence. Seedman said, "So you shot him on purpose, right? You felt he was the weak sister, and if you all got caught he'd blab everything. So to keep him quiet you killed him?"

Brown said, "I shot him by accident."

So Seedman knew at last that Brown had been the one with Laurie's gun.

Seedman said, "The bullet entered the left nipple of Carter. What do you mean you shot him by accident? How did you shoot him by accident?"

Brown mumbled, "When the cops started shooting at us, I scrunched down in the back seat on the floor, and I guess the gun went off by accident."

Seedman wanted to make Brown admit that he had been in Brooklyn the night of the assassinations. For a long time Brown claimed he had never been in New York or Brooklyn ever, but Seedman had questioned him too adroitly for too many hours. Brown came to the conclusion that Seedman must have proof. At last Brown admitted having been in Brooklyn, and even mentioned the specific apartment where a witness had seen him after the shootings.

Seedman thought, Got you, you bastard.

A warrant was made out in New York charging Henry Brown with the murder of Patrolmen Foster and Laurie.

Shortly after Seedman returned to New York, Bottom and Washington were convicted in San Francisco of the attempted machine-gun murder of Sergeant Kowalski there. They were sentenced to from five years to life. But Seedman was still thinking about his many hours of conversation with Henry Brown. Seedman said, "You think these guys sit around between holdups smoking marijuana and getting laid. It's just not true. They're reading Chairman Mao. This guy Brown could quote you long passages from Chairman Mao."

Seedman remarked that now Bottom and Washington could be extradited to New York to stand trial for the murders of Patrolmen Jones and Piagentini. However, the prosecution's two principal witnesses, the two women who had testified under oath before the grand jury as to the conduct of those two men and the three others on the night of the murders, now could no longer be found. Seedman had detectives out looking for them. The grand jury testimony was not admissible evidence in a murder trial. If these two women could not be found, a jury might acquit Bottom,

Washington, and the others, or perhaps there might never be a trial. A jury today wouldn't convict Bottom just because he had Jones' gun, or Henry Brown just because he had Laurie's gun. Seedman talked about vicious criminals such as this beating the law on legal technicalities and he foresaw the day when cops would start taking matters into their own hands. If they cornered Herman Bell or Andrew Jackson and were really convinced that the guys would get off in court, they would go in there guns blazing, and this was as much a menace to society as the existence of the Black Liberation Army itself. Seedman mused, "With the courts it's getting so bad now—"

But then his sense of humor got the better of him. The Chief of Detectives suddenly said, "Let's you and me write a short story. A guy gets stuck up, and the stickup man takes his wallet, and he tells the police that not only did he get stuck up, but that he would recognize the guy again, because the guy was a midget. So a little distance away the cops capture a midget carrying the guy's wallet and they say, 'Alright, now you've got to identify the midget in the lineup.' Now the midget's lawyer comes in and says, 'You can't have a lineup with my midget and five detectives. My midget would stand out. He would be conspicuous.' " Seedman said with a grin. "The punch line is this. We get a table and we stand the midget on the table in the midst of five detectives, so they are all the same height. How's that for a short story?"

5 / Narcotics Undercover

Narcotics, the scourge of the city and of the times. New York was without any question the biggest market for what was apparently the single most lucrative business in the world. The Federal Bureau of Narcotics and Dangerous Drugs estimated that Americans consumed six to ten tons of heroin a year. It guessed that half a million Americans were addicted—and put up to 300,000 of these people in New York. If these figures were even slightly accurate, this meant that several tons of narcotics were being sold on New York street corners every year. Most years, when the day came for the Police Department to burn all confiscated heroin which was no longer needed as evidence in court—that is, a whole year's seizures—this blaze amounted to less than 100 pounds worth. The rest of the tonnage had already disappeared into people's veins.

The previous year there had been 41,266 narcotics arrests, 68 percent for heroin, 12.7 percent for marijuana and hashish, and only 2.7 percent for cocaine. Other drugs and paraphernalia made up the rest. Only 35 percent of those arrested on felony narcotics charges admitted to being addicts. The rest were merely in the business, like bartenders who did not drink themselves. Almost half of those arrested were less than 16 years old.

Overall, more than 100,000 persons had been arrested for felony crimes, 17 percent of whom admitted to being addicts. There had been 181,000 reported burglaries in the city, and not quite 16,000 arrests for burglaries. Almost 22 percent of the burglary prisoners admitted to being addicts. There had been almost 89,000 armed robberies in the city and 17,500 arrests for robbery; 18.1 percent of the robbery prisoners admitted being addicts. Ten percent of arrested murderers admitted they were addicts.

The Police Department did not classify narcotics criminals or narcotics users according to race, but the trade flourished most openly and most widely in the ghettos, especially the black ghettos. Black leaders cried out in pain and toward the vast narcotics conspiracy leveled the terrible charge of genocide.

Against this ghastly business the New York Police Department mobilized only 800 full-time cops, of whom 40 worked as undercover narcotics buyers. Of the 40, six were girls, and one of the girls was Kathleen Conlon.

In a country jealous of its civil liberties, citizens could not be searched or arrested on mere suspicion of possession of narcotics. Anguished mothers could denounce each corner pusher preying on the community, but no cop for that reason alone could lock the suspected pusher up. There had to be evidence.

That evidence in most cases was supplied by undercover agents making registered buys. Usually, before an arrest was made, two separate buys spaced several days apart had to be made by the same agent from the same dealer. The arrest would be made by the agent's back-up team—usually two plainclothes cops—on still a third day. The back-up cops, called "field teams," made observations—they sometimes were close enough to watch the buy effected, but principally they were the ones who made the arrests afterwards. They were the muscle of the Narcotics Division. But the undercover agents were the division's eyes and ears and heart.

For undercover agents, police work was theater. They dressed like addicts and/or dealers themselves, and they talked the jargon of the streets. Day after day they passed themselves off for what they were not, criminals instead of cops. Day after day they wrote their own acts on the spot. Like bullfighters, they wore costumes and they had each memorized a few tricks which had saved them in the past, but each day they confronted a beast more deadly than they were, and it obeyed no rules. Day after day they brazened their way in and out of sleazy bars and tenement hallways, in and out of street-corner encounters with dangerous men. Each could be betrayed by any slip of the tongue or hand, or merely fall victim to the irrational suspicion of the professional lawbreaker. They were actors in a deadly play.

And six of them were girls. And one of the girls was Kathleen Conlon.

Chief Grubert's Intelligence Division employed undercover agents too, but these were different men, for they played only one role at a time, and they played it for months or even years on end.

Most Intelligence Division detectives gathered evidence in much the same way reporters did. They made phone calls, they looked up legal documents on file somewhere, they went to the library to read through back issues of newspapers and books. Day after day they gathered intelligence on every group that operated inside New York City, nearly all of which operated legally.

Were the Knights of Columbus or Jehovah's Witnesses having a rally? Then it was the Intelligence Division's job to find out when and where the rally would take place, how long it would last, and how many people could be expected to attend. This information was needed by the Chief Inspector before he could decide how much crowd control would be necessary.

Intelligence detectives came back with information of all kinds, for instance, that the Jehovah's Witnesses always cleaned up the stadium after themselves.

But Grubert also had 35 undercover agents in a super hush-hush category. Information about them was extremely closely guarded. Probably even the Police Commissioner himself did not know who these men were or where they were working.

These were the undercover men (possibly a woman or two) who attempted to infiltrate organized crime and also certain political groups, such as the Black Panthers. They were all cops, though not one had ever publicly graduated from the Police Academy. In general, all were young men who had passed the examination for patrolman and were awaiting appointment on the Civil Service list. They had been interviewed by Grubert or one of his associates. Only about one in 50 of those interviewed were accepted as undercover agent.

Once sworn in, they quit their classes in the Police Academy and had no further contact of any kind with cops, except for their one of possibly two liaisons with the Intelligence Division itself.

Intelligence Division undercover agents were paid through dummy corporations. Recently, several who had infiltrated the Panthers had been surfaced to testify at the trial of the Panther 21. Although they testified as witnesses to criminal acts, and to the existence of a criminal conspiracy, the jury refused to believe them and every one of the Panther 21—which by trial time had shrunk to the Panther 13—was acquitted. The undercover agents were then reabsorbed into the Police Department as cops. Attempts to infiltrate organized crime had not, so far, been very successful. One undercover agent had managed to make himself chauffeur to a Mafia overlord, but one day the Mafia hoods realized they had no idea where he had come from, or who he might be, and they beat him up and told him to get out of there, and not come back.

At the present time a certain Intelligence Division under-

cover agent of Spanish ancestry was attempting to infiltrate
the pornography industry, and another was attempting to
get himself accepted by black thugs who might or might
not be related to the Black Liberation Army. To improve
his credentials it had been necessary for this man to commit a crime of violence in their presence, and so a holdup
was arranged. The undercover agent stuck up another detective and robbed him of $178.50 of city money.

Narcotics undercover agents were in no sense in this
super-secret category. They carried guns and shields, they
walked in and out of station houses, they were present
when arrests were made, they testified to grand juries, and
probably all of them were known by sight and name by
every other narcotics patrolman or detective.

However, most drove cars outfitted by the Police Department with phony out-of-state license plates, and all
were given a street name. This was the name by which they
identified themselves to their criminal contacts, and it was
also the name by which they would be addressed on the
street, if necessary, by their back-up teams. Kathy Conlon's
street name, was, let us say, Annabelle.

She was born September 20, 1943. Kathy grew up in
Queens and went to high school there. In high school the
idea came to her that she would be a policewoman, and she
remained faithful to this idea for nearly ten years.

For she grew up tiny. She was not quite 5 feet 2 inches
tall, and she weighed less than 100 pounds when she took
the test for the Police Department in 1964—as soon as she
was old enough. But they measured her and found her a
quarter of an inch below the minimum height requirement,
and her hemoglobin was too low as well, whatever that
was. Diet could correct her hemoglobin. It could do nothing for her height.

She went home, and for two years slept on a board in
order to lengthen her spine a quarter of an inch. And so
she was accepted into the Police Academy in a class of just
under a thousand recruits, ten of whom were girls. This
was in June of 1968. Kathy Conlon was not quite 25 years
old.

Policewomen received the same pay and allowances as
men, and were sworn peace officers just like men. Other-

wise, they were second-class cops. There were about 350 in all, and the highest ranking of their number at that time was a lieutenant.

The first policewoman had been appointed in 1888, when she was known as a "matron." Most policewomen still were matrons, whatever the book said, and their primary function was to deal with females. This meant searching live female junkies for narcotics possibly concealed in intimate places; and it meant searching the bodies of deceased females who perhaps had dived under trains. Male cops were not allowed to touch female bodies even when dead, and although this was often ignored, it was often observed, too.

A good many policewomen served in station houses as telephone operators. Many others served as secretaries to police brass—among the hierarchy it was considered a real coup to have one's office door guarded by a policewoman. The Youth Aide Division was composed largely of policewomen, and especially in summer it was their job to cope with lost kids.

And a very few policewomen worked as detectives. It had been found useful to send female detectives into the stores to catch shoplifters. In rape investigations female detectives had their advantages too, for they could talk to victims as woman to woman, could ask intimate questions about the MO of the rapist: How did he do it, and was he circumcised or not? Victims often would not talk to a man. Some would talk to another woman, and sometimes it became possible as a result to link together a chain of rapes by the same suspect. On the whole, rape victims did not like to talk about it, and female detectives had some success, and male ones had almost none.

But nowhere else in the Police Department were male and female cops as integrated as in the Narcotics Division. The six undercover girls operated in all the boroughs, and with numerous field teams. Wherever an undercover girl went she was the leader. She led and men followed. Without her they were nothing, and they knew it. Between boys and girls inside the Narcotics Division there existed the same camaraderie as on a good ski team. They had all been down the same slopes together, very fast and at great risk.

In 1968 Kathy Conlon and nine girl classmates had gone through normal Police Academy training surrounded by nearly a thousand young men. Kathy Conlon, five feet two inches tall, had learned judo, stop and frisk, and all the other physical instruction all the other young cops were getting; and then she was asked if she wanted to go into undercover.

Altogether two girls and two young men had been invited into undercover from that class, having been chosen principally for their appearance. To say that they did not look like cops was an understatement. Narcotics undercover cops were simply not believable as cops. Kathy was not only tiny, she had the smooth, pretty face of a high school girl. Certain of the boys were either baby-faced or exceptionally pimply. A certain undercover girl looked the part of a middle-aged matron; still another one was a beauty.

The four in Kathy's class were told that they could go to the graduation ceremony if they liked, but they would have to sit behind a screen. Kathy said she would rather not be there if she couldn't be a part of her class. So, privately, she was given a gun and a shield and sworn in.

Now she went out into the field and spent eight weeks at the side of an experienced undercover cop named Denis Roberts. She watched Roberts make new contacts, she watched Roberts make buys, she listened to Roberts make jive talk—the jargon of the streets.

With Roberts at her side she made one or two buys of her own.

Police work was a team effort, and a cop was seldom alone. But an undercover agent, once the breaking-in period ended, was always alone; and there were few lonelinesses like it. Consequently there was no set time after which a rookie undercover agent had to operate on his or her own. Instead there were two criteria, and two only. The new undercover agent had only to "feel ready," and to be passed by the person breaking him or her in. Some new agents were ready in a few weeks, others in a few months, and some never. There had been girls eager to make buys almost at once, and others who quit after investing half a year, explaining to the commanding officer, "It came to me when I was sitting down to dinner last night. Is this the type of people I want to mix with? Do I want to take the chance of getting raped, getting molested, getting killed? No, it's not for me."

Such girls—or boys—left undercover, and this was no disgrace.

Most buys were made through the use of an informant. Selling heroin was illegal, and few dealers would sell to people they didn't know—after all, the buyer could be a cop. So informants were used to introduce the undercover cop to the dealer. Usually the informant was a criminal himself, and he was doing this in exchange for a lesser plea, or time off from a sentence. He would bring the undercover agent to a dealer and say, "This is my friend Annabelle; she wants to cop a half load off you. You can trust her."

A half load usually was 15 decks of heroin. A deck, enough for a single shot in the arm, cost from $2 to $8, and each deck was sold in a thin glassine envelope such as gauze bandages sometimes came in. A bundle was 25 to 30 decks. A spoon amounted to about 35 decks of heroin. A quarter was 50 to 55 decks. A piece was 437 grains, and usually it was sold in a plastic bag at between $250 and $1800, depending on its potency.

This was only part of the street jargon that had to be learned by every novice.

Kathy Conlon's first buy was to occur in the 20th Precinct on the upper West Side. Kathy was provided with an informant, and the informant presently introduced her to the dealer.

The dealer said, "Come with me."

He led her into the Stratford Arms Hotel, the informant trailing behind. On the second floor hallway, rooms gave off from each side. Suddenly the dealer opened a door, and at the same time collared her with one big arm and dragged her into a room. Before the door had slammed shut he had dragged the informant in too.

Kathy Conlon, scared, realized she was in the hotel men's room. The informant quickly disappeared into a stall, and just as quickly the dealer dropped his pants. Kathy's first thought was that she was about to be "taken off"—robbed—on her first buy. She had her gun in her pocket, and wondered, Do I pull it now, or do I wait?

She had no idea what she was expected to do.

The dealer's pants were on the floor and Kathy decided that the danger of being robbed was past, even if the danger of being raped was not. She spun around to see what had happened to the informant, and there he stood with an open switchblade the size of a butcher knife.

It was a run-down hotel, and the men's room had not been cleaned or even properly aired for a long time.

The dealer said, "What's the matter?"

Kathy said, "This place stinks."

The dealer said, "Don't change the dope none."

With that remark, he removed a plastic bag which had been secreted between his legs. Taking out a quantity of narcotics, he extended this toward Kathy.

She said, "I ain't touching that." Ripping off a handful of toilet paper, she gave this to the informant saying, "You get the stuff, I ain't touching it."

The dealer not only looked filthy, but he seemed to have scabs and abscesses on his body. Now he brought out what junkies call a set of works, and said to Kathy, "Do you want to get off?"

Kathy said, "God no, this place is terrible."

She dashed out of there. Several days later she made a second buy from the man and then had him arrested. Ever afterwards Kathy thought this the most horrifying thing that could happen to a young girl. "It was so—so degrading," she said.

Soon Kathleen Conlon was one of the stars of the Narcotics Division.

One Friday night, when she was at home, off duty, Kathy's phone rang. A certain Captain Nelson suggested that she make herself available for a special assignment at once.

So she went into the night to meet with Captain Nelson and three other superior officers, and after that she met with a troubled young girl who had agreed to serve as her informant on this particular case. Kathy was about to try to make narcotics buys from this girl's boyfriend. The boyfriend was a New York City patrolman, John Gardellis, who was attached to the Central Park Precinct.

The case had started with a letter from the girl's parents to the Police Department. The girl had just done several weeks in a hospital because of LSD administered by her boyfriend who, she claimed, was a cop. She had been living with this individual off and on for some time. The parents were distraught.

The letter was checked out and the girl interviewed. She agreed to cooperate. That is, she would introduce a police undercover agent to Gardellis. Her motive was obscure. Perhaps she saw no other way to untangle the trouble and confusion of her life. Or perhaps she was thinking only of revenge.

And so Kathleen Conlon was summoned in the night and introduced to the girl, call her Winnie, who led her to the door of John Gardellis' apartment. Kathy was supposed to be there as a blind date for Gardellis' brother Artie; Winnie, as always, was the date of John Gardellis.

The operation had been hurriedly conceived, and hurriedly set up. Kathy Conlon had entered the Police Academy in June 1968, Gardellis in October 1968. So there was the chance he would recognize her. Perhaps he had seen her in the halls. How many five-feet-two-inch policewomen were there in those halls at that time?

Being a cop, Gardellis was of course armed. If he made Kathy Conlon for an undercover agent, would he panic and blow her head off? Or would he simply throw her out, claiming that he had never used narcotics in his life? For Kathy the two alternatives were almost equally chilling. If Gardellis made her as a cop, she would be suspected of having warned him, as one cop to another. She might even be accused of corruption herself.

She wanted nothing to do with this job, and had so informed Captain Nelson, saying, "This is a job for the Internal Affairs Division. It's their job to catch corrupt cops, not the job of undercover narcotics agents."

But Nelson told her bluntly, "You are it."

Now the apartment door opened, and Gardellis and Kathy smiled at each other for the first time. Kathy wore no electronic gear. Her back-up team would not hear what was happening to her. They would be no closer than the hallway or the street.

The hi-fi was playing loudly. In the living room sat Kathy, Winnie, and the Gardellis brothers. Marijuana cigarettes were passed around. Kathy, who did not smoke, had an ordinary cigarette in one hand so that each time it came her time to put the reefer to her lips, she could blow real smoke out of her mouth while pretending to smoke the reefer. She did not dare put the marijuana cigarette in her mouth, for she had no idea what it would do to her. Besides, perhaps the whole job was a setup of some kind. Perhaps there had been allegations against her, and Gardellis was not a crooked cop but an honest one assigned to test out Kathleen Conlon. But presently Gardellis began to pass around LSD tablets, and Kathleen Conlon relaxed. He was a crooked cop, all right.

Soon the other three were not only smoking reefers, they were also swallowing LSD. Kathy took this to mean that there would be traces of LSD on the tip of the reefer. After that she couldn't even make herself put it close to her mouth, for she feared going off on a trip herself.

Gardellis began to brag that he was a cop. He said he was hoping to undermine the foundation of the Police Department. He was going to take and pass all the tests, and become a boss himself. He wanted to turn on as many cops as he could, make this a swinging department. Everybody was so square they didn't know where their heads were at. He was going to show them all.

Kathy's attitude changed. Now she was ready to hang him if she could. She saw herself laying him out for the slaughter.

She asked how he could have made arrests in Central Park. Since he used narcotics himself, how could he arrest others for narcotics? Wasn't he being a hypocrite? Gardellis answered that he arrested narcotics users when he had to, but when the case came up in court, he either wouldn't show up or would change his testimony, and the defendant would always go free.

Suddenly Gardellis stood up, and yanked his girl friend into the bedroom. He had forced her to swallow two tabs of acid by now, and she was pretty well out of it. They had sex in the bedroom with the door open. In the living room, Kathy had been left on the sofa with the brother, and now as the bed squeaked, she jumped up and began moving about the room, looking at the records, reading the titles on the books, trying to keep away from him.

Winnie came out of the bedroom. Kathy said, "Do you have any more cigarettes?"

The girl said, "No."

Kathy said, "Why don't you go out and buy a pack?" But the disheveled Winnie declined.

Kathy had wanted to get the other girl out of the apartment, so as to calm the back-up team. Kathy had been in the apartment nearly three hours, and the back-up team must be frantic.

In fact, she learned later, they were so frantic they were ready to blow the entire operation. Earlier she had told one of her partners, "If anything happens and I can't get out, I'll throw something through the window." That partner had been waiting in the next apartment ever since, straining to hear the sound of broken glass. It was summer, all the windows were open, and the hi-fi was making so much noise that perhaps glass had been smashed and he hadn't heard it.

Down in the street, the other partner and the lieutenant were equally frantic. The other partner suggested they send a radio car on a noise run. They could send a uniformed cop to the door claiming there had been complaints from the neighbors.

The lieutenant said, "She's on her own now. What happens, happens."

After three hours, Kathleen Conlon purchased five tabs of LSD from Patrolman John Gardellis. She confiscated a roach (a burned-down reefer), and Gardellis gave her two reefers as a present. She also confiscated two other tabs of LSD. The confiscations had taken place prior to the sale, because she couldn't be sure Gardellis would ever sell her anything.

By the time Kathy Conlon met Patrolman John Gardellis two days later, she knew that Gardellis had been growing marijuana in a patch of weeds behind the station house in Central Park, an item which would soon titillate and/or scandalize the city.

Kathy's second visit occurred in the middle of the afternoon. She wore an electronic transmitting device—what cops call a "body set"—and before rapping on Gardellis' door she told her back-up team that under no circumstances would she remain in that apartment. If she were

not out in a few minutes, they were to come in after her.
Because Gardellis had taken a shine to the somewhat prud-
ish Miss Conlon. He had told her to come back without
Winnie and at that time he would make Kathy his sex kit-
ten. He was quite a ladies' man, and she would enjoy it, he
said.

So she rapped on his door. She was going to buy LSD if
she could, and she was going to transmit to a nearby recording device any incriminating statements she could trick him
into making. But if he grabbed her, she was going to blow
her cover and take action.

Gardellis now bragged that he had about 100 tabs of
LSD secreted in his apartment, and he sold Kathleen Conlon 30 of them. He explained how she could resell these
drugs at a profit. If she chose to go into business for herself, he could even give her some tips. He had a connection
up on Columbus Avenue near the Central Park precinct
station house.

Kathy paid him, thanked him, and left. She found her
back-up team in a car nearby. "Did you get all that down
on tape?"

The cop with the tape recorder on his lap said, "Every
word."

Gardellis pleaded guilty and was sentenced to five years
in jail.

And Kathleen Conlon went on to her next job.

The back-up teams changed, and the site and the time of
day, but the job remained the same: to pose as a criminal,
to buy narcotics from other criminals. She worked with
back-up teams she knew well and trusted, and with others
she didn't know and instinctively did not trust. However
close the back-up team might be, they would not be close
enough if anything went wrong. Kathleen Conlon stepped
into alleys with addicts and pushers. She stepped into
apartments, and doors closed behind her. She was always
armed—the gun would not give her away if found, for
nearly everybody involved in the drug business was armed.
Most times she carried her shield pinned to her panties. A
good search would find it, but it was safer than being without it, for she might need to demand assistance from uniformed cops, and she needed protection from them if she
got caught in a raid.

More crime took place by night than by day; criminals seemed to feel a safety in darkness. But for Kathy Conlon the danger was the same whatever the hour, for she was dealing with minds and emotions warped by narcotics. Once she said, "It's a weird thing. You're geared for the inevitable. You're alone and death is near. You accept it. That's the risk of undercover. You're dealing not only with pushers and addicts, but with your own informant. You're dealing with people who would give you up for a nickel bag. People ask me if I have second thoughts when I'm on the street. I have second thoughts every day."

On the day that the attack she had been dreading finally came, she was working on the South Bronx with a back-up team she did not know. She did not know the informant either. The back-up team had produced the informant. He was white, and in this racially mixed slum she felt that a white informant was wrong. She sensed it.

Kathleen Conlon asked herself, "Who is this guy? Am I taking too big a risk to go with him?"

In the pocket of her jeans, she had a .25-caliber Browning automatic.

The informant led her along the sidewalk. Outside 1484 Howe Avenue, the informant introduced her as a prostitute to one Sanford Johnson, a 6-feet 2-inch, 225-pound black man. The informant's own fear was obvious. The introduction completed, the informant scurried away.

Johnson eyed her.

It was 2:30 in the afternoon. There were kids sitting on the stoops, and mothers hanging out the windows. Some of the tenements looked half demolished. Next door stood the Union Grove Missionary Baptist Church, the Reverend F. C. Crawford, Minister. There was litter in the gutters, and six garbage cans against the wall.

Kathleen Conlon's back-up team was nowhere in sight.

Suddenly she found herself three steps down in a dark alley littered with garbage. Johnson had lifted her by the elbows and carried her in, and she knew her back-up team hadn't seen it happen.

In the alley were two other black men.

She had money for the buy in her hand, but one of the men grabbed it. Another demanded the rest of her money.

A hand ripped her blouse half off and reached into her bra.

She was being held from behind by one of the men, but she was fighting and struggling to get loose. She felt a knife slash her shoulder. She got her right arm into the pocket of her jeans, and came out with her automatic. She put the barrel against someone's chest and pulled the trigger, but the gun did not fire. There was no shell in the chamber. She had neither time nor room to cock the automatic.

One of the men nearly broke her fingers off, tearing the gun from her hand. He put it to her head, saying, "Now I'm going to kill you."

Out in the street women stood with baby carriages. She did not scream, for she had been taught not to scream. "If you panic, he panics." Her mouth was tightly shut as the trigger at her head was pulled.

There was an empty click. The automatic had not fired again. Now one of their own guns was pressed to her head. Voices yelled they would kill her.

It was the middle of the afternoon. This couldn't be happening.

Where was the back-up team?

The second trigger was pulled, and the click in her ear sounded as loud as buildings falling down.

This gun too had misfired.

Kathleen Conlon was still struggling. The men had gone through all her clothing, had found her money and grabbed it, $130 in all. They had her gun. She was thrown against the bricks. All three men sprinted out of the alley.

Kathleen Conlon sprinted out after them and now, spying the first member of her back-up team, screamed at last. What she screamed was, "Get the tall one, he's got my gun."

But the three fugitives split up and vanished.

All Kathy could think about was her missing gun. It was a disgrace for any cop to lose his or her gun. She would be brought up on Departmental charges probably and fined five days' pay.

The search through the streets lasted most of the rest of the afternoon. Superintendents were interviewed. Door bells were rung. There was a brief struggle when Johnson was found and caught. Then Kathleen Conlon's gun was slipped back into the pocket of her jeans, and the relief she felt to have it there was, in a moment, succeeded by wave after wave of terror.

Within a few hours the other two fugitives were in custody also. Kathleen Conlon went home, took off her clothes, and found that her legs were black-and-blue all over.

The next morning she sat beside Commissioner Murphy at a press conference at headquarters. Murphy remarked that this was "a very happy occasion." Policewoman Conlon was present, Murphy noted, "because a gun misfired—a gun that was pointed at her head."

To preserve her cover, Kathleen Conlon wore a long, dowdy dress, a cheap wig, sunglasses, and a double thickness of veil around her head. Asked why she, such a small and apparently very pretty young woman, was willing to undertake the risks of such a job, she replied enthusiastically that she loved being a policewoman. If she had her life to live over, she would be a policewoman again. Somebody had to get out there and do the job. Everybody couldn't say, Why doesn't somebody else do it? Somebody had to do it herself, and that was her.

The next question was directed to Commissioner Murphy. Why had he invited Policewoman Conlon to this press conference?

"To make her a third grade detective," said Commissioner Murphy, and he pulled a detective shield out of his pocket and pinned it to the front of her dress.

The irrepressible Detective Conlon then remarked, "If some junkie rapes me, and I get pregnant, my mother's going to come down here and make the P.C. marry me."

Murphy laughed. "What's the most important function of the Police Department?"

Kathleen Conlon said, "The detectives."

The amused Murphy started to give her a lecture: "You people all think alike, don't you? Well, the most important function of the Department is the patrol force. Now let me ask you that question again. What's the most important function of the Police Department?"

Kathleen Conlon grinned at the Police Commissioner and said, "The detectives."

There were plenty of soft, safe jobs for girls; and this

particular girl, who had had guns pressed to her head and triggers pulled twice, could have had her pick of them. Instead she went out into the field again. At Far Rockaway High School she registered as a teen-age student, walked into a class in session, and called out loudly to her teacher, "You're supposed to sign this."

The teacher took the card from Detective Kathleen Conlon. "Where did you come from?"

"From another school. Where do you think I came from?" snapped Detective Conlon.

"All right, please sit over there."

Detective Conlon said, "I'm not gonna sit over there all by myself. I'm going to sit here."

The teacher sighed.

Detective Conlon looked around at the other students, grinning. If one of them was pushing narcotics in this high school, he would, after this performance, soon make himself known to her.

She studied arts and crafts, social studies, and English. After several days she turned up in the station house and announced, "That school looks pretty clean. I think I'll cut the rest of my classes."

One day I followed Detective Kathleen Conlon into Queensborough College in the 111th Precinct. Detective John Carlson and Patrolman Carl Schroeder formed her back-up team. They told me that previously the highest-ranking officer ever to go on a buy operation with them or any other team they knew of was a lieutenant. Narcotics policy was being made at headquarters by men who never went out into the field at all. Which was reason enough, it seemed to me, for me to go with them.

The three of them had left the station house carrying attaché cases three inches thick, like those carried by every downtown businessman.

In Detective Conlon's attaché case were handcuffs, a box of bullets, testing devices for narcotics, and all the various forms and envelopes for sealing each batch of evidence. Detective Conlon was wearing a red sweater, and she was carrying two guns, one of them in a belly holster under her sweater. If you knew the gun was there, you could see the point of the handle thrusting into the material just below and between her breasts. In her pocket she carried her .25-caliber Browning.

She wore a ski hat—red with white stripes—and I saw why just as soon as she had entered the college lounge: She could be picked out instantly in that crowd by her hat. The back-up team didn't have to peer about for her, all they had to do was scan the room.

She moved from the lounge into the science building, into the cafeteria, back into the lounge, into the poolroom there. She was pacing nervously back and forth like someone who needed a fix bad. We, her back-up team, pretending to be inconspicuous, trailed her through corridors that reeked of marijuana smoke. In one corner a group of students were snorting coke, and in another corner another group was rolling reefers. Two campus security guards walked by holding their noses, grinning at the students.

Kathy was trying to find a black youth known as Pal from whom she had bought narcotics in the past; if she could find him, the back-up team planned to arrest him. But there was no sign of this Pal. Kathy paced, hoping to make some other connection. After two hours, directly behind me, she made her buy. I was facing in the wrong direction when the connection was made, and was afraid to turn around to watch it. This often happened. Back-up teams were rarely close enough to see the event take place. I could hear Kathy talking loudly, clearly, but could not hear what the connection was saying to her.

Suddenly she strode by me, putting her coat on, and out the door she hurried. A minute or two passed, then the three of us from different corners of the lounge followed her out. When, some blocks from the college, we pulled alongside her car, she rolled her window down, and thrust out her hand. In it rested four bags of heroin.

Back at the station house she opened her attaché case and withdrew a knife. With the point, she picked under the scotch tape which sealed the glassine envelopes. The tip of the blade entered the first bag and withdrew a few specks of heroin which Detective Conlon dropped into her test kit. The test kit resembled a toy thermometer inside a plastic case. The specks of heroin were dropped into the ball at the end of the thermometer, and then she snapped the tube inside its plastic envelope so that the acid ran down the tube into the heroin in the ball. It turned the heroin a kind of bluish green.

After each of the four glassine envelopes had checked out as heroin, Detective Conlon marked each, then inserted the four of them into the evidence envelope, sealed it, wrote her initials along the seal, and then watched while her back-up team countersigned the envelope.

The evidence envelope went into her attaché case. In a few minutes she would drive to the police lab for formal testing. In her notebook she was writing a physical description of the man she had bought the heroin from. She did not know his name. This was the second buy she had made from him, and now he could be arrested anytime, and Detective Carlson and Patrolman Schroeder would attempt to do this in a day or two—not right away, lest he connect his arrest to Detective Conlon.

Kathleen Conlon remarked, "Some people think that narcotics detectives are often users. That's ridiculous. We have carried stuff to the lab too many times for analysis. I've bought heroin which contained rat poison, and also heroin which contained lye. All narcotics agents know this, and there isn't one of them who would use the stuff."

She also remarked that a good many dealers would assume she had no money, and would attempt to get her into bed in exchange for heroin. Detective Conlon, pretending to be an addict, flirted with each until he had produced the stuff. Then she would whip money out, pay for it, and leave.

Kathleen Conlon believed the relationship between junk and sex to be very strong.

A number of newly promoted sergeants began courses at the Police Academy before being assigned to Narcotics. Lieutenant William Ballner, commanding officer of the undercover agents, addressed the new sergeants from the stage. He said, "Gentlemen, gold is worth $45 an ounce. You think that makes gold pretty valuable, don't you? Well, let me tell you how valuable heroin is. One ounce equals about 440 grains. Pure heroin can be hit nine times, scrambled, mixed with milk sugar and stretched. That means that one ounce of pure heroin can be stretched to about 4000 grains. Each grain makes one bag of heroin for sale on the street. If you sell each bag even at $2 a bag, then that means you get $8000 per ounce. If you get $6 a bag for it, you take in over $24,000 per ounce. Compare that to gold at $45 an ounce. That, gentlemen, is what narcotics is all about. Money, money, money!"

Heroin was all around you, Lieutenant Ballner told the new sergeants. "We locked up a guy who was selling it on the steps of the Treasury Building. We locked up a paraplegic in a hospital who was selling it from his wheelchair. It has infected every area. I don't know a single high school where heroin is not being sold."

A number of undercover agents were present, including Detective Kathleen Conlon. Ballner now asked each to recount to the class the funniest experience of their careers. A black female detective presently described how a certain dealer had ordered her killed. He had put a price on her head of $500. The girl made this sound amusing.

When her turn came Detective Kathleen Conlon recounted the story of her first buy in the men's room at the Stratford Arms Hotel: "He showed me all his wares."

Everybody laughed.

Raising his hand, a sergeant asked, "Would you be able to identify him if you saw him again?"

Detective Conlon answered, "I could identify him, if I had a yardstick."

Beginning at 6 A.M. on a Friday in March, raids were conducted in Queens and Staten Island, and 24 students from five schools were arrested, one of them Pal, the boy Detective Conlon had been looking for at Queensborough College.

His name was Walt Okum and he lived on Farmers Boulevard in Queens. He was under indictment, and we had a warrant for his arrest. It was just daylight when his stepfather came around the corner of the building with the garbage pail in his hand and bumped into us, and looked surprised. We showed our shields, at which point he became very nervous. We told him we wanted his stepson. "Well, he's there. He's in bed. I'll go get him for you."

Detective Carlson said, "No, we'll go down. Where is he sleeping?"

So we trooped down into the darkness of the cellar and found a little room the size of a jail cell, constructed of partitions, beside the furnace. Pal slept naked to the waist, a lovely brown, tightly muscled young body in pajama bottoms. He woke up groggily, and was shown the warrant. He found his bed surrounded by policemen, and he seemed unable to speak. The stepfather and mother now pushed their way into the little room. So did the little sister, who must have been 10 or 12, with her hair in rag curlers.

Patrolman Schroeder now read the youth his rights, sentence by sentence, ending each sentence with the question, "Do you understand that?"

"Yes," said Pal.

The parents were told where the boy was being taken and what would happen to him. They were told how their lawyer was to make contact with him.

Pal got dressed. It was a shabby, poor house, but Pal was dressed in very nice tight-fitting clothes. The mother said to me, "What are you taking him in for?"

I said, "Selling drugs."

She bowed her head. We went out of there with Pal.

Kathy Conlon was parked about 100 yards away, slouched down in the seat so she could not be seen. When Pal came out of the house in handcuffs, Kathy spoke by walkie-talkie with Detective Carlson. "That's him," she said.

As we entered the station house with Pal, there came a number of other young people in handcuffs. One of them was the undercover agent Bobby Gullo, with a cigarette in his mouth and his hat down over his eyes. Apparently he had been needed to identify the other suspects, and as a result it had been necessary to arrest him too. Now he sat in the cage with the others and somehow he had to be got out of there with no one knowing he was a policeman.

He was taken out of the cage as if to be fingerprinted, and the fingerprinting actually was begun, a nuisance to everybody, when Lieutenant Ballner started hollering, "Watch that guy, that's a real bastard!"

A minute or two was allowed to elapse before Lieutenant Ballner marched by again and cried, "That guy's got to go over to the 105th Precinct and stand in a lineup. Handcuff the son of a bitch and get him over there as fast as you can. Watch him. Don't take your eyes off him, he's dangerous."

Patrolman Gullo was at the sink in the corner washing the fingerprint ink off his hands, silently laughing his head off. In the cage the young prisoners sat dully on the floor. Gullo was handcuffed again and marched past the cage and downstairs, and then released. He and Detective Conlon spent the rest of the morning hiding in an anteroom down there, watching the prisoners come and go.

Kathy's back-up team now went out to make a second arrest, this time a boy named Willy. Kathy had said, "He's such a nice guy, I hate to bust him." The plan was to arrest him, hoping to make a registered informant out of him. Willy lived in a gray shack which might have been a garage at one time. It stood in back of another shack, beside and about ten feet below the railroad tracks and also in the glide path of LaGuardia airport.

We went inside. There were patches of decayed linoleum on the floor and a butane gas heater burning in the living room. On the wall hung an old picture of the Sacred Heart, plus some framed patriotic pictures cut from the *Daily News* color section many years ago. The doorway into Willy's room had no door. A tattered blanket was nailed to the top of the doorway to serve as a door. Willy looked up. He was sitting on the edge of his bed, pulling on socks and sneakers. He was a nice-looking young man, 21 years old.

We took him out to the car in handcuffs, and in the car Detective Carlson kept telling him what trouble he was in. He could get seven to 15 years. Selling drugs was a Class C felony. Willy previously had been on heroin, but now he was in a methadone program. He didn't say anything. He just stared out the window with his hands handcuffed behind his back, and every once in a while Detective Carlson would say, "Your lawyer will know what trouble you're in; he'll tell you what to do. We can do a lot for you."

Willy would nod, and then turn and look out the window again. He looked terribly hurt.

This time, when we got back to the station house, all sorts of confiscated drugs lay on the table. There were also various pipes for smoking marijuana, some of them home-made.

We went back out to Queensborough College and made more arrests. I got the impression we could have gone on making arrests all day, or even all week. There were that many young people buying and selling drugs.

Two nights later we cruised the streets of the upper West

Side, Detective Conlon in one car, the backpup team in the trailing car. Detective Conlon wore a body-set transmitter. The transmitter was the size of a cigarette package and was tucked into the center of her bra. The aerial was a wire that ran down inside her sleeve. The receiver was attached to a tape recorder that lay on the lap of Patrolman Martin Hogan in the front seat.

Detective Conlon, accompanied by an informant named John, a burglar with two pending cases over his head, visited a number of bars, trying to make a narcotics connection. Normally, in bars where narcotics were sold, lookouts were stationed outside. It was the job of the lookouts to smell cop.

So we could not keep any of the places she entered under observation. We cruised, relying on the body set to tell us where she was, and that she was safe.

We heard her say, "I'm going to the bar at Broadway and 93rd Street."

Then we heard some mumbled conversation surrounded by dim music. A few minutes later we heard her loud and clear in the street. "There's nobody in there. I'm going to the Parkview Hotel on West 96th."

We drove to this hotel, and circled the block. From the radio receiver on Patrolman Hogan's lap we heard nothing. After about ten minutes we began to get extremely nervous. We drove by the hotel but did not see Kathy's car. Now we began searching in an ever-widening circle, trying to pick up signals from her body set. There was no way we could contact her. She could transmit, but not receive, and we couldn't have tried to contact her anyway—suppose she was in conversation with a narcotics dealer at the very moment one of us called, "Detective Conlon, come in please."

The upper West Side was replete with dead areas—atmospheric voids in which radio signals, or at least our radio signals, did not exist.

Round and round we drove. A tense silence filled the car.

Suddenly we heard Kathy's voice. It was weak and distant. Patrolman Hogan said, "Try the Rey Noble."

As we came down Columbus Avenue, we saw Kathy getting out of her car. Patrolman Hogan sighed. The driver, Patrolman Bob Kotraba, muttered, "She's so little. It would be so easy to kill her, and these guys don't care about the consequences. They're all on coke anyway. They could do it in a bar in front of other people. They could hustle her back into the kitchen and throttle her and stuff her in a garbage can. The kitchen is where all the junk is being sold anyway."

The bar called the Rey Noble was run by a middle-level narcotics dealer known as Bert. Detective Conlon had made buys in there before. Now Patrolman Kotraba circled the block, and as we came out onto Columbus Avenue at 78th Street, he drove straight across the street and down the ramp into the driveway behind the Museum of Natural History. There we parked and waited. We were about 100 yards from the Rey Noble and out of sight. Kathy's transmitter was working perfectly. We could hear her voice, and we could hear loud music in the background.

The night was dark and the car was cold. From time to time Patrolman Kotraba started the engine to get some heat up.

A door into the basement of the museum opened. Someone peered out at us. A little later, two people carrying briefcases walked up the ramp to the street past us. They gazed in at us, but no one questioned us, and they did not stop. One or another of these people might phone the police, and we could have a radio car down on top of us any minute. That could blow Kathy's cover in the bar. However, no radio car ever turned up.

We waited in that driveway nearly three hours in the cold winter night. Across the street we heard Kathy sipping gin and orange juice. She was pretending to be the wife of a dealer who was in jail; she was carrying on his business for him. We had to reconstruct what was said to her, for although Kathy spoke loud and clear, wanting her transmitter to pick up every word, those she talked to tended to mumble, and the music drowned them out. At one point someone must have tried to fondle her, for we heard her say decisively, "I'm faithful to my old man. I'm here strictly on business. I never mix business with pleasure."

She was trying to fight off hands and still make a buy. Later she got into conversation with the owner, Bert. We heard Kathy say, "Nothing here? I don't believe it."

The longer she stayed, the more dangerous it got. All of

us were aching for her to come out of there. We began to discuss one of us going in after her.

A long time passed during which all we heard was music, and the noise of glasses. It occurred to us that one of those hands fondling her might have found her transmitter, or her gun. It would have been easy enough to clamp a hand over her mouth, rip the transmitter out of her bosom, and lay it on the bar where it would continue to pick up all of the normal bar noises, while Detective Kathleen Conlon was disposed of elsewhere.

Suddenly the bar noises stopped, and we heard Kathy's voice in the street, "I'm getting back into my car, I'll meet you at 88th Street and Riverside."

This was the rendezvous point for jobs in that area.

We pulled into the curb there behind Kathy's car. She got out and sat with us. She had been able to buy nothing.

It was past midnight when she drove me home. She was not off duty yet, for she had to return the body set to Internal Affairs headquarters in Brooklyn before going home herself. The Police Department did not have all the equipment in the world. There was only one body set in the entire Department, and Internal Affairs owned it. She—or any other narcotics undercover agent—could borrow it only on special occasions; that is, especially dangerous occasions.

Detective Conlon's two principal quarries in that neighborhood were Bert, owner of the Rey Noble, and a South American known as Juan, from whom she had once bought $600 worth of cocaine. After that first buy, Kathy had fallen ill for several days, and when she went back into the area to make a buy on Juan, she could no longer find him. For days she kept asking for him, but everyone seemed to think Juan had gone back to South America. As for Bert, he controlled the flow of narcotics in and out of his bar. However, the actual selling was done by his bartender, a black man named George. Bert himself was a white man, apparently Jewish, about 40 years old.

Several days later, Kathy went back into the Rey Noble. She was wearing raspberry-striped pants and a dark-brown rabbit's-fur coat. It was about 4:30 in the afternoon.

When Kathy came out, she had $60 worth of marijuana in a white envelope which she had just bought from

George, the barman. She said, "Bert is there. The shipment has come in."

While buying the marijuana, Kathy had said, "I'd really like to buy some cocaine. Juan always supplied me with cocaine but I never can find the guy."

George said, "Well, he's back. I just saw him yesterday."

Kathy said, "Well, if you see him, tell him I'm looking for him and that I'll come back later."

Now we were parked on Riverside Drive in the sunlight, while Kathy did her paper work. The evidence was sealed and signed. She noted that she had bought it from a male Negro, six feet two inches tall, dressed in a blue shirt and blue dungarees, who went by the name of George.

Pen in hand, Detective Conlon remarked, "He was wearing the same clothes the last time I bought off him. I wish he'd buy some new clothes."

Since Juan was back in the city, we went looking for him. There was a once-handsome apartment building on 89th Street between Riverside Drive and West End Avenue which had been taken over by the Welfare Department and was filled with welfare families. Juan had lived there at one time, or so Kathy had been told.

I went into the building with the back-up team ahead of Detective Conlon. We rode the elevator as far as the fourth floor, and then walked the rest of the way up. Juan's apartment was on the seventh floor, just below the roof. We went up past it and hid in the stairwell between the seventh floor and the roof.

Presently the elevator door opened, and we heard Kathy Conlon, accompanied by her informant, John, rap on the door to Juan's apartment. The rest of us waited crouched in the stairwell.

But nothing happened. She rang the bell, then banged on the door a few times. A moment later we saw her face, grinning, peering up the stairwell at us. She shrugged, and with that all our guns went back into the holsters. That was the first I realized that everybody, not just me, had had a gun ready.

Detective Conlon went down in the elevator with her informant, came out into the street, got into her car, and drove away. We three went over the rooftop into the next building and downstairs from there. We didn't want anybody to notice so much traffic coming out of the same doorway. Perhaps Juan would be back later. We didn't want to scare him off. The adjoining building smelled even worse than the one we had been in. People apparently urinated in the hallways in these buildings, and the ceiling of the tiny elevator was covered with grease, as if someone had been cooking in there.

Back we went to the Rey Noble. There was a lookout in the doorway, and so we in the back-up car drove right on past. Kathy parked and went in. We circled the block until we saw that she had come out again and driven away.

Back at the rendezvous site on Riverside Drive, Detective Conlon said, "The Rey Noble was really jumping this time. But still no Juan." Then she said, "Bert is the one I would really like to nail, but I can't get close to him. Everybody deals for Bert, but Bert doesn't deal for himself."

Patrolman Hogan said, "The one I would really like to get is Juan."

Patrolman Kotraba said, "We'll get him. We'll get him on Easter Sunday. He'll be standing on the street corner with an Easter basket, and he'll be eating a chocolate bunny."

Patrolman Hogan said, "That's the type of collar I like to make."

Detective Conlon now drove off toward the laboratory with the marijuana she had bought from the barman. The barman now could be arrested; and probably the bar itself, as a result of repeated narcotics arrests in there, could be closed.

We watched Kathy drive off. Patrolman Kotraba said, "The time when sweat really comes out on your brow is when she goes into somebody's apartment. One time there was one of us on the roof, and one of us in the stairwell. We gave her three minutes there, and then we began to get really nervous and started to rush the door. As we got close to the door, we could hear her inside chatting normally. So we did nothing, and presently she came out and walked away. But if they ever made her for a cop, even now in daytime, they'd be liable to kill her on the spot and worry about what to do with her body afterwards."

Detective Conlon was under increasing pressure to find and arrest Juan. There was a $600 buy outstanding on him.

That was a lot of money wasted. Orders were to find him and arrest him.

So she kept going back into the same neighborhoods on the upper West Side: "Have you seen Juan?"

At last she found him in a coffee shop. She got him in a corner and bought $300 worth of cocaine from him. Juan had his back to the plate-glass window. In the street Kathy saw Patrolman Kotraba mouthing the words, "Is that Juan?" Almost imperceptibly, Detective Conlon nodded her head, Yes.

Juan was allowed to walk some distance down the street before he found a plainclothes patrolman on either side of him. When they told him he was under arrest, Juan said, "That girl, she mistaken. I not Juan."

So Juan had connected Kathy Conlon to his arrest. Therefore Kathy Conlon was The Man. Her cover was blown as far as Juan was concerned, and possibly now it would be widely blown all over the upper West Side.

Juan was booked and arraigned, made bail, and was out on the street again. The next morning Kathy went looking for him to make another buy. She was convinced that she could convince Juan that she was not The Man at all. Her confidence in her ability as an actress was supreme. But she couldn't find him.

After the Rey Noble was closed down, its windows boarded up, Bert simply opened another club elsewhere. Kathy Conlon went looking for this club. She found it some nights later at Broadway and 120th Street. As she waited outside for her back-up team, three teen-agers stopped to ask her in Spanish what her price was.

"You're only a kid," said Detective Conlon. "You're too young for sex. Besides, I'm waiting here for my husband."

One kid said, "Too bad." Eyeing her up and down, all three youngsters strolled away.

After advising her back-up team of her plans, she walked up the staircase, and on the first floor attempted to enter Bert's new club. At the top of the staircase was a landing, and as Detective Conlon stepped onto it a steel grating slammed shut behind her. Ahead was a steel door. She was trapped. She rang the bell. She could smell marijuana smoke. There was a cutout in the wall with a mirror in it, and through the mirror she could see a card table inside. On the card table were packets of tinfoil—cocaine, she supposed.

But Bert and his bouncer came out onto the landing.

"You're in more trouble than you know," said Bert. To his bouncer Bert said, "I know she's The Man."

Detective Kathleen Conlon thought, I must be burned.

She laughed and said, "If I was The Man, would I be here?"

She showed no panic.

Bert looked puzzled.

Detective Kathleen Conlon grinned at him, but she was thinking, Bert is known to have had people killed.

After a moment, Bert said, "I want your address and telephone number. I want to check you out."

"Are you kidding me?" said Detective Kathleen Conlon, and casually, showing no sign of panic, she talked her way out through the gate.

Later I asked her, "Why did he let you go?"

She said, "It didn't surprise me. Whenever Bert would have people thrown out of his place, they would never do the dirty work in the bar itself. They would drag somebody out, take them up the block, and beat the living daylights out of them. I had seen this happen. I had seen his boys at work. He himself would escort them out, but once outside, someone would be waiting who either took the customer for a ride, or for a walk. The number was done to him on the outside. Now he had a new club, and he didn't want it raided. He didn't want any problems at all unless he was calling the shots. And he looked at me and he wasn't sure, so he let me go. I took him by surprise, and I got outside before he could decide to do anything awful."

One day I asked her about her life. She was 29 years old, and lived with her mother in a private house in a residential neighborhood. Her mother was ill with diabetes, and it was Kathleen Conlon, detective third grade, who did the cooking, the gardening, who fixed the roof when it needed fixing. She had had two years at Baruch College, and she would like to have got a degree; but how could she go back to any college, she asked herself, when tomorrow or next week she might be sent into that very place to make buys?

She loved to dance, but didn't dare go into clubs with a boyfriend. Suppose she was sent into that club to make buys?

She was a vivacious girl, but very serious underneath. She hated drugs, all drugs. She hated marijuana almost as much as heroin, and believed that kids who started on the one soon graduated to the other. She was a practicing Catholic, believed in discipline, believed in love and marriage, in children and a house in the suburbs. Maybe some day . . .

But in the meantime she was a cop, and she loved being a cop. She had recently testified in Washington before the Select Committee on Crime of the House of Representatives on the subject of drugs in the schools. She appeared wearing a hood over her head, and a gun stuck into her belt where the shocked congressmen could see it.

Once she talked to me about the new policy in the Narcotics Division. She and the other undercover agents had been told to concentrate on major buys. They were to leave the street dealers pretty much alone, and go looking for people who would sell them half loads and bundles. "The higher up the ladder you go, the easier the burn," Detective Conlon said. "Because the higher up you go, the fewer people this guy sells to. So it's easier for him to narrow it down to you. Someone sooner or later is going to get hurt."

Now when she went out on buys another undercover sometimes went with her. The second undercover sometimes carried a shotgun in plain view. "It's very common when you're dealing at that level," said Detective Conlon. "You bring your heat along, because you're carrying a lot of money. That's just what they say on the street: 'I see you've got your heat.' "

Previously, her biggest buy had been the $600 one, and most times she operated with $100 or less in her handbag along with her gun. But now she was involved in buys of many thousands of dollars. Sometimes there was a helicopter coverage, but it was impossible to wear transmitting devices because, as she put it, "When you're making a buy this heavy, they'll search you. You can't carry your shield in case you are padded down. You can carry your gun. To find a gun means nothing when you're dealing with buys of eight or nine thousand dollars or better. It's getting pretty hairy."

One day she ran into Bert in a coffee shop outside Manhattan Criminal Court. He was with another policeman who had arrested him. In a few minutes he would go before the judge, post bail, and then he'd be out on the street again. Detective Kathleen Conlon spied him, and attempted to duck out of sight, but too late. Bert saw her.

"I know she's The Man," said Bert to the cop he was with.

Kathy told me that she was working in Queens these days, but soon she would go up onto the West Side again, and she would go to see Bert. She would convince Bert that she was not The Man after all, and eventually she would make a big buy off him. She said, "I would like to push him and push him for all it's worth, and push him to the breaking point. Then, when he goes to do something, nail him. And nail him right. He's one of the names on my hate list. He's one of the guys who must do time."

6 / The Stake-out Squad

The small liquor store owned by an old man and his ailing wife had been stuck up 13 times. One of the armed robbers, before looting the place, had amused himself by holding a gun to the back of the old man's head and remarking, "If you turn your head, you're dead." Another had sat on top of the old man, holding a bottle over his head, promising to bash his brains out if he uttered a sound. The old man had had guns rammed into him, he had been poked with switchblade knives and slashed at with a machete— before giving up his cash. Once he and his wife were led into the store's small bathroom at gunpoint, where the gunman had promised to kill them. But this was just a joke, and after cleaning out the cash register, the gunman and his accomplice left.

This small liquor store was in the Jamaica section of Queens and the desperate owner now placed an ad in *The New York Times* addressed to Mayor Lindsay. The ad outlined some of the preceding details and perhaps exaggerated a little. But the Mayor saw the ad and so did the Police Commissioner, then Howard Leary, who ordered an investigation. Presently it was decided to give stake-out coverage to this liquor store.

January 1969. The stake-out unit, forty men, four sergeants and one lieutenant, was at that time only eight months old.

The normal procedure was followed; a sergeant came to survey the store. He found that there was a rear stockroom in which two patrolmen could hide. With a hole cut in the wall and covered by a see-through mirror, the stake-out team would be able to watch the whole store from one spot. Fields of possible fire were plotted. A transmitter was placed near the cash register so that the two patrolmen hiding in the back could hear what was going on.

If there had been no rear stockroom in which to secrete the two patrolmen, there would have been no stake-out; if potential fields of fire had promised to involve too many customers or pedestrians in the street, there would have been no stake-out. The transmitter was necessary because some armed robbers would speak so softly and hide their weapons so well that a robbery could take place with literally no one knowing about it but the man handing over the money and the robber.

Each stake-out was given a code number. This one was No. 51Q. It began at 4:00 P.M. on February 3. Stake-outs were only manned during business hours, and each two-man team worked five straight hours without a break. One man or the other was always peering through the one-way mirror. He was called the "man on point." The second man was the back-up man. They switched jobs every 30 minutes, for to be on point demanded absolute concentration. The man on point must be ready to step out at any moment. He must know exactly who was in the store at all times and where each person was standing. He must determine if any two were known to each other. He must guess whether or not two apparent customers were instead partners in a robbery that was about to take place.

Stake-out men wore their patrolman's uniform cap and a bullet-proof vest, with the word "POLICE" emblazoned in three-inch yellow letters across both the hips and shoulders. Each team each day was delivered to each stake-out plant in an unmarked police car, and once inside the stake-out plant they were sequestered in the back room there; they had no latitude whatsoever until such time as they stepped forward to interrupt a robbery in progress. They could not move from that room.

The old man and his sick wife, owners of the liquor store that was stake-out No. 51Q, were told to behave normally at all times; to forget that two heavily armed patrolmen were hiding in the back of their store; to make no sign of any kind if and when robbers did appear.

This particular stake-out ended after only three days. Some of them went on for months. At 7:00 P.M. on February 6, a man came into the store and asked the owner for a half pint of Park and Tilford Scotch. The old man, lifting the bottle down from the shelf, turned back into the muzzle of a white metal automatic. A second man now entered the store, ran behind the counter, and began scooping money out of the cash register. The first man had his gun at the owner's head and he forced him to the wall. "If you turn around, I'll blow your brains out," he said. Reaching down, he jerked the owner's wallet out of his right rear pocket.

Secreted in the stockroom, the two stake-out men felt they could not move while that gun was at the owner's head. There were general guidelines for stake-out work— the safety of innocent people was paramount—but no one went into a stake-out with the important answers. The definitive confrontation was new each time. The men in the back room had to decide each time when and how to step out into the light of the store.

Now the first gunman was in front of the counter and the second behind the counter. This seemed the best moment the two patrolmen were likely to get, so they sprang out of the darkness with service revolvers drawn, shouting, "Police. Don't move, drop your gun." Most gunmen at such an instant would whirl to face the patrolmen. "This is the classic pattern," admitted Lieutenant James Brady, the commanding officer of the stake-out unit. "The guy turns with his gun pointed at us. If he does this, the guy is dead. My men are experts. If you run into my men, you don't have a chance."

However, these two men dropped to the floor and, concealed by the counter, began to crawl out of the store. Nearing the door, the first gunman jumped to his feet to aim his gun at one of the patrolmen. The patrolman shot him. Later he was arrested outside, badly wounded. The second gunman, unhurt, was handcuffed while lying on the floor behind the counter. The old man who owned the store, his eyes filled with tears of rage or fear or relief or whatever it was, ran over and began kicking the gunman in the side.

From May 1968 to midwinter 1972, there were 212 requests by store owners through their local precincts for stake-out coverage. Some requests were rejected because the site was wrong: The physical configuration did not lend itself to a stake-out, or it was too dangerous to outsiders. Lieutenant Brady said, "We set up a highly dangerous situation each time, a potential gun battle." Some were rejected in favor of other stores which had been robbed more frequently, or more recently. If the choice were between a site robbed six times in the last two years and a site robbed three times in the last month, stake-out coverage would go to the second.

And so only 182 of these requests were implemented. The results: 24 armed robbers killed, 19 wounded, 53 arrested. Two of the gunmen, before being killed, managed to fire at the policemen, striking them in the vest, and afterward one of the patrolmen kept the blunted bullet on his dresser, next to his brush and comb.

That winter alone, a total of seven robbers entered five staked-out stores. Six of them were killed and the seventh captured. There were two separate attempts to hold up the same store, Fannie Farmer's on 42nd Street, next to Grand Central Station. The first attempted robbery occurred on January 26; the two gunmen were killed. On February 18, in another robbery, a third was killed. Candy stores were favorites with stickup men because usually they were manned by one 65-year-old woman and/or one 16-year-old girl. For the same reason, candy stores were also a favorite of the Stake-out Squad.

Another favorite target of stickup men was finance companies. One on 32nd Street, off Sixth Avenue, had been robbed five times in seven months. The first gunman robbed it three times, which, for him, turned out to be one too many. Because the third time the stake-out unit was there and when the gunman put his cocked weapon to the head of a cashier, a stake-out patrolman fired through the one-way mirror and shot him dead. When the finance company was robbed again, shortly after, the Stake-out Squad was put back in, and soon a fifth robbery was attempted. This gunman was captured alive.

"We do robbery work," said Lieutenant Brady, "and that's all we do. There are 42,000 in-premises armed robberies a year. One out of every 2000 robbers bumps into us. I realize that we are controverisal with all these killings, but we deal with a particular type of criminal. They come to us; no one goes out looking for them. No one pulls them in there. These people are not victims; they are the aggressor. Most times it is the same guy or team robbing the same place again and again. We have to get them; these are people who terrify, beat, pistol-whip store owners. One of them once put a rifle barrel inside a storekeeper's mouth, and that gunman is dead now. If a gunman is going to kill a storekeeper or if innocent people are involved, we don't have much choice. You have to put him out of the picture. You have to neutralize the guy, and to neutralize him you have to hit him in the heart or the brain. If there was a large area in the shoulder that would neutralize him, we would shoot him there, but there is no such area. So we shoot for dead center. We capture as many as we can. If an armed man runs, even though maybe he plans to turn and shoot, my men have orders to lower their guns to shoot him in the upper leg or backside. We don't shoot men with knives, or men who have already put their guns away, or who surrender."

Before taking command of the Stake-out Squad, Lieutenant Brady worked for more than ten years in Police Emergency Service, rescuing people trapped in elevators, bringing oxygen to cardiac victims.

"My men all carry service revolvers of course, but their primary weapon usually is a shotgun, loaded with one-ounce slugs. If a gunman is hit with that, it is devastating. He's completely disoriented. We have never accidentally shot a bystander. It would be better if we didn't have to shoot; but as soon as we step out, these gunmen normally point their guns right at us and so we must shoot. We don't have the luxury of waiting to see whether they intend to shoot at us or not. It's a problem. We had a lieutenant come here from Los Angeles, and a captain from Philadelphia. There are stake-out units in both places. Both these men said to me, 'Do you have this problem too?'

"No one gets killed because he stole money from a cash register, but because he menaced one or more innocent persons with a deadly weapon and the next time—or even this time—he may kill a shopkeeper or a customer. He is a potential killer. I have surveyed the records of 13 of the most recent gunmen we have run into and found that they had previously been arrested a total of 142 times."

An ordinary New York City policeman was obliged to practice his shooting twice a year. Members of the stake-out unit practiced once a month, and they must score "expert" with both hands. In their training, combat shooting was stressed. Their targets were much smaller than normal and they were advised to practice dry firing at home every day.

There were only five members of the Police Department rated as expert shots. Four were in the Stake-out Squad. One of these was second in the National Championships. Three were in the Olympic tryouts. One patrolman in a recent Washington, D.C., tournament, shot the only perfect 1,200 score ever shot.

Their average age was 29, and in general they were conservative, religious, short-sideburn-type men. They tended to be devoted to hunting when off duty or on vacation. They were the type of men who could sit all day in a tree waiting for a deer.

Lieutenant Brady, when selecting new men, tended to choose hunters: "They have the patience and judgment—the infinite patience—that the job requires."

The names of members of stake-out teams were never revealed, even after a shoot-out that brought press and cameras to the scene. And the Stake-out Squad had received no notoriety whatever, making them, perhaps, less of a deterrent to stickup men than they should have been. However, some word did get around. One stickup man, arrested by detectives, recently said, "I can tell you're not from the Stake-out Squad. If you were, I'd be dead."

In addition to rigorous selection, followed by rigorous training with guns, stake-out men had to attend seminars twice a year where they studied the full ramifications of their specialized job, principally the rights and restrictions of a police officer as to the use of deadly force. During the summer seminar they sat around a fire at night at the Police Department's outdoor range near Orchard Beach. They ate charcoal-broiled steaks and aired their gripes, and if any man was troubled by having had to kill—one patrolman had killed six gunmen, another five—it should have come out here, but it never did. Apparently these men had no emotional problems. One stake-out sergeant brought into the unit his young patrolman son.

Stake-out men were not allowed to use unauthorized guns. Lieutenant Brady told them, "If you kill a gunman with an unauthorized gun, no one is going to make too much of it, but if a shot goes wild and you kill Mary Jones, 42, with seven children, we don't want to have to explain an unauthorized gun too."

On the whole, the Stake-out Squad did not go into ghetto areas. One day a request came in from Captain William Bracey, commanding officer of Harlem's 32nd Precinct. Lieutenant Brady refused the job, saying, "If we kill somebody there you might end up with a public disorder of some kind." Captain Bracey, who was black, insisted, saying, "We have good people in this precinct and they're entitled to police protection too."

So the stake-out plant was maintained in Harlem for a month, during which time nothing happened. Captain Brady theorized that word had spread through the community and no stickup man went near that particular store, or for that matter, any other store in the neighborhood.

Sometimes a stake-out team was composed of three men, not two, especially in certain vast stores. Three-man teams operated in supermarkets where there were normally 150 customers on hand. In stores like this they sometimes installed a partition or hung a curtain to hide behind.

"The important thing," Stake-out Sergeant Pete Milo said, "is that we are the ones who decide when to start the shooting, not the hoods. Because they don't care who they shoot.

"We have made a science of stake-outs," he added. "Our

expertise is matched nowhere else in the Police Department." And he began to talk of the Air Host Motel, near Kennedy Airport, which had had a rash of stickups. One occurred while two off-duty patrolmen were moonlighting as clerical help inside the office. These were real cops, not security guards, but the gunmen disarmed both of them, escaping with two extra guns as well as the loot.

Shortly after this, detectives from the 103rd Precinct received a tip that an adjacent motel would be robbed that night. They staked the motel out. They did it their way. The result was that some 20 shots were fired; one gunman was killed, but the other three escaped, with the money. The detectives had had one man inside the motel posing as a clerk, and the rest hidden outside. "This probably seemed very sophisticated to them," said Milo. "We would never have permitted that kind of a deployment. Naturally their inside detective wound up as a hostage in the middle of the holdup, the outside detectives didn't find out soon enough that a holdup was even taking place, and then they couldn't shoot until their inside man was clear."

And so at last a stake-out team was assigned to the Air Host Motel. Within three months, there were two more attempted robberies there. During the first of these the lone gunman fired two shots at the patrolmen, who then shot him four times. He made it outside and fell dead on the ground near the right rear wheel of his stolen car.

The next time, two gunmen entered, one of them carrying a loaded rifle which was at first concealed by a coat over his arm. The second man, without provocation, jumped behind the counter and punched the telephone operator in the middle of his glasses. Blood flowed. The two stickup men then forced the cashier and the telephone operator to the floor behind the counter, and began kicking them. At this point the two hidden patrolmen stepped forth.

"Police. Don't move, drop your guns."

The rifleman spun in their direction, and both patrolmen opened fire with shotguns. Both gunmen ran toward the door, but fell to the floor in the hallway. The patrolmen's shotguns were empty. The patrolman who had been on point came forward with his service revolver in one hand and his back-up Colt automatic in the other. The gunmen were attempting to regain their feet; the rifle was lifted toward the patrolmen. The second gunman thrust his hand into his coat as if searching for a revolver. The man on point discharged six rounds from his service revolver and eight from his automatic, then stooped to retrieve the rifle which lay near one gunman, and the opened knife near the other.

All of the operations of the Stake-out Squad took place in full view of innocent witnesses, often dozens of them. Each confrontation was over in a few seconds, but each was subject to terrific review. Hours and even days were spent documenting them.

Lieutenant Brady, who had disarmed a number of criminal and psychotic individuals but never shot anyone, responded to the scene of each incident. Usually Sergeant Milo, who had never shot anyone, did too. So did Chief Arthur Hill, commanding officer of the Special Operations Division, whose command included the Stake-out Unit, and so did a dozen or so superior officers and detectives. A district attorney was always called in, and testimony from civilian witnesses was taken at great length. There had never been a charge of unnecessary force and/or unnecessary gun fire against any member of the Stake-out Squad.

Of course some confrontations ended differently. A stake-out unit was on duty at the Pitkin Avenue A&P, in Brooklyn. It was three in the afternoon and the supermarket was full of shoppers, mostly housewives, when in sauntered a stickup man. He walked straight up to the checkout counter where stood the manager of the store and said, "You know what I want, give it to me." Indeed the manager did know what he wanted, because this chap had already robbed that same store seven times, always armed with a gun. He was why the stake-out team was there. This time he showed no gun, but when he patted the bulge in his coat, the manager handed over the money. The robber thanked him, nodded, and started out of the store, with the two stake-out men walking swiftly behind him. In the street they grabbed him, disarmed him, took the stolen money out of his pocket, and charged him with first-degree robbery. Later he was charged with having committed two other robberies elsewhere in Brooklyn, making a minimum of nine that could be documented, by this one man.

Nor was this such an isolated case. Another stake-out team was secreted in the back of Praisner's Drug Store in Brooklyn, when a man walked up to the prescription counter and said to the owner, "Okay, Doc, give me the stuff." The owner cried out, "Oh, no, not again," and slowly backed away from the intruder. Then he screamed, "That's him!"

As the two patrolmen leaped from hiding, guns drawn, the robber ran, only to be tackled and handcuffed near the door. However, when the patrolmen searched him, they found that he was carrying no weapon whatsoever. It was his eighth robbery of the same drug store, and perhaps he had decided, as a lark, to knock the store off this time with words alone. If so, this decision probably saved his life. Since no weapon was showing, the stake-out team could afford themselves the rare luxury of tackling a robber instead of having to shoot him.

Every man in the unit knew what the stakes were. One of them once killed two gunmen with two shots. The proprietor of the store was pinned between the two gunmen, a gun to his head, when the patrolman stepped forth. Three shots rang out. The first bullet missed the patrolman. The second struck one gunman in the head. The third struck the second gunman in the heart. This was at 3:05 in the afternoon, in a liquor store in Queens. The owner, still alive after being caught in the middle of a shoot-out, broke open a bottle from his shelf and took a long drink. "I will never be sober again," the owner said.

7 / Durk and the Model Precinct

Finally Murphy realized that Durk wouldn't simply go away. Durk would have to be dealt with.

It always seemed to me that Murphy was not really interested in individuals, but rather in concepts. Murphy declined to meet other human beings on any sort of an emotional level. If he had an antipathy to Durk, then, this was why: Durk was trying to force Murphy to meet him on even terms, human being to human being, and Murphy met no one this way except perhaps members of his immediate family.

Instead, Murphy often seemed to me a kind of Thomas Aquinas of the police departments of our times. Murphy was as cool and detached as a philosopher. He would have been happier in a medieval cloister dealing ideas off the deck at the rate of one card a day, formulating an entire system to send down through the police forces of the ages.

It never occurred to him to fit one of his ideas to Durk, or Durk to one of his ideas. The conjunction, when it happened, would occur almost by accident.

Murphy never claimed that all the ideas he was currently floating through the building were purely his. In the same way that Aquinas had built upon a system originally formulated by Aristotle, Murphy now built upon previous police ideas. It was his conceit that many ideas, some old, some new, could be integrated into a new system which would be purely his.

For instance, there was the concept of the "residential policeman." Standard police theory had always preached that no policeman should serve in his own neighborhood, for a policeman was supposed to be a dispassionate dispenser of justice, and how could he be dispassionate when coping with friends and neighbors? However, the British had used the resident constable idea in a number of ways, and it had worked.

The Police Commissioner determined to install New York's first residential policeman in some cop's own neighborhood somewhere in the city, but which cop and where?

He suggested "C" precincts (low-crime precincts) should be considered for the experimental period, and he wanted the resident cop, whoever he might be, to volunteer. He should be an experienced, high-quality patrolman, and a college graduate. His home would become the "sector office." He would wear his uniform nearly all the time. He would get to know everybody in his neighborhood. He would be their cop. Some kind of insignia identifying him as the residential policeman should be provided.

The Police Commissioner one weekend at home scribbled a brief outline of these ideas and sent them to Inspector Henry Morse, commanding officer of the Planning Division. Morse was to drop in for a chat and after that he was to staff the project.

A second memo was afloat on the subject of the Model Precinct. It was Murphy's notion that the best way to change the attitudes of, and establish higher standards of productivity for, more than 30,000 policemen would be to concentrate on one or a limited number of units at a time. Why not pick out one precinct and load it with the best young patrolmen, the best superior officers, and all the new ideas, and perhaps lift it so high above all other precincts that the entire Department would suddenly be striving to reach that same level? Especially Murphy wanted a model precinct that would serve as a kind of monastery for new recruits—a place that would isolate them from existing evil influences within the Department while they learned their jobs.

Murphy had sent around a memo early in December. It asked questions. Should we begin with one or more precincts? If more, how many more? When should we begin? Should we announce our plans or not? If we announce, when? Before the next Knapp hearings? During the next Knapp hearings? After the next Knapp hearings?

If the concept were to be tried, it should start with the careful selection of the captain or deputy inspector who would command the model precinct. He would be allowed a short period to learn about the precinct and its personnel, and once he knew which men he wanted to get rid of, these would be transferred out and replaced with handpicked people. Obviously only 20 to 25 percent of the precinct complement at a time could be transferred out, for the streets could not be left to the protection entirely of rookies. However, close to a total turnover could be accomplished within a few months.

Up in the Fifth Division Inspector Bonacum had been begging for permission to rid the precincts of his division of what he referred to as "superior officers with negative backgrounds." Murphy now suggested that Inspector Bonacum's enthusiasm, and his desire to improve his division, merited the choice of one of his precincts—perhaps the 24th—as the first model precinct.

Again Inspector Morse was advised, "Please staff this, and report to me in two weeks' time."

Police Commissioner Murphy did not invent the idea of a model precinct; versions had been tried before. One such occurred during the last four months of 1954, when Frank Adams was commissioner, and it involved the 25th Precinct in Harlem, diagonally across the island from the 24th. That experiment had had a less grandiose name. They called it Operation 25. At 8 A.M. on August 31, the commanding officer had turned out 27 men for foot and radio car patrol. The following day at the same hour, 99 men were turned out. Operation 25 had begun.

Previously the precinct had been divided into 55 foot posts, which were, in the main, irregular—a typical one being four blocks north and south on an avenue and one-half block east and west on intersecting streets, an average of about ten blocks. But since only about 15 foot patrolmen were available on each tour, each inevitably was responsible for more than one post. But once Operation 25 had begun, all posts were laid out in grid fashion in straight lines. Now the average patrolman—and there was one to each post—could see his entire post, or nearly his entire post, at one time.

The 25th Precinct complement was 206 men on August 31. For Operation 25, 276 more were thrown in there, 252 of them probationary patrolmen fresh out of the Police Academy. All other units which covered the 25th Precinct also were increased: Emergency Service, Narcotics, Traffic, Juvenile Aid Bureau. Some cops were assigned to a fourth platoon which went on duty at 6 P.M. and worked until 2 A.M.—a new concept then, giving double coverage to high-crime hours. Supervision was increased. There were many more sergeants, many more lieutenants, even extra captains.

Commissioner Adams later published a booklet about Operation 25, which called it an unqualified success. During the four months that the experiment lasted, major crime diminished by 55 percent.

At midnight December 31, 1954, Operation 25 came to an end. Statisticians went to work on the results, and Commissioner Adams went to see the Mayor to request more manpower. Inside five months the Mayor had approved the expansion of the Police Department by 1663 new cops.

Meanwhile the 25th Precinct reverted to its former complement. And crime there reverted to its former patterns.

Cynics, of which the Police Department was so full, noted two facts: (1) Any special effort that chased criminals out of one precinct merely chased them into the adjoining precincts, and (2) The Police Department tended to call every experiment a success. "If we want it to be a success, we simply announce it as a success, and that makes it a success," a veteran sergeant explained to me one day.

So Commissioner Adams 17 years ago had tried much of what Commissioner Murphy proposed now: increased supervision, the addition of presumably uncorrupted and idealistic recruits, a more careful and accurate deployment of men. But Murphy planned to add much more: a residential patrolman; a policewoman sergeant as station house supervisor, neighborhood police teams in each sector, increased use of auxiliary policemen who hopefully would be integrated into the precinct structure to an extent never before attempted, and, as the *pièce de résistance*, Sergeant David Durk as coordinator of all the neighborhood police teams.

Some of these ideas Murphy had envisioned from the start, others developed at high-level conferences, and the insertion of Durk was the brainstorm of yours truly, for Murphy still didn't know what to do with Durk, and Durk was still hoping for rank and responsibility that Murphy had no intention of giving him. I saw the installation of Durk in the model precinct as a possible solution that would suit both of them. Durk would be thrown once more into the limelight, which he would not disdain, and Murphy would seem to be illuminating the project with the brightest beacon in the Police Department. Then, if Durk did well, the rank and responsibility that he coveted would be forthcoming. Murphy would have no choice but to accord them.

The trouble would be to sell the idea to both sides.

I sent a memo about Durk to the Police Commissioner, but no answer came back.

Durk's speech to the Knapp Commission ending with his own tears apparently had not impressed Murphy at all. Nor did it impress Murphy when the *New York Post* ran a transcript of the speech. I never heard one word of praise for Durk by Murphy at that time, even in private. However, nine days after the speech *The New York Times* printed excerpts on its Op. Ed. page. Murphy, reading Durk there, at last was impressed.

When he told me so, I said carefully, "What impressed me most was that Durk said, 'I'm a cop, and I intend to remain a cop.' That's a hell of a commitment."

Murphy said, "Right." Then he added, "I'm really enthusiastic about your idea to put Durk in the model precinct. We can invent a new position for him, call him a personnel sergeant or something. We could make him into a kind of super sergeant. He could be responsible for seeing to it that there was no corruption in that precinct. It's an idea with a lot of possibilities."

Now to sell the idea to Durk.

I talked it over with him that night in his apartment on the West Side. We sipped Johnny Walker Scotch-on-the-rocks out of wine glasses.

Durk was not interested.

Nonetheless, we went forward with the idea of using Durk, and with other ideas too. There were meetings between Deputy Commissioner Ward and myself during which we made grandiose plans for the auxiliary police. These were unarmed, unpaid part-time civilians who wore blue uniforms much resembling police uniforms, but on their breasts they wore a kind of star, like a western sheriff. They patrolled certain areas in their own cars. Some patrolled Central Park on horseback. They held ranks such as colonel. A great many were old and wealthy gentlemen, and almost all were police buffs.

They were objects of derision to real cops.

However, Ward and I saw the chance in the model precinct to recruit young businessmen as auxiliary police, particularly men who spoke Spanish. We could begin to integrate bilingual young men into normal patrol operations. We could start with one such auxiliary riding in the back of a radio car. Whenever the car responded to the call of a Spanish-speaking citizen, the auxiliary cop could stand as surrogate for the real cops. Carefully supervised, such a squad of auxiliary cops could earn the respect of patrolmen. Eventually, hopefully, we would wind up with one cop and one auxiliary in many cars, as was currently done in Washington. With a citizen on hand to settle disputes, and to perform many police services, we might even succeed in integrating the police back into society.

These were heady notions even to talk about.

In the meantime, a captain and some sergeants from the Planning Division were making the decisions and arrangements involving the Model Precinct project. They were working on the assumption that Durk would be available to them, but when I next checked, they had penciled in Durk as a neighborhood police sergeant, one among five others, performing the duties of an ordinary sergeant.

So I spoke to Chief of Patrol Cawley, telling him I had promised Durk something special if he would take the job, which he hadn't even agreed to take yet. He was supposed to be, in the Police Commissioner's own words, a "super sergeant." But nobody was watching how the Planning Division was setting up the model precinct, and the chances were that nobody in the Planning Division had a clue how Durk could or should be used, or what the Model Precinct was supposed to be about, either.

As always, high-level executive conferences often brought out new ideas, great enthusiasm, and even great idealism. Then there were the cops in the radio cars, responding day after day, night after night to routine emergencies. In between stood police middle-management, totally divorced both from the street and from the executives. It was the habit not only of the Police Commissioner but of everybody else simply to dump projects on these people. When at last the structured project struggled to the surface, it often bore no resemblance to the needs in the street, and none to the inspired scheme originally conceived by the executives either. This was true not only of staff work performed by the Planning Division—which was, in effect, the personal staff of the Police Commissioner—but also by staffs working for the Chief Inspector, or the Chief of Patrol, or anybody else. For the most part, no police executive ever followed one of his own projects from conception to application on the sidewalk.

Cawley now said, "Okay, we'll do it over. We'll make Durk Coordinator of the Neighborhood Police Teams. How's that?"

Cawley was obliged to be amenable because I outranked

him, and because apparently I spoke for the Police Commissioner.

So Durk was penciled in as Coordinator of the Neighborhood Police Teams.

The model precinct concept was too big to keep quiet for long. Newspaper stories began to appear. To force Durk to join the project, I mentioned to Federici of the *News* that Durk had been offered a big role, and the next morning Durk's name appeared in headlines. He called up, cursing.

"Alright," he said finally, "I'll do it." In fact, he had no choice. He could not reject such a job without losing the allegiance of many of those who believed in his idealism.

I went in to see the Police Commissioner: Durk would take the job. That day Murphy was presiding at the graduation of 150 recruits, most of whom would be assigned to the Model Precinct. I suggested that he invite Durk to this ceremony, and introduce him there to the recruits and to the press.

Murphy stared at me for a moment. He had not once met with Durk since the second Knapp hearings, and he had never before appeared with Durk in public.

Presently Murphy said, "Alright, send him down."

So I sent a radio car to get Durk. I told him to report to the office of Chief Downer, the C.O. of the Police Academy, so that we could talk to him before the ceremony. The police brass always met in that office, waiting for the appearance of Mayor Lindsay. As soon as Lindsay showed up—and he was almost always late—we would all ride down to the auditorium on the second floor and the ceremony would begin.

Ignoring my order, Durk went directly to the auditorium and mingled there with other cops. The auditorium was connected to the C.O.'s office by walkie-talkie, and when I learned that Durk was down there I summoned him upstairs. He was wearing civilian clothes. He looked into the office and saw Chief Codd, Chief Cawley, a number of deputy commissioners and high-ranking chiefs.

Murphy and the Mayor entered almost simultaneously. Murphy shook hands with Durk and kept moving. Mayor Lindsay, denounced so many times by Durk, seemed to have to force himself to shake Durk's hand. As he did so, he remarked, "I'm glad to meet you, I've admired you from afar."

Chief Cawley then went over and said, "I was with you all the way, Dave."

Durk spun on his heel and, in the anteroom, began chatting with a sergeant with whom he had once shared a radio car.

Drawing Murphy aside, I suggested that in his speech he announce to the graduating recruits that many of them would serve in this model precinct under Sergeant Durk. At this point he might call Durk forward and shake hands with him in front of the recruits. Murphy said nothing. A few minutes later, in the elevator going down, Murphy leaned across to Durk and said, "When I mention your name, Dave, you could rise and remain standing in your place for a moment." Murphy nodded at Durk, as if he had just awarded him a notable assignment.

The ceremony began. The Police Commissioner introduced Chief Lonergan, who had recently got his second star, and with it command of Manhattan North—which included the 24th Precinct; and Chief Kendall, who here received his third star as the new chief of personnel. Then Murphy said, "Now I want to introduce to you another superior officer who has shown you what dedication is, and what integrity is. I'm referring of course to Sergeant David Durk. Will you stand up, please, Sergeant Durk?"

Durk rose in his place, in the third and final row of the guests on the stage. Murphy continued for another sentence or two on the subject of Durk, but seemed to be forcing each word out. There was no spontaneity, and no enthusiasm.

But when the ceremony ended, the press and TV reporters wanted to interview Durk and Murphy together. So they stood side by side in front of cameras and microphones.

"Commissioner, will you say what you hope for from Sergeant Durk?"

Murphy mentioned the integrity for which Durk was famous and which he hoped Durk would now instill into new patrolmen in the 24th Precinct.

"What about you, Sergeant Durk? What do you hope to accomplish in the model precinct?"

They were standing on the floor beside the edge of the

stage, and First Deputy Commissioner Smith, Chief Inspector Codd, and I were sitting on chairs on the edge of the stage just above Murphy's right ear, for we were anxious about this interview. As Durk prepared to answer, all of us, Murphy included, sucked in a deep breath: What was this nut liable to say?

Even I had forgotten that Durk was no nut at all. Fanatic, yes. Idealist, yes. But he was also an experienced and hypnotic speaker, as well as a pragmatic cop. He said his aim was to help reduce crime and tension, to help increase both integrity and productivity. He wanted to show the people of that precinct what good police work meant. He wanted to give summonses to landlords who polluted the atmosphere, not just to illegally parked cars. Beside him, Murphy was beaming, and in the car afterward Murphy was euphoric, saying to me, "Having Durk there was an act of genius."

Soon a memo came from Murphy. Durk had great credibility with the public. Murphy's own image as a corruption-fighting police commissioner could be enhanced if he appeared in public with Durk at his side. What could be arranged?

So the Police Commissioner and Durk appeared together on the Dick Cavett talk show. However, Durk dominated the interview. It was Durk who answered whatever question Cavett threw out.

Murphy found himself the supporting actor, with Durk the star, and he didn't like it.

When, a few days after that, they were due to appear on another television panel show, Murphy sent one of his secretaries, Lieutenant Doyle, down to my office. Doyle remarked that the P.C. was worried that the Cavett show might have left viewers with "erroneous impressions." Doyle never used the word "upstaged," but that's what this present conversation was about. The Police Commissioner certainly wanted to guard against similar results this time.

And guard against them he did. Each time this new interviewer threw out a question, it was Murphy who lunged for it before the surprised Durk had had a chance to react.

I had seen this syndrome before. There had been a luncheon, and Murphy, on the dais, found himself paired with James Ahern, the former Police Chief of New Haven. The gray-haired, 40-year-old Ahern proved a more vibrant and vital public performer than Murphy, and he was a liberal cop much in Murphy's own image. The only difference was that Murphy had more fame, more rank, and therefore spoke with more weight. Murphy had opened proceedings with a brief, bland address. Then Ahern began to speak so dynamically, with such force and emotion that he captivated the audience. A question-and-answer period followed. At first nearly all questions were directed to Ahern. Seeing this, Murphy began to snatch them out of the air himself, like a pass receiver snagging balls thrown to somebody else. Before long, because Murphy's ideas, if not his delivery, were dynamic, the bulk of the questions were directed where Murphy thought they belonged, to himself; and it was Ahern who found himself ignored.

The model precinct concept was formally launched. All elements were present: the six neighborhood police team sergeants; the new and handpicked commander, Deputy Inspector Norman Andersson; the new station house supervisor, Sergeant Margaret Powers; the residential patrolman, John R. Juris, a 28-year-old bilingual college graduate; Sergeant David B. Durk, wearing a uniform for the first time in some six years; and of course the enthusiastic Police Commissioner himself.

When he left there that day, Murphy considered his own role terminated. He had breathed forth the model precinct full-blown, like a Greek god giving birth to thunder or flame. Murphy knew the quality of the police soil—had he not rooted around in it 25 years after all? And this soil was never hospitable to new ideas. Nonetheless, the model precinct existed. He would go on to something else. He was a man who scattered acorns around the base of the tree and apparently he cared little more about what happened to them than an oak did. Many months before he had installed his first neighborhood police team in Brooklyn, the birth of another noble idea; and there were now some 40 teams scattered through the city including the new ones here in the 24th Precinct. But Murphy himself, once the first inaugural ceremony was over, had never looked back to see how any were doing, not even to ask whether the idea was sound: Were the flowers blooming or had someone cemented over the garden? He had commissioned a study. That seemed the extent of his personal interest and apparently he had no personal interest in the model precinct either, once his car had driven him away on the first day.

Within a week, Detective Sergeant David Durk was disgusted with his new job and a few days after that he stopped going back there for good.

After only a few days as residential patrolman, John Juris had had enough too, and asked to be relieved. Presumably Juris had volunteered for this job—had not the Police Commissioner directed that the job go only to a volunteer? So what had gone wrong?

But there are volunteers, and there are volunteers. The Planning Division staff had culled Personnel Bureau statistics for a bilingual college graduate living in the 24th Precinct, and had come up with Juris. Juris was called in and told, "You are it."

And so against his will, Juris volunteered. It took him a very few days to learn that special pressures came with the job. The phone calls in the evening, in the early morning, and in the middle of the night were more than his shaky marriage could stand. John Juris wanted out at once.

Apprised of these facts and others, the Police Commissioner suggested that meetings be held. I should get together with Chief of Patrol Cawley and subordinate commanders. We should "work something out."

Model Precinct Commander Andersson was then 45 years old and he had been a policeman for 23 years. He had been an instructor and later executive officer at the Police Academy, and Murphy had known him there. He held a teacher's license and was a lawyer, and he had even stepped out of the New York Police Department for a year and a half to serve as superintendent of the Long Island Railroad Police. He was married and had four children ranging in age from 24 to 10. On paper he had had all the credentials needed to head the Model Precinct, but in person he was a mild kind of man, certainly no idealist, certainly no dynamic leader either. At top-level conferences he seldom offered an opinion. He preferred to let higher-ranking officers do the talking. After a week in the 24th Precinct, Durk had said of Andersson, "He's a nice guy, but he sees this as a nine-to-five job."

Andersson also saw David Durk as a sergeant. He thought Durk should behave like a sergeant and be treated like a sergeant.

Far from seeing the Model Precinct as something special, Andersson sought to snuggle it into its quiet little niche inside the Fifth Division, which in turn fit inside Manhattan North. He was not interested in innovations, and he sent all reports, requests, and recommendations up through the chain of command as a loyal subordinate should.

It took Durk only a week to realize that there was no special role for him in the 24th Precinct, and that the job created especially for him, that of Neighborhood Police Team Coordinator, not only didn't exist, but couldn't exist, for it sought to make him the commander of sergeants who, according to the Neighborhood Police Team concept, were supposed to be autonomous.

Durk hung around long enough to see there was no job for him, that no one intended to use him, and then he simply ceased to show up. Being the acknowledged expert on police recruitment and police corruption, he had a heavy calendar of speaking engagements before civic groups and police departments throughout the state and country. In addition, his phone rang night and day with people who wanted to give him information on crime and criminals. (His number was listed in the book though almost no other cop's was, from patrolman to Murphy.) Chief of Intelligence Grubert, one of the few commanders who believed in Durk, was closing out an investigation that would result in nearly a score of arrests. The information had come to Grubert from Durk, and it had been impeccable.

Durk, believing himself invulnerable to ordinary discipline, began to concentrate on collecting and funneling out such information, and on meeting his informants, and on his speeches.

And so Cawley and I called a conference which was supposed to be chaired by Cawley. But Cawley didn't show up, and the meeting was chaired by Deputy Chief Louis Cottell, Cawley's thin, bespectacled 58-year-old Chief of Staff. Later Cottell would be jumped two ranks and named Chief of Detectives. But at the time he rated as a minor figure, and I accepted his presence as proof that Cawley's own commitment to the Model Precinct was small. Also present were Chief Lonergan, the new commander of Manhattan North; Inspector Bonacum, commander of the Fifth Division; Deputy Inspector Andersson, commanding officer of the 24th Precinct; and a Lieutenant Murphy from the Planning Division.

There were serious problems to discuss, including the future of the residential patrolman idea, the future of Sergeant Durk, and especially the future of the 24th Precinct as a Model Precinct. But Inspector Andersson's mind was on furniture. He needed an extra desk here, an extra table there. He wanted partitions put up in various parts of his station house. He was sending requests up through channels, but the stuff still hadn't come.

I said, "Look, this is supposed to be a model precinct. You shouldn't have to come in here to a conference like this and ask for such stuff. You shouldn't have to go up through channels if you need a desk or 20 portable radios. You should be able just to pick up the phone and say you want it, and get it. That's the whole point of your being in command of a model precinct."

But Inspector Bonacum said, "Wait a minute. What about me? I'm Commanding Officer of the Fifth Division; Inspector Andersson works for me. Any requests of any kind should come up through me for approval. And what about Chief Lonergan here? He's Commander of Manhattan North. He's my superior. After I endorse a request it's got to go up through him."

I said, "Even a request for a new table?"

"Even a request for a new table."

Chief Lonergan added, "I can get Inspector Andersson anything he wants in ten minutes. All he has to do is come up through channels to me."

Now Bonacum and Lonergan both declared that Durk had to go. He didn't put any time in the 24th Precinct, and they didn't want him there. He served no purpose. He was just a sergeant, but refused to behave like one. Why should he be in the 24th Precinct, anyway? Yes, it was true that Murphy had told them to give Durk room to breathe, and they had given him all the breathing room they thought he merited. But now he didn't even come there anymore. It was an untenable situation. The commanding officer of the division never knew where Durk, a sergeant, was. The commanding officer of the borough never knew where Durk, a sergeant, was.

I explained about Durk's lectures, which were of great value to the Department, and about the criminal information that people would give only to him personally.

Chief Lonergan said, "If you or anybody else wants Durk to make a speech somewhere, sir, your request should go through channels. You shouldn't just call Durk, you should call Inspector Andersson. Everything should be cleared through Inspector Andersson."

What they were all saying was so reasonable that I couldn't even argue. But it was also ridiculous. A special project, a concept as strange and as potentially glorious as the model precinct could not be run through channels and according to stale regulations. It had to be something special or it couldn't exist. And why wasn't Chief Cawley even at this meeting?

I tried to solve the Durk question at least temporarily. If I got Durk to agree to work in the 24th Precinct two days a week, would they accept him on that basis?

All agreed they would be happy to have him, though I saw they didn't mean it.

I pointed out that Durk was one of the stars of the Police Department. If we failed to find a way to use Durk, then we were hurting not so much Durk as the entire Police Department.

A number of them nodded at me, as if they not only understood what I was saying but believed it.

I said, "You've got to give Durk a meaningful job to do."

After the meeting I went straight to the Police Commissioner and informed him that the model precinct concept was foundering. I suggested that the only way to save the ideas that he had conceived and embodied in this precinct was to yank the precinct out of the chain of command, get it out from under Bonacum and Lonergan and Cawley and the Chief Inspector. I suggested he assign it to an executive committee composed of Deputy Commissioner Canick of Administration (for he would be able to handle the budgetary aspects of it); Deputy Commissioner Ward of Community Affairs (for our basic task was to serve a specific community more thoroughly and efficiently than it had ever been served before); and myself (for our long-range hope was to integrate the precinct into its own community, and as a result show the way toward integrating the Police Department into society as a whole).

Murphy never responded directly to the idea of this three-man executive committee.

Some weeks later I expressed to him my disappointment. The Model Precinct had subsided back into the mass of the Police Department. It was indistinguishable from any other precinct. "We could have really made it into something," I said. "We should be doing something new there at least once a month. We should be creating belief in it. People should be hearing of it every time they turn around."

Murphy said, "Well, if we can just eliminate corruption there I'll be satisfied."

"But we could have done so much more than that. That was the place to put policewomen in radio cars and—"

But he wasn't really listening.

Book Six / **SPRING**

1 / The Gallo Hit

A .32-caliber slug cut through the aorta of Crazy Joe Gallo at 5:30 in the morning in a restaurant in Little Italy that would have closed 30 minutes later. Gallo, who was celebrating his 43rd birthday and also his three-week-old marriage, was full of pasta and tomato paste at the time, for an hour later I stood over his table contemplating his plate. He had evidently mopped up with bread, and perhaps was contentedly munching when the gunmen came through the door shooting. There were bullet holes along the opposite wall and below the bar, and what looked like pools of gore on the floor, and my first impression was that it must have been a massacre. At the moment Gallo lay naked on a table at Beekman Downtown Hospital, while in another room doctors worked on his bodyguard, Pete the Greek Diapoulis, who, during the fusillade, had caught one in the backside. Pete the Greek had refused to give even his name, though he was under arrest for possession af an illegal gun.

Though I had got there soon after the murder, the restaurant was already crowded. Ballistics men were digging bullets out of the wood that paneled the underside of the bar, and also out of paneling behind the bar. They had chalked spots in the floor where deformed bullets had come to rest, and uniformed cops carefully moved chairs and tables about, looking for other spent bullets. Fingerprint technicians worked on the glass door which gave onto Mulberry Street. About a dozen detectives moved about, making notations in notebooks, and presently the door onto Hester Street opened and in walked Chief of Detectives Seedman. He had come in through the crowd outside, like a film star arriving at a premiére.

The restaurant occupied the corner of Hester and Mulberry Streets, and this entire corner had been roped off and hung with "Crime Scene" placards. Behind the ropes waited two dozen or more newsmen and cameramen plus mobs of curious citizens. Although it was a cold, gloomy morning. other citizens hung from the windows.

The restaurant was called Umberto's Clam House—

within three weeks *New York* magazine's food critic would write a gourmet review of the place under the headline "Clamming up at Umberto's." Joey Gallo might have appreciated the humor. Then again he might not. He was noted for being crazy, not funny.

What had looked like blood as I came into Umberto's that morning was not blood at all, but pools of ketchup. There had been about 20 people in the place, including the six at Gallo's table; and as the shooting started, most must have jumped to their feet. Their suddenly straightened knees had struck the undersides of the tables, toppling ketchup bottles whose contents, upon impact with the floor, spread into pools of cinema gore. Umberto's Clam House was like the movie set of a Mafia killing, ketchup everywhere.

This was not the first time a gangland assassination had occurred in Little Italy; doubtless it would not be the last. And police headquarters was only three blocks away, which was embarrassing; in addition, witnesses in Little Italy never saw anything—invariably they had their backs turned and were never curious enough to turn around when gunfire erupted—which was downright annoying.

Among those who unfortunately hadn't got a good look at anything or anybody earlier that morning, was a part-owner of Umberto's Clam House.

Now he refused to let the press inside his restaurant, and he was anxious that we should all leave too.

He said to Chief Seedman, "How soon do you think I can reopen?"

"Why don't you shut up?" said Seedman.

"I mean—"

"If we get any trouble from you, we'll stay here a week."

"I'm sorry. I mean—I didn't mean anything by it."

To me Seedman muttered, "Treat a guy like that politely and he'll bug you all day."

Gallo had been seated at a table near the door onto Mulberry Street. On one side, backs to the wall, had sat Joe's 11-year-old stepdaughter, his wife, Sina, and Edith Russo, Pete the Greek's girlfriend. Opposite, facing the door, sat Pete the Greek on the left, Crazy Joe in the middle, and Joe's sister, Camilla Fiorello, on the right.

Suddenly the glass door opened, and gunfire commenced. One of the first shots caught Pete the Greek in the left buttock, presumably as he sprang to his seat to get his .25-caliber gun out of his pocket. The shot must have been aimed at his head, but he sprang up too fast, replacing his head with his behind as the first ketchup bottle went over onto the floor. Gallo was shot in the buttocks also, a second shot hit his left elbow; but by now he was sprinting away from the bullets, racing the length of the restaurant toward the door out into Hester Street, bullets tracking him. Later we dug eight slugs out of the bar and out of the paneling behind the bar, two groups of four, all of them .38-caliber slugs. That is, two .38's were searching for him but missing as he dashed for the street and for his Cadillac parked there. A .32-caliber slug which missed him fell to the floor just inside the Hester Street door. Another .32-caliber slug went into the back of his left shoulder, presumably just as he got the door opened, and he lurched out into Mulberry Street and dropped dead.

By chance a radio car containing Patrolmen Philip Agosta and Robert Barnes happened along Hester Street just at that moment. The two cops scooped up Joe and threw him in the back. Pete the Greek, having run out the Mulberry Street door to fire shots at the escaping assassins, had reentered the restaurant and run through it and out the other door to see what had happened to Gallo. Once in Hester Street, Pete the Greek also collapsed. The same radio car team scooped him up too, speeding both to Beekman Downtown Hospital.

Crazy Joe Gallo's black Cadillac remained parked outside, its windows plastered with black-and-orange stickers proclaiming the "Americans of Italian Descent," an organizations which Gallo was backing in direct competition with the Colombo mob's Italian-American Civil Rights League.

It was nine and a half months since the Colombo hit. During that lapse an occasional mobster had died, most of them shot in the back of the head, although one of the deceased had been garroted by a silk necktie.

But there had been no gang war, no spate of revenge, and perhaps in some measure this was due to many pronouncements by Chief Seedman and myself that detectives knew everything about the Colombo hit, including who had ordered it and how, and that shortly all evidence would go before the grand jury.

Because now within hours of the Crazy Joe Gallo assassination there would be Italians lying dead all over town. There would be at least 20 victims in the next two months, some of whom would die spectacularly, and in midsummer a hired assassin would walk into a midtown restaurant called The Neapolitan Noodle, and gun down four Jewish businessmen, killing two. The businessmen had moved into places at the bar vacated only moments before by four Mafia hoods.

2 / Sergeant Weber's Last Stand

So if this was war, and if the Colombo hit was at the root of it, where exactly were we in the Colombo investigation?

Colombo himself still lay in a coma. His Italian-American League was as moribund as himself. Its president and also its secretary-treasurer had been indicted by a federal grand jury for having obtained a fraudulent loan. Its midtown office had been abandoned in order to save $16,000 annual rent. Its officers had admitted a 1971 cash flow of one million dollars but this had flowed no one knew where. The league was heavily in debt. Its summer camp would not reopen. All its officers, those under indictment and those not, were now supposedly operating without pay.

All through the winter, Sergeant Weber, his squad now down to ten detectives, had labored on the Colombo investigation. It was a case of hallucinating and unexplainable images: of Jerome Johnson moping across the plains of the Canadian West, of Jerome Johnson joining and professing his faith in a bizarre religious sect out on the West Coast.

How did he get to these places? Why did he get to these places?

Two informants had placed Johnson in the frequent company of black radicals. But Weber was now reaching different conclusions from heretofore: that Johnson enjoyed the company of black radicals not because he was a black radical himself, but because he was a nut, drawn to any oddball group he came upon in his travels. Jerome

Johnson, far from being the key to the Colombo hit, had turned into a point of no return for Sergeant Weber. He was the permanent red herring in the case. Hundreds of hours of detectives' time had been wasted trying to follow the trail backward from Jerome Johnson to Crazy Joe Gallo, but the only real progress had been made when following the same trail in the opposite direction.

By now Weber knew that there were four individuals between Joe Gallo and Jerome Johnson—three men and a woman. He knew the names of each of them. One was a black thug willing enough to talk to Weber. Possibly this thug could even be induced or forced to testify in court. But unfortunately he was a professional stickup man who had been shot on five different occasions, by friend and by foe. There was no chance any jury would believe a word he said, though Weber did. A second intermediary was the Jewish shopkeeper on Delancey Street—the one who began every conversation by snarling, "You fuckin' cops," into the tapped phone in his store. This man, who had been in the hotel room in Roxbury when Jerome Johnson was hired, was in hijacking and narcotics. Weber wanted to tap his home phone too. But the guy lived in a series of seedy hotels, changing hotels every two or three days, so that it was impossible to get a court order on any specific place.

On the day Joey Gallo was killed, it was hoped that this man, or somebody, would be shocked into incriminating conversation over one of the tapped phones. Instead, all Weber's men heard was, "Get down here right away. Something's happened.

Weber had brooded long and hard over the characters and personalities of these people. He had come to the conclusion that the minds of Carlo Gambino and Joey Gallo were diabolical. Weber believed Gambino had sent Gallo to kill Colombo, knowing sooner or later the Colombo mob would retaliate. Gambino would kill two birds literally with one stone, get rid of Gallo and Colombo both, and take over all of Brooklyn. Gambino was a 72-year-old man with a heart condition, a semi-invalid confined for long periods to bed, who had been rushed to intensive care wards in hospitals in the past, whose deportation order back to Italy had already been signed by the court—if he ever got well enough to travel he would be gone within hours. Nonetheless, Gambino had all of Brooklyn now, he was the number one Mafia don in the country, and presumably he was a happy man.

As for Gallo, he had invented a scheme unlike every other Mafia hit of this century. As Weber saw it, Gallo had expected the Colombo mob to go off hunting blacks within minutes after Joe Colombo hit the ground. Colombo hoods would race up to Harlem hunting. This would turn into a race riot which would totally obscure the Colombo hit. "That's the kind of scheming Gallo did," Weber said. "Why do you think they called him crazy?"

Weber had reconstructed the entire scenario. He had seen it develop, detail by detail, not wanting to believe much of it. But every piece now interlocked like chain mail. It surrounded the case. The case could not escape. Weber had it cold. He had cross-checked every bit of information he could possibly cross-check, and the rest of it he took not so much on faith as on 20 years' experience as a detective. He could see a lie in a man's eyes, and hear it in his voice. Not always. But often enough.

In February Weber had got sick. He was out for weeks, and the Police surgeon thought he was too sick ever to return to duty. However, Weber fought to stay in the Police Department just a little bit longer. He wanted to present the Colombo case to a grand jury. He begged Seedman to put in a word for him, and Seedman did. Sergeant John Weber, ill with heart disease, was granted six more weeks as a cop.

One day Seedman said, "I'll tell you how these mob contracts work. Gambino calls in Joey Gallo and says, 'I want Colombo hit. I'll pay $40,000.'

"So Gallo goes out and calls in another guy, and says, 'I want Colombo hit. I'll pay $20,000.'

"So that guy goes out and finds another guy and says to him, 'I want Colombo hit. The job is worth $10,000.'

"And so it goes down through a few more guys. The last guy, he's the one who finds Jerome Johnson. He says to Jerome Johnson, 'I want Colombo hit. Furthermore, I want him hit in the middle of a crowd in broad daylight in Columbus Circle in the midst of 1500 cops. I'll pay you $40.' "

Seedman looked up at me and grinned. He said, "And

that dummy Jerome Johnson says, 'Yeah, I'll take it.' "

But now the grin faded from Seedman's face and he said, "Now how are you going to prove something like that in court, even though you know that's the way it happened?"

Seedman still was confident that the case would break. He kept saying that detective work required above all things patience. You had to be willing to wait. Judging from conversations over the tapped telephones, it was possible that the Jewish shopkeeper meant to kill somebody, or try to. Seedman said, "Even if he got killed himself, that might be the break we're waiting for."

A group of us met in the office of First District Homicide in the 13th Precinct to discuss the Gallo hit, which was now almost one week old. The detective who made architectural drawings of crime sites was there. He had brought new drawings of Umberto's Clam House which the rest of us were staring at. The scale drawings showed where the tables were placed, how the bar fitted in, and where bullets or parts of bullets were recovered—there were marks all over the drawing which corresponded to code explanations on the bottom: B stood for bullet, S for shell, C for casing. From this drawing it was possible to plot the position and the subsequent movements of nearly everybody.

By now Gallo had had an elegant funeral, and so, subsequently, had about six other hoods.

By now the patrons and employees of Umberto's Clam House on the night of the hit had been interrogated and reinterrogated. Certain of them had identified one of the assassins from photos, and the purpose of the current meeting was to decide if we felt confident enough of this identification to make an arrest. The answer was that we didn't.

One detective made a joke about the behavior of the Gallo hoods in Brooklyn now that their leader had passed away. Unlike most murders, we could all laugh about Gallo's.

Captain Bob McDermott said, "There isn't one of those guys on President Street that could count to three without making a mistake. They are what you might call real shitheads."

Chief Kinsella said, "We know they're not smart. They

wouldn't have tried this if they were smart."

A cop who drove an injured citizen to a hospital filled out what was called an aided card. Now Chief Seedman said, "Why don't we make out an aided card on Gallo and call the case closed?"

"We've never been this far ahead at this point in my memory," said Chief Kinsella.

A hoodlum named Ciprio had that day been found shot-gunned through the top of the head from an upstairs window. Seedman said, "I have a suggestion on the Gallo case. We pin it on this guy Ciprio. Who will know the difference? And call it closed."

Though he made jokes, Seedman was suddenly thoroughly perplexed.

A man named Joseph Luparelli had just turned himself in to the FBI in California. He had spoken to Chief Seedman by telephone, and Seedman had been gruff with him. "What kind of crap are you trying to tell me? How do I know what you're saying is true? You dummy, what do you take me for?"

For Luparelli had just confessed to having been a participant in the Gallo hit. He had named the other participants, who were not the same men the eyewitnesses had named. Luparelli was a thick-necked, thick-waisted chunky man. The highest he had ever got in the mob was chauffeur. He was terrified, and he wanted to sing.

Presently Luparelli was on a plane back to New York. When the plane door opened, Seedman was waiting at the foot of the stairs.

Luparelli was hidden out in series of hotels, moving to a new one every couple of days, guarded night and day by two detectives. Luparelli's very existence became one of the most closely guarded secrets in the history of the Police Department.

Meanwhile, Sergeant John Weber's final six weeks dwindled and disappeared, with the Colombo case no closer to a conclusion. Ten months almost to the day after Joe Colombo was gunned down in Columbus Circle, Sergeant Weber turned his squad over to another man and retired from the Police Department. Even so, he had outlasted the tenure of Chief of Detectives Seedman, and he had come with a few days of outlasting me.

3 / A Solution to the Colombo Case

Weber was replaced by Sergeant Paul Reilly, 18 years a cop, who had been brought over from the Auto Squad. With Seedman gone, I went up to the 18th Precinct, still the headquarters of the Colombo investigation, to be briefed by Reilly. He had been on the case two months, and Weber had been ill so much of that time that Reilly, in effect, had long since taken over the case.

We met in a small crowded room on the second floor of the dilapidated old station house. The place was crowded with filing cabinets and other clutter, detectives' guns lay here and there, and there were only a few chairs. The investigation was now down to eight men, all of whom were present in that small room. They were all very discouraged.

They had had three wiretaps going at the high point of the investigation. Now they had none. The three tape recorders lay on a shelf, attached to nothing. The court-ordered wiretaps had had to be renewed every 30 days, and for a while this was no problem, and then suddenly it was a problem, and one by one the taps had run out.

Reilly was inclined to blame this on a technical failure by the District Attorney's office; but Assistant DA Keenan explained that the courts had accorded the three wiretaps in conjunction with the investigation into the homicide of Jerome Johnson, and the attempted homicide of Joe Colombo. Right up until the last day, solid evidence relating to other crimes kept coming over those wires, but the Colombo hit was so far in the past that no one spoke of it anymore. Therefore, according to the rules—and both the District Attorney's office and the Police Department were constrained to play according to the rules—those wiretaps could no longer be supported as essential to the Colombo investigation.

Reilly and his men had listened to evidence of three other homicides. They knew exactly who had shotgunned Ciprio in the top of the skull, they knew that the murderer had then jumped down onto the sidewalk and broken his leg—he was still hobbling around in a cast at this moment.

No good, said District Attorney Keenan. Legally this evidence was inadmissible.

If we can't support the wire on the homicide case, Reilly suggested, why couldn't we support it as a narcotics wire? The narcotics information coming across it was outstanding.

The Appeals Bureau of District Attorney Hogan's office studied this possibility and ruled that any such wiretap would be illegal.

The frustrated Reilly had even listened to hoodlums planning the next hit—on Joe Colombo Jr. Why couldn't we support the wire on that?

No good, said Keenan.

(In fact, the attempted hit on a Colombo son took place almost exactly a month later, but it was on Anthony, not Joe Jr. Somebody fired at Anthony as he drove his Cadillac up in front of the Colombo home in Brooklyn at 1:15 in the morning. He was supposed to have been accompanied only by Joe Jr.; instead he was accompanied by Phillip Rossillo, whom the police still believed had killed Jerome Johnson, and by Santo Vingo. These men later claimed to have been unarmed at the time. However, the cops found that 18 bullets had smacked the building across the street, all apparently fired from inside the Colombo car.)

Sergeant Reilly said to me, "Anyway, we got no more wires."

The Jewish shopkeeper had moved to a different flea-bag hotel nearly every night. Finally he stayed put, and Reilly had raced to court to get a wiretap order. But it was refused.

"Our only hope now," Reilly said, "is to get somebody to roll over." Reilly said that the Jewish shopkeeper was in "hijacking up to his eyeballs. If we could get him with a heavy hijacking load—"

Would the hijacker then turn state's evidence and confess his part in a murder? I doubted it, and I saw Reilly doubted it too.

The other detectives in the room didn't say much, but all were as gloomy as Reilly.

I saw that there was one other possible solution, though it had never been tried before in a case of this kind. Was Reilly ready to face a grand jury? He said he was.

But, Reilly said, I would have to be the one to speak to

Assistant District Attorney Keenan and also to Acting Chief of Detectives Kinsella. A sergeant had no clout with such personages. The idea was to subpoena approximately 20 Mafia hoods and throw them in front of the grand jury. Our pictures from Columbus Circle on the day of the hit plainly showed two of them with guns. A good deal of other evidence was in our possession as well. None of the hoods could be sure what we knew and what we didn't know. Once in front of the grand jury they would be granted immunity. At that point, they would either refuse to talk at all, in which case they would go to jail for contempt; or else they would talk, but being hoodlums and not knowing how much we had on them, they would lie. Once they had lied we would charge them with perjury.

As Reilly then pointed out, once charged, they could be arrested. If we arrested them in their cars, we would get to search their cars. If we arrested them at home, perhaps we could search at least part of their homes.

I saw that we could make the grand jury hearings last perhaps three weeks. We could keep these guys sitting in the hallways. We could get new mug shots on all of them, gather a good deal of intelligence, and in addition we would drive them crazy.

We would also tell the public all. The public should see what a fine job our detectives had done. The Colombo case would have a solution.

Back at headquarters, I explained Reilly's idea to Chief Kinsella. He said, "It sounds fine to me. Why don't you try it out on the DA?"

So I phoned Assistant District Attorney Keenan and met him for lunch at Sweets, a seafood restaurant down on Fulton Street. I outlined our solution to the Colombo case, and Keenan began nodding thoughtfully. We agreed to meet to see all the films shot at Columbus Circle, and after this we would make our decision.

Then we began to speak of the Gallo case, and Keenan was furious. The existence of the informant, Luparelli, was supposed to be top secret. Hardly anybody in his office knew of Luparelli's existence, only a few people in the Police Department knew, only a few in the FBI; but this morning, spread out across page one of *The New York Times* was an account of the Gallo murder as Luparelli had told it to the cops. The story had been written by Nick Gage. Where had Gage got his information from?

Keenan claimed that *The New York Times* had ruined the case, that finally law enforcement had been in position to deal a stunning blow to organized crime, but it would all fall apart now. Gage had named Phillip Gambino and Carmine DiBiase as two of those involved in the shooting. Keenan noted that DiBiase had been charged with murder before, and had even been convicted and sentenced to the electric chair. However the conviction had been reversed on appeal, and at the second trial DiBiase was acquitted. In any case, before being caught for that murder he had stayed underground seven years. How many years would he stay underground this time, Keenan asked. As for Phillip Gambino, he had been scheduled to meet his parole officer in two days time. Plans had been laid to put him under surveillance at that point, and tail him to wherever he might go. Now he would never show up to meet his parole officer at all.

Keenan had been up since 5:30 A.M. worrying. He had already ordered Luparelli moved from a midtown hotel to one further uptown. Luparelli was terrified, and calling up all the time. As Keenan saw it, the guards on Luparelli would probably have to be doubled, which would cost a fortune. Already the cost of paying for the room for Luparelli and meals for all the detectives came to $65 per day. The detectives were eating high. The District Attorney's office was already $49,000 over budget for the fiscal year ending June 30.

Luparelli had admitted helping to bury a body in the basement of a service station at the corner of Elizabeth and Kenmare Streets, and, after leaving the restaurant, Keenan and I drove there. Luparelli had made a detailed diagram, even noting how the pipes were placed under the earth. The burial had taken three hours, he said. The body had been murdered by an ice pick about 18 months ago.

Now as Keenan and I stepped downstairs into the cold and gloom, we saw two FBI agents stripped to the waist digging in a hole that was already about six feet deep and nearly ten feet across at the widest point. Pipes crossed this hole exactly where Luparelli had said they would be. Patrolmen from Emergency Service had done the digging

A Solution to the Colombo Case 553

until a few minutes before, at which time a steam pipe had burst in an office building at 80 Pine Street, scalding seven people to death. The Emergency Service men were needed there. Gratefully, they jumped out of the hole, washed, and disappeared; and from then on the FBI had had to do the spade work, literally.

Keenan and I looked down into the hole. Dr. Milton Helpern, the city's chief medical examiner, and also Dr. Michael Baden, his chief assistant, stood with us on the edge. Other FBI agents and cops waited nearby.

One of the FBI diggers handed up what might have been the remains of a human pinky. Dr. Helpern studied it a minute, then broke it in half and pronounced it a stick.

The digging went on. The earth was not as hard-packed as it should have been, and Keenan surmised that the body Luparelli had helped bury had since been dug up by somebody else—presumably during the hours immediately after Nick Gage's story broke. Keenan, looking down into the hole, cursed softly.

Back at police headquarters, I set up plans for the screening of all of the confiscated Colombo films for a few days hence.

Meanwhile, another meeting was called on the Gallo case. About ten of us, men from the FBI, the District Attorney's office, the Chief of Detectives' office and myself met in police headquarters. The two subjects under discussion were Luparelli and Nick Gage. Thanks to Gage, 50 to 60 detectives were tied up just guarding Luparelli, and the other witnesses. Gage had got his story, but at tremendous cost to the taxpayers. It was difficult for me to believe that he had done any other harm, for Phillip Gambino had reported to his parole officeer on schedule that very morning, and had been arrested. DiBiase had probably gone underground shortly after the crime. We wouldn't have found him anyway.

Keenan remarked that our only hope now was to put Pete the Greek on trial for felonious possession of an illegal handgun. If we could convict him on that charge, if he saw himself going away for seven years, he might panic and agree to identify the murderers of Joey Gallo—obviously he knew who they were. And just as obviously, his life wouldn't be worth a thing if he went to jail.

(And in fact, Pete the Greek would be convicted later in the year; but the jury would cop out at the last minute, convicting him only of possession of an unloaded handgun, a misdemeanor, maximum sentence one year. Pete the Greek accepted his one year, and said nothing.)

One of the FBI agents now pointed out to us that Luparelli was an illiterate. He had signed certain statements both for the FBI and for the Police Department, but all of them had had to be read back to him before he affixed his signature—he could not read them himself.

Captain McDermott commented, "You don't have to know how to read and write in his line of work, which is knocking people off and then burying them."

But my days in the Police Department were running out. The Gallo case would be dealt with by others. There was time left only for the Colombo case, or perhaps not even that.

The final meeting on the Colombo case occurred high up in a midtown skyscraper in the offices of *Radio Italiana,* because some of the footage of the Colombo rally had been shot by them, had since been transferred to television tape, and they owned virtually the only equipment in town that could show their tape back to us. They gave us a big room with a big, expensive viewing machine along one wall, and a big-busted Italian girl to work the machine for us. While we watched this film and the others, normal business was conducted all around us, and through an open doorway we could hear somebody telephone Rome.

"Pronto, Roma. Roma, pronto."

Rome must have answered, for the next phrase was, *"Qui New York. New York che parla."*

Present were Assistant District Attorneys Keenan, Dan Fitzgerald, and Robert Tannenbaum; Acting Chief of Detectives Kinsella, Sergeant Reilly and a number of detectives from his squad; Deputy Chief Thomas Reid, who had grabbed Jerome Johnson's gun hand; and myself.

The Italian TV film had already proven a major disappointment. Earlier, Sergeant Weber had plotted exactly where the Italian cameraman must have been standing. Probably the black girl who had accompanied Jerome Johnson to the rally had escaped by running directly past the Italian cameraman. Surely her face would be visible in a few frames of this film. Weber had waited months for the film to come back from Rome, but when it arrived it had been transferred to tape, and cut down to a few seconds of viewing time. The black girl was nowhere in sight.

Now we watched this short film, frame by frame, while Reilly pointed out who the various arms and shirts belonged to. Rossillo was wearing a blue shirt. Miccio, the muscle man, was wearing a purple body shirt; not only were his muscles showing, but in his belt under his shirt in the frames before the shooting, one could plainly see his gun. Later, after the shooting had started, he ran frantically about waving his gun in the air.

We studied the Italian film, and all the other films, frame by frame. It was almost impossible to tell what was happening—without Reilly's explanations it would have been completely impossible.

Was that a gun being held in that hand? Was that a cop's hand grappling with that gun hand? If so, which cop? Was this before Johnson was shot, or afterwards?

The work was slow and painful.

John Keenan kept shaking his head.

I said, "You'll never get a jury to understand what's happening on that film, or to agree to what they've seen. They'd have to study it as long as Reilly's studied it."

Keenan said, "You're telling me."

Finally we all sat down on leather sofas and armchairs in the room. "What's your plan, John?" said Keenan to Chief Kinsella. "Do you want to put them before a grand jury, bust their chops?"

We went over all the arguments in favor of doing just this.

Keenan then instructed Sergeant Reilly and Assistant District Attorney Fitzgerald to work out exactly which hard questions would force these hoods into perjuring themselves when they were subpoenaed to appear before the grand jury. Their appearance should be set up for June, after the trial season was over. He didn't want to bring any cops before the grand jury, just Mafia figures.

"The papers will have a field day," he remarked.

I thought, Yes, and this frog in the throat of the Police Department will be gone at last.

"Frog in the throat" was what Commissioner of Orga-

nized Crime Control McCarthy had called the Colombo
case, when I had met with him and with First Deputy Commissioner Smith shortly before. Both had announced themselves in favor of the solution which Sergeant Reilly, District Attorney Keenan, and I had worked out, and both had
promised to come to the screening in order to be in on the
final decision. However, neither had shown up, and perhaps I should have feared the worst right then.

In fact, none of these hoods would ever be summoned to
appear before any grand jury to answer any questions
about the Colombo hit. For over three weeks Reilly and
Fitzgerald would work over the evidence and prepare the
questions. But one day Captain McDermott, homicide
coordinator for Manhattan South, would appear in Fitzgerald's office to announce that the Police Department was
abandoning the Colombo case.

Sergeant Reilly's squad was disbanded. Reilly was given
a squad working on the Foster-Laurie homicide—eventually it would be Reilly himself who arrested Ronald Anderson, accused of murdering the two patrolmen, on a street in
Brooklyn.

Why would the Police Department decide to abandon
the Colombo investigation at the door to the grand jury
room, and who gave the order?

Later I spoke to those who thought it was done out of
petty jealousy. Indictments of any kind might have reflected credit toward Seedman and toward myself. Why should
the Police Department pursue minor indictments—perjury
and contempt—to bring major credit to the two of us? If
the case remained unresolved, perhaps both of us would be
embarrassed.

Other detectives told me it was a simple economy move.
Too much detectives' time was being wasted on an insoluble case.

McDermott had told Fitzgerald only that the decision to
close out the Colombo case had been made higher up than
himself, in order to throw that manpower into the Gallo
case, which seemed more hopeful.

However, the eight detectives were not assigned to the
Gallo case but were sent back to their commands.

One day I asked Sergeant Reilly if he knew who had ordered the Colombo case closed out. The frustrated Reilly

said he didn't know and he hadn't been able to find out.

Assistant District Attorney Fitzgerald, naming no individual, blamed the Police Department, and believed that the police decision was a mistake.

One day at lunch I questioned Deputy Commissioner McCarthy, but he said he knew nothing about who had closed down the Colombo case.

I never asked the Police Commissioner anything. He had not previously got involved in any criminal case. It seemed inconceivable that he would have got involved in this one, one way or the other.

I might have telephoned First Deputy Commissioner Smith, and perhaps he might have told me something or at least sung me a high note. But I never did it. I was out of the Police Department now. I had no right to ask hard questions of Smith or anybody else. It was their police department now, not mine.

Some months later, the Gallo case reached the exact dead end the Colombo case reached. But this time Mafia figures were thrown in front of the grand jury—our solution indeed—where some refused to talk, and some talked too much. The results: four indictments for criminal contempt, two for perjury; six hoods, unless they elected to cooperate, were headed for jail. The case stayed open.

4 / Murphy for Mayor

One morning each month the Police Commissioner had himself driven directly from his home on Staten Island to the offices of WCBS, where he would spend most of the next two hours recording answers to questions received from listeners. During the ensuing month CBS would broadcast these, using up one a day, and when all were gone Murphy would come in and record some more. The station liked to get its money's worth; although each question was used only during a single day, they were thrown into news broadcasts at odd hours, and it was possible for a citizen to hear Murphy answer the same question—and possibly a dull question—four or more times within 24 hours.

One morning when we were leaving this radio station the Police Commissioner asked what I thought of these questions.

"Why do you ask?"

"Somebody came up to me at a dinner last night and said, 'Get off that program, those questions are ruining you.'"

"Ruining me?" Murphy had asked.

"You've got to start thinking about 1973."

"1973?"

"That's right, all the way in '73."

The Police Commissioner had asked, "What do you mean, 1973?"

"1973 is when you get elected mayor. The only thing that can stop you is that stupid program. That program will ruin you for 1973."

Murphy was not the man to tell anecdotes, not about himself, not about anything.

"So I just wondered what your opinion was of that program?"

Was he asking my opinion about the program, or my opinon about 1973?

There was a luncheon on the second floor of a restaurant in Harlem. About 60 people attended. The police delegation numbered about ten. The rest of the faces, all black, belonged to Harlem businessmen and politicians.

The Police Commissioner was late. He was almost always late these days. Upstairs the rest of us sipped cocktails, waiting. Out in the street Murphy's security forces were deployed as inconspicuously as possible; though in a black neighborhood, it was clear enough who these men were. Unmarked cars were parked here and there along the street, and other detectives stood carefully in doorways.

Harlem was not police territory, and these detectives were the proof of it.

Upstairs, conversation abruptly stopped, and all eyes turned toward the door. The Police Commissioner was suddenly among us. A television crew rushed to his side and glaring lights came on. As Murphy moved through the crowd, shaking hands, the television crew moved along at his side, tracking him. The lights and the lens were a yard from his face, and the excitement he had just brought into that room was palpable. The community leaders of Harlem reached to touch him, to listen to any polite words he might have for them.

Later Murphy spoke without notes. He talked of ending corruption among policemen. He talked of reducing street crime, and reducing fear. He talked about the need for more black cops. He made no jokes, but he spoke no platitudes either. Then he stopped, and asked questions from the floor.

The president of the Uptown Chamber of Commerce rose: "You're the best Police Commissioner we've had here in my lifetime."

A few minutes later a second black businessman declared: "I don't know whether you're the best, but we trust you more than any we've ever had."

A police commissioner beloved in Harlem?

This was heady stuff, though not so heady as the television lights and camera tracking him through crowded rooms, wanting only to show the city his face, and how well he shook hands.

There was a press conference at police headquarters.

A question from the floor: Was he running for mayor?

The Police Commissioner proved as nimble as any politician. "I may run the Police Department, but my wife runs my family, and she hasn't given me permission yet to run for mayor or any other public office."

A TWA airliner returned immediately to Kennedy Airport, because a letter had been delivered from an extortionist announcing that a bomb was aboard. Now a German shepherd named Brandy, which belonged to the Police Department and which had been trained to sniff out bombs, went through the airliner and found the suitcase containing the device.

While the plane was still in the air, Inspector Devine, who was Murphy's chief secretary, had come down to my office. Devine said the Police Commissioner was willing to go out to Kennedy Airport if I thought this was the thing to do. Later I was called to Murphy's office. He was very friendly and began to make idle conversation, something which almost never occurred in that office. He was waiting for a phone call from Inspector Lane, who was at the airport. While waiting, Murphy and I sat gossiping, wasting time. This was so unlike Murphy, and I became so uncomfortable, that presently I went back to my own office.

It was clear Murphy wanted to drive out to the airport and hold a press conference there, and presently he summoned me back, and we rode out together. In the car he remarked that the reporters were all picking up the notion that he was running for mayor.

I asked only how long he thought he could last as Police Commissioner. The job demanded tremendous stamina after all.

He said he thought he could finish out his five-year mandate, that physically the job was getting easier month by month. Whether he would be allowed to last five years was another story, for Lindsay's term ended in 1973. If somebody else became mayor, perhaps this person would get rid of him. Or perhaps the new mayor, whoever he was, would feel that Murphy was so strong that he had to keep Murphy on. Perhaps, Murphy remarked, he himself could even be a casualty in the Presidential campaign coming up. "Suppose Nixon decided it was to his advantage to attack Murphy," the Police Commissioner said. "Suppose the President started denouncing Murphy, Murphy is soft on crime."

It was odd to hear him talk of himself as Murphy.

"Nixon could well decide that it would be valuable politics to go after Murphy's head."

It was also possible that Nixon had never heard of Murphy.

Then Murphy remarked that all of this could end within 48 hours. Anything could happen. One had to be philosophical. If you were worried about the future all the time, you would never take any chances—meaning that you would never try anything. You would never accomplish anything either. And you might not last anyway. You'd just be waiting around to make the mistake that would end it for you.

It was a long ride. We talked about Police Commissioner Murphy all the way.

At the airport, we waded through journalists into an office where Murphy talked to authorities representing the Port of New York Authority, the FBI, the airport, and TWA itself. No one had planned to make any public statements, but as soon as they saw Murphy they realized he would hold a press conference. He said quietly, "Of course we'll have to tell the press what's going on."

Someone said, "Yes, sir, of course. We knew you would want to do that."

We were supplied with a room; and as soon as Murphy, Detective Schmidt, who had defused the bomb, the dog Brandy, and I were in place at a table, a horde of journalists was admitted.

In 20 minutes the press conference was over—and Murphy had grabbed himself thousands of dollars worth of publicity. He had praised Detective Schmidt, patted the German shepherd on the head. He had smiled and spoken briefly for the benefit of every TV station in town, and then he was back in his car on his way home. Twenty minutes. A virtuoso performance.

I had not seen him so avid for headlines before, never realized to what extent he could now create headlines just by appearing somewhere. I did realize that he was now less and less receptive to criticism of any kind, and that his instincts for publicity were very keen, as keen as mine, perhaps keener.

He read his own importance in the headlines. In addition, he now listened to, and believed, any and all optimistic reports from his police commanders, as if it was only normal that everyone of his programs was working beautifully.

Adverse comments came to him only from Lacovara and myself. One day Lacovara accused him of being paranoiac on the subject of the Knapp Commission—for Murphy believed that Michael Armstrong was out in the streets making observations of corrupt policemen even now, months after the commission hearings were over.

"Paranoiac?" inquired Murphy.

To me Lacovara later remarked, "I knew I had made a mistake the minute I saw the way he stiffened."

I never heard Lacovara offer a critical comment of any kind after that.

I was still urging Murphy to put the Model Precinct under the command of the three-man executive committee, including myself; that in fact, an executive committee was needed to make things happen.

I said, "Because, as things are now, some of your ideas just don't get done. They keep going down through the chain of command, and when they get to the bottom they just sit there. We need a committee that can make things happen."

The Police Commissioner said stiffly, "Well, a great deal has been done. It's so slow just to get top management changed. To get top management moving is hard."

Occasionally I tried to push him a little further on this subject or another. But as soon as he saw he was being even mildly criticized, he would look up at the clock and say, "Well, I'm running a little late. Thanks, Bob, appreciate it." And he was gone.

At length, strictly for my benefit it seemed, a high-level conference was laid on. Subject: The Model Precinct.

The fourth-floor conference room was full. Inspector Andersson, commanding the Model Precinct, had brought members of his staff. The other conferees included every member of the chain of command from Andersson up to the Police Commissioner. Several of the deputy commissioners were present as well. I sat at Murphy's right hand, while Andersson read a five-page progress report. The Model Precinct had been in operation two and a half months, and Andersson's report was rosy. The community was delighted, morale was excellent, crime was down.

Andersson then noted the defections of Durk and of the residential policeman, but both had already been replaced by better men. Anderson could use a few more sergeants, and he also wanted six new radio cars, and 63 additional portable radios. Radio car teams were finishing each job in an average of 26.4 minutes, as opposed to 30.8 minutes in pre-Model Precinct days; the precinct had been 42nd best in this important statistic, and now it had jumped up to the eighth best.

Beside me, the Police Commissioner sat beaming.

"What about corruption, Norm?"

"I'm nearly perfectly certain there are no pads," Anderson replied. "Maybe one or two of the cops cadge a meal here and there. But if there were pads, too many people would have to know, and we have strong supervision."

"Cadge a meal?" Murphy said with a grin. "In the Model Precinct, no one's supposed to get a pretzel."

The report had told him exactly what he wanted to hear.

He turned to me as the conference neared its end and said, "Was there something you wanted to say, Bob?"

During the past hour not a single doubt had been expressed. The Police Commissioner had been repeatedly praised for having thought up the idea. Andersson had been praised for having done such a fine job.

It was going to sound churlish to express reservations. A man could not have asked for a less receptive audience.

I said, "I don't see where the Model Precinct differs very much from any other precinct. I thought it was supposed to be something really special. We were going to try out new concepts. But I don't see—"

Voices around the table assured me that the model precinct was "moving right along."

The Police Commissioner turned to me and shrugged. The model precinct was a success, and there was nothing further to be discussed.

Nothing had been decided on the future of Sergeant David Durk.

Durk called, "What's he going to give me?"

The answer was, nothing. Murphy was not interested in the subject of David Durk. No special job or responsibility would be offered him.

Durk was crushed. "Then that's the end of it. I'm quitting the Police Department. I'm gonna go to the newspapers. Murphy owes his job to me, and he knows it. If it hadn't been for me, Murphy would still be in Detroit. You can tell him that for me."

Presently I did tell him, knowing he wouldn't like it, but believing that someone had to tell him unpleasant truths occasionally, and there was no one else but guess who.

He owes his job to me, and he knows it. If it wasn't for me he'd still be in Detroit.

Executive conferences were held monthly, and on all levels. A Police Academy lieutenant was the moderator, and each month to our top-level executive conference he would bring the problems, proposals, and gripes that he had previously heard from lower-ranking commanders. One day he brought up the subject of expense accounts for precinct captains. At present they received not one dime, and many were inviting community leaders and businessmen to lunch to discuss community problems. This was costing the captains plenty. Was there no way they could have a small expense account?

That meeting was chaired by First Deputy Commissioner Smith. Smith announced himself as opposed to expense accounts for anybody.

No one was for them except Deputy Commissioner Ward and myself. While Ward spoke Smith wrote a note and passed it to me. The note read, "Those people that he wants to take to lunch, what do they want back from him?"

Seated beside Smith, I explained in a whisper that in our modern expense-account society, more business probably was transacted at lunch than any other time or place. In addition, how could a precinct captain summon some influential citizen to the station house? Most station houses were outstandingly old, ugly, and dirty. Visitors would come in fear, for nearly every citizen was afraid of what could happen to him inside a station house. On the other hand, no precinct captain could invite himself to a citizen's house for lunch. His only alternative was to offer to meet the citizen in a restaurant, and no self-respecting man could let the other guy pay all the time. The captain had to pick up some of these checks, and a way should be found to reimburse him for these expenses.

Smith kept shaking his head. I was wrong. He didn't want any precinct captain taking anybody to lunch.

One entire top-level conference was devoted to the problem of internal communication, lack of which was hampering many of Murphy's ideas and reforms. He recognized this himself, and had sent out memos on the subject. How was information, not to mention faith and enthusiasm, to be disseminated down through command and out into the radio cars?

Murphy was aware that his message was not getting through. He was aware also that cops had no use for him, and as a result he recoiled from them. He had long since ceased making any effort to ingratiate himself with policemen.

Chief Neil Behan, commanding officer of the Police Academy, opened the conference by remarking that internal communication was difficult because the average policeman had no respect for himself. Because he had no respect for himself, he wasn't going to listen to, or pay any attention to, people telling him how good he was, and that he could be better. He wasn't going to be receptive to requests to do some things differently, or more efficiently, or more effectively. Chief Behan declared that all large organizations had this communication problem, and he wasn't sure that it could be solved at all, which didn't mean that we shouldn't try to solve it.

The second speaker was myself. In front of each place lay two memos which I had written to the Police Commissioner. The first, sent on December 15, had noted the low morale of the Department, and had suggested that Murphy start a regular program of attempting to win over members of the force. There were a number of rules and procedures of the Department that Murphy could change with a stroke of the pen, causing every cop on the force to say, That's nice, I'm glad he did that.

I suggested that once a week he should eliminate with said stroke one or more stupidities or anachronisms in the rules and procedures; furthermore, he should start with Christmas amnesty for cops facing disciplinary charges.

He agreed in principle, and Departmental amnesty was granted. However, no action was ever taken on any of the other suggestions in my first memo. My second memo was similar, and had resulted only in this conference.

Now I began to explain to him and to the others that if he wanted to communicate with the troops, if internal communication was really important to him, then it seemed to me he had to start by winning the allegiance of the cops. The only way to do this was via specific acts and decisions designed to make their lives better and easier. Once he had won them over, then they would be willing to listen to him, and to follow him. Or at least some of them would, some of the time.

I was talking about leadership through communication.

Deputy Commissioner Ward broke in, saying that internal communications was a management problem: "Our managers are patrolmen with stars on their shoulders. They don't communicate with anybody above or below them."

With that the conference swung onto the far more popular subject of management. Everyone there had taken a management course at one time or another, and all understood that Murphy saw quick, efficient management as the solution to all problems.

Once or twice I tried to swing the discussion back to its origins.

Chief Inspector Codd and Chief of Patrol Cawley were both against trying to win over the patrolmen by giving them things. There was no sentiment in the room for trying to make their lives a little easier and thereby obtaining their cooperation.

A number of commanders now pointed out that cops were always griping. But if you examined their gripes, they had nothing to gripe about. One commander spoke of sitting down with cops only a week ago.

"Come on, tell me your gripes," he had said.

But they didn't have any, he said.

A number of commanders now began bad-mouthing cops in general.

It came as a surprise to me to see that no one in that room was fond of cops.

Each time the Police Commissioner appeared at a communion breakfast or a dinner sponsored by one of the line organizations, I suggested next, he should take that opportunity to win over the hundreds of cops present. It would be especially easy on such an occasion to give them something that they wanted, and which cost him nothing. If he addressed the traffic patrolmen's group, why not tell them that from now on they were allowed to wear mittens on frozen winter nights? It was an old police cliché that no one could shoot a pistol wearing mittens, but one couldn't shoot one with frozen fingers either. Give them such a boon, and you would have their total attention. They would then listen to most of the rest of what the Police Commissioner had to tell them that day.

First Deputy Commissioner Smith declared that the line organizations were all, in effect, labor unions. They were not sympathetic to bosses. Whatever Murphy might say, they would take the opposite position.

I said I thought the Police Commissioner could win the men over, and it was worth a try.

Murphy said quietly that sometimes he thought he could too, but most of the time he believed it was impossible, and not worth the try.

I almost had the feeling that he had called this conference to convince me that none of the things I was proposing were possible.

Suddenly Chief of Inspections Anthony Bouza, whom Murphy had promoted twice in the last few months, remarked that the Police Commissioner should be speaking directly to the men, should be saying specific things to them, that it was time all of us cut out the bullshit. "Furthermore, you ought to be writing that newsletter that you distribute to the troops. You shouldn't let some lieutenant do that. That's your job. You should talk directly to the men."

The Police Commissioner said stiffly, "Well, I'd like to if I had the time. But I don't really have the time."

Presently the conference broke up. Nothing whatever had been decided.

I wrote another memo: "Your changes, improvements, reorganizations, will be accepted better and, therefore, will work better, if the men are basically pleased with you and trust you or at least are not hostile to you. Some people say your reforms can only work if the men accept them and you. I believe that you can win the men over if you try. I believe that you can appear to them twice as tough as you appear now and still win them over."

Murphy waited two and a half weeks, then sent another memo back. It's easy to be critical, he noted. The basic problem was very poor leadership from top to bottom, a climate of corruption. Until leadership from sergeant on up was better, it would not be easy to sell himself to the men. It would take some doing to obtain respect and loyalty for the guy who had killed Santa Claus, and taken food out of the mouths of cops' kids by depriving cops of the "legitimate" fringe benefits that Murphy's anti-corruption stance had deprived them of.

Negotiations for a new contract for patrolmen had been under way for more than a year. Once when agreement was near, negotiations had been broken off because Deputy Commissioner McCarthy announced that henceforth he planned to polygraph all cops accused of corruption. Another time an agreement collapsed when Chief of Patrol Cawley's so-called master plan leaked to the press. The master plan numbered about 100 ideas to be studied for possible future use, everything from one-man patrol cars to forcing non-productive cops out of the job. But Murphy considered both men "tough" and did nothing except to praise them.

Later, negotiators had agreed to terms once again—but the rank and file voted to reject the contract. There was talk of another job action or strike. The Police Commissioner appeared unworried.

"The single word which best decribes the P.C.," Lacovara said one day, "is 'unflappable.' He just doesn't get upset. I don't think he's personally committed to any of this. I think that to him his job is a hobby. Sometimes on weekends I call him up and ask what he's doing, and he tells me he's watching TV with his kids. That's what he cares about. Being Police Commissioner is a hobby with him."

Hobby?

One day, in the middle of a luncheon that a number of us attended, he leaned across me to speak to Chief Cawley. "Don, who would you rate as your two weakest division commanders?" A fork load of meat then went into his mouth. He worked even when chewing.

Rising to speak, Murphy looked to where District Attorney Mackell sat sipping Scotch. Murphy said, "I'll keep it short, because Commissioner Daley has advised me that that is the way to do it, and also because if I don't keep it short, the distinguished District Attorney of Queens County will be carried out of here on a stretcher."

This brought down the house. Murphy could be funny at times.

One day, a new police harbor launch was dedicated to the memory of Patrolman Miguel Sirvent, who had interrupted a holdup in a hamburger joint late at night while off duty. He had pulled his gun on one holdup man, only to be shot in the head by another, whom he had not seen, and now the new launch bobbed in the swells, and the wind blew off the water at us, and the young blonde widow, not more than 23 years old herself, was asked to speak into the microphone.

She managed to say: "Thank you—very—much," then started to bawl. In her seat beside the Police Commissioner, she hid her face, weeping. Murphy started to put his arm around her, hestitated, let his hand drop to the back of her chair. At last he did put his arm around her, and his hand cupped her shoulder until she had stopped crying. But it had been a hard thing for him to do.

He wanted to be considered tough. He sent me a memo demanding three "tough Murphy" stories a week. He wanted to hit hard on the corruption issue. I suggested that we group all our corruption investigations, and release this news once a month. If we tried to make publicity out of each individual case, we'd merely give the city the impression that every single cop on the street was corrupt.

Murphy replied, "Steve Kennedy stayed on top for five years as the feared head who month after month fired crooked cops. Let's put more stories out, and I'll judge whether we are making our point."

Sergeant Durk did not quit the Police Department, and he did not "go to the papers." Instead he was assigned to my office. It was up to me to supervise him. And perhaps I would fail. Meanwhile, once a week for three weeks, men from the Chief Inspector's office entered my office in the middle of the night trying to catch my duty sergeant asleep. This would presumably prove I could not supervise my men; was not "tough."

I phoned the Chief Inspector.

"What's going on here? Is there something I don't know? Have there been complaints?"

"Absolutely not," said Codd. "If there had been complaints, you'd be the first to know. It's just a routine check on offices that are open 24 hours a day. Your office checked out fine."

I said, "The Chief of Detectives' office was not checked."

"Don't you believe it. They checked there too."

But I verified they hadn't.

One day I got into a radio car in Harlem. We rode along. The cop who was the recorder turned in his seat and said, "Commissioner, I just want to know one thing. Does Murphy hate cops?"

5 / The Harlem Mosque Murder

At 11:41 that spring morning, a man dialed 911, the police emergency phone number. The connection was made—and a tape recording began—at 11:41:20 A.M.

OPERATOR: "Police operator."

CALLER: "Hello, this is Detective Thomas of the 28th Precinct."

OPERATOR: "Yeah?"

CALLER: "I have a 10-13, 102 West 116th Street."

OPERATOR: "102 West 116th?"

CALLER: "Right. That's on the second floor."

OPERATOR: "Second floor?"

CALLER: "Right."

OPERATOR: "Hold on."

However, the caller hung up.

The operator, one of many cops sitting at banks of electronic machines in a vast, brightly lighted room on the fourth floor of police headquarters, began tapping out signals on the keyboard in front of him. These signals reappeared in a smaller, adjoining room in front of the radio dispatcher operating on the frequency received by Sixth Division—Harlem—radio cars. The dispatcher now spoke into his headset.

DISPATCHER: "Signal 10-13, 102 West 116th on the second floor. 102, 116, second floor, signal 13."

It was precisely 11:42 A.M. There was no immediate acknowledgment from any radio car.

DISPATCHER: "Units receive assist patrolman 102 West 116. K."

UNIT: "28 Frank on the way."

UNIT: ". . . (distorted) . . . David will respond."

DISPATCHER: "That's second floor hallway, 102 West 116. K."

UNIT: "28 Sergeant responding."

Thirty-five seconds had gone by.

UNIT: ". . . (distorted) . . ."

DISPATCHER: "10-5. *(pause)* Is there a footman requesting assistance?"

UNIT: "Said something about 116th Street, Central."

Two minutes and ten seconds had gone by.

DISPATCHER: "Any unit on the scene at that assist patrolman, 102 West 116?"

UNIT: "That a 13, Central?"

DISPATCHER: "Any 28 car on the scene of that assist patrolman, 102 West 116th Street? K."

UNIT: "No further, 102 West 116, scooter post two of the 28."

According to scooter post two, no further assistance was required.

DISPATCHER: "Units in the 28 Precinct, no further, 102 116th authority 28 scooter patrolman on the scene, 11:45 hours."

So three minutes had now gone by.

Ten more seconds passed.

UNIT: "10-13, 102 West 116th Street."

DISPATCHER: "102 West 116th, a signal 13, 101 West 116th, a signal 13, what units to respond?"

UNIT: "25 anti-crime, Central."

DISPATCHER: "10-4. Any other units, 102 West 116th assist patrolman?"

UNIT: "10-13, get additional units, Central."

DISPATCHER: "Units in the 25 to respond to 102 West 116th Street, 102 116. K."

UNIT: "25 . . . *(distorted)* . . . Gonna respond there."

DISPATCHER: "10-4. Any other units in the 25, 102 West 116?"

UNIT: "32 available, Central. 32 Adam available."

DISPATCHER: "Adam respond forthwith 102 West 116th. K."

UNIT: "25 Henry, 25 Sergeant, we're also responding."

DISPATCHER: "10-4. Any unit in the 30, 32 or 25 Precincts, 102 West 116th, 102 116th."

UNIT: "32. . . *(distorted)* . . . is responding, Central."

DISPATCHER: "10-4. Be advised you have numerous plainclothes units also responding, numerous plainclothes units also responding. Use caution."

UNIT: "Shots are being fired, Central."

DISPATCHER: "Shots fired, shots fired, shots fired. 102

West 116th, repeating units responding, 102 116th shots fired at this time."

It was 11:46 A.M. Four minutes had gone by.

UNIT: ". . . *(distorted)* . . ."

UNIT: "10-5 that last transmission."

DISPATCHER: "That's shots fired, assist patrolman, 102 West 116th in the 28 Precinct."

UNIT: "Patrolman shot, Central . . . *(distorted)* . . ."

It was 11:46:20 A.M. Four minutes and 20 seconds had passed since the signal 10-13 first went out on the Sixth Division frequency.

UNIT: "10-5 that last transmission. K."

DISPATCHER: "We have reports of a patrolman shot at this time, 102 West 116th, reports of a patrolman shot, 102 West 116th."

UNIT: ". . . *(distorted)* . . . Patrolman shot at this location, Central."

DISPATCHER: "Affirmative, affirmative, units be advised we have reports of a patrolman shot, 102 West 166th. K."

UNIT: "10-5."

UNIT: "What have you got there, Central?"

DISPATCHER: "That's 102 West 116th, 102 West 116th, report of a patrolman shot."

UNIT: ". . . *(distorted—possibly—*two cops shot at this location) . . ."

DISPATCHER: "An ambulance is on the way."

Nearly 40 seconds of silence now followed.

DISPATCHER: "Any further assistance required at this time, 102 West 116th?"

UNIT: "Send emergency service. I understand that they have the perpetrators in the building with the cops' guns."

DISPATCHER: "10-4."

UNIT: "No further . . . *(distorted)* . . . West 116th. There's enough units on the scene. Authority Sixth Division lieutenant."

UNIT: "Central, has that been a definite shooting of a police officer?"

DISPATCHER: "That's affirmative. Report of two patrolmen shot at this time."

It was 11:49 A.M., seven minutes had gone by since the

first transmission over Sixth Division radio.

DISPATCHER: "Any supervisor on the scene 102 West 116th? K."

UNIT: "Inspector's here, Central. Hold on, I'll get him."

UNIT: ". . . *(distorted—possibly—*close that building. Don't let anybody out.) . . ."

UNIT: *(distorted)* . . . to Central K."

DISPATCHER: "Unit with a message?"

UNIT: ". . . *(distorted)* . . ."

UNIT: "Any description on the perpetrators, Central?"

UNIT: "28 John to Central, K."

DISPATCHER: "28 John."

UNIT: "The inspector of the division is here. They are going to set up a temporary headquarters here, and there have been two patrolmen shot, removed to the hospital, no further information."

It was 11:49:55 A.M.

DISPATCHER: "10-4. We have emergency service on the way up."

UNIT: "No further, 116th and Lenox. All units resume patrol but the 28 units. All units resume from 116th and Lenox."

DISPATCHER: "Who's that on the air, by what authority?"

UNIT: ". . . *(distorted)* . . . Sergeant's car report to front of . . . *(distorted)* . . ."

UNIT: "Was there any description on the perpetrators?"

DISPATCHER: "All we have at this time reportedly the perpetrators still trapped in the building in possession of the patrolmen's guns, K."

Police radios could be monitored by anyone with the proper equipment, and the news media did monitor them so as to be fast on the scene of any interesting catastrophe. 102 West 116th Street was the site of the Harlem Mosque of the Black Muslim sect. By the time I got there, after a siren-blowing ride up from headquarters, scarcely 20 minutes had elapsed, but hundreds upon hundreds of people already milled in the streets, drawn to see the shoot-out which the news broadcasts were already promising. Television cameras rode on the shoulders of cameramen, above the sea of heads. I plunged through to the double steel doors and passed inside the mosque, which swarmed with cops. In the entrance hall, chairs were upturned, and a police service revolver lay on the floor between the legs of the cop who was guarding it, and the walls were pocked with bullet holes. There was blood on the floor and on the staircase. Downstairs was a kind of lounge. It too was crowded with cops, and with a dozen or 20 blacks who were evidently being detained.

I was the highest-ranking commander on the scene, and I now began interrogating people, trying to piece together what had happened, and what was happening.

There was no shoot-out in progress. Although two cops had been removed by ambulance, only one was shot, no one knew how badly. The other had evidently been slugged over the head. Only one police gun was missing. There were no perpetrators holed up in the building, for cops had been through every inch of it by now. The perpetrators had not been one or two men, but dozens of men.

This was enough information with which to rush out into the street to try to calm down the mob. As I exited, I was surrounded by microphones, cameras, and reporters.

I kept repeating, "There is no shoot-out. No one is trapped inside. Everything is under control. One cop has been shot. Two have been removed to the hospital. One gun is missing. We're trying to find out what happened now."

A kind of Sunday school had been in progress inside, and rumors swept the street that cops had fired in on people and/or kids at pointblank range. I explained that the shots fired in through the doors were aimed high. The bullet holes were high up in the walls and in the ceiling. There had been a terrific fight in there between three cops on one side and 20 or 30 or more men on the other. And the other cops outside could not get through the barred steel doors. So they had fired through the glass high up in the doors, trying to gain admittance.

I went back inside for more information. I interrogated cops. I interrogated superior officers.

Among the first detectives to reach the mosque were Sonny Grosso, formerly the partner of Eddie Egan, and Grosso's current partner, Randy Jurgensen. Jurgensen had been staked out a block from the mosque in a fake gypsy cab with three anti-crime patrolmen, watching a building where Robert Vickers, wanted in the Foster-Laurie assassinations, was believed holed up. Ten blocks away, Grosso was watching for Twyman Meyers, another of the Foster-Laurie fugitives.

Now they were close to these fugitives, and knew that such men sometimes called in false 10-13s to clear an area of cops. While cops rushed elsewhere, the fugitives could move in or out with impunity. Grosso and Jurgensen hesitated, then both responded to the mosque, for a cop in trouble took precedence.

Outside the crowd swelled and swelled, fed by rumors. A young woman television reporter was slugged and trampled. Certain boys moved through the mob spraying white reporters with lighter fluid, and then touching a match to the saturated clothing. Part of the mob came upon the fake gypsy cab belonging to Jurgensen. The car was thrown onto its roof and set afire. From the rooftops, bottles, bricks, and other objects sailed down onto the crowd, but cops, one of them Jurgensen, were being sent up onto all the rooftops to clear them. A police helicopter whirled overhead, sweeping down close to the rooftops and then rising swiftly. The noise was such that radio transmissions in the street were virtually unreadable. Faces kept gazing upward at the helicopter, some showing excitement, some fear, and I found Inspector Thomas Mitchelson, the black commanding officer of the Sixth Division, and suggested he call that helicopter off. He was hollering into a walkie-talkie. He said, "I've been trying to, but I can't get through."

I estimated about 1200 people in the street within a one-block area. These people seemed to me on the edge of violence. Any incident could touch off a riot.

Groups of blacks surrounded me, shouting angry questions. I tried to calm them.

I also kept moving. It was the only way to stay safe in a situation this explosive.

I kept begging radio broadcasters, some of whom had already broadcast misinformation, to go on the air with accurate information as soon as possible. There was no shoot-out. No one was holed up. No blacks were dead.

The crowd had now attacked a number of reporters. I began begging the reporters to leave the scene, particularly the TV cameramen who, with bulky gear on their shoulders, were so easily identifiable.

Jurgensen got clubbed with a stickball bat. As he fell, the cop trying to support him fired a gun into the air.

How much would it take to ignite all of Harlem?

With the rooftops cleared, a loaded bus entered 116th Street, then was immobilized by the mob. Burning newspapers were rammed in the open windows. Passengers screamed.

A radio car was surrounded and its windows bashed in.

Chief of Detectives Seedman had entered the mosque, and his investigation had begun.

Two Black Muslims were taken out through the crowd, handcuffed, and driven away. The mob had barely failed in its attempt to free the prisoners.

At St. Luke's Hospital the wounded patrolman, Phillip Cardillo, lay on an operating table. As always, Mayor Lindsay and the Police Commissioner waited in a small room. Whenever a cop was shot, both always drove directly to the hospital, and there they sat, sometimes for three hours or more, waiting. It was never clear to me what purpose this served, but it was always done.

Now as I entered this room, neither of them asked me a single question, though presumably I had come directly from the scene and would have the freshest information.

Presently I said, "It certainly was delicate there. It came so close to a riot. So close. It was still delicate when I left, five minutes ago."

Lindsay looked up sharply. "Riot?" he demanded. "What do you mean, riot? There can't be any riot. There won't be any riot. It never came close to being a riot. How can you say such a thing?"

"I've been around riots before. This was as close to one as I've ever seen."

"How many people were there?" asked Lindsay angrily. "There weren't many people in the street."

He hadn't been there, and any information he might have on the subject would, by now, be old information.

"Well," I said, "there are at least 1200 people in the streets."

"What's a thousand people, 1200 people?" demanded Lindsay. "You can't have a riot with a thousand people or 1200 people."

If he thought not, there was nothing I could do to change his mind.

Murphy drew me aside. "We had reports it wasn't so bad there."

"It was pretty bad."

I began to relate some of the details to the Police Commissioner, but he cut me off, saying, "No, we're not sure of anything yet. We better check into it a little further."

I said, "I interrogated most of the cops involved."

But he shook his head, and went back and sat down beside Lindsay. A long time passed. They neither moved nor spoke. At length Lindsay said with a sigh, "I sure hope that fella pulls through."

Seedman arrived. He and I went upstairs to interview the second injured cop. We found him groggy and half sedated. He explained that he had been struck on the head, apparently with a blackjack. He could not remember anything after that.

A little later we moved into a kind of auditorium on the ground floor of the hospital, Lindsay and his entourage, the Police Commissioner with his police entourage. The press was admitted and a short press conference began.

In response to questions, both the Mayor and the Police Commissioner claimed that nothing was known yet of what had happened. Most of the reporters had come directly from the Harlem Mosque and knew some details if not all, having been told them by me. But no specific answer of any kind was forthcoming from either the Mayor or the Police Commissioner.

This tended to repudiate my previous statements.

Headquarters for the investigation was set up in the 24th Precinct—the model precinct. Seedman and I went there, and during the rest of the afternoon each of us separately interrogated all of the cops involved. Seedman worked in one office, I in another. At some point the Police Commissioner dropped by and I briefed him. He said again, "No, we're not sure yet. We better check into it a little further."

About 5 P.M. I phoned him at headquarters and told him that I had put together a coherent story, and that this story ought to be released to the press and the people before rumors, mistakes, and deliberate misinformation not only formed the basis for tonight's news broadcast and tomorrow's newspapers, but also acquired such weight, such inherent truth even, that we would never be able to refute it.

Murphy, cautious, told me to dictate an account to one of my secretaries. Murphy would then appraise this account, and decide whether or not to make it public.

So I got Patrolman Znaniecki, one of my stenographers, on the phone. In the other office Chief Seedman was dictating a similar account to one of his stenographers. Later Seedman and I talked. Seedman said, "What do you know that I don't know?" We seemed to be the only two in the Police Department who cared to know exactly what had happened.

Ballistics details were not available at that time. All of the other details dictated by Seedman and myself that first night matched not only what I had told reporters outside the mosque, but also the eventual official police report.

The first radio car to reach the Harlam Mosque had contained Patrolman Phillip Cardillo, of the 28th Precinct, and his partner, Patrolman Vito Navarra. These two cops entered the hallway of the mosque—which looked exactly like a hallway in any office building in the city—and heard what they took to be scuffling on the second floor. The 10-13 to which they were responding had specified second floor, and now Navarra ran up to the second floor, where he was confronted by 15 to 20 men. He attempted to go downstairs again, but was cut off by additional men coming up the stairs.

Within a few minutes a number of radio cars responded to the same emergency call, and some of these men succeeded in forcing their way into the building. One was Patrolman Victor Padilla, 25th Precinct, who was almost immediately blackjacked. He fell to the floor and his gun was taken. It was never recovered.

The entrance hallway measured only about eight feet square. Twenty or more men may have been crowded into this enclosed space, including a number of patrolmen. All but Cardillo, Padilla, and Ivan Negron, who was Padilla's partner, were forced out into the street again, and the metal door was locked against them. This was a double door, with foot square glass windows in each side. Inside the hallway, Cardillo and Padilla were on the floor.

Negron had his back to the door and was struggling to retain his gun from men trying to wrench it away from him. He now heard one or more shots, drew his gun, and fired three times in the direction of a man who had a gun in his hand, who seemed to be getting up from the floor where Cardillo lay shot. Apparently these shots hit no one. It was possible that Negron's arm was forced high even as he pulled the trigger, and that his shots were the three which stitched the wall above the reception desk, one of them perforating the oil portrait of Elijah Mohammed which hung there.

Out on the street, Patrolman Navarra, who had previously fought his way out of the building, and Patrolman Rudy Andre of the 28th Precinct, smashed the glass in the doors with their revolvers and fired high into the hall. Andrew fired three times, and Navarra twice. The 20 or more men assaulting the police officers jumped up and fled down the corridor. The shaken Negron now unbolted the door, and a number of patrolmen entered the building.

These cops never noticed Cardillo's gun on the floor as they surged inside; later speculation suggested that the gun was returned to the entrance hall and dropped there sometime later.

So nine shots had been fired from four police guns, not including Padilla's gun, which was missing and may or may not have been fired. Ballistics men recovered only four bullets. Three were mutilated, and the fourth so badly damaged that it was useless too. Powder burns on the jacket of Patrolman Cardillo proved that the gun muzzle was held against his jacket. He was not shot from a distance by another policeman. He may or may not have been shot with his own gun, for the bullet passed completely through him.

When my report had been typed up, it was carried in and placed before the Police Commissioner, who summoned Chief Inspector Codd and Deputy Commissioner Benjamin Ward, the only black man among the police hierarchy, for advice.

This advice was to release only the names of the injured cops, and the fact that they were responding to an apparently legitimate call for assistance, which call later proved unfounded. Patrolman Cardillo had been operated on and was in critical condition in St. Luke's Hospital.

Apart from this, the official police posture should be absolute silence.

A number of phone calls ensued between the Police Commissioner and me, and between Codd, Ward, and me; and Ward especially declared that Harlem was on the edge of a riot. This was no time to give out any information that conceivably could provoke a reaction—and possibly violence. Silence was the thing.

"This is Friday," explained Ward. "Let's get through the weekend, and on Monday or next week we can reveal what actually happened."

After arguing briefly that an information void would probably be filled by misinformation, by tales of attempted slaughter of Muslims by police, I concurred. Ward was supposed to be the expert on Harlem, not I.

In the 24th Precinct, Chief of Detectives Seedman muttered, "It was a cowardly assault on police officers, but nobody's gonna have the stomach to say it."

I was summoned to the phone to take a call from the Mayor's office. I thought it might be Lindsay himself, but it was a secretary. The message was, When the cop dies, let us know immediately so the Mayor can get up to the hospital.

Cardillo had been shot only once, but it was hard to imagine a more damaging wound unless he had been killed outright. The bullet had entered his right side slightly to the rear of the midline, passing between his sixth and seventh ribs. It proceeded through the right leaf of the diaphragm, through the right lobe of the liver in the area of the gall bladder, through the transverse colon, and exited through the seventh and eighth ribs on his left side, slightly forward of the midline. During its 13-inch trajectory, the bullet had changed shape considerably. After penetrating between four to six inches, it must have looked like a mushroom, and probably it began to tumble. During the first five-hour operation on Cardillo, and during a second operation performed three days later, the right lobe of his liver was excised, his spleen and gall bladder were excised, and a colostomy and tracheostomy were performed.

Cardillo was 31 years old and married. He stood five feet eight inches tall and weighed 172 pounds. He was not expected to live.

The day following the shooting was Saturday. There had still been no statement from the Police Department as to what had happened or why; Harlem was still in a turmoil, and after multiple phone calls between the Police Commissioner and myself, Murphy agreed to release only a brief communiqué, which clarified nothing.

Deputy Commissioner Ward called me to protest even this communiqué. He said he was trying to sit on this thing, to keep Harlem from blowing up, and Murphy and I with our communiqué were making his job difficult. Ward said he agreed with what all of Harlem was saying at this time: that the cops had no legal right to enter that mosque. 10-13 or no 10-13. That mosque was a place of worship. Cops never would have entered a synagogue or St. Patrick's Cathedral in the same manner. The Muslims had a rule about firearms in their temples. Firearms were not allowed. Cops were not allowed.

Ward did not describe the incident as a deliberate attack on Muslims by police, but he said it certainly looked that way in Harlem, and he couldn't blame people for thinking so.

Ward was a big man, six feet one, 210 pounds. He was 45 years old. Appointed a patrolman on June 1, 1951, he began his higher education then, and eventually graduated from Brooklyn College magna cum laude. Brooklyn Law School followed, and after graduation Ward was admitted to the New York State Bar. His highest rank as a cop was lieutenant. While still a cop, he had worked as a lawyer prosecuting other cops in Departmental trials; and later he was named Deputy Commissioner of Trials by Commissioner Leary. Commissioner Murphy had switched him to Deputy Commissioner of Community Affairs. Murphy respected Ward, and once, while Murphy and First Deputy Commissioner Smith were attending a conference in California, Murphy had named Ward acting Police Commissioner in his absence, even though certain other deputy commissioners had seniority over Ward.

At this time black cops constituted only 7 to 8 percent of the force. Almost all black patrolmen were assigned to black precincts, or else they were on special assignments. A number worked as undercover agents for Narcotics or Intelligence; and a number had made splendid records as anti-crime plainclothesmen or as detectives, for they could move into places white cops could not. Very few black men had reached the hierarchy at all. One, Arthur Hill, was a two-star chief. Another, Tom Mitchelson, was a full inspector. And Ward, who had spent much of the last ten years as a prosecutor or judge of corrupt and/or brutal cops, and whose view of cops was perhaps somewhat harsh, was a deputy commissioner.

Technically the mosque called itself Mohammed Temple Number 7, and its leader was Minister Louis Farrakhan. At the height of the disturbance the day before, Farrakhan had demanded that white policemen be withdrawn from the scene, and this was done. He had demanded that Seedman and the other detectives end their investigation and clear out of the mosque; and when Farrakhan also promised that he would personally escort all Muslims waiting to be interrogated to the 24th Precinct later that day, Seedman had agreed and had left the mosque.

The disturbance in the street was as great as ever as Seedman came out onto the sidewalk—he was alone, and the crowd surged in around him. For a moment he felt fear, but nothing showed on his face. His teeth clenched upon his cigar, and he pushed his way through the mob to his car.

In Seedman's wake the disturbance swelled again in intensity, and it ended only when Farrakhan, a tall, eloquent young man wearing a white coat, climbed upon a car and appealed to the crowd to "just be cool."

When Farrakhan showed up at the 24th Precinct later, he was accompanied not by the suspects Seedman wished to interrogate, but by Charles Rangel, the black congressman from Harlem, and by a number of other black dignitaries. They were there to demand the release of the two Muslims already in custody, claiming that they could not be responsible for street disturbances in Harlem that night if this was not done. We actually discussed releasing the two prisoners in Farrakhan's custody, but presently decided against it.

But Farrakhan had flexed his muscles and found himself strong, and now the next day he called a press conference at which he denounced the "unprovoked, wanton, and possibly premeditated attack" by the police on a place of worship.

"We are here to voice our anger, outrage, and bitter resentment," Farrakhan declaimed. He was surrounded by newsmen and cameramen in the dining room of the restaurant adjacent to the mosque, and this crowd hung on every word.

The police had not simply made a mistake, Farrakhan said. "They said the Bay of Pigs invasion was a tragic mistake because it didn't bring off the intended results." The two policemen had come "charging into our temple like criminals, and they were treated like criminals. Muslims are people without weapons, but we fight to the death when we are attacked."

Farrakhan charged that one of the policemen "ran past our man on the desk and rushed up the stairs to the second floor." The act, the minister said, was "disrespectful and provocative. The brothers had to bring the policeman back down the steps, and shortly after that six other patrolmen tried to gain entrance." Farrakhan said that the police were "expelled from the temple."

Later, other cops had arrived with "submachine guns, automatic weapons, every kind of handgun imaginable, and they were wearing bulletproof vests."

Such swift arrival of vast numbers of cops proved, according to Farrakhan, premeditation.

Farrakhan demanded an apology from the Mayor, an apology from Commissioner Murphy, a dismissal of charges against the Muslims arrested, and the replacement of white cops and their commanding officers by black men in Harlem.

The official police silence was being read only one way: The cops must have committed some sort of atrocity, and were trying to hush it up.

By Monday it was clear that the Muslims did not intend to give up either the missing service revolver or whichever of their number was responsible for shooting Patrolman Cardillo.

Still the official police posture was silence.

I pointed out both to the Police Commissioner and to Deputy Commissioner Ward that we now knew all we were ever likely to know about last Friday's tragic events. We owed an explanation not only to the public, but also to over 30,000 cops, for there was pressure from that quarter too. Whose side was the brass on, cops had begun to demand: on the side of Patrolman Cardillo, or on the side of the Muslims who had assaulted and shot him?

I was informed by the Police Commissioner that there would be no statements issued by the Department that day.

In fact, the Harlem Mosque incident seemed to be one of Murphy's lesser preoccupations. After lunch I was summoned to his office.

"Well," he said, "the phone's been ringing all day. That article on you this morning."

He was shaking his head.

"The Mayor, everybody, is uptight about the remark about me," said Murphy.

That morning *The New York Times* had run a long profile about me. The reporter, Eric Pace, had asked what my future plans were. I told him I sometimes daydreamed about becoming director of the FBI—"in the administration of President Murphy, of course."

By the time I appeared before Murphy, I had begun to hear all over the building that this remark had done a great disservice to Murphy. Now he appeared to be running for president.

I said to Murphy, "That was a joke. That was one of the few things that I rather liked about the article, because anyone who can make a joke can't be a total idiot."

The Police Commissioner did not smile. He said, "Well, The Mayor's been on there—" He pointed to his phone.

He brooded a minute then said, "The Mayor said to me, 'What's this about Bob holding a press conference out in front of the mosque?'"

I reminded Murphy of the first meeting I had ever attended at Gracie Mansion, when the Mayor had explained how quickly wrong information could blossom into a disturbance or even a riot, and that it was the duty of all of us to make sure that correct information was disseminated as widely and as quickly as possible.

"The police radio had already announced that two cops were shot, their guns taken, and that the perpetrators were holed up inside the mosque," I reminded Murphy. "All I did was go out into the street and try to calm down the mob by describing what the actual situation was at that time."

Murphy nodded, then he said, "Lindsay was very uptight with what you said about a riot when you came into the hospital."

I said, "Well, there nearly was a riot, and he's got to face the facts. Perhaps I shouldn't have said that to him, but to you. The fact is that it was a riotous situation. It was very close to a riot. I've seen riots in other countries. I know about riots."

"When you came into the hospital," Murphy said, "we had other information that there was no danger."

"Well, that was wrong information. There definitely was a danger."

Murphy now remarked that Lindsay had never asked him to promote anybody, or even obliquely suggested that he do so. Lindsay really gave him quite a free rein.

"I've been in four cities now," the Police Commissioner said, "and you learn something each time. You learn that you have to give a little to get a little. This is really the best situation that I've ever had. He doesn't tell me what to do, and so when he does call up about something, about this matter, it has that much more importance."

"I was the one in the street at the time," I said. "I was the one who had to make the decision on what to do. No one else was there. I did what I thought was right in a riotous situation such as that one."

Murphy nodded.

That night Murphy, Bill Smith, and I were due to attend a banquet, but there would be journalists there, and Murphy canceled. Smith and I went alone, and after Smith had had a drink or two he remarked that the *Times* article on me was not so bad. He said everyone had been telling him all morning how awful it was. One of the men claimed to have read it with breakfast, and after that he got up and vomited, Smith said.

That day, as ordered, I had referred all questions on the Harlem Mosque to Deputy Commissioner Ward—who had refused to take any calls from anybody. Meanwhile, in Harlem the Muslims were entertaining journalists. One Muslim led press photographers into the mosque and pointed out bullet holes in the inner wall less than six feet above the floor. These bullet holes contradicted, according to the next morning's newspaper, earlier assertions by me that a cop had "fired high" into the mosque.

According to that day's press, two patrolmen had entered the mosque "under circumstances that are still unclear." Also according to the press, Cardillo possibly had been shot accidentally by another policeman.

Reporters now found Minister Farrakhan in a dimly lit inner dining room, together with the Reverend Jesse Jackson, an important Civil Rights leader. Farrakhan declared that the black community was rallying to support the Muslims against the police, and that the black community was in agreement with Muslim demands. A second Harlem clergyman, the Reverend Dr. Henry Dudley Rucker, called upon the Mayor and the Police Commissioner to apologize for what he called the "reckless, disrespectful, anti-religious manner in which one of our religious temples and groups was rudely and crudely shot up."

Farrakhan suggested again that the cops had entered the Mosque as part of a deliberate and premeditated attack on the Muslims.

The next morning I sent a memo to the Police Commissioner.

It was my advice last Friday afternoon to give out a two-page detailed sequence of events on the shooting in the Harlem Mosque. This advice was rejected for reasons which seemed to have some weight at the time even to me. I am sorry now that I did not push my views more strongly and force us to release the detailed sequence of events. The result of not doing this is today's story in *The New York Times* which attacks not me but the credibility of this department.

Whenever anything is held back for what may seem a good reason at the time the primary result is to establish suspicion in the minds of every working journalist in the city, not to mention close to 100 percent of the thinking population. The natural impulse of nearly everyone in this Department is to keep everything secret. This instinct is wrong and must be fought against at all times. My sequence of events from Friday afternoon would have made it clear where these extra bullet holes in the mosque came from. We are now placed in the position four days later of defending ourselves from doubt and suspicion that is so deep that any defense is virtually impossible.

One other effect of holding back information last Friday is to keep this damn story alive for four days when we could have killed it in one. I propose that this afternoon we make everything we know public.

This memo came back within 30 minutes bearing the margin handwritten message from the Police Commissioner: "I strongly disagree. We've been burned several times for saying too much too soon. I understand we take certain risks to overcome criticism we are hiding facts."

And so another day of silence was ordained.

The following day Ward wrote a memo to go out to the press at once: Murphy would meet with Minister Farrakhan.

Before I had had a chance to consider this memo, an order came down from Murphy canceling it.

By this time none of us knew what Murphy was thinking, nor who was advising him, nor why he was behaving this way. Absolute silence for five days.

The following morning, Thursday, an envelope arrived on my desk written by hand by Murphy and marked "personal and confidential." In it was an anonymous typewritten letter addressed to the Police Commissioner which denounced me for my "comments about the occurrence on West 116th Street."

The typewritten signature read: "A Citizen."

The letter contained many strikeovers and three misspelled words.

Below the signature Murphy had scrawled, "The flack re Bob's TV performance on Friday is heavy."

I wrote Murphy an angry note, stating that to send along an anonymous misspelled letter was a cheap shot and he knew it—but this note I never sent.

That night Patrolman Cardillo died. Murphy didn't go to the hospital. He said he didn't feel well.

Friday morning, a week after the shooting, the mystery was still there. What awful conduct was the Police Department hiding? And why?

The Police Commissioner released a brief statement, then flew to England with his wife. "While all of the facts concerning the shooting have yet to be determined by our investigation, it is clear that this officer responded to a call for assistance which was later found to be an anonymous unfounded call. Shortly after entering the location the officers encountered resistance and a struggle ensued. While there is considerable discussion concerning the struggle itself, the fact remains that the officer, responding in uniform and in the performance of his duty, sustained a gunshot wound resulting in his death."

David Burnham, *The New York Times*' corruption reporter, phoned to ask who was paying for Murphy's trip to Europe. He had phoned all around, but no one would tell him. So I told him. Victor Green Publications Ltd. was paying, for this organization was sponsoring the so-called International Security Exhibition and Conference, and the attendance of the Police Commissioner of the City of New York was of course an important exhibition in itself. Murphy would be gone from New York two weeks. When this conference ended, he would go on to Paris for the weekend with his wife, and then to Rome for a week with his wife. The City of New York was paying for those portions of his travels, for he said he was going to research both police departments while there.

His wife's portion of the trip he was paying himself.

Burnham thanked me and hung up.

Perhaps all week the Police Commissioner had attempted to smother the Harlem Mosque case rather than risk having it swell to proportions that would oblige him to cancel his trip to Europe with his wife. Who knew? Speculation was Burnham's job, not mine.

First Deputy Commissioner Smith was acting police commissioner now, and that afternoon there was a meeting in his office. Present were Deputy Commissioner Ward, Chief Inspector Codd, Chief of Patrol Cawley, Chief of Detectives Seedman, and myself.

I began to speak about the terrible silence of the past

week. There was no reason why all details could not be told. There never had been. But silence had become a normal Police Department crutch. When in doubt, tell the people nothing. That was why the police were hated and distrusted everywhere in this country today. That was why the people so seldom cooperated with the police. That was why the police found it so difficult to do the job most policemen wanted to do.

Secrecy was wrong, and it was especially wrong in this case. Secrecy here had made the police appear guilty, when in fact they were not. Secrecy had allowed the Muslims to fill the void with accusations of racism. Secrecy had made Farrakhan into a personage of stature, and now we would have to deal with him in the future; you could count on it. Secrecy had hardened the black community against us once again; and it had accentuated the distrust of the white community. It had earned us the contempt of everybody.

It had crushed the cops who knew the true story, and who wanted us to stand behind Cardillo and behind them.

Chief Cawley said, "That's why we're here, to discuss what to do to show some support for the men."

Ward said, "Those cops had no legal right to enter that mosque."

I said, "Every lawyer I've talked to says they did."

Seedman watched me carefully. I had lost the support of all the others when I had lost Murphy's support, however long ago that was. Apart from Seedman, they were solidly against me. I could feel it.

I had come into the Police Department to open it up, I told them, to tell the people what the police were doing, to win back the people for the cops. Police credibility was what counted. If we could once establish that, then the fear and hatred and contempt would diminish by themselves. But the silence of the past week had probably destroyed all the credibility I had sought to build up during the past year. "You do what you want," I told them. "Always in the past I talked of 'us' and of 'we.' But now it's 'you'. I'm not with you on this any longer."

Ward commenced a diatribe against the press.

I said, "If you want to curse the press out, you have to curse the people out too, for the press and the people are the same. The press is merely asking questions the people want answered."

"They're not," said Ward. "The press is just trying to sell papers. They don't care what the people want to know; they tell the people what the press wants them to know."

I answered him with some heat, and suddenly they all retreated, urging me to calm down.

"We're here to talk about a statement that will show some support for the men," said Chief Cawley.

"You've opened the Department up more than anybody ever did before," said Ward, "and it was necessary, but is it necessary now?"

I said, "It's five against one."

Smith said, "I haven't said a word yet."

Chief of Detectives Seedman sat quietly, saying nothing.

Ward talked about another weekend to be got through. It was better to keep quiet three more days. On Monday we would tell all.

As we were leaving the conference room, Ward said to me, "The trouble with you is you've begun to see everything from a police point of view. You've been hanging around these hair bags too long."

"Hair bag" was one of the most derogatory words in police argot. Almost any older commander was subject to being called a hair bag.

That day orders were tapped out on the police teletype. "To all commands—the pallbearers of the second platoon police escort company will be directed to report to the Thomas Quinn and Son Funeral Home Long Island City . . . 0900 hours said date for duty in connection with the funeral of the late active Patrolman Phillip W. Cardillo assigned to the 28th Precinct. Uniform—summer blouse, white shirt, trousers, cap and white gloves will be worn."

Squads from 52 different precincts were ordered to form outside the church. Deputy commissioners, chaplains, commanding officers and heads of line organizations were invited to attend.

On Monday morning it was raining. We stood outside the church. Not only was Murphy far away, but so was the Mayor. Mary Lindsay was there in her husband's place, as was Deputy Mayor Hamilton. Commissioner Smith stood in for Murphy.

As I had got out of my car outside the church, all the television crews converged on me, cameras rolling. Smith, Cawley, and the rest stood on the street corner.

"Give them your best profile."

"Comb your hair."

"Turn around. Your public wants to look at you."

Inside the church I knelt next to Deputy Inspector Jack Haugh, commander of Cardillo's precinct, and during the Mass I showed him the transcripts of the Sixth Division radio during the period of the shooting. In exchange he showed me a hand-written paper, which he had composed. It talked about the cowardly Muslims who had killed Cardillo who was performing in accordance with the highest traditions of the police service. Cardillo had had an absolute right to be inside the mosque, to answer that emergency call.

I didn't realize that Haugh was about to order this read to all his men, and at the same time resign from the Police Department.

Outside, taps was not played. The widow was dry-eyed. Cardillo's three small children, none older than seven, had not attended the funeral.

Riding back to headquarters with Smith, I showed him the transcriptions both of the original call to 911 from the so-called Detective Thomas, and of the transmissions on the Sixth Division frequency. I suggested to Smith that we release these transcriptions to the press. There were two strong reasons why we should *not* do so, and I explained these first: We don't sound very professional on those tapes; and we might encourage others to phone in 10-13s. Look at the excitement this one had caused.

Nobody would pull false alarms if the fire engines didn't come.

But for the following reasons I suggested that we release not only the transcriptions, but copies of the tapes themselves: (1) Few citizens realized that every call to 911 was taped, and to hear a recording of the voice of this Detective Thomas would deter others from making similar calls; (2) There was some possibility that the voice of this Detective Thomas would be recognized, and that as a result we would catch him; (3) To throw his voice onto every radio station in town would enhance police credibility—we had been claiming for days that this call had been made, and now we were proving it; (4) The voice of this Detective Thomas was a black man's voice, which would tend to prove not only that the Harlem Mosque incident was no police plot, but also that a black man was responsible for it; (5) We would dramatize the awful results of what was possibly only a prank.

Smith listened thoughtfully.

I asked Smith if Murphy had left him with instructions. He said, "Absolutely not. How could he, when he had no way of knowing what the situation would be like here?"

So Smith was in charge.

It was difficult not to think somewhat bitterly that each time something sticky came up Murphy arranged not to be there.

At three o'clock we met in Smith's office: Ward, Codd, Cawley, Seedman, Smith, and myself.

I had had tapes made, and now a cop from the communication division started the machine. We listened to the voice of this Detective Thomas. Then the Sixth Division traffic came on. Some were frantic, some unintelligible. In those transmissions were all the lurid emotions one would expect: excitement, panic, curiosity, fear, horror.

When the tape stopped and the operator had been dismissed, there was general agreement around the table—excepting myself—that we were not going to release the tapes. There followed conversation about how unprofessional all the Sixth Divison cops had sounded when faced by this emergency. I remarked that I thought the tape showed them not as unprofessional, but as human, and that it might be a significant accomplishment to let the city know that its police department did not own the kind of flawless radio instruments one found on TV cop shows and in the cinema, and that if the citizenry knew better what cops were faced with, perhaps there would be more understanding of cops.

These arguments were quickly shouted down, so next I maintained that we had an obligation now at last to give out all details: how many bullets were fired and by whom, where the powder burns were found, and so forth.

"We can't do that," said Chief Inspector Codd. "We

can't tell everything. We may need some of this information as evidence."

"That's not true. We've got to tell the people what's going on. We've waited too long already."

But we were there to write and release a statement, and eventually we began this work. It took us three hours and ten minutes to hammer out a statement which, basically, was exactly what I had written on the night of the tragedy, ten days before. However, nearly every one of my phrases now was twisted by someone.

Nearly every sentence was a fight.

I wanted to describe where the bullets had smacked into the walls, for I had made my statement in the street, Farrakhan had contradicted it several days later, and my statement had been correct. I wanted to describe how the patrolmen had fired in through the doors, deliberately firing high. I saw this as important. It proved that cops outside weren't wantonly trying to slaughter Muslims inside.

"How do you know they were firing high?" demanded Ward.

"They told me," I said.

"I'll tell you what happened," said Ward. "Those cops were shooting to kill at point-blank range and the bullets went into the ceiling because they were scared. Their hands were shaking so hard the bullets went into the ceiling. Admit it, you were wrong."

The people who did most of the shooting were standing outside the doors, in no danger whatsoever. It was inconceivable that their gun hands could have been shaking through fear. But I was quickly losing my calm.

Ward said, "Those cops had a perfect right to shoot at these people who were assaulting police officers. So we don't need to put in where the bullets went. Admit it, you made a mistake."

Chief Cawley attempted to put our meeting in perspective. "We're here to write a statement explaining what happened. We owe this to the men. We're doing this for the sake of the men."

Smith kept ranting about the lack of proper management techniques at the scene of the incident. The cops went busting in there, not using their guns properly, not following proper procedure. Cops always raced to respond to 10-13s, and that was wrong.

"Where is our training and our management?" demanded Smith. "Those cops didn't follow proper procedure."

I had written that Cardillo was not shot from a distance by another policeman.

Ward said, "How do you know he wasn't?"

Seedman looked up from across the table and said, "Because there was nobody else near him, Commissioner."

"What about that phrase, 'the powder burns prove—' " Ward said. "What powder burns?"

Seedman picked up the ballistics report off the table and read it in a low voice. "Powder burns prove that he was shot at point-blank range with the gun pressed against his jacket."

Even then, Ward said, "You can't use the word proved. Put indicated."

So I put "indicated."

Ward, Smith, Codd, and Cawley fought over every line.

"How do you know that? Did you get inside the man's head or something?"

"Because I asked him, and he told me. I talked to every one of those cops except Cardillo himself. Chief Seedman and I are the only ones here who talked to every one of them."

Ward said, "If they told you that, it's because they knew that's what you wanted to hear."

"I've interviewed people before, you know. With the possible exception of Chief Seedman, I dare say I have interviewed more people in more languages in more countries than all the rest of you people in this room put together."

Chief Cawley said calmly, "What we need to do now is write something that will show support for the men."

I had written, ". . . the assailants fled . . ."

Ward said, "You can't call them assailants. They're not assailants until they have been proven assailants in court."

"They were assaulting police officers. That makes them assailants. Look, they killed one cop and they put another one in the hospital. They're assailants."

I had written that Patrolman Padilla had been black-jacked.

Smith demanded, "How do you know that?"

"Because I went up to his hospital room, and he told me."

Perhaps Seedman was sick of all of them. He was sitting there almost with his eyes closed, not saying anything.

At one point Smith said to him, "What do you say, Al? You haven't opened your mouth."

"That's the way you learn something," said Seedman. "That's the way you conduct an interrogation. You keep your mouth shut and listen."

Somebody said, "All that shooting at point-blank range, and they didn't even hit anybody. That's how good their training is."

Even so, the statement we prepared that night was held one more day.

The next day I addressed a girls' college in Troy, New York. In my absence there was another meeting about this statement, and I was represented by Lieutenant Paul Murphy. This meeting was attended by Deputy Inspector Bill Devine, who was the Police Commissioner's chief secretary by my Lieutenant Murphy, and by another Lieutenant Murphy from the Planning Division. The chief topic seemed to be Inspector Haugh, who had resigned the night before. Inspector Devine charged that Haugh had quit only in order to enhance the value of his school—Haugh was part-owner of Police Tutorial Service Inc., which tutored cops studying for promotion exams. Chief Inspector Codd mentioned that Haugh's income from this school alone was supposed to be $50,000 a year.

After convincing each other that Haugh's defection was of no significance, they got down to business. My Lieutenant Murphy remarked that the cops had had a perfect right to enter the mosque; the police radio in effect was almost an order to go in there. Once they were inside and heard scuffling on the second floor, that constituted probable cause to search the second floor. The other Lieutenant Murphy from Planning agreed with Paul Murphy.

Deputy Commissioner Ward cried that the cops had had no legal right to enter that mosque.

The Chief Inspector attempted to make a joke. He said, "You Murphys don't know anything, do you? Anybody named Murphy doesn't know anything."

Inspector Devine said curtly, "You mean two out of

three Murphys don't know anything."

Everyone gave a dry laugh.

The statement from the night before was studied one last time, and that paragraph describing where the police bullets had struck the walls was deleted.

Driving back to headquarters from Troy, I phoned in several times, found this out, and dialed Smith's number. I told him that the position of the bullet holes should go back in. It was one of the disputed points, therefore it was important. Its inclusion would prove that we weren't just spraying bullets in there, another good point. It would refute Farrakhan, who had called us a liar on this. Since I had made my statements in the street outside the mosque as the official spokesman of the Police Department, it was the Department he was calling a liar, not me personally.

Smith said, "That's all you're worried about. You don't want to look bad. I don't think it's important. Anyway, it's already done. The statement's already gone out."

"I think it's very important," I said.

"Well, it's too late."

"No, it's not too late. I've spoken to my office, and it hasn't gone out."

"Well, I have a conference to go to and I don't consider it important."

I said, "I'm going to have to put it out anyway."

"Well, you do that if you feel you have to."

"All right, I will."

Then Smith said, "If you can get the Chief of Detectives to go along with you, then you can do it."

So I phoned Seedman. I was standing in a glass booth beside the New York State Thruway.

Seedman said he didn't think that the point of impact of the bullets was particularly important.

I said, "Look, it's important to me."

"Go ahead and do it then, I don't care."

"I'm just about ready to walk away from all this," I said.

Seedman laughed. "Will I see you in the morning?"

"Yes," I said.

"You will come in in the morning?"

"Yes."

The Chief of Detectives said, "I'll see you then. We'll talk about it then."

That night on the TV news broadcasts I watched Deputy Inspector Jack Haugh resign from the Police Department several times. "When Patrolman Cardillo was killed, he was doing his job properly," Haugh said. "That is the only issue here. All we wanted was a clear, unequivocal statement during the week that he lay in the hospital, or when we were waking him, saying that he was in that mosque doing his job, and doing it properly. I don't like leaving this job and the men. My father was a cop for 32 years, and my my father-in-law was a patrolman for 27 years. The job has always been in my family." Haugh was 43 years old and a lawyer. He had been promoted to Deputy Inspector only 40 days before by Murphy, who at the time considered him one of the brightest young officers in the Department. What Murphy thought of him now was unknown. Murphy was in England, and presumably had not even heard of Haugh's defection yet.

"The most important thing isn't if we catch Patrolman Cardillo's killer," said Haugh. "What is important is that his wife and his children firmly believe that he was doing the right thing, and he was. Somebody had to say it and I did. That's it."

The TV cameras then closed up on the face of some of Haugh's cops. All supported him vehemently. One said, "If the brass won't stand behind you, if you know that you're not going to be supported afterwards by the brass, then you can't take any action in the street whatsoever."

A petition was being drawn up in the 28th Precinct; all the cops were signing it. It would be sent to Commissioner Murphy. It would ask Murphy to prevail upon Haugh to reconsider his resignation.

Murphy, when he returned, would take no notice of this petition.

A new precinct commander was in the 28th Precinct the next day.

The next morning the halls of headquarters were full of rumors.

That Haugh had retired not on a matter of principle, but so the cops would consider him a stand-up guy and flock to his school. Haugh was not a good commander, never had been. Now he had polarized the Department. The Department was lucky to get rid of him.

The second rumor was that Seedman was retiring.

Pretty soon there would be a third: Seedman also had never been any good.

I went in to see Seedman.

He was sitting behind his big desk with his cigar in his mouth. When he shot his sleeves, I saw again the embroidered "Al" on his cuffs, and his jeweled cuff links. When he opened his drawer to get out a match, I saw his hammerless revolver lying in it.

I said to him, "I don't know if you agree with me, but I feel that you do. There's just no support for the patrolmen. Smith, Codd, Cawley, Ward—Murphy—none of them like patrolmen."

"I do agree with you," said Seedman quietly.

There had been talk for months that Seedman would retire; Alexander's department store had offered him a big job as vice-president for security.

After New Year's Day, Seedman had returned from a week's vacation to find that he no longer commanded the Narcotics Division. In his absence the Police Commissioner had transferred those 800 men to the command of Deputy Commissioner McCarthy. When, shortly afterwards, Seedman had been approached by Alexander's, he had listened.

Rumors that he was listening had reached Murphy, who sighed, saying, "Al is such an able man."

Murphy had asked me if I knew what Seedman's plans were. Why hadn't Murphy asked Seedman himself?

Sometimes I had the impression that no one talked to anybody at the top of the Police Department.

Meeting with Seedman at that time, I had attempted to talk him out of quitting. We needed him, Murphy needed him. Given a little time, all of us together could change the Police Department into what it ought to be.

I quoted Murphy's words: "Al is such an able man."

"I'm glad he feels that way," Seedman had said.

He had requested an audience with the Police Commissioner and asked, "Do I still have your confidence?"

When Murphy assured him of this, Seedman had declined Alexander's offer.

About three months later the rumors had started again: Seedman was about to put his papers in.

Again I asked him: "What's this about quitting?"

"I think I have to."

"I don't want you to."

"I know you don't. But look at this." He handed me a report which had just been forwarded by the Inspections Division. A copy had gone to the Police Commissioner. Inspections had been investigating the Bureau for weeks. The report proposed that the Police Commissioner eliminate first and second grade detective pay. Detective stature should be reduced. There should be only a single grade, and these men should be called not detectives but investigators.

Seedman said the detectives were thoroughly demoralized. They were ready to go out on strike.

"Who saved the Department during the job action last year?" asked Seedman. "The detectives, that's who. Who solved the Foster-Laurie homicides within two weeks? The detectives, that's who."

"Have you told the Police Commissioner any of this?"

"No."

"Why not?"

"He knows what my feelings are."

"I think you should go in and talk to him. It's your duty to talk to him. You're the Chief of Detectives. Nobody ever dares tell him anything around here."

Now, two days after the funeral of Patrolman Phillip Cardillo, hours after the resignation of Deputy Inspector John Haugh, with the Police Commissioner in England, Chief of Detectives Seedman told me that he meant to quit the Police Department before the end of the week.

I said, "Previously I urged you to stay out of loyalty. But I don't feel that loyalty anymore."

"I know," said the Chief of Detectives. On his desk lay an advance copy of *The New York Times Magazine*. The lead article was a profile of Albert Seedman, and on the cover stood Seedman with his hands in his pockets and a big cigar in his mouth. It was the first time in over ten years that he had allowed himself to be photographed smoking a cigar.

This article would not appear for four more days, and the Police Commissioner would not return to New York for ten more days. Albert Seedman did not intend to wait for either event. It was as if suddenly, after 30 years, he couldn't wait to walk away from all of this. Two more days and it was over. He asked me to arrange an audience with the Mayor for Friday at noon. The Mayor often met publicly with men of Seedman's rank as they went off into retirement. Seedman wanted this send-off if he could get it.

I did call the Mayor's office, and I did arrange this.

Seedman had been obliged to inform Acting Police Commissioner Smith of his plans, for there were a good many papers to be signed. Also Seedman had had to be examined by a medical board, and this board ruled him eligible for retirement under what cops called the Heart Bill. According to this technicality, most of Seedman's pension would be tax free.

A reporter got through to Smith. How did Smith explain the sudden retirement of Chief of Detectives Seedman?

Smith replied that Seedman was not in good health, and was leaving because of physical disability.

Smith reported this to me somewhat proudly. "That's the category Seedman is going out under. The important thing is not to lie to reporters. What else could I tell them?"

When he heard about this, Seedman began cursing.

About noon on Friday, his last day as a cop, Chief of Detectives Albert Seedman met with the Mayor at City Hall. After that he returned to his own office, which was already crowded by those detectives who had been close to him. On the table where we had held conferences on the Colombo and Gallo hits stood bottles of liquor and soda. Treated paper bags filled to the top with ice stood on a chair. There was a vat of potato salad and trays of sandwiches. The sandwiches were cut in half. As we drank Scotch out of paper cups, the bread was already beginning to curl.

It was a pleasant party. Calls kept coming in for Seedman, who sat at his desk taking them.

Someone must have asked him why he was resigning now. Why not wait a few more days until Murphy came back, for he answered into the phone, "Remember when I was out of town on that cruise? When I came back I found he had transferred Narcotics, 800 of my men, to the Organized Crime Bureau. Well I owed him one while he was out of town."

Although Seedman had invited all deputy commissioners and high commanders to his party, none attended except myself. The highest-ranking policeman present was Deputy Chief Sy Silver, Chief of Detectives in Brooklyn.

Silver came up to me. "I wonder who's going to get his job?" said Silver. "I would hope that I would be given the highest consideration. You'll put in a good word for me, won't you, Commissioner?"

"Sure I will, Sy, if I'm still here."

He said, shocked, "You're not leaving too?"

Sergeant Reilly tossed a tape down on Seedman's desk, saying, "This is tape No. One of nine on the Colombo case."

Seedman had asked all the Colombo detectives to sit around and just talk into a microphone. The Colombo case was fantastic, he had told them, and he wanted a complete report to take with him into retirement.

At his desk, between sips at the Scotch, Seedman was filling out forms for a pistol permit.

"Are you going to keep your gun?" I asked him.

"Are you crazy?" he laughed. "I wouldn't walk around this city unarmed."

"How many of your guns are you going to keep?"

"All of them."

He looked up at his party and beamed. Then he laughed and said, "All them rats are running around trying to get my job, and they have no one to run to. Those guys are going to have a heart attack before he gets back."

We sipped from our paper cups. Inspector Nicastro looked across at Seedman. "He'll miss it. Any guy, who, when he's in Florida, he says call, when he's up in the Catskills at the Concord, he says call. That's a guy who will miss it."

A white-haired man, one of the top executives from Alexander's, stood near Seedman's desk. Seedman had introduced him, but none of us had bothered to catch his name. He was an outsider. He wasn't one of us. He wasn't a cop.

As I walked back to my own office, I brooded. I remembered First Deputy Commissioner Smith criticizing me for having made statements in front of the Harlem Mosque, so that I said to him, "I was the one in the street making the decision. I didn't see you in the street. I didn't see Murphy or Cawley, I didn't see Codd."

He had answered, "Well, maybe you shouldn't have been there either."

I had said, "If that's the way you feel, maybe we ought to talk about that."

"Well, maybe we should."

"It's about time you stood up for the guy in the street making the tough decision," I said. "It's about time somebody around here did."

And I remembered Seedman in the 9th Precinct station house in the hours after Foster and Laurie were assassinated. Patrolman James Liedy, who had driven the shattered Laurie to the hospital, had cornered Seedman on the staircase in the middle of the night in the midst of this terribly tense investigation. Liedy was distraught, and he didn't make all that much sense. Besides which, he was only a patrolman. He told Seedman how much it meant to him to be a policeman, how hard he worked at the job, how he was one of the leaders in the precinct in summonses, and also arrests. He complained about a sergeant who made life difficult for other patrolmen.

Seedman had listened patiently. Liedy must have talked ten minutes, and when he had finished the Chief of Detectives had patted him on the shoulder and gone on his way.

Would any of the other commanders have listened to Patrolman Liedy?

Later Liedy had said, "Seedman's a cop. Those other guys, they're not cops."

Back in my own office I stared down at my desk. On it lay a memo sent to me by Patrick V. Murphy, Police Commissioner of the City of New York, only an hour or two before he had taken off for England.

The memo concerned itself with the length of my hair. It suggested that if I sacrificed my "locks" it might enhance the Police Commissioner's image in the eyes of the men.

I decided to go home. I went down the stairs into the rotunda, and there ran into Chief Cooper. Syd's beefy face broke into a grin. He didn't know what had gone on during these recent meetings. He did know that within the councils of power my advice was now as unwelcome as his. His grin seemed to extend from under his big nose to the top of his bald head, and he shook my hand, saying, "Now that you're among the damned too, I guess we can talk to you again."

I gave a rather pained laugh.

Cooper socked me in the arm. "Don't worry about it. I told you when you came in here, take one year and run. Remember the first day when we had lunch together? Take one year and run. Don't worry about it. Two years from now they'll be saying, 'Patrick who? Was that the tap dancer?' "

6 / Resignation

That very day, Xaviera Hollander, the Happy Hooker, who in her way had been as responsible for the Knapp Commission as Sergeant Durk, was deported. She was wearing the same red, white, and blue mini-dress she had been wearing the last time she was arrested.

Before boarding the plane she was given a farewell champagne party by a group of friends and admirers. The party started aboard a London-style, red double-decker bus, which picked her up at her plush penthouse apartment and drove her with her friends to Costello's bar on Third Avenue at 44th Street. Xaviera, who did not drink anything alcoholic, sipped orange juice, while her friends and admirers got smashed. Later the party went on to Umberto's Clam House, where glasses were raised to the memory of Joe Gallo. Xaviera said, "The Mafioso kill each other, and I get thrown out of the country."

By this time Patrolman William Phillips was under indictment on two counts of murder, and two tow-truck operators, George Burkert and Vincent Wright, were under indictment, charged with having given perjured testimony to the Knapp Commission. Claiming that certain cops had tried to shake them down, they had been star witnesses too.

Knapp himself was about to be named a federal judge.

That summer, Detective Frank Serpico would be awarded the Medal of Honor, the Police Department's highest decoration, and then he would retire on three quarters disability pension. He would collaborate in the writing of his life story, and then sell that story to the movies, and after that he would be lionized by the literary set. He turned up for one party in his honor wearing a T-shirt on which was stenciled the head of a pig.

Detective Sergeant David B. Durk, Amherst '57, would be awarded an honorary degree of Doctor of Laws by his alma mater. The citation would read, "Your college greets you with the proudest title of all, 'A good cop.' You expand our imagination of what a man educated here might do to achieve a more decent and a more humane society."

But all this was in the future.

One night I was in my car, coming back from Brooklyn. I had the habit of tuning my radio to the frequency of whichever division we happened to be driving through, and now as we came into the First Division the voice on the radio said, "We have some additional information on that job at 217 Avenue A. That was called in by an 8-year-old boy who says his mother and his brother are lying in a pool of blood on the fifth-floor hallway. What car is responding?"

So I looked up, searching for a street sign to see where we were.

We were close, I said to my driver, "Let's go there."

As we pulled up in front, I saw that three or four radio cars had arrived before us.

The building had a narrow entryway, and a narrow staircase. It was a walk-up. It was a little better than a tenement, not much. Halfway between the second and third floors stood a cop. He wouldn't let anybody else up. I didn't know him. I showed my shield and went on up.

At the end of the hallway on the fifth floor, her head into the corner, lay a young woman. She lay face up. The soles of her naked feet were very white. She was wearing a red blouse that was absolutely soaked with blood. Below the blouse she wore only white panties. They were spotless, except for where there was blood on them.

There was deep blood on the narrow hallway. I had to put my hands to both walls to move along the hallway without slipping. I stepped over the woman into the apartment. When I looked back at her, I saw that her head had been nearly cut off. She was young, and very pretty, and although she had been dead only about ten minutes, her skin had already gone white and waxy.

I looked down at her. Well, there was nothing that could be done there. Inside the little apartment was a narrow bed. There were posters scotch-taped to the walls.

Five or six cops were already inside. They were face-to-face with still another ghastly scene, but they hadn't come to grips with it yet. They kept looking at the young woman in the hallway, at the white soles of her feet which crossed the doorsill and extended into the apartment, and no one knew yet what to do, or what to say.

One of the cops was Patrolman James Liedy.

He came toward me with a broad grin and his hand outstretched. He said, "You can't stay out of the 9th, eh?"

But then his grin faded and he stared at the murdered young woman and bit his lip, and looked away.

No one knew what had happened, or why. No one knew who she was.

A nine-year-old boy suffering from multiple knife wounds, presumably her son, had already been rushed out of there and to Bellevue Hospital by radio car. The other boy, the one who had called in the alarm, was downstairs in a second radio car.

I stepped over the young woman into the blood, balanced myself with my hands against the walls of the hallway, and moved away from her. I stood on the landing with several cops, looking back at her.

There were other doors along the hall, and a black man's face stared out at us. One of the cops said, "I was up on this very floor only a few nights ago. It was a family fight. That black guy whose face is sticking out of the door there, he was going after his wife with a machete. I calmed them down, and took the machete away from him, and then I left. Tonight as I came up the stairs, he stuck his head out of the door and said, 'I bet you thought it was me, didn't you?'

"I said, 'I did. How are you getting on?'

"The guy said, 'Everything's fine. Couldn't be better.' "

I looked back down the hall at the pretty, frozen face, at the spotless white panties with blood on them, at the red shirt or blouse that was absolutely soaked.

I went downstairs into the street again with Liedy.

In a radio car parked outside the door a hulking young cop sat with the little boy who had just discovered his mother and brother murdered. The cop had his arm around the kid. The kid had his head against the cop's chest.

No superiors, no detectives had got there yet. These were just cops, confronted night after night by routine horror.

Seedman once said, "You've got to have some kind of love for these guys. You can't lead them unless you have that."

I didn't think they could be led from headquarters by men who never went into the street with them. They deserved better.

Who would have thought I could learn to care so much about cops?

I phoned in my resignation at noon on a Sunday, having brooded about it all the preceding week, still not wanting to go. Counting accrued vacation time, I had served as Deputy Police Commissioner of the City of New York for seven days longer than one year.

Nationwide Bestseller!
#1 Thriller!

THE TAKING OF PELHAM ONE TWO THREE

a novel by
John Godey

"Reads faster than the speed of light!"
—*Saturday Review*

"Absolutely tops!"—*The New York Times*

"Can the hijackers get away with it? The answer will have you speed-reading . . . a taut and crackling novel."
—*Newsweek*

"A spellbinder that hurtles along like a runaway express train . . . harrowing, terrifying."
—*Business Week*

"A cliffhanger, fast moving and believable!"
—*New Yorker*

Soon to be a major UNITED ARTISTS movie
A DELL BOOK $1.75

HOW MANY OF THESE DELL BESTSELLERS HAVE YOU READ?

1. **THE TAKING OF PELHAM ONE TWO THREE**
   by John Godey — $1.75

2. **A DAY NO PIGS WOULD DIE**
   by Robert Newton Peck — $1.25

3. **QUEEN VICTORIA** by Cecil Woodham-Smith — $1.75

4. **ELEPHANTS CAN REMEMBER**
   by Agatha Christie — $1.25

5. **TREVAYNE** by Jonathan Ryder — $1.50

6. **RAMBLING ROSE** by Calder Willingham — $1.50

7. **THE MAN WHO LOVED CAT DANCING**
   by Marilyn Durham — $1.75

8. **MEAT ON THE HOOF** by Gary Shaw — $1.50

9. **SOLDIER** by Anthony B. Herbert — $1.75

10. **11 HARROWHOUSE** by Gerald A. Browne — $1.50

11. **THE CAR THIEF** by Theodore Weesner — $1.50

12. **THE GREAT EXECUTIVE DREAM**
    by Robert Heller — $1.75

13. **TARGET BLUE** by Robert Daley — $1.75

14. **THE GLOW OF MORNING**
    by Irving A. Greenfield — $1.50